A

Philip E. Lilienthal (signature)

. . .

B O O K

The Philip E. Lilienthal imprint
honors special books
in commemoration of a man whose work
at University of California Press from 1954 to 1979
was marked by dedication to young authors
and to high standards in the field of Asian Studies.
Friends, family, authors, and foundations have together
endowed the Lilienthal Fund, which enables UC Press
to publish under this imprint selected books
in a way that reflects the taste and judgment
of a great and beloved editor.

The publisher gratefully acknowledges the generous
contribution to this book provided by the Philip E.
Lilienthal Asian Studies Endowment Fund of the
University of California Press Foundation, which is
supported by a major gift from Sally Lilienthal.

A History of
Modern Tibet,

Volume 2

A History of
Modern Tibet,
Volume 2

The Calm before the Storm: 1951–1955

Melvyn C. Goldstein

UNIVERSITY OF CALIFORNIA PRESS

Berkeley   Los Angeles   London

University of California Press, one of the most distinguished
university presses in the United States, enriches lives around the
world by advancing scholarship in the humanities, social sciences,
and natural sciences. Its activities are supported by the UC Press
Foundation and by philanthropic contributions from individuals
and institutions. For more information, visit www.ucpress.edu.

University of California Press
Berkeley and Los Angeles, California

University of California Press, Ltd.
London, England

Library of Congress Cataloging-in-Publication Data

Goldstein, Melvyn C.
    A history of modern Tibet, vol. 2. The calm before the
storm, 1951–1955 / Melvyn C. Goldstein.
        p.   cm.—(Philip E. Lilienthal Asian studies imprint)
    Includes bibliographical references and index.
    ISBN 978-0-520-24941-7 (cloth : alk. paper)
    1. Tibet (China)—History.   I. Title.

DS786.G635   2007
951'.5055—dc22   2006038083

Manufactured in the United States of America

15   14   13   12   11   10   09   08
11   10   9   8   7   6   5   4   3   2

This book is printed on Natures Book, which contains 50%
postconsumer waste and meets the minimum requirements
of ANSI/NISO z39.48-1992 (R 1997) (*Permanence of Paper*).

To CMB

CONTENTS

ILLUSTRATIONS

FIGURES

MAPS

PREFACE

This volume is part 1 of a two-part study of the 1951–59 era, which continues the story of modern Tibet begun in my *A History of Modern Tibet, 1913–1951: The Demise of the Lamaist State* (University of California Press, 1989). The narrative in this volume starts with the events leading to the Tibetan government's signing of the Seventeen-Point Agreement for the Liberation of Tibet in May 1951.[1] In that agreement, Tibet grudgingly accepted Chinese sovereignty for the first time in its history, and Chinese Communist troops and officials quickly entered Lhasa. For Tibetans, a new, albeit unwanted, era began. How both sides dealt with this new situation is the focus of this study.

This book ends four years later in mid-June 1955, when the Dalai Lama returned from a year-long trip to China, enthusiastic about starting to modernize Tibet as an integral part of the People's Republic of China. At this juncture, Tibet was calm, religious and secular institutions were intact, and innovations such as primary schools were increasing. This was the high point in Sino-Tibetan cooperation and rapprochement.

However, within months of the Dalai Lama's return, Sino-Tibetan relations began to spiral downhill, ending four years later with the uprising of 1959 and the flight of the Dalai Lama into exile. Part 2 of this history will examine the second four-year period, from the Dalai Lama's return to Lhasa in 1955 to the uprising in 1959.

The history of Tibet in the 1950s has not been studied in depth,[2] despite

---

1. There is some overlap between the first few chapters in this volume and the final four chapters of the previous history. In cases of such overlap, the discussions of events in this volume supersede those of the previous book.

2. There are, however, several useful brief accounts of the period (or parts of it), such as Grunfeld 1996, Knaus 1999, Shakya 1999, and Smith 1996. There is also an earlier monograph

being a critical transitional period between the traditional society and the new socialist society that was implemented after the failed uprising in 1959. In general, the period has been viewed simplistically as a confrontation in which *Tibetans* faced *Chinese Communists* in a showdown doomed to fail because the Chinese were intent on destroying Tibet. As with most stereotypic generalizations, there is some truth to this view, but new primary data have revealed that neither the Chinese nor the Tibetan side was as homogeneous as previously thought. Not only did each side have significant internal factions representing conflicting points of views, but these internal factions allied themselves with factions on the opposite side, creating a far more complex situation than had been previously realized. The current study, therefore, attempts to examine this period, taking into account the complexity that existed on both the Tibetan and Chinese sides with the aim of presenting a detailed and balanced history of this important era of modern Tibet.

SOURCES AND METHODS

A multiple methodology was employed for this study, utilizing five sources of data: (1) primary materials, including government records, unpublished letters, and diaries from individual Tibetans; (2) oral history data from interviews conducted specially for this project with Tibetan, Chinese, and American participants; (3) firsthand "memoir" accounts written by former Tibetan, Chinese, European, and Indian officials (in Tibetan, Chinese, and English); (4) restricted circulation (ch. neibu) books from China that include citations from documents and interview data; (5) newspapers, books, and academic monographs and articles, some of which quote primary political documents.

Primary Materials: Government Records and Documents

Although a study such as this would normally be rooted in an analysis of government documents, access to such materials was difficult to secure. The Tibet Autonomous Region (and other parts of China) refused to give access to any documents in its extensive archives, as did the Government of India.

The United States government provided limited access to its records. Some State Department documents were available in the National Archives and via the United States Foreign Relations publication series, but many more documents, presumably important, were withheld from the archives and not

---

on the period: Ginsburgs and Mathos 1964. It was good for its time but now is known to contain too many inaccuracies to be usable.

released despite my "freedom of information" requests and appeals. The CIA and the National Security Agency released virtually no documents, stating that to do so would be detrimental to the United States' national interests. As absurd as this may sound fifty years after these events occurred, it was part of the reality I encountered while conducting this research.

The British national archives (the Public Records Office) contained some materials on this period, but this corpus was limited in quality and quantity, particularly for the years after 1953, when the Government of India stopped sending London copies of its Lhasa Mission's monthly report to Delhi.

Nevertheless, a series of very important Chinese documents was obtained from India (Dui xizang gongzuo de zhongyao zhishi [wei chuban de shouji] [Important Instructions on Work in Tibet]), where they had been taken at the end of the Cultural Revolution. Other important Chinese documents were cited in secondary books on the period and in compilations of official documents published in China, for example, a compendium of Mao's statements on Tibet. Similarly, a number of important documents held by the Tibetan government in exile and by the Library of Tibet Works and Archives in Dharamsala were made available to me, as were important primary materials written by the famous Tibetan official Tsipön Shakabpa.

Taken together, these primary materials are an invaluable window to the history of the 1950s. There are, to be sure, still gaps and confusions whose clarification will have to wait until the remaining archival materials are released, particularly those in the Tibetan archives in China, but the corpus of primary materials that were available for this history are important and substantial. When possible, I have included full texts of relevant documents so that readers can see the full content of the documents and not have to depend on only one- or two-sentence summaries.

Oral Historical Data

Oral history—the collection of primary historical data by interviewing eyewitnesses concerning some period or event—can provide invaluable information when government records are not readily available or as a supplement to such records. Oral historical research, however, is not without problems. Memory is often selective, participants' accounts are sometimes self-serving, and current political issues can affect the quality and quantity of the accounts. Consequently, such accounts need to be evaluated carefully in terms of the background of the subject and checked against other interviews and archival sources when available. I tried diligently to do this.

Funding from the National Endowment for the Humanities (RO-22251–91 and RO-22754–94), enabled interviews to be conducted with over one hundred individuals in China, India, Nepal, England, and North America. The subjects included important Tibetans such as the Dalai Lama, Ngabö, Lhalu, and Takla (Phüntso Tashi), and important Chinese officials such as Li Zuo-ming and Fan Ming. Parts of interviews conducted for my previous history of modern Tibet (with funding from the National Endowment for the Humanities, RO-20261–82, and RO-20886–85) were also utilized. Several former members of the CIA who were involved with Tibet were interviewed as well.

Permission was also kindly granted to utilize transcripts of important interviews conducted in Dharamsala by the Tibetan Government-in-Exile's Publicity Office and by the Library of Tibet Works and Archives, some of which were from key Tibetan officials who had died by the time this project was started.

Most of our interviews were conducted between 1991 and 1995. In general, interviews involved multiple visits, almost all of which were recorded on audio tape. Follow-up visits were often made to clarify information in the initial interviews or to cover events not discussed initially. On many occasions, six to ten hours of interviews were conducted with a single person. The English transcripts of these interviews compose a corpus of over six thousand pages. Dr. Paljor Tsarong conducted most of the interviews in India either alone or with me, and I did the interviews in England, Hong Kong, Tibet, and other parts of China. Both Dr. Tsarong and I conducted interviews in the United States.

When contradictory versions of important events were collected, these were evaluated in accordance with (1) understanding of how the traditional system operated; (2) other accounts; (3) the source of the subject's information (hearsay or firsthand); (4) the relationship of the subject to the event— for example, whether he was a relative or ally of the actors in the event—and (5) the subject's reputation for duplicity or honesty. On many important issues a decision had to be made regarding which version to accept, and I spent a great deal of time trying to clarify issues by reinterviewing and conducting interviews with new individuals. Although alternative explanations of incidents are sometimes presented, usually in footnotes, it was not always possible or desirable to do so.

All these interviews are currently being compiled for inclusion in the Tibet Oral History Archive and are being prepared with support from Henry Luce Foundation by the Center for Research on Tibet (Case Western Reserve University). They eventually will be housed permanently in the Asian Division of the Library of Congress and will be available to scholars and students on the Internet as a Web archive.

Restricted Circulation (Neibu) Publications from China

I was fortunate to obtain several important sources of data from China that were published on a restricted circulation basis, that is, not available to the general public. One of these is the official *Zhonggong xizang dangshi dashiji*

(Chronology of Major Events of the Chinese Communist Party in Tibet) in several versions. It is organized as a chronological diary of events and includes citations from documents, telegrams, and so forth. In addition, I was able to utilize a number of important books published in China that were also either neibu or had been published briefly but then withdrawn from circulation.

Eyewitness and Other Written Accounts

An important source of information on the period derived from the substantial number of published accounts on the period written by participants. These "memoir" materials were published in China and India in both Tibetan and Chinese languages. They range from books such as those written by Alo Chöndze, Shenkawa, Kundeling, and Namseling to articles in journals/ magazines and collected volumes, such as the invaluable series *Bod kyi lo rgyus rig gnas dpyad gzhi'i rgyu cha bdam bsgrigs pa* (Selected Materials on the History and Culture of Tibet) and the *Gsar brje'i dran tho* (Revolutionary Memoirs).

Newspapers, Books, and Articles

Published magazine articles from China during this period were utilized via the *Survey of Mainland China Press* series. Newspapers from Western countries and India were also consulted, as was the Tibetan-language newspaper published in Kalimpong called *Yul phyogs so so'i gsar 'gyur me long* (the Mirror of World News, better known in English simply as the Tibetan Mirror). Books published in China and the West were, of course, also consulted. Many of these included some primary interview data or, on the Chinese side, government records otherwise unavailable to me. A set of the *Bod ljongs nyin re tshags pa* (Tibet Daily Newspaper) from the 1950s was also utilized.

Consequently, despite the lack of full access to official governmental records, the primary information on which this study is based provides a level of detail and understanding not heretofore attainable.

CITATION CONVENTIONS

Throughout the book, square brackets are used for comments or clarifications that I have added. For example, in the following quotation:

> [If this occurs] we absolutely will fight back militarily and contend for victory according to the principle of "reasonable, moderate and beneficial to us" (ch. youli youli youjie).

In this quotation, I added "[If this occurs]" for clarification: By contrast, the words in parentheses "(ch. youli youli youjie)" represent the original Chinese phrase that was translated as "reasonable, moderate and beneficial to us."

ACKNOWLEDGMENTS

This study would not have been possible without the assistance of many individuals in and outside China who helped point me to key questions and issues as well as to the still-living actors who could shed light on these questions. They, and the many individuals who agreed to be interviewed on tape, did this not for money or fame but because they felt strongly that future generations of Tibetans and Chinese should know what happened in the 1950s. I have no way to repay their advice and assistance and regret that in many instances their names will have to remain cloaked in anonymity. But their wish—that future generations have access to an objective and nonpartisan account of what happened—was the guiding light throughout the project.

Four very different Tibetan scholars, colleagues, and assistants warrant special mention here. In India, Dr. Paljor Tsarong worked together with me on the project in Cleveland until he moved back to India, where he became involved in his own research. He conducted outstanding interviews with key figures in India and did the initial translations of these. His knowledge of Tibetan modern history is superb, and he has served as an invaluable source of constructive criticism for me about the events of this period. This book would be far less balanced were it not for his perspective and insights.

In China, Dr. Tenzin Lhundrup of the Beijing Institute of Tibetology has been a valued colleague since I began to conduct research in the Tibet Autonomous Region in 1985. His knowledge of Tibetan society and modern history is truly outstanding, and he, too, has offered me constructive criticism when he thought my views and interpretations were not valid. In addition, in Lhasa, my long-time friend and classmate from the University of Washington, Professor Tashi Tsering of Tibet University, provided invaluable assistance in the fieldwork and interview phase of the study in Tibet. As someone who lived in the old society and became part of the new society, he provided extremely helpful knowledge and insights from both.

Lastly, I am deeply indebted to my research assistant, the late Trinley Dorje. Trinley Dorje was not a scholar or an academic. He was part of the common people, but he was also a true intellectual; extremely bright and amazingly knowledgeable about modern Tibet. Until his untimely death, he accompanied me on all my field trips, including the one taken in conjunction with this book. Born and raised in Lhasa, he was as comfortable in nomad tents at sixteen thousand feet as in sweet tea shops in Lhasa, and I regret that he is not able to see this book in print.

The perspectives of these Tibetan scholars and intellectuals are not identical, but I respect their viewpoints and was very fortunate to have such outstanding Tibetans to turn to when I was confused and to set me straight when I did not know enough to recognize my confusion. In the end, of course, I listened to what they (and others) had to say but ultimately made my own decisions about the history of this period. I hope they are not too disappointed because in many cases my own views ended up different from theirs.

Since the first time I conducted research in Tibet in 1985, I have collaborated with the Tibet Academy of Social Sciences in Lhasa, and I owe its researchers and staff a tremendous debt of gratitude for their support and gracious cooperation over the past two decades. I have always felt welcome as a foreign scholar and have been very fortunate to work with so many of their excellent researchers.

This book contains a number of photographs of people involved in this period, and I would like to thank a number of individuals and families for allowing me to use their images: in China, the Janlocen family, the Demo family, Fan Ming, and Phünwang; in North America, the Yuthok and Surkhang families. In addition, I want to specially express my gratitude to Chen Zonglie, a famous, award-winning, photo-journalist who worked as a photographer for the *Tibet Daily Newspaper* for twenty-five years. He very kindly showed me his magnificent photographic collection and gave me permission to use images from it in this book.

I also want to express my deep appreciation to the Shakabpa family for giving me access to invaluable letters and documents from one of the great figures in modern Tibetan history, the late Tsipön Shakabpa.

My sincere thanks also go to Reed Malcolm, my editor at the University of California Press. As in the past, he and his staff have supported this project and made it easy for me to focus on finishing the manuscript.

And last, but certainly not least, I want to thank the many excellent students who worked for the Center for Research on Tibet on this project.

NOTE ON ROMANIZATION

Tibetan written and spoken forms diverge considerably in that the written form contains consonant clusters that are not pronounced. For example, the written Tibetan word *bsgrubs* is actually pronounced "drub," and the bisyllabic word *rtsis dpon* is pronounced "tsipön."

Throughout the text of this book, Tibetan terms are spelled according to their spoken (phonetic) pronunciation, and the proper Tibetan spellings (romanization) are cited in the "List of Correct Tibetan Spellings" (appendix D) according to the system of T. V. Wylie (1959).

References to an article or book written in Tibetan cite the author's name in romanization. However, given the divergence between spoken and written Tibetan, when the name of the Tibetan author also appears in the narrative, the phonetic version of his name is included in the reference to enable readers to connect the person in the text to the author of the book or article.

The phonetic rendering of Tibetan names has no universally accepted standard, so sometimes Tibetan names and terms cited in quotations will vary considerably from those I use in the narrative; for example, Dzongpön is spelled in some quotations as Jongpoen, and Lobsang Samden is sometimes written as Lopsang Samten.

Chinese names are cited with the family name before the personal name; for example, in "Zhang Guohua," Zhang is the family name and Guohua is the personal name. Tibetan names are also cited with the family name first and the personal name following. In these instances, the personal name has been clarified with parentheses, since not all Tibetans have family names. For example, in "Changöba (Dorje Ngüdrub)," the family name is Changöba, and the personal name is Dorje Ngüdrub. However, in "Tsering Dolma," there is no family name; Tsering Dolma is entirely the personal name.

LIST OF ABBREVIATIONS

CCP	Chinese Communist Party
ch.	Chinese language
chi.	Chinese
CHMC	Culture and Historical Materials Committee of the Political Consultative Conference of the Tibet Autonomous Region
cld	could
congen	consul general
coop	cooperate
CPPCC	Chinese People's Political Consultative Conference
cpr	Chinese People's Republic
cro	Commonwealth Relations Office
del	delegation
DL	Dalai Lama
emb	embassy
embtel	embassy telegram
evac	evacuate
FO	Foreign Office (British)
fyi	for your information
gen	general
GMD	Guomindang
GOI	Government of India
HMG	His Majesty's Government
IOR	India Office Records
KMT	Kuomintang
ltr	letter
MAC	Military Administrative Committee
MEA	Ministry of External Affairs

mil	military
msg	message
negots	negotiations
NWB	Northwest Bureau
PCTAR	Preparatory Committee for the Tibet Autonomous Region
PLA	People's Liberation Army
pls	please
PRC	People's Republic of China
qte	quote
reftel	referenced telegram
rpt	repeat
rptd	repeated
shld	should
sm	same as
SWB	Southwest Bureau
syg	secretary-general
TAR	Tibet Autonomous Region
tel	telegram
tib.	Tibetan language
Tib	Tibetan(s)
TWC	Tibet Work Committee
unqte	unquote
ur	your

Alo Chöndze	a leader of the second People's Association
amban	Imperial commissioners sent by the Qing dynasty to Tibet
Big Three Monastic Seats	see "Three Monastic Seats"
Chamdo	the town in Eastern Tibet that was the headquarters of the governor of Kham, or Eastern Tibet, and the target of the PLA's invasion in 1950
chandzö	a manager working for a monastery, labrang, or aristocratic family
Che Jigme	one of the two top officials in the Panchen Lama's Administrative Council
Chömpel Thubden	one of the four heads (trunyichemmo) of the Ecclesiastic Office; a major spokesman in 1951 for the Dalai Lama's returning to Lhasa rather than going into exile
Coocoola	an English-speaking Sikkimese princess married to a Tibetan aristocrat from the Phünkang family. She was a frequent source of information for the United States.
dayan	a Chinese silver coin from the old society used by the PLA in Tibet in the 1950s, because Tibetans did not accept Chinese paper currency
Deng Xiaoping	one of the two main leaders of the Southwest Bureau during 1950–52. In 1953 he moved to Beijing to

	serve as the secretary-general of the Central Committee.
depön	commander or general in charge of a regiment in the traditional Tibetan army. If a regiment had only five hundred troops, there was usually only one depön, but if there were a thousand troops, there were usually two.
divine lottery (senril)	a type of divination frequently used by the Tibetan government to make major decisions. The lottery was based on two or more alternative answers being written on paper and rolled into dough balls of exactly the same size and weight. These were placed in a bowl and shaken before the statue or icon of a deity until one ball rolled out, which was the one believed to contain the answer chosen by the deity.
dobdo	a kind of deviant fighting/punk monk found in many larger monasteries
Dombor (Kyenrab Wangchuk)	an acting Kashag minister in the 1950s
dotse	a Tibetan unit of currency that was equal to fifty ngüsang
dzasa	(1) a high rank in the Tibetan government; (2) a title of some Labrang managers, such as Kundeling Labrang
Ecclesiastic Office (Yigtsang)	the highest office in the monk official side of the Tibetan government. It was headed by four officials called trunyichemmo.
Fan Ming	a senior Northwest Bureau cadre who was the representative to the Panchen Lama and a major official in the Tibet Work Committee in Lhasa
geshe	an advanced degree earned by scholar monks
Guomindang (GMD)	the Nationalist Party that ruled China until the CCP defeated it and established the PRC in October 1949. Prior to the language reforms of the People's Republic of China, it was normally romanized as "Kuomintang" (KMT).
gyagpön	a noncommissioned officer in charge of a unit of one hundred in the traditional Tibetan army
Gyalo Thondup	the second oldest brother of the Dalai Lama and one of the leaders of Jenkhentsisum

Jenkhentsisum — the informal name of the anti-Chinese exile group in India. The term is an acronym of the titles of its three leaders, Gyalo Thondup, Tsipön Shakabpa, and Khenjung Lobsang Gyentsen—literally, jen (older brother), khen (khenjung), tsi (tsipön), and sum (word for the number three).

jigyab khembo — the highest monk official in the government. His responsibilities included oversight of the Dalai Lama's personal attendants and private treasury (tib. dzöbu). The jigyab khembo was also entitled to sit with the Kashag but typically went there only on special occasions, for example, if the Dalai Lama had something to tell the Kashag. Between 1952 and 1956, the jigyab khembo was the Dalai Lama's brother Lobsang Samden.

kadrung — important administrative aides to the Kashag ministers. There were usually two of these, both aristocratic lay officials. Their job was to assist the ministers in any way needed, but their usual work involved writing whatever drafts, letters, documents, orders, or recommendations the Kashag sent to the Dalai Lama and other offices and the edicts the Kashag sent to counties. By custom, the seal of the Kashag could be applied only by the two kadrung, even if the ministers were present.

kalön — the title for a Kashag minister

kandrön — administrative aides to the Kashag. There were usually three of these, all aristocratic lay officials. They were in charge of petitions to the Kashag.

Kashag — the highest office in the Tibetan government

khe — a basic Tibetan measure of volume. One khe of barley weighed about thirty-one pounds.

Kheme Dzasa (Son- — one of the commanders-in-chief of the Tibetan
am Wangdü) — army. He was a part of the Tibetan delegation that went to Beijing and signed the Seventeen-Point Agreement. He was also the uncle (father's brother) of Surkhang, one of the Kashag ministers.

khenjung — a rank and title for monk officials that was equal to fourth-rank (rimshi) officials in the lay side of the traditional government bureaucracy

labrang — (1) the common name of the Panchen Lama's

	government (sometimes referred to as Tashilhunpo Labrang); (2) name of a large Gelugpa monastery in Gansu; (3) the corporate property-holding entity of any incarnate lama
Le Yuhong	an important cadre who came with Zhang Jingwu in 1951. He worked in the Tibet Work Committee in Lhasa and maintained a valuable diary. (Also known as Alo Budrang.)
Lhalu	Kashag minister and governor of Chamdo until replaced by Ngabö in the fall of 1950
li	a Chinese measure of distance equal to about half of a kilometer
Li Jingquan	the first party secretary of Sichuan Province
Ling Rimpoche	the senior tutor of the Dalai Lama
Liu Bocheng	the commander of the Second Field Army and a major Southwest Bureau official
Liu Geping	an ethnic Hui (Muslim) who was deputy director of the United Front Work Department and the State Nationalities Commission in Beijing
Liu Shaoqi	one of the top leaders in the CCP in the 1950s. He served, among many positions, as president of the People's Republic of China.
Liushar (Thubden Tharba)	the codirector of the Tibetan government's Foreign Office and one of the two government liaison officers assigned to the Chinese
Li Weihan	a key official in Beijing dealing with minority nationalities. He was the director of the United Front Work Department and the State Nationalities Commission.
Lobsang Samden	the third oldest brother of the Dalai Lama. He was a monk official in the Tibetan government. In early 1952, he was appointed the jigyab khembo.
Lobsang Tashi	the monk official who was one of the two sitsab during 1950–52
lord chamberlain	a monk official in the Dalai Lama's court who was in charge of access to the Dalai Lama
Lukhangwa	the lay aristocratic official who was one of the two sitsab during 1950–52
mendredensum	a type of religious offering given to lamas that represents the body (via a statue), the speech (via a text/scripture), and the mind (via a stupa)

miser	a term that can refer to a serf or a bound subject as well as a citizen, depending on the context. For example, "miser of a lord" connotes the serfs of that lord, whereas "miser of Tibet" connotes citizens of Tibet.
Mönlam	in this book, a short form of Mönlam Chemmo
Mönlam Chemmo	the Great Prayer Festival held in Lhasa at the start of the first Tibetan lunar month
Mullik	the head of Indian Intelligence Bureau for most of the 1950s
Mu Shengzhong	one of the senior cadre from the Northwest Bureau who came with Fan Ming to Lhasa
Namseling	an anti–Chinese nationalist aristocratic official who was one of the four heads of the Revenue Office (Tsigang)
Ngabö (Ngawang Jigme)	the Tibetan governor-general at the time of the Chinese invasion of 1950. He was the head of the Tibetan negotiating team in Beijing for the Seventeen-Point Agreement talks and then returned to Tibet in September 1951 and resumed his activities as one of the Kashag ministers. The leading progressive in the Tibetan government.
ngüsang	a Tibetan unit of currency, fifty of which equaled one dotse
Peng Dehuai	the first secretary of the Northwest Bureau and the commander of the First Field Army. He also commanded the PLA troops in the Korean War.
Phala	a powerful monk official from an important aristocratic family. During the period of this history, he was the lord chamberlain.
Phüntso Tashi	See "Takla (Phüntso Tashi)"
Phüntso Wangye	a Tibetan cadre in the Southwest Bureau who was the only Tibetan on the Tibet Work Committee in Lhasa
Phünwang	abbreviation of "Phüntso Wangye"
Ragasha (Phüntso Rabgye)	member of the Kashag in the 1950s
Ramba (Thubden Güngyen)	the elder member of the Kashag, who was a monk official
Reting	the regent from 1933 to 1941. He sought unsuccessfully to return to power in 1944–45 and then plotted

	a coup against the sitting regent, Taktra. He was arrested and imprisoned, where he mysteriously died. Most believe he was poisoned.
rimpoche	title for an incarnate lama
rupön	a military officer in the traditional Tibetan army just under a depön; usually in charge of half of a regiment
sang	same as ngüsang
sawangchemmo	term of address for Kashag ministers
senril	see "divine lottery (senril)"
Shakabpa (Wang-chuk Denden)	the key Tibetan official dealing with the United States and India in 1950–51; later a leader of Jenkhentsisum, the anti-Chinese resistance organization in India
Shasur (aka Shen-kawa) (Gyurme Dorje)	one of the acting Kashag ministers in the 1950s
shondrön	monk official aides in the secretariat of the regent
sitsab	the two officials appointed in 1950 to head the government while the Dalai Lama was in Yadong.
Surjong Kashag	the special three-minister "little Kashag" office that had the authority to streamline implementation of the Seventeen-Point Agreement
Surkhang (Wang-chen Gelek)	one of the Kashag ministers in the 1950s
Tan Guansan	a Southwest Bureau official who was one of the leading officials in the Tibet Work Committee in Lhasa
Takla (Phüntso Tashi)	a Tibetan from Amdo who married the Dalai Lama's sister and became an official of the Tibetan government. He was one of the few officials who knew Chinese.
Taktra (Rimpoche)	the regent of Tibet from 1941 to 1950
Taktse Rimpoche	the eldest brother of the Dalai Lama. He was an incarnate lama from Kumbum Monastery in Qing-hai Province who came to Lhasa in 1950 and then went to the United States, where he was a important source of information for the State Department and the CIA.
Three Monastic Seats	the name of the three great Gelugpa monasteries around Lhasa: Ganden, Sera, and Drepung. To-

gether these housed about twenty thousand monks in 1959.

Tibet Work Committee	the main Chinese administrative office in Tibet in the 1950s; called "Xizang gongwei" in Chinese
Trijang Rimpoche	the junior tutor of the Dalai Lama
Tromo	the Tibetan name for Yadong
trungtsi	an acronym that refers to heads of the Ecclesiastic Office (trunyichemmo) and the Revenue Office (tsipön)
trungtsigye	an acronym that refers to the four heads of the Ecclesiastic Office (trunyichemmo) and the four heads of the Revenue Office (tsipön). It is constructed from the first syllable of *trunyichemmo*, the first syllable of *tsipön*, and the word for "eight." These heads held the most important office apart from the Kashag and often met with the Kashag to discuss important issues. They also chaired the meetings of the Tibetan Assembly.
trunyichemmo	the title for the heads of the Ecclesiastic Office (Yigtsang)
tsamba	parched barley flour, the Tibetan staple food
tsendrön	monk official aides in the Sectretariat of the Dalai Lama
Tsigang	the Revenue Office
tsipön	the title for the heads of the Revenue Office
Tsondu	the general name for the several levels of assemblies that were sometimes convened by the Kashag to render an opinion on important issues
Tsuglagang	the main temple in Lhasa that is surrounded by the circular Barkor Road. The Jokhang is located within it.
Wang Qimei	a senior commander and official from the Southwest Bureau. He led the advance troop of the Eighteenth Army Corps to Lhasa in September 1951.
Xikang (Province)	the province immediately north of Sichuan, which was predominately ethnic Tibetan (Khamba) in composition. It was merged into Sichuan in 1955.
Xi Zhongxun	a senior leader from the Northwest Bureau (vice chairman of the Northwest Military-Administrative Bureau) who was called to Beijing and became the vice premier of the PRC

Xu Danlu   an important cadre in the Tibet Work Committee. He
                    was the Central Committee's liaison to the Dalai Lama
                    on his trip to and from eastern China in 1954–55.

Yadong   a town on the border with Sikkim. The place to which
                    the Dalai Lama fled in 1950–51 after the Chinese took
                    military control of Chamdo. In Tibetan it is called
                    Tromo.

Ya Hanzhang   a senior Northwest Bureau official in Tibet in the early
                    1950s

Zhang Guohua   the top Southwest Bureau official in Tibet and the com-
                    mander of the Eighteenth Army Corps; also the first
                    deputy secretary of the Tibet Work Committee in Lhasa

Zhang Jingwu   representative of the Central Committtee to the Dalai
                    Lama and first secretary of the Tibet Work Committee

Zhou Enlai   the premier of the People's Republic of China

Zhu De   the commander in chief of the PLA

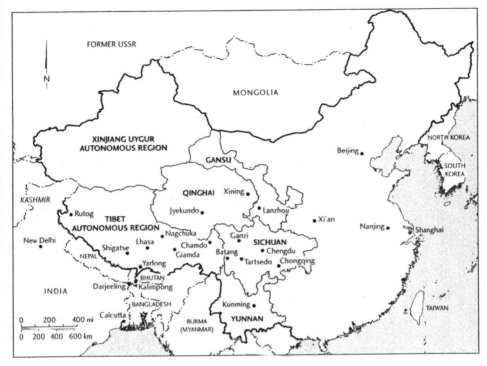

Map 1. China

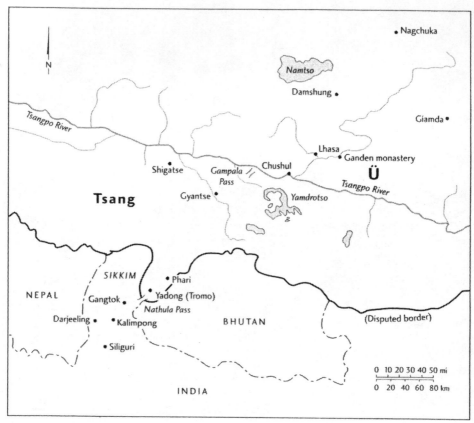

Map 2. Central Tibet

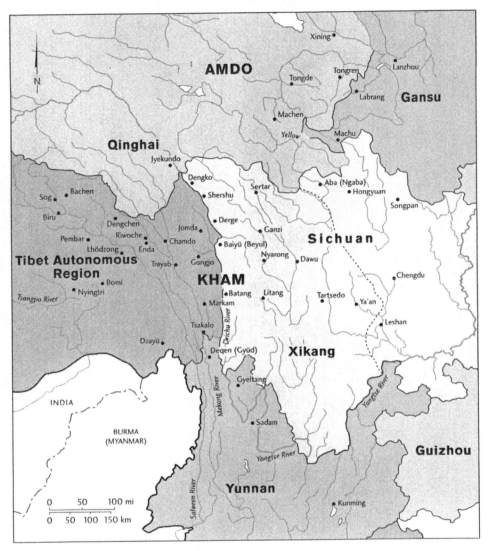

Map 3. Kham

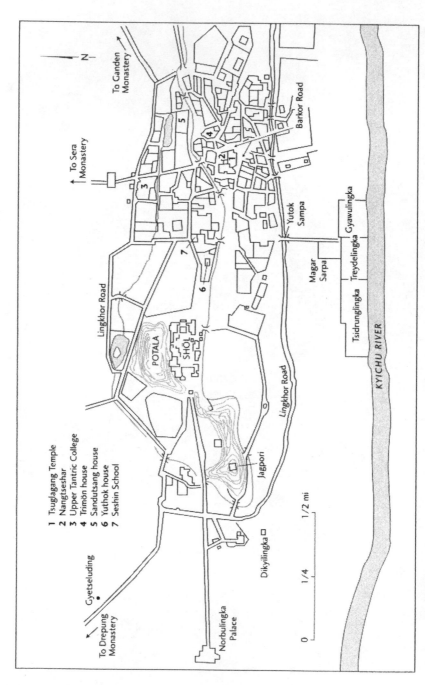

Map 4. Lhasa City, ca. 1950s. Source: adapted from a sketch map by Zasak J. Taring, 1959 (in Nakane 1984).

Introduction

Tibetan Society on the Eve of Incorporation into China

Political systems have ideologies that summarize and rationalize their basic premises. In Tibet, society and government were based on a value system in which religious goals and activities were paramount. The Tibetan state as headed by the Dalai Lama was founded in the mid-seventeenth century after decades of bitter sectarian conflict. The new theocratic government saw its mission as the support and enhancement of Buddhism, particularly its own "yellow hat" (or Gelugpa) sect. Tibetans conceived of this as a system of "religion and government joined together" (tib. chösi nyiden), because the ruler, the Dalai Lama, was an incarnation of the Bodhisattva Avalokitesvara, and monks served alongside laymen to administer the country. Moreover, beginning in the eighteenth century, the regents who ruled during the dalai lamas' minorities were also incarnate lamas. Tibetans considered their country unique because of this "dual system" of government. The depth of this belief was conveyed in a letter the Tibetan government sent to Chiang Kai-shek in 1946: "There are many great nations on this earth who have achieved unprecedented wealth and might, but there is only one nation which is dedicated to the well-being of humanity in the world and that is the religious land of Tibet which cherishes a joint spiritual and temporal system."[1]

To understand twentieth-century Tibetan history, therefore, it is necessary to understand that Tibet was, in many fundamental ways, a premodern theocratic polity, and this was not because of any unusual isolation. In the twentieth century, Tibet looked modernity straight in the eyes and rejected change and adaptation. Its leaders saw Tibet's greatness in its religious in-

---

1. Goldstein 1989: 816.

stitutions and held strongly that these should be continued without competition or contamination from "modern" institutions such as public schools or a professional army.[2]

THE GOVERNMENT

The Tibetan government in 1951 consisted of a system of hierarchically arranged offices staffed by a bureaucracy of roughly five hundred officials, about half of whom were monk officials and half lay aristocratic officials.[3] Virtually all offices and positions in that government were headed by lay and monk officials jointly sharing power. This tiny bureaucracy was able to administer a country the size of western Europe, because the Tibetan government operated under a minimalist philosophy in which most governmental functions were performed by local lords who held manorial estates.

The lay official segment of the government was recruited from a hereditary aristocracy that consisted of about two hundred families. Each aristocratic family held at least one manorial estate with attached peasant families and in return was required to send at least one male family member to serve as a government official (with no salary). Serving the government as a lay official was technically an obligation but in reality was a carefully guarded prerogative. With the exception of the families of the successive dalai lamas and, in the twentieth century, a few very rich trading families, nonnobles could not become lay government officials.

The monk official segment of the government was recruited primarily from a small number of monasteries, principally the three huge monasteries around Lhasa (Sera, Drepung, and Ganden) but also a few others such as Muru and Shide. These monk officials were required to be celibate but did not live in monasteries and were not active in the affairs of their original monasteries. Instead they were specially trained for administrative service in the Tselabdra, a government school located in the Potala. They became bureaucrats much like their lay aristocratic counterparts, although, unlike the aristocrats, they were celibate monks and had no estates.

The Tibetan government was headed by a ruler, the Dalai Lama, or in his minority, a regent. The ruler ideally had ultimate authority over all decisions and appointments, and, theoretically, all recommendations for action had to be submitted to him for approval.

The Dalai Lama himself is recruited by incarnation. In other words, within one to three years after a Dalai Lama dies, he chooses his successor by incarnating his "essence" into the fetus of a boy. The task of the traditional Tibetan

---

2. The history of the first half of the twentieth century is examined in detail in Goldstein 1989.

3. The Tibetan government was known in Tibetan as Ganden Phodrang or Dewashung.

government and regent, therefore, was to identify that child from among the tens of thousands of boys born within a few years of the death of the last Dalai Lama.

To do this, the Tibetan government or regent examined dreams, visions, miraculous events, and the like to focus the search geographically and then sent out a series of search teams to try to discover young boys who might be the new incarnation. As potential candidates for the new Dalai Lama were identified, the small children were tested by showing them pairs of items—one personally owned by the late Dalai Lama and another that was identical but new. The correct child was expected to choose the things he had used in his previous incarnation, not the new and shiny ones. Ultimately, the next Dalai Lama was chosen from the pool of several "candidate-children" who had been identified by the different search teams; then he was brought back to Lhasa, where he studied religion with tutors. This system effectively transferred the charisma of the previous incarnation to the new one and legitimized the selection.

During the Dalai Lama's minority, Tibet was ruled by a regent, who held power until the Dalai Lama reached age eighteen. At this time, the Dalai Lama assumed political power for the remainder of his life. However, even after a dalai lama formally assumed power, how much he was really able to exercise has varied according to circumstances and the particular dalai lama involved.

The Dalai Lama was surrounded by a small number of monk attendants and government monk officials who served him in his personal household and his secretariat office (called the Tse ga).[4] One of the most important of these was the jigyab khembo. He was a high monk official who was in charge of the Dalai Lama's personal treasury and his three chief personal attendants.[5] The jigyab khembo had a high status and was entitled to sit with the Kashag, although he usually did so only if the Dalai Lama had something to say to the Kashag or vice versa.

The other major monk official in the Dalai Lama's secretariat was the lord chamberlain (tib. drönyerchemmo). He was the conduit to the Dalai Lama for such things as private petitions and requests for audiences, so although lower in rank than the jigyab khembo, he could be extremely powerful, because he controlled access to the Dalai Lama. In the period covered by this history, Phala was the influential and powerful lord chamberlain.

Also important in the Dalai Lama's entourage were his senior and junior tutors (and their assistants). They had constant access to the Dalai Lama and

---

4. The Dalai Lama's secretariat was small. It was headed by the lord chamberlain and staffed by sixteen tsendrön and four singga, all of whom were monk officials.

5. These were the chief attendant for food (tib. söpön khembo), the chief attendant for clothes (tib. simpön khembo), and the chief attendant for rituals (tib. chöpön khembo).

were also influential. Ling Rimpoche and Trijang Rimpoche were, respectively, the senior and junior tutors during the 1950s.

A number of factors affected the Dalai Lama's ability to wield power effectively. One of the most circumscribing factors was his physical isolation from virtually everyone in his kingdom. The Dalai Lama was cloistered in his palaces and had no informal contact outside of those immediately around him. The Dalai Lama, therefore, was dependent on information coming to him from other offices and officials, particularly those in his immediate entourage, and it actually took an active effort on the part of a dalai lama to overcome this institutionalized isolation. This problem was exacerbated by the tactics of the bureaucracy, especially the Kashag, the highest office in the Tibetan government.

The Kashag (Council of Ministers) traditionally consisted of four ministers (tib. kalön), one of whom was a monk official, but in modern times this number was not strictly adhered to. In 1951, for example, there were eight (full and acting) ministers.[6] These were appointed by the ruler for life from a short list of nominees prepared by the Kashag itself. Although the ruler was not limited to choosing from the Kashag's list, normally he did so. Supporting these ministers was a small staff of six or seven junior aristocratic officials.[7]

The Kashag was the administrative center of the Tibetan government for secular affairs and also functioned as the Tibetan equivalent of a paramount court of appeals. It was the only office that could send secular items to the ruler for approval and, therefore, was the only secular office that could have direct contact with him. All other secular offices had to go through the Kashag to obtain a decision from the ruler. The Kashag also was responsible for making nominations for appointments and promotions (of lay officials).

Under the Kashag, a hierarchy of offices handled the business of government. Most were headed by both monk and lay officials, but the two most important, the Revenue Office (tib. Tsigang) and the Ecclesiastic Office (tib. Yigtsang), were headed, respectively, by four lay officials (tib. tsipön) and four monk officials (tib. trunyichemmo). The Ecclesiastic Office dealt with religious affairs and the government's monk officials; and the Revenue Office, with issues of revenue, taxes, and secular affairs.

Traditionally, there were no portfolios in the Kashag, and decision mak-

6. The five full Kashag ministers in 1951 were Ramba (Thubden Güngyen) (monk official), Surkhang (Wangchen Gelek), Ragasha (Phüntso Rabgye), Lhalu (Tsewang Dorje), and Ngabö (Ngawang Jigme). The three acting ministers were Thubden Ramyang (monk official), Shasur (also known as Shenkawa) (Gyurme Dorje), and Dombor (Kyenrab Wangchuk) (monk official).

7. The staff of seven junior officials comprised two kadrung, two kandrön, and three Kashag shöpa, all of whom were aristocratic officials.

ing was done collectively, with consensus required for action. The fundamental power of the Kashag was that no secular matter could reach the ruler
for settlement without first passing through its hands. Tibetans, therefore,
often spoke of it as the throat through which all governmental matters must
pass.

The following example will illustrate how recommendations for action
were framed. This example was sent as a hypothetical from a county governor to the Revenue Office to the Kashag to the Dalai Lama, then back to the
Kashag, from there to the Revenue Office, and finally to the county in question.[8] In Tibet, the Kashag and Dalai Lama used different colors of ink, so
it is immediately clear to a reader which changes each made on a document.
For the purpose of illustrating the different inks, the Kashag's emendations
are presented in square brackets, and the underlining and strike-through
reflect the Dalai Lama's decision:

> It was examined (by me the Dalai Lama) on the 5th day of the 9th month of
> the Wood-Tiger year.
> Wood-Tiger year. A report has arrived from the Gyantse county governor. This
> year because of heavy rains, the fields of the people of Samada have become
> covered with water and they were not able to harvest a crop. Based on the great
> difficulties caused by that [which others have no means for imitating] after
> doing their corvée taxes, for three, four, five years we are requesting a con-
> cession of taxes in kind. [and on top of that, to make up for the loss, ~~silver
> coins 200, 250, 300~~ and barley khe 70, 80, 90 to be given as a gift].[9]
> Please instruct whether it is __all right__ or not to do this.[10]

As is seen in this example, proposals submitted to the Dalai Lama for his
action were cast in the form of a decision coming from him. Thus, the first
sentence of this petition indicates that the Dalai Lama (or, in his minority,
the regent) examined the request on such and such a date, and the underlining in the final sentence indicate his approval.

The Kashag, in this example, had first altered the Revenue Office recommendation by adding the phrase "which others have no means for imitat-
ing" and the phrase "and on top of that, to make up for the loss, silver coins
200, 250, 300 and barley khe 70, 80, 90 to be given as a gift." The Dalai Lama
then chose to cross out the recommendation for payment in silver coins, while
choosing seventy khe and a tax concession of five years.

This hypothetical example reveals some of the basic ways that the politi-

---

8. This example was constructed by a former Kashag minister, the late Surkhang (Wangchen
Gelek) (Goldstein 1968: 175–76).

9. A khe is a traditional measure of volume equivalent to about thirty-one pounds (for
barley).

10. Goldstein 1968: 176.

cal system restricted the Dalai Lama (or regent). While the ruler unquestionably held ultimate authority over all decision making, his power was limited by his lack of information. In the above incident, for example, the Dalai Lama knew only what was in the recommendation, and since recommendations for action were supported by the Kashag, he would almost always leave the basic notion intact, even though, as he did here, he might well alter some points within the decision. On major issues, the Dalai Lama could summon the Kashag for a meeting and discuss the issue in question in person, but for most recommendations he based his decision on what was given him. The Dalai Lama was also limited in seeing only those issues that the Kashag decided to send to him.

The control of the Kashag was further enhanced by its long-established practice of unilaterally settling many issues without first sending these to the ruler. This was possible because the Kashag's seal was the official government seal. Even items that went to the ruler for approval were issued with the Kashag's seal. Consequently, in cases when the Kashag did not send an issue to the Dalai Lama for approval, the council simply wrote the decision as if it had already been seen by the Dalai Lama (i.e., as above) and then sent it out for implementation using the council's seal.[11]

The Kashag's internal rationalization for bypassing the ruler was usually that an issue was too inconsequential to bother the sacred ruler or, alternatively, that it dealt with matters unsuitable for an incarnate lama, for example, decisions that ordered corporal punishment. However, the Kashag normally would not withhold several clear-cut types of issues from the ruler: (1) decisions that involved the expenditure of government funds, (2) decisions that involved the transfer of land from one owner to another or confiscations/awards of land, (3) decisions granting permanent tax exemptions or adding new taxes, (4) promotions and demotions, (5) decisions involving border relations and foreign affairs. The majority of other issues were generally settled unilaterally by the Kashag.

One Kashag minister, the late Surkhang (Wangchen Gelek), estimated that in the late 1940s about 70 percent of incoming requests were settled by the Kashag without approval of the ruler. During the government's six-day work week, the Kashag sent about one hundred pieces of business to the ruler for final confirmation, according to Surkhang's estimation. As one would predict, he indicated that the percentage of items approved unilaterally by the Kashag increased considerably during the reign of a regent and a new dalai lama and decreased during the era of a strong dalai lama. However, in the history of the institution of the Dalai Lama, only a few dalai lamas were

---

11. The Kashag seal was called kadam. The Dalai Lama had his own seal, called bugdam, which he used to issue decrees in his own name.

able to exercise extensive autocratic power. The 13th Dalai Lama was one of these, and an important issue for the history of the 1950s was whether the 14th Dalai Lama, who ascended to official authority in late 1950, would continue that style of active rulership.

The Kashag, therefore, controlled the daily operation of the government and was the critical link between the ruler and the bureaucracy. However, the Kashag's dominance of the Tibetan government occasionally was lessened by the creation of another office above it—the Office of the Silön. Such was the case during 1950–52.

THE SILÖN OR SITSAB

The Office of the Silön was created in 1904 when the 13th Dalai Lama fled to exile in Mongolia and China as a result of a British invasion of his capital. At that time the Dalai Lama appointed three Kashag ministers to govern in his absence, calling them silön, which literally means "minister of political administration." Unlike regents who ruled after the death of a dalai lama and during the minority of the successor dalai lama, the Silön were in charge of the country when the ruler was alive but in exile. However, when the Dalai Lama returned to Lhasa from India in 1913, he resumed his authority but chose not to disband the Office of the Silön, which continued to function, forming a new layer in the bureaucratic hierarchy that sat between the Kashag and the Dalai Lama. The Kashag, heretofore the highest office in the government, then had to send all its petitions, requests, and decisions to the ruler via the silön, who exercised the same power over the Kashag's requests as the Kashag did over the other governmental offices subordinate to it. For example, the silön could unilaterally decide not to forward a Kashag recommendation to the ruler.

By the early 1930s, only one of the original three ministers appointed in 1904 was alive, but the Dalai Lama kept the office going by appointing his nephew, Langdün, to serve jointly with that last silön, and by the time the 13th Dalai Lama died in 1933, only the Dalai Lama's nephew Langdün remained as silön.

The Dalai Lama's death required the appointment of a regent to oversee the selection of the new Dalai Lama and rule in his minority. Since the late eighteenth century, this had been an incarnate lama, but in 1933 there was some sentiment favoring the appointment of Langdün, a lay aristocrat, to perform this function. Ultimately, a lama—Reting—was selected as regent with the proviso that he share power equally with Langdün. This arrangement lasted for only a few years, because Reting quickly managed to force Langdün to resign. From then until December 1950, the Office of Silön was vacant. In that year, the Dalai Lama appointed two acting silön (called sitsab), to oversee governmental affairs from Lhasa while he fled to Yadong, on the border of Sikkim, to wait to see whether the Chinese would continue their invasion into Central Tibet.[12]

THE (NATIONAL) ASSEMBLY, OR TSONDU

The institution of the Assembly (tib. Tsondu) appears to have arisen during the 1860s when the lay aristocrat Shatra convened an ad hoc meeting that called itself "the great Ganden Monastery, Drepung Monastery, and the government officials" (tib. gandredrungche). It deposed the regent and replaced him with Shatra. After Shatra's death, the Assembly, or Tsondu, as it came to be called, selected the regents and came to play an important role in national affairs. In the modern period (1913–51), assemblies met irregularly at the request of the Kashag to consider and give an opinion on a specific question supplied by the Kashag. They were, therefore, consultative rather than legislative and were convened to broaden the base of support for some sensitive or difficult decision that the Kashag did not want to make unilaterally. By tradition, the Kashag ministers themselves did not participate in the Assembly discussions or even attend.

The configuration of the Assembly with respect to size and composition varied according to the topic under consideration. The smallest of these Assembly configurations was a type of elite government committee consisting of the Council of Ministers and the heads of the two most important offices under them, the Ecclesiastic Office and the Revenue Office. Together they were known as the Kashag Trungtsi Lhengye and met at the Kashag's request. Sometimes, the sitting abbots of the three major Gelugpa monasteries were added to this assembly to expand its representativeness.

The largest of the assemblies was called the Full Assembly (tib. Tsondu Gyendzom). It consisted of (1) all the abbots and ex-abbots of the three major Gelugpa monasteries, Ganden, Sera, and Drepung; (2) the eight heads of the Revenue and Ecclesiastic offices (tib. trungtsigye); (3) all the lay and monk officials present in Lhasa at the time; (4) representatives from a number of incarnations and other monasteries such as Reting, Kundeling, Tshomöling, Tshechöling, Ditru, Tashilhunpo, the Ganden Tri Rimpoche, and Sakya; (5) the captains (tib. rupön) and lieutenants (tib. gyagpön) of the army who were stationed in Lhasa; (6) the approximately twenty minor officials (tib. tshopa) who were in charge of collecting house taxes and arranging corvée taxes in Lhasa; and (7) about thirty clerks and craftsmen (tib. drungtog). It was convened only for extraordinary issues, such as the confirmation of the discovery of a new Dalai Lama.

The Full Assembly, furthermore, rarely remained in session for more than

---

12. Sikkim was a Tibetan kingdom that was part of India.

a day or two, normally adjourning in favor of the third main type of assembly, the Abbreviated Assembly (tib. Tsondu Hragdu). This assembly consisted of twenty to fifty members, usually the abbots and ex-abbots of the three major Gelugpa monasteries and representatives of the government ranks chosen by the Kashag and the Ecclesiastic Office, for example, two from the fourth rank and two from the fifth rank. The Abbreviated Assembly was the type of assembly usually convened. It used the same seals as the Full Assembly and operated in the same manner.

The Abbreviated and Full assembly meetings were presided over by the trungtsigye, one of whom opened the meeting by reading the topic to be discussed. Since votes were not taken, the final decision was generally reached when one of the trungtsigye summed up the feelings expressed by the Assembly members. If there were no dissenting views, a draft was written, and if there were no objections to the wording of this, the trungtsigye took it to the Kashag. If the Kashag disagreed or had questions, the Assembly discussed these and generally rewrote the draft. In the end, four seals were affixed to the Assembly's documents: one representing all the government officials and one for each of the three great Gelugpa monasteries.

None of these assemblies could initiate action, nor could they ultimately determine administrative action. Whether or not their advice was heeded and converted into policy depended on the Kashag and the ruler. The assemblies, in short, were consultative bodies that represented primarily the monks of Sera, Drepung, and Ganden and the mass of government officials. Nevertheless, as will be seen, the influence and power of these three monasteries in the assemblies gave them a kind of veto power over issues in Tibet.

THE ESTATE SYSTEM

Tibet's estate system was roughly analogous to the manorialism found in medieval England and western continental Europe in the sense that both were characterized by lands held by lords who were supported by a legally bound peasant population. In Tibet, estates (tib. shiga) could be held by aristocratic families, monasteries, incarnate lamas, or the government itself. Such estates were granted by the ruler (the Dalai Lama or regent), who had the right to confiscate such estates and occasionally did so, although in reality the estate holders held their land hereditarily across generations. The Tibetan ruler also had the right to grant new estates, as he did for the families of new dalai lamas, thus ennobling them and making them part of the lay aristocracy.

Tibet's estates combined the means of production—economically productive land—with a hereditarily bound peasant labor force. The estate's land was made up of two sections—the lord's land (in European manorialism called demesne land) and the peasant's land (called tenement or villein land). The lord's land typically constituted about one-half to three-fourths of the total arable land on the estate and was cultivated entirely by the estate's hereditarily bound peasants as a corvée obligation (tib. ula), that is, as a labor tax with no reimbursement. On most estates, peasant families had to provide their lord one worker *every* day and two or more at peak agricultural times.[13] If there was no agricultural work to be done, the lord could have his corvée workers do other things, such as collect firewood or spin wool. All of the yield from the demesne land went directly to the lord.

The remainder of the estate's land was allocated to the estate's hereditarily bound peasants and was the means by which they derived their subsistence. They did not own this land in the sense of having the right to sell it, but they normally held hereditary usufruct rights so long as their corvée obligations were fulfilled.

The defining feature of the Tibetan estate system was that the peasants did not have the right to relinquish their land and seek their fortunes elsewhere. They were not free; they belonged to their estate hereditarily, and if they ran away, the lord had the right to pursue and forcibly return them to the estate.[14]

The peasants' linkage to an estate and lord was transmitted hereditarily by parallel descent; that is, a man's sons became subjects of the estate/lord to which *he* belonged, and a woman's daughters became subjects of the estate/lord to which *she* belonged (if they were different). If an estate changed hands as sometimes happened, its bound peasants remained with the land and became the subjects of the new lord.

The authority of estates over their peasants was political as well as economic. Lords adjudicated disputes, meted out punishments, and controlled the movement of their peasants. The permanent subservience—bound status—of peasants to their estates/lords was manifest clearly when individuals sought to leave their estate permanently, for example, to marry a person from a different estate or to join a monastery. In both such cases, permission from the lord was required.

In marriage, the simplest method of securing such permission was via "person exchange" (tib. mije). This involved the replacement of the person marrying out with someone marrying in from the other estate. Each in-marrying spouse then became the subject of his or her spouse's estate and lord. This option was ideal for lords, since neither estate lost a subject—a free worker.

If there was no in-marrying spouse to serve as the exchange for the bride

13. Land was calculated in basic units called "tax land units" (tib. tregang). Households holding one such unit had to provide the customary one person per day for work on their estate. Households holding half such a unit had to send a worker every other day, and so forth.

14. This right was called "retrieving people from an area" (tib. mitsa yüügug or mitsa yüügong).

who left, occasionally a servant or landless peasant was sent by the receiving lord as a substitute. That person would then physically move to the other lord's estate and become part of it.

Another common practice for handling an out-marrying situation involved the bride or groom leasing his/her physical freedom from the estate by paying a fee in perpetuity to his/her lord that was called "human lease" (tib. mibo). In such cases, the human-lease holder remained the subject of his/her lord but was free to marry or live and work where he/she chose so long as the fees specified in the human-lease agreement were paid annually. Under this arrangement, even though a woman was living on the estate of her husband, she would still be a subject of her original lord, as would all of her female children (and their female children in perpetuity). Her male offspring, however, would belong to their father's lord.

Human lease status fees varied significantly in size and nature. The fee was typically money but sometimes also labor or goods, or even both. Lords kept detailed records of their subjects, including household births and deaths and annual human lease payments.[15] In essence, therefore, virtually the entire Tibetan peasantry was hereditarily tied to estates/lords either directly or through "human lease" status.

Monks and nuns, however, were partly an exception to this. Peasants seeking to become monks or nuns required the permission of their lord.[16] This was invariably granted, and so long as the person remained in the monastic order, he/she had no obligations to the estate/lord. Jurally, however, the lord retained residual ownership rights over the person such that if he/she was later expelled from or voluntarily left the monastic community, his/her previous subject status was reactivated.[17]

The authority of lords over their subjects also included the right to transfer them unilaterally to other individuals, both other lords and rich peasants, although this was not common in Tibet. For example, lords sometimes sent house servants (tib. yogpo; nangsen) or poor landless peasants as "tax appendages" (tib. trenön) to larger taxpaying peasant households that were short of labor.[18] Similarly, aristocrats often sent one of their maid-servants as part of the dowry of their daughter when she went as a bride to another family, even if this meant breaking up the maid-servant's family. Lords could also physically move their peasants to other locations in accordance with their own labor requirements.

An example of this occurred in the late 1940s on one of Drepung Mon-

---

15. An examination of this institution is found in Goldstein 1971b,d.

16. This was called chödrö, or literally, "religion release."

17. This residual right of lords was called gyatsa rangdag ("revert to original lay status and lord").

18. See Goldstein 1986 for a discussion of such peasant transfers.

astery's estates. Drepung required large quantities of firewood for the daily "mangja" tea it served its ten thousand monks and decided to use its corvée peasant labor force to provide this at no cost to the monastery. It did so by moving twelve young unmarried men from one of the monastery's estates to a noncontiguous mountain area, where they lived in tents and were responsible for cutting and transporting firewood for a ten-year period. These youths were drafted on the basis of their families' obligation to provide corvée labor to the lord, so they received no salary or food during the ten years the monastery kept them there, although their families did receive credit for providing one corvée laborer per day to the estate. The peasant households, of course, did not have the option to refuse to send their son for this task.[19]

The Tibetan political economy, therefore, not only provided elites with productive resources but critically guaranteed them a "captive" labor force. From the lords' vantage point, this was an extremely efficient system that required miniscule expenditures of their money or time. Lords did not have to compete for workers in a labor market, nor did they have to worry about the feeding, clothing, and housing of the workers as in a slavery system. The lord, whether an incarnate lama, a monastery, an aristocrat, or the government itself, needed only to supply a manager or steward to organize the hereditarily bound labor force on its estate. It is this feature of Tibet's traditional society that has led many, including myself, to classify it as a variant of European manorialism and to refer to these peasants as serfs.[20] I will use this term in the subsequent chapters rather than repeatedly using *bound peasants* or Tibetan terms such as *miser, treba, düjung,* and *nangsen.*

Despite this structural rigidity, rural life at the ground level was simultaneously characterized by considerable flexibility. Lords were concerned exclusively with their estate's economic output—with transforming their land into economically valuable products. Beyond extracting the full measure of corvée labor and fees from their serfs, they were unconcerned with exercising control over the other aspects of their lives. How a peasant spent his or her time outside corvée labor was of no concern to them. And since the tax obligations actually fell on the household rather than on its individuals, household members were free to do as they wished, including travel to other areas, for example, on a pilgrimage or for a visit to relatives, so long as the household fulfilled its corvée obligations. Being bound to an estate and lord, therefore, meant subjects were not free to relinquish their corvée labor obligations unilaterally by returning their land to the lord, but in another sense, peasant households retained substantial individual freedom of day-to-day ac-

19. Samdrup (interview, 1989, Lhasa, Tibet Autonomous Region, China). Samdrup was a monk working under the overall manager of Drepung (tib. jiso) and was personally in charge of this operation.

20. See Goldstein 1971b and 1986 for data on and analysis of this institution.

tion, so long as all the obligations owed to the estate were performed when the lord demanded it.

Finally, the fact that virtually the entire peasantry was hereditarily bound to an estate and lord did not mean that the peasantry was homogeneous in terms of standard of living and status. First, government-owned estates differed significantly from aristocratic- and monastic-owned estates in that they generally had only tenement land; that is, all of a government-owned estate's land was divided among the peasants, who in turn had heavy obligations not only in labor but also in kind. Second, significant differences existed within the general category of serf, which included (1) the subcategory "taxpayers," who held land from their estate and had heavy obligations, (2) the subcategory called düjung, who were tied to estates but did not possess taxable arable land and therefore had fewer obligations to the estate, and (3) the subcategory of hereditary servants of the lord, called nangsen. Consequently, being a serf—a bound peasant—did not necessarily mean poverty. Many taxpayer families were actually wealthy and had their own servants.

In summary, the Tibetan feudal politico-economic system was based on estates, each of which had hereditarily bound serfs who provided free labor and often other taxes in kind. The monasteries, incarnate lamas, aristocrats, and the government itself all depended on this system of relations.

THE MONASTIC SYSTEM AND MASS MONASTICISM

Monasticism is fundamental to both Mahayana and Theravada Buddhist philosophies and is found wherever Buddhism exists. However, in contrast to the systems of other Buddhist countries, the Tibetan monastic system supported a staggering number of monks before the Chinese takeover. Surveys showed that there were already 319,270 monks in 1733,[21] and estimates for the 1930s and '40s claim that between 10 and 20 percent of males were lifelong, celibate monks. By contrast, at about the same time in Thailand, another prominent Buddhist society, only about 1–2 percent of the total number of males were monks.[22]

In 1951 there were approximately twenty-five hundred monasteries in Tibet, the three largest around Lhasa (Drepung, Sera, and Ganden) alone containing twenty thousand monks. The state supported these religious institutions, having allocated over the centuries large amounts of arable and pasture land for their subsistence along with the serfs to work the land. In 1951, between 37 and 50 percent of the best, most fertile land in Tibet was held by monasteries and incarnate lamas (and another 25 percent, by lay aristocrats). The government held the rest. The government, in addition,

21. Dung dkar (Dunggar) 1983: 109.
22. Tambiah 1976: 266–67.

provided generous subsidies to important monasteries for prayer ceremonies and for religious rites, such as the annual Great Prayer Festival in
Lhasa. The vigor with which the state supported religious activities and institutions contrasted markedly with its lack of provision of even rudimentary
services to its lay population. Countrywide, for example, it operated no
schools, no medical public health system, no police force, no banks, and no
newspapers.

This is not surprising, because Tibet's monks, abbots, and incarnate lamas
believed that the real measure of Tibet's superiority and uniqueness as a nation was not individual monks' intellectual or spiritual virtuosity, one holy
monk meditating in the mountains for years on end, or the authorship of
one brilliant new religious text on Buddhist dialectics, but rather monastic
quantity, or what I refer to as mass monasticism. Tibetans felt that Tibet's
greatness lay in its development of a system wherein tens of thousands of
young boys were constantly being taken away from the mundane world of
inevitable suffering and thrust into a purer alternative culture—the organized community of celibate monks. In traditional Tibet, every monk, good
or bad, was considered superior to every layman, because by virtue of having renounced marriage and family, monks took the mandatory first step to
a higher level of spiritual development (although this journey would inevitably take many rebirths and many lifetimes).

However, to be successful generation after generation, mass monasticism
required powerful and effective mechanisms for recruiting large numbers
of monks, retaining them in lives of celibacy and supporting them materially. The Tibetan monastic system was unusual in the Buddhist world in that
the overwhelming majority of monks were placed in monasteries by their
parents when they were just children, usually between the ages of seven and
ten or eleven, without regard for their personality or wishes.

Parents made a son a monk for many reasons. Some, perhaps most, were
motivated by their deep religious belief that being a monk was a great privilege and honor. Others were motivated to fulfill a solemn vow previously
made to a deity when their son was very ill or because an older established
monk who was a close relative asked them to allow their son to join his monk
household. In still other cases, recruitment was simply the result of a corvée
tax obligation: in some areas, monastic serfs with three sons often had to
make one a monk.[23] Poor families, moreover, frequently made their sons
monks because it was a culturally valued way to reduce the number of mouths
they had to feed while also ensuring that their son would never have to experience the hardships and poverty of village life. And sometimes the decision to make a son a monk resulted from parents strategizing about how to

---

23. In Tibetan this is expressed as phusum pharma ("the middle of three sons").

organize their family's human resources; for example, the parents of a family with four sons might decide to make one or two a monk and marry the rest polyandrously, since four brothers sharing a wife was considered difficult, whereas two or three was considered ideal.

Parents sometimes broached the subject with a son but usually simply told him of their decision. For parents, whether or not the child wanted to become a monk was irrelevant. The child's wishes were also not important to the monastery, although its rules required that monks enter of their own volition and its officials formally asked the child whether he wanted to be a monk. This is seen clearly in the phenomenon of runaway young monks. When a new child monk ran away from the monastery, as many did, the situation did not result in his dismissal on the grounds that his actions were clear evidence that he did not want to be a monk. To the contrary, it typically resulted in monks from the monastery going out to search for the child and bringing him back forcibly. And even if the runaway child monk managed to reach his home, he typically received a beating from his father, who immediately returned him to the monastery. However, the many monks who related these incidents about themselves in interviews did not see this as abusive.[24] Rather, they laughed at how stupid they had been to want to give up being a monk. Tibetans traditionally felt that young boys could not comprehend the wonder of being a monk, and it was up to their elders to see to it that they had the right opportunities.

However, since monks had the right to leave the monastic order and had the ability to do so once they became young adults in their twenties, powerful mechanisms were needed to retain young monks who were unsure about living a lifetime of celibacy. The monastic system was structured to facilitate this. For one thing, while monks enjoyed high status, ex-monk were somewhat looked down on. For another, the great large monasteries generally did not place severe restrictions on comportment or demand educational achievement. Rather than diligently weeding out all novices who seemed unsuited for a rigorous life of prayer, study, and meditation, the Tibetan monastic system expelled monks only if they committed murder or engaged in heterosexual intercourse.[25] Novices or monks were not required to pass any exams in order to remain in the monastery (although exams were required to attain higher statuses within the monastic ranks). Monks who had no interest in studying or meditating were as welcome as the virtuoso scholar monks. Even totally illiterate monks were accommodated, because, like the

---

24. I interviewed several hundred Drepung monks in Tibet as part of an oral history of the Drepung project.

25. While Tibetan monasteries enforced heterosexual celibacy, homosexual intercourse was generally overlooked so long as no orifice was penetrated. Thus, if a monk engaged in homosexual intercourse, it was typically done between the thighs of the partner.

great monks, they too had made the critical break from the attachments of secular life. The monks of Drepung conveyed the great diversity in their monastery with the pithy saying "In the ocean there are fishes and frogs."

Furthermore, leaving the monastery posed economic problems. Monks lost whatever rights they might otherwise have had on their family farm when they entered the monastery, so monks who left the monastery had to find some new source of income. They also reverted to their original serf status when they left and were liable for service to their lord. By contrast, if they remained monks, their basic economic needs were met without their having to work too hard. All these factors made it both easier and more advantageous for monks to remain in the monastery.

As mentioned above, the monastic leadership espoused the belief that since the Tibetan state was first and foremost the supporter and patron of religion, the needs and interests of religion should take primacy. And since mass monasticism represented the greatness of Tibetan religion, the leadership believed that the political and economic system existed to facilitate this and that *they*, not the government, could best judge what was in the short- and long-term interests of religion. Thus, it was their religious right, even duty, to intervene whenever they felt the government was acting against the interests of religion. This, of course, brought them into the mainstream of political affairs and into potential conflict with the Dalai Lama or regent and the government. And while the Dalai Lama and the rest of the government agreed with mass monasticism in principle, disagreement on specific issues often occurred. For example, in 1946 when the government hired an English teacher and opened a modern school in Lhasa to better prepare Tibet to deal with the modern world, the monks in Lhasa perceived this as a threat to the dominance of religion and protested, threatening to kidnap students. The government quickly backed down and the school was disbanded after a few weeks.

The political interests of the monastic segment were conveyed not only by the threat of thousands of monks taking to the streets but also institutionally through the government's monk official segment and by the participation of the abbots and ex-abbots of the great Gelugpa monasteries around Lhasa in the Full and Abbreviated assemblies. Through their voice in these assemblies, the abbots exercised a kind of de facto veto on major government decisions. Consequently, as Tibet attempted to adapt to the rapid changes of the twentieth century, the power and prestige of religion and the interests of the great monasteries played a major role in limiting the options of the Tibetan government and thwarting change, because these monasteries consistently equated modernization with secularism and a decline in the unique greatness of Tibet—the efflorescence of mass monasticism and the system of manorial estates that supported it.

PART ONE

The Road to a Sino-Tibetan Agreement

Chapter 1

Chinese Perspectives

Radio Beijing

On 27 May 1951, the sixteen-year-old Dalai Lama was living in Yadong, a small town on the Sikkimese border, where he and his leading officials had moved a few months earlier so that they could easily cross into India if the People's Liberation Army (PLA) were to invade Central Tibet suddenly. A group of top officials headed by the Kashag ministers Ramba and Surkhang accompanied him, while the remainder of the government stayed in Lhasa, headed by two acting chief ministers (sitsab) and two acting Kashag ministers who were specially appointed to remain in Lhasa just before the Dalai Lama left.[1]

The Dalai Lama was relaxing in his quarters, listening to Beijing's Tibetan-language radio broadcast, when he suddenly heard the Xinhua News Agency announce that a "Seventeen-Point Agreement for the Peaceful Liberation of Tibet" had been signed on 23 May by the People's Republic of China (PRC) and the "local" government of Tibet.[2] Tibet, the announcer enthusiastically said, was returning to the "motherland." The Dalai Lama was further shocked when he heard the list of points, because they included items the Tibetan government had explicitly instructed its negotiators not to accept, for example, that the local government of Tibet would actively assist the People's Liberation Army in entering Tibet, and because they reported that something ominously called the Military-Administrative

---

1. The officials who went with the Dalai Lama to Yadong were known as the "traveling government" (tib. cheshung), and those who remained in Lhasa were known as the "home government" (tib. shishung).

2. "Local government" (tib. sane sishung) was the name the Chinese Communist Party used for the Tibetan government of the Dalai Lama in order to avoid referring to it verbally as an independent political entity.

Committee would be set up in Tibet. The Dalai Lama's reaction was instant and visceral.

> I could not believe my ears. I wanted to rush out and call everybody in, but I sat transfixed. The speaker described how over the last hundred years or more aggressive imperialist forces had penetrated into Tibet and "carried out all kinds of deceptions and provocations." It added that "under such conditions, the Tibetan nationality and people were plunged into the depths of enslavement and suffering." I felt physically ill as I listened to this unbelievable mixture of lies and fanciful clichés.[3]

MAO ZEDONG'S PERSPECTIVE

This Seventeen-Point Agreement dominates the history of the 1950s and even today continues to have an impact in Sino-Tibetan relations. It came about through a shrewd Chinese policy that was crafted and personally directed by Mao Zedong and applied a combined diplomatic and military pressure against an ill-prepared and weak Tibetan government.

No Chinese internal documents are available in which the issue of liberating Tibet was specifically discussed, but two fundamental reasons clearly appear to have informed the PRC's decision to do so. The most important was the issue of national honor. Over the past hundred years, China had become weak as a result of the corruptness of the previous Chinese regimes and the interference of Western and Japanese imperialists. The Chinese Communist Party was committed to expelling all the vestiges of foreign influence and power that had humbled China for so long and to reversing what it considered its national humiliation. A part of this restoration of national dignity was restoring full sovereignty (actual control) over all that had been China during the Qing and Guomindang periods.

Tibet was one of the most visible examples of China's decline from greatness. From Beijing's reading of history, British imperialism had played a major role in splitting off that vast territory from the Chinese state. The Chinese felt that the British invasion of Tibet in 1903–4 and Britain's subsequent support for Tibetan autonomy played a major factor not only in influencing the Tibetan government to desire independence from China but also in preventing China from reasserting its control over Tibet.[4] Restoring Tibet to the People's Republic of China, therefore, had deep nationalistic and symbolic value, especially since another vast minority territory, Outer Mongolia, had already been lost during the Guomindang period.[5] An exposition

---

3. Dalai Lama 1990: 63.
4. The history of this period is covered in detail in Goldstein 1989.
5. The history of this is discussed in Goldstein 1997: 40.

of some of these views occurred some years later in a 1954 internal party report on problems within the party in Tibet.

Tibet and the motherland have had a close, inseparable relationship since a long time ago. Tibet is one part of the territory of our great motherland. However, after the Republican Revolution (1911), Tibet's rulers, who were controlled and manipulated by imperialists, abandoned the motherland and went to rely on the imperialists. To a great extent, imperialists controlled Tibet, signed unfair treaties and gained great privilege in the spheres of politics, economics, and military. Also they took numerous pieces of territory from the border area of Tibet. Because of the development of the anti-imperialist struggle of the entire Chinese people and the existence of an anti-imperialist force within the Tibetan nationality (among them, including a part of the upper-class lamas and aristocrats), they failed to conquer the whole of Tibet. During this period of time, Tibet was semicolonial, and mainly took an independent attitude toward us.[6]

In addition to this set of powerful historical and nationalistic issues, and in a sense inextricably intertwined with them, was the geopolitical significance of Tibet for China's national security. Losing Mongolia was not a great security risk, because it was a loyal Communist satellite of the USSR. Tibet, on the other hand, was a religious theocracy in which the elite aristocracy was influenced by British customs and language. When the elite wanted to give their children a modern education, they sent them to British missionary schools in India. They clearly valued British education and the English language, not Chinese. Consequently, it was obvious that Western and Indian interests would play a major role in Tibet should it continue to be, as it then was, a de facto independent state. And more dangerous, it was also likely that the United States would come to play a significant role in Tibet, given the Cold War and U.S. support of Chiang Kai-shek against the Chinese Communist Party. The Tibetan government, in fact, had already sent a state mission to America in 1948, and the Tibet situation had received a great deal of publicity and sympathy in the United States as a result of the well-publicized visit of the famous journalist Lowell Thomas.[7] For China, the possibility that countries hostile to it could influence or secure bases in Tibet was an unacceptable risk, given that Tibet bordered on Xinjiang, Qinghai, Yunnan, and Sichuan provinces—and, of course, on India, Nepal, Sikkim, Bhutan, and Arunachal Pradesh. Mao alluded to this in conversations he had with the Panchen Lama and the Dalai Lama in 1954, saying to the Panchen, "Now that the Tibetans are cooperating with the Han, our national defense

6. Dui xizang gongzuo de zhongyao zhishi (wei chuban de shouji), n.d. All translations from foreign sources are my own unless otherwise noted.

7. For his account of the trip to Tibet, see Thomas 1959.

line is not the Upper Yangtse River but the Himalaya Mountains."[8] And to the Dalai Lama, "If you had chosen to cooperate with the imperialists and made the Upper Yangtse River as the border with us and made us your enemies, things would be very difficult for us."[9] Thus, for both of these reasons, Mao and the leaders of the Chinese Communist Party were convinced that Tibet had to be liberated and reintegrated into the Chinese state and that this was best done at once.

Mao was realistic in undertaking this and believed military force would be needed to some degree. He was, in fact, prepared to achieve Tibet's liberation entirely by force if China had to. However, he also believed that to do so could have serious international consequences for the legitimacy of the People's Republic of China's assertion of sovereignty over Tibet, as well as for the attitudes and loyalty of the Tibetans, who would become part of the new Chinese state. Because of this, he felt the ideal solution for China was to accomplish Tibet's liberation peacefully, in other words, with Tibet voluntarily accepting Chinese sovereignty and allowing the People's Liberation Army to enter Tibet uncontested. Military liberation was to be used as the last resort when "persuasion" failed or as a tactic to gain leverage with Tibet's leaders. From early 1950, therefore, work proceeded both on military preparations for an invasion and on diplomatic and public relations activities to persuade Tibetans to accept peaceful liberation (ch. heping jiefang).

Mao's emphasis on peaceful liberation stemmed from his realization that the situation in Tibet was fundamentally different from that encountered in the other areas the PLA had liberated and was potentially far more dangerous to the long-term interests of China. So while straight military liberation was the simplest and quickest approach, peaceful liberation was the safest and most advantageous strategy for China's long-term interests. There were several major reasons for this.

First, unlike in other large minority areas such as Xinjiang, where tens of thousands of ethnic (Han) Chinese resided, virtually no Han Chinese were living in Tibet, and almost no Tibetans spoke Chinese. Therefore, no obvious internal cohort was likely to provide overt or covert support.

Second, not only was Tibet homogeneously non-Han, but also it had been operating totally independently of China for at least the past thirty-five years and had secured an international identity of sorts. It had conducted relations with, among others, India, Britain, Nepal, and, most dangerously,

8. Zhonggong zhongyang wenxian yanjiu shi; zhonggong xizang zizhiqu weiyuanhui; zhongquo zangxue yanjiu zhongxin 2001: 117–22.
9. Dui xizang gongzuo de zhongyao zhishi (wei chuban de shouji), n.d.

China's Cold War enemy, the United States. Conquering Tibet militarily, therefore, could easily become an international issue. Mao himself alluded to this in a telegram he sent from Moscow to the Central Committee on 2 January 1950, saying, "Although the population of Tibet is not large, its international position is extremely important."[10]

Moreover, Tibet clearly wanted to continue to be independent from China. This was stated clearly in a letter sent by the Tibetan Foreign Affairs Bureau to Mao on 2 November 1949

To:

The Honourable Mr. Mautsetung,
Chairman of the Chinese Communist Govmt., Peiping

Tibet is a peculiar country where the Buddhist religion is widely flourishing and which is predestined to be ruled by the Living Buddha of Mercy or Chenresig [Avaloketisvara, i.e., the Dalai Lama].[11] As such, Tibet has from the earliest times up to now, been an Independent Country whose Political administration had never been taken over by an [sic] Foreign Country; and Tibet also defended her own territories from foreign invasions and always remained a religious nation.

In view of the fact that Chinghai [Qinghai] and Sinkiang [Xinjiang], etc. are situated on the borders of Tibet, we would like to have an assurance that no Chinese troops would cross the Tibetan frontier from the Sino-Tibetan border, or any military action. Therefore please issue strict orders to those Civil and Military Officers stationed on the Sino-Tibetan border in accordance with the above request, and kindly have an early reply so that we can be assured. As regards those Tibetan territories annexed as part of Chinese territories some years back, the Government of Tibet would desire to open negotiations after the settlement of the Chinese Civil War.[12]

Third, Tibet was a traditional religious theocracy in which Buddhist ideology and values dominated the population's worldview and the state's raison d'être. The authority and stature of incarnate lamas and monastic leaders

10. Zhonggong xizang zizhiqu dangshi ziliao zheng ji weiyuanhui 1990, entry for 10 January 1950.

11. The Dalai Lama is an incarnation of Avaloketisvara. He explained the predestination idea in English in an interview: "Of course, firstly the Tibetans believe, almost believe, that we Tibetans are a chosen people. . . . Like the Jewish people [the Tibetan people are] the chosen people of Chenrezi. I think that that is our general conception" (Dalai Lama, interview, 1994, Dharamsala, India). (Unlike most of the interviews, which were conducted in Tibetan or Chinese, the Dalai Lama sometimes spoke in English. In these cases, I have left the syntax uncorrected.)

12. British Foreign Office Records, FO371/76317, copy of letter from the Tibetan Foreign Affairs Bureau, Lhasa, to Mao Zedong, dated 2 November 1949.

were enormous, and the underlying theoretical framework of Tibetan Buddhism effectively inculcated political passivity among the lower classes and the poor. The masses were not at all clamoring for change. Tibetan Buddhism taught that life is characterized by inherent suffering, so the harsh lives of the poor and down-trodden did not seem unusual, especially since Tibetan Buddhism also taught that the cause of suffering is one's own bad behavior in past lives transmitted to the present via the laws of karma and reincarnation. The impoverished poor in Tibet, therefore, were suffering not because of the inherent oppression of their lords and the estate system but, rather, because of their own deficiencies in a past life or lives. The way to improve one's current circumstances, moreover, was to perform religiously meritorious actions so as to amass karma in this life and thereby secure a better rebirth in the next life; it was not to kill the lords and change the current sociopolitical system. Consequently, in Tibet, even the poorest strata—those who would normally constitute the core constituency of the Communists—were unlikely to be receptive to a call to rise up and struggle against the lay and religious landowners, at least initially.

Fourth, Tibet's physical geography and climatic circumstances posed serious logistical obstacles to a military invasion. The absence of *any* motor roads or airfields in Tibet meant everything would have to be brought in and resupplied by pack animals on crude and difficult dirt trails that stretched for hundreds and hundreds of miles over high mountain passes, which were often blocked by snow for long periods of time in winter.[13]

Tibet, moreover, had a regular army, half of which, about thirty-five hundred to four thousand, were deployed on the Chinese border. These troops were supported by several thousand local militia, and there was a system for calling up still more militia.[14] And although these troops were generally ineptly led and poorly trained, the Tibetan army in fact had some modern weapons—bren and sten guns, mortars, hand grenades, cannons, and machine guns.[15] Moreover, the Tibetan government had started increasing the size of its army and was in the process of creating a new regiment (the Trongdra Regiment) because of the Chinese threat.[16] Tibet's army, of course, was no match for the PLA in traditional combat, the latter having several mil-

---

13. The distance from Chamdo to Lhasa is roughly equivalent to the distance between New York City and Detroit (650 miles).

14. Goldstein 1989: 638–39; Lhalu, interview, 1992, Lhasa.

15. These had been bought from India in 1947 and 1949 (Goldstein 1989: 618–19). Khreng (Cheng Bing) (1981: 185) says that in 1958 the Tibetan army still had 490 sten and bren guns, 13 machine guns, and 48 cannons. However, it certainly had many more in 1950, before all the weapons with the main Tibetan army in Chamdo were captured in the war.

16. Lodrö Chönzin, interview, 1993, Lhasa.

lion battle-hardened and well-equipped troops, but as the letter to Mao in-sinuated, Tibet was saying it was prepared to fight the Chinese, and the Chi-nese side could not, given the terrain and climate, take for granted that the Tibetan army would not try to employ guerrilla tactics to cut the PLA's long and exposed supply lines, particularly if Tibet secured assistance from China's enemies, such as America. In turn, given Tibet's international rela-tions and the realities of the Cold War, there was a danger that extended guerrilla warfare might internationalize the conflict with regard to the po-litical status of Tibet.

Consequently, "peaceful liberation" for Tibet was the strategy Mao pur-sued. This type of liberation had already been achieved in Beijing and Xin-jiang, but Mao felt an even more peaceful approach was required in Tibet because of its international identity and its de facto independent status. So in Tibet, peaceful liberation was to be effected with a formal written agree-ment in which the Tibetan government/Dalai Lama accepted Tibet's return to the "motherland" under Chinese sovereignty. Chinese troops and officials would then enter Tibet peacefully with the consent and assistance of the Dalai Lama. The presence of such a formal document would, of course, preclude any international attempt to challenge China's assertion of sovereignty over Tibet and would also preclude the need to launch a full-scale military inva-sion. This was to be the first time that the Chinese Communist Party (CCP) incorporated a polity via a written agreement with the local government.[17]

However, since Tibet considered itself independent and did not want to be part of a communist Chinese state, achieving a peaceful liberation was not go-ing to be easy, and to overcome this difficulty Mao pragmatically articulated a dual "carrot and stick" strategy. China would, on the one hand, offer the Dalai Lama very attractive terms to return to the "motherland" and, on the other hand, simultaneously threaten a full-scale military invasion if he did not.

MILITARY PREPARATIONS

It is not certain how early formal discussions started in Beijing regarding the liberation of Tibet, but it is clear that Mao had Tibet on his mind as early as August 1949, when the Northwest Bureau's (ch. xibei ju) First Field Army (ch. diyi yezhanjun), under the command of Marshal Peng Dehuai, was mov-ing to liberate Qinghai and Gansu provinces.[18] Mao's concern with winning over Tibetans was conveyed in a 6 August 1949 telegram to Peng, warning

17. It was also the only time. Even the case of Hong Kong, four decades later, was not anal-ogous, because the CCP was dealing with the British.

18. At the Second Plenary Session of the Seventh Central Committee, held 5–13 March 1949, China was divided into five large regions, each based on a "field army" (ch. yezhanjun)

him to be sure his troops were very careful about how they treated Tibetans in these areas, because this would have implications later for China's success in Tibet. The telegram said: "The Panchen [Lama] is in Lanzhou now. When you attack Lanzhou, please pay close attention to the Panchen and the Tibetans in Gansu and Qinghai provinces. Protect and respect them so as to lay the groundwork for solving the Tibet problem."[19] Similarly, both of the Panchen Lama's 1 October 1949 telegrams to Mao and Peng Dehuai, congratulating them on the founding of the PRC, explicitly mention the liberation of Tibet. (They are cited in chapter 10.)[20]

At the same time, it was obvious to Mao that military planning for invading Tibet had to begin immediately, and on 23 November 1949, Mao contacted Marshal Peng about this. Mao's assessment of the military situation in China had led him to conclude that the Northwest Bureau's First Field Army seemed the best choice to take the lead, because military activities in the northwest had basically come to an end by October-November, whereas the military campaigns of the Second Field Army of the Southwest Bureau, under Liu Bocheng and Deng Xiaoping, had just started.[21] The southwest was the last major territory held by the Guomindang, the Nationalist Party of Chiang Kai-shek. The nationalists still had almost a million troops deployed there, so at that point it was not clear how much time Liu and Deng would need to defeat those forces. Consequently, Mao sent Peng Dehuai the following telegram, laying out his wish to liberate Tibet the following year (1950).

---

and each run by a bureau (ch. ju) representing the Central Committee of the Chinese Communist Party. Each also had a military-administrative committee (tib. magsi uyön lhengang; ch. junzheng weiyuanhui), all of which functioned as transitional civil governments operated by the military until they could be replaced by people's governments. The Northwest Bureau was responsible for Qinghai, Xinjiang, Shaanxi, and Gansu. The Southwest Bureau (ch. xinan ju), based on the Second Field Army (ch. dier yezhanjun), was responsible for Yunnan, Guizhou, Sichuan, Xikang, and Tibet. By 1954, all these military-administrative committees had been replaced by people's governments.

19. Zhonggong zhongyang wenxian yanjiu shi; zhonggong xizang zizhiqu weiyuanhui; zhongguo zangxue yanjiu zhongxin 2001: 1.

20. British Foreign Office Records, FO371/83325, enclosure in Nanjing dispatch to the British Foreign Office, dated 27 December 1949. The enclosure was taken from the *New China Daily News*, Nanking, 25 November 1949.

21. Liu Bocheng and Deng Xiaoping were the leaders of the Second Field Army and the Southwest Bureau. Liu Bocheng, fifty-seven in 1949, was commander of the Second Field Army. He also served as second secretary of the Southwest Bureau, chairman of the Southwest Military-Administrative Committee, and vice-chairman of the Central Military Commission. Deng Xiaoping, forty-five years old at this time, was the first secretary of the Southwest Bureau, vice-chairman of the Southwest Military-Administrative Committee, and political commissar of the Southwest Military command and Second Field Army.

Comrade Peng Dehuai. Please pass [this on to] He [Long], Xi [Zhongxun], and Liu [Bocheng]:[22]

. . . (2) (Peng) Please raise and discuss the question of managing Tibet at a meeting of the Northwest Bureau. . . . Try to solve the problem of Tibet by the fall or winter of next year [1950]. On the basis of the current situation, we should let the Northwest Bureau take the major responsibility for this task. The Southwest Bureau should take secondary responsibility for Tibet.

[The reasons for this are that] The war in the northwest finished earlier than that in the southwest, and some people say that the road from Qinghai to Tibet is flat and easy. In addition, the Panchen and his group are in Qinghai. We will not be able to settle the Tibet issue without sending troops (ch. jiejüe xizang wenti, bu chubing shi bu keneng de). [However] The northwest route is not the only way to send our troops. There is another route in the southwest. So after the Southwest Bureau finishes its tasks in Sichuan and Kham [of liberating them], they should start to manage things in Tibet. We probably will need three armies to attack (ch. da) Tibet.

It is hard to decide on the distribution of tasks and the nomination of commanders. However, the Northwest Bureau should make plans to train Tibetan cadres and also make preparations. What is your opinion? Please let me know.[23]

This led the Northwest Bureau to conduct a detailed investigation of the feasibility of taking the lead in militarily liberating Tibet. Peng asked the head of his Liaison Office, Fan Ming, to research this, and after intensive examination of archival materials (from the Qing and Guomindang periods) as well as interviews with traders from Qinghai who had actually made the trip to Tibet, Fan Ming reported twenty days later that logistically it would be extremely difficult and time consuming to move militarily from Qinghai to Lhasa. Although Peng Dehuai was prepared to accept the task if Mao insisted, his reply to Mao and the Central Committee (sent on 30 December 1949) was based on and reflected Fan Ming's negative conclusions, saying, in part:

Generally speaking, it is very difficult to enter Tibet from Qinghai and Xinjiang. The difficulties are very hard to overcome. . . . If the task of entering Tibet is given to the northwest, we must gather soldiers and grain supplies in Yutian and Yushu [Jyekundo] and build roads; the preparation work may take two years. . . . If the task of entering Tibet is given to the southwest military region, we can try to send some of the Tibetans from the [Northwest Bureau's] training classes to enter Tibet with troops of the Second Field Army.[24]

---

22. He Long was the second commander in the Second Field Army and the third secretary of the Southwest Bureau. Xi Zhongxun was vice chairman of the Northwest Bureau.

23. As cited in Ji 1993a: 4.

24. As cited in Ji 1993a: 7.

By this time, Mao was in Moscow trying to secure a defense treaty with the USSR, so he received Peng's reply there. Mao thought about this rather negative answer for two days and then took Peng Dehuai's advice. At 4 A.M. on 2 January 1950, he sent the following detailed telegram to the Central Committee, giving the Southwest Bureau the task of liberating Tibet. The Northwest Bureau would now play a secondary, supporting role.

[To] The Central Committee and Comrade Peng Dehuai:

Please pass this on to Comrades [Deng] Xiaoping, [Liu] Bocheng, and [He] Long

(1) I have received the telegram of 30 December from Comrade Dehuai regarding the situation in Tibet and the routes leading into Tibet. The Central Committee should pass this telegram to Comrades Liu, Deng, and He.

(2) The population of Tibet is not big, but the position of Tibet in the international arena is very important. We must liberate Tibet and change it into a Tibetan people's democracy. There are great difficulties in sending troops into Tibet from Qinghai and Xinjiang, so the task of sending troops into Tibet and of later managing Tibet should be given to the Southwest Bureau.

(3) There are only four months each year, from May to September, when roads to Tibet are passable. During the other eight months, heavy snow makes roads impassable. If that is the case, I am afraid that the time to enter Tibet from Kham (ch. Xikang) is probably the same.[25] [Thus] If we cannot send troops to Tibet between mid-April and mid-September this year [1950], we will have to postpone it until next year. My point is that if there are no unconquerable difficulties, we should try to start marching into Tibet this coming April and liberate Tibet before this October. Thus, I suggest:

(a) Comrades Lui, Deng, and He should please convene a meeting soon (e.g., mid-January) to decide which troops should be sent to Tibet and which cadre will be responsible for the leadership in managing Tibet. Start making such arrangements immediately.

(b) Immediately occupy Tachienlu [in Xikang Province], and make it a base for planning and preparing to enter Tibet.

(c) From now on, build a road for trucks or carts that goes from Kham to Tibet as preparation for entering Tibet this April.

(d) Recruit Tibetans and train cadres.

(e) I heard that there are only six thousand officers and soldiers in the Tibetan Army and that they are scattered, so it seems that we do not

---

25. Xikang was the Chinese province that consisted primarily of the ethnic Tibetan Khamba areas east of the Upper Yangtse River that were not under the control of the Dalai Lama's government. It was called Kham in Tibetan, although the name Kham also included the Khamba areas west of the Yangtse River. The province was officially created in 1938 and was dissolved and merged into Sichuan Province in 1955. Its initial capital was Tartsedo (also known as Kangding or Tachienlu), but this shifted to Ya'an in the early 1950s.

need three army corps (ch. jun) as I suggested in my last telegram. We need only one army corps or four divisions with a total of about forty thousand troops. This will be enough. They will need special political training and superb arms.

(f) We can make it a rule that troops in Tibet will be changed every three years in order to create high morale among them.

(4) Sending troops into Tibet and managing Tibet are glorious tasks for our Party but they are hard tasks. The southwest has just been liberated, and our comrades in the Southwest Bureau are extremely busy. Now there is the additional task of liberating Tibet for you. I make the above suggestions, because this is an important task, and it has time limitations. The Southwest Bureau should reply to me by telegram, indicating whether my suggestions can be applied in practice.

Mao Zedong

4 A.M., 2 January, from a distance [from Moscow][26]

The Southwest Bureau responded on 7 January, agreeing to take the main responsibility for Tibet. It designated the Eighteenth Army Corps (ch. shiba jun) to take the lead (that telegram is not available). On 10 January 1950, Mao sent them the following telegram in reply:

[To] The Central Committee. Please pass this on to Lui, Deng, He, and the Northwest Bureau:

(1) I completely agree with Lui and Deng's plan to march into Tibet as conveyed in their telegram of 7 January. Great Britain, India, and Pakistan have all recognized us [the People's Republic of China]. This is favorable to our action of advancing into Tibet.

(2) According to Comrade Peng Dehuai's information, the four months during which it is possible to march into Tibet start from mid-May (I made a mistake and [previously] wrote three months). If Liu and Deng push Zhang Guohua and the Eighteenth Army Corps, we have the time to do it this year.

(3) To manage Tibet, we need to establish a party leadership committee (ch. dang de lingdao ji guan) there.[27] As to what name it should have and the nomination of its members, the Southwest Bureau should make a plan and send a telegram to the Central Committee for approval. This committee should be set up immediately and should do all the planning and design of the practical work plans. It should then send the plans to the Southwest Bureau for approval. The Southwest Bureau should examine the committee's work once or twice a month. The first steps of the new office should be to complete investigative work [on Tibet], train cadres and troops, build roads, and march the

26. As cited in Ji 1993a: 3.

27. This, as we shall see, later became the Tibet Work Committee (ch. xizang gongwei; tib. phö leydön uyön lhengang), which was the leading Chinese administrative office in Tibet.

troops to the border between Kham and Tibet. This should be done within three and a half months. Some of the work of training cadres and troops and road construction should be completed after our occupation of the border areas of Kham and Tibet. In order to foster internal divisions among the people of Kham, please make sure to occupy the border area of Kham and Tibet by mid-May.

(4) As to cooperation from the Northwest Bureau, the Southwest and Northwest bureaus should discuss things among yourselves when specific issues arise. The Northwest Bureau should please make plans and cooperate with the Southwest whenever possible, and please ask the offices below you to do the same.[28]

While still in Moscow twelve days later, on 22 January 1950, at the end of a discussion between Mao and Stalin, Mao casually mentioned his plan to liberate Tibet when Stalin asked him if he had anything else to talk about. Mao thanked Stalin for sending an air regiment to China and then asked that it be allowed "to stay a little longer, so that it could help transport provisions to Liu Bocheng's troops, currently preparing for an attack on Tibet." Stalin replied, "It's good that you are preparing to attack. The Tibetans need to be subdued." He said he would discuss the air unit request with his military personnel and get back to Mao.[29]

Meanwhile, in Sichuan, Liu Bocheng had already set about organizing a strike force but, along the way, had to overcome a surprising series of problems with his troops. The Second Field Army's Sixty-second Army Corps should have been the unit chosen to go to Tibet, since it was based in Ya'an, in Xikang; that is, it was situated closest to Tibet, and this proximity would have facilitated the transport of men and materials.[30] However, the Sixty-second Army was part of the Eighteenth Large Army (ch. bingtuan),[31] under the command of He Long, and it had become part of the Second Field Army only a short time before. Because of this, Liu Bocheng worried that if he selected it to go to Tibet, He Long might think that Liu was giving a very difficult and unwanted task to these "newcomers." Liu was reluctant to do this. The next logical unit to send was his own Tenth Army Corps. It had the strongest fighting capacity in the entire Second Field Army, but here too there was a problem: its commander, Du Yide, was then in bad health. So Liu discussed this with Deng Xiaoping, the political commissar of the Sec-

28. As cited in Ji 1993a: 11–12.

29. "Record of Conversation between Comrade I. V. Stalin and Chairman of the Central People's Government of the People's Republic of China Mao Zedong, January 22, 1950," cited in Cold War International History Project 1995–96: 9.

30. Ji 1993a: 8.

31. A bingtuan in the PLA military structure of that time was a unit larger than an army corps and smaller than a field army.

ond Field Army, and they both agreed that it would be best to replace Du with a young commander called Zhang Guohua.[32]

Zhang Guohua was born in Jiangxi Province in 1914 and had joined the guerrilla forces in March 1929, when he was only fifteen years old. He joined the Communist Party two years later and became part of the Fourth Red Army, participating in the Long March. In November 1946, he became commander of the Yu Wansu Region, which had the hardest and toughest conditions among all the war zones in China. It was an isolated guerrilla region and did not have a rear area for supplies among other problems. When this region was included in the jurisdiction of the Second Field Army, Zhang became commander of the Eighteenth Army Corps and had a successful career in the war. His extensive experience working within an enemy-occupied region and opening up new regions led Liu and Deng to decide he was the best commander to replace Du Yide and head the Tenth Army Corps.

Liu Bocheng, therefore, sent Zhang a telegram on 7 January 1950, ordering him to come to Chongqing immediately. However, no sooner had Liu sent the order than he started worrying if replacing Du Yide would have a negative impact on the morale of the Tenth Army Corps and make it difficult for Zhang Guohua to lead it effectively. Consequently, he and Deng Xiaoping decided it was best not to send the Tenth Army Corps with a new commander but, rather, to allow Zhang to choose three of the best divisions (ch. sri) within the Second Field Army to form a new army corps that he would head. Zhang, however, did not like the thought of leading new officers and troops in the difficult task of liberating Tibet so asked to be allowed instead to take his own Eighteenth Army Corps, which had been with him for years. Although its fighting capacity was not as good as that of the Tenth Army Corps, he argued that since Liu and Deng did not expect major battles in Tibet, the Eighteenth Army Corps's experience in functioning in new regions would be particularly helpful. They agreed.[33]

The decision to send the Eighteenth Army Corps, however, did not sit well with that army's rank and file and noncommissioned officers. In fact, a minirebellion occurred. After the campaign for Chengdu had been won (on 27 December 1949), the troops had been promised that they would be permanently stationed in Luzhou, a beautiful part of southern Sichuan Province, so the news that they were going to Tibet was an unpleasant surprise. The amazing story of what happened after this is detailed in Ji Youquan's *Bai xue* (White Snow), a book based on interviews with the soldiers involved as well as on otherwise unavailable primary documents. It was briefly published in China but was then banned and taken off the shelves.

32. Ji 1993a: 8.
33. Ji 1993a: 9–10.

All the officers and soldiers were very happy indeed [about being stationed in Luzhou]. The soldiers said, "We in the Eighteenth Army Corps have experienced the worst hardships and the leaders of the [Second] Field Army know this. So this time they are taking good care of us." Veteran soldiers were thinking of getting married and settling down.

According to Chen Jingpo, then the director of the Eighteenth Army Corps's Department of Enemy Work . . . , "When we moved into the rich 'heaven's province' of Sichuan, our task was to take over southern Sichuan. The army commander, Zhang Guohua, was given the position of the director of southern Sichuan administrative office. . . . I was the general secretary. Most of the directors of our political departments were named head of various bureaus, and some of our political commissars became county mayors or party secretaries. After years of extreme hardship, all the troops were thinking of having a peaceful life. Nothing could be better for the officers and soldiers than to settle down in the rich and beautiful Luzhou area.

"[Before that] While we were marching south, there were rumors that we would end up settling in Guizhou. Most of our officers and soldiers had never been to Guizhou, but we all knew that it was a very poor place and all had heard that 'the sky doesn't have three sunny days [in a row], the land doesn't have three li of flat ground, and people don't have three liang of silver.' Some rumors even said that mountain folks in Guizhou had tails. From such a place, we were suddenly ordered to Sichuan, a province rich like heaven, so who would not be happy? Everyone was conjuring up beautiful images of building a new socialist China there." The whole Eighteenth Army Corps was soaked in this happy atmosphere. Nobody dreamed that a hard task [such as Tibet] would be given to them. . . .

Wei Ke recalled, "We of the [Eighteenth Army Corps's] Fifty-second Division . . . were in good spirits. We had never felt so delighted. It was like everyone was embracing a beautiful wish that would soon be carried out. . . . On the morning of the 8th, after we finished breakfast and were preparing to start, we suddenly received an order that the troops should wait for further orders. At first, we thought we were simply being given a day's rest, but later on there were rumors that . . . we would be getting a new mission. People asked what kind of task it would be and why it was so urgent. Why couldn't we wait till we got to Yibin and take a break? Why did we have to stop on the way? We were all guessing and speculating. Soon we heard that an emergency telegram had been sent from the Field Army's headquarters ordering our division's commander to accompany the Eighteenth Army's commander, Zhang Guohua, and go by boat . . . to Chongqing to accept a new mission." . . .

Wu Zhong, the commander of the Fifty-second Division . . . , recalled, "It came so suddenly that we were not in the least prepared. So all sorts of guesses began circulating—if the commanders of both the army corps and the division were going to Chongqing to accept a new mission, it must be an unusual task. What could it be? To guard the city of Chongqing? It did not look like it. We had just left Chongqing. Besides, that would not need one entire army corps. Maybe we were going to be sent to take over Xikang Province. But that was also unlikely, as we had heard that this task had already been given to the Eighteenth Large Army, which had moved down from the northwest.

"Then some people thought about the New Year's Day editorial of Xinhua News Agency, which they had just finished studying. The editorial talked about things to be done during 1950, specifically 'liberating Taiwan, Tibet, and Hainan Island to complete the unification of the whole of China.' It was obvious that the tasks of liberating Taiwan and Hainan Island belonged to the Third and Fourth field armies, but what about liberating Tibet? Could it be ours? The more they analyzed, the more people believed that this could be right. Some officers rushed to me and asked, 'Commander, can you leak some news to us? It is better to let us know earlier so that we don't feel like we are hanging in the air.'"

When the commanders returned from Chongqing and announced that the task of marching into Tibet had been given to the Eighteenth Army Corps, chaos erupted. Wu Zhong recalled, "The response was very strong. It was truly a sharp turn. Many issues had yet to be resolved, for example, the practical issue of [the men] getting married and starting families. During all the years we were fighting, we had no time to consider such issues and problems, but now we had defeated Chiang Kai-shek, and the hope of solving such problems was close at hand. Marching into Tibet would make such things totally out of the question. Even aside from these other things, it was not easy to send a letter home from Tibet. Though there were not going to be tough battles in Tibet, everything would be 'tough.' It was really difficult to straighten things out in the soldiers' minds. Although things were very difficult when the troops were marching into the Dabie Mountains, such chaos never occurred." . . .

[Consequently] It was very difficult for the officers to persuade the soldiers about this. Former deputy chief of staff of the Tibetan Military Region, Wu Chen recalled, "The commander of the 160th Regiment . . . had guaranteed his soldiers that they could look for lovers if they wanted to, and they could start to prepare for their weddings if they so desired. He said that he had never imagined that he and his soldiers could end up settling down and enjoying the rest of their lives in the rich province of Sichuan. This was called 'bitterness first, and sweetness afterward' (ch. xianku houtian). If you have to move again, you soldiers can curse me (he said). He never imagined that in another few days the order to march into Tibet would be sent out. [After the order came] He hit his own head and said fuck it. I will never mobilize the troops."

According to Liu Zhenguo, the former director of the political department of the Tibetan Military Region, "From information reported by all our troops, many people felt the order to march to Tibet came too suddenly. Particularly resistant to the new order were those who were ready to enjoy life in cities after the victories and those who already thought weapons could be left in warehouses and horses could be let loose in the mountains. They complained, asking why the hardest task was given to us. They even said that they were knocked down from the place of heaven to hell. Some people started to manifest their complaints by sleeping, running to the hospital for small ailments. . . . In a word, they were afraid to go to Tibet."

The number of sick people increased day by day, and the number of those who were "too sick to get out of bed" increased day by day too. It was mealtime, but nobody came to eat. Company commanders and political instructors got worried and ordered company quartermasters to make good meals. The standard of meals was suddenly raised. Tofu and pork were [served] in container after container. Five-course meals plus soup [were served], and still nobody wanted to eat. The military camps were filled with complaints. Company commanders could not order platoon leaders, platoon leaders could not order squad leaders, and soldiers did not listen to squad leaders.

For example, a company commander once thought killing a pig would help improve the situation so one morning ordered a platoon leader to send four soldiers to kill a pig. Later that afternoon, however, no one had come with the pig, so the company commander summoned the platoon leader and said, "Are you still a platoon leader? You can't even command four soldiers." The platoon leader responded, saying, "I couldn't get them to move." The company commander then said, "You cannot even do that? What kind of a platoon leader are you? Why don't you just quit?" The platoon leader said, "That is exactly what I am thinking. If you think you can get these soldiers to obey, try it yourself." The commander said, "If I get them here, you will be placed in confinement for three days. [Then he asked,] Which ones did you order to come to me?" The commander got the names, rushed to the platoon, and found that the soldiers who had been asked to do the job were all lying in bed with quilts over their heads. None paid any attention to him. The company commander got angry and threatened he'd shoot them right away. The soldiers then sat up and roared in one voice, "Who did you say you would like to shoot?" The commander was stunned and said, "OK, OK, you enjoy your sleep." Then he and his platoon leader killed the pig themselves to make a meal for the soldiers, but while he was doing this he kept muttering, "Rebels, rebels."

Some of the soldiers called going to Tibet "being buried." [In Chinese, *bury* is *xia zang,* and *Tibet* is *Xi zang.*] They said that they did not lose their lives when they fought the Japanese and the Guomindang, but this time they would lose their lives in Tibet. It would be the end for them. Some started crying at hearing the term *being buried.*

Following the complaints, unthinkable things occurred in the Eighteenth Army Corps, which had heretofore been known as the iron troop when it had been fighting the Japanese and the Guomindang. . . . But this time, there were deserters, and more and more of them. In some squads, only squad leaders and deputy squad leaders were left; everyone else had disappeared. Company commanders and political commissars panicked and were afraid to sleep at night. They took turns watching the soldiers. Battalion commanders got upset, and regimental commanders got upset too. There were fewer and fewer soldiers they could command. If there was a battle, how could they fight without soldiers? They called company headquarters all the time, and every evening they asked each company for the number of deserters. . . .

The increase in the number of deserters made the leaders of the Eighteenth Army Corps upset. Its commander, Zhang Guohua, got angry and banged the table saying, "These deserters are terrible. Why are they so bad? Why? Catch all of them for me!"

So action was taken in each troop. A strong force made up of Communist Party members, Communist League members, and activists was organized to catch deserters. They were called "deserter catchers," and most of the deserters were caught. . . . Their shirts were first taken off, and then they were completely tied up by coir ropes. It was unbearable to be tied up for a long time, so they cried and begged company commanders for a pardon. The officers would roll up their sleeves, pick up a whip, raise their voices, and roar, "Let me see if you are still running away." When they got really angry, they would whip the deserters hard on their arms and behinds, which were already bruised and swollen. Afterward, the deserters had to listen to criticism and education, make self-criticisms, and write confessions. Only then would they be counted as having regretted their mistakes and returned to the ranks of revolutionary troops. They would [be expected to] make achievements in wars to make up for their mistakes and become new persons.

Not only were there deserters among the soldiers, but even among officers there were requests not to go to Tibet. Lui Jieting, political commissar of the artillery battalion of the Eighteenth Army Corps, for example, . . . informed Zhang Guohua and Tan Guansan (the Eighteenth Army Corps's political commissar) that he was not in good health and did not want to go to Tibet. Zhang got so angry when he heard this that he bit his lower lip, which started bleeding. He said over and over, "This Lui Jieting is very bad. I did not know that he could be this bad. How could he be so bad?" Tan Guansan also was furious. He banged the table and started yelling, "He is not going to Tibet? How can he decide that? Tie him up and bring him to me. So he doesn't want to go. I will tie him up and take him to Lhasa. If he cannot walk, I will tie him to the tail of my horse and drag him, even dead, even in small pieces, to Lhasa." Zhang and Tan were really tough this time. Lui . . . was tied up and brought back. . . .

The Eighteenth Army Corps then started a large rectification campaign. . . . From 27 to 30 January (1950), they first held a meeting of the twenty-four party officials above the division level. These leaders committed themselves to accomplishing the sacred historical task of marching to Tibet to raise the five-star red flag on top of the Himalaya Mountains, whatever price they had to pay. . . .

Afterward, the Eighteenth Army Corps held a mobilization meeting in each division called—"Marching into Tibet, the border area of our country." The leaders of the army attended these meetings. From 5 to 10 February, Zhang Guohua attended the mobilization meeting of the Fifty-second Division. . . . In Zhang's mind, the Fifty-second Division would be the major force in the march to Tibet. If they could not do a good job with the ideological work in this division, it could have a very large negative impact for the entire army corps. So not only did Zhang attend, but he made a [two-hour] speech himself. . . . Again on 9 February, Zhang made another down-to-earth speech . . . saying, "Regarding personal questions, there is an old saying that 'since ancient times beautiful women love heroes.' We will carry out the great historical task of liberating Tibet, and we can say that all of you are heroes. If we study hard, work hard, and happily accomplish the task, it will not be a problem for you to find a wife. Girls from cities or rural areas will fall in love with you. Some people asked if they could consider marrying Tibetan girls. Everyone knows that more than one thousand years ago during the Tang dynasty, Princess Wengcheng married the Tibetan king Songtsen Gambo and [later] Princess Jincheng married the Tibetan king Tride Tsugtsen. When we get to Tibet, you can consider marrying Tibetan girls. Tibetan girls are very hard working and kind. They are pretty too.

"In the past, because of wartime restrictions, we had strict regulations for marriage. In one or two years, when we set up our salary system in the country, we will loosen up our regulations. We will allow officers' wives to live in our military camps, and as the voluntary system is carried out, soldiers can solve their problem of marriage too. We must see that our march to Tibet is different from the Long March made by the Red Army. At that time, we were making a strategic move. Chiang Kai-shek sent his troops to block us at our front and attack us at the rear. Their planes were following us and bombing us. This time, we have the support from people in the entire country. In addition, we have the support and help of people in the USSR. Our conditions are hundreds of times better than those during the Long March. They are better than the conditions during the anti-Japanese war and the Liberation War. Our weapons and supplies will be better than at any time since the founding of our army. We know that those comrades who are a little older do not want to go. They think they already have two or three of those glorious medals, and they want to sleep on their past glories. This is wrong. Officers should take a leading role, and everyone has to truly accept the task. We will go to Tibet happily." The two speeches of Zhang were printed and distributed to the whole army.[34]

Gradually, the leaders of the Eighteenth Army Corps regained control and created enthusiasm among the troops slated to go to Tibet. Ji's *Bai xue* explains,

> There was excitement again in the Eighteenth Army Corps. . . . everybody asked to go to Tibet. Letters expressing determination and letters written in blood [to show their determination] flew like snowflakes into the hands of commanders of companies, battalions, and regiments. Even those who had deserted asked the leaders to let them go to Tibet. Those who were not in good health also asked to go. . . . The Eighteenth Army Corps had now made the sharp turn from "settling down in southern Sichuan."[35]

China's military preparations also included a cavalry unit from the Northwest Bureau, which, although numerically small, ultimately played a major role in the Chamdo campaign. As we shall see, throughout the 1950s, the ideas of the Northwest Bureau troops about how to deal with Tibet were very

---

34. Ji 1993a: 18–25.
35. Ji 1993a: 26.

different from those of the Southwest Bureau, and conflict between the two units' leaders plagued the CCP in Tibet throughout that decade. This will be discussed in detail in later chapters.

PUBLIC RELATIONS (UNITED FRONT) WORK

During the spring and summer of 1950, while military preparations were underway, China tried to persuade the Dalai Lama to send representatives to Beijing to negotiate.[36] Prominent lamas and leaders from the already incorporated ethnic Tibetan areas outside Tibet (in Xikang and Qinghai provinces, i.e., in Kham and Amdo) were sent to try to assure Lhasa that Tibet's religion and monasteries would not be harmed.

Phünwang, a Tibetan cadre in the Southwest Bureau, recalled,

> We were trying to do two things at once. On the one hand, we were organizing for a military attack. On the other, we were doing what we could to persuade the Tibetan government to accept peaceful liberation. We sent religious leaders like Geda Trulku to Chamdo to talk with Lhalu, the governor general. . . . And I went to see Panda Tobgye and persuaded his brother, Raga, also to go to Chamdo and try to influence Lhalu.[37]

Furthermore, a ten-point document laying out terms for what a peaceful liberation agreement might look like was distributed. This document, initially drafted by the Southwest Bureau, is important because it embodies the core of Mao's thinking on how to incorporate Tibet—what we can think of as Mao's "gradualist" strategy. It contained the following points:

1. The Tibetan people will unite and drive the invading British and American imperialists out of Tibet. The Tibetan people will return to the big family of the motherland.

2. Tibet will become an ethnic autonomous region.

3. The existing political system in Tibet will stay, and there will be no changes in this area. The power and prestige of the Dalai Lama will remain the same, and officials at various levels will remain in their positions.

4. Religious freedom will be implemented, monasteries will be protected, and the religious beliefs and customs of Tibetans will be respected.

5. The existing Tibetan military system will not change. The Tibetan armed forces will become part of the national armed forces of the PRC.

---

36. "United Front work" refers to the Chinese Communist Party's strategy of building a broad consensus among non–party members and minorities for party-supported programs and goals. The party's United Front Work Department is responsible for this.

37. Quoted in Goldstein, Sherap, and Siebenschuh 2004: 138–39.

6. The Tibetan oral and written language will be developed, as will a school system.

7. Agriculture, animal husbandry, industry, and commerce will be developed in Tibet. The living standard of the Tibetan people will be improved.

8. Various reform issues in Tibet will be fully decided according to the will of the Tibetan people. The Tibetan people and leaders will discuss and make decisions regarding reforms.

9. Officials who were pro-British and American imperialists and pro-Guomindang may remain in their positions if they break their relationship with the imperialists and the Guomindang.

10. The PLA shall station troops in Tibet for the purpose of national defense. The PLA shall observe the above policies. The Central People's Government shall be responsible for the expenses of the PLA in Tibet. The PLA shall purchase/sell fairly in Tibet.[38]

Mao's gradualist strategy, therefore, gave primacy to pragmatism over ideology and had two primary goals. The immediate goal was to induce the Dalai Lama to accept an agreement that would allow for the peaceful liberation of Tibet. To facilitate this, as the Ten-Point document outlined, Tibet could continue to operate much as in the past, as an autonomous region, at least for some unspecified period of time. Despite the ideological foundation of the Chinese Communist Party, according to this document, the theocratic political system headed by the Dalai Lama would continue to operate without changes. Similarly, there would be no attempt to impose reforms, for example, to end the exploitive feudal system via socialist land reforms. Reforms of all kinds would happen only with the agreement of the Dalai Lama's government and the Tibetan people. And there would be religious freedom, including the protection of monasteries. This was the carrot that Mao dangled.

Mao's longer-term goal was to incorporate Tibet in a way that would generate cooperation and friendship. In today's language, it sought to win over Tibetans to willingly become loyal citizens of the new multiethnic China. However, given the attitudes and realities of 1950 Tibet, the focus was to be on winning over the aristocratic and religious elites, especially the Dalai Lama. Winning these elites over, however, would take time and require much more than just holding meetings and giving propaganda speeches; it would require correct behavior on the part of the PLA and the slow and gradual development of a cooperative relationship between Tibetans and the "new Chinese"

---

38. Zhonggong zhongyang wenxian yanjiu shi; zhonggong xizang zizhiqu weiyuanhui; zhongquo zangxue yanjiu zhongxin 2001: 20–21 fn. 2. This was officially approved by the Central Committee on 27 May 1950.

Figure 1. Eighteenth Army Corps troops training for the Chamdo campaign, Xikang, 1950. Source: Chen Zonglie

(tib. gyami sarpa), as they called themselves, who would be committed to help Tibetans modernize and develop, not to exploiting and abusing them. At some point Tibet ultimately would be administratively incorporated and undergo socialist reforms, but not immediately. Mao, therefore, ordered the CCP cadre in Tibet not to rush change but to do things gradually and steadily. And while there were obvious risks in allowing the feudal secular and religious elites to retain real power, so long as the risk of *losing* Tibet was nil—which would be the case, because the Chinese army would be stationed there—the long-term benefits of winning over Tibetans were so huge that Mao was willing to make extraordinary concessions. It was a shrewd strategy that traded short-term negatives (permitting the theocratic government and the feudal manorial estate system to continue) for the achievement of long-term national interests (Tibetans' genuine acceptance of being part of China and their own conclusion that major reforms were needed).

At the same time, as indicated above, the "stick" was also at play, namely, the well-trained, well-armed military troops of the People's Liberation Army. In the spring and summer of 1950, the Eighteenth Army Corps began intensive training at high altitude. At the same time, the Southwest Bureau launched a crash program to build roads toward Tibet from the areas that it already held outside Tibet (in Kham [Xikang]) and to recruit Tibetans to provide thousands of their yaks to transport supplies for an invasion if the "carrot" failed. Phünwang, who was responsible for organizing transport in one part of Kham, recalled it was not difficult to do this. "Everyone was happy to do this because the PLA was paying in silver dollars (dayan) [ch. da yang]. Many Tibetans made a lot of money from this."[39] Mao, therefore, gave the Dalai Lama and his elite a clear choice of how they would be incorporated—peacefully via negotiations or militarily via invasion.

39. Quoted in Goldstein, Sherap, and Siebenschuh 2004: 138.

Chapter 2

Tibetan Perspectives

Contacts with the Chinese Communists

The Tibetan government, for its part, was also pursuing a two-track approach. On the one hand, its main effort was focused on securing military and diplomatic support for its de facto independence. To this end Tibet sent appeals to Western nations such as Britain and the United States and started reinforcing its army along the Chinese border (in Eastern Tibet).[1] In December 1949, for example, it decided to send three high-level missions to the United States and India, Great Britain, and Nepal to explain its precarious situation and seek assistance.

On the other hand, it also decided to make contact with China and formed a fourth mission for this purpose.[2] This mission, led by Tsipön Shakabpa and the monk official Mindrubu (Thubden Gyebo), arrived in Kalimpong on 7 March 1950 with instructions to discuss four topics:[3]

1. The unanswered letter to Chairman Mao Tse-tung from the Foreign Bureau of the Government of Tibet [the 2 November letter cited earlier];

2. The atrocious radio announcements from Sining [Xining] and Peiping [Beijing];

---

1. Eastern Tibet, known in Tibetan as Kham, was the homeland of the subethnic Tibetan group known as Khambas. At this time in history, Khambas were divided into two segments, one living under direct Chinese rule in Xikang Province and the other under the Tibetan government. The latter was administered by a senior Lhasa official known as the domey jigyab, or governor, of Eastern Tibet. He was stationed in the town of Chamdo. It should be noted that Chamdo was frequently used in speech and documents to refer not just to the town but also to the larger administrative unit of Eastern Tibet.

2. For a more detailed discussion of these efforts, see Goldstein 1989: 625–37.

3. The China Mission included Taring Dzasa and Takla (Phüntso Tashi) as English and Chinese translators.

3. Securing an assurance that the territorial integrity of Tibet will not be violated; and;

4. Informing the Government of China that the people and Government of Tibet will not tolerate any interference in the successive rule of the Dalai Lama, and they will maintain their independence.

The delegation is instructed to negotiate on the above subjects with a Chinese representative at a place close to China.[4]

These internal instructions reveal the tremendous gap still existing between the views of the leaders of Tibet and those of China.

Contact was made with the Communists through the brother of the Dalai Lama, Gyalo Thondup, whose Chinese father-in-law (Chu Shihkuei) was a retired Guomindang general with close ties to the new communist government.[5] In response to a letter from Chu, the Tibetan Mission contacted Lhasa and, on 8 April, received instructions from the government authorizing them to tell the Chinese to send a representative with authority to a place near to China. To this, the Chinese replied through Chu that they would send someone to Hong Kong to meet with the mission delegates and that the representatives of the Tibetan government should come quickly. They also stated that it was not okay for them to come as foreigners.[6] In his conversations with British diplomats in India, Shakabpa referred to this Chinese person as a "guide" rather than the actual negotiator, implying that he was being sent solely to take them to China.[7] The head of the Indian Mission in Lhasa reported to New Delhi on this connection:

---

4. Shakabpa 1967: 299–300; Zhwa sgab pa (Shakabpa) 1976: 412–13. The choice of Shakabpa to head this was the result of a divine lottery rather than his suitability to deal with the Chinese. Shakabpa, in fact, did not want to go to China, since he had deceived the Chinese in 1948, when he was in Beijing with a Tibetan trade delegation that was secretly en route to the United States (about this, see Goldstein 1989: 582, 627).

5. Gyalo Thondup stated in a video interview (in the Dalai Lama's private office, ca. 1991) that Marshal Zhu De, the commander-in-chief of the PLA, sent him a letter in 1949 saying, "Please report the following to the Tibetan government's Kashag. Please make relations with the new Chinese Communist government. The Communist Party does not have any thought of making changes to the political power of the Dalai Lama and the status of Tibet. So please send a delegation to China. We will hold talks." Gyalo said he reported this to Khenjung Thubden Sangpo, who was in Kalimpong under orders from the Kashag to report information about foreign countries. If this date is correct, then this occurred before the public announcement of the plan to liberate Tibet on 1 January 1950 but was likely to have occurred after Mao contacted Peng Dehuai on 23 November 1949. It would be the earliest example of Mao's gradualist strategy.

6. Zhwa sgab pa (Shakabpa) 1976: 413.

7. British Foreign Office Records, FO371/84468, report of conversation with Shakabpa in a telegram from the U.K. deputy high commissioner in Calcutta to the U.K. high commissioner in Delhi, dated 4 May 1950.

Gyalo Thondup has had some correspondence with his father-in-law in an effort to settle the Sino-Tibetan problems; and he wants to go to China with the Tibetan mission there. Mr. Chu is believed to have advised him that the Tibetan government should be told not to send missions to the U.K. and U.S.A. and that if a Tibetan mission is sent to Peking, Tibet's case will be favourably considered.

The Tibetan Mission to China are now on their way through India and so far as is known the decision that they should open negotiations with the Chinese Government from Hong Kong or Singapore still stands.[8]

The Tibetan Mission now made arrangements for visas and foreign currency, but when they tried to send two of their team for advance work, they were not allowed to board the plane at the Calcutta airport.[9] The visas they had obtained were, they were informed, considered invalid by the British, who, to their amazement, would not grant them new visas to visit Hong Kong or Singapore. After several months of complicated discussions, the Tibetans decided to pursue a British suggestion that they hold their talks in India. The Chinese were notified of this by Shakabpa, who said they told the mission to wait and hold talks with the new Chinese ambassador when he arrived in New Delhi in early September 1950.[10] However, from other documents, it appears that the Chinese plan was really to hold the negotiations in Beijing and that the arrangements in Delhi were meant only as preliminary conversations.[11]

In Beijing, Mao was not certain whether the Tibetans would really come to negotiate and was not willing to let this issue drag on to the point where the PLA would lose the seasonal window of opportunity for a 1950 attack. Consequently, as September approached, he instructed Zhou Enlai to pressure the Tibetan side through the India Government and Chinese embassy in Delhi. The first communication to Zhou on this issue said:

Zhou [Enlai]:

Please pay attention to the time to attack Chamdo. Please let an appropriate official pass on to the Indian Embassy the information that we hope a Tibetan delegation can arrive in Beijing in mid-September for negotiations and that

8. British Foreign Office Records, FO371/84453, monthly report of the Indian Mission, Lhasa, for the period ending 15 March 1950.

9. Zhwa sgab pa (Shakabpa) 1976: 413.

10. Shakabpa, interview, 1983, New York City; Zhwa sgab pa (Shakabpa) 1976: 413–14. Also, for a detailed discussion of the British decision, see Goldstein 1989: 644–75.

11. U.S. National Archives, 793B.00/8–2350, telegram from U.S. ambassador in India to the U.S. secretary of state, dated 23 August 1950. The telegram reports on the ambassador's conversation with the Indian foreign secretary, in which he conveyed that this is what the Chinese had said to the Indian ambassador in Beijing.

our troops will march to Tibet soon, so if the Tibetan delegation truly wants to negotiate with us they should come soon. Please pass on the message that we hope the Indian government will provide necessary help to the Tibetan delegation during their journey.

Mao Zedong
29 August[12]

On the same day, Mao also instructed Zhou to contact the new Chinese Embassy in New Delhi.

Zhou:

It is very necessary to telegram Shen Jian and ask him to urge the Tibetan delegation to come to Beijing soon.[13] Please make it clear in the telegram that we hope the Tibetan delegation will quickly start their trip to Beijing soon after they receive the telegram. They will travel by air to Hong Kong, and then travel by train to Beijing. . . . They should arrive in Beijing by mid- September.

Mao Zedong
29 August[14]

Soon after this, on 4 September, the Tibetan Mission returned to New Delhi and on 6 September 1950 met with the chargé d'affaires, Shen Jian (because the new ambassador had not yet arrived). The Tibetans said they were ready to begin negotiations as soon as the ambassador arrived and that in the meantime Beijing should refrain from doing anything in Kham (Chamdo). Shen informed them that talks had to be conducted in Beijing, not in India, and that they had to arrive by mid-September.

Two days later, on 8 September, the Tibetans met with Prime Minister Nehru for more than two hours. Their hope had been to secure his assistance, but the meeting did not go well. The Tibetans told Nehru they would not go to Beijing unless the Chinese guaranteed Tibetan independence in advance. Moreover, they said they did not trust the Chinese and asked that India guarantee any outcome between Tibet and China. Nehru responded that India would continue its policy of outwardly recognizing Tibet as a part of China but would also continue to consider Tibet to be internally autonomous. However, he also said bluntly that if the Tibetan delegation insisted on saying that Tibet is completely independent, then reaching an agreement with the Chinese would be difficult. And he added, "As to India acting as

12. Zhongguo zangxue yanjiu zhongxin keyan chu zhuban 1993: 7.
13. Shen Jian was the interim chargé d'affaires in the Chinese Embassy in India. Later on he became counselor of government affairs and was responsible for handling various issues regarding the journey of the Tibetan delegation to Beijing via India.
14. Zhongguo zangxue yanjiu zhongxin keyan chu zhuban 1993: 7.

a guarantor to any agreement, that is talk from thirty years ago and is not acceptable in this day and age."[15] When the Tibetans objected, saying that the 1914 Simla Convention, signed between Britain and Tibet, was proof of their independence, Nehru immediately called his Ministry of External Affairs and asked them to check whether there was such a separate treaty that stipulated this. Then he replied, showing some anger:

> There is no separate treaty like this, and China never accepted the Simla Convention. The Chinese believe that Tibet is a part of China. Tibet thinks that because China didn't accept Simla it is independent, but at that time Tibet did not make any clear decisions. That was a mistake. And later when you had the time and opportunity to do something [about "independence"] you did nothing and that was a mistake. During this time China has been very clever and has proclaimed widely in the international community that Tibet is a part of China. Now you, the representatives, have to be very careful [with what you say and claim] when you begin your talks with the Chinese.[16]

After the meeting with Nehru, Shakabpa and his associate met with the British acting high commissioner, F. Roberts. As with Nehru, they asked for British assistance with the Chinese but were told that, since Indian independence in 1947, all responsibilities regarding Tibet had now passed to the Government of India.[17]

The next day the Shakabpa mission visited the U.S. Embassy. According to Ambassador Henderson's report,

> Shakabpa stated that Tibetan Government has taken firm decision to meet any Communist Chinese incursion with force. He said that his government wished him to express its deep appreciation of US offer of military assistance.[18] As had been suggested, the Tibetan Government would approach the GOI [Government of India] to solicit its cooperation. A separate mission comprising Surkhang Depön and Khenjung Lobsang Tsewang had been dispatched from Lhasa and would arrive in New Delhi in a few days. To allay suspicion this mission had been designated as trade mission, but its real purpose was to bring full instructions from Lhasa Government and to conduct conversations re mil-

---

15. Zhwa sgab pa (Shakabpa) 1976: 418.

16. Zhwa sgab pa (Shakabpa) 1976: 417–18.

17. British Foreign Office Records, FO371/84469, report of conversation with the Tibetan Mission, dated 8 September 1950.

18. In early August, the United States had agreed to help Tibet by providing "war materials and finance" but not troops. However, at the same time it said that India's cooperation was essential in this so that delivery could be effective. The United States urged the Tibetans first to ask the Government of India to give Tibet additional aid, and if India refused (as expected) then to ask it to permit passage of aid if Tibet itself secured this from abroad (U.S. National Archives, 693.93B/8–750, telegram from U.S. ambassador in India to the U.S. secretary of state, dated 7 August 1950) (see also Goldstein 1989: 669–71).

itary aid with GOI. Detailed information re types and quantities of additional military equipment desired would presumably be supplied by new mission. As yet this question had not been raised with GOI by Shakabpa. . . . As regards the aims of the Tibetan Government in the forthcoming negotiations, he was at first reluctant to make a positive statement, but finally stated that what Tibet wanted was independence.[19]

A week later, on 16 September, the Tibetans finally met the new Chinese ambassador, Yuan Zhongxian. Shakabpa has written that the Tibetan side began by reiterating its traditional position, saying, "Tibet will remain independent as it is at present, and we will continue to have very close 'priest-patron' relations with China. Also, there is no need to liberate Tibet from imperialism, since there are no British, American, or Guomindang imperialists in Tibet, and Tibet is ruled and protected by the Dalai Lama (not any foreign power)."[20]

Ambassador Yuan responded that it was completely unacceptable to talk of Tibetan independence, but if there really were no foreign influences in Tibet, he was very glad. Then the ambassador gave them a pamphlet explaining the Chinese government's policy and told them to examine points 50–53 carefully.[21] He also told them that the Chinese side considered three issues key: (1) Tibet must accept that it is a part of China; (2) Tibet's defenses must be handled by China; and (3) all political and trade matters concerning foreign countries must be conducted through China. The ambassador said that if Tibet accepted these points, there would be peaceful liberation; otherwise, the PLA forces would liberate Tibet militarily.

These points far exceeded Shakabpa's instructions, so he told Ambassador Yuan that he would have to consult with his government about this. He asked Yuan to ensure that no Chinese troops would alter the status quo on the border until his mission received a reply.[22] Yuan did not give him such an assurance and, in fact, emphasized that it was very important that the Tibetan Mission arrive in Beijing before the end of September.[23]

Three days later, the Shakabpa mission sent a detailed telegram to the Kashag explaining the mission's conversations with the Indian government

19. U.S. National Archives, 793B.00/9–1050, telegram from the U.S. ambassador in India to the U.S. secretary of state, dated 10 September 1950.

20. Zhwa sgab pa (Shakabpa) 1976: 419.

21. Shakya notes that this was a copy of the "Common Programme," the PRC's precursor constitution. Points 50–53 dealt with minority nationalities (Shakya 1999: 446 fn. 141).

22. Zhwa sgab pa (Shakabpa) 1976: 419–20.

23. Chinese documents on this exchange are not available, but the former head of Indian intelligence wrote that the Chinese said they should come by the end of September (Mullik 1971: 66). A note from the Chinese to the Government of India dated 16 November 1950 also said this is what they told the Tibetans (cited in Carlyle 1953: 550–51).

and the Chinese embassy and asking for instructions.[24] The Shakabpa mission recommended that it would be very difficult to get an agreement with the Chinese if the Tibetan government did not compromise a little bit. Specifically, the delegates suggested that Tibet accept being a part of China, albeit in name only. They also suggested that Tibet seek to maintain trade and cultural relations with foreign countries such as India and Nepal, meaning it should accept that China would handle political relations with the remaining foreign countries. And with regard to China stationing Chinese troops in Tibet (to defend the border), Tibet should suggest that, since there were no likely threats, Tibetan troops would do this, and, in the future, should there be danger from India and Nepal, Tibet would ask for military assistance from China. Finally, they asked permission to go to Beijing to hold discussions.[25] In essence, then, Shakabpa and Mindrubu recommended that Tibet partly accept Ambassador Yuan's point 1, reject his point 2 about military occupation, and partly accept point 3.

The Tibetan government, however, was not yet prepared to compromise and, after a lapse of twelve days, informed Shakabpa on 28 September that it had not yet reached any decision. Its telegram explained that this was a critical issue for Tibet, and since the Chinese seemed determined to achieve their points, it had to discuss all of this in detail and would let the mission know its decision later. In the meantime, it told the mission delegates to try their best to talk with the Chinese so as to maintain cordial relations.[26] In other words, it instructed Shakabpa to stall the Chinese until a decision on these matters could be reached in Lhasa.

When days passed with no response, the Chinese side became anxious and impatient. As mentioned earlier, launching a military invasion of Tibet in winter ran the risk of being hit by snowstorms or having troops cut off by the months-long closure of passes. That meant either beginning an offensive in the summer and fall of 1950 (the Chinese considered October the latest date they could start an attack) or waiting until 1951. The latter option was tactically less attractive, because there was no telling whether the Tibetan government would be able to use the additional time to attract international support, or be more effective in preparing for war, or both. Therefore, the

---

24. Regarding the transmission of this telegram, in 1950, Tibet had a small, but functioning, communication system manned by Nepalese, Indians, and Englishmen. Telegrams could be sent to Gyantse, Lhasa, Yadong, and India from the Tibet government's telegraph office in Lhasa, and wireless stations existed between Lhasa and Chamdo and other places along the frontier of Eastern Tibet. For a short time in 1950, a broadcast station was set up in Lhasa (Radio Tibet). (See www.tibet.com/Status/kazi.html, "A brief account of Mr. Sonam T. Kazi's experience in Tibet before the Chinese Invasion.")

25. Zhwa sgab pa (Shakabpa) 1976: 421.

26. Zhwa sgab pa (Shakabpa) 1976: 421.

Chinese contacted Shakabpa and the delegation several times after the meeting on 16 September, asking whether he had received a reply from Lhasa.

Thus, when the Kashag's telegram of the 28th arrived, the Tibetan Mission immediately went to the Chinese Embassy and, following the instructions of the Tibetan government, tried to stall by inventing a story that Lhasa was still waiting to receive a detailed letter sent from India by special *horse* messenger (since telegraphic communication was poor in Tibet). It would, therefore, they said, take a few more weeks before the Kashag's response would arrive. There is no record of what the Chinese said, but it must have frightened the Tibetans, because on 30 September, they again cabled Lhasa urging the government to act. The Chinese Embassy, they said, was continually urging them to give an answer, so if Lhasa delayed answering any longer, war might break out on the border, and if it did, it would not be a good situation, even if the mission delegates then went to Beijing. So they urged that an answer be sent as soon as possible.[27]

On that same day, the Tibetan government finally informed the Shakabpa mission by cable that the government's smallest assembly (the Kashag Trungtsi Lhengye) had decided that it would be difficult to accept Yuan's three points, because to do so would mean that Tibet would lose all its political and religious power. On the other hand, the telegram said, China was strong militarily and had many troops massed on the border, so it was difficult to respond negatively to these terms. Consequently, it instructed the mission to continue to stall with the hope of delaying a Chinese attack until such time that Lhasa could reassess the world situation and convene a meeting of the Full Assembly. The Tibetan Mission in India was disappointed and frustrated by this delaying strategy, which not only put them in an awkward situation in Delhi but also, they felt, might push the Chinese to invade Eastern Tibet. The delegates telegraphed back almost immediately, saying that while they understood that the decision was crucial, the time for procrastination was over. The international situation, they said, would not improve, so Lhasa should answer immediately.[28]

In the meantime, the "Trade Mission" the Kashag had sent to discuss military assistance arrived in Delhi on 4 October, but as Shakabpa had feared, time had run out. Mao decided not to wait any longer and ordered the Eighteenth Army Corps to launch the attack on Chamdo. On 7 October, PLA troops crossed the Upper Yangtse River (the de facto border) in a number of places and started a multipronged campaign.[29]

From the start, however, this attack was not intended as an invasion of

27. Zhwa sgab pa (Shakabpa) 1976: 421–22.
28. Zhwa sgab pa (Shakabpa) 1976: 422.
29. See Goldstein 1989: 648ff., for a detailed discussion of the campaign.

Tibet per se. The Chinese plan was to encircle and capture the Tibetan army deployed in Chamdo by means of a blitzkrieglike attack, striking simultaneously from five directions.[30] This, they felt would psychologically demoralize both the Tibetan government in Lhasa and the remaining Tibetan army units defending Central Tibet and would, thereby, exert powerful pressure on Lhasa to send negotiators to Beijing. In essence, the real goal of the Chamdo campaign was to induce the Dalai Lama to accept the peaceful liberation that Mao considered important for China's long-term interests (and, of course, preclude the need for a major invasion of Central Tibet). Mao's 23 August instructions to the Southwest Bureau about the military attack conveys this:

[To] The Southwest Bureau. Please pass this message on to the Northwest Bureau:

Your telegram of 20 August was received.

(1) Your plan to occupy Chamdo this year and to keep three thousand of our people there after taking it over is very good. You can make preparations according to this plan. By the end of this month or early next month, when you make sure that roads to Ganzi [a major Tibetan area in Xikang Province] are open, you may start the march to Chamdo. Your goal is to take Chamdo in October. This is favorable to our work in winning political changes in Tibet and to our march into [the rest of] Tibet next year.

(2) India has made an announcement acknowledging that Tibet is part of China. They hope that we will solve the Tibetan question through peaceful means instead of military means. The British did not allow a Tibetan delegation to come to Beijing in the past; now they have given permission. If our troops can occupy Chamdo by October, it will pressure a Tibetan delegation to come to Beijing for negotiations, and then we can solve the Tibetan question through peaceful means. (Of course, other possibilities also exist.) We are now trying to get Tibetan representatives to come to Beijing and we are trying to reduce Nehru's fear.

When Tibetan representatives arrive in Beijing, we will use the Ten-Point [statement] as our terms in the negotiation and try to get the Tibetan representatives to sign a joint agreement based on these ten points. If we can achieve these, our march into Tibet next year will be smooth. *After you take Chamdo, leave only three thousand of our people there during the winter. Do not get to Lhasa this year. Withdraw our main forces to Ganzi. From the Tibetans' point of view, they may take this as a friendly gesture by us.* . . .

Mao Zedong
23 August[31]

30. One of the battle slogans, for example, was "Fight and do not let a single Tibetan escape. No matter how hard it becomes, you must do it."

31. Zhonggong zangxue yanjiu zhongxin keyan chu zhuban 1993: 6 (emphasis added).

The PLA military campaign in Chamdo was completely successful, and the PLA quickly captured Chamdo. However, as the Tibetans retreated toward Lhasa, a PLA cavalry unit from Qinghai pushed south far to the west of Chamdo and was able to cut the single road to Lhasa, trapping almost all of the Tibetan troops and officials fleeing from Chamdo. The retreating Tibetans actually outnumbered this small force, but the Tibetan governor-general, Ngabö, had no stomach for trying to fight his way through. On learning that a small Chinese force had arrived at the road, he and all the Tibetan army troops with him stopped their retreat and literally sat down, waiting to be captured. This occurred on 19 October.

Twelve days after the attack began, therefore, the Tibetan Chamdo army was destroyed as a fighting force, and the road to Lhasa was virtually open to the PLA. However, as Mao had ordered, the PLA did not take advantage of their total victory and advance into Central Tibet. Instead, they stopped and gave Beijing another opportunity to persuade the Tibetan leadership to start negotiations and agree to peaceful liberation.[32]

In India, Shakabpa received no news of the events in Chamdo until 17 October, ten days after the invasion had started and the day before Ngabö physically fled from Chamdo. At this point Lhasa informed Shakabpa that Chamdo would soon fall and instructed him to contact the Chinese ambassador immediately to try to stop the invasion from moving farther into Tibet.[33] Shakabpa went at once to meet Ambassador Yuan and accused China of flagrantly ignoring international law by attacking without warning while peaceful negotiations were in progress.[34] The Chinese ambassador disagreed vigorously, telling Shakabpa that the blame for the attack fell on the Tibetan government itself, because it had failed to authorize his mission to go to Beijing to negotiate. Shakabpa wrote that Ambassador Yuan told him:

> We also know about the attack on Chamdo. However, since we gave you terms to respond to, almost a month has passed, so we are not in violation of any laws. Whatever people may say throughout the world, it is our firm decision that we will liberate Formosa and Tibet. Now if you accept Tibet as part of China and if your delegation goes to Beijing, there will be no further military suppression.[35]

32. This is discussed in detail in Goldstein 1989: 638–773. It should be noted, though, that some small elements of the PLA gradually moved into Lho dzong and Pembar (west of Chamdo) when Tibetan troops and officials moved back farther west toward Kongpo and Lhasa (see Lha Klu [Lhalu] 1993: 246–47).

33. Ngabö left Chamdo early in the morning of 18 October without telling his British wireless operator, so he was unable to send a final message informing the Kashag that Chamdo was being evacuated. Lhasa, therefore, could only surmise from the absence of subsequent wireless messages that Chamdo had fallen.

34. Zhwa sgab pa (Shakabpa) 1976: 423.

35. Zhwa sgab pa (Shakabpa) 1976: 423–24.

The loss of Tibet's large Chamdo army and the presumed capture of the governor-general (Ngabö) with all the Lhasa officials serving under him had the effect the Chinese had hoped for: it demoralized Lhasa.[36] Although several Tibetan regiments were still intact between Chamdo and Lhasa, these were poorly trained and led and, inexplicably, had no contingency plan for opposing the Chinese by beginning guerrilla warfare against the PLA's supply lines. Nor did they immediately begin to devise such a plan. Over the past three decades, conservative views had dominated in Lhasa, and Tibet had consciously chosen to deemphasize its military and refrain from modernizing.

As late as 1946, for example, an attempt by the government to hire an English principal and open a government-run English school in Lhasa was stopped by the Big Three Monasteries, whose fighting dobdo monks threatened to kidnap and rape the boy students and physically attack the teachers. An official's recollection of the government's talks with monastic leaders over this illuminates how entrenched the opposition to change was in the monastic segment at that time.

> About thirty-five monk and lay officials attended that school. The idea was that when these students were ready, they would be sent abroad [for further studies]. . . . [However] After a while, the monks came and said, "Why have you started such a school?" The teachers became afraid for their lives. . . . The Big Three monasteries wanted the school completely closed. They were powerful and refused to listen to us at all. At the meetings [with the Revenue Office] we told them, "You have to look at the world as it is now. The world is changing and you have to change. You are just wearing your robe on your head and holding your eating bowl in your hand. You shouldn't act like this. Look to the future; this school will not harm religion and politics. If you don't allow the school, you won't be able to stand on your own." But they insisted and wouldn't listen. They would talk always about the deities and the lamas. We had meetings and tried to convince them, but they refused and the school was closed. Had it been left open, it would have been excellent.[37]

And although the Tibetan government took note of the increasing Chinese threat in 1947–49 and started to increase the size of its army and buy new

---

36. The Tibetan "Trade Mission" of Surkhang Depön and Khenjung Lobsang Tsewang had met with the U.S. Ambassador on 16 October to discuss Tibet's military aid needs and were told to return on the 18th. However, after the telegram about Chamdo arrived from Lhasa on the 17th, they decided this was too risky under the circumstances and sent Ambassador Henderson a cryptic note saying they were unable to make their appointment due to "urgent works." (U.S. National Archives, 793b.00/10–2650, telegram from the U.S. ambassador in India to the U.S. secretary of state, dated 26 October 1950).

37. Chabtsom, interview, 1992, Lhasa.

weapons from India, it was too late to raise and train an effective army.[38] Tibet now was paying the price for its conservative short-sightedness. By preventing the emergence of a well-educated and professionally led army, Tibetans now found their country defended by "generals," who were simply regular aristocratic officials assigned to their military positions with no special training and without regard to the appropriateness of their personality for warfare.

In Lhasa, the debacle in Chamdo meant the PLA was now in control of Tibet's easternmost province, and a full-scale invasion of Central Tibet seemed imminent if they did not act. As a consequence, Tibet finally addressed Ambassador Yuan's three points. A Full Assembly meeting was convened to discuss the options, and its members decided that there was no longer any choice but to accept Tibet as part of China. Soon after this, on 21 October, with the regent Taktra's approval, a telegraphic message was sent informing Shakabpa of this. However, the assembly and regent still took a tough line with the Chinese, specifying that this acceptance meant that Tibet would be completely independent internally and instructing him additionally to reject China's other two points. Shakabpa has written what the instructions he received said:

1. Proceed immediately to China for negotiations.

2. Regarding point 1—that Tibet is a part of China—if you have to accept this, it is permissible if you are able to guarantee that the Dalai Lama's name and authority will remain intact and the Tibetan government will continue to function as it is now, making decisions and acting independently.

3. Regarding point 2—that all foreign trade and political dealings will be done through China—you have to convey to the Chinese that Tibet will continue to handle all its foreign dealings by itself.

4. Regarding point 3—that Chinese soldiers will take over security/defense forces in Tibet—this is a very dangerous issue, and we do not accept this. Tibet will appoint its own soldiers to protect our own territory.

5. Impress on the Chinese that no harm should befall the Tibetan government officials who were captured in Eastern Tibet and that all Tibetan prisoners should be returned home speedily.[39]

Shakabpa and his colleagues were disappointed by this hard-line response, feeling that it was too little too late, but they immediately called the Chinese Embassy and arranged for a meeting with Ambassador Yuan the following day, 22 October.

---

38. For a relevant assessment of the appalling state of the Tibetan army in 1936 by a British military officer, see Goldstein 1989: 280–89.

39. Zhwa sgab pa (Shakabpa) 1976: 425.

In Lhasa, however, even this mild compromise went too far for some key figures who believed that once Tibet admitted it was part of China, Tibet's legal status would be transformed and its planned appeals for international aid (e.g., from the United Nations) would have little weight. The officials holding this view felt that even if this led to the Chinese invasion of Central Tibet, the Dalai Lama could seek refuge in a foreign country and continue to struggle for independence from abroad, as the 13th Dalai Lama had done forty years earlier. The main forces opposing the compromise appear to have been the Kashag minister Surkhang, Lord Chamberlain Phala, and the Dalai Lama's tutors (Ling Rimpoche and Trijang Rimpoche). When they failed to persuade the Full Assembly to reject point 1, they took action on their own. In a risky gambit that bypassed the regent, they turned to the other, heretofore uninvolved, source of power in Tibet, the Dalai Lama.

The fifteen-year-old Dalai Lama was still three years away from assuming political authority so had not been involved in political affairs at all. However, given the seriousness of the situation facing Tibet, these officials felt that he was their only hope. If they could get him to intervene on an important issue like this, the impact would be tremendous. His views could not be ignored. Thus, on 21 October, someone with easy access to him, presumably his tutors or Phala, informed him about the assembly and regent's decision, giving it a negative spin. As hoped, the Dalai Lama reacted strongly against this decision and ordered that a divine lottery be consulted.[40] The very next morning, in the presence of other top officials and, of course, the protector deities, this was held. The deities' answer via the lottery was that Tibet should not accept being part of China. A telegram was immediately sent to Shakabpa countermanding the previous telegraphic instructions.[41]

Meanwhile, in Delhi, on the morning of 23 October, as the Tibetan delegation was preparing to leave for a luncheon meeting at the Chinese Embassy to discuss their new instructions (from the first telegram), they learned that another urgent telegram had been received from Lhasa. Keeping the car the Chinese had sent to pick them up waiting, the mission members spent the next hour decoding the new telegram, which was dated 22 October. Shakabpa recalled that he was surprised when he read the open-

---

40. Zhwa sgab pa (Shakabpa) 1976: 426–27. A divine lottery (tib. senril) was a common method of making difficult or contentious decisions. It operated as follows: Answers to a question, such as "accept" or "not accept" being part of China, were written on small pieces of paper, which were then rolled inside tsamba (flour made from roasted barley) dough balls that were weighed and measured to be exactly the same size and weight. These were placed in a bowl and shaken around in front of the statue (or image) of a protector deity until one of the balls fell out. The message in that dough ball was taken to be the answer chosen by the deity.

41. Zhwa sgab pa (Shakabpa) 1976: 426–27.

ing line of this new telegram, "By the order of His Holiness the Dalai Lama," because at that time the Dalai Lama had not yet assumed power, and this phrase was normally not used until he formally became the ruler.[42] The new instructions further shocked him because they countermanded the previous telegram's concessions. According to what Shakabpa has written, the telegram said:

> Regarding the reply to China's three points, we have had meetings between the regent and Kashag and also discussed this with the Assembly and have communicated our decisions to you, which we hope you have received. I am sure you are planning to leave [for Beijing]. However, with regard to point 1, concerning Tibet's acceptance of being a part of China externally [in name only], the Dalai Lama ordered, "Since this is an important matter related to the welfare of Buddhism and politics, if we pray to the three jewels and do a divine lottery, there will be no harm for the present and the future." Since this idea had great advantages, we did such a divine lottery in Norbulingka in the chapel of the protector Gombo in the front of the [protector] deities Gombo and Lhamo. The lottery answered that if you accept that Tibet is part of China externally, then this will be harmful for Buddhism and politics. Since the divine lottery will never let us down, do not accept any of the three Chinese points. However, you should all leave for Beijing by 26 October.[43]

Shakabpa and Mindrubu were in a difficult position, since they now had nothing concrete to report to Yuan. They made the best of it, however, by telling the ambassador that they had just received instructions from Lhasa ordering them to leave for Beijing. The ambassador responded by asking Shakabpa what reply he had received concerning the three points he had laid out. Shakabpa answered that there had been no reply to this, but later wrote that he felt the ambassador could tell from his expression and demeanor that this was not the truth. Shakabpa told Yuan that the mission would leave the next day for Kalimpong to pick up their winter clothes and would then go directly to Calcutta. Yuan replied that all documents for their trip would be issued by the Chinese Consulate in Calcutta.[44]

However, a week later, Lhasa again changed its mind. On 2 November, while Shakabpa and the others were making final arrangements to leave from Calcutta, the delegation received another telegram from Tibet, dated 31 October, which said, "Since we began peaceful discussions with the Chinese, the Chinese have invaded our territory, so now you should postpone your trip to Beijing to continue negotiations. This was the decision of the Tibetan Assembly, so you should not yet proceed. We will let you know when you can

42. Shakabpa, interview, 1983, Dharamsala.
43. Zhwa sgab pa (Shakabpa) 1976: 426–27.
44. Zhwa sgab pa (Shakabpa) 1976: 426–27.

leave." The next day the delegation received yet another telegram postponing their departure indefinitely.[45]

The reason for this sudden change was the continued success of the anti-compromise faction in Lhasa, which now had convinced the Dalai Lama and other key figures to make an to appeal to the United Nations. These officials felt an attempt should be made to secure support from the United Nations, which had recently come to the support of South Korea with tens of thousands of troops. Consequently, they did not want a delegation in Beijing negotiating while the United Nations was considering their plea for help against Chinese aggression.[46] Shakabpa was instructed to forward the appeal to the United Nations.

These events also appear to have marked a shift in attitude by some of the supporters of the regent, such as Phala and Surkhang, in favor of new leadership—the Dalai Lama. Not surprisingly, just two weeks later, on 17 November, in the midst of this political chaos, the regent Taktra was forced to resign, and the Dalai Lama assumed political power at the age of fifteen.[47]

While Shakabpa was in Kalimpong preparing to leave for Beijing, the Trade Mission in Delhi discussed the possibility of securing Indian assistance with a United Nations appeal. The Indians were not encouraging, suggesting that the Chinese might regard their appeal as further provocation. Lhasa, however, was not to be dissuaded and, on 29 October, asked India directly if it would bring an appeal from Tibet before the United Nations. India responded that Tibet itself must make the appeal but also said that India would support the appeal on the grounds that the Chinese should not have used force but should have continued peaceful negotiations.[48] This was the weakest support India could have offered, but it was more than a complete rejection.

Meanwhile in Lhasa, the views of the anti-compromise officials were reinforced when the older brother of the Dalai Lama, Taktse Rimpoche, arrived in Lhasa from Qinghai, a province that had been liberated by the Chinese First Field Army the previous year.[49] Taktse Rimpoche had been the abbot of Kumbum Monastery and was being pressured by the Chinese officials to go to Lhasa and persuade his brother to accept peaceful liberation. He finally decided he had to get out of Qinghai, so he lied and said he would talk with his brother and the Tibetan government about this. However, he

45. Zhwa sgab pa (Shakabpa) 1976: 429–30.
46. Zhwa sgab pa (Shakabpa) 1976: 429–30.
47. See Goldstein 1989: 704–7 for a discussion of this event.
48. British Foreign Office Records, FO371/84457, report of conversation with G. S. Bajpai cited in a telegram from the U.K. high commissioner in India to the Commonwealth Relations Office in London, dated 5 November 1950.
49. The Tibetan name for this area is Amdo.

Figure 2. The Surkhang family, left to right: front row, Surkhang Khenjung (Khenrab Wangchuk), Surkhang Depön (Lhawang Tobden); back row, Kheme Dzasa (Sonam Wangdü), Surkhang Dzasa (Wangchen Tseden), Minister Surkhang (Wangchen Gelek). Source: The Surkhang family

instead conveyed a very negative account of what had been transpiring in Qinghai Province (Amdo) and told his brother and the government that they should go into exile. He recalled,

> Then I stayed with the Chinese for six months [in Qinghai]. During this six-month period, as I listened to what the Chinese were saying, all the signs pointed to making things worse for Tibetans, and there wasn't a single thing about doing anything good. Within five years, starting from 1949, they said that they were going to destroy the Tibetan culture and ways. They said that the Tibetan custom of offering butter lamps was bad. That the butter was being wasted and that, instead of doing this, if this money was collected and sent to China it could support the war against the Americans in Korea. One soldier could be supported. They said that if you have no food to eat, do you think that praying to god is going to get you bread? Then there was this talk about killing His Holiness. . . .
>
> They said that I had to convince His Holiness and the government officials to work with the Chinese. At that time they were very scared that His Holiness

and the officials would escape to India. So they told me to tell them to cooperate with the Chinese, and as a reward they would offer me the governorship of Lhasa.

Q: And did they say anything else?

They said that His Holiness has five years to cooperate with the Chinese. If he does not, then I have the power to kill him. So I had such talks. . . .

So with all this . . . I used to think that I had to get out of this situation. So that is how I got to Lhasa.[50]

However, much of this seems an exaggeration. For example, in another part of his interview Taktse Rimpoche recalled that Marshal Peng Dehuai, the commander of the First Field Army and head of the Northwest Bureau, came to Kumbum and told him, "The Chinese and Tibetans are brothers from one big family who got separated. The reason why we got separated is that the imperialists came—the Americans and the English interfered. Now we have to bring [Tibet] into the fold, and it won't be good if one kills the other. So without bloodshed Tibet must be peacefully liberated, and toward that end you have to help us. So please go to Lhasa."[51] It is, therefore, hard to assess the significance of Taktse's report, since it is not clear whether this was said by anyone with authority, but clearly this was not the policy of either the Northwest Bureau or the Central Committee.

In these confusing and tense circumstances, Tibet sent a brief note to Mao Zedong in the name of the newly empowered Dalai Lama. The Dalai Lama has written about this:

So I wrote to the Chinese Government, through the commander of the army which was occupying Chamdo. I said that during my minority, relations had been strained between our countries, but that now I had taken over full responsibility and sincerely wanted to restore the friendship which had existed in the past. I pleaded with them to return the Tibetans who had been captured by their army, and to withdraw from the part of Tibet which they had occupied by force.[52]

The actual note is not available, and so far as we know, the Chinese side never responded.

But the real hope of the Tibetan government was now the United Nations. On 3 November, the Government of India was notified that Tibet would appeal directly to the United Nations and other Buddhist countries in South Asia (apparently referring to Ceylon, Thailand, and Burma).[53] It was at this

50. Taktse, interview, 1993, Bloomington, IN.

51. Taktse, interview, 1993.

52. Dalai Lama 1962: 84–85.

53. British Foreign Office Records, FO371/84457, report of conversation with G. S. Bajpai cited in a telegram from the U.K. high commissioner in India to the Commonwealth Relations Office in London, dated 5 November 1950.

time that the Tibetan government instructed Shakabpa not to proceed to Beijing and instead to make its appeal to the United Nations. Shakabpa, having already been shocked twice by changes in orders from Lhasa, was so unsure whether the new instructions were genuine that he actually went to Gangtok in Sikkim in order to confirm the order directly with the Kashag by wireless phone.[54] There he learned that the instructions were correct, so he returned to Kalimpong and on 7 November forwarded Tibet's appeal to the United Nations' secretary-general. This appeal is the subject of the next chapter.

54. Shakabpa, interview, 1983.

Chapter 3

Tibet Appeals to the United Nations

Although Tibet had no experienced diplomats, its first appeal to the United Nations was surprisingly sophisticated and eloquent, and it effectively presented the Tibetan government's view of Tibet's historical relationship with China and of the events from 1911 to the present.[1]

Appeal to the Secretary General of the United Nations

The attention of the world is riveted on Korea where aggression is being resisted by an international force. Similar happenings in remote Tibet are passing without notice. It is in the belief that aggression will not go unchecked and freedom unprotected in any part of the world that we have assumed the responsibility of reporting through you [the secretary-general] recent happenings in the border area of Tibet to the United Nations Organisation. As you are aware the problem of Tibet has taken on alarming propoitions in recent times. The problem is not of Tibet's own making but is largely the outcome of unthwarted Chinese ambition to bring weaker nations on her periphery within her active domination. Tibetans have for long lived a cloistered life in their mountain fastness remote and aloof from the rest of the world except insofar as His Holiness the Dalai Lama, as the acknowledged head of the Buddhist Church, confers benediction and receives homage from followers in many countries.

In the years preceding 1912, there were indeed close friendly relations of a personal nature between the Emperor of China and His Holiness the Dalai

1. The British high commissioner informed London that he had been told in strict confidence that the Tibetan appeal had been drafted by Sinha, the Indian representative in Lhasa (British Foreign Office Records, FO371/84454, the U.K. high commissioner to the Commonwealth Relations Office, dated 14 November 1950). Shakabpa confirmed this in a discussion with me.

Lama. The connection was essentially born of belief in a common faith and may correctly be described as the relationship between a spiritual guide and his lay followers; it had no political implications. As a people devoted to the tenets of Buddhism, Tibetans had long eschewed the art of warfare and practiced peace and tolerance, and for the defense of their country relied on its geographical configuration and in non-involvement in the affairs of other nations. There were times when Tibet sought but seldom received the protection of the Chinese Emperor. The Chinese, however, in their natural urge for expansion, have wholly misconstrued the significance of the time of friendship and inter-independence that existed between China and Tibet as neighbors. To them, China was suzerain and Tibet a vassal state. It is this which first aroused legitimate apprehension in the mind of Tibet regarding the designs of China on her independent status.

Chinese conduct during their expedition in 1910 completed the rupture between the two countries. In 1911–12, when Tibet under the thirteenth Dalai Lama declared her complete independence—even as Nepal simultaneously broke away from allegiance to China—the Chinese revolution in 1911 which dethroned the last Manchurian emperor snapped the last of the sentimental and religious bonds that Tibet had with China. Tibet thereafter depended entirely on her isolation, her faith in the wisdom of Lord Buddha, and occasionally on the support of the British in India for her protection. No doubt in those circumstances the latter could also claim suzerainty over Tibet. Tibet, notwithstanding Anglo-Chinese influence from time to time, maintained her separated existence, in justification of which it may be pointed out that she has been able to keep peace and order within the country and remain at peace with the world. She continued to maintain neighborly goodwill and friendship with the people of China but never acceded to the Chinese claim of suzerainty in 1914.

It was British persuasion which led Tibet to sign a treaty which superimposed on her the nominal (non-interfering) suzerainty of China and by which the Chinese were accorded the right to maintain a mission in Lhasa though they were strictly forbidden to meddle in the internal affairs of Tibet. Apart from that fact even the nominal suzerainty which Tibet conceded to China is not enforceable because of the non-signature of the treaty of 1914 by the Chinese. It will be seen that Tibet maintained independent relations with other neighboring countries like India and Nepal. Furthermore, despite friendly British overtures, she did not compromise her position by throwing in her forces in world war two on the side of China. Thus she asserted and maintained her complete independence. The treaty of 1914 still guides relations between Tibet and India, and the Chinese, not being a party to it, may be taken to have renounced the benefits that would have otherwise accrued to them from the treaty. Tibet's independence thereby reassumed *de jure* status.

The slender tie that Tibet maintained with China after the 1911 revolution became less justified when China underwent a further revolution and turned into a full-fledged Communist state. There can be no kinship or sympathy between such divergent creeds as those espoused by China and Tibet.

Foreseeing future complications, the Tibetan Government broke off diplomatic relations with China and made a Chinese representative in Lhasa depart from Tibet in July, 1949. Since then, Tibet has not even maintained formal relations with the Chinese Government and people. They desire to live apart uncontaminated by the germ of a highly materialistic creed, but the Chinese are bent on not allowing Tibet to live in peace. They have, since the establishment of the Chinese People's Republic, hurled threats of liberating Tibet and have used devious methods to intimidate and undermine the Government of Tibet.

Tibet recognises that she is in no position to resist. It is thus that she agreed to negotiate on friendly terms with the Chinese Government. It is unfortunate that the Tibetan Mission to China were unable to leave India, through no fault of their own but for want of British visas which were required for transit through Hong Kong. At the kind intervention of the Government of India the Chinese People's Republic condescended to allow the Tibet Mission to have preliminary negotiations with the Chinese Ambassador to India who arrived in New Delhi only in September. While these negotiations were proceeding in Delhi, Chinese troops, without warning or provocation, crossed the Dre Chu [Upper Yangtse] River, which has for long been the boundary into Tibetan territory, at a number of places on 7th October, 1950. In quick succession places of strategic importance like Demar, Kamto, Tunga, Tshame, Rimochegotyu, Yakalo, and Markham fell to the Chinese. Tibetan frontier garrisons in Kham, which were maintained not with any aggressive design but as a nominal protective measure, have all been wiped out. Communist troops in great force converged from five directions on Chamdo, the capital of Kham, which succumbed soon after. Nothing is known of the state of a Minister of the Tibetan Government posted there. Little is known in the outside world of this sneak invasion. Long after the invasion had taken place the Chinese announced to the world that they had asked their armies to march into Tibet.

This unwarranted act of aggression has not only disturbed the peace of Tibet, it is in complete disregard of the solemn assurance given by the Chinese to the Government of India. It has created a grave situation in Tibet and may eventually deprive Tibet of her long cherished independence. We can assure you, Mr. Secretary-General, that Tibet will not go down without a fight, though there is little hope of a nation dedicated to peace resisting the brutal effort of men trained to war, but we understand the United Nations have decided to stop aggression whenever it takes place.

The armed invasion of Tibet for the incorporation of Tibet within the fold of Chinese Communism through sheer physical force is a clear case of aggression. As long as the people of Tibet are compelled by force to become a part of China against the will and consent of her people, the present invasion of Tibet will be the grossest instance of the violation of the weak by the strong. We therefore appeal through you to the nations of the world to intercede in our behalf and restrain Chinese aggression.

The problem is simple. The Chinese claim Tibet as part of China. Tibetans feel that, racially, culturally, and geographically, they are far apart from the Chinese. If the Chinese find the reactions of the Tibetans to their unnatural claim not acceptable, there are other civilised methods by which they could ascertain the views of the people of Tibet, or should (settle) the issue (by) purely judicial (means). They are open to seek redress in the international court of law.

The conquest of Tibet by China will only enlarge the area of conflict and increase the threat to the independence and stability of other Asian countries.

We Ministers, with the approval of His Holiness the Dalai Lama, entrust the problem of Tibet in this emergency to the ultimate decision of the United Nations and hope that the conscience of the world would not allow the disruption of our state by methods reminiscent of the jungle.

The Kashad [Kashag] (The Tibetan Cabinet) and the National Assembly of Tibet, Tibetan delegation Shakabpa (house Kalimpong)

Dated Lhasa the 27th day of the 9th Tibetan month of the Iron Tiger year, 7 November, 1950.[2]

The United Nations secretariat immediately ruled that since Tibet was not a member of the United Nations[3] and the telegram was from a delegation outside Tibet rather than from the Tibetan government itself, it would simply record its arrival in its routine list of communications from nongovernmental organizations. The secretariat also decided that the Tibetan telegram would not be issued as a Security Council document unless a member of the Security Council requested that it be issued or unless a member of the United Nations asked for the subject to be placed on the council's agenda.[4] To that end, they gave copies of the appeal to delegations on the Security Council. Both Britain and India could easily have clarified this mistaken interpretation concerning the "nongovernmental" origin of the appeals, since they knew that the Tibetan government sometimes sent official messages from Kalimpong because of communication limitations in Tibet. Neither chose to do so.

The Tibetan government, again through Shakabpa and Mindrupu, also requested support from Britain, Canada, and the United States for its appeal, as the following letter sent to the United Kingdom's high commissioner in India reveals:

According to the information received by wireless from the Government of Tibet the Chinese Communists have made sudden invasion into Tibet from number of different places in Eastern Tibet on 7th October, 1950 while negotiations were proceeding in Delhi. Now the Cabinet [Kashag] and the National

2. British Foreign Office Records, FO371/84454, telegram from the United Kingdom's U.N. delegation to the British Foreign Office, dated 14 November 1950. Words in parentheses appeared in the *New York Times* version and fill obvious blanks in the copy supplied by the secretariat.

3. It is interesting to note that in 1948 while the Tibetan Trade Mission was in the United States, some lawyers in New York who heard Shakabpa speaking about Tibetan independence urged him to have Tibet try to join the United Nations. He wired to Lhasa about this but was told, "Keep quiet (about this.) Don't do a lot of different things. Do your [original] publicity and return home" (Shakabpa, interview, 1983, New York City).

4. British Foreign Office Records, FO371/84454, telegram from the United Kingdom's U.N. delegation to the British Foreign Office, dated 13 November 1950.

Assembly of Tibet have appealed to the United Nations for ultimate judgment of this treacherous action by the Peking Government, a copy of which is enclosed herewith for your information. Tibet being a religious country is naturally weak in political and military activities. Thus we request Your Excellency to approach your Government for effective support in the United Nations so that the peace-loving religious country may be saved from destruction of war. Your kind advice and acknowledgment will be greatly appreciated.[5]

The letter sent to the United States was almost identical.

Tibet found support for its appeal from a most unlikely source—El Salvador. On 14 November, Hector David Castro, the chairman of El Salvador's delegation, telegraphed the U.N. secretary-general requesting that the "invasion of Tibet by foreign forces" be added to the agenda on the basis of the United Nation's primary responsibility "to maintain international peace and security," as cited in paragraph 1 of Article 1 of the United Nations Charter. El Salvador had hoped that this issue could be brought directly before the General Assembly, but the secretariat instead ordered that the issue first be brought up before the General Committee for a discussion of whether it should be referred to the General Assembly.[6]

The draft resolution proposed by El Salvador asked not only for condemnation of the Chinese but also for the creation of a special committee to develop proposals for the United Nations regarding actions that could be taken:

The General Assembly,

Taking note that the peaceful nation of Tibet has been invaded, without any provocation on its part, by foreign forces proceeding from the territory controlled by the Government established at Peking.

Decides,

1. To condemn this act of unprovoked aggression against Tibet;

2. To establish a Committee composed of (names of nations) . . . which will be entrusted with the study of the appropriate measures that could be taken by the General Assembly on this matter.

3. To instruct the Committee to undertake that study with special reference made to the United Nations by the Government of Tibet, and to render its report to the General Assembly, as early as possible, during the present session.[7]

The Tibet issue would now be discussed by the General Committee and, if its members agreed, would be heard by the General Assembly.

5. British Foreign Office Records, FO371/84454, letter sent by Shakabpa, dated 12 November, to the U.K. high commissioner in India, cited in a telegram from the U.K. high commissioner in India to the Commonwealth Relations Office in London, dated 16 November 1950.

6. The General Committee made recommendations regarding items to be included in the agenda. United Nations Document A/1534, cited in Bureau of His Holiness the Dalai Lama, n.d. The motivation behind the El Salvador initiative is unclear.

7. Ibid.

On the international front, these events—the invasion of Tibet in October, the Tibetan government's appeal to the United Nations in November, and El Salvador's action on behalf of Tibet—compelled India, Britain, and the United States to weigh their own national interests carefully against their historical connections with Tibet and their moral and legal obligations to assist Tibet at this critical time.

BRITISH AND INDIAN REACTIONS TO TIBET'S APPEAL

The British Foreign Office found it difficult to establish a course of action with regard to Tibet's appeal to the United Nations. The office began by examining Tibet's eligibility to appeal in the light of Article 35, paragraph 2, of the United Nations Charter, which stipulated that the appealing party must be a "state."[8] At question was whether Tibet could qualify as a state. The British Foreign Office's legal examination concluded that it could easily be argued that Chinese suzerainty was so amorphous and symbolic that it did not preclude Tibet's possession of its own international identity. The reasoning supporting this position was stated in a telegram from the Foreign Office to the British high commissioner in India:

> The actual control which China in virtue of her suzerainty excercised over Tibet varies at different times. In 1911 Tibet threw off Chinese control and expelled all Chinese troops from her territory. By 1913 she had established independence of China and she participated in a tripartite Conference in Simla in 1914 in her own right. As a result of this Conference, representatives of Britain, China and Tibet drew up a Convention recognizing Tibetan autonomy under Chinese suzerainty but expressly precluding China from incorporating Tibet as a Chinese province or from sending troops into Tibet other than an escort of 300 men for the representative in Lhasa. It was made plain by this Convention that Tibet was entitled to conduct foreign relations directly and not through China. The Convention was signed by Britain and Tibet but only initialed by China. The Chinese Government subsequently repudiated the initialing of the Convention by their representative but on occasion they have stated that they accept the terms of the Convention apart from the clauses fixing the boundary between China and Tibet. Though China did not sign the Convention, it was only on the faith of the conditions in it that Tibet agreed to accept Chinese suzerainty again. If, therefore, China repudiated the Convention in its entirety, as her present actions clearly show she has done, she has no rights whatever over Tibet, not even to a nominal suzerainty. Since 1913 Tibet has

8. Article 35 said: "A State which is not a member of the United Nations may bring to the attention of the Security Council or the General Assembly any dispute to which it is a party if it accepts in advance, for the purposes of the dispute, the obligations of pacific settlement provided in the present Charter" (British Foreign Office Records, FO371/84454, given in a letter from the British Foreign Office to the attorney general, dated 25 November 1950).

not only enjoyed full control over her internal affairs but also has maintained direct relations with other states. She must therefore be regarded as a state to which Article 35 (2) of the Charter applies.

2. It is important to stress that the right enjoyed by Tibet to engage in foreign relations on her own account distinguishes her case from, for example, that of British protected states with internal autonomy but no right to engage in foreign relations.

3. Our recognition of Chinese suzerainty over Tibet after 1914 was conditional on the recognition by China of Tibetan autonomy; in other words the suzerainty which we recognized was of the nominal kind envisaged in the Simla Convention, and we have since 1914 accepted the right of Tibet to enter into direct relations with other states.[9]

The Foreign Office also examined the meaning of suzerainty and, in particular, the status of any vassal state or territory that was subordinate to a suzerain. It concluded that situations lumped under this rubric were so divergent that the status of a vassal state under a suzerain depended in a large measure on the facts of the specific case. Two factors in particular were critical: first, whether all international treaties concluded by the suzerain state are ipso facto concluded for the vassal; and, second, whether war of the suzerain is ipso facto war of the vassal. On both these counts the research division of the Foreign Office concluded that all the evidence showed that Tibet was not a part of China but, rather, had a clear international identity of its own.[10]

On the basis of these briefs, the British Foreign Office decided that Tibet had the right to bring its case before the United Nations and, on 10 November (three days before the Tibetan appeal even reached New York), sent the following telegram to the British high commissioner in India and the British United Nations delegation in New York:

We are considering what attitude to adopt should the Tibetan appeal come up in the United Nations. We are already committed in a general way to India's support and this will doubtless extend to [the] line she adopts at Lake Success. Though we fully acknowledge preponderance of Indian interests in this matter and recognise that initiative must lie with her, we consider it of utmost importance to have a preliminary exchange of views with her on account of grave implications of discussion of Tibetan issue in United Nations on our relations with China.

2. For your personal information we view present situation on following lines:

9. British Foreign Office Records, FO371/84454, telegram from the British Foreign Office to the U.K. high commissioner in India, dated 9 November 1950.

10. British Foreign Office Records, FO371/84454, minute by R. H. Scott, Southeast Asia Department of the British Foreign Office, dated 2 November 1950.

(a) We consider that Tibetan autonomy is sufficiently well established for her to be regarded as a "state" within the meaning of the United Nations Charter. My immediately succeeding telegram gives our views on the legal aspect: these are also for your information only at this stage and not for communication to Government of India. Whether we shall be prepared to support this interpretation of Tibet's international status in the course of preliminary debate in United Nations on validity of her appeal remains for decision. Assuming that India takes this attitude we should be prepared to do so too, though the implications are far reaching.

(b) If this view of Tibet's status is conceded and validity of her appeal is upheld in debate, it follows that Chinese action constitutes aggression against Tibet, and in the Security Council [meeting] which would presumably follow two obvious possibilities would present themselves:

> (i) the Council might content itself with a condemnation of the Chinese action;
> (ii) it might call on China to withdraw her forces from Tibet and to restore the status quo.

(c) We should hope that Security Council action would be restricted to (i) above. We should particularly wish to avoid action on lines of (ii) above, which would at best be likely to lead to a resolution which China would defy and which could only be enforced by armed action which neither we, nor we assume India or anyone else, e.g., the United States, would be prepared to take. In the result the United Nations would lose prestige.[11]

The British Foreign Office at this stage, then, was leaning toward supporting Tibet in some fashion and preventing China's aggression from going completely unnoticed, but it did not want to go counter to the policy of the Indian government, whom it now considered had the primary responsibility for Tibet.[12] And it especially did not want the United Nations to pass resolutions it could not enforce.

---

11. British Foreign Office Records, FO371/84454, telegram from the Commonwealth Relations Office in London to the U.K. high commissioner in India, dated 10 November 1950.

12. In some ways, the Indian government resented Britain acting as if it no longer had interests in the area. India conveyed this resentment to the British Foreign Office in its answer to Britain's request for India's opinion to a draft response, which the British wanted to use in a parliamentary question about whether Britain would press for the inclusion of the Tibetan problem in the Security Council: "The situation in Tibet is one which primarily concerns the Government of India and for this reason we would not ourselves wish to take the initiative. We are however in close consultation with the Government of India on this matter" (British Foreign Office Records, FO371/84454, the Commonwealth Relations Office to the U.K. high commissioner in India, dated 11 November 1950). The Indian government informed Britain that it preferred the first sentence of the statement to read, "The situation in Tibet is one which primarily concerns the Government of India *although His Majesty's Government are also interested.*" The reason India gave for this was that it was worried that the statement in the original British

The British delegation to the United Nations, however, felt that the position presented in Foreign Office telegram was far too strong. The head of the delegation, Sir Gladwyn Jebb, responded that whatever opinion one might hold about the Chinese aggression, the reality was that no one could possibly give effective aid to Tibet. He argued that the Indians themselves had doubts about Tibet's status as a state and that Britain should therefore modify its views on the matter. He recommended that the best line to take in the United Nations would be to argue that the Tibetan issue was wrapped in "legal obscurity." This was conveyed in a telegram he sent to the Foreign Office on 14 November 1950:

> . . . Since Indian Government themselves seem to have strong doubts regarding the "absolute independence" of Tibet, I feel that we should do well to modify our own legal views on this subject. If indeed we are to argue that Tibet is fully independent, there seems no doubt that an act of aggression has occurred and in these circumstances there might be strong pressure brought on us to support some far reaching resolution in the Security Council and when that is vetoed, transfer the whole matter to the General Assembly under the terms of the recent resolution "Uniting for Peace."
>
> 2. I greatly hope therefore that I shall be instructed, when and if the Indians raise this matter in the Security Council, to argue to the general effect that the legal situation is extremely obscure and that in any case Tibet cannot be considered as a fully independent country.[13]

This response prompted the Foreign Office to ask the British attorney general for a ruling on Tibet's international status. It also led to an attempt to ascertain more clearly the policy of the Indian government toward the Tibetan appeal, since its views were considered primary to those of Britain.

INDIA'S RESPONSE TO THE CHINESE INVASION

Although India had decided that friendship with China outweighed obligations inherited from Britain regarding Tibet, it initially had been unwilling to back China's claim of sovereignty openly. India had addressed this dilemma by helping to foster conditions that would compel Tibet to accede to China's terms and thereby preclude India's having to make a difficult or embarrassing decision unilaterally. News of the Chinese invasion, therefore, came as a shock to Delhi, which responded by sending a note on 21 October

---

draft suggested that the initiative lay completely with India (British Foreign Office Records, FO371/84454, telegram from the U.K. high commissioner in India to the Commonwealth Relations Office in London, dated 13 November 1950, Emphasis added).

13. British Foreign Office Records, FO371/84454, telegram from the U.K. delegation in New York to the British Foreign Office, dated 14 November 1950.

criticizing the Chinese government's actions. The note, however, was extremely weak and argued not that China's actions were morally or legally unacceptable but rather that its actions would harm India's efforts to assist China in gaining admittance to the United Nation and the Security Council. The note said:

> The Central People's Government are fully aware of the views of the Government of India on the adjustment of Sino-Tibetan relations. It is, therefore, not necessary to repeat that their interest is solely in a peaceful settlement of the issue. My government are also aware that the Central People's Government have been following a policy of negotiations with the Tibetan authorities. It has, however, been reported that some military action has taken place or is about to take place, which may affect the peaceful outcome of these negotiations.
>
> The Government of India would desire to point out that a military action at the present time against Tibet will give those countries in the world which are unfriendly to China a handle for anti-Chinese propaganda at a crucial and delicate juncture in international affairs. The Central People's Government must be aware that opinion in the United Nations has been steadily veering round to the admission of China into that organization before the close of the present session.
>
> The Government of India feel that military action on the eve of a decision by the (General) Assembly will have serious consequences and will give powerful support to those who are opposed to the admission of the People's Government to the United Nations and the Security Council.
>
> At the present time when the international situation is so delicate, any move that is likely to be interpreted as a disturbance of the peace may prejudice the position of China in the eyes of the world. The Government of India's firm conviction is that one of the principal conditions for the restoration of the peaceful atmosphere is the recognition of the position of the People's Republic of China, and its association with the work of the U.N. They feel that an incautious move at the present time even in a matter which is within its own sphere will be used by those who are unfriendly to China to prejudice China's case in the U.N. and generally before neutral opinion. The Government of India attach the highest importance to the earliest settlement of the problem of Chinese representation in international organizations and have been doing everything in their power to bring it to a successful conclusion. They are convinced that the position of China will be weakened if through military action in Tibet those who are opposed to China's admission are now given a chance to misrepresent China's peaceful aims.
>
> The Government of India feel that the time factor is extremely important. In Tibet there is not likely to be any serious military opposition and any delay in settling the matter will not therefore affect Chinese interests, or a suitable final solution. The Government of India's interest in this matter is, as we have explained before, only to see that the admission of the People's Government to the U.N. is not again postponed due to the causes which could be avoided

and further that, if possible, a peaceful solution is sought while military action may cause unrest and disturbance on her own borders.[14]

This Indian note is interesting in that it does not indicate or question China's right to incorporate Tibet and accepts the Chinese position that Tibet was a matter within its own sphere. It also ignores the Indo-Tibetan Agreements of 1914, through which India held rights regarding Tibet's status.[15]

India received no response to this communication, so on 28 October, three days after the Chinese publicly announced that their troops had liberated Chamdo, it sent another, somewhat stronger, note. This letter stated that because China had given assurances that its intentions were peaceful and that negotiations in good faith were going on between Tibet and China, the advance of China's troops into Tibet appeared "most surprising and regrettable." It also said India *deplored* the invasion, but in part negated the force of this language by saying that her advice to China had been "friendly and disinterested." The note read:

> We have seen with great regret reports in newspapers of official statements made in Peking to the effect that "People's Army units have been ordered to advance into Tibet."
>
> We have received no intimation of it from your Ambassador here or from our Ambassador in Peking.
>
> We have been repeatedly assured of the desire of the Chinese Government to settle the Tibetan problem by peaceful means and negotiation. In an interview which our Ambassador recently had with [China's] Vice-Foreign Minister, the latter, while reiterating the resolve of the Chinese Government to "liberate" Tibet had expressed the continued desire to do so by peaceful means.
>
> We informed the Chinese Government through our Ambassador of the decision of the Tibetan delegation to proceed to Peking immediately to start negotiations. This delegation actually left Delhi yesterday. In view of these facts the decision to order Chinese troops to advance into Tibet appears to us most surprising and regrettable.
>
> We realise that the Tibetan delegation has been delayed from proceeding to Peking. This delay was caused in the first instance by their inability to obtain visas for Hong Kong, but the delegation can in no way be held responsible for this.
>
> Subsequently, the delegation returned to Delhi because of the wish of the Chinese Government that preliminary negotiations should first be conducted in Delhi with the Chinese Ambassador.
>
> Owing to the lack of knowledge on the part of the Tibetan delegation on how to deal with other countries and the necessity of obtaining instructions

14. Carlyle 1953: 550–51.
15. Jain 1960: 45–46.

from their Government, who in turn had to consult their assemblies, certain further delays took place.

The Government of India does not believe that any foreign influences hostile to China have been responsible for the delay in the departure of this delegation.

Now that the invasion of Tibet has been ordered by the Chinese Government, peaceful negotiations can hardly be synchronised with it, and there naturally will be fear on the part of Tibetans that the negotiations will be held under duress. In the present context of world events the invasion of Tibet by Chinese troops can only be regarded as deplorable and in the considered judgement of the Government of India, not in the interest of China or of peace.

The Government of India can only express their deep regret that in spite of the friendly disinterested advice repeatedly tendered by them, the Chinese Government should have decided to seek the solution of the problem of their relations with Tibet by force instead of by the slower and more enduring method of peaceful approach.[16]

Two days later, China responded in a most disparaging and unequivocal manner, stating that Tibet was a part of China and that whatever China did there was an internal matter of concern to no foreign country. It went on to insult Nehru and India by charging that India had been "affected by foreign influences hostile to China in Tibet." It was a strong statement, especially in contrast to the relatively mild Indian notes.

The Central People's Government of the People's Republic of China would like to make it clear:

Tibet is an integral part of Chinese territory. The problem of Tibet is entirely the domestic problem of China. The Chinese People's Liberation Army must enter Tibet, liberate the Tibetan people, and defend the frontiers of China. This is the resolved policy of the Central People's Government.

The Central People's Government has repeatedly expressed the hope that the problem of Tibet may be solved by peaceful negotiations and it welcomes, therefore, the declaration of the local authorities from Tibet to visit Peking at an early date to proceed with peaceful negotiations.

However, the Tibetan delegation, through outside instigation, has intentionally delayed the date of its departure for Peking. Nevertheless, the Central People's Government has not abandoned its desire to proceed with peaceful negotiations.

But regardless of whether the local authorities of Tibet wish to proceed with peaceful negotiations and whatever results may be achieved by negotiations, the problem of Tibet remains a domestic problem of the People's Republic of China and no foreign interference will be tolerated.

The particular problem of Tibet and the problem of the participation of the People's Republic of China in the United Nations are two entirely separate problems.

16. Union Research Institute 1968: 11–12.

Therefore, with regard to the viewpoint of the Government of India on what it regards as deplorable, the Central People's Government of the People's Republic of China can only consider it as having been affected by foreign influences hostile to China in Tibet and therefore expresses its deep regret.[17]

Angry at this insulting note, the Indian government made its strongest response on 1 November in a third note that openly articulated the cause of Tibetan autonomy (within the context of Chinese suzerainty), arguing that its previous note was not unwarranted interference in Chinese internal affairs "but well-meant advice by a friendly government which has a natural interest in the solution of the problems concerning its neighbours by peaceful means." India, however, still unilaterally relinquished its traditional rights regarding Tibet. The Government of India wanted to maintain its missions in Tibet, as well as the McMahon border delimitation, and apparently felt that the best way to accomplish this end was by renouncing the very legal rights on which these were based:

The Indian Ambassador in Peking has transmitted to the Government of India a note handed to him by the Vice-Foreign Minister of the People's Republic of China on October 30. The Government of India have read with amazement the statement in the last paragraph of the Chinese Government's reply that the Government of India's representative to them was affected by foreign influences hostile to China and categorically repudiates it.

At no time has any foreign influence been brought to bear upon India in regard to Tibet. In this, as in other matters, the Government of India's policy has been entirely independent and directed solely towards the peaceful settlement of international disputes and the avoidance of anything calculated to increase the present deplorable tension in the world.

The Government of China is equally mistaken in thinking the Tibetan delegation's departure for Peking was delayed by outside instigation. In previous communications, the Government of India have explained at some length the reasons why the Tibetan delegation could not proceed to Peking earlier. They are convinced that there has been no possibility of foreign instigation.

It is with no desire to interfere or gain any advantage that the Government of India have sought earnestly that a settlement of the Tibetan problem should be effected by peaceful negotiations adjusting legitimate Tibetan claim to autonomy within the framework of Chinese suzerainty. Tibetan autonomy is a fact which, judging from reports they have received from other sources, the Chinese Government were themselves willing to recognise and foster.

The Government of India's repeated suggestions that China's suzerainty [over Tibet] and Tibetan autonomy should be reconciled by peaceful negotiations were not, as the Chinese Government seems to suggest, unwarranted interference in China's internal affairs, but well-meant advice by a friendly gov-

17. Union Research Institute 1968: 13.

ernment which has a natural interest in the solution of the problems concerning its neighbours by peaceful methods.

Wedded as they are to ways of peace, the Government of India had been gratified to learn that the Chinese Government were also desirous to effect a settlement in Tibet through peaceful negotiations. Because of this the Government of India suggested sending their delegation to Peking, and were glad that this advice was accepted in the interchange of communications which had taken place between the Government of India and the Government of China, and the former had received repeated assurances that a peaceful settlement was the goal.

In the circumstances, the surprise of the Government of India was all the greater when it learned that military operations had been undertaken by the Chinese Government against peaceful people. There has been no allegation of any provocation, or any report on non-peaceful methods on the part of the Tibetans. Hence there was no justification whatever for such military operations against them. Such a step, involving an attempt to impose a decision by force, cannot possibly be reconciled with a peaceful settlement. In view of these developments, the Government of India is no longer in a position to advise the Tibetan delegation to proceed to Peking unless the Chinese Government thinks it fit to order their troops to halt their advance into Tibet and thus provide a chance for peaceful negotiations.

Every step that the Government of India has taken in recent months has been to check the drift to war all over the world. In doing so they have often been misunderstood and criticised, but they have adhered to their policy regardless of the displeasure of great nations. They cannot help thinking that the military operations of the Chinese Government against Tibet have greatly added to the tensions of the world and to the drift towards general war, which they are sure the Government of China also wishes to avoid.

The Government of India has repeatedly made it clear that they have no political or territorial ambitions toward Tibet and do not seek any novel privileged position for themselves or for their nationals in Tibet. At the same time, they pointed out, that certain rights have grown out of usage and agreements which are natural between neighbours with close cultural and commercial relations.

These relations have found expression in the presence of an agent of the Government of India in Lhasa, the existence of trade agencies at Gyantse and Yatung and the maintenance of post and telegraph offices along the road route up to Gyantse over the last forty years. *The Government of India is anxious that these establishments, which are to the mutual interests of India and Tibet and do not detract in any way from Chinese suzerainty over Tibet, should continue. The personnel at the Lhasa mission and the agencies at Gyantse have accordingly been instructed to remain at their posts.*

It has been the basic policy of the Government of India to work for friendly relations between India and China, both countries recognising each other's sovereignty, territorial integrity and mutual interests.

Recent developments in Tibet have affected friendly relations and the interests of peace all over the world; this the Government of India deeply regrets.

In conclusion, the Government of India can only express their earnest hope

that the Chinese Government will still prefer the method of peaceful negotiation and settlement to a solution under duress and by force.[18]

While this exchange was occurring, the Tibetan appeal to the United Nations
reached Lake Success. India's reaction was particularly important, because
Britain, and to a lesser extent the United States were committed to following India's lead, as mentioned earlier.

For several weeks, India did not inform Britain of its official position but
informally seemed to indicate it would support a Tibetan appeal. For example, on 13 November, G. S. Bajpai, secretary in the Ministry of External
Affairs, said that India would support the Tibetan appeal and that he hoped
support would be forthcoming from other powers on the Security Council.[19]
And again on 17 November, he told the British that the head of the Indian
delegation to the United Nations had been instructed to make inquiries to
see if some nonsuperpower would present the Tibetan appeal to the United
Nations Security Council. Bajpai said, however, that if no other country could
do so, he thought it more than probable that the Indian government would
be prepared to act.[20]

However, in mid-November, a Chinese reply to the last Indian note arrived in New Delhi. Dated 16 November, it is important because it led the
Government of India not to support the Tibetan appeal.

> On November 1, 1950, the Ministry of Foreign Affairs of the People's Republic
> of China received from His Excellency Ambassador Panikkar a communica-
> tion from the Government of the Republic of India on the problem of Tibet.
>
> The Central People's Government of the People's Republic of China, in its
> past communications with the Government of the Republic of India on the ques-
> tion of Tibet, has repeatedly made it clear that Tibet is an integral part of Chi-
> nese territory and that the problem of Tibet is entirely a domestic problem of
> China. The Chinese People's Liberation Army must enter Tibet, liberate the
> Tibetan people and defend the frontiers of China. This is the firm policy of the
> Chinese Government. According to the provisions of the common programme
> adopted by the Chinese People's Political Consultative Conference, the regional
> autonomy granted by the Chinese Government to national minorities inside
> the country is autonomy within the confines of Chinese sovereignty.
>
> This point has been recognized by the Indian Government in its aide mé-
> moire to the Chinese Government dated August 28 this year. However, when
> the Chinese Government actually exercised its sovereign rights and began to
> liberate the Tibetan people and drive out the foreign forces and influences in

18. Union Research Institute 1968: 13–16 (emphasis added).

19. British Foreign Office Records, FO371/84454, telegram from the U.K. high commissioner in India to the Commonwealth Relations Office, dated 13 November 1950.

20. British Foreign Office Records, FO371/84454, telegram from the United Kingdom high
commissioner in India to the Commonwealth Relations Office, dated 17 November 1950.

order to ensure that the Tibetan people would be free from aggression and would realise regional autonomy and religious freedom, the Indian Government attempted to influence and obstruct the exercise of its sovereign rights in Tibet by the Chinese Government. This only causes great surprise to the Chinese Government.

The Central People's Government of the People's Republic of China sincerely hopes that the Chinese People's Liberation Army may enter Tibet peacefully to perform the sacred task of liberating the Tibetan people and defending the frontiers of China. Therefore, it long ago welcomed the delegation of the local authorities of Tibet which still remains in India to come to Peking at an early date to proceed with peace negotiations. Yet the said delegation, obviously as a result of continued external obstruction, has delayed its departure for Peking. Further, taking advantage of the delay in starting negotiations, the local authorities of Tibet have deployed strong armed forces at Chamdo in Sikang [Xikang] province and in the interior of China, in an attempt to prevent the Chinese People's Liberation Army from liberating Tibet.

On August 31, 1950, the Chinese Ministry of Foreign Affairs informed the Indian Government through Ambassador Panikkar that the Chinese People's Liberation Army was going to take action soon in west Sikang [Xikang] according to set plans, and expressed the hope that the Indian Government would assist the delegation of the local authorities of Tibet so that it might arrive in Peking in mid-September to begin peace negotiations. In early and mid-September, the Chinese Chargé d'Affaires, Shen Chien [Jian], and later Ambassador Yuan Chung-hsien [Zhongxian], both in person, told the said delegation that it was imperative that it should hasten to Peking before the end of September, otherwise the said delegation should bear the consequences and be responsible for all the subsequent events resulting from the delay.

In mid-October, the Chinese Ambassador Yuan again informed the Indian Government of this. Yet still owing to external instigation, the delegation of the local authorities of Tibet fabricated various pretexts and remained in India.

Although the Chinese Government has not given up its desire of settling the problem of Tibet peacefully, it can no longer continue to put off the set plan of the Chinese People's Liberation Army to proceed to Tibet. The liberation of Chamdo further proved that through the instrument of Tibetan troops, foreign forces and influences were obstructing the peaceful settlement of the problem of Tibet. But regardless of whether the local authorities of Tibet wish to proceed with peace negotiations, and regardless of whatever results may be achieved by negotiations, no foreign intervention will be permitted. The entry into Tibet of the Chinese People's Liberation Army and the liberation of the Tibetan people are also decided.

In showing its friendship toward the Government of the Republic of India, and in an understanding of the desire of the Indian Government to see the problem of Tibet settled peacefully, the Central People's Government of the People's Republic of China has kept the Indian Government informed of its efforts in this direction. What the Chinese Government can only deeply regret is that the Indian Government, in disregard of the facts, has regarded a domestic problem of the Chinese Government—the exercise of its sovereign rights in Tibet—as an international dispute calculated to increase the present deplorable tensions in the world.

The Government of the Republic of India has repeatedly expressed its desire to develop Sino-Indian friendship on the basis of mutual respect for territory, sovereignty, equality and mutual benefit, and of preventing the world from going to war. The entry into Tibet of the Chinese People's Liberation Army is exactly aimed at protecting the integrity of the sovereignty of China. And it is on these questions that all those countries who desire to respect the territory and the sovereignty of China should first of all indicate their real attitude towards China.

In the meantime, we consider that what is now threatening the independence of nations and the world peace is precisely the forces of these imperialist aggressors. For the sake of maintaining national independence and defending world peace, it is necessary to resist the forces of these imperialist aggressors. The entry into Tibet of the Chinese People's Liberation Army is thus an important measure toward maintaining Chinese independence, to preventing the imperialist aggressors from dragging the world towards war, and to defending world peace.

The Central People's Government of the People's Republic of China welcomes the renewed declaration of the Indian Government that it has no political or territorial ambitions in China's Tibet and that it does not seek any new privileged position. *As long as our sides adhere strictly to the principle of mutual respect for territory, sovereignty, equality and mutual benefit, we are convinced that the friendship between China and India should be developed in a normal way, and that the problems relating to Sino-Indian diplomatic, commercial and cultural relations with respect to Tibet may be solved properly and to our mutual benefit through normal diplomatic channels.*[21]

Although the response was still completely unequivocal concerning the Chinese attack on Chamdo, the Indian government saw positive aspects in this more diplomatic letter with regard to Indian commercial rights in Tibet and India's interest in achieving a peaceful settlement. Menon, the Indian foreign secretary, told the British high commissioner in India that the Chinese note did not specifically question India's right to maintain its trade agencies and so forth in Tibet, and he made mention of discussions through diplomatic channels of Indian interest in Tibet. Menon commented that this contrasted favorably with the Chinese ambassador's preceding statement.[22] Consequently, the Indian government now decided to pull back from support of the Tibetan appeal, sending the following somewhat disingenuous instructions to its U.N. delegation:

21. Union Research Institute 1968: 16–18.

22. British Foreign Office Records, FO371/84454, telegram from the U.K. high commissioner to the Commonwealth Relations Office, dated 21 November 1950. Menon, however, also commented that he thought the Chinese would, in fact, try to clear the Indians out of Tibet as

(a) the Government of India did not like the El Salvador resolution and Rau was not to support it.

(b) the question of timing of the handling of the Tibetan appeal needed careful consideration. Korea was obviously of first importance and it was therefore desirable that nothing should be said or done which was likely to embitter relations with China at this critical state, and it would be preferable therefore *for no action to be taken on the Tibetan appeal for the present.* Little good could come out of any condemnation of the Chinese action in Tibet and at this stage such a condemnation might conceivably do a great deal of harm.[23]

THE UNITED NATIONS DEBATE ON THE TIBETAN APPEAL

On Friday, 24 November, a mere week after the Dalai Lama became ruler of Tibet, the issue of whether to include "the invasion of Tibet by foreign forces" as an additional item in the United Nations General Assembly was debated by the General Committee at the request of El Salvador. The U.N. summary report of the ensuing debate (written in the third person) is cited below. The move to defer action on Tibet's appeal was suggested by none other than the British representative, K. Younger, and was strongly supported by India. Tibet's two traditional friends now pulled the rug out from under its appeal for help from the United Nations.

The debate began when Hector David Castro, from El Salvador, read his proposal, which follows:

Two weeks ago the El Salvador delegation had asked the Secretary-General for a copy of the appeal forwarded to the United Nations by the Government of Tibet. The Secretary-General had agreed to that request but so far had taken no action in the matter. In pursuing the aims of the Charter, however, the United Nations should be careful not to isolate itself and lose all touch with governments which were not members of the Organization. Every important communication sent to the United Nations by the government of a non-member State should be made known to all member states. He [Castro] regretted that the Secretary-General had not distributed to delegations the appeal from the Government of Tibet. He asked the President of the General Assembly to do everything possible to see that communications and documents sent by non-members, like those sent by member States, were distributed to members of the United Nations when those members were called upon to take an important decision. The invasion of Tibet by Chinese armed forces had been an-

---

soon as they were in a position to do so and indicated general agreement with the British interpretation of Tibet's legal position (ibid.)

23. British Foreign Office Records, FO371/84454, instructions related by G. S. Bajpai in a conversation with the U.K. high commissioner in India, cited in a telegram from the U.K. high commissioner to the Commonwealth Relations Office, dated 30 November 1950 (emphasis added).

nounced by the press of the whole world. As the Government of Tibet had refused to comply with the orders of the Government of the so called People's Republic of China, the latter had decided to send a military expedition to Tibet. It should be borne in mind that the Government of Tibet had always shown readiness to enter into peaceful negotiations with the so-called People's Government of China. A delegation from the Government of Tibet had been on the point of proceeding to Peking when the invasion occurred.

Little information was available; it was known that Tibet was invaded by a foreign army but the extent of the territory won by the army was not known.

Before submitting its proposal to the General Committee, the Salvadorean delegation had had rather peculiar questions put to it. It had been asked whether its government was not, in the present case, acting under the influence of another government. The Government of El Salvador had always exhibited the fullest independence and the delegation of El Salvador had always complied with its Government's instructions. No other government therefore could have influenced the Government or the delegation of El Salvador. He [Castro] then recalled the terms of the telegram and the letter sent on 14 November 1950 to the President of the General Assembly by the Chairman of the delegation of Salvador (A/1534).

The delegation of El Salvador had hoped that the General Assembly could make a decision on that question without referring it to the General Committee. This was a case of international aggression which the General Assembly could not overlook. Under the terms of Article 1, paragraph 1, of the Charter, the United Nations must "maintain international peace and security." Tibet, of course was not a member of the Organization, but the United Nations must maintain peace not only between member states, but throughout the whole world.

The aggression committed against Tibet should be of particular concern to the great powers. He recalled that a permanent member of the Security Council has accused the other permanent member of dealing with questions only in so far as their own political interests were concerned. There was no basis for that accusation, but, if the General Assembly refused to consider the proposal of El Salvador, some weight might attach to that charge.

Mr. Dulles had stated, in regard to threats to the independence and territorial integrity of China, that if the General Assembly took no action in that matter, it would disappoint the whole world. It would be equally disappointing if the General Assembly disregarded an act of international aggression on the pretext that consideration of that question would complicate still further the present situation. It might also be asked whether there was any basis for such an argument. Representatives of member States frequently made strong statements before the General Assembly and charged certain other Governments with pursuing a dangerous policy. Such statements showed the complete freedom of expression of delegations, but were more likely to complicate the international situation than was consideration of the aggression committed against Tibet.

Some claimed that Tibet was not autonomous at all and that it was a province of China, so that its invasion by a Chinese army would be an internal affair which came within the competence only of the Chinese Government. He [Castro] wished to submit certain information to members of the General

Committee to show that that argument was unfounded. He then read an extract from *Chambers Encyclopedia* (Volume XIII). . . .

. . . He [Castro] did not think the General Assembly could disregard the aggression against Tibet on the mere pretext that that country was isolated and had but a few means of communication with the outside world. Tibet was a particularly important strategic position; the high plateaus of Tibet dominated India. These were facts which the General Assembly could not disregard.

The representatives of the Tibetan Government were coming to New York to lay a complaint before the General Assembly or the Secretary-General. The General Assembly could not dismiss their case unheard.

The Government of El Salvador had done its duty by drawing the attention of the General Committee to the aggression against Tibet. If the General Assembly disregarded that aggression, it would be neglecting its responsibilities.

Finally Mr. Castro read the draft resolution submitted by his delegation (A/1534) and concluded by saying that the General Assembly should at least condemn the unprovoked acts of aggression against Tibet.[24]

Following this, the British representative, Younger, spoke. As we saw earlier, the U.K. delegation preferred to avoid debate on the Tibetan issue, while the Foreign Office was in favor of supporting some form of the Tibetan appeal. On 18 November 1950, London in fact had sent relatively clear interim instructions to its U.N. delegation. These instructions stated:

You should maintain that Tibet is entitled to submit an appeal under Article 35 (2) of the Charter for the reasons contained in Commonwealth Relations Office telegram No. 2539 to New Delhi [discussed above]. If the point is raised you should explain that, even if a nominal Chinese suzerainty subject to Tibetan autonomy is recognized, Tibet's right of appeal is not thereby invalidated. But you should not commit us either to continuing or to repudiating recognition of Chinese suzerainty in the new circumstances. You should deplore the Chinese resort to force and stress that it was taken without provocation and while peaceful negotiations were in progress. You could, if necessary, support a resolution condemning Chinese action on these lines. You should not, however, without further instructions, support any resolution which calls for or implies that threat of military action of the United Nations.[25]

Although the British archives show no subsequent telegrams contravening these instructions, it appears that the general British policy of following India's lead gave Younger enough leeway to recommend taking no action at this time, because, as was seen, India wanted to prevent a United Nations General Assembly debate. Thus, as soon as the General Committee discussion was opened to the floor, Younger said that he

24. As given in Bureau of His Holiness the Dalai Lama, n.d.: 7–10.
25. British Foreign Office Records, FO371/84464, telegram from the Foreign Office to the British U.N. delegation, dated 18 November 1950.

did not think he could participate at that time in a general discussion on the question of Tibet. That did not mean that the United Kingdom delegation was attempting to shirk its own responsibilities or to prevent the United Nations from assuming its full responsibilities. The question before the Committee was one of procedure. The point was to decide what was the best way of considering the question of Tibet. Consideration of the question was not an end in itself, but rather a way of trying to settle the problem.

The Committee did not know exactly what was happening in Tibet *nor was the legal position of the country very clear.* Moreover, it could still be hoped that the existing difficulties in Tibet could be settled amicably by agreement between the parties concerned. In those circumstances, before taking a decision the members of the General Committee would be wiser to wait until a better idea could be formed of the possibilities of a peaceful settlement. He proposed, therefore, that the Committee should defer decision on the request made by the delegation of El Salvador.[26]

Although the British Foreign Office did not consider the matter closed at this time and saw Younger's statement to the United Nations as a procedural postponement, news of this speech devastated the Tibetan pro-West leadership, who were stunned to find that Britain, of all countries, could say that the legal status of Tibet was unclear.[27]

Younger was followed by the Indian delegate, the Jam Saheb of Nawanagar, who made a very strong speech stating that India, the country most closely involved, felt there was a chance for a peaceful settlement and argued that the United Nations could aid this, not by discussing the Tibetan plea, but rather by abandoning it. According to the same official U.N. report, he said,

His Government [India] had given careful study to the problems raised by the proposal of El Salvador to place the question of the invasion of Tibet by foreign forces on the General Assembly agenda. That was a matter of vital interest to both China and India. The Committee was aware that India, as a neighbor of both China and Tibet, with both of which it had friendly relations, was the country most interested in a settlement of the problem. That was why the Indian Government was particularly anxious that it should be settled peacefully.

He had no desire to express an opinion on the difficulties which had arisen between China and Tibet, but would point out that, *in the latest note received by his Government, the Peking Government had declared that it had not abandoned its intention to settle those difficulties by peaceful means.* It would seem that the Chinese forces had ceased to advance after the fall of Chamdo, a town some 480 kilo-

26. Bureau of His Holiness the Dalai Lama, n.d.: 11 (emphasis added).

27. Because the British attorney general had not yet commented on the Foreign Office's interpretation of Tibet's legal status, the United Kingdom U.N. representative was, from the British point of view, technically not completely deceitful when he said that the British government felt Tibet's legal status was not clear.

meters from Lhasa. The Indian Government *was certain* that the Tibetan Question could still be settled by peaceful means, and that such a settlement could safeguard the autonomy which Tibet had enjoyed for several decades while maintaining its historical association with China.

His delegation considered that the best way of obtaining that objective was to abandon, for the time being, the idea of including the question in the agenda of the General Assembly. That was why he supported the United Kingdom representative's proposal that consideration of the request for inclusion should be adjourned.[28]

However, notwithstanding the Indian arguments, the Government of India knew very well that the Chinese and Tibetans were not negotiating at that time and that they were far apart in their aims. And India's assertion that it was *certain* of a peaceful outcome is hardly credible. In fact, a British Foreign Office minute of 28 November expressed the thought that the last Chinese note to India "holds little hope of peaceful settlement."[29]

After the Indian delegate's speech, all the other countries fell into line. Australia's representative, Keith Officer, said that he "agreed with the representatives of the United Kingdom and India. In view of the statement made by the Indian representative, he would unreservedly support the United Kingdom proposal that consideration of the request for inclusion by El Salvador should be adjourned."[30] And the Russian representative

agreed with the United Kingdom proposal. However, he wished to explain his delegation's view on the substance of the question. It was an extremely simple question; Tibet was an inalienable part of China and its affairs were the exclusive concern of the Chinese Government.

The representative of El Salvador had referred to newspaper articles and encyclopedia, but he had not cited any international instrument in support of the argument that Tibet was in independent country, which had been invaded by Chinese troops. Chinese sovereignty over Tibet had been recognized for a long time by the United Kingdom, the United States and the U.S.S.R.

The question was therefore one which came essentially within the national jurisdiction of China; the United Nations could not consider it. If it did so, it would be guilty of unwarranted intervention in the internal affairs of the Chinese people, who had been liberated after centuries of foreign domination. That being so, his delegation would vote the adjournment of consideration of the request submitted by the representative of El Salvador and even for its outright rejection.[31]

---

28. As given in Bureau of His Holiness the Dalai Lama, n.d.: 11–12 (emphasis added).

29. British Foreign Office Records, FO371/84454, Foreign Office minute by R. H. Scott, dated 28 November 1950.

30. As cited in Bureau of His Holiness the Dalai Lama, n.d.: 12.

31. Bureau of His Holiness the Dalai Lama, n.d.: 12.

Finally, after a long speech by the representative of the Chinese Guomindang government of Taiwan, it was unanimously decided to adjourn consideration of the El Salvador proposal. Following this, the United States' representative, Ernest Gross, spoke. According to the U.N. report, he said,

> [Gross] had voted for adjournment in view of the fact that the Government of India, whose territory bordered on Tibet and which was therefore an interested party, had told the General Committee that it hoped that the Tibetan question would be peacefully and honourably settled. In accordance with its traditional policy the United States would in any other circumstances have voted for the inclusion of the item in the General Assembly agenda. His government had always supported any proposal to refer to the United Nations international disputes or complaints of aggression, which could thus be aired, considered and settled at international hearings. That was the principle applied by the United States Government even in the case of accusations made against the United States and despite the illogical and fraudulent nature of the accusations.
>
> However, in the present case, the United States delegation wanted to support the proposal made by the States most directly concerned in the subject matter of the request submitted by the delegation of El Salvador.[32]

Tibet's first appeal to the United Nations, therefore, had failed. The response from the international community was a terrible disappointment. Western nations, such as the United States and Britain, had refused to support Tibet's appeal or even to allow the Tibetan delegations to enter their countries. And despite the unprovoked invasion of Tibetan territory by China, the United Nations showed little interest and facilely tabled Tibet's urgent appeal for assistance. India played a singularly unhelpful role in this by, on the one hand, arguing strongly in the international arena that it would be best if Tibet and China settled their differences alone and, on the other, by refusing to allow India to be used as a base/conduit of support to Tibet. And on the home front, Tibet's protector deities also proved to be useless. So as the winter of 1950 began, Tibet's leaders faced bleak prospects.

32. Bureau of His Holiness the Dalai Lama, n.d.: 12.

Chapter 4

Negotiations with Beijing

Tibet's first appeal to the United Nations had failed, undercut not by communist countries such as the Soviet Union but by friendly democracies such as Britain and India. However, since the Tibet appeal was technically only tabled, the United Nations had not completely shut the door on it, and the Kashag, desperate to secure international support, immediately tried to widen the remaining opening with a new appeal and campaign. However, at the very same time that the Kashag was appealing again to the United Nations, the Chinese side made a new push to use its Chamdo victory as leverage to persuade Tibet to send delegates to start negotiations. The Kashag, therefore, found itself in very difficult straits. How long could it wait for the United Nations to respond before having either to negotiate an unwanted "peaceful liberation" agreement or, alternatively, to take the last resort and send its top officials and the Dalai Lama into exile?

· · · · ·

By the end of November, many officials in Lhasa feared that the PLA would soon launch another attack that would quickly overwhelm the remaining Tibetan army forces and capture Lhasa, despite the winter climate. And the PLA forces in Chamdo were not the only threat. PLA troops from the Northwest Bureau were also in far Western Tibet. They had moved down from Xinjiang during the summer of 1950 and had captured Rutog and the surrounding areas. If they moved east and took Shigatse and Gyantse, they could cut off the normal escape routes to India from Lhasa. Consequently, in December 1950, it was decided that the safest course of action was to move the young Dalai Lama to Yadong, a town on the Sikkim border. He would still be on Tibetan territory, but from there he and his top officials could easily flee to India if China continued its invasion into Central Tibet.[1]

After new officials were appointed in Lhasa to replace those accompanying the Dalai Lama to Yadong, the Dalai Lama departed Lhasa on 18 December 1950. He arrived in Yadong on 2 January 1951. He was now beyond the reach of the Chinese no matter what they did militarily. At the same time, the Tibetan government also sought to protect its wealth, moving hundreds and hundreds of mule loads of gold, silver, and other precious valuables to Gangtok (the capital of Sikkim), where the ethnically Tibetan maharaja of Sikkim agreed to store them for safekeeping.

While this was going on, the Chinese side again began to take steps to attain its real goal—an agreement with the Dalai Lama for the peaceful liberation of Tibet. Not only was the invasion, as mentioned, halted, but great care was taken to treat the captured Tibetan soldiers and officials as "brothers," not as enemies. For example, after giving the thousands of captured Tibetan troops some propaganda (in the terms of the Chinese, "education") about the Communist Party's policies on religion and nationalities, the Chinese sent them home on their own with a gift of a few Chinese silver dayan (ch. da yang) coins to cover their travel expenses. Beijing also continued to assure Tibetans by radio broadcasts, pamphlets, and posters that China would not alter the traditional social and religious systems. One such poster, dated 9 November 1950, said,

> With serious concern for the people of Tibet who have suffered long years of oppression under American and British imperialists and Chiang Kai-shek's reactionary Government, Chairman Mao Tse-tung of the Central People's Liberation Army ordered the People's Liberation Army troops to enter Tibet for the purpose of assisting the Tibetan people to free themselves from oppression forever.
>
> All the Tibetan people, including all lamas, should now create a solid unity to give the People's Liberation Army adequate assistance in ridding Tibet of imperialist influence and in establishing a regional self-government for the Tibetan people. They should at the same time build fraternal relations, on the basis of friendship and mutual help, with other nationalities within the country and together construct a new Tibet within the new China.
>
> *With the entry of the People's Liberation Army into Tibet, the life and property of the Tibetan lamas and people will be protected. Freedom of religious belief will be safeguarded and Lama Temples will be protected. Assistance will be rendered to the Tibetan people in the direction of developing their educational, agricultural, pastoral, industrial, and commercial enterprises, and their living conditions will be improved.*
>
> *No change will be made in the existing administrative and military systems of Tibet.*

---

1. See Goldstein 1989: 737–40 for a more detailed account of this period.

Existing troops will become a part of the National Defense Forces of the People's Republic of China. All lamas, officials and chieftains may remain in their posts. Matters relating to reforms in Tibet will be handled completely in accordance with the will of the Tibetan people and by means of consultations between the Tibetan people and Tibetan leaders.

Pro-imperialist and Kuomintang officials concerning whom there is definite evidence that they severed relations with the imperialists and Kuomintang and who will not carry out any sabotage or put up resistance may remain at their posts irrespective of their past history.

The People's Liberation Army is a strictly disciplined army which will faithfully carry out this policy of the Central People's Government. They will respect the Tibetan people's religious beliefs, as well as their traditional habits and local customs. They will be polite in their speech, fair in business transactions, and will not take a single thread from the people. In borrowing any articles, they will obtain the owner's consent; in cases of damage, compensation will be paid at market price of the article concerned. In hiring hand or animals, appropriate remuneration will be paid. No person will be drafted; no livestock taken away.[2]

The captured Lhasa officials were also treated with respect. Ngabö was moved back into the governor-general's quarters and ate in the same canteen that the top Chinese officials used. Phünwang, the leading Tibetan cadre in the Eighteenth Army Corps, was given the full-time task of talking with Ngabö and his top aide, Tsögo, about the Communist Party's nationality and religion policies. He explained in detail the general policies and the specific arrangements the CCP was offering Tibet and, at the same time, emphasized how futile it would be to try to resist the Chinese militarily. Phünwang told Ngabö bluntly that it would be like the old Chinese proverb "Whether the rock hits the egg or the egg hits the rock, the result is the same."[3]

The Chinese desire for a negotiated settlement fell on receptive ears, since Ngabö, from the start, had wanted to negotiate with China, not try to fight.[4] Even when he was first captured, he is reported to have said, "We have been defeated, and we are now your prisoners. Whether you keep me under arrest or not, my hope is that we can have a good negotiation and a peaceful settlement. That's all I can say."[5] Phünwang explained what happened next.

2. U.S. National Archives, 693.93B/11–2250. This translation of the poster was included in a memorandum from the U.S. State Department's Office of China Affairs to its Office of Far East Affairs, 22 November 1950 (emphasis added).

3. Phünwang, interview, 2000, Beijing. For an interesting account of early missteps on the part of the Chinese, see Goldstein, Sherap, and Siebenschuh 2004: 143.

4. His predecessor, Lhalu, in fact, had criticized him for deliberately weakening the border defenses. He said that Ngabö actually began to dismantle existing mountain fortifications because he feared these could provoke the Chinese to attack (Lhalu, interview, 1992, Lhasa).

5. Horsur, interview, 1992, Dharamsala. This is his recollection of a conversation he had with his relative Ngabö.

As the efforts to improve relations with Ngabö and the other Lhasa officials began to bear fruit, we discussed an idea that we thought might persuade Lhasa to negotiate. Ngabö should write a letter to his colleagues on the Council of Ministers [Kashag] explaining what happened to them and the realities and opportunities—and to urge that they agree to send representatives.

Ngabö agreed, and we considered the contents of the letter with great care. After Tsögo wrote a first draft, he, Ngabö, and I discussed and revised it several times. Then I took it to Wang Qimei, and he and Ngabö went over it carefully and revised it several more times. Finally Ngabö and all the other Tibetan officials signed it, and it was sent on its way to Lhasa.[6]

Ngabö's account of this differs slightly in the process by which this letter was produced but not in the outcome.

During the two months we had contact with the Communists after Chamdo, we found them excellent; nothing like the rumors that were said of them in Lhasa. Even if there were rainstorms, they lived in tents and didn't stay in monasteries and people's houses. And when they traded, they did so honestly and didn't take even a needle from the people. They strictly followed the "three main rules of behavior and the eight things that must be done." They put these into practice. Whatever work they did, the PLA did it to serve the people. They gave medical care to the people, and they started a school and helped alleviate the people's difficulties.

So because we saw this ourselves, *we took the initiative* and had a meeting at which the thirty-six Lhasa officials in Chamdo discussed the situation. According to reports, many false rumors are being circulated in Lhasa and everyone has become frightened and doesn't know what to do. Chairman Mao has decided to liberate Tibet. If Central Tibet were liberated by force, a war would certainly arise, and the people would experience the suffering of war. And there is a danger that the religious and secular leaders headed by the 14th Dalai Lama would flee to India, and if that occurs, it would not be good. Consequently, everyone at the meeting decided that it would be good if we sent a message to the Dalai Lama recommending that he and the Chinese Central Government hold discussions. In the letter it said that if Tibet is peacefully liberated, the monks and lay people will not have to experience the suffering of war, and monasteries and villages will not be destroyed, and everyone will not have to become separated and dislocated and will be able to live together. Because we have seen and experienced the good behavior of the PLA and the policies of the Chinese Communist Party, we do not believe the rumors said of them, and we sincerely recommend that you start peaceful talks with the Chinese central government. After this was written, we sent a message to Wang Qimei, who said this is good.[7]

6. Goldstein, Sherap, and Siebenschuh 2004: 142–43.
7. Nga phod (Ngabö) 1989: 4.

To give this initiative maximum credibility, the letter from Ngabö and his officials was hand-carried to Lhasa by two of Ngabö's officials—the monk official Gyentsen Phüntso (a tsendrön) and the lay aristocratic official Samling (a kandrön). On 5 December 1950, these two left without any accompanying Chinese officials. Ngabö was not sure who was in charge in Lhasa so addressed the letter simply "To whoever in Lhasa is holding political authority."[8]

These two officials rode hard and made it back to Lhasa in seven days, arriving on 12 December, soon after the Dalai Lama had assumed political power and six days before he left for Yadong. Gyentsen Phüntso recalled the trip and his reception in Lhasa.

> Ngabö and Wang Qimei gave us some money for the road and Wang gave me a gun. . . . We also had a Tibetan government lamyig [a road pass which permitted the holder to requisition corvée horses] for the road. But only some of the areas honored the lamyig. Some would not give us anything. After Shopando, there was a mountain pass that we had to cross, and the serfs (tib. miser) said, "We have been liberated, so we don't do the tawu (horse corvée tax) anymore." Consequently, we had to carry the saddles and rifle on our backs and cross the pass on foot. After that, we bought horses with Tibetan paper money (about 128 ngüsang per horse). I reached Lhasa in seven days and nights on horseback. Two horses died. We were worried about getting the message to the Dalai Lama and Kashag, so we rode hard.
>
> Lhalu was at Lharigo. He asked how were things at Chamdo, so I told him what I knew. . . . I stayed two hours at Lhalu's. From Lharigo, Lhalu sent a cable to Lhasa saying we were coming.
>
> Q. What was in the message you were carrying?
>
> The essence of the message was that there is no way to compete with the Communists through warfare. If we fight, the Tibetan people will suffer a lot. So it is best to have peaceful negotiations. The Chinese captured me, and I (Ngabö) am at Chamdo. If you want to hold talks, please send a representative.
>
> We went on, and at Thomora, we met a government messenger coming from Lhasa. He at once dismounted, took off his hat, and said, "Honorable two sirs, hello" (tib. Gungö nyi Tashidele). He said he was specially sent by the government to welcome us and gave us a message from the Kashag telling us to come directly without changing clothes. So as soon as we arrived, we immediately went to the Kashag, which was meeting in the Tsuglagang. We dismounted at Sungjör (Tsuglagang's south side). There were a lot of people there waiting to see us. Some said, "Poor things (tib. nyingje), they came from so far." Others said, "They sold us out." I didn't get angry when they said that.
>
> When we went to meet the Kashag ministers, Ramba, Surkhang, and Thubden Ramyang were present. Usually officials of our rank can't just go in, but

8. Lha sa'i bzhugs mkhan chab srid kyi gan 'kher mkhan gto su yin nas der 'bul rgyu (Nga phod [Ngabö] 1989).

this time they said, "Come in, Come in." We gave them the letter . . . and explained the situation and events of Chamdo. . . . In the Kashag there were two types (of ministers), those who were stubborn and militant (tib. leba drago) and those not. Ramba said, "Oh my, the other side was iron, but we were "bag" (kneaded tsamba); how did we come to this state [read: iron is tough, but bag can be made into any shape, i.e., it's too malleable]. He didn't like this and wanted to fight. He was leba drago and wanted to fight. We didn't answer him but just said, "Yes, yes, yes" (tib. lo, lo, lo). Surkhang was clever [and did not let on what he was thinking], saying, "Oh, you have had a hard time. It's not your fault. It is good that Ngabö and his staff are all right." So the Kashag ministers told us, "You two take it easy and rest up for a few days."[9]

Discussions about Ngabö's letter began at once. An Assembly meeting was convened at which the two competing views clashed. Some said Tibet should not submit to the Communists and should continue to fight, but the majority felt that Tibet should follow Ngabö's recommendation and proceed with negotiations. It was, therefore, agreed to send two representatives to Chamdo to assist Ngabö in talks with the Chinese. Gyentsen Phüntso recalled the day the Dalai Lama left and he learned of representatives being sent to Chamdo.

At 11:00 A.M. I got a message saying Samling and I should come to the Kashag at 4:00 P.M. At this time Shasur and Thubden Ramyang were there. They told us, "The Dalai Lama has gone to Yadong to avoid danger, and now the Sitsab are in charge. We are under them. It has been decided to pursue peaceful negotiations, and we are sending Khenjung Thubden Lengmön and Sambo Rimshi (Tenzin Thundrup) from Lhasa. . . . You have had a hard time, but it has been for the defense of religion. So today please go with these two representatives to Chamdo." . . . So we went back to Chamdo. It took us twenty-six days [to reach there].[10]

Sambo himself recalled his appointment and the general situation in Lhasa.

When I was told to go to China, I didn't think much about it. Life in Lhasa was very uncertain and tense. It was full of rumors. I expected that the Chinese would not harm us, since we were coming as a delegation, and I felt it was better to be doing something than just sitting in Lhasa apprehensively, waiting to see what transpired. My parents had already left for India with all of our valuables [in July 1950], so I was not worried about them. At this time, all the higher-class aristocratic families such as Tsarong and Surkhang had made arrangements to send their wealth to India. . . . [Moreover] people at this time felt that even

9. Gyentsen Phüntso, interview, 1992, Lhasa.

10. Gyentsen Phüntso, interview, 1992. Meanwhile, since Ngabö had heard no word from these first two officials, he sent another two officials (Jarong Jija and Khenjung Lodrö Kesang) to Lhasa.

though Chamdo had fallen they would not have to stay in India a long time. I made hurried preparations to leave [for Chamdo] with my wife and arranged to send the remainder of our possessions in Lhasa to one of our estates.[11]

Sambo and Thubden Lengmön arrived in Chamdo the day before the Tibetan New Year, in the third week of February 1951.

However, the apparent willingness to negotiate was deceptive. In reality, Tibet's leaders were still not ready for peaceful liberation. The United Nations remained their hope, and they had actually sent a new appeal to Shakabpa for transmission to Lake Success. Sending Sambo and Thubden Lengmön to Chamdo was meant primarily as a stalling tactic, as is apparent from the instructions these two representatives were given.

Sambo recalled his reaction when he initially read the written instructions given to him in Lhasa.

> I had a look at the list of five points, wondering what they contained, but after reading them I realized that if we based our work on this list, successful peaceful negotiations were not possible. So I thought that maybe these were just written for external consumption and that we would be given different verbal instructions. I made it a point, therefore, to go to see each of the acting Kashag ministers and the two sitsab individually, ostensibly to bid them good-bye—but really hoping that they would give me some additional instructions. But they did not say a word about them. . . .
>
> Q. What were the five points?
>
> They were more like answers to questions than negotiating points. One that I recall was a response to Chinese Guomindang statements that the five different ethnic groups in China were part of the same race and that all these must unite. It said that we are Tibetans and are different from the Chinese. We don't know anything about any other ethnic groups or races [nationalities]. . . . I have forgotten all the other points, but I remember that there was no way negotiations could be based on them. None were substantive positions that you could discuss and work out a compromise. It was impossible. . . . The only thing they said to me was, "Ngabö will be your leader, and you must obey him." That is all.[12]

After Sambo arrived in Chamdo and met Ngabö, the latter asked him what orders he brought from Lhasa and then went to his room to read them. After a short time, he came back and said to Sambo,

> "These five points are useless. Don't you have other verbal instructions?" When he heard there were none, he said, "What are we supposed to do now? How do they expect us to negotiate with such points?" I had no answer.[13]

---

11. Sambo, interview, 1981, Rajpur, India.

12. Sambo, interview, 1981.

13. Sambo, interview, 1981.

It was obvious to Ngabö, therefore, that no agreement would be forthcoming with these instructions. The Chinese Communists had decided to liberate Tibet and incorporate it into the People's Republic of China, but the Tibetan government was holding on to the idea that the new relationship between Tibet and the new Chinese government could be as it was during the Guomindang or Qing periods. It still did not accept that Tibet was to be an integral part of China. To Ngabö, who did not know about the new U.N. appeal, it seemed a continuation of Lhasa's flight from reality. Ngabö discussed this extensively with the other Tibetan representatives and staff, and in the end they decided that it was not possible to hold negotiations in Chamdo on the basis of these instructions.

As a result, Ngabö went to Wang Qimei and suggested that Wang lead a small delegation of a few Chinese officers to Lhasa (with him accompanying) to hold discussions there. This was in late February/early March 1951. Wang agreed, so Ngabö immediately sent two of his officials—the monk official Thondrub Namgyal and the lay official Dingyön Surpa—to inform the sitsab in Lhasa that negotiations could not be held in Chamdo with the instructions brought by Sambo. Moreover, given the distances and difficulties of communication between Chamdo and Lhasa, he suggested that the sitsab permit a Chinese representative to come to Lhasa to hold talks there. He received a positive reply, but just as he and Wang Qimei were about to leave for Lhasa, Ngabö suddenly received a telegram from Yadong (via the Chinese Embassy in Delhi) that said, "It is confirmed that the negotiation between the local Tibetan Government and the Central Committee will be held. So you and the representatives sent from Lhasa who are in Chamdo should go to Beijing right away. Kheme and Lhautara will come from Yadong via the sea route. You are appointed as the leader of the five person delegation."[14] Faced with two sets of contradictory orders, Ngabö decided to follow the one from Yadong, since that was where the Dalai Lama resided. This was in late March 1951. Meanwhile, the Tibetan government's new appeal to the United Nations had arrived.

TIBET'S SECOND UNITED NATIONS INITIATIVE

The Tibetan government's response to the United Nations' initial decision, again beautifully written with Sinha's help, expressed surprise and regret at the United Nations' action and emphasized that organization's moral duty to uphold the rights of small powers against more powerful neighbors. It invited the United Nations to send a fact-finding mission to investigate Tibet's claim "to a separate Tibetan culture and existence apart from

14. Ngabö 1989.

China," and it indicated Tibet would send its own delegation to Lake Success. It said,

Kalimpong, 8 December 1950

We have heard with grave concern and dismay of the United Nations' decision setting aside the discussion of our appeal regarding the unwarranted violation of our national territory by armed forces of the Central Peoples Government of the People's Republic of China. The agony and despair which prompted us to seek for the assistance of the United Nations Organization at a critical stage of the invasion will be better appreciated by those nations whose liberty is always at the mercy of being jeopardized by the aggressive designs of their more powerful neighbors. We who are completely secluded by a natural barrier from easy contact with the rest of the world have come to acknowledge that the only secure foundations of international peace and order can lie on the firm determination of all peace loving nations of the world to resist aggression and on their frank disapproval of all violent methods of settling inter-state disputes.

It is therefore a matter of great surprise and regret to us that the United Nations on whom solely rests the responsibility of maintaining the peace and well being of all nations should have so indifferently treated the peace appeal of a weak and peace loving people, hardly exceeding 3 million, beleaguered by their powerful neighbors, who are a mighty host of 450 million and whose resources are incomparably vaster than those of Tibet. Are we to believe in the justice of Chinese demands over our liberty merely because they happen to be strong in arms?

It is today a matter of common knowledge that there have been hostile incursions into our territory by Chinese troops and that we have had to surrender a good portion of our land to the invaders. We have earlier reported how by surprise and force they seized the town of Chamdo and captured the large garrison we maintained there. Our liberators have not made much progress since then but their armed soldiers are roving over weakly held areas in both eastern and western Tibet. In consequence, the constant threat of being overpowered hangs ominously over us and our meager resources, so long devoted to peaceful ends and to our religion, now strained by the need of protecting our country from being submerged by a force that is lethal to the values long cherished by our people, we are convinced that it would be the height of cowardice to bow to superior force. We would rather be overpowered by its blind rage than accept it with a show of reverence.

We have already made known our decision to abide by any settlement advocated by the United Nations. We do not wish the world to be convulsed into an armed conflict for our sake and yet we would like to know that the world has given thought and consideration to the issue that we have so humbly brought before them and advised the Chinese not to indulge in murder and intimidation of our peaceful lands. There can be no better opportune moment than the present when Chinese delegates have arrived at Lake Success in connection with other matters to have a full and frank discussion of the Tibetan issue. We have decided if necessary to dispatch a small delegation to the United Nations to assist the Assembly in their deliberations.

Should there be any doubt or hesitation on the part of any of the various delegations to the United Nations regarding our claim to a separate Tibetan culture and existence apart from the Chinese we should be happy to welcome a United Nations fact finding commission to carry out investigation in Tibet

His Holiness the Dalai Lama graciously consented to assume full power for the administration of Tibet at the unanimous request of all his people on 17 November. It is with his consent and blessing that we venture to place this fresh appeal before the United Nations for consideration.

Dated Lhasa, 3 December 1950,
Tibetan delegation, Shakabpa (House, Kalimpong)[15]

A few weeks after this, on 21 December, the Tibetan government's newly appointed U.N. mission sent appeals to Britain, the United States, and Canada, informing them of their plans to go to the U.N. headquarters in Lake Success and requesting their support for this action.[16] Their letter to the United States said,

We would like to inform Your Excellency we three, Foreign Secretary Dzasak Surkhang, Dzasak Gyaltakpa and Khencung Choepel Thubten, together with Tsjchag Thubden Gyalpo and Tsepon Shakabpa, have instructions from our government to go to Lake Success [to] agitate and enforce [the] appeal which Kashag Cabinet [and] National Assembly Tibet submitted [to the] UN re hostile incursions into Tibet by Chinese Communists and we are all now here [in] Kalimpong.

Though [the] Government [of] Tibet recently submitted fresh appeal [to the] UN for early discussion on Tibetan issue, it is presumed no decision has yet been reached for discussion and further we have also had no information from [the] UN [to] attend [the] Assembly which keeps us waiting here.

[The] Government and people [of] Tibet have great hope [that] your government will afford effective help in any problems Tibet [has] and therefore they earnestly hope your government will help bring [the] question of Tibet under discussion in UN Assembly soonest.

15. British Foreign Office Records, FO371/84455, copy of U.N. file A/1658, original English version of Tibetan appeal, dated 11 December 1950. (The inconsistency in dates reflects when the letter was drafted and when it was translated and sent from Kalimpong. The third date, the 11th, is when the document was received in London.) After the first U.N. appeal, Shakabpa informed the Kashag about the United Nations' uncertainty about whether the appeal had actually come from the Tibetan government or from a private group, so the second appeal clearly mentions in the last sentence that the appeal comes from the Dalai Lama as ruler of Tibet.

16. U.S. National Archives, 793B.00/12-2250, telegram from the U.S. ambassador in India to the U.S. secretary of state, dated 27 December 1950. This is discussed in more detail in Goldstein 1989: 746–57.

We hope your Excellency will give us your valuable advice so that it will make matter of Tibet a success.[17]

The letter to Great Britain was identical. London initially instructed its high commissioner in New Delhi to respond positively to the new Tibetan appeal as follows:

Unless Indian Government have strong objections, we should be glad if you would now reply to Tibetan communication on following lines.

. . . Government of United Kingdom continue to maintain the friendly interest which they have taken in the maintenance of Tibetan autonomy since August 1947, when the rights and obligations arising from the existing treaty provisions devolved on the Government of India. Since the Government of the Chinese People's Republic have resorted to force instead of seeking to reach agreement on the question of Sino-Tibetan relations through the peaceful methods of discussion and negotiation, the Government of the United Kingdom are prepared to afford their general support to the Tibetan Government's appeal to the United Nations.[18]

However, the United Kingdom's high commissioner in India disagreed strongly with making even this mild statement of support:

I would strongly deprecate making this communication to Government of India and would also recommend against making any reply on proposed lines to Tibetan letter at this juncture.

2. The Foreign Secretary [of the Government of India] this morning confirmed our impression that things are at present quiet in Tibet and that there is no sign of any early resumption of Chinese advance toward Lhasa. He said in confidence that Panikkar had reported from Peking recently that he had heard that talks were proceeding at Chamdo between Chinese representatives and representatives of Tibetan Government. . . .

3. As regards United Nations angle the Foreign Secretary said that Tibetan Delegation were still in India and had not so far as he knew made any definite plans to leave for New York. The Indian view which he understood was shared by us was that in the absence of any further forward movement by Chinese and given many other issues now under discussion at Lake Success, it was preferable to postpone any hearing of Tibetan appeal. In these circumstances our suggested reply to Tibetans some five weeks after their letter to us would probably be interpreted by them as a direct encouragement to become more active at Lake Success. If it came to the ears of Chinese they would

17. U.S. National Archives, 793B.00/12–2650, cited in a telegram from the U.S. Embassy in India to the U.S. State Department, dated 27 December 1950.
18. British Foreign Office Records, FO371/84455, telegram from the Commonwealth Relations Office to the U.K. high commissioner in India, dated 16 December 1950.

surely regard it as further evidence of British interference. The Government of India would certainly consider such reactions from both Chinese and Tibetans as probable and would ask why we thought it necessary to make such a reply at all and if so deprecate our action. Incidentally there has been no hint that Tibetans are expecting any further reply from us.[19]

The British U.N. delegation replied similarly, and this prompted London to do nothing.[20] It ultimately instructed the high commissioner in India.

We are unable to give Tibetans this assurance [that Britain would help put the Tibetan appeal on the U.N. agenda] since in view of other issues now under discussion in United Nations, we do not consider that time is opportune for raising question of the Tibetan appeal, nor, if it were, should we be willing to take the initiative ourselves in view of Government of India's more immediate interest and responsibility in this matter. We are of course prepared to afford our general support to the Tibetan appeal to United Nations when question is raised . . . but it is considered that even an assurance of this nature to Tibetans might be misleading at this stage in the context of their last communication and we should not wish to do anything which would tend to raise their hopes unduly.[21]

London did, however, instruct the high commissioner that he could issue transit visas for the Tibetan delegation to the United Nations.[22]
The attitude of the Indian government, as reported to the U.S. ambassador and the British high commissioner, was even more negative. On 18 December, Bajpai said that India's attitude regarding the Tibetan case remained unchanged; that is, it was opposed to supporting the United Nations taking up Tibet's appeal. He said, the "GOI was still interested in Tibet case before UN but had delayed action pending outcome its efforts assist in achieving cease-fire in Korea. GOI had decided that criticism by it of Communist China in UN just now might adversely affect India's ability exert influence on China in direction cease-fire."[23] A few weeks later Bajpai offered the same reasons to the United States: "If GOI should press Tibetan case just now in UN Communist China would be alienated to such extent GOI would lose all amelio-

19. British Foreign Office Records, FO371/84455, telegram from the U.K. high commissioner in India to the Commonwealth Relations Office, dated 18 December 1950.

20. British Foreign Office Records, FO371/84455, telegram from the British Foreign Office to the United Kingdom U.N. delegation, dated 7 December 1950.

21. British Foreign Office Records, FO371/93002, telegram from the Commonwealth Relations Office to the U.K. high commissioner in India, dated 2 January 1951.

22. British Foreign Office Records, FO371/8469, telegram from the Commonwealth Relations Office to the U.K. high commissioner in India, dated 9 December 1950.

23. U.S. National Archives, 793B.00/12–1850, telegram from the U.S. ambassador in India to the U.S. secretary of state, dated 18 December 1950.

rating influence on Peping re Korea and related problems. Therefore Tibetan case should remain temporarily in abeyance as far as GOI concerned."[24]

The United States, however, in the interim, had become more interested in and sympathetic to the Tibetans' plight. On 14 December, the State Department sent the following telegraph to the U.S. ambassador in India:

> DEPT desires explore possibility of joint US-UK-India position aiming at obstructing or halting CHI COMMIE assault Tibet, which now seems slowed or stalled. . . .
>
> Prior to DEPT approach to BRIT UR [your] views requested on (1) possibility of getting active Indian support of Tibetan case in UN; (2) probably reaction of GOI to a proposal for quiet US support of more positive measures designed to stiffen Tibetan resistance; and (3) suggestions as to possible measures and means of implementation of both measures.[25]

Ambassador Henderson's reply on 30 December tended toward nudging Washington to decide to provide assistance to the Tibetans.

> We have been giving considerable thought this end to problem Tibetan case before UN. Thus far seemed preferable India take lead this matter. UN representatives GOI had repeatedly assured us it intended do so. Now appears views B. N. Rau and other India officials who do not wish India make any move in present world contest which might offend Communist China have prevailed and GOI continues postpone taking initiative re Tibet in UN. Seems likely Communist China will have taken over Lhasa and have fastened firmly its grip on Tibet before GOI prepared take lead in UN. We seem faced with choice supporting some power other than India taking initiative or of continuing postpone hearing Tibetan pleas until autonomous Tibet ceases to exist. We are wondering whether this would be to credit [of] UN. Is it logical for UN which gave Indonesia which was under Dutch sovereignty hearing to ignore Tibet? Will India, for example, have greater respect for UN if merely out of deference to it, UN gives Tibet no opportunity present case? We do not feel qualified make any fast recommendation because we are not acquainted with all ramifications international situation this particular moment. Nevertheless, we suggest Tibetan question be revived before substantive reply is made to letter from Tibetan delegation.[26]

Four days later, the State Department informed Henderson that the Tibetans could be given visas for temporary entry to the United States and that while

24. U.S. National Archives, 793B.00/12-2550, conversation reported in a telegram from the U.S. Embassy in India to the U.S. State Department, dated 27 December 1950.

25. U.S. National Archives, 793B.00/12-1450, telegram from the U.S. secretary of state to the U.S. ambassador in India, dated 14 December 1950.

26. U.S. National Archives, 793B.00/12-3050, telegram from the U.S. ambassador in India to the U.S. secretary of state, dated 30 December 1950.

the United States position on the Tibetan United Nations appeal was not yet formulated, the State Department was "hopeful [that the] presence [of the] Tibetan DEL[egation] in [the] U.S. may precipitate earlier consideration by interested countries."[27] At this stage, however, the Tibetan mission to the United Nations was informed only that their appeal was being forwarded to Washington. But ironically, while the United States was quietly moving toward more active support of Tibet, the Tibetans were once again disheartened by the lack of support and encouragement and began to contemplate whether it was time to abandon the U.N. approach and enter into real negotiations with the Chinese.

By the time the Dalai Lama and his attenuated government arrived in Yadong, intense debate had already taken place regarding the advantages and disadvantages of compromising with the Chinese and, if the decision was not to accept being part of China, for the Dalai Lama to go into exile. A key element in this debate was whether the Dalai Lama could expect any serious assistance from India and the Western democracies. In Yadong, this discussion continued. Two days after arriving in Yadong, all Tibetan officials in India were ordered to report there for an Assembly meeting at which their experiences in India with the Government of India and with the British and the U.S. diplomats would be discussed.[28] At this meeting it became obvious that, on the one hand, no positive feedback had come from the United Nations, Britain, or the United States in support of Tibet's new appeal and that, on the other, Ngabö and the other lay and monk officials with him were expressing positive opinions of the Chinese and their intentions. So after days of discussions, it was decided that Tibet's best option was now to start serious negotiations with the Chinese Communists.

The Kashag immediately sent two senior officials, the foreign minister Surkhang Dzasa and the monk official Chömpel Thubden, from Yadong to Delhi to discuss the site for the talks with the Chinese ambassador and to secure his agreement for additional representatives to be sent from Yadong to join Ngabö. Under the pretext of making a pilgrimage, Surkhang and Chömpel Thubden arrived in Calcutta on 25 January 1951. From there they went to Delhi and met the Chinese ambassador, who insisted the talks take place in Beijing rather than in Chamdo or Lhasa. Ambassador Yuan, however, readily agreed to Tibet's request to send more representatives from Yadong via India. He also said that China would halt its military invasion while the talks were going on and that, if Tibet accepted it was part of China, China

27. U.S. National Archives, 793B.00/12–2650, telegram from the U.S. secretary of state to the U.S. ambassador in India, dated 3 January 1951.

28. U.S. National Archives, 793B.00/1–851, telegram from the U.S. Embassy in India to the U.S. secretary of state, dated 8 January 1951.

would not change the politico-religious system in any way. After only a week in Delhi, the two Tibetan officials returned to Yadong. The Kashag, with the Dalai Lama's approval, then appointed two additional negotiators, the army commander-in-chief, Kheme Dzasa (Surkhang's father's brother) and one of the Ecclessiastic Office heads, Trunyichemmo Lhautara. They left for India in March with Takla (Phüntso Tashi), the Dalai Lama's brother-in-law (as the Chinese interpreter), and Sandutsang (Rinchen), as the English interpreter. It was at this point that the Kashag sent Ngabö the telegram mentioned above.[29]

NEGOTIATIONS IN BEIJING

Ngabö, Sambo, and Thubden Lengmön arrived in Beijing from Chamdo on 22 April. Kheme and Lhautara arrived from Yadong on 26 April. Ngabö's general frame of mind is revealed by his decision to demonstrate his modernity visually by cutting the long hair that was a prerequisite for service in the Tibetan government. In a sense, this was the first sign of a new Tibet.[30]

The delegation from Yadong brought a new and different set of external and internal instructions, as Ngabö recalled.

> They brought a note with instructions from Yadong for me. The note had an external part to show others and an internal one that we would use as we saw fit. The external one said that China and Tibet had a relationship of priest-patron and we hope that the relationship can become better than in the past. The internal one said if you have no choice but to accept Tibet as a part of China, you can accept that, but you can't accept them sending troops to Tibet. If about 50–100 Chinese representatives reside in Lhasa, that is all right, but they cannot bring soldiers with them. And among the representatives, it is best if they would send representatives who have faith in religion.[31]

The negotiators coming from Yadong had also been given verbal "instructions" from the Dalai Lama, who had told them, "Here are ten points. I have faith that you will not do anything bad [for Tibet], so you should go and achieve whatever you can."[32] The Dalai Lama also told them to use their best judgment according to the situation and circumstances and report back to the Kashag in Yadong. These officials brought a secret codebook so that

---

29. Goldstein 1989: 758–59.

30. Chabtsom (interview, 1992, Lhasa) recalled seeing a letter Ngabö had written to the Kashag in Lhasa about this; it told them, "I'm going to China to negotiate, so it's not appropriate to go with long braided hair. Therefore, I am cutting my hair."

31. Ngabö 1989; also Nga phod (Ngabö) 1989: 4.

32. Sambo, interview, 1981.

Figure 3. The five Tibetan negotiators, left to right: Sambo (Tenzin Thondrup),
Kheme Dzasa (Sonam Wangdü), Ngabö (Ngawang Jigme), Lhautara, Thubden
Lengmön, Beijing, 1951. Source: Chen Zonglie

they could establish a wireless link with Yadong and discuss issues as they
arose.[33] As we shall see, they did not do so.

Ngabö and the other delegates discussed these instructions, which, while
better than those sent from Lhasa, were still woefully unrealistic. They were
frustrated that after all this time the instructions still revealed a glaring lack
of understanding. They thought it ridiculous to say the Chinese should send
representatives who are believers in religion, since everyone knew that Communist Party members are atheists. Ngabö also knew from his talks with the
Chinese in Chamdo and from the Ten-Point document they discussed with
him that not accepting Chinese troops in Tibet was an instruction impossible to follow, and if Yadong insisted on this, the Tibetan delegates had no
way to negotiate an agreement with the Chinese.[34] Consequently, they sent

33. Sambo, interview, 1981.
34. Sambo, interview, 1981.

a coded telegram to the Kashag and the Dalai Lama in Yadong that said, "With the exception of the sending of PLA troops to Tibet and the border, there is not much problem on the other issues. However, if we do not accept [the Chinese troops], there is absolutely no way of negotiating." The answer from Yadong was naive and disappointing, instructing them as follows: "Sending PLA troops to the border is unacceptable. If there is no other way [to block this], then we can convert our Tibetan soldiers into Communist Party troops and then send them to the border [thus satisfying the Chinese demand to have PLA troops on the border]. But it is not okay for Han Chinese troops to come."[35]

This reply placed Ngabö in a very difficult situation. As mentioned earlier, he was committed to negotiating even before he arrived in Chamdo to replace Lhalu. He believed that Tibet was too weak to oppose China militarily on its own and, given the absence of outside intervention on its behalf, was convinced that Tibet's best hope was to compromise with the Chinese and try to find a way to create a modern Tibet as part of China that would preserve the Dalai Lama's status and authority together with Tibetan religion and monasticism. Having been with the Chinese Communists for half a year, he felt confident he could secure an agreement that would genuinely meet the needs of Tibet, but now he realized that the only way to achieve this was to do it on his own, since there was no way the PLA would not move into Tibet. If he tried to resolve every issue like this by sending telegrams to Yadong, nothing would ever get settled.[36] Gridlock would quickly ensue, and with summer approaching, this would precipitate a renewal of the Chinese invasion. As he saw it, the end goal for Tibet, an effective agreement, outweighed the means—disregarding instructions to discuss the issues with Yadong. Ngabö felt that since the Dalai Lama had already accepted the key issue—that Tibet was a part of China—the rest of the issues, such as allowing Chinese troops to be stationed in Tibet, were small by comparison. And in any case, if the Dalai Lama did not approve of the resulting agreement, he, Ngabö, would accept the blame, and the Dalai Lama could reject the agreement on the grounds that he had not been consulted.[37] Ngabö discussed this with the other members of the delegation, who unanimously agreed.[38] So just like that, the sitsab in Lhasa and the Kashag/Dalai Lama in Yadong were excluded from these historic negotiations.

35. Nga phod (Ngabö) 1989: 5.
36. Nga phod (Ngabö) 1989: 5.
37. Nga phod (Ngabö) 1989; also Sambo, interview, 1981.
38. Sambo, interview, 1981; Nga phod (Ngabö) 1989. It is interesting to note that although Takla (Phüntso Tashi), the brother-in-law of the Dalai Lama, was the delegation's Chinese translator rather than one of the five full delegates, the Tibetan delegation included him in all their discussions so that he could later report firsthand to the Dalai Lama (Sambo, interview, 1981).

Ngabö was undoubtedly correct in his assessment of the mindset of his colleagues in Lhasa and Yadong, but this decision is indicative of the enormity of the problem Tibet faced in coming to grips with the realities of its new situation vis-à-vis China at this critical time. As in the 1920s, the majority of the Tibetan elite were still unable to accept that their world would have to change.[39] With Eastern Tibet occupied militarily and the People's Liberation Army poised to continue its invasion to Lhasa, the ostrich-head-in-the-sand mentality of the conservative religious and lay elites now rendered Tibet unable to function effectively after having stood still in a world that had changed over the past half century. For those like Ngabö, who loved their country but understood that change was critical, these dangerous times would require difficult and risky decisions.

THE SEVENTEEN-POINT AGREEMENT

The Seventeen-Point Agreement was signed on 23 May 1950. As Mao had planned, it was based on the Chinese Ten-Point document and was carefully crafted to meet China's core aim—inducing Tibet to accept Chinese sovereignty and the military occupation of Tibet—while also giving the Tibetan side a number of major concessions regarding the continuation of the traditional theocracy under the Dalai Lama. It set the framework for Sino-Tibetan relations in the 1950s and is cited in full below.

THE AGREEMENT OF THE CENTRAL PEOPLE'S GOVERNMENT AND THE LOCAL GOVERNMENT OF TIBET ON MEASURES FOR THE PEACEFUL LIBERATION OF TIBET, 1951

Preamble
   The Tibetan nationality is one of the nationalities with a long history within the boundaries of China and, like many other nationalities, it has performed its glorious duty in the course of the creation and development of our great Motherland. But over the last one hundred years or more, imperialist forces penetrated into China, and in consequence also penetrated into the Tibetan region and carried out all kinds of deceptions and provocations. Like previous reactionary governments, the Guomindang reactionary government continued to carry out a policy of oppressing and sowing dissension among the nationalities, causing division and disunity among the Tibetan people. And the local government of Tibet did not oppose the imperialist deceptions and provocations, and adopted an unpatriotic attitude toward our great Motherland. Under such conditions, the Tibetan nationality and people were plunged into the depths of enslavement and suffering.
   In 1949, basic victory was achieved on a nationwide scale. In the Chinese

---

39. Regarding the situation in the 1920s, see Goldstein 1989: 89–139.

People's War of Liberation, the common domestic enemy of all nationalities—the Guomindang reactionary government—was over-thrown, and the common foreign enemy of all the nationalities—the aggressive imperialist forces—was driven out. On this basis, the founding of the People's Republic of China and of the Central People's Government was announced. In accordance with the Common Programme passed by the Chinese People's Political Consultative Conference, the Central People's Government declared that all nationalities within the boundaries of the People's Republic of China are equal, and that they shall establish unity and mutual aid and oppose imperialism and their own public enemies, so that the People's Republic of China will become a big fraternal and cooperative family, composed of all its nationalities, that within the big family of all nationalities of the People's Republic of China, national regional autonomy shall be exercised in areas where national minorities are concentrated, and all national minorities shall have freedom to develop their spoken and written languages and to preserve or reform their customs, habits, and religious beliefs, while the Central People's Government shall assist all national minorities to develop their political, economic, cultural and educational construction work. Since then, all nationalities within the country, with the exception of those in the areas of Tibet and Taiwan, have gained liberation. Under the unified leadership of the Central People's Government and the direct leadership of higher levels of People's Government, all national minorities are fully enjoying the right of national equality and have established, or are establishing, national regional autonomy.

In order that the influences of aggressive imperialist forces in Tibet might be successfully eliminated, the unification of the territory and sovereignty of the People's Republic of China accomplished, and national defense safeguarded; in order that the Tibetan nationality and people might be freed and return to the big family of the People's Republic of China to enjoy the same rights of national equality as all other nationalities in the country and develop their political, economic, cultural and educational work, the Central People's Government, when it ordered the People's Liberation Army to march into Tibet, notified the local government of Tibet to send delegates to the central authorities to conduct talks for the conclusion of an agreement on measures for the peaceful liberation of Tibet.

In the latter part of April 1951, the delegates with full powers of the local government of Tibet arrived in Peking. The Central People's Government appointed representatives with full powers to conduct talks on a friendly basis with the delegates with full powers of the local government of Tibet. As a result of these talks, both parties agreed to conclude this agreement and guarantee that it will be carried into effect.

There was no discussion regarding the preamble. The Tibetan delegates concerned themselves only with the actual points of the agreement.

Point 1. The Tibetan people shall unite and drive out imperialist aggressor forces from Tibet: the Tibetan people shall return to the big family of the Motherland—the People's Republic of China.

This point ended Tibet's de facto independence. The Tibetans initially denied that any imperialist forces were operating in Tibet, but the Chinese insisted that such forces were there—the Tibetans were just not aware of them. In the end, the Tibetans agreed to the point, saying, "If they are there, then you send them out."[40] The Tibetans understood that this point meant they accepted that Tibet was part of China; however, they also believed that the overall agreement left Tibet's internal administration in Tibetan hands.

> Point 2. The Local Government of Tibet shall actively assist the People's Liberation Army to enter Tibet and consolidate the national defense.

The Tibetans tried to no avail to persuade the Chinese side not to station troops there permanently but instead to send troops only if a threat should arise. The Tibetans also discussed the meaning of the term *local government* but did not worry much about it, because, on the one hand, the term translates in Tibetan literally as "the government of an area" (tib. sane sishung) thus obscuring the meaning of *local,* and, on the other hand, it uses the standard Tibetan word for government—*shung.*

> Point 3. In accordance with the policy toward nationalities laid down in the Common Programme of the Chinese People's Political Consultative Conference, the Tibetan people have the right of exercising national regional autonomy under the leadership of the Central People's Government.

There was discussion concerning the meaning of "regional autonomy," but since *autonomy* was translated into Tibetan as "self rule" (tib. rang gyong), the Tibetans had no real objections to this. Note should also be taken that the term used for "Central People's Government" was not the Tibetan word for "central government" *(üshung)* but the phonetic rendering of the Chinese term *zhongyang,* which the Tibetans took to mean "China."

> Point 4. The central government will make no change with regards to the existing political system in Tibet. The central authorities also will not alter the established status, functions, and powers of the Dalai Lama. Officials of various ranks shall hold office as usual.

The Tibetans considered this point extremely important and of course, agreed with it.

> Point 5. The established status, functions and powers of the Panchen Erdini shall be maintained.
> Point 6. By the established status, functions, and powers of the Dalai Lama and of the Panchen Erdini are meant the status, functions and powers of the Thir-

40. Sambo, interview, 1981.

teenth Dalai Lama and of the Ninth Panchen Erdini when they were in friendly and amicable relations with each other.

These two points created a major dispute that will be discussed in a later chapter.

Point 7. The policy of freedom of religious belief laid down in the Common Programme of the Chinese People's Political Consultative Conference shall be carried out. The religious beliefs, customs, and habits of the Tibetan People shall be respected, and lama monasteries shall be protected. The central authorities will not effect a change in the income of the monasteries and temples.

The Tibetan side also strongly agreed with this point. However, the wording of this point initially bothered the monk official Lhautara, since it originally said the central authorities would not change "the root for continuing religion" and did not precisely specify income. When Lhautara raised this issue, the Chinese side's Tibetan cadre-translator, Phünwang, suggested replacing this phrase with a term that clearly meant "income" in Tibetan, and the Tibetan delegation was then satisfied with the guarantees offered regarding religion.[41]

Point 8. Tibetan troops shall be gradually reorganized by stages into the People's Liberation Army, and become a part of the national defense forces of the People's Republic of China.

The question of the future of the Tibetan army was discussed in detail, with the Tibetans objecting strenuously to its disbandment. The Chinese side finally agreed to a compromise in which the agreement would say the Tibetan army was to be incorporated gradually in stages, but a secret codicil would say more specifically that three thousand troops of the Gyajong Regiment (i.e., the Trapchi and Bodyguard regiments) would be allowed to continue after the rest of the Tibetan forces had been disbanded. This avoided embarrassing the Chinese government by not forcing it to reveal that it would permit an autonomous part of China to have its own army force. This was the first of seven points in a secret codicil, which, to this day, has never been published.

Point 9. The spoken and written language and school education of the Tibetan nationality shall be developed step by step in accordance with the actual conditions in Tibet.
Point 10. Tibetan agriculture, livestock raising, industry, and commerce shall be developed step by step, and the people's livelihood shall be improved step by step in accordance with the actual conditions in Tibet.

41. Takla (Phüntso Tashi), interview, 1993, Dharamsala.

There was no disagreement regarding points 9 and 10.

Point 11. In matters related to various reforms in Tibet, there will be no compulsion on the part of the central government. The local government of Tibet should carry out reforms of its own accord, and when the people request reforms, they shall be settled by means of consultation with the leaders of Tibet.

This was seen by the Tibetans as another of the most important points in the agreement. In the discussions, the Chinese side assured the Tibetans that the Chinese government would not force any changes, and the Tibetan delegation believed that the Chinese could *never* get the Tibetan people to demand reforms that would alter the basic religious nature of the Tibetan polity. Consequently, they felt satisfied that the essence of the traditional system would continue.

Point 12. In so far as former pro-imperialist and pro-Guomindang officials resolutely sever relations with imperialism and the Guomindang and do not engage in sabotage or resistance, they may continue to hold office irrespective of their past.

Point 13. The People's Liberation Army entering Tibet shall abide by all the above-mentioned policies and shall also be fair in buying and selling and shall not arbitrarily take a single needle or thread from the people.

There was no disagreement regarding these points.

Point 14. The Central People's Government shall conduct the centralized handling of all external affairs of the area of Tibet; and there will be peaceful coexistence with neighboring countries and establishment and development of fair commercial and trading relations with them on the basis of equality, mutual benefit, and mutual respect for territory and sovereignty.

The Tibetans disliked this point but felt they had to agree.

Point 15. In order to ensure the implementation of this agreement, the Central People's Government shall set up a military and administrative committee (tib. magsi uyön lhengang) and a military area headquarters (tib. magükhang) in Tibet, and apart from the personnel sent there by the Central People's Government, these two organs shall include as many local Tibetan personnel as possible to take part in the work.

Local Tibetan personnel taking part in the military and administrative committee should include patriotic elements from the Local Government of Tibet, various districts, and leading monasteries and temples. This committee should include representatives appointed by the Central People's Government. The list of members shall be drawn up after consultation between the representatives designated by the Central People's Government and the various quarters concerned and shall be submitted to the Central People's Government for appointment.

This point raised a bitter argument and almost terminated the negotiations. It will be discussed later.

> Point 16. Funds needed by the military and administrative committee, the military area headquarters, and the People's Liberation Army entering Tibet shall be provided by the Central People's Government. The local government of Tibet will assist the People's Liberation Army in the purchase and transport of food, fodder, and other daily necessities.

This was accepted with no argument.

> Point 17. This agreement shall come into force immediately after signatures and seals are affixed to it.[42]

There was also the seven-point secret codicil, which included a statement on Chinese troop size (one army corps, or jun), the earlier-mentioned statement on the Tibetan army, a statement specifying that the Tibetan government would send two top-level officials to serve as deputy commanders of the new Tibet Military Area Headquarters, a statement on ending Tibet's own currency, and a statement that was critical for the Tibetans about the right of the Dalai Lama to return to Tibet and resume his full authority should he initially flee to India but later change his mind and want to return.

The Seventeen-Point Agreement was a stunning victory for Mao's peaceful liberation Tibet policy.[43] Carefully crafted in accordance with Mao's gradualist strategy, it allowed the Tibetan side to feel that its government and social system would be able to continue in the immediate future and, by not specifying when full implementation should occur, that it had control over the pace of changes and reforms. At the same time, however, the agreement clearly gave Mao everything he wanted.

In addition to acknowledging Chinese sovereignty for the first time in Tibetan history (point 1), the Tibetans would now assist the troops and cadres of the PLA to occupy Tibet peacefully (point 2). The Tibetans also agreed to give up all control over Tibet's foreign affairs, border defense, and com-

---

42. Basically from Goldstein 1989: 763–70; Dangdai zhongguo congshu bianjibu 1991: 162–65.

43. It was also a victory for Prime Minister Nehru, who had encouraged the Tibetans to accept being part of China and had worked to prevent the Tibet Question from being internationalized in the United Nations. India's assertion in the United Nations that the two parties were able to settle their differences internally had been vindicated and the danger of Sino-Indian relations deteriorating over Tibet averted. Britain's total support for India's Tibet policy and its thorough opposition to American encouragement of Tibetan resistance to the Communists was also validated. The United States, however, now found itself isolated, as its anti-communist mission in China was without support from either the victims (the Tibetans) or the relevant diplomatic players (India and Britain). It had frittered away an excellent opportunity to create a situation in which it had a great Asian Buddhist leader attacking Communist China.

merce (point 14) and agreed that the Tibetan army would be gradually incorporated into the PLA, albeit with no set deadline (point 8). They also accepted the return of the Panchen Lama to Tibet (points 5 and 6) and, in point 15, the creation of a new administrative entity, the Military-Administrative Committee, separate from the Tibetan local government and under the Central People's Government. This was explained as functioning to oversee the implementation of the agreement, but for the Chinese it was seen as eventually being the core of a new "autonomous region" government.

For the Tibetan side, the Seventeen-Point Agreement offered a number of important rights and authorities. First, it gave Tibet a unique status as the only political entity with which the Chinese Communist government signed a written agreement on the terms for liberation. In addition, points 3 and 4 state that Tibetans would have the right of exercising regional autonomy and that the central government in Beijing would not alter either the existing political system in Tibet or the "established status, functions and powers of the Dalai Lama" or his officials. Point 7 said religious freedom would be protected, and the income of the monasteries would not be changed by the central government. The agreement also commented in a moderate manner on change. Point 10, for example, said that commerce would be developed step by step but with no direct mention of socialist changes. Point 11 said there would be reforms but stipulated, "In matters related to various reforms in Tibet, *there will be no compulsion on the part of the central authorities.* The local government of Tibet should carry out reforms of its own accord, and when the people raise demands for reform, they shall be settled by means of consultation with the leading personnel of Tibet." All in all, for the Tibetans this seemed to create an agreed-on basis that would allow much of the old system to continue if not indefinitely then at least for some considerable time.

The agreement, however, clearly was not what the Tibetans would have preferred, since it meant thousands of Chinese Communist troops and officials would be coming to Tibet, and the new Military-Administrative Committee would be created, but the Tibetans did not have enough leverage to block this or to argue for a very different kind of relationship, for example, something similar to what existed during the Qing dynasty. The Tibetan side played an active role in the discussions and on several occasions either threatened to pull out of the negotiations or made plans to leave as a result of Chinese intransigence. Their tough stance over the issue of the Panchen Lama, for example, forced the Chinese to compromise, as will be discussed in a later chapter. However, on the major issues for the Chinese, such as stationing troops in Tibet, the threat of China continuing its military advance into Central Tibet compelled the Tibetan delegates to agree reluctantly.

Overall, however, given Tibet's hopeless situation on the ground, the Tibetan delegates were satisfied with the terms of the Seventeen-Point Agreement. Although everything could not stay the way it had been and key traditional institutions that symbolized Tibet's de facto independence, such as its own army, currency, and foreign affairs office, would cease to exist as separate entities at some point, the delegates focused on the positive aspects of the agreement. The Tibetan government, monasticism, and especially the position of the Dalai Lama would be preserved. Given the initial fear of the Tibetan elite that the Chinese Communists would destroy religion and the authority of the Dalai Lama, the negotiators felt they had done a good job for Tibet.

Since this agreement was to provide the legal basis for China's incorporation of Tibet, its signing was a major concern for the Chinese side. Sambo explained how the final signing came about.

> They [the Chinese] said: "Do we all agree now? If we all agree, then we have to put the terms down on paper and we will sign it on the 25th [actually 23 May]." This was said on the 19th or 20th of that month.
>
> Q: At that point, did anyone ask all of you whether you had the authority to sign the treaty?
>
> Oh. I forgot to tell you earlier that at the beginning of the discussions, the Chinese side told us, "If you agree and settle on terms, you will have to sign an agreement. In that case, do you have the authority and power to sign?" Ngabö said, "I have the power to agree to and sign a treaty." . . . Then the Chinese further asked, "Can you write 'Ngabö Ngawang Jigme, possessing full power and authority' [plenipotentiary powers]?" Ngabö said yes.
>
> Q: Was this discussed in front of all the delegation members, and did Ngabö consult the other members before saying yes?
>
> Ngabö answered straightaway [without consulting us].
>
> Q. Did Ngabö really have the power to sign the agreement?
>
> It's like this. I think he based his statements on the Dalai Lama's verbal statement [to go and achieve the best you can].[44]

The signing of the Seventeen-Point Agreement has often been contested as invalid in the West and in the Tibetan exile community because of a charge that the Tibetan delegates were forced to sign under duress and because the Chinese used forged Tibetan government seals. However, the facts do not support this assertion.

The Chinese did make new seals for the Tibetans, but these were just personal seals with each delegate's name carved on them. Other than this, there were no forged government seals. Part of the confusion derives from the fact that Ngabö had in his possession the seal of the governor of Eastern Tibet but chose not to use it. That seal, however, was not the official seal of the Tibetan government, so not using it did not lessen the validity of the agreement.[45]

---

44. Sambo, interview, 1981.

45. Ngabö later explained to the Dalai Lama why he did this: "I (Ngabö) had the seal of the governor of Eastern Tibet, but the Chinese themselves were not taking any interest, and so

In his autobiography, the Dalai Lama states that the Tibetan delegates claimed they were forced "under duress" to sign the agreement, but this is clearly incorrect in the sense of any personal duress.[46] The Chinese did not threaten the delegates with physical harm to make them sign. The delegates were free not to sign and to leave Beijing. Their feeling of duress derives from the general Chinese threat to use military force again in Central Tibet if an agreement was not concluded. However, according to international law, this does not invalidate an agreement (for example, America's use of atomic bombs to induce Japan to surrender). So long as there is no physical violence (or threat of violence) against the signatories, an agreement is valid. However, the validity of the agreement is premised on the signatories' full authority to finalize an agreement, and this, as we saw, was clearly not the case. So in this sense, the Dalai Lama actually had grounds to disavow it.

THE AFTERMATH OF THE SIGNING

Back in Yadong, as mentioned above, the news that an agreement had been signed stunned everyone. No one had any idea what had been discussed or how the seventeen points mentioned on the radio had come about, for example, whether the delegation had been mistreated or what? In fact, it was only on 31 May, eight days after the signing, that the Dalai Lama received a telegram from Ngabö informing him of the terms of the agreement and mentioning the presence of a secret codicil but not its contents.[47]

The Yadong Kashag responded to Ngabö's communication by telling him he had signed this agreement rashly, because his instructions stated he should consult with Yadong. It instructed him to wire the contents of the secret codicil to Yadong and wait in Beijing for the Kashag to examine them in detail and send further instructions.[48]

Ngabö and the other delegates, however, again chose not to comply. On the one hand, they felt that they had done the best they could, and on the other hand, they knew full well that the Chinese would not stand for reopening the negotiations, since they had already been assured by Ngabö that he had complete authority to conclude the agreement. He waited so long to cable Yadong in part to avoid something like this happening before the signing.

---

they made the [other] seals. If there should ever come a time in the future when we can say we did not voluntarily agree to sign, for this reason I did not use the seal of the governor of Eastern Tibet, though I had it" (Dalai Lama, interview, 1993, Dharamsala).

46. Dalai Lama 1990: 65.

47. Zhonggong xizang zizhiqu dangshi ziliao zhengji weiyuanhui 1990, entries for 28 May 1951 and June 1951.

48. Lha'u rta ra (Lhautara) 1981: 111; Le (1981: 136–37, entry for 28 May 1951) says that the telegram from Yadong was received on 28 May.

Moreover, an elaborate signing ceremony had already been held, the agreement had been publicly announced, and Mao Zedong himself had attended a grand banquet honoring the achievement. Ngabö, therefore, responded negatively, saying, "Telegraphic connections between Beijing and Yadong are difficult, and on top of that it is not possible to wire the content of the separate secret codicil because of the danger that its content will leak out. Consequently, we will bring them with us when we return, which we are doing as planned. However, if you in Yadong ultimately do not like the content of the agreement and want to renegotiate it, you should send a new delegation."[49]

The public announcement of the agreement created a great dilemma for the Kashag and the Dalai Lama. They had no idea what had really transpired in Beijing or what was included in the secret codicil. And while they knew it was much less than they had expected or authorized, particularly regarding Chinese troops coming to Tibet, it was difficult for them to evaluate what anything meant until they could confer with members of their delegation. To publicly denounce the agreement as illegal might mean losing the best opportunity they would get and would certainly precipitate the full invasion of Tibet. Not surprisingly, they chose to say nothing about it for the time being, making no public statements at all.

The Chinese government also found itself in a somewhat awkward situation. From Beijing's vantage, Chinese officials and troops could now enter Tibet "legally," beginning a new era in Sino-Tibetan relations. Internationally, the Tibet Question, the question of the status of Tibet vis-à-vis China, appeared to have been settled. But from another perspective, the Chinese knew well that the Dalai Lama quite possibly would reject the agreement and flee into exile. In fact, as mentioned, this possibility was so real that the Tibetan delegation had insisted that language be included in the Seventeen-Point Agreement stating that if the Dalai Lama fled abroad he could later return to Tibet and resume his role as head of the Tibetan government. The Chinese side had agreed to this, although it refused to place this statement in the main agreement (since it would obviously raise questions about the legitimacy of the agreement). It was one of the points in the secret codicil.[50] Because of this, the Chinese understood that the Dalai Lama might denounce the agreement as illegal and might even order the remaining Tibetan military (and militia) forces to man a new defense line east of Lhasa or to begin guerrilla operations against the PLA or both. And with the Korean War underway, there was always the possibility that the Dalai Lama might be able to secure U.S. assistance to challenge the international validity of the agreement itself and even to provide military support.

49. Lha'u rta ra (Lhautara) 1981: 111.
50. Sambo, interview, 1981; Nga phod (Ngabö) 1989; Stag lha (Takla) 1995.

The Chinese government decided, however, that whatever happened, it would treat the agreement as a legal document signed by valid plenipotentiaries and move at once to incorporate Tibet physically into the PRC. Two days after the agreement was signed, the PLA was ordered to move into the rest of Tibet.[51] Mao, however, still believed that the long-term national interests of China would be best served by trying to persuade the Dalai Lama to accept the terms of the agreement and return to Lhasa. To facilitate this, he immediately appointed Zhang Jingwu, a senior military administrator, as the Central Committee's "representative" to Tibet (ch. zhongyang fuzang "daibiao") and instructed him to leave quickly to meet with the Dalai Lama in Yadong.[52] There, he was to present the Dalai Lama with a letter from Chairman Mao as well as gifts from the Central Committee. In particular, Zhang was to try to allay any fears the Dalai Lama might have concerning the agreement and its implementations and persuade him to accept it and return to Lhasa.

However, traveling overland to Lhasa and then down to Yadong would take months, raising fears in Beijing that this would give the enemies of China (and the agreement) too much time for mischief. Consequently, Zhang suggested that he travel to Yadong via Hong Kong and India, and this was approved.[53] The members of the Tibetan negotiating delegation were given the choice of returning to Tibet with Zhang via India or going overland. All opted for the quicker (India) route, but as it turned out, the Chinese decided to have Ngabö return overland. Politically, it is not difficult to understand Beijing's concerns. If the Dalai Lama decided not to return to Tibet, Ngabö, as a Kashag minister and the head of the negotiating team, was critical to asserting the validity and legitimacy of the agreement. Should something happen to him in India or should he defect, the validity of the agreement itself could be compromised. In the end, therefore, Ngabö and one other member of the team, Thubden Lengmön, returned overland with the PLA, carrying the original Tibetan version of the agreement. Sambo, Kheme, Lhautara, Takla, and Sandutsang (Rinchen) returned via India with Zhang. Ngabö notified Yadong in his telegram that Zhang Jingwu was traveling to Yadong via India and verbally told the other Tibetan representatives going via India to tell the Tibetan government not to worry about him being in Chinese hands when they deliberated over whether to accept the agreement or flee into exile.[54]

51. Zhonggong xizang zizhiqu dangshi ziliao zhengji weiyuanhui 1990, entry for 25 May 1951.

52. *Zhongyang* technically means the Central Committee of the Chinese Communist Party, but it also commonly connotes the "central government."

53. Ha'o 1986: 117.

54. U.S. National Archives, 793B.00/7–951, memorandum of conversation on 6 July 1951 among Shakabpa, Thacher, and Tering.

Zhang Jingwu was an interesting choice to represent Mao and the Central Committee. He was an experienced military administrator who had been a member of the Chinese delegation at the Seventeen-Point Agreement talks and a signatory to that agreement.[55] He was born in Hunan in 1906 and was a Long March veteran who worked in military and administrative positions for over twenty years. At the time the PRC was founded in 1949, he was a commander (ch. can mo zhang) of the Southwest Bureau's Military Committee, but after the inauguration of the new government, he was called to Beijing and appointed director of the General Office (ch. ban gong ting) of the Military Committee and also the director of the People's Armed Forces Department (ch. renmin wu zhung bu).[56] Zhang, therefore, was no longer associated with the Southwest Bureau and clearly was chosen as someone working for the central Chinese government.

Zhang and the others on his staff spent a few weeks in Beijing getting passports, visas, vaccinations, and some supplies before going to Guangzhou, where they spent another two weeks making clothing and buying supplies and gifts.[57] From Guangzhou, Zhang and the others took the train to Hong Kong, where they stayed seven or eight days, organizing the shipment of their gifts and things by sea. To expedite meeting the Dalai Lama, Zhang, three staff members, and the Tibetans went by plane to Calcutta, stopping overnight in Singapore.[58] They arrived in Calcutta on 1 July 1951.[59]

Zhang Jingwu's instructions were simple. If the Dalai Lama decided to return, he was to return with him. However, if the Dalai Lama opted to go into exile, Zhang was still to go on to Lhasa and wait for the troops of the PLA's Eighteenth Army Corps to arrive overland.[60] After they arrived in Lhasa, Zhang was expected to return to his job in Beijing.[61] However, for reasons

55. The lines between civilian and military leadership and institutions in China at this time were indistinct. Military personnel had party positions and commonly worked in what we would call civil administrative functions.

56. Zhao 1995: 8–10.

57. Le 1981: 137. Stag lha (Takla), in his 1995 autobiography, adds that Zhang Jingwu came to visit him when they were ready to leave and suggested that he (Takla) stay in Guangzhou until he recovered from a bad eye infection while the rest went ahead to Yadong. Takla declined. He says he was afraid he would be left behind in China so insisted he would leave with the others even though he was still ill (Stag lha [Takla] 1995: 65).

58. Ha'o 1986: 118; Dangdai zhongguo congshu bianjibu 1991; Phündra, interview, 1993, Beijing.

59. U.S. National Archives, 302 Tibet, telegram from Wilson in consulate in Calcutta to embassy in New Delhi, dated 2 July 1951. Le (1981: 138) gives a date of 8 July, but that appears to be incorrect.

60. Zhonggong xizang zizhiqu dangshi ziliao zhengji weiyuanhui 1990: 5, entry for 25 May 1951.

61. Jambey Gyatso, interview, 1992, Beijing; Takla (Phüntso Tashi), interview, 1993, London.

that will be explained in a later chapter, Zhang ended up remaining in Tibet as the highest Chinese official throughout the 1950s.

While Zhang was preparing to leave for Yadong, elements of the PLA's Eighteenth Army Corps began to march from Xikang to Tibet, as did a cavalry force from the Northwest Bureau in Qinghai. The Eighteenth Army Corps left Ganzi in Xikang on 1 July 1951 and arrived in Chamdo on 17 July.[62] The Northwest Bureau's cavalry unit left Lanzhou for Xining also on 1 July.[63] Since it was important for Ngabö and the original Tibetan-language copy of the agreement to reach Lhasa promptly, Ngabö was sent with an advance unit of the Eighteenth Army Corps (of five hundred to six hundred troops) under the command of Wang Qimei. Phünwang, who accompanied them, explained the preparations: "Since Zhang Jingwu was not accompanied by soldiers, our advance force was going to be the first PLA troops encountered by Tibetans in Lhasa, and great care was taken to select the best soldiers from among the thousands of troops in the Eighteenth Army Corps. All the advance unit's troops were young and fit, well disciplined, and equipped with the finest weapons."[64] They left Chamdo for Lhasa on 25 July.[65]

THE TIBETAN RESPONSE TO THE AGREEMENT

The announcement of the agreement set off major debates in both Yadong and Lhasa about what the agreement meant for Tibet and how best to respond. For most, the questions were simple: Would the agreement enable the Dalai Lama and Tibetan religion to persevere, or would it be the vehicle for their quick demise? Could the Chinese Communists be trusted to abide by the terms of the agreement, or would they ignore it once their troops were in Lhasa? How much would the Chinese Communist's archenemy, the United States, assist Tibet if the Dalai Lama fled into exile rather than accept the agreement? Was it better to reject Chinese sovereignty at all costs or to work to secure as much autonomy as possible within the PRC? These were not new issues, but now they took on an urgency not felt previously.

Militarily, Tibet, in fact, still had several thousand troops in the field, as well as perhaps a thousand more in Lhasa. These theoretically could have been organized to set up a new defense line or reorganized to engage in guerrilla operations in the rough mountain terrain between Chamdo and Lhasa. But no such plans existed or were discussed, and morale was terrible.

---

62. Zhao 1998: 57–58.
63. Fan Ming 1987.
64. Goldstein, Sherap, and Siebenschuh 2004: 155.
65. Tshe ring don grub and O rgyan chos 'phel 1991: 43–44; Zhao 1998: 59.

One official in Giamda, with reinforcement troops sent from Lhasa, recalled that they were thinking of fleeing, not fighting!

> I was one of the new staff officials of Ngabö, . . . but I came a bit later, so by the time I went to join him, Lhalu was at Giamda, and Chamdo had been lost, so I was told to stay with Lhalu. However, neither I nor Lhalu wanted to remain. My whole family—my wife, children, etc.—were already in India, and I received many telegrams from my family [from Yadong] telling me to come to India. . . . When I was at Giamda, we kept horses saddled by our house so that if the Chinese suddenly arrived we could run away at once. We all had the same thought. If the Communists came, we would run.[66]

Lhalu had a similar recollection.

> At this time they [the government] said I should stay in Giamda, and they would send more troops. So I had to stay, but if we had to fight with the PLA, I could not have lasted even a day. When people asked what I was doing there, I said I was guarding the area. I had one to two thousand troops, but I couldn't have really made a fight of it.[67]

Moreover, the troops returning from Chamdo said there was no hope of overcoming the PLA in battle. One monk official who worked in the Tibetan Military Headquarters recalled the discussions in his office on the Chamdo debacle: "People were saying that first the Chinese sent five, then ten, then one hundred, and then one thousand and that even if we fight them they come at us endlessly (tib. gyashi tonglang).[68] So people lost enthusiasm and hope."[69]

Militarily, therefore, the Tibetan government had no plan to use its remaining troops should it reject the agreement. In Yadong the only issue was whether to accept the agreement or go into exile. No one saw a military option. Opinion about the other two options, however, was still seriously divided. Some important officials were strongly in favor of the Dalai Lama going into exile and opposing the Chinese, but the majority opposed the Dalai Lama living in exile and favored his returning to Lhasa. Coming to a decision about this was complicated by the intervention of the United States, which immediately tried to persuade the Dalai Lama to denounce the agreement and flee to exile. This, of course, enhanced the viability of fleeing to exile vis-à-vis simply accepting peaceful liberation. An important decision obviously had to be made, and there was very little time to make it, for Chinese officials and troops were already departing for Tibet under the terms of the agreement.

66. Shatra, interview, 1992.
67. Lhalu, interview, 1992, Lhasa.
68. Literally, "If one hundred die, one thousand rise up."
69. Lodrö Chönzin, interview, 1993, Lhasa.

A key issue for the Tibetans, therefore, was the extent to which they had real external support for their cause. Shakabpa, the Tibetan government official in India who had taken the lead in communicating with the United States and India, argued strongly that America was sympathetic and that Tibet would receive strong support from it. However, his verbal optimism was met with considerable incredulity from the officials in favor of returning to Lhasa, which will be examined in the next chapter.

Chapter 5

The United States Intervenes

In March 1951, at the same time that the Yadong negotiating team was en route to Beijing, James Burke of Time-Life brought Heinrich Harrer to see Loy Henderson, the U.S. ambassador in India.

Harrer was an Austrian who had fled to Tibet from internment in India in 1943 and had worked there for the Tibetan government for the next seven years. He had just returned to India from Yadong and was close to the Dalai Lama and his family. He was seeking to secure American support for the Tibetans and told Henderson that the Dalai Lama very much needed advice and that he trusted the United States more than any other country. Harrer said that the Dalai Lama had been frustrated by Tibet's inability to establish close relations with the United States and was sending the mission to Beijing only with great reluctance, because he feared that the delegates might yield to Chinese pressure. Harrer also said that the young ruler (then fifteen years old) had doubts about the wisdom of returning to Lhasa but that he was under constant pressure from some of the monks around him, who insisted he come to terms with China. Harrer said that the Dalai Lama did not know which way to turn for advice and that officials in the United States should try to convey their interest to him.[1] Harrer's account fell on receptive ears.

The Cold War in Asia was then in full swing. China had become communist and the neighboring communist state, North Korea, had invaded South Ko-

---

1. U.S. National Archives, New Delhi Post File, lot 58F 95, telegram from the U.S. ambassador in India to the U.S. State Department's director of the Office of South Asia Affairs, dated 29 March 1951.

rea the year before (on 25 June 1950), quickly bringing in a U.S.-led United Nations army to defend South Korea. The bloody Korean War became a proxy war between the United States and the Communist bloc, including China and the Soviet Union. The PRC, of course, also entered this war in mid-October 1950, when almost two hundred thousand PLA troops under Marshal Peng Dehuai crossed the Yalu River. The People's Liberation Army initially achieved dramatic successes that included not only driving the U.S. troops out of North Korea in a matter of weeks but also capturing Seoul, the South Korean capital, at the start of January 1951. However, by the summer of 1951, the U.S./U.N. force had stopped the Chinese advance and pushed them back to the thirty-eighth parallel, where a stalemate occurred. In this context, the invasion of Eastern Tibet by the PLA in October 1950 was seen as yet another negative Communist step in the Asian Cold War.

In Ambassador Henderson, Harrer found a hard-line, anti-communist, Cold War warrior. Henderson believed what Harrer said about the Dalai Lama, in no small part because he was already convinced that the United States should play a closer and more active role in Tibet. Long before this, in January 1949, Henderson had recommended that the State Department review U.S. policy regarding Tibet in light of the changing conditions in Asia, especially the Chinese civil war, and proposed "that if for example, the Communists succeed in controlling all of China . . . we should be prepared to treat Tibet as independent at all intents and purposes."[2] As a result of this, Ruth Bacon, of the State Department's Office of Far Eastern Affairs, laid out the pros and cons of such a shift in America's Tibet policy in a carefully reasoned memorandum to the Division of China Affairs dated 12 April 1949:

Arguments in Favor of the Embassy Proposal

1. If the Communists gain control of China proper, Tibet will be one of the few remaining non-Communist bastions in Continental Asia. Outer Mongolia is already detached. Communist influence is strong in Burma and Communists are infiltrating into Sinkiang [Xinjiang] and Inner Mongolia. Tibet will accordingly assume both ideological and strategic importance.

2. If Tibet possesses the stamina to withstand Communist infiltration—and the Embassy in New Delhi seems to feel that it does—it would be to our interest to treat Tibet as independent rather than to continue to regard it as part of a China which has gone Communist.

3. The Government is relatively stable. The people are conservative and religious by nature and disposed to oppose Communism as in conflict with the tenets of Buddhism. The Dalai Lama's authority extends beyond Tibet over

---

2. U.S. Department of State 1974: 1065, memorandum of Bacon, of Office of Far Eastern Affairs, to Sprouse, chief of China Affairs Division, 12 April 1949.

persons who practice the lamaist form of Buddhism in Nepal, Sikkim, Bhutan, Mongolia, etc.

4. The Chinese Government cannot now assert—and there currently appears little likelihood that it ever again will be able to assert—effective *de facto* authority in Tibet.

5. The Tibetans are showing increasing interest in establishing trade and other relations with the outside world. It is to our interest to see that these efforts are oriented to the West and not to the East.

Arguments against the Embassy Proposal

1. A decision to recognize Tibet involves a reconsideration not merely of our policy toward Tibet but also of our policy toward China. A basic principle of our policy toward China has been respect for China's territorial integrity. This principle has retarded while not entirely preventing the gradual dismemberment of China and it helped China emerge from World War II with the status of a great power. This policy should not be abandoned unless it is clear that a permanent breakup of China is inevitable and that we have a substantial stake in Tibet.

2. Adoption of such a policy would lessen the weight of our objection to current Soviet efforts to detach additional northern areas from China. It would also complicate our position that we are not sufficiently sure of the Mongolian People's Republic's independence to favor the MPR's admission to the UN.

3. Such a policy might lead to intensified efforts on the part of the USSR to take Tibet into the Communist camp. If we carry on toward Tibet much as at present, the Communists might also be content to let the present situation there ride. By recognizing Tibet as independent while we are not in position to give Tibet the necessary practical support, because of its remoteness, we may in fact be pointing the way for Communist absorption of the area.

4. As a political matter Tibet's importance both ideologically and strategically is very limited. Because of its geographical remoteness, the primitive character of its Government and society and the limited character of its contacts with the outside world Tibet's orientation toward the West cannot be counted upon to endure on an ideological basis unless supported by far-reaching practical measures. If we cannot take these practical measures, recognition in itself would not hold Tibet in an alignment with the West and might in fact work against our long-run interests. Similarly, efforts to utilize Tibet strategically for example as an air base or for the discharge of rockets would encounter not merely formidable difficulties of terrain and weather but also Tibet's objections on religious grounds to the passage of planes over its territory. Unless rare minerals are found in Tibet, the Army does not regard Tibet as of strategical significance.

5. The answer to what measures of a practical nature can be taken appears to lie largely with India which now controls Tibet's access to the West. If India cooperates with the West the importance of Tibet both ideologically and strategically will be considerably less. If India does not cooperate with the West the difficulties in the way of utilizing Tibet as a bastion for the West would be enormously magnified.

Chinese Sovereignty or Suzerainty over Tibet

It is to be noted in the files that there are references to China's "sovereignty" or "suzerainty" over Tibet. As is, of course, known the two terms are not synonymous. It is difficult, however, to draw a precise line of demarcation between them. In general "suzerainty" implies less of Chinese authority and more of Tibetan autonomy than "sovereignty." "Suzerainty" would accordingly appear to fit the case quite closely in some respects. "Suzerainty" however carries the connotation of a vassal state and does not fit as well into customary American concepts as into British usage. It is suggested that it might be desirable to avoid a possible controversy over "sovereignty" versus "suzerainty" by referring in future to Chinese *de jure* authority over Tibet or some similar comprehensive term.

Conclusions

A. Under Present Circumstances

1. Without placing too great reliance upon Tibet's ideological or strategic importance, it is believed to be clearly to our advantage under any circumstances to have Tibet as a friend if possible. We should accordingly maintain a friendly attitude toward Tibet *in ways short of giving China cause for offense.* We should encourage so far as feasible Tibet's orientation toward the West rather than toward the East.

2. For the present we should avoid giving the impression of any alteration in our position toward Chinese authority over Tibet such as for example steps which would clearly indicate that we regard Tibet as independent, etc. We have recently given renewed assurances to China of our recognition of China's *de jure* sovereignty or suzerainty over Tibet. Any decided change of our policy might give China cause for complaint, might necessitate embarrassing explanations, might stimulate Soviet efforts at infiltration into Tibet and might not itself be sufficient to hold Tibet to our side. We should however keep our policy as flexible as possible by avoiding references to China's sovereignty or suzerainty unless such references are clearly called for and by informing China of our proposed moves in connection with Tibet, rather than asking China's consent for them. Ambassador Henderson's statement of our policy in his

conversation with the head of Tibetan Trade Mission on January 5, 1949 would seem to cover the situation quite adequately. . . .

3. Our information with regard to Tibet comes for the most part from third parties—China, India, Tibet—and is colored according to the aims and purposes of its source. To secure first-hand information and as an indication of our friendly interest, it would be desirable to send a suitable official or officials to Tibet if this can be done inconspicuously and without giving rise to speculation that we may have designs upon Tibet.

B. For the Future

The nature of developments will affect the policy which we should adopt toward Tibet in the future. If for example the Communists should take over all of China proper and the National Government should disappear we would be faced with the alternatives of (1) treating Tibet as under the authority of the Communist Government—which we should clearly wish to avoid or (2) dealing with Tibet as for all intents and purposes independent. The latter policy would clearly be to our advantage. If however the Communists take over China proper but an *émigré* Nationalist Government should continue to exist, we would then have to decide our policy toward Tibet partly in light of our policy toward the émigré Government. The question would arise whether we should place emphasis on Tibet's independence by formally recognizing it and by sponsoring its application for membership in the UN or whether we should avoid stressing the matter of independence but should merely maintain direct relations with Tibet without a public change of policy. Decision on this question would involve (1) our estimate whether open recognition of independence might stimulate Soviet activities to take over Tibet; (2) whether we have the practical means to afford sufficient assistance to Tibet to make probable its continuance in a western alignment; and (3) our estimate whether China's dismemberment is likely to be on a fairly permanent basis.[3]

In early July 1949, Henderson followed up to Bacon's comment about the lack of reliable information by recommending to Washington that the United States send a mission to Lhasa that would arrive no later than September 1949.[4] Washington liked this idea, and less than a week later, on 8 July 1949, Secretary of State Acheson asked Henderson's thoughts on the following two alternatives on how to operationalize this:

a) Minimum expedition undertaken immed [immediately] by Jefferson Jones, perhaps accompanied by similar rep [representative] Brit High Commissioner's Office New Delhi ostensibly personally arranged unofficial and dur-

3. U.S. Department of State 1974: 1065, ibid. (emphasis added).
4. U.S. Department of State 1974: 1076, ambassador in India to secretary of state, 2 July 1949.

ing Fon-Serv [foreign service] leave. Actually time not to be counted against Jones' leave and expedition financed by US in whole or in partnership with Brit. This expedition to remain Lhasa perhaps 2 weeks having as its objective survey current polit [political] situation and recommendations re feasibility eventual establishment Consular representation after Chinese suzerainty question no longer obstacle.

b) Expedition headed by experienced explorer-scholar, such as Schuyler Cammonn, University of Pennsylvania, with established reputation and *prima facie* justification trip. This expedition also to be accompanied by Jones ostensibly on leave who wld return earliest with prelim report. Cammonn to remain major portion year under scientific cover but observing polit trends.[5]

Nothing, however, came of this. By the end of July 1949, it was clear to the U.S. Embassy in India that there was not enough time to organize something for the current year, and once the Chinese Communist Party inaugurated the People's Republic of China on 1 October 1949, it was deemed too provocative to Beijing to send such a mission.

However, the situation changed radically when the PLA captured Chamdo in mid-October 1950 and the Dalai Lama fled to Yadong in late December. The United States now had to decide how to respond. Although it opted not to play a leading role in assisting Tibet in the United Nations, the presence of the Dalai Lama on the verge of flight into exile generated a more immediate and proactive response. Taking the lead in the United Nations had serious international ramifications, whereas persuading the Dalai Lama to flee into exile and become an important Asian symbol/voice of anti-communism was low risk and high gain.

The United States, of course, was interested in Tibet because American foreign policy at this time was focused on combating and containing communism, which it felt had replaced Nazi fascism as the main enemy of freedom and democracy. Tibet, therefore, was a potent example of Communist aggression against a small, peaceful country. Ambassador Henderson agreed that "unless someone in whom this young man might have confidence should give him advice, he will fall into the Chinese Communist trap, or he will be in an extremely unenviable position in India."[6] In the spring of 1951, therefore, he decided that the United States should send the Dalai Lama an unofficial and unsigned letter that would be accompanied by a verbal message saying the letter had come from the U.S. ambassador. To protect the United States in case the letter fell into the hands of the Chinese, he used paper purchased in India whose origin could not be traced, and he included

5. U.S. Department of State 1974: 1079, secretary of state to ambassador in India, 8 July 1949.

6. U.S. National Archives, New Delhi Post File, lot 58F 95, telegram from the U.S. ambassador in India to the U.S. State Department's director of the Office of South Asia Affairs, dated 29 March 1951.

nothing in the text that would indicate that the letter came from Henderson or the United States. Henderson justified this strategy to Washington by contending that it was better to take this risk than to see the "Chinese Communists succeed by trickery in taking over Tibet and in gaining control of the Dalai Lama."[7] Henderson's supportive letter to the Dalai Lama, which follows below, strongly urged the Dalai Lama to oppose the Chinese and seek asylum abroad. It suggested Ceylon as a place of asylum for the Dalai Lama but also mentioned the United States as a possible asylum site. Although it was too late to stop the Tibetan negotiating delegation from going to Beijing, it was the kind of explicit evidence of U.S. support wanted by the Tibetan officials favoring exile over communism.

[NEW DELHI, undated] A high foreign official who has recently visited Asia and who has sympathy for Tibet and deep concern for the welfare of His Holiness and His people sends the following message:

1. The Peiping Communist regime is determined to obtain complete control over Tibet. No concession made to that regime by His Holiness can change this determination. The Chinese Communists prefer to gain control through trickery rather than through force. They are therefore anxious to persuade His Holiness to make an agreement which would allow them to establish a representative in Lhasa.

2. The establishment of a representative of Peiping Communist regime in Lhasa would serve only to speed up the seizing of all of Tibet by the Chinese Communists.

3. Until changes in the world situation would make it difficult for the Chinese Communists to take over Tibet, His Holiness should in no circumstances return to Lhasa or send his own treasures or those of Tibet back to Lhasa. [A section of the letter has been excised by the U.S. State Department.] Any treasures which might be returned to Lhasa would eventually be taken over by the Chinese Communists.

4. His Holiness should not return to Lhasa while the danger exists that by force or trickery the Chinese Communists might seize Lhasa. He should leave Yadong for some foreign country if it should [seem?] like the Chinese Communists might try to prevent his escape.

5. It is suggested that His Holiness send representatives at once to Ceylon. These representatives should try to arrange with the Government of Ceylon for the immediate transfer to Ceylon of the treasures of His Holiness. They should also try to obtain permission for His Holiness and His Household to find asylum in Ceylon if His Holiness should leave Tibet. After the Government of Ceylon has granted permission for asylum, His Holiness should ask the Government of India for assurance that if he and His Household should leave Tibet they could pass through India to Ceylon.

7. Ibid.

6. If His Holiness and His Household could not find safe asylum in Ceylon he could be certain of finding a place of refuge in one of the friendly countries, including the United States, in the Western Hemisphere.

7. It might also be useful for His Holiness to send a mission to the United States where it would be prepared to make a direct appeal to the United Nations. It is understood that His Holiness is already aware that favorable consideration will be granted to the applications made by members of a Tibetan mission to the United Nations for United States visas.[8]

In early April 1951 the State Department approved Henderson's letter with the important proviso that paragraph 7 be deleted because a recent survey by the State Department had revealed that there was little support among member countries for U.N. action on behalf of Tibet.[9] The ramifications of the United States going the U.N. route were still too high given the relative low value of Tibet. Henderson sent duplicate copies of this letter to the Dalai Lama on 6 April. This U.S. interest, of course, was precisely why Mao felt that Tibet was very different from other parts of China and required a different long- and short-term strategy.

A month later, on 13 May, at least one copy still had not been sent to Yadong, for on that day the U.S. Embassy's first secretary, Fraser Wilkins, apparently personally handed a copy to Liushar, one of the heads of the Tibetan Foreign Affairs Bureau, who was then in Kalimpong.[10] Wilkins had been sent to meet Liushar and directly convey America's interest in Tibet. In a memorandum of conversation about that meeting, Wilkins says that he assured Liushar that the United States was greatly interested in Tibet, not only economically, but also politically. Wilkins told Liushar that the United States was interested in the continuance of Tibetan *autonomy* and that America viewed Tibet's appeal to the United Nations sympathetically and was willing to consider the issuance of visas to the Tibetan delegation, which had been

8. U.S. National Archives, 791.00/4–451, telegram no. 2673 from the U.S. ambassador in India to secretary of state, dated 4 April 1951; and telegram no. 1633 from the director of the U.S. State Department's Office of Southeast Asia Affairs to the U.S. ambassador in India, dated 6 April 1951. Henderson sent a copy of this to the U.S. ambassador to Ceylon, who replied that he thought Ceylon would grant asylum and safeguard Tibet's treasures (U.S. Department of State 1983: letter from Satterthwaite to Henderson, dated 13 April 1951).

9. U.S. Department of State 1983: telegram from Mathews to Henderson, dated 6 April 1951. A recent book on the CIA and Tibet (Conboy and Morrison 2002: 12) states that one copy of the letter was taken to Yadong by Heinrich Harrer, but this is implausible, because there is no indication elsewhere that he personally was in Yadong at this time, and the authors provided no source for this.

10. U.S. National Archives, 793B.00/5–2951, chargé in India to secretary of state, dated 29 May 1951. In this document Shakabpa said that Liushar had shown him the letter a few days earlier and was taking it to Yadong.

scheduled to proceed to Lake Success. Wilkins recalled that Ambassador Henderson had written letters to this effect on 5 and 11 January.[11]

Liushar was not overly impressed with this and diplomatically replied that the Tibetan government appreciated America's interest but, on the advice of India, the United Kingdom, and the United States, had already *begun* negotiations with the Chinese. He explained that his government feared that sending a delegation at this sensitive juncture to Lake Success might have adverse effects on these talks, so they had placed that plan in abeyance.[12]

Wilkins countered that the United States had not advised Tibet to negotiate with the Chinese and suggested that a Tibetan U.N. delegation at Lake Success might focus world attention and possibly deter Communist Chinese activity.

Liushar's reply conveys the skepticism about American support and sympathy that pervaded much of the Tibetan elite—for good reason. He clarified his comment, saying that while the United States had not advised Tibet to negotiate in so many words, it and other Western countries had refused to help when Tibet requested assistance. He also pointed out that the United Nations had not invited Tibet to appear and present its case and said that this was seen as a further indication that Tibet's best hope for maintaining her independence was through negotiation with China.[13]

Two days later, on 13 May, Liushar and Wilkins again met. This time Liushar conveyed something of Tibet's hopes and fears regarding the Beijing negotiations. Wilkins wrote of this meeting,

> The Foreign Secretary indicated that [if necessary] they would probably settle for autonomy in internal affairs but that what Tibet really desired was the maintenance of the status-quo which had existed prior to the Chinese invasion of Tibet. They hoped they would not have to retreat to their minimum position but if they did he believed they would in the course of time again be able to assert complete Tibetan supremacy over all of their affairs. The Foreign Secretary recalled that in the past, whatever the legal situation might have been, Tibet was in effect independent. It had all the attributes of sovereignty except recognition by foreign powers. They hoped one day to recover their full sovereignty and recognition from foreign powers as well.[14]

11. U.S. National Archives, memorandum of conversation between F. Wilkins and Liushar on relations between Tibet and the United States, dated 11 May 1951, enclosed with 611.93B/5–2451, letter from F. Wilkins, U.S. Embassy in India, to the U.S. Department of State, dated 24 May 1951.

12. Ibid.

13. Ibid.

14. U.S. National Archives, memorandum of conversation among F. Wilkins, Liushar, and G. Patterson, dated 13 May 1951, enclosed with 611.93B/5–2451, letter from F. Wilkins, U.S. Embassy in India, to the U.S. Department of State, dated 24 May 1951. The interpreter was Lhundrup, the son of the well-known official Kapshöba.

At the same time, however, when asked whether Tibet had ever approached India about obtaining additional arms from India or from overseas, Liushar told Wilkins that "they had not done so formally and at the present time, in view of the fact that they were discussing matters with the Chinese, did not believe it would be wise to take action in this respect."[15]

Soon after this, on 21 May, two days before the signing of the Seventeen-Point Agreement, the Dalai Lama responded to Henderson in a letter (the date of its delivery to Henderson, however, is unknown). In this response, the Dalai Lama was cautious and evasive but friendly. He stated only that peace negotiations between China and Tibet were proceeding in Beijing and that if Tibet should have to approach the United States again, the Dalai Lama hoped the United States would do its best to help.[16]

About a week after Liushar's second meeting with Wilkins, a meeting took place in Calcutta between Wilkins and Shakabpa. Shakabpa told Wilkins that he had been sent by the Dalai Lama to ascertain precisely what kind of help Tibet could expect from the United States.[17] This, of course, was the crucial issue, since the pro-exile officials understood that it would be difficult to convince the conservative elite to agree to have the Dalai Lama flee without proof of strong external support.

Shakabpa also informed Wilkins that on 13 May the talks in China had become almost deadlocked and asked him for the U.S. government's advice on what Tibet should do "when Tibetan-Communist talks at Peking broke down." Shakabpa said that the Chinese wanted control over all of Tibet, including the military and external affairs, and that while the Tibetan government was willing to concede this for Inner Tibet (the area east of the Upper Yangtse River, then the Chinese province called Xikang), they were not willing to do so for Outer Tibet (political Tibet), the area controlled by the Dalai Lama's state. Shakabpa went on to say that the Dalai Lama was adamant about not ceding control over Tibet's defense and that if he were forced to leave Tibet, he would do so immediately. Shakabpa added that Liushar had returned

15. Ibid.

16. U.S. Department of State 1983: 1721, chargé d'affaires in India to the U.S. secretary of state, dated 28 June 1951.

17. It is unlikely that Shakabpa was instructed by the Dalai Lama to ask this, as the U.S. report of the meeting implies. The Dalai Lama was then not actively involved in running the Tibetan government, and even if he had been, Shakabpa, as a government official, would have been contacted by the Kashag or the Tibetan Foreign Affairs Bureau. However, in this and subsequent discussions with the United States, Shakabpa frequently used the name of the Dalai Lama. This is likely to have been Shakabpa himself deciding it would be more effective to use the Dalai Lama's name, since the issue for the United States was what the Dalai Lama was going to do. It is clear, therefore, that we cannot take this mention of the Dalai Lama's name in U.S. records to mean he was actually giving these instructions. More will be said of this issue later.

to Yadong to discuss the letter Ambassador Henderson had sent to the Dalai Lama. Shakabpa then listed six specific operational questions he and Liushar needed to have answered. These queries cut right to the heart of the matter:

(1) Should Tibet report to the UN when current talks break down and how should they do it? Was the UN still interested in Tibet and could it be of any help? What would the US do? Would it be willing to grant visas?

(2) As Tibet had no official relations with Ceylon, would the US be willing to approach the Government Ceylon re asylum for Dalai Lama and his followers?

(3) Would the US be willing grant asylum to the Dalai Lama and approximately 100 followers? How would he be received? As head of state? Would the US be willing provide for their expenses?

(4) If Dalai Lama leaves Tibet would the US be willing supply the Dalai Lama with military assistance and loans of money when the time was ripe for the purpose enabling of Tibetan groups to rise against the Communist Chinese invader? Money was needed to encourage groups.

(5) Would the US be willing establish some form of representation at Kalimpong for liaison between US officials and Tibetan authorities? Shakabpa stressed the necessity for representation which would be informal and covert in character.

(6) The Dalai Lama wished his elder brother, Taktser [Taktse] Rimpoche, to leave Tibet and visit India. Taktser's opposition to Communist China following his arrival in Lhasa from Kumbum monastery has made it difficult for him to remain in Tibet and face possible Communist Chinese criticism. In the event Taktser could not remain India for similar reasons, could Taktser and Tibetan servant proceed to the US in an unofficial capacity?[18]

Shakabpa was told that Ambassador Henderson would be consulted immediately and that answers would be sent to him in Kalimpong. Virtually simultaneously with this, on 26 May the Chinese announced that the Seventeen-Point Agreement had been signed in Beijing on 23 May 1951.

A few days after Beijing's announcement, the Department of State asked the U.S. Embassy in Delhi to find out from Tibetan officials in Kalimpong whether such an agreement had actually been reached and, if so, what course the Tibetan government proposed to take regarding its acceptance and implementation.[19] A week later, on 1 June, Shakabpa did not comment on this

---

18. U.S. National Archives, 793B.00/5–2951, telegram no. 3398 from the U.S. chargé d'affaires L. V. Steere, in India, to the U.S. secretary of state, dated 29 May 1951.

19. U.S. National Archives, 893B.13/5–2651, telegram no. 2015, from the U.S. secretary of state to the U.S. Embassy in India, dated 29 May 1951.

but told the U.S. consul general in Calcutta that the Tibetan government was anxiously awaiting the U.S. reply to the Dalai Lama's six questions. He also explained how a U.S. representative could meet him secretly after dark in Kalimpong. The Americans saw this as a good sign, since it indicated that the Tibetan government was still considering opposing the Chinese.[20]

The following day, Secretary of State Dean Acheson replied cautiously to the Tibetan questions. After indicating that the State Department would reserve final judgment until it had received conclusive information on the Beijing agreement, Acheson instructed Henderson as follows:

> Tibet SHLD not RPT [repeat] NOT be compelled by duress accept violation its autonomy and that Tibetan people SHLD enjoy certain rights self determination, commensurate with autonomy Tibet has maintained since Chi revolution [1911]. DEPT believes further that cause world peace WLD be served if gen support CLD be mustered for this point of view, and agrees with EMB that US RPT US itself SHLD demonstrate its interest in case in every practical POLIT and ECON way. Assuming Peiping terms inacceptable established Tibetan GOVT and combined POLIT and MIL pressure may be exerted on Tibet, DEPT accepts EMB suggestions contained REFTEL, SUBJ GEN proviso US is not RPT NOT assuming responsibility guidance Tibetan GOVT, with fol qualifications.[21]

These so-called qualifications were the responses to the Tibetan's six questions. Acheson instructed Henderson that it was okay to issue a visa for Taktse Rimpoche, that the United States was willing to contact Ceylon on the Dalai Lama's behalf, and that establishing informal liaison in Kalimpong was acceptable. On the key issues he instructed:

> [1. Regarding the United Nations]
> US believes that when complaint is made to UN, there SHLD be opportunity have it heard and considered in proper UN forum. US RPT US has not however been chief moving party in every case, and degree US initiative necessarily has taken into account attitude other UN members and their special relation to issue raised. In this case GOI [Government of India] interests particularly involved. While US RPT US willing support consideration new Tibetan appeal, US believes attitude other UN members important factor in situation. Tibet might consider setting forth in new MSG [message] to UN SYG [secretary-general] circumstances NEGOTS Peiping and nature Commie threat re Tibet. US believes new Tibetan appeal to UN, followed promptly by Tibetan efforts interest other leading States such as UK, India, Pakistan, France, USSR in support WLD probably be more fruitful approach than first sending DEL to UN RPT UN (this especially in view importance time element). If Tibet CLD

---

20. U.S. National Archives, 793B.00/6–151, telegram no. 3439, from the U.S. Embassy in India to the U.S. secretary of state, dated 1 June 1951.

21. U.S. National Archives, 793B.00/5–2951, telegram no. 2051, from the U.S. secretary of state to the U.S. Embassy in India, dated 2 June 1951.

mobilize some influential world opinion in support its case, this might create POLIT environment favoring UN consideration. US WLD agree issue visas to Tibetan DEL to UN RPT UN. Whether and when Tibetan DEL might undertake travel UN is for them determine. . . .

[3. Regarding asylum and financing for the Dalai Lama and hundred followers (and their families)]

US unable commit itself to providing for expenses Dalai Lama and retinue. Note precedents such as Tsarist refugees and, more recently, CHI Vice President Li Tsung-jen, all of whom unsupported by US. Note Tibetan GOVT by all reports possesses much treasure including gold and silver. We assume those assets ample for purpose and Dalai Lama himself WLD arrange to EVAC from Tibet such treasure as required for support his GOVT in exile. Omit in UR reply any suggestion US willing consider what financial assistance CLD be given or that US WLD QTE do utmost help Tibetans solve financial problems, UNQTE but suggest Dalai Lama WLD probably best be able serve cause Tibetan freedom if he remained nearby as in India or Ceylon.

[4. Regarding willingness to supply the Dalai Lama with military assistance and funds to enable uprisings against the Chinese]

US prepared provide limited assistance in terms light arms depending upon POLIT and MIL developments in Tibet proper, and depending also on whether GOI attitude WLD make such supply feasible. US GOVMT feels aid CLD effectively be given only while there may be within Tibet POLIT and MIL forces willing and able resist, that complete collapse within Tibet and offering of POLIT campaign from outside wld render undertaking probably fruitless. Strong stand by Tibetan Govt against any clear aggression WLD encourage world support for its position, whereas surrender in Outer Tibet WLD almost certainly be followed by collapse interest elsewhere. US unwilling commit itself to support any such undertaking from outside, but if resistance maintained in Tibet from beginning WLD contribute insofar as attitude GOI makes it possible. Have Tibetans recently approached GOI re providing arms or permitting shipment through India and if so with what results?

Dean Acheson ended with the following instructions and observations:

DEPT agrees it important at this stage particularly that US respond in cooperative manner Shakabpa's questions. PLS evince that sympathetic attitude, indicating US GOVT prepared do everything feasible assist Tibet maintain autonomy, but note high importance which position GOI bears re developments.

Tibetans themselves will appreciate high desirability, in view historical and actual POLIT relations, that if possible Tibet enlist support GOI. US under no illusions that current attitude GOI is more sympathetic to Tibet cause than shown by actions to date. Dept does not RPT not propose Tibetans approach GOI or accept GOI opinion against better judgment. US itself WLD be guided by own judgment re situation and possibilities, is sympathetic to Tibetan cause as indicated above but WLD merely note ineluctable fact India by reasons of traditional relationships and geographic position plays very important role. Tibetans SHLD be under no RPT no illusions likewise that MIL assistance can be obtained for them through UN RPT UN action. Tibetans must necessarily be guided by consideration all factors and by their interests as autonomous people.

FYI although considering resistance WLD bear promise of fruits only if Tibetan POLIT organization can be caused make stand in OUTER Tibet, believe it important Dalai Lama not RPT not let himself come under control Peiping. US RPT US is sympathetic to Tibetan position and will assist insofar as practicable but can help only if Tibetans themselves make real effort and take firm stand.[22]

This new U.S. position did not offer much additional concrete support. Tibet was in no position to muster support from other countries in the United Nations, so for the secretary of state of America to suggest that they do this first was ridiculous if not insulting. It reflects how poorly Washington understood what was going on or how little it cared. Moreover, the U.S. response gave Tibet no assurance that the United States would spearhead a coalition to demand Chinese withdrawal from Tibet. And even the limited offer of light arms was meaningless, since it was contingent on "whether GOI attitude WLD make such supply feasible" and on the continued presence of political and military forces in Tibet willing to resist the Chinese after the Dalai Lama and his top officials left. The Tibetan government had no contingency plans for anything like this, and the cooperation of the Government of India was totally unrealistic—and the United States knew that. Finally, the United States quite clearly was still willing to recognize Tibet only as an *autonomous* part of China, that is, not independent with the Dalai Lama as head of state. To do more would have meant confronting the position of Chiang Kai-shek on Taiwan, and the benefits of helping Tibet were not worth the costs.

The U.S. Embassy in Delhi sent Wilkins to Kalimpong to report these answers to Shakabpa and to ascertain the status of the Seventeen-Point Agreement. He arrived there on 7 or 8 June and, after explaining the position taken by the United States, impressed on Shakabpa that this position was predicated on the assumption that the Seventeen-Point Agreement was unacceptable to the Tibetan government and would be disavowed. Shakabpa then told Wilkins that he had received a telegram from the Dalai Lama that had said that he and the Tibetan government did not recognize the Sino-Tibetan agreement and that the Tibetan delegation had been forced by pressure and threats to sign it. He also informed Wilkins that the Tibetan delegation in Beijing had been instructed to refer all important points to Yadong and thus had no authority to ratify such an agreement. Shakabpa further speculated that after all of the delegation members had left China and were

22. Ibid. For a brief discussion of the policymaking context in Washington, see Knaus 2003: 58–60.

out of danger, the Chinese would be informed that the agreement was unacceptable.[23] Shakabpa was probably ad-libbing or massaging reality about
the last part to keep the United States interested.

When Shakabpa and Wilkins met a second time the next day, Shakabpa
told Wilkins that he had just received an urgent message from the Dalai Lama
indicating that all these issues were currently being discussed in Yadong. Shakabpa's discussion of the message, as reported in U.S. documents, said, "If
US willing to help, you [Shakabpa] shld make arrangements for my departure from Yadong, for India immediately; if US unwilling to help, you should
return Yadong at once." Shakabpa told Wilkins that he was very pleased with
the U.S. replies and was certain that the Dalai Lama and the Tibetan government would also be pleased. He said he would inform the Dalai Lama at
once of the U.S. offer and that he thought it could affect the outcome of
the debate in Yadong.[24]

Shakabpa also told Wilkins that the Tibetan government considered it
preferable to postpone any further appeal to the United Nations until after
the Dalai Lama's public disavowal of the Seventeen-Point Agreement and
until after the Dalai Lama had reached India. Shakabpa again asked the
Americans to contact the Ceylon government regarding asylum for the Dalai
Lama, because Tibet had no relations with Ceylon and it would be difficult
for Tibet to contact Ceylon without the Indian government immediately hearing about it and possibly taking offense. Wilkins agreed.

Shakabpa then reiterated that the Dalai Lama and one hundred to two
hundred followers and their families would prefer asylum in the United
States, and he said that he considered the willingness of the United States
to receive the Dalai Lama as one of the most important points in the U.S.
response. Shakabpa also pressed Wilkins again for more specific information on military assistance and on the issue of possible U.S. help through
loans. Finally, Shakabpa asked Wilkins whether it would be possible for a
representative of the United States to remain in Kalimpong for the next
few weeks, since many important questions were likely to arise. Wilkins
replied that he would try to arrange something, and the U.S. Embassy soon
afterward sent Vice-Consul N. G. Thacher from the Calcutta Consulate,
with his wife and son, ostensibly on a vacation but actually to deal with the
Tibetans.

Shakabpa's optimistic reading of the U.S. response and Tibetan opposi-

23. U.S. National Archives, 793B.00/6–1151, telegram from the U.S. ambassador in India
to the U.S. secretary of state, dated 11 June 1951.

24. The message is reported in U.S. National Archives, 793B.00/6–1151, telegram from
the U.S. ambassador in India to the U.S. secretary of state, dated 11 June 1951. As mentioned
in an earlier footnote, it is again highly unlikely that these instructions actually came from the
Dalai Lama directly. This should probably mean the Tibetan government.

tion to the agreement does not appear to have been the dominant view of the Tibetan government, let alone the Dalai Lama. It was not shared, for example, by the head of the Foreign Affairs Bureau, Liushar, who told the Americans at the same time that he was pessimistic about the likelihood of any strong opposition to the Seventeen-Point Agreement.[25]

A few days later, on 15 June, Thacher met with Shakabpa in Kalimpong, and Shakabpa now told Thacher that he had received no new word about the Dalai Lama denouncing the Seventeen-Point Agreement. Thacher, in turn, passed on to Shakabpa the news that the Chinese delegation from Beijing could arrive in Tibet as early as 22 June and stressed that it was important that the Dalai Lama disavow the Sino-Tibetan agreement before then.[26]

Thacher's recollection of that meeting gives some idea of the gap between Tibetan aspirations for U.S. help and American intentions. In a later interview, he said of this meeting, "There was a sense of the absurd. . . . They were talking wistfully in terms of America providing them with tanks and aircraft."[27] While Thacher found the Tibetans hopes absurd because he understood that Washington was not interested in making a major commitment to helping Tibet maintain its freedom against the Chinese Communists, the Tibetans were still unsure what exactly the United States was willing to do. They knew Washington wanted the Dalai Lama to renounce the agreement, go into exile, and criticize the Communists, but they were trying to figure out whether the United States would assist Tibet in stopping Beijing from taking over their country or, if this were not possible, give real assistance eventually in throwing the Chinese out.

In the meantime, in early June 1951, the thirty-one-year-old brother of the Dalai Lama, Taktse Rimpoche, arrived in Kalimpong carrying a secret letter for the United States from the Dalai Lama. Shakabpa, as mentioned above, had already asked the U.S. Embassy in New Delhi on 24 May to allow the Dalai Lama's brother to go to America if India would not allow him to remain there.[28] On 8 June, Shakabpa told Wilkins, "The Dalai Lama wished him [Taktse] to go to the United States because although he would proceed in an unofficial capacity he would be able to speak for the Dalai Lama."[29]

25. U.S. National Archives, 793B.00/6–1151, telegram no. 3576, from the U.S. ambassador in India to the U.S. secretary of state, dated 11 June 1951.

26. U.S. National Archives, 793B.00/6–1951, telegram no. 3687, from the U.S. Embassy in India to the U.S. secretary of state, dated 19 June 1951.

27. Conboy and Morrison 2002: 14.

28. U.S. National Archives, 611.93B/5–2651, memorandum of conversation between Shakabpa and F. W. Wilkins, first secretary of U.S. Embassy, India, 26 May 1951.

29. U.S. National Archives, memorandum of conversation on 8 June 1952 among Wilkins, Shakabpa, and Taring, attached to 611.93B/6–1451, dispatch from U.S. Embassy, India, to Department of State, 14 June 1951.

The U.S. Embassy quickly recommended that the State Department approve Taktse's visit to the United States and asked Washington to permit him to enter the United States with an affidavit in lieu of a passport, since further documentation from Yadong would take months. The U.S. Embassy also recommended that it should help Taktse financially, since he was reluctant to go to the Indian government to request foreign currency. It similarly indicated that the United States should provide funding for him also after he arrived in America. As the U.S. Embassy wrote, "Tak-tse Rimpochi is . . . a person who might prove to be a valuable link between the United States and the Dalai Lama and a means whereby close and friendly relations might be maintained between the U.S. and Tibet."[30] The United States was eager to make an overture of friendship, and this was approved on 18 June.[31] The funds for Taktse were ultimately provided by the CIA via the Committee for a Free Asia, an organization that it supported financially.[32]

The secret letter Taktse brought was dated 29 May and appears to have been sent by the Dalai Lama personally without knowledge of his government. It began by asking for U.S. help for his brother Taktse, saying, "My brother Tak-Tse is on his way to America. He is worthy to be protected from all fear of attack. Whatever it is the custom to give please give help to him."[33] The remainder of the letter has been excised from the document, but discussions about it in State Department documents suggest that it said that Taktse was empowered to speak for the Dalai Lama and that, although he would go to the United States as a private citizen, he would also serve as an unofficial representative of the Dalai Lama himself. The letter also mentioned political issues. The Dalai Lama not only said that he desired close relations and help from the United States but also raised the idea of a secret agreement between the United States and Tibet, which the embassy referred to as an exaggerated hope.[34] It commented on that idea, saying, "In spite of exaggerated hopes therein expressed Emb can inform Tak-Tse prior [to his] departure re difficulties in [the] way [of] any such agreement as mentioned; and that US through Tak-Tse can render practical advice and assistance to

30. U.S. National Archives, 611.93B/6–1451, dispatch from U.S. Embassy, India, to U.S. Department of State, 14 June 1951.

31. U.S. National Archives, 793B.00/6–1351, telegram no. 3616, from U.S. Embassy in India to U.S. secretary of state, dated 13 June 1951; and ibid., telegram no. 2194, from U.S. State Department to U.S. Embassy in India, dated 18 June 1951.

32. Conboy and Morrison 2002: 15.

33. U.S. National Archives, 793B.00/6–1651, telegram from Steere, U.S. Embassy in India, to U.S. secretary of state, 16 June 1951.

34. Regarding the desired close relations and help from the United States, see U.S. National Archives, memorandum of conversation on 8 June 1952 among Wilkins, Taktse Rimpoche, Y. Pandatsang, and George Patterson, attached to 611.93B/6–1451, dispatch from U.S. Embassy, India, to U.S. Department of State, 14 June 1951.

Dalai Lama."[35] Taktse asked that the letter be treated with utmost confidentiality because of the views expressed by his brother and said he had not shown it to other members of the Tibetan government.[36] This appears to be the first instance of the Dalai Lama or his family or both operating a U.S. foreign policy independent of the rest of the government. It will not be the last.

However, the reality of the situation was puzzling. Almost a month had passed since the agreement was announced, and the Americans had received no indication from the Dalai Lama that he planned to denounce the agreement, despite the repeated assertions of Shakabpa and Taktse Rimpoche that they were in communication with the Dalai Lama and that he was in favor of the denunciation. With the Chinese delegation due to arrive in India imminently, the Americans decided to sweeten their offer to the Dalai Lama by indicating more clearly than before that they would render public support for him if he denounced the agreement. This was conveyed by the State Department to the acting ambassador in India on 16 June.

> You may inform Tibetans, if and when you consider desirable, that upon disavowal Sino-Tibetan agreement US official reference to this action, indicating sympathy for Tibetan position, cld be expected. Tenor and timing of any comment wld depend on character Tibetan announcement.
>
> It is considered undesirable that US GOVT publicly introduce UN question in advance Tibetans own action this regard.[37]

The United States also informed the British that America was not ready to "appease" India and was content to suffer a deterioration in relations with that country, if need be. This action, it felt, was justified by the need to counter Communist aggression.[38] This could have been a major step forward in U.S. thinking, but at this time it was just rhetoric unsupported by concrete actions.

Thacher again met with Shakabpa and conveyed the new information,

35. U.S. National Archives, 793B.00/6–1651, telegram from Steere, U.S. Embassy in India, to U.S. secretary of state, dated 16 June 1951.

36. Taktse's request for the letter's confidentiality is documented in U.S. National Archives, 793B.00/6–1151, telegram from Ambassador Henderson to U.S. secretary of state, dated 11 June 1951; and U.S. National Archives, 611.93B/6–1451, memorandum of conversation among Taktse, Yangpel Pandatsang, George Patterson, and F. Wilkins, dated 8 June 1951. On the issue of his withholding the letter from other members of the Tibetan government, the U.S. Consulate in Calcutta, for example, reported that Taktse had not shown the letter to Wilkins in their meeting on 8 June 1951, because another Tibetan official, Pandatsang, was present (U.S. National Archives, 793B.00/6–1751, telegram from Wilson, Calcutta Consulate, to secretary of state, dated 17 June 1951).

37. U.S. National Archives, 793S.00/6–1551, telegram from the U.S. State Department to the U.S. Embassy in India, dated 16 June 1951. Chinese sources say Zhang Jingwu arrived in Calcutta on 26 June.

38. British Foreign Office Records, FO371/92997, telegram from U.K. Embassy in Washington, D.C., to the British Foreign Office, dated 25 June 1951.

which Shakabpa said he would pass on to Yadong at once. He also informed Thacher that almost all high Tibetan officials in India had been summoned to Yadong for an important meeting.[39]

On 26 June, Shakabpa and Thacher had a lengthy conversation about which Thacher wrote a detailed report. It conveys some of the concerns of the Tibetans at Yadong as well as a lack of diplomatic and military planning on the Tibetan side:

Conversation with Shakabpa and Jigme Tering [the latter was the translator]

I had called earlier in the day on Shakabpa and we arranged for him to come with Tering to Rinking Farm that evening. I told them first about the message I had received that afternoon from Calcutta. This message stated that the Chinese and Tibetan delegations had been delayed by floods and were still in China.

Next I touched on our eagerness to receive all available information from Yadong or Lhasa, whether of major importance or not. I pointed out that the more of such information we had to relay to Washington, the more convincing evidence we would have of the Tibetan Government's genuine desire to cooperate and resist. Shakabpa declared, however, that he still had no definite information as to what the Tibetan Government would do. I then asked him whether he had yet been able to send to Yadong the declaration regarding the U.S. Government's intentions which I had given him on June 19. Shakabpa stated this message had already gone to Yadong. When I inquired whether he knew what definite plans the Tibetan Government had for notifying the government of India in anticipation of the issuance of a statement by the Dalai Lama, he stated he did not know what arrangements had been made. I asked whether perhaps this might be done through Dayal [political officer in Sikkim] but Shakabpa had no clear idea that Dayal would be the proper person. I repeated again the suggestions made in our discussion of June 19 re: the desirability of working out means for prior notification of the Chinese, American, Indian and British Governments prior to the issuance of the statement as means of stirring the GOI into awareness of the Chinese Communists' aggressive intentions toward Tibet.

Shakabpa then mentioned that he had received requests from the Tibetan Government in Yadong for information on five points. We discussed these at some length and I gave my answers on the questions involved and in each case Shakabpa declared that the answers he had already sent to Yadong were in substantial agreement with my views.

(1) The first question raised inquired whether it was thought that the GOI would not allow the Dalai Lama to transit India on his way to the U.S.A. I said I did not see how India could possibly object to the Dalai Lama's passing through on his way somewhere else. I could not of course say whether or not the GOI would permit the Dalai Lama to stay in India. I took the opportunity of mentioning that we felt the Dalai Lama should consider India as the most

39. U.S. National Archives, 793B.00/6–2851, telegram no. 548, from the U.S. consul general in Calcutta to the U.S. secretary of state, dated 28 June 1951.

desirable refuge, then Thailand, then Ceylon. If the Dalai Lama could stay in none of these places then the United States Government would be glad to have him. I pointed out that our attitude on this [was] dictated by the desirability of having the Dalai Lama stay near his own territory and in areas where his religious position would provide him with a reverent and sympathetic reception from the local residents. I explained the Department of State's reasons for suggesting Thailand as preferable to Ceylon. I emphasized that our views did not denote any unwillingness or reluctance to receive the Dalai Lama, but simply that we felt his influence and effectiveness would be greater if he stayed among persons who revered him for his religious leadership and where he was closer to his own people.

(2) The second question raised by the Tibetan Government was whether aid from the U.S. Government would be directed simply toward assisting the Dalai Lama's flight or whether some aid might also be forthcoming for resistance. I replied that certainly the U.S. Government was willing to help both. I emphasized, however, if the Tibetan Government could provide definite evidence that some of its and the Dalai Lama's private resources were being drawn upon and that definite efforts were being made to translate this treasure into usable assets, then the U.S. Government would be more willing to help. However, I pointed out that it was not reasonable to expect the U.S. Government to carry the whole burden if the Dalai Lama had some means to help himself. Our intention, however, was definitely to give assistance [to] the Tibetan people if it could be worked out.

(3) The Tibetan Government had inquired of Shakabpa whether he thought aid would be given "openly or surreptitiously." To this I replied that it was conceivable that aid could be arranged to reach the Dalai Lama in whatever place of refuge he chose, without public knowledge. *It was difficult, however, to imagine how the Tibetan Government and people could be aided without the knowledge and consent of the GOI. This brought us back once more to the whole question of the vital nature of India's position and the necessity of securing its consent before the U.S. Government could do anything really effective.*

(4) The Tibetan Government had inquired whether the U.S. Government would give any assistance if the Tibetan Government should announce that it would accept the Chinese Communists' terms. I stated that we regarded the Tibetan Government's disavowal of the terms as the first and most important step in opening the way for U.S. assistance and toward arousing India to dangers involved. I was not prepared to say that the United States would give no assistance if Tibet accepted the Chinese terms but it seemed that the chances of aid materializing under such circumstances were rather slight. Shakabpa stated that he had informed the Tibetan Government there would be "no hope" of aid if Tibet accepted the Chinese terms.

This opened the entire question of the Tibetan action with regard to the Chinese terms. Shakabpa pointed out that necessarily the Tibetan Government was fearful of a strong reaction from the Chinese Communists and of danger to Tibet were it to disavow the Chinese announcement re the terms. *I pointed out that Tibet was faced with two difficult alternatives: one was to make vigorous resistance to China, while the other alternative involved an attempt to cooperate with China.*

I outlined as clearly as I could the fate of people who tried to cooperate with the Communists, and emphasized that the Panchen Lama, who was now trying to cooperate with the Chinese, would eventually be brushed aside as would the Dalai Lama himself if he stayed in Tibet. That I should think such a fate awaited the Panchen Lama surprised Shakabpa considerably. I outlined as vividly as I could what had happened where the Communists had taken over in other areas (mentioned events in Czechoslovakia, China, Poland, etc.).

I wondered whether the Tibetan government was seriously considering acceptance of the Chinese terms and whether this was connected with some other scheme of hidden resistance. Shakabpa said he knew of no such scheme.

(5) If the Dalai Lama should decide to go to the U.S.A., how would he be received?

I emphasized again our feelings about where the Dalai Lama should go — Thailand, Ceylon, etc., but said the Dalai Lama would be received as great religious leader and as temporal leader of autonomous state, but without deciding question of Chinese suzerainty over Tibet. We could make no action in this respect until Tibet decided to declare its own complete independence from China. This gave me an opportunity to emphasize again that some signs of vigorous action and vigorous resistance by the Tibetan Government was of the utmost importance. The U.S. Government's policy must be one of only helping those who would help themselves.

I asked Shakabpa what would happen if the U.S. Government suddenly placed 50,000 rifles at the disposal of the Tibetan Government in Kalimpong. *Shakabpa talked of using them [in] guerrilla warfare rather than in open fighting.*

Finally I asked Shakabpa about relationship between Taktser and the Dalai Lama. He endorsed former highly—said he was very much in confidence of the latter.[40]

Two days later, Thacher informed Shakabpa that the Chinese and Tibetan delegations had arrived in Hong Kong on 26 June; Shakabpa promised to relay the news at once to Yadong.[41]

Despite the Dalai Lama's continued failure to reply positively to the U.S. overtures, Taktse Rimpoche, now in Calcutta, told the U.S. consul general there that the Dalai Lama (1) certainly did not approve of the Sino-Tibetan agreement; (2) would very likely make a statement disavowing the agreement before the Chinese arrived in India; (3) would definitely leave Tibet before the Chinese and Tibetan delegates arrived there; and (4) preferred to seek asylum in the United States.[42] He raised the same set of questions that Sha-

---

40. U.S. National Archives, 793B.00/7–251, report of conversation of Vice-Consul N. G. Thacher with Shakabpa and Jigme Tering [Taring] on 26 June 1951, dated 2 July 1951 (emphasis added).

41. U.S. National Archives, 793B.00/7–2951, extract from letter from N. G. Thacher, dated 29 June 1951.

42. U.S. National Archives, 793B.00/6–2651, telegram no. 541, from the U.S. consul general in Calcutta to the U.S. secretary of state, dated 26 June 1951.

kabpa had asked earlier regarding the nature of U.S. support in the event that the Dalai Lama left Tibet, and he commented freely that many around the Dalai Lama were opposed to such a move.[43]

The United States asked Taktse to convey the complete U.S. position to the Dalai Lama once again through a trusted messenger.[44] On 28 June, Taktse sent a coded telegram as well as a secret letter, in which he urged his brother to act and denounce the agreement.[45]

The Dalai Lama recalled this letter in his book, saying, "He suggested that if I were to go into exile, some arrangement for assistance could be negotiated between our two Governments [United States and Tibet]. My brother concluded his letter by saying that it was imperative that I should arrive in India as soon as possible, adding that the Chinese delegation was already in Calcutta, en route to Tromo [Yadong]. The implication was that if I did not make a move immediately, it would be too late."[46]

In the meantime, the United States discussed the issue with Britain and India.

THE UNITED STATES TALKS WITH BRITAIN AND INDIA

The American ideas regarding assistance to Tibet met with little enthusiasm in India and Britain. On 11 June 1951, G. S. Bajpai informally expressed the Indian position, reiterating India's earlier decision to avoid any military or diplomatic confrontation that could prove prejudicial to Indian relations with China. Bajpai also indicated that if the Dalai Lama decided to leave Tibet and ask for asylum in India, his request would be granted but that this asylum would *not* be "political asylum" of a sort in which the Dalai Lama could function as the head of a government in exile.[47] It would, rather, be a "humanitarian" gesture to an *individual* who would *not* be allowed to engage in

43. U.S. National Archives, 793.00/6–1151, State Department internal memorandum, dated 2 July 1951; and U.S. National Archives, 793B.00/7–951, comment in telegram from the U.S. consul general in Calcutta to the U.S. secretary of state, dated 9 July 1951.

44. U.S. National Archives, 793B.00/6–2651, telegram no. 541, from the U.S. consul general in Calcutta to the U.S. secretary of state, dated 26 June 1951.

45. U.S. National Archives, 793B.00/7–351, telegram no. 13, from the U.S. consul general in Calcutta to the U.S. secretary of state, dated 3 July 1951; and U.S. National Archives, 793B.00/7–351, U.S. consul general in Calcutta to the U.S. secretary of state, cited in U.S. Department of State 1951: 7:1728 fn. 1. Taktse Rimpoche declined to comment to me on these dealings with the United States.

46. Dalai Lama 1990: 64–65. The Dalai Lama also received a letter from Heinrich Harrer from Kalimpong urging him to flee into exile.

47. Regarding the Indian grant of asylum, see British Foreign Office Records, FO371/92996, telegram from the U.K. high commissioner in India to the Commonwealth Relations Office, dated 11 June 1951.

political activity while in India. India had written off Tibet and planned simply to watch the ensuing events with regret. The British high commissioner also reported that the Indian government was strongly opposed to the United States' involvement.[48]

The British Foreign Office continued its policy of yielding all initiative to India and trying to discourage the United States from supporting Tibet. For example, on 18 June, in response to the U.S. willingness to issue a statement of support for a Tibetan disavowal of the Sino-Tibetan agreement, the British told the State Department that they hoped Tibet would not appeal to the United Nations and that the United States would consult the Indian government about U.S. plans and attitudes. The British told the State Department that continued failure to consult India would further strain relations and might even "result in Nehru washing his hands entirely of [the] Tibetan problem."[49] R. H. Scott, head of the British Southeast Asia Department of the Foreign Office, thought the American suggestions were cynical from the Tibetan point of view and dangerous from the point of view of American-Indian relations. Scott argued acerbically that "the result of encouraging the Tibetans to denounce the Sino-Tibetan agreement would be to provide American publicists with some propaganda points, but not aid the Tibetans effectively." He thought that the U.S. Embassy should consult the Indian government and weigh the Indians' views carefully before embarking on this "propaganda stunt."[50]

Furthermore, on 25 June the British Embassy in Washington informed the State Department of the feelings of the British high commissioner in Delhi, Sir Archibald Nye: "(1) No resistance on the part of Tibet could possibly be successful. (2) One of the principles which motivated GOI was opposition to any action which might worsen relations with Communist China. . . . (4) GOI would not be pleased to see a US involvement in Tibet. (5) India would not be likely to think an appeal to the UN on the part of the Dalai Lama useful and therefore would not support making such an appeal."[51]

The significance of the United States' apparent willingness to support the

48. British Foreign Office Records, FO371/92997, telegram from the U.K. high commissioner in India to the Commonwealth Relations Office, dated 18 June 1951. See Goldstein 1989 for an examination of India's position on Tibet since India's independence in 1947. See also Garver 2001.

49. British Foreign Office Records, FO371/92997, telegram from the U.K. high commissioner in India to the Commonwealth Relations Office, dated 18 June 1951.

50. British Foreign Office Records, FO371/92997, comment by R. H. Scott on minute by J. A. Murray, dated 21 June 1951.

51. U.S. National Archives, 793B.00/6–255 1, memorandum of conversation between R. H. Belcher, first secretary of the British Embassy, and D. D. Kennedy, acting director of the Office of South Asian Affairs, dated 25 June 1951.

Tibetan cause regardless of British and Indian desires or attitudes was not missed by the perceptive Scott of the British Foreign Office, who wrote: "This is an important landmark in Tibetan history. If, under American encouragement, the Dalai Lama repudiates the Peking agreement, a heavy responsibility will fall on the United States authorities and we should at least try to secure that the Dalai Lama goes into voluntary exile in India rather than that he should attempt a futile resistance campaign without Indian support."[52]

While this was unfolding, a great final debate was occurring in Yadong on how the Dalai Lama should respond.

52. British Foreign Office Records, FO371/92997, minute by R. H. Scott, dated 27 June 1951.

Chapter 6

The Dalai Lama Returns to Lhasa

THE FINAL ASSEMBLY DEBATE

The final decision about whether the Dalai Lama should return to Lhasa came after a three-day Assembly meeting of all government officials present in Yadong in early July 1951.

The largest group in Yadong was composed of officials who felt strongly that the Dalai Lama should return to Lhasa. This included virtually all of the monk officials. They were supported by the sitsab and other top officials in Lhasa, who also wanted the Dalai Lama to return, as did the abbots of the Three Monastic Seats (Drepung, Sera, Ganden). Chabtsom, the aristocratic government official who was the Lhasa Kashag's secretary (tib. kadrung), recalled the sitsab and Kashag's efforts to achieve this even before the Yadong meeting.

> When the Dalai Lama was in Yadong, the sitsab said we [the Kashag in Lhasa] must write to the Dalai Lama. The Lhasa Kashag agreed, and we sent letters several times urging him to return. The letters argued, "The situation in Lhasa is now different from when you left. Previously there were a lot of lies and rumors, but now we have checked everywhere and ascertained that there is no danger at all. Earlier, we didn't have any custom of sending spies out, but after you left we did. We collected lots of intelligence; for example, we sent spies to keep an eye on the lamas from Amdo [Qinghai Province]."
>
> We sent several letters like this, but I don't recall sending any delegations. We also received several petitions from the Big Three Monastic Seats, who came to us saying, "Some government officials and a group from Kalimpong led by Shakabpa are trying to get the Dalai Lama to go to India, so you must try to ensure that this doesn't happen and that he returns to Lhasa."
>
> So we wrote a letter to the Dalai Lama saying, "You went suddenly to

Tromo [Yadong], and the people feel empty, so please return. We will watch carefully [in Lhasa], and if later you have to leave again, you can do this gradually."[1]

In addition, the Three Monastic Seats sent several delegations to Yadong, imploring the Dalai Lama to return to Lhasa quickly.

Then, after news of the agreement reached Lhasa, the top officials there again urged the Dalai Lama to return. Thubden Sangye, a Tibetan official who was there, recalled a meeting in Lhasa called by the sitsab.

> They informed the meeting that the Seventeen-Point Agreement had been signed and that such and such were the points in the agreement. Then they asked us what we thought about it.
>
> Everyone thought it was reasonable in the sense that the Dalai Lama's position would not be changed, and the practice of religion would not be disturbed, but they also expressed their concern about PLA troops coming to Tibet. We also said that there was nothing to do until the negotiators returned and we found out in detail what actually happened, but we also sent a request to the Dalai Lama to return to Lhasa as soon as possible, and we sent three separate groups to Yadong to invite the Dalai Lama back in person.[2]

On the other hand, the anti-agreement, pro-exile group, also included important officials, the most senior of which was the Kashag minister Surkhang. Other prominent opponents of returning to Lhasa were the senior lay officials Shakabpa and Namseling, the Dalai Lama's lord chamberlain Phala, and the Dalai Lama's relatives (e.g., his brothers Lobsang Samden and Taktse Rimpoche). Both sides held strong views on this issue, which they all saw as a decision that would likely change the history of Tibet.

The Tibetan Assembly meeting in Yadong was chaired, as always, by the trungtsigye, namely, the eight heads of the Revenue and Ecclesiastic offices, or in this case as many of these as were present in Yadong. The Kashag ministers did not attend Assembly meetings.

One of the Revenue Office heads, Namseling, was the main speaker in favor of rejection of the agreement. He was angry and bitter about the Chinese attack and began by arguing that the Seventeen-Point Agreement was flawed because it was signed without consultation and because it accepted that Tibet was completely a part of China.[3] He expressed the views of Shakabpa, Surkhang, and others that, for one thing, the agreement gave up too much, and for another, the Chinese Communists, although they now pro-

---

1. Chabtsom, interview, 1992, Lhasa.

2. Thubden Sangye, interview, 1991, Dharamsala.

3. His wife said he was so upset by the news of the Chamdo invasion and defeat that he could not sleep (Mrs. Namseling, interview, 1994, Dharamsala).

claimed a moderate policy promising to leave Tibet as it was, would change their demeanor and destroy religion and communize everything after large numbers of their troops reached Tibet.[4] Once that started, no foreign country would be able to help Tibet, and the Dalai Lama himself would be at risk and helpless.

Namseling also argued that by going into exile they would not only refute Chinese claims to sovereignty over Tibet and keep the flame of Tibetan independence alive but would also facilitate securing assistance from the United States and other democratic countries and, with their help, work to regain Tibet's independence. This, he said, had worked out well for the Thirteenth Dalai Lama in 1910–13 and would do so again now. Conversely, accepting the agreement and going back to Lhasa meant the end of Tibet as an independent entity, not just for then, but forever.[5]

The main person speaking in favor of return (and opposing Namseling) was the trunyichemmo Chömpel Thubden, a senior monk official from the Ecclesiastic Office. He argued with emotion, saying that the Seventeen-Point Agreement was a good document because it left the position of the Dalai Lama intact and preserved monastic life and income. The items in the agreement he looked to were points 3, 4, 7, and 11:

> Point 3. In accordance with the policy toward nationalities laid down in the Common Programme of the Chinese People's Political Consultative Conference, the Tibetan people have the right of exercising national regional autonomy under the leadership of the Central People's Government.

> Point 4. The central authorities will not alter the existing political system in Tibet. The central authorities also will not alter the established status, functions, and powers of the Dalai Lama. Officials of various ranks shall hold office as usual.

> Point 7. The policy of freedom of religious belief laid down in the Common Programme of the Chinese People's Political Consultative Conference shall be carried out. The religious beliefs, customs, and habits of the Tibetan People shall be respected, and lama monasteries shall be protected. The central authorities will not effect a change in the income of the monasteries and temples.

4. On 20 July 1951, the Dalai Lama's brother and brother-in-law (Lobsang Samden and Takla [Phüntso Tashi]) visited the Chinese cadre Le Yuhong in Yadong. Le wrote that during the course of that visit, Takla told him that Surkhang thought the Communists would be mild at first but later harsh (tib. ngönjam jedzub) and feared this (Le 1981: 142, entry for 20 July 1951).

5. Gyentsen Tempel, interview, 1993, Lhasa; Panden, interview, 1992, Dharamsala; Sambo (Tenzin Thondrup), interview, 1981, Dharamsala.

Figure 4. Tsipön Namseling (Penjor Jigme). Source: Chen Zonglie

Point 11. In matters related to various reforms in Tibet, there will be no compulsion on the part of the central authorities. The local government of Tibet should carry out reforms of its own accord, and when the people request for reform, they shall be settled by means of consultation with the leaders of Tibet.

Chömpel Thubden said, "We sent five excellent representatives to China and I have faith they would not exchange the entire nation for a cup of beer [would not sell out Tibet]. We have requested foreign help and are dependent on it, but what have we received from our appeals? Nothing. And in the future we will receive no more than we have up to now. The Dalai Lama must go back to Lhasa. We cannot let him go to a foreign land."[6] Others made similar comments, saying things such as, "The Chinese are communists, but their face is the same as ours. It will be hard to live and mix with the white-faced ones."[7]

Pandenla, a personal attendant of Trijang Rimpoche, the Dalai Lama's junior tutor, recalled that both of the very influential tutors of the Dalai Lama also were in favor of not going into exile: "Most of them [monasteries and the Dalai Lama's tutors] thought that it is better to return, because if we went abroad we would have a small refugee government and they were pessimistic about receiving help. So that is what they were thinking, judging by the conversations of Trijang Rimpoche and Ling Rimpoche [which he had heard]."[8] The Dalai Lama also says in his autobiography that Ling Rimpoche was adamant that he should not go into exile.[9]

Within the segment favoring a return to Lhasa, most officials thought Tibet could live with the terms of the agreement. Like the negotiators, they thought that the neologism *regional autonomy,* invented by the Chinese, sounded good, because the component words meant "a region/area ruled by oneself" (tib. rang gyong jong). Similarly, the above-mentioned items in the Agreement about the continuation of the Tibetan government, the protection of monasteries and estates, and especially the Dalai Lama's status sounded excellent. All of this had come as a relief to the religious and lay leaders who initially feared that the Chinese would be committed to destroying the traditional system and implementing atheistic communism. And although they disliked being absorbed into China and the eventual arrival of Chinese troops and officials in Tibet as an army of what they considered occupation, the moderate Chinese terms and the gradual policy were an unexpected re-

---

6. Gyentsen Tempel, interview, 1993. This was also mentioned by Panden (interview, 1992) and Sambo (interview, 1981).

7. Takla (Phüntso Tashi), interview, 1992, Dharamsala.8. Panden, interview, 1992.

8. Panden, interview, 1992.

9. Dalai Lama 1990: 65.

lief, given Tibet's helplessness, and made it easy for them to ignore the agreement's sections that talked about reforms and the Military-Administrative Committee. Moreover, among those who favored the Dalai Lama's return to Lhasa, some, led by the sitsab, still hoped that once in Lhasa they could persuade the Chinese to change some of the terms they did not like, in particular the need for large number of Chinese troops remaining in Tibet.[10]

Namseling then rose to rebut this, stating forcefully that unless the Assembly denounced the agreement before the Chinese arrived, Tibet would become a communist country and all would be lost. Tibet could never be independent again. So His Holiness must go to exile. To this Chömpel Thubden angrily retorted, "I have lived in a foreign country [China] and know very well how difficult it is to live abroad if no one pays you attention and helps you. What will we do in India if this happens? We have seen that the Indian government does not want to support or assist us in any way, so how can you say the Dalai Lama should leave Tibet and live under such circumstances in an alien non-Buddhist country? What do you know about this."[11]

Then Shölkang Jedrung, a monk official who was the son of a well-known aristocratic family, spoke in support of Chömpel Thubden, saying, "First Shakabpa had told us that India would welcome us with great dignity and honor, but now when we have come to the very doorstep of India we see no signs of welcome. Seeking help and trying to rely on foreign countries has had no result. It is better that we rely on the Chinese. I am going back, whatever you decide."[12] Then still others said things such as, "It is not the same as in the 13th Dalai Lama's time. In the past, China wasn't as strong as it is now. Now China is strong, so it is better if we stay in Tibet."[13]

Shölkang is interesting because of his love for things new and modern and the trouble it caused him. Tsarong Rimshi recalled:

> Shölkang Jedrung was very fond of things like riding bicycles and motorcycles and playing football. So it appears that the trunyichemmo heard about Shölkang Jedrung doing all of these things . . . and called him to the Ecclesiastic Office and probably kind of scolded him, saying, "You can't act like this. It is a disgrace for the monk officials to do this." They didn't like this, but Shölkang Jedrung was very fond of these things, and he also played tennis well. In winter, he also used to ice skate. So they probably criticized him again.
>
> At the time of Regent Taktra, people were not allowed to play football and ride bicycles. So people didn't like this, even though they didn't dare say anything against it openly.

10. Dalai Lama, interview, 1993, Dharamsala.

11. Sambo, interview, 1981. Chömpel Thubden had served in the Tibetan government's Bureau Office in China.

12. Sambo, interview, 1981.

13. Takla (Phüntso Tashi), interview, 1993, Dharamsala.

There was also a problem when Shölkang Jedrung took a photo. I was with him at that time. This was the first time that the Dalai Lama went to Drepung for the ceremony to enter the monastic order. At that time, there were many people in the procession, and he took photos of it. I also took photos, but I did it surreptitiously. . . . He probably took the photos conspicuously. So I heard that Taktra and those people who didn't like him [Shölkang] saw that, and they told him that he is not allowed to take photos and confiscated his camera. After that, the lord chamberlain . . . called him to the secretariat of the Dalai Lama (tib. Tse ga) told him, "You have done a very serious thing for which you will be punished by prostrating during the monk official's morning tea ceremony (tib. trung ja) for seven days. So he had to prostrate for seven days, and I think he was also demoted to the status of an ordinary monk official. Therefore, he might have been frustrated.[14]

Anti-Indian feeling was running very high at this time, because the Tibetan officials in Yadong were insulted that Harishwar Dayal, the Indian political officer in Sikkim, made no attempt to pay even a courtesy call on the Dalai Lama, despite residing only two days away in Gangtok (in Sikkim) and despite having been warmly welcomed in Lhasa only a little more than a year before. The Dalai Lama expressed it this way:

Even though he was just a mountain pass away, he did not come to Tromo [Yadong]. So from our side this was taken as a testing ground to examine what the Indian government's [position/attitude] was. So if things were loose and easy, the political officer would definitely have come. All he had to do was go over one pass. But he did not come. So there was some question as to the predictability of the Indian position.[15]

Shölkang was followed by others who argued that if the Dalai Lama renounced the agreement and fled into exile he might never again return to Tibet and certainly would not be able to use his position to help his people. If he remained in Lhasa, however, many opportunities were likely to develop in which he could use his influence to moderate the Chinese occupation of Tibet.[16] Clearly, an important consideration for those opposed to going into exile was apprehension of what the Chinese Communists would do to religion and monasticism should the Dalai Lama flee. The overriding fear was that without the Dalai Lama in Lhasa, the Communists would destroy everything.

In addition to such political and strategic assessments, the material and practical thought of trying to live abroad with no estates or subsidies also frightened many officials. Consequently, although the elite distrusted and feared the Chinese Communists and considered themselves independent of

14. Tsarong Rimshi, interview, 1991, Kalimpong.
15. Dalai Lama, interview, 1993, Dharamsala.
16. Sambo, interview, 1981; Gyentsen Tempel, interview, 1993.

China, they were inclined to return to Tibet, since the Seventeen-Point Agreement, if adhered to, would allow them to continue their style of life—at least for the foreseeable future.

After a long and heated debate, the consensus was clearly on the side of return, and the Assembly recommended to the Kashag that the Dalai Lama should return to Lhasa. Council minister Surkhang, however, completely opposed accepting Chinese sovereignty and returning, so he made a last-ditch attempt to thwart the Assembly's recommendation by suggesting that a divine lottery be held before making a final decision, since that gave him a fifty-fifty chance that exile would be selected.[17] His Kashag colleagues agreed, and the next day, amid sacred prayers and incense, the lottery balls were shaken in a bowl before the image of the protector goddess Lhamo. When a dough ball popped out and was opened, it said that the Dalai Lama should return to Lhasa. From the Tibetans' perspective, that meant the deity Lhamo had prophesied in favor of return. Surkhang, distraught and suspicious, is said to have opened the remaining dough ball in the bowl just in case the lottery had been rigged by putting identical answers in both balls. It had not been tampered with.[18] The gods had spoken.

One element underlying the majority's decision to return was the belief that the U.S. offers of support were far too limited to justify making the complete break that denouncing the agreement would entail. While the United States was the only outside country that had offered Tibet any support, it had not offered a real hope of preventing the Chinese takeover or of Tibet regaining control in the near future. The United States was not willing to recognize Tibet's claim to independence, let alone give substantial financial and military assistance to help Tibetans regain their land, so it was feared that they would end up having to live the rest of their lives in exile in someone else's country. As the Tibetans saw it, the United States had sent tens of thousands of troops to Korea to contain communism, yet it was unwilling to make a similar commitment to prevent the Communists from taking over Tibet and to preserve Tibetan "freedom." America could serve as a haven where the Dalai Lama could decry Chinese aggression, but little else.

A second problem with the Americans' offers was that they were invariably contingent on the cooperation of the Government of India. The constant reference to having to do things through the Government of India particularly irritated Tibetans and negated the positive elements in the U.S. position, since

17. Surkhang was actually skeptical about all these supernatural manipulations. Once when a shaman came to his home to "suck out" the illness from a family member through a cord, he conducted an experiment. Instead of tying the cord to the ill person, he tied it to a banister and watched as the shaman sucked a bloody mass signifying the illness from what he thought was the patient but was really the banister (Surkhang, personal communication, 1963).

18. Panden, interview, 1992.

Tibetans felt that Nehru was pro-Chinese and was not going to support Tibet. And they were correct. The Indian contingency made all the U.S. claims of sympathy and support seem empty and meaningless or at least unlikely to be effective. Mao's "carrot" seemed attractive vis-à-vis the modest U.S. alternative and the hostile attitude of the Government of India.

An official from the U.S. Consulate in Calcutta recalled a conversation he had with Pandatsang (Yambe), the Tibetan trade agent in Kalimpong, several months later on about 17 September, in which he expressed this attitude clearly.

> Pandatsang emphasized that he and many other Tibetans felt that they had been completely deserted by the rest of the world in their efforts to reach a settlement with the Chinese Communist Government. He argued that the Tibetan Government was deeply discouraged by the rebuffs received by its emissaries to New Delhi about a year and a half ago, and by the failure of any other country to come out strongly for the maintenance of Tibetan autonomy. Most Tibetans felt that India was seriously to blame [for] Tibet's apparent isolation. He reviewed recent events which had made the Tibetans particularly bitter and had strengthened the resolve of many never again to seek the assistance of India in any way. He pointed out that Mr. Harishwar Dayal, Indian Political Agent of Sikkim and representative designated by the Indian Government for official contact with the Tibetans, had failed to convey to the Tibetans any willingness on the part of the Government of India to receive the Dalai Lama should he wish to leave Tibet.[19]

So in the end, most officials, along with the gods, saw the Dalai Lama's return as Tibet's best hope of preserving the essence of their lamaist state and way of life. However, this decision did not mean that the Tibetans were ready to accept the agreement formally. On this issue, for reasons discussed below, the Dalai Lama and the Kashag stalled, insisting that, since all officials were not in Yadong, that decision could not be made until they were back in Lhasa.

THE CHINESE ARRIVE IN INDIA

On 1 July, while this debate was going on, Zhang Jingwu and his staff arrived in Calcutta.[20] Two days later, they flew to Bagdogra Airport and drove from there to Kalimpong, the Indian border town that was the heart of the Tibetan wool export trade. There Zhang was welcomed on 4 July to the blaring of traditional horns and clarinets (tib. dung, gyaling) at the Teesta Bridge

19. U.S. National Archives, 611.93B231/9–1751, enclosure to dispatch 119, from the U.S. consul general in Calcutta to the State Department, dated 17 September 1951.

20. U.S. National Archives, 302 Tibet, telegram from Wilson in Calcutta Consulate to embassy in New Delhi, dated 2 July 1951. A Chinese source gives the arrival date as 26 June 1951.

by a reception committee organized by the Kalimpong Tibetan Traders' Association and resident representatives of the Tibetan government.[21] Zhang spoke briefly, summarizing the agreement and the Communist Party's religion and nationalities policies. He emphasized that the Dalai Lama would retain his title and authority as before and asked the reception committee to pass this information on to those close to the Dalai Lama.[22]

A few days later, Kheme and Lhautara, two of the Tibetan negotiators from Beijing, left for Yadong to report to the Tibetan government while Zhang and the others stayed in Kalimpong, waiting for the arrival of the gifts for the Dalai Lama.[23] By the time Kheme and Lhautara arrived in Yadong, however, the decision to return to Lhasa had been made, and two officials— Shölkang Sey (Sonam Dargye) and Nanggar (Ngawang Tsempel)—had been appointed as liaison officers to the Chinese. Shölkang Sey was sent to Kalimpong to meet and assist Zhang Jingwu in traveling to Tibet.[24]

Kheme and Lhautara explained to the Kashag what had happened in China and overall spoke positively about the agreement, which they felt was the best Tibet could have hoped to achieve. Lhautara recommended that the government accept the agreement, but the Kashag was noncommittal.[25]

Interestingly, Lhautara and Kheme were denied permission to report firsthand to the Dalai Lama about the negotiations. They were informed that the Dalai Lama was too busy getting ready to return to Lhasa, so they should ask for an audience after he returned.[26] That the leading officials in Yadong did not permit these two negotiators from Beijing to explain to the ruler in person what had transpired in China illustrates how isolated the Dalai Lama was from what was occurring on a day-to-day basis. At this time, neither the Kashag nor the religious tutors and officials in the Dalai Lama's entourage wanted him too intimately involved, and, as will be discussed in the next chapter, he himself was not inclined to take such a role.

The Kashag instructed Kheme and Lhautara to inform Zhang Jingwu of the Dalai Lama's decision to return to Lhasa soon. The two negotiators immediately called Zhang in Kalimpong and told him that if he was able to come quickly he could meet the Dalai Lama in Yadong; otherwise he would

---

21. Alo Chöndze, interview, 1993, Cleveland, OH. He described the welcome in that interview: "There was a Traders' Association (tib. tshongpa gidu) in Kalimpong, and I was in this. So the Nepalese traders were making preparations to welcome Zhang. Shakabpa said we should make preparations to welcome Zhang. We should prepare horns and clarinets for this. I and Gowa Chöndze watched the welcome from a ridge. Shakabpa had made a big welcome with cymbals and horns. They also gave Zhang a banquet."
22. Ha'o 1986: 119.
23. Sambo, interview, 1981; Stag lha (Takla) 1995: 65.
24. Lha'u rta ra (Lhautara) 1981: 114–15.
25. Lha'u rta ra (Lhautara) 1986b: 45.
26. Lha'u rta ra (Lhautara) 1986b: 45.

have to wait until Lhasa.[27] Zhang decided to leave Kalimpong at once without waiting for the gifts. He arrived in Yadong on 14 July.[28]

CONTINUING U.S. EFFORTS TO PERSUADE THE DALAI LAMA TO FLEE TIBET

The U.S. expectation that the Dalai Lama would take a strong stand against the Chinese Communists received a severe setback when Shakabpa informed U.S. officials on 1 July that the Dalai Lama planned to hold further discussions with the Chinese Communist delegation in Yadong before he issued a statement on the agreement or went to India. Shakabpa also indicated that the Chinese would encounter a friendly reception in Yadong.[29] Wilson, the American consul general in Calcutta, clutching at straws, tried to add a positive spin to this bad news, telling Secretary of State Acheson, "This of course [is a] serious blow *although [it is] still possible in our view for DL [Dalai Lama] to act after Chi del [arrives] in Yadong.*"[30]

At about the same time (on 2 July), the Dalai Lama sent a reply to Taktse Rimpoche's 28 June cable, but it was not what Taktse expected. The Dalai Lama *now advised him not to go to the United States,* because this would create problems for the Dalai Lama and the Tibetan government with the Chinese. Taktse, however, refused to follow these instructions, and from Calcutta telegraphed back again, urging the Dalai Lama to disavow the agreement and leave Tibet at once.[31] Taktse put his own spin on events when he spoke with the Americans saying that the Dalai Lama was surrounded by Communist sympathizers and agents who might obtain control of the Dalai Lama and Tibetan Government at any time.[32] Taktse finally left for the United States with his servant on 5 July 1951.

Notwithstanding this disappointing news, in early July the United States made another attempt to contact the Dalai Lama and persuade him to flee Tibet. A secret letter was sent by Ambassador Henderson providing the Dalai Lama with a "concise and clear statement of the attitude of the United States." For security reasons, this letter again was unsigned, undated, and contained no mention of the United States. It was believed to have reached the Dalai Lama by 6 July and said,

27. Phündra, interview, 1993, Beijing.

28. Zhonggong xizang zizhiqu dangshi ziliao zheng ji weiyuanhui 1990, entry for 15 July 1951.

29. U.S. National Archives, 793B.00/7–1251, telegram from the U.S. consul general in Calcutta to the U.S. secretary of state, dated 2 July 1951.

30. Ibid. (emphasis added).

31. U.S. National Archives, 793B.00/7–351, telegram no. 13, from the U.S. consul general in Calcutta to the U.S. secretary of state, dated 3 July 1951.

32. U.S. National Archives, 793B.00/7–95 1, telegram no. 28, from the U.S. consul general in Calcutta to the U.S. secretary of state, dated 9 July 1951. This, as was seen above, was untrue.

We sent you a letter two months ago about the dangers of the Chinese Communists. Some of your advisors probably think that they understand the Chinese Communists and can make a bargain with them. We do not think they understand Communism or the record of its leaders. . . . Your Holiness is the chief hope of Tibet. If the Chinese Communists seize control of Tibet, you will be the recognized leader and will symbolize the hopes of the Tibetans for the recovery of Tibet's freedom.

We do not know whether you received our letter about the Chinese Communists. We would like to know.

Since sending the previous letter we have read in the newspapers your delegation to Peiping signed an agreement with the Chinese Communists. We do not believe they signed it with your permission but [that they] were forced to do so. However, the world is beginning to think that you do not object to the agreement because you have made no statement about it. We think you should make this statement soon because the Chinese Communists are sending a delegation to Yadong through India. If you make your statement before they reach India, it should make it difficult for the Chinese delegation to come to Tibet. If you do not make such a statement, we think that Tibetan autonomy is gone forever. *The only access we have to Tibet is through the country of India. It is therefore important that Tibet tell India what you now want to do and persuade India to help you or permit other countries to help you. We don't know for sure but we think it is possible India will permit help because although India now seems friendly with the Chinese Communists we know many Indians are fearful of the Communists near India.* We ourselves are willing to help Tibet now and will do the following things at this time:

1) After you issue the statement disavowing the agreement which your delegation signed with the Chinese Communists in Peking, we will issue a public statement of our own supporting your stand.

2) If you decide to send a new appeal to the United Nations, we will support your case in the United Nations.

3) If you leave Tibet, we think you should seek asylum in India, Thailand or Ceylon in that order of priority because then you will be closer to Tibet and will be able to organize its resistance to the Chinese Communists. Although we haven't consulted India, we think it would let you come to India because it said you could come last year.[33] We haven't consulted Thailand or Ceylon but we will ask them if you can come if you want us to talk to them. If you are unable to remain in any of these countries, you may come to our country with some of your followers.

4) If you leave Tibet and if you organize resistance to the Chinese Communists, *we are prepared to send you light arms through India. We think, however, that you should first ask India for arms and, if they cannot give them to you, ask India for permission for other countries to send them through India.* If you are able to organize resistance within Tibet, we will also give consideration to supplying you with loans of money to keep up the resistance, spirit and morale of the Tibetan

---

33. As we have already seen, the United States knew that India was willing to accept the Dalai Lama only as an individual refugee but not as the head of a government in exile.

people. This is important if Tibet's autonomy is to be maintained or regained in the event you should feel impelled to seek asylum outside of Tibet. We will discuss plans and programs of military assistance and loans of money with your representatives when you tell us who your representatives are.

5) We have already told your brother, Taktse Rimpoche, that he can go to our country and we are making arrangements for his departure.

We are willing to do all these things. We have sent you many messages to this effect. We do not know if you have received them. Therefore we ask you to write us whether you have received this letter. We ask you also to send us a personal representative or to write us which Tibetan representatives in India have your confidence.[34]

This letter is interesting because it offers more concrete political and military support than previous communiqués did. It is also interesting that U.S. officials were finally questioning who of all the Tibetans they were talking with actually represented the Dalai Lama and the Tibetan government. The disjunction between what they were being told and what was happening had by this time become very evident. Six weeks had passed since the announcement of the agreement, and Washington still did not know what the Dalai Lama was really thinking about the agreement and the previous U.S. communiqués to him.

This new U.S. communiqué, however, did not sway the Dalai Lama and Kashag, and on 11 July, Shakabpa reported that he had received word from the Dalai Lama that he would meet with the Chinese delegation and return to Tibet in ten days. The Kashag, moreover, had instructed all Tibetan officials in Kalimpong to return to Yadong with the Chinese delegation. A large number of officials left with Zhang Jingwu on the 11th.[35]

ZHANG JINGWU IN YADONG

On 15 July, the day after Zhang had arrived in Yadong, the Kashag ministers came to meet him and discuss the arrangements for a meeting with the Dalai Lama the next day. A Chinese account describes the encounter as follows:

> On 15 July, in Yadong, the Kashag ministers (Ramba, Surkhang, Ragasha, and Dombor)[36] together with several other people came to visit Zhang Jingwu and discuss arrangements for his meeting with the Dalai Lama. They said, "The

---

34. U.S. National Archives, 793B.00/7–1151. The letter forwarded to the Dalai Lama was included in a dispatch from the U.S. Embassy in India to the U.S. State Department, dated 11 July 1951 (emphasis added).

35. U.S. National Archives, 793B.00/7–1251, from the U.S. consul general in Calcutta to the U.S. secretary of state, dated 12 July 1951.

36. Ramba (Thubden Güngyen), Surkhang (Wangchen Gelek), Ragasha (Phüntso Rabgye), and Dombor (Kyenrab Wangchuk).

Dalai Lama will ascend the throne and all the [Tibetan] officials will stand in rows. After Representative Zhang comes in, the Dalai Lama will descend from his throne and will receive the letter from Chairman Mao. Then the Dalai Lama will ascend the throne again. Next, Representative Zhang will be seated in the first spot in the row on the right side."

This, however, was the feudal custom for a king meeting his ministers, so of course we could not at all agree to this. Zhang Jingwu recognized that the seating arrangement is not only a personal issue but also represents the relationship between the central government and the local government. Therefore we had to show the subordination of the local government. We had to work on this principle. However, because of the special status of Tibet, Zhang understood that he had to look at the whole situation and make an appropriate compromise. . . .

Le Yuhong then said to the Kashag ministers, Zhang Jingwu is the representative of the Central People's Government, and when he meets the Dalai Lama, the Dalai Lama should not be sitting on the throne. After climbing the mountain [to where the Dalai Lama was residing], first he should rest briefly in a tent. Then he will go directly to the Dalai Lama's apartment to meet and give him the letter from Mao Zedong and have a discussion.

Le Yuhong [further] explained . . . that when the Tibetan delegates came to Beijing, Deputy Chairman Zhu De and Premier Zhou Enlai went to receive them at the railway station. When Chairman Mao met the delegation, their seats were equal in height, and they talked warmly. Le pointed to Kheme and Lhautara saying they [were delegates so] have experienced this and know. Kheme and Lhautara said it was like that. So the Kashag ministers had no response and agreed.[37]

Phündra, the Amdo Tibetan who served as Zhang Jingwu's translator, recalled this discussion.

On the day after he arrived [in Yadong], the Kashag met with Zhang to discuss the forthcoming meeting with the Dalai Lama. According to the ministers, the 14th Dalai Lama would sit on his throne and Zhang would be introduced to him.

Zhang smiled and said nothing, but Le Yuhong, who had accompanied Zhang, got angry and said that Zhang has come on behalf of Chairman Mao, so how could the Dalai Lama refuse to greet him [appropriately]? Discussion on this procedure went on and on for two hours. In the end, it was agreed that the 14th Dalai Lama would place two chairs in his living room. When the two met, they would sit on these chairs.[38]

Both sides, therefore, compromised. The Chinese had to accept that the local government, in the person of the Dalai Lama, would not have to demon-

---

37. Zhao 1995: 19. Le (1981: 139, entry for 15 July 1951) gives a similar account of the meeting arrangement agreement.
38. Phündra, interview, 1993.

strate its subordination to the representative of the central government, but the Tibetans had to accept the Dalai Lama would not sit higher on his platform and throne.

Zhang's audience with the Dalai Lama took place on the 16th. Zhang Jingwu's biography relates the meeting:

> After resting in the tent for a while, Zhang Jingwu went to the Dalai Lama's living room. As soon as he entered, the Dalai Lama stood up and walked a few steps and welcomed him, saying, "Please sit down." The Dalai[39] and Zhang Jingwu were seated in two chairs made of sandalwood, and Zhang Jingwu warmly greeted the Dalai, asking about his health. The Dalai politely asked about Chairman Mao's health and asked General Zhang whether he had many difficulties on his trip.
>
> Zhang Jingwu said, "You sent the delegates to Beijing for negotiations, and they signed the Seventeen-Point Agreement for the Peaceful Liberation of Tibet. Chairman Mao is very appreciative and glad for your patriotic attitude."[40]

Zhang Jingwu then delivered a copy of the agreement (with the codicil) and the letter from Chairman Mao, which clearly picked up on a comment in the Dalai Lama's November letter that indicated his hope, since he had now come into power, that Sino-Tibetan relations would improve.

> Mr. Dalai Lama,
>
> Thanks for your letter and the gifts [you sent] through Mr. Ngabö (Ngawang Jigme).
>
> The Tibetan government has changed its former attitude since you took control. The Tibetan government responded to the call for the peaceful liberation of Tibet by the Central People's Government and sent the plenipotentiaries headed by Ngabö (Ngawang Jigme) to Beijing for negotiations. What you have done is totally correct.
>
> The plenipotentiaries of the Central People's Government and the plenipotentiaries of the Tibetan local government have signed an Agreement on Measures for the Peaceful Liberation of Tibet on the basis of friendship and repeated negotiations. The agreement is in the interest of the Tibetan nationality (ch. minzu) and the Tibetan people and at the same time in the interests of the people of all nationalities in our country.
>
> From now on, the Tibetan local government and Tibetan people will be able to rid themselves of the shackles of imperialism and the oppression of foreign countries and be a gentle nationality within the grand family of the motherland and under the united leadership of the central government. The Tibetan people can stand up and strive for their own causes.

---

39. Chinese sources generally refer to the Dalai Lama only as "Dalai" (and the Panchen Lama only as "Panchen").

40. Zhao 1995: 20.

I hope you and, under your leadership, the Tibetan local government, can genuinely implement the Agreement on Measures for the Peaceful Liberation of Tibet and try hard to assist the PLA to enter Tibet peacefully. I have specially sent Zhang Jingwu with your delegates to contact you. If you need my help, you should feel free to contact Zhang. Please accept my gifts for you.

> Chairmen of the Central People's Government
> Mao Zedong
> 24 May 1951[41]

Zhang explained the agreement, emphasizing that the Tibetan government could remain as it was. Zhang then asked the Dalai Lama what he thought about the agreement, hoping he had persuaded the Dalai Lama to express his acceptance of it publicly.[42] The Dalai Lama, however, gave only a noncommittal answer.[43]

The Dalai Lama's written description of the same meeting is similar to the Chinese account in the essentials.

> On 16 July 1951, the Chinese delegation reached Dromo [Yadong]. A messenger came running to the monastery to announce its imminent arrival. At this news, I felt both great excitement and great apprehension. What would they look like, these people? I was half convinced they would all have horns on their heads. I went out onto the balcony and looked out eagerly down the valley towards the town, scanning the buildings with my telescope. . . . Suddenly I spied movement. A group of my officials was heading in the direction of the monastery. With them, I could make out three men in drab grey suits. They looked very insignificant next to the Tibetans, who wore the traditional red and gold silk robes of high office.
>
> Our meeting was coldly civil. General Zhang Jingwu began by asking me whether I had heard of the Seventeen-Point "Agreement." With the greatest reserve, I replied that I had. He then handed over a copy of it, together with two other documents. As he did so, I noticed that he was wearing a gold Rolex watch. . . .
>
> Next, General Chiang [*sic*, Zhang] asked me when I intended to return to Lhasa. "Soon," I replied not very helpfully, and continued to act as aloof as possible. It was obvious by his question that he wanted to travel back to Lhasa with me so that we could enter the city together, symbolically. In the end my officials managed to avoid this and he set off a day or two after me.[44]

---

41. Zhao 1995: 21. Since the Dalai Lama did not know Chinese, this letter was translated by Zhang Jingwu's translator, Phündra. Zhonggong xizang zizhiqu dangshi ziliao zhengji weiyuanhui 1990, entry for 14 July 1951, summarizes the content similarly.

42. Le 1981: 140–41, entry for 16 July 1951; Phündra, interview, 1993.

43. Phündra, interview, 1993.

44. Dalai Lama 1990: 66–67.

In a later interview, the Dalai Lama elaborated more on his reluctance to say anything about the agreement in Yadong.

> I was shown the copy and asked what opinion I had. I remember that. What I said in reply was that I had not had the time to look at it in detail. I remember saying that clearly. That meant that I had hopes to think about it and discuss it [later]. At that time in Lhasa, as I mentioned to you last time, the two sitsab were taking the responsibility [for the government]. They said that we have to discuss the agreement and relations between Tibet and China [i.e., reopen issues]. So they had strong hopes for that. The Seventeen-Point Agreement was already signed at Beijing, but we did not immediately say yes, that is it [i.e., we accept it]. So if one examines the way most of the officials thought at that time, there was a section who sort of felt that there is still something to discuss. At that time Ngabö had yet to come [back], and it seemed that things were not clear and there was some confusion. So I sort of recall this feeling.[45]

This first meeting of a Chinese Communist official and the Dalai Lama also had a positive effect on the thinking of the Dalai Lama. In contrast to the endless rumors about how terrible the Chinese Communists were, Zhang was rational, respectful, friendly, and mild-mannered. The Dalai Lama has written about his initial impression: "Regardless of all the suspicion and anxiety I felt beforehand, during our meeting it became clear that this man, although supposedly my enemy, was in fact just another human being, an ordinary person like myself. This realization had a lasting impact on me. . . . Having now met general Chang [Zhang], I was a bit happier about the prospect of returning to Lhasa."[46]

Zhang had also informed the Kashag that a statement was needed regarding the agreement, but the Kashag sent Kheme and Lhautara the next day to tell Zhang that they would not make any comment on the agreement until they returned to Lhasa, met with Ngabö, saw the original of the agreement, and consulted with the other religious and government officials in Lhasa.[47]

Le Yuhong tried to push the Tibetan government to respond then, saying, "The terms of the agreement were sent by telegram, and we have brought a copy of the original agreement. They [the Kashag ministers] have also met with Zhang, who is the representative of the Central Committee, and have seen Mao's letter. Therefore, there is no reason to wait until all the Kashag

45. Dalai Lama, interview, 1993.
46. Dalai Lama 1990: 67.
47. On the need to see the original of the agreement, see Le 1981: 141, entry for 17 July 1951. On consulting with the other religious and government officials in Lhasa, see Lha'u rta ra (Lhautara) 1981: 113.

ministers meet in Lhasa. If they indicate their attitude about the agreement early, it will help the reputation of the Dalai Lama throughout China. To this Zhang Jingwu added immediately that, because the Panchen Lama has great love for the Dalai Lama, the Dalai Lama also should show his attitude in order to create harmony. Kheme said only that he would pass along these comments to the Kashag."[48]

The declaration that the Kashag and the Dalai Lama needed to wait until Ngabö came was obviously a ploy, since one member of the negotiating team then in Yadong, Kheme, was Surkhang's uncle, and another, Takla, was the Dalai Lama's brother-in-law. Thus, there was no "confusion" about the meaning of the various points in the agreement, nor could Ngabö clarify anything about how the discussions had proceeded better than these two could relate them. The real reason for delaying, therefore, was the view of the sitsab in Lhasa that nothing should be decided until everyone was back in Lhasa and pressure could be placed on the Chinese to revise some of the points.

The sitsab, as mentioned above, felt that the treaty had been poorly negotiated and that the Tibetan negotiators had gone beyond their brief in signing it, especially with regard to allowing the PLA to enter and remain in Tibet.[49] Shatra, a lay aristocratic official, recalled attending a meeting in Lhasa convened by the sitsab after news of the agreement had surfaced.

> The sitsab . . . said that because the agreement was made in another's territory,[50] Ngabö became powerless, and the Seventeen-Point Agreement that has been signed does not contain the same points as the instructions the Tibetan government gave to the delegation. This agreement is not what we wanted, so we all must now take control of the situation and in unity sign a statement opposing it. And we did that. There was no discussion [about this] at the meeting. The sitsab simply informed us. . . . So we sent a petition to the Dalai Lama saying that we wanted to discuss the terms of this agreement. . . . Their [the sitsab's] idea was to reassess and revise the agreement in Lhasa.[51]

The Dalai Lama also recalled Lukhangwa's strong views on this.

> The two sitsab were thinking and saying that it was a big mistake to have the agreement signed in Beijing. They were saying that one can't finalize an agreement on the enemy's territory. In the petition they sent after the agreement

---

48. Le 1981: 141, entry for 17 July 1951.

49. Lukhangwa is also said to have told Ngabö after his arrival in Lhasa, "You have brought darkness on your own country while bringing daylight to the others' country" (Mrs. Lukhang, interview, 1993, Dharamsala).

50. In Tibetan, rang sa mi sa thug pa yin tsang.

51. Shatra, interview, 1992, Lhasa.

was already signed, they said that while the talks [renegotiations] were underway in Lhasa, the Tibetan people would support us. The old folks carrying prayer wheels instead of guns in their hands would say things like "Ours is a small country, so if a lot of Chinese come up there will be famine and stuff." I remember so vividly Lukhangwa and Lobsang Tashi saying this.[52]

The pro-exile people were not sanguine that the terms could be changed, let alone that the Chinese would honor the actual terms. But they had lost the debate about going into exile, and it was advantageous to stall, since dealings with the United States were ongoing and something might change in the near future. Surkhang, in fact, is said to have sent the sitsab a cryptic telegram implying that something could still be done in Lhasa: "It is hard to defeat an enemy by confronting him face-to-face with force. [But] Using clever methods, one can [still] attain one's goal."[53]

So in the end, the sitsab's urging to say nothing until everyone was back in Lhasa was adopted as the "public" response to the agreement, and the Tibetan government adopted the strategy of welcoming the Chinese to Tibet but refusing to accept the agreement publicly. The Dalai Lama perhaps missed an opportunity to use going to exile as leverage to negotiate directly with the Chinese through Zhang in Yadong, but this option was never raised, because the Tibetan government was not ready to discuss anything. On 20 July, therefore, the Kashag asked the Chinese to translate a letter from them to the Central Committee in Beijing. It repeated what they had already said verbally, namely, that after Ngabö and the original copy of the agreement arrived in Lhasa a meeting would be convened to discuss the agreement and that only after that could implementation occur.[54]

However, not only did the Kashag stall acceptance of the agreement, but also they took a tough line regarding the return trip, not permitting the Dalai Lama and Zhang Jingwu to travel back to Lhasa together, since that would have given too great an appearance of solidarity. Since the Dalai Lama had not officially accepted the agreement, the Tibetan side wanted to give the impression that the exact nature of Sino-Tibetan relations was still an open issue. Consequently, the Kashag told the Chinese that conditions and facilities along the road were poor, so it would be better if each, the Dalai Lama and Zhang's group, went separately.[55] Zhang Jingwu had no choice but to agree.

52. Dalai Lama, interview, 1993.

53. Dongtug tragbö drawo dül khagbe/ nosam thabgi dünpa drubar che//. Chabtsom, interview, 1992. Chabtsom said this was originally composed by the 5th Dalai Lama. An alternative second line for this is: natsog thabgi dradülwar che.

54. Le 1981: 142, entry for 20 July 1951.

55. Lha'u rta ra (Lhautara) 1981: 113.

Figure 5. Zhang Jingwu riding from Yadong to Lhasa, July 1951.
Source: Chen Zonglie

The Dalai Lama left for Lhasa on 22 July, and Zhang left two days later.[56]
Most Tibetans who had left when the Dalai Lama fled Lhasa in 1950 now
also had to decide whether to return. Many of these had moved all or most
of their movable wealth to safety in India or Sikkim, so they also had to decide about this. Almost all opted to return, but often the decision was not
straightforward. One aristocrat, Mrs. Taring,[57] recalled her discussions about
this with her husband.

56. Le (1981: 142–43, entries for 21 and 23 July 1951) says the 21st and 23rd.
57. Mrs. Taring and her husband were both aristocrats who spoke fluent English.

When His Holiness left [Lhasa] for Yadong, most of the aristocrats brought their things out to Kalimpong. So when we went back [to Lhasa], we left most of our belongings with the Tibetan government official in Phari [in southern Tibet]. However, we took a lot of things back, like silverware, chests, and others.

When my husband and I were in Kalimpong, Taktse Rimpoche was telling us, "There's no use in us going back. Would you two like to come with me to America?" My husband asked me, "What do you want to do? It would be nice to go with Taktse Rimpoche." I replied, "Whatever may be the case, His Holiness has already returned, and I can't leave my family, children, and relatives. I'm not going. Your parents are also there, and you can't just leave. So no matter what, let's go back." So we decided to return. When we got there, the Chinese had already arrived.[58]

But not all officials and prominent Tibetans decided to return. A few, such as Shakabpa, chose to remain in India, whereas the Dalai Lama's elder brother, Taktse Rimpoche, ignored the request from the Dalai Lama to return and went to the United States. The Dalai Lama's mother also remained in India, as did the Kashag minister Surkhang and several other officials such as Yuthok. Surkhang had traveled with the Dalai Lama as far as Gyantse but then returned to Kalimpong, ostensibly for medical treatment but in large part because he feared retribution from the Chinese because of his strong opposition to the agreement in Yadong. His sister, Mrs. D. Yuthok, recalled, "Our mother sent me to Gyantse to try to convince him [Surkhang] to return to Lhasa, but he went back to Kalimpong. He said that his life would be in danger if he returned to Lhasa."[59]

Surkhang's wife, who was with him, provided more details about this.

Sawangchemmo said [of the deliberations in Yadong], "We did whatever we could, but some of the officials can't think straight and were stubbornly stupid (tib. gugpa utsu).[60] If His Holiness is taken to Tibet, the moment he comes under the Chinese it will be very difficult. The Chinese are politically clever and very tricky. Although there is this so called Seventeen-Point Agreement, you just watch, they won't stick to it. There is no way it will last. Their main enemies are the leaders/lords, the religion, and the monks—the feudal elements. These will never be left alone. Therefore, I question what [they] will do." Sawangchemmo knew about the communist system from long ago. He had learned a lot from some Mongolian monks [he knew in Lhasa].

[When Sawangchemmo came back to] Kalimpong, he went to Calcutta for medical treatment. It took about a month. Then he [returned to Kalimpong and] said that he wanted to stay there. However, while there, a lot of letters came from Tibet. Sawangchemmo's father and mother were telling him that

58. Taring (Rinchen Dolma), interview, 1991, Rajpur.
59. Yuthok (Dorje Yüdrön), interview, 1994, Dharamsala.
60. *Sawangchemmo* is a term of address used for Kashag ministers.

he should return to Tibet and that it was not good if he stayed like that [in India]. Letters were sent one after another. They said that the way things had been going [in Lhasa], it didn't look as if the Chinese would do anything bad. It was better to return. The leading Chinese cadres had also approached Sawangchemmo's parents, telling them things such as "Kashag minister Surkhang is an educated man, so what is the use of his staying in another person's country? He should return and not stay in a foreign country. We are only helpers and developers here in Tibet and have not come to cause trouble. So there is absolutely nothing to fear. You are his mother, and it seems that he cares a lot for you, so please write him and ask him to return." They also told [Surkhang's] father [his parents were divorced] to ask him to return, and letters kept coming one after another. [They wrote things such as] "Parents will not give poisoned water to a son, so there is no need to be suspicious. These days things are good. Even His Holiness has returned, and so it seems that in the future things will not get bad." . . . Sawangchemmo still was saying that he would not go. [He said], "I will resign [from the Kashag]. I'm not keeping too well, and all the children are here in India [in school, and so was his wealth in India]." So we sent a letter stating these things, but instead they [the family] sent people to accompany us back [to Lhasa]—servants and horses and mules, everything. Then he went. That was in 1952 [February].[61]

As the Dalai Lama and Zhang were traveling to Lhasa, Chinese troops and administrators were also moving or making final preparations to move to Lhasa. The advance force of the Eighteenth Army Corps, under Wang Qimei, was already en route together with Ngabö and would arrive in early September, and the main Eighteenth Army Corps force, under the command of Zhang Guohua, would arrive at the end of October. From the Northwest Bureau's First Field Army, a cavalry unit under the command of Fan Ming was also preparing to march to Lhasa, as was the Panchen Lama, who was then residing in Qinghai Province.

The United States, meanwhile, was still unwilling to accept that the Dalai Lama did not want to go into exile and further intensified its efforts to undermine the agreement.

WASHINGTON TRIES AGAIN

As Zhang Jingwu was about to arrive in Yadong, officials of the United States were still scrambling to persuade the Dalai Lama to go into exile by further sweetening their offer to him. To a large degree, they were influenced by his brother Taktse Rimpoche, who was assuring them that the Dalai Lama was really opposed to the agreement and wanted to go into exile.[62] In July 1951,

61. Mrs. Surkhang, interview, 1992, Dharamsala.
62. They were also fed misleading information by two Westerners, Heinrich Harrer and George Patterson, who were then in India.

State Department officials met with Taktse Rimpoche in Washington and orally presented a much improved offer, which they also sent to Ambassador Henderson in Delhi on 12 July. It stated that if the Dalai Lama disavowed the agreement and fled into exile, the United States was willing to support (1) Tibetan "self-determination," (2) the Dalai Lama as the head of an autonomous Tibet, and (3) the Dalai Lama's ultimate return to Tibet to head a noncommunist state. The United States, through friends of Tibet in the United States, also would now arrange to fund the movement of the Dalai Lama and an entourage of one hundred to Ceylon, as well as fund the Dalai Lama's other needs in Ceylon. Acheson's cable said,

US Govt believes Tibet shld not be compelled by duress accept violation its autonomy and that Tib people shld enjoy rights self determination commensurate with autonomy Tibet has had many years. This has consistently been position US. US therefore will indicate publicly its understanding of the position of DL as head of an autonomous Tibet.

US similarly will endeavor to persuade other nations take no action adverse DL's position as head autonomous Tibet.

US will support Tib request for refuge in Ceylon; it believes that cost chartering planes for journey DL and entourage from India to Ceylon cld be met by US CITS [citizens] having strong and friendly interest Tibet; if requested by DL, US will use its best efforts persuade GOI assure transit DL and retinue. (It was pointed out here that in view practical considerations, approach GOC [Government of Ceylon] and GOI shld be made in first instance by representative DL; that assurances thus given based on assumption refuge wld be taken Ceylon; and that if refuge shld be taken India financial assurances wld have to be reexamined.)

To extent required and as long as mutually satisfactory purposes served, friends of Tibet in US will provide appropriate support for DL, his family and entourage of 100 or slightly more in Ceylon, it being our hope that among considerations DL wld have in selection wld be polit influence and effect persons chosen.

Resistance in Tibet must be viewed as long range problem limited by physical polit conditions in Tibet and in adjoining areas, over which US of course has no control. [A key section here was excised from this file.] The assurances conditioned on withdrawal DL from Tibet, his public refusal accept Tibet CHI COMMIE agreement, his continued opposition COMMIE aggression, and his continued willingness coop generally; implicit in this understanding however is US support DL's return Tibet at earliest practical moment as head autonomous non- COMMIE country. Recommended Tibet urgently approach GOI for informal discussion India attitude toward departure DL from Tibet. This approach SHLD include firm statement that DL seeks transit rights through India. US through Emb New Delhi will use good offices support this request.

It made clear to Taktser that our position basic and longstanding is not related to CHI COMMIE involvement in Korea and not to be affected by developments there.

REF item 5 Calcutta's 28 Jul 9, RPTD New Delhi 29th, Taktser has indicated he will prepare Tib language MSG to DL, including above info, to be forwarded DIPL pouch ETD WASH JUL 15. You will be further advised channel communication MSG from Taktser to DL. Meanwhile you SHLD endeavor pass substantive portions this TEL to DL by best available means . . .

Acheson[63]

This was still not U.S. support for Tibetan independence, but it was the strongest offer of support to date. The Americans urged Shakabpa, then still in Kalimpong, to delay his planned departure to Yadong until the Tibetan-language letter prepared by Taktse had arrived, but Shakabpa said he could not.[64]

On 13 July, the day before Zhang Jingwu arrived in Yadong, the U.S. Consulate in Calcutta received two telegrams from R. H. Linn in Kalimpong saying that Shakabpa had followed up on this new proposal. Shakabpa had told Linn that the Dalai Lama himself approved coming to India, but his advisers favored his going to Lhasa. He said that the Dalai Lama requested more information on the discussion between the United States and India regarding India's willingness to receive him and facilitate his stay. Since the Dalai Lama had already decided to return and had communicated that to Zhang Jingwu, it is not clear what the source of Shakabpa's comments were, but those in favor of exile, such as Surkhang, were certainly eager for new ammunition to try to reverse the decision.

Linn, misunderstanding the nature of the debate in Yadong, suggested to the Calcutta Consulate that the Dalai Lama had delayed deciding to come to India because he believed that India was unwilling to receive him and because he feared that the Chinese would take reprisals if he accepted U.S. support and disavowed the agreement in advance. Linn, therefore, suggested that the U.S. government should attempt to persuade the Indian government to assure Shakabpa that it was willing to receive the Dalai Lama.[65]

The State Department agreed with this suggestion and instructed the U.S. Embassy in Delhi to urge the Indian government to invite the Dalai Lama to India, explaining that Tibet was unwilling to approach the Indians directly because of their pro-Chinese tilt. The U.S. Embassy in London was instructed to ask the British also to urge this invitation.[66] However, when the British

---

63. U.S. National Archives, 793B.00/7–1251, telegram no. 107, from the U.S. secretary of state to the U.S. Embassy in India, dated 12 July 1951.

64. U.S. National Archives, 793B.00/7–1351, telegram no. 108, from the U.S. State Department to the U.S. consul general in Calcutta, dated 13 July 1951.

65. U.S. National Archives, 793B.00/7–1451, telegram no. 43, from the U.S. consul general in Calcutta to the U.S. secretary of state, dated 14 July 1951.

66. U.S. National Archives, 793B.00/7–1651, telegram no. 335, from the U.S. State Department to the U.S. Embassy in London, dated 16 July 1951.

Foreign Office consulted its high commissioner in India about approaching the Indian government, he responded instead that the Foreign Office ought to try to persuade the Americans to drop the whole idea.[67] London then told the Americans that the Tibetans should contact the Indians themselves, making reference to India's offer of asylum given in October 1950, and asking them if India would still honor this offer.[68]

On the American side, Linn and William Gibson, the vice consul of Calcutta, persuaded Shakabpa to discuss this informally with Dayal, the Indian political officer in Gangtok, when he passed through Sikkim on his way to Yadong.[69] And on 17 July, U.S. officials in Delhi met S. Dutt of the India Foreign Office and brought this up, making an unofficial suggestion that it would be useful if the Indian government were to instruct Dayal about asylum, since the Dalai Lama was seriously considering the matter. The next day the U.S. Embassy informed Dutt that a representative of the Dalai Lama was about to contact Dayal at any moment. Dutt responded that Dayal had already been instructed regarding granting asylum.[70]

However, when Shakabpa met Dayal in Gangtok, the latter said he had received no instructions from Delhi regarding asylum for the Dalai Lama in India. Gibson, who had gone to Gangtok to facilitate communications, confirmed Shakabpa's report by talking directly to Dayal. On receipt of this news, the U.S. Embassy in Delhi notified Dutt, who admitted with embarrassment that Dayal had not been instructed about asylum until the evening of the 18th. Dutt then explained to embassy counselor L. Steele that "in accordance with international law, [India] was prepared to grant asylum upon the condition that DL did not engage in political activities while in India."[71] At Steele's suggestion, Dutt said he would take steps to assure that this information was passed on to the Dalai Lama in Yadong.[72] That was four days before the Dalai Lama left for Lhasa. India, however, had again demonstrated its lack of commitment to support Tibet politically or diplomatically.

At the same time, the U.S. Embassy in India worked out a truly bizarre es-

67. British Foreign Office Records, FO371/92998, letter from J. A. Murray, of the British Foreign Office in London, to Tomlinson, of the British Embassy in Washington, dated 18 July 1951.

68. British Foreign Office Records, FO371/92998, telegram from the U.K. Foreign Office's South Asia Department to the U.K. high commissioner in India, dated 20 July 1951.

69. U.S. National Archives, 793B.00/7–17511, telegram no. 52, from the U.S. consul general in Calcutta to the U.S. secretary of state, dated 17 July 1951.

70. U.S. National Archives, 793B.00/7–1951, telegram no. 269, from the chargé d'affaires in India to the U.S. secretary of state, dated 19 July 1951.

71. Ibid.; and U.S. National Archives, 793B.00/7–1951, telegram no. 61, from the U.S. consul general in Calcutta to the U.S. secretary of state, dated 19 July 1951.

72. U.S. National Archives, 793B.0–2151, telegram no. 302, from U.S. ambassador in Delhi to the U.S. secretary of state, dated 21 July 1951.

cape plan for the Dalai Lama that was based on the fanciful notion, suggested by interlocutors such as Harrer, Patterson, and Taktse Rimpoche, that the Dalai Lama was being physically prevented from seeking asylum by pro-Chinese elements surrounding him. Consequently, a letter was sent to Yadong on 17 July by Harrer, urging the Dalai Lama to adopt one of three options:

a. Choose small group of faithful followers and leave quietly with them. This wld presumably involve leaving at night in effort to avoid deputations which have come to Yadong from principal monasteries and from govt at Lhasa to persuade Dalai Lama to return to Lhasa.

b. Order [name redacted from file] bring him surreptitiously to India. [section redacted from file]

c. If neither (a) nor (b) feasible, Dalai Lama to send msg to [name redacted from file] requesting [name excised from file] send Harrer and Patterson secretly and in disguise to meet Dalai Lama near Yadong in accordance with prearranged plan and bring Dalai Lama back. Detailed plan for this operation also being conveyed by [name redacted from file] but he is to make it clear to Dalai Lama it is to be adopted only as a last resort.[73]

The Dalai Lama recalled that letter: "When I was in Tromo [Yadong], Harrer wrote me from Kalimpong with a plan of escaping through Bhutan, where there would be some Americans. He said he would also come. . . . I was sort of supposed to go for a walk and then to meet trained Americans. So we had such communications. . . . There were connections with Harrer and Taktse Rimpoche."[74]

On 20 July, the U.S. Consulate in Calcutta passed along Taktse Rimpoche's Tibetan translation of the new U.S. proposal that been had sent from Washington. An unnamed person was to see that it reached Yadong and the Dalai Lama. Almost simultaneously, the U.S. Consulate received telegraphic word from Yadong by prearranged code that the Dalai Lama was returning to Lhasa in a few days,[75] although that decision, as we have seen, had been made over a week before.

This episode reveals how poorly the United States understood what was really going on in Lhasa and Yadong. It would not be the last time that Tibetans (and Westerners) who opposed the policy of Tibet seeking accommodation with the Chinese would attempt to manipulate U.S. policy by hyperbole and distortions and by freely using the name of the Dalai Lama.

---

73. U.S. National Archives, 793B.00/7-1751, telegram no. 52, from the U.S. consul general in Calcutta to the U.S. secretary of state, dated 17 July 1951.

74. Dalai Lama, interview, 1993.

75. U.S. National Archives, 793B.00/7-2251, telegram no. 68, from the U.S. consul general in Calcutta to the U.S. secretary of state, dated 22 July 1951.

In the end, the United States failed to undermine the agreement and convince the Dalai Lama to mount an anti-Chinese publicity campaign from exile, because what it offered was less persuasive than the offer of Mao Zedong. The United States, to be sure, was the only country to exhibit any support for the Tibetans in their hour of dire need, but the support was perceived as too little. It did not offer a real hope of preventing the Chinese takeover nor of facilitating Tibet's recovery of its independence in the near future. As the Tibetan government was making this decision, thousands of American troops were dying in Korea in a fight against communist expansion, yet Washington was never willing to make a similar commitment to Tibetan "freedom." Instead, Washington repeatedly insisted that all military aid (meaning guns, not troops) had to go through India, which was, if not outright hostile to Tibetan interests vis-à-vis China, then at least not supportive.[76] The

76. Gyalo Thondup, the Dalai Lama's second older brother, however, has said that the Government of India was willing to provide strong support for Tibet. In interviews with Kenneth Knaus, Thondup asserts that the Indian ambassador to China, Panikkar, visited him in Kalimpong in the summer of 1949 and informed him that "Tibetans could use India as a base and a supply of arms," and Nehru confirmed this commitment to him soon after. A recent book suggests that Lhasa had missed an opportunity there, which the author summed up by saying, "Thondup did not receive instructions from Lhasa to follow up with the Indians on these surprisingly bold pledges" (Knaus 1999: 51). However, it is difficult to take this assertion seriously, because no such interest on the part of the GOI is in evidence in the diplomatic records of the period. To the contrary, the British and American archival materials reveal the opposite, as has been demonstrated above. Also, the memoirs of senior Indian government officials from that period do not support Thondup's assertion. For example, S. Dutt, the secretary of the Commonwealth Relations Department of the Indian Foreign Office at that time, has written, "When the first Indian Political Officer in Sikkim, H. Dayal, visited Lhasa in 1949, the Tibetans formally requested him for arms and ammunition from Delhi. The Government of India was not keen on getting involved in Tibet's internal affairs and showed no interest in the proposal" (Dutt 1977: 80). And in early 1950, when the Tibetans sent a delegation to Delhi seeking support and aid against a threatened Chinese invasion, Dutt commented, "The Government of India advised the Dalai Lama's Government to try to reach an understanding with the new Chinese Government by peaceful negotiations" (Dutt 1977: 30). And B. N. Mullik, director of the GOI's Intelligence Bureau from 1950 to 1965, has written about a 1950 Indian government meeting on Tibet at which the question of Indian military intervention in Tibet was raised and rejected, because India was in no position to intervene. Mullik writes that General Cariappa, head of the Indian army, "categorically said that he could not spare any troops or could spare no more than one battalion for Tibet, so hard-pressed was he with his commitments on the Pakistan front and with the internal troubles raised both by communal and Communist forces. . . . Moreover, he explained that the Indian army was not equipped or trained to operate at such heights and would be at a serious disadvantage against the Chinese army which had much better training and experience in fighting in these extremely cold plateau and were even better armed, having acquired all the arms which the USA had poured into China to bolster the KMT army." Mullik concluded that Cariappa was correct, and it would have been "suicidal for India to send a couple of battalions" (Mullik 1971: 80–81).

Tibetans, as we have seen, considered anything based on their having to secure Indian approval a meaningless gesture.

Ruth Bacon, in a State Department memorandum on Tibet in 1949, stated
perceptively that if the Communists were victorious in China and an émigré
Nationalist government was established, the United States would have to decide its Tibet policy partly in light of its policy toward that exile government.
As she put it, "The question would arise whether we should place emphasis
on Tibet's independence by formally recognizing it and by sponsoring its
application for membership in the UN or whether we should avoid stressing the matter of independence but should merely maintain direct relations
with Tibet without a public change of policy."[77] By the end of 1949, this was
in fact the choice Washington faced, and the United States clearly opted for
the latter approach. Deferring to Chiang Kai-shek's sensibilities, it refused
to break with the past and support Tibetan independence even in the face
of Communist aggression against Tibet. An autonomous Tibet was the best
the United States was willing to offer the Dalai Lama.

Thus, the U.S. offers of concern and support, though gradually enhanced, ultimately were too weak to offset Mao's "carrot." Mao's gradualist
policy would allow the Dalai Lama (and his government) to continue to rule
Tibet for the present and would also preserve the social and religious institutions that were considered critical to this. The Tibetan political elite, of
course, had serious doubts about the trustworthiness of the Chinese Communists and thus the value of the agreement and were totally opposed to a
large Chinese military force occupying Tibet, but they could not bring themselves to go into exile for only what the United States was willing to provide
them, given the alternative encompassed by the agreement.

The Dalai Lama's immediate future, therefore, was now committed to dealing with Zhang Jingwu and his comrades in a way that would preserve his
authority and the integrity of Tibetan religion and society, albeit as an integral part of China. The challenge was to develop a strategy for Tibet to coexist successfully as part of the People's Republic of China. A new era in Tibet was clearly beginning, but it was not at all clear how Tibet would best
achieve its goals.

77. U.S. Department of State 1974: 1065. See chapter 5, pages 115–18, for the full text of
the memorandum.

PART TWO

The First Two Years

Confrontation and Adjustment

Chapter 7

Initial Contacts and Strategies

When the Dalai Lama arrived in Lhasa, the pressing issue facing his government was whether conciliation was the right course. If so, should the Tibetan side make every attempt to develop a friendly and collaborative partnership with the Chinese as a means of persuading them to interpret the Seventeen-Point Agreement in a manner favorable to Tibet? Or alternatively, should a tougher, less conciliatory approach be adopted to try to pressure the Chinese side to change key aspects of the agreement, and, if so, how should they be pressured? Or even more extreme, should a course of active or passive resistance be developed, for example, fostering guerrilla operations against Chinese personnel and troops? Something clearly had to be done to relate, good or bad, to the Chinese side, for at stake was nothing less than the future of Tibet.

. . . . .

Zhang Jingwu departed Yadong on 24 July, two days after the Dalai Lama, but caught up with him in Gyantse, where he had stopped to give religious teachings.[1] There Zhang tried again without success to elicit a statement of acceptance of the agreement from the Kashag ministers traveling with the Dalai Lama.[2] Zhang then headed on to Lhasa, where he arrived on 8 August 1951, nine days ahead of the Dalai Lama. He was the first Chinese Communist leader to enter Lhasa.

The atmosphere in Lhasa was ostensibly calm, but there were deep under-

---

1. Phündra, interview, 1993, Beijing. The Dalai Lama gave a Kalachakra teaching (tib. dükhor wangchen) in Pegaw Chöde Monastery.

2 Le 1981: 144, entry for 12 August 1951.

currents of apprehension and anger. People were curious and anxious about Zhang and his staff because of the many negative things they had heard about the Communists; everyone wondered what these Red Chinese would be like and how they would behave. At the same time they were angry at their government's incompetence and inability to prevent this situation from coming to pass. And although there were no newspapers in Tibet in which to express such feelings, at important times like these, information and opinions were conveyed through anonymous satiric "street songs" that wickedly criticized and ridiculed the high and mighty—this was no exception.

The following three street songs convey different aspects of opinion in Lhasa as Zhang was about to arrive and inaugurate a new era in Tibet. The first song pokes fun at the Tibetan government for making a big show of toughness when it expelled the Guomindang officials in 1949 but then two years later was powerless to stop the Chinese Communists from coming to Lhasa. The second song chides the Kashag for expelling the moderate and harmless Chinese (the Guomindang of Chiang Kai-shek) and then bringing in the violent and dangerous Red Chinese.[3]

> By their power, they expelled them,
> By their powerlessness, they were brought here.
> Whether they are peaceful or violent
> We shall see gradually.[4]

> The Lhasa government's Kashag
> Please realize the essence of the matter.
> You have expelled the peaceful white ones [Guomindang],
> (and have) brought in the violent red ones [Communist Chinese].[5]

A third song commented on how the Chinese Communists had been able to outsmart the Tibetan government by utilizing gentle (peaceful) methods to get their troops and officials to Lhasa without fighting.

---

3. These street songs were a traditional and beautiful genre of secular poetry in Lhasa. Traditionally, the Great Prayer Festival was the time when new lyrics emerged, sung to traditional melodies by the women who carried water for the festival. Tibetan lore holds that these new songs were divinely inspired and a kind of a prophecy sent to the water carriers by an emanation of Be Lhamo, the main protector deity of Lhasa. Actually, they appeared whenever an important event stimulated someone in the elite to anonymously compose one. See Goldstein 1982 or www.case.edu/affil/tibet/moreTibetInfo/street-song.htm.

4. In Tibetan, yod pa'i dbang gis spid [phud] nas / med pa'i dbang gis khrid byung / zhi dkar drag dmar yod med / ga ler ga ler gzigs dang. Cited in *Yul phyogs so so'i gsar 'gyur me long* (Tibetan Mirror), 1 August 1951, 5.

5. In Tibetan, lha ldan gzhung gi bka' shag / rdo la ngo 'dzin gnang dang / zhi dkar phyi la spid nas / drag dmar nang la khrid byung. Cited in *Yul phyogs so so'i gsar 'gyur me long* (Tibetan Mirror), 1 August 1951, 5.

The "nine-eyed" slingshot[6]
That is made of soft wool
Was shot by the Beijing government
And has landed on the Lhasa government.

Zhang's entrance to Lhasa went well but at the same time was not without problems. Ceremonial etiquette was very important to the Tibetans as well as to the Chinese, since it reflected relative power and status relations. How Zhang would be welcomed in Lhasa, therefore, was important, and while still in Yadong, Zhang sent a letter about this to the two sitsab, who headed the government in Lhasa. As the "representative" of the Central Committee, he said that he should be met and greeted at the traditional welcoming site in the suburbs of Lhasa by a committee (tib. phebsu) that included the highest Tibetan government officials, the two sitsab.[8] The two sitsab disagreed. As Zhang would soon learn, they were angry and hostile about the war, the agreement, the loss of independence, and now the actual presence of the first Communist officials in Lhasa. So while the sitsab organized a welcome ceremony at the appropriate site outside Lhasa, they refused to attend personally, thus snubbing the Chinese, to their irritation. Interestingly, they based their decision on past precedent from the Qing dynasty, in the early twentieth century.[9] This was not by accident. In looking for a model of how to relate to Beijing, the sitsab were looking back in history to a China that was long gone, not to the realities of the present new China.

Notwithstanding the sitsab's snub, Zhang's welcome reception otherwise went surprisingly well. One young Tibetan aristocrat who was present recalled that Zhang and his colleague Le Yuhong were both dressed in light blue "Mao jackets" (i.e., not in military uniforms) and were riding mounts saddled with the best-quality European leather saddles. They were greeted by a large number of Tibetans lining the road, most of whom, like the young Tibetan, had

6. This is a well-known type of slingshot that has nine designs woven into it that look something like eyes from a distance.

7. In Tibetan, 'jam po'i bal gyis sles pa'i / 'ur rdo chu mig dgu sgril / pe cing gzhung nas rgyab pas / lha ldan gzhung la babs song. Cited in *Yul phyogs so so'i gsar 'gyur me long* (Tibetan Mirror), 1 August 1951, 5.

8. It was considered respectful to go to welcome visiting high officials and dignitaries at some distance outside Lhasa, much as in the United States one would go to meet someone at the airport. *Phebsu* is the term used by the Tibetan government when officials are sent outside the city to welcome the Dalai Lama or some high dignitary, for example, the Qing amban. How far from Lhasa the phebsu occurs reflects the status of the person arriving. Gyetseluding was the standard reception site for this. It was located on the main road west of Lhasa between Drepung and the Norbulingka Palace (see map of Lhasa).

9. Drakten, interview, 1992, Dharamsala. His comments were based on discussions with Samjöla, the aide (tib. nendrön) to the sitsab at this time.

just come out of curiosity, not friendship or support.[10] But they had come, and no hostility was shown. In fact, the reception was so warm that Alo Chöndze, a Lhasa trader from Kham, took offense and set about organizing a special (and better) phebsu from the common people of Lhasa for the Dalai Lama's coming arrival.[11]

Zhang's entrance into Lhasa, therefore, was a great victory for Mao and the CCP, whose strategy had so far worked just as planned. Zhang and his small staff now set up their office and residence in the heart of Lhasa in Trimön, in a house formerly owned by an aristocrat that the Tibetan government had given them. They were now ready to start the next phase in the incorporation of Tibet. However, Zhang would quickly learn that the two sitsabs' snub was not an isolated aberration. It was a reflection of their deep hatred and a portent of what would come.

Of the two sitsab, the lay aristocratic official Lukhangwa was the dominant personality. He was fifty-three-years old and had previously served as one of the four heads of the Revenue Bureau (tib. Tsigang). He was respected as a straightforward person of high integrity and ethics whose loyalty to the traditional system was unquestioned and admired. But he was also notoriously one of the most conservative and rigid officials in the government bureaucracy, especially among the aristocracy. He was also almost totally ignorant of world history and current affairs and had the arrogant and at the same time naive notion that Tibet should handle its own problems and not worry about or depend on foreign countries.[12] Chabtsom, a Tibetan lay aristocratic official who at that time was one of the Lhasa Kashag's secretaries (tib. kadrung) and had close contact with Lukhangwa, described him: "Lukhangwa was always hard-headed and stubborn. He wanted to do things his own way and did not listen to other's opinions. He was a person who really liked the old customs and also had great loyalty and devotion to the Dalai Lama and the government. But he did not have much foresight or vision."[13]

Lukhangwa's conservative views went beyond government affairs and politics. His daughter-in-law, for example, recalled that he ran their household in the same way.

> At that time our household was run in the traditional Tibetan style, so we had no chairs. When the Chinese officials came to visit, Lukhangwa's wife and son [the subject's husband] expressed some concern for them and suggested borrowing chairs from a neighbor, but the sitsab refused, insisting there was no need to do this. He would say things like, "We have our own mattresses and cushions. We can pile them up for them. If they sit on these that is fine, and if

10. Shelling (Tsewang Namgye), interview, 2002, Cleveland, OH.
11. Alo Chöndze, interview, 1993, Cleveland, OH.
12. Chabtsom, interview, 1992, Lhasa.
13. Chabtsom, interview, 1992.

not, then its too bad. We have to do things in accordance with our own customs."... The sitsab was very strict and would not stand for any [new things].

Similarly, we did not serve any of the new snacks, such as [Indian-style] biscuits or candies at home. We served only traditional snacks, such as popped barley and popped lentils, and some walnuts, et cetera. We young people used to eat [the modern foods outside the house] on the sly, because we were not allowed to keep them at home. So when the Chinese came to meet the sitsab, he made a point of not serving them any candy or biscuits [as was fashionable in aristocratic Lhasa society].

We were also not permitted to wear leather (Western style) shoes. The sitsab would say these are foreign things we don't need. We were young and thought differently, so we would keep a pair of Western shoes with our shopkeeper tenants [downstairs on the first floor of their house], and when we went to town would first go to their apartment and secretly change into the modern shoes.[14]

Among the aristocracy in Lhasa, that kind of strictness was unusual enough to be considered eccentric. Lukhangwa, therefore, was a not only an ultraconservative traditionalist but also someone who did not believe in compromise and was not particularly open to alternative modes of thought.

Lobsang Tashi, the other sitsab, was somewhat more knowledgeable of the world despite being a monk official since he had spent several years in the Tibetan government's Bureau Office in China during the Guomindang period. He even knew some spoken Chinese. However, he wasn't a forceful person and invariably followed Lukhangwa's lead, saying, as one official recalled, "Yes, yes," whenever Lukhangwa turned to him at meetings asking, "Isn't that so?"[15]

While many Tibetan officials had deep doubts about the reliability of the Chinese Communists' assurances of religious freedom and so forth, Lukhangwa was visceral in his distrust. Chabtsom recalled a meeting held in Lhasa before the Dalai Lama and Zhang Jingwu arrived from Yadong at which some Tibetan officials casually commented that the religion and nationality policies of the Chinese Communists seemed quite good. Lukhangwa immediately responded angrily, saying that the Communists have no religion, so their so-called religious policy was just a trick to fool the people. "Formerly during the Qing emperors' (time)," he said, "the Chinese had faith in Buddhism, so if they proclaimed a religious policy we would believe it. But we cannot believe a religious policy coming from these atheists."[16]

Lukhangwa, therefore, from the start did not trust the Chinese Communists' assurances and, as mentioned earlier, also did not agree with the Yadong Kashag's decision to send the representatives to Beijing. He had strongly fa-

14. Mrs. Lukhangwa, interview, 1993, Dharamsala.
15. Chabtsom, interview, 1992.
16. Chabtsom, interview, 1992.

vored holding negotiations with the Chinese in Lhasa, where the atmosphere would have been supportive and had been working on the final aspects of the plan to bring Ngabö and Wang Qimei to Lhasa from Chamdo. Holding the talks in Beijing was, he felt, a major mistake, which he incorrectly thought was the Yadong Kashag's decision, when it actually was a demand of the Chinese side.

Not surprisingly, when Lukhangwa heard the terms of the agreement, he not only was angry and disappointed but, in a sense, also vindicated: his worst fears of negotiating in Beijing had been realized. Ngabö and the others had exceeded their instructions by agreeing to a substantial Chinese military presence in Tibet and by allowing the gradual absorption of the Tibetan army into the PLA as well as the creation of the ominous-sounding Military-Administrative Committee to implement the agreement. Lukhangwa interpreted the words used for that office—"military" (tib. mag) and "administrative/political" (tib. si)—to imply that Tibet would be ruled by the Chinese military and that the traditional head of the "political" sphere, the Dalai Lama, would be pushed out.[17] What he saw as the "flawed" Seventeen-Point Agreement, therefore, confirmed his opinion that he, not the Kashag ministers, knew best how to handle the situation with the Chinese. But subtle diplomacy was not on his mind when Zhang Jingwu arrived in Lhasa. He and Lobsang Tashi, instead, began to pursue a tough, confrontational stance that explicitly showed the Chinese that they, the highest officials in the Tibetan government, were bitter about the invasion and did not accept parts of the agreement, such as the large Chinese army force coming to occupy Tibet. They were angry and had no compunction about conveying that clearly to the Chinese.

Zhang Jingwu, however, was not ready to start discussing the implementation of specific parts of the agreement. The Chinese side did not understand the depth of the sitsab's hostility but understood in general the difficulties they faced and had already decided to go slow and wait until Ngabö and the original of the agreement arrived in September before trying to implement parts of the agreement. For the next month, therefore, Zhang was content to undertake what can be thought of as a public relations campaign aimed at getting to know the Lhasa elite and letting the elite get to known them. Zhang Jingwu began a series of visits to all the higher Tibetan officials as well as to monastery leaders and lamas. At all these visits they handed out copies of the agreement (in Tibetan) and explained in very general terms the Communist Party's nationality and religious policies and the agreement. Most of these visits were polite and uneventful, as the Tibetan aristocracy was noted for its exquisite manners and grace in face-to-face

17. Chabtsom, interview, 1992.

interactions—even with enemies. Open arguments and crude comments were considered to be in very poor taste. Consequently, when Le Yuhong visited high officials there were no arguments. And even when he visited the sitsab Lobsang Tashi and gave him a copy of the Seventeen-Point Agreement, Lobsang did not argue. He merely said he didn't know much about politics and let it pass without comment, changing the subject.

But the same was not true of Lukhangwa, who chose to be adversarial every chance he had. For example, soon after Zhang Jingwu and his staff arrived, the two sitsab invited Zhang to the Tsuglagang Temple for a formal reception, following the protocol for the Imperial commissioners (amban) during the Qing dynasty era. The sitsab used this ceremony to demonstrate once again their superiority by seating Zhang lower than themselves. Zhang's Chinese biography reveals that the Chinese clearly understood the insult but chose not to create an incident over it.

> On the third day after Zhang Jingwu's arrival,[18] the sitsab and Kashag ministers entertained Zhang Jingwu in the Jokhang Temple [in the Tsuglagang]. However, the hosts, Sitsab Lobsang Tashi and Lukhangwa, were still extremely conceited and arrogant and were seated in the highest place. Zhang Jingwu thought he was a newcomer and didn't know much about the whole situation, so in keeping with [the saying that warns against] "trying to gain a little only to lose a lot" (ch. yin xiao shi da), he did not let this rude reception provoke him. . . . However, he foresaw the difficulties he would face in implementing the agreement. He even saw very serious obstacles.[19]

Zhang Jingwu's Tibetan translator, Phündra, recalled this same first meeting vividly, because it placed him in a difficult situation. Some of Lukhangwa's comments were so confrontational and insulting that Phündra thought an argument might break out if he translated them correctly. Fearing this would negatively affect the course of Sino-Tibetan relations, he decided on his own not to translate these. Phündra summed this up, saying, "In general, Lukhangwa seemed like someone who wanted to insult the Chinese any way he could."[20]

A few days later, on 15 August, when Zhang Jingwu and Le Yuhong formally went to visit Sitsab Lukhangwa at his home, the meeting was anything but cordial. There is no official transcript of this meeting, but most people on both sides agree about what happened. First Zhang Jingwu made some general propaganda-like comments about how good it is that Tibet has returned to the motherland and how the PLA will now defend the borders and so forth, and then Lukhangwa answered angrily, indirectly attacking the agreement and threatening the Chinese:

18. Le 1981 says the seventh day.
19. Zhao 1995: 30.
20. Phündra, interview, 1993.

I have a lot to say today about the (Chinese) troops marching into Tibet. When Ngabö went to Beijing, his charge concerned making peace. He was not given any authority to discuss military affairs [read: PLA troops entering Tibet]. As for the Seventeen-Point Agreement, it is beyond anything I could have imagined; I will discuss its points later after Ngabö returns and reports how they really came about.

While we were in the process of taking steps to begin peaceful talks [with you Chinese], I heard about the liberation of Chamdo [read: China attacked us while we were trying to make peace talks]. Tibet is a religious country that likes peace. All the dalai lamas in sequence have done whatever they could to maintain peace. The 14th Dalai Lama also is doing everything he can to maintain peace. Even though the people were feeling militant, he sent a delegation to Beijing and was completely committed to holding peaceful talks. Therefore, because Tibet is a religious country where religion has spread widely, rather than your sending military troops here, it would be better to send capable and knowledgeable [nonarmy] officials.

As for China, it is a country that has many people and is very powerful. Nevertheless, whatever things it does must be done in the correct way/amount. If it doesn't do that, even people who are asleep [Tibetans] will get up and oppose it. . . . As for me, I am an old man with a white beard at the point of death, but as for the Tibetan people, if they are oppressed, even though they are not powerful, they will pray to the Three [Buddhist] Jewels, and karmic cause and effect will occur [China's bad deeds will be punished].[21]

In addition to his thoughts about the agreement, what he saw as Chinese hypocrisy also angered Lukhangwa,— who said the Chinese were coming as friends and brothers to help Tibet when in reality they had invaded Chamdo and killed many Tibetan troops. Whether he could not control this anger or did not care to, it became a hallmark of Lukhangwa's interaction style with the Chinese leadership.

Zhang had to endure another insult from the sitsab when the Dalai Lama arrived in Lhasa on 17 August.[22] Zhang wanted to participate in the welcome ceremony but was thwarted by the sitsab. Shatra, an aristocratic official who was there, recalled,

Zhang Jingwu and Le Yuhong were planning to participate in the welcome [for the Dalai Lama], but there was a disagreement over the seating arrangements. The two sitsab said that Zhang Jingwu could not sit in the same line as the Dalai Lama. The Dalai Lama would face straight ahead, and the sitsab would sit on one side facing another direction. Zhang [therefore] had to sit facing the two sitsab.

21. Le 1981: 150–51, entry for 15 August 1951. Stag Lha (Takla)'s 1995 account of this must have come from Le Yuhong's account, for the words are virtually identical.

22. Zhonggong xizang zizhiqu dangshi ziliao zheng ji weiyuanhui 1995, entry for 8 August 1951; Phündra, interview, 1993.

The Chinese, however, refused. Although they were willing to have Zhang sit on a Western chair rather than on raised cushions [thus avoiding the issue of the height of their cushions], they argued that Zhang had to sit facing the same direction as the Dalai Lama, since he was the representative of the Central Committee. The sitsab refused, so in the end Zhang chose not to attend and sent his associate Le Yuhong.[23]

On another front, the arrival of the Dalai Lama also produced the first example of nonelite Tibetans organizing to make a political statement. As mentioned above, Zhang's welcome to Lhasa had irritated Alo Chöndze and given him the idea that the Lhasa "people" should organize a special welcome committee for the Dalai Lama's arrival (in addition to the traditional welcome from government officials and the religious sector). Alo Chöndze recalled his thinking.

> There was a big welcome for Zhang. . . . Many aristocrats, such as Shölkang Jedrung and Maya and some ordinary lay officials and many Nepalese, went to welcome him. Zhang Jingwu came in an imposing manner, and as we were watching him, I got very angry and argued with the Nepalese [from Lhasa] and said, "You live here [in Tibet] but have no taxes, and you don't have to abide by the law.[24] You should be very grateful to the [Tibetan government], so why are you now welcoming the Chinese like this? You had better watch your step (tib. temo tö a)." I really fought with them verbally.
>
> The very next day I called people like Gyabing Chöndze to my house and we started organizing. . . . We discussed the Chinese [welcome] and then made a list of appropriate people among the Khambas, Amdowas, and Central Tibetans. The day after this, we went to tell them that the [Lhasa] people should organize and send a welcome committee to greet the Dalai Lama [when he returns]. I said, "Look how they welcomed the Chinese. We can't just stay like this [and do nothing]."
>
> For two days we went to the homes of roughly forty people who were important . . . and discussed sending a welcome committee from the people for the Dalai Lama. They agreed and signed their names. They were very glad and said this was a good idea and that we should think about what we should do. . . .
>
> The first meeting was held in Tresur's house. Andrug Gompo [later the head of the Chushigandru guerrillas] was there, and people had different opinions, saying things such as, "If we [common people] go to do a welcoming committee for the Dalai Lama, it will be the first time in Tibetan history, so the [Tibetan] government may be angry at this action on our part." So one group [at the meeting] said we shouldn't do it. I argued that they wouldn't be angry. I said, "I know about this. Sandutsang Lo Gendün organized a group of people to accompany the Dalai Lama when he went to Yadong, and I also had a group. We

23. Shatra, interview, 1992, Lhasa.
24. Nepalese in Lhasa had extraterritoriality rights.

went to see him off, so now if we welcome him back nothing will happen. It would, in fact, be good if we went farther from Lhasa to welcome him, say to Gyantse or Tashilhunpo. . . .

Then others said that if we do something like this we had better first request permission from Phala, the Dalai Lama's lord chamberlain. In those days, the Tibetan government had a phone in the telegraph office in Lhasa, as well as one in Chushur, Paldi, Nangkarste, and one in Phari. . . . They were thinking about the rules and said that we should first make a request. . . . So we contacted Phala by phone, and he replied that our plan was very good but coming to Gyantse was too far. "It will be hard for you, and there also will not be enough time. So do it nearer to Lhasa."

. . . We did the welcome committee ceremony at Nyetang [a location about forty kilometers south of Lhasa], where the big statue of the Buddha (tib. Nyetang lhachenpo) is carved on a rock. There were probably a hundred people in our group. All of us were important persons. . . . I told everyone that they had to wear Tibetan clothes and that they had to ride horses not mules.

Before we reached Nyetang, [we met] the advance guard of the Dalai Lama, which was coming up [from Yadong]. We thought that if we kept on riding like this we might encounter the Dalai Lama on a narrow path [making a welcome ceremony difficult to do], so I stopped and we got off our horses and took our ceremonial scarves in our hands. I knew the Dalai Lama would be coming soon. I said we should do three prostrations and then offer the scarves, which would be put back on us by the lord chamberlain or one of the aides of the Dalai Lama's secretariat (tib. tsendrön), who would be coming ahead of the Dalai Lama. After that we would mount up and ride at the front of the Dalai Lama's procession with the scarves on our necks. . . .

So we waited by the big statue at Nyetang with scarves in hand. At that time . . . Ngawang Rigdrol, an aide, arrived, and when he saw us he asked, "What are you people doing here?" I said we are the People's Association (tib. mimang tsogpa). He then took the scarves [we offered] and gave them back to us. At this time they had stopped the Dalai Lama's group. I said we should now travel in front of the Dalai Lama. Others in the group said no. . . . Then the Dalai Lama spoke to the lord chamberlain, who said to us, "The representatives of the people should go ahead of the Bodyguard Regiment [of the Dalai Lama]." So I told the others [with me], "Didn't I tell you this? Now let's go." So we went ahead in the procession. . . .

. . . At the Trisum Bridge, there was a welcome committee from Nechung Monastery, and preparations had been made for the Dalai Lama to stay there three nights. . . . When I asked Phala what we should do, he said, "Your coming today is very good, but you should return to Lhasa, and on such and such a day and time you should come back and be part of the Great Procession accompanying the Dalai Lama back into Lhasa (tib. chibgyur chemmo). . . .

The day after that, we returned at the specified time and were part of the procession from the Trisam Bridge. This time there were three hundred of us. I thought the more that came the better. I asked Phala, "There are many people with us, so what should we do?" He said, "It's okay. Its fine. You can all go ahead of the Dalai Lama." So we were all dressed in our finest. All the Lhasa people were waiting at Gyetseluding. The Lhasa people were very happy to see a people's association leading the way.[25]

This, of course, was not a formal people's association, but it reveals that the idea that the common people should be involved in Tibetan politics was in the air. In the traditional Tibetan polity, the people had no say in political affairs and were prohibited even from publicly criticizing the government. But times were changing, and, as will be discussed later, six months hence a real people's association would become a political player, confronting the Chinese and almost precipitating a deadly outbreak of violence in Lhasa.

THE INITIAL CHINESE STRATEGY FOR TIBET

Getting the Tibetan local government to sign the Seventeen-Point Agreement and allow Chinese troops and officials to enter Tibet peacefully was only the first step in Mao's Tibet strategy. Mao wanted more—to integrate Tibet harmoniously into the Communist Chinese state. As mentioned in chapter 1, Mao and the Central Committee, however, had no illusions about the Tibetan government and elite. It was clear that they did not want to be part of China, let alone the atheist Communist China, so persuading them to accept the new reality and become loyal citizens of the new multiethnic Chinese state was going to be extraordinarily difficult. However, avoiding the converse—the creation of a sullen, bitter, and hostile conquered people—was clearly in China's long-term interest, so that avoidance, in fact, was Mao's long-term goal.

To try to achieve that, Mao employed his pragmatic "gradualist" strategy, which focused on slowly winning over the elite in general and the Dalai Lama in particular and then, with and through them, ultimately the common Tibetans. Li Weihan, the minister of the United Front Work Department, succinctly commented on this to a group of Northwest Bureau officials in Beijing in 1950, telling them, "Winning over the Dalai will be our greatest victory."[26] Similarly the Central Committee sent Zhang Jingwu similar instructions (on 18 August 1951): "Your principal task on arrival in Lhasa is to get close to the Dalai Lama and the upper strata personages and to propagandize and explain the policies to dispel their worries. Do not propagandize too heavily with regard to obtaining assistance with the entry of the PLA into Tibet. It is important to wait for Ngabö and after that to work together [with him] on that issue. With respect to making donations to the monks, it is appropriate to donate more than what the Guomindang had done."[27]

25. Alo Chöndze, interview, 1993.
26. Fan Ming 1987: 26.
27. Zhonggong xizang zizhiqu dangshi ziliao zhengji weiyuanhui 1995, entry for 18 August 1951; and Zhao 1995: 31.

Central to this approach was Beijing's emphasis on reversing the decades of Tibetan-Han enmity. Mao understood that propaganda alone would not be enough. Not only did the Communist Chinese need to present themselves to Tibetans as "new" Chinese, who were, they believed, totally unlike the Han Chinese the Tibetans had known before, but they also assiduously had to behave in a way that reflected this ideology. An editorial published in the *People's Daily* right after the signing of the agreement conveyed this.

> *Endorsement to the Agreement for the Peaceful Liberation of Tibet*
> *(26 May 1951)*
>
> . . . Among Tibetans, Buddhism enjoys very high prestige. Tibetans highly worship the Dalai Lama and the Panchen Lama Erdini Chökyi Gyaltsen. Thus, in the peaceful agreement, it is not only specified to respect religion and to protect monasteries but also to respect the power and prestige of the above two Tibetan leaders. Not only is this for the purpose of resolving this internal dispute among Tibetans; it is also for the purpose of getting necessary respect for Tibetan leaders from different nationalities in China.
>
> All troops and civilian workers entering Tibet must strictly observe our ethnic and religious policies, must observe the peaceful agreement, must obey discipline, must trade fairly with Tibetans, which means to trade according to equal value principle, *and must prevent and correct the tendency of big nationality chauvinism. They have to truly respect the Tibetan people and serve them in order to get rid of the huge gap left by history between Hans and Tibetans and to win trust from the Tibetan local government and Tibetan people. If any of the military or civilian members do things contrary to the peaceful agreement, if they do not obey discipline, if they cheat Tibetans or show disrespect to Tibetan leaders who have a good relationship with the people, if they make the mistake of big nationality chauvinism, our leading organs and leaders should be responsible for correcting such mistakes.*[28]

Proper behavior and attitude on the part of the PLA and cadres was, therefore, essential to winning over Tibetans, since many of them obviously doubted the sincerity of the Communists. The top leaders in Beijing emphasized this over and over in their instructions to the Chinese officers going to Tibet. For example, just before Zhang Guohua, the commander of the Eighteenth Army Corps, left Beijing for Lhasa, Mao told him, "Signing the Seventeen-Point Agreement was only the first step. The second step is implementing it. . . . After you arrive in Tibet, whatever comes up, first keep in mind our nationality and religion policy. You must do all work steadily and gradually (step by step)."[29] And once when Zhang Guohua mentioned to Mao that some of his comrades are impatient and think that the work in

---

28. *Renmin ribao (People's Daily)*, 28 May 1951 (emphasis added). *Steadily* here conveys not rashly or too fast.

29. Zhang 1983: 199–200; Phünwang, interview, 1991, Beijing. See also Zhonggong xizang zizhiqu dangshi ziliao zhengji weiyuanhui 1990, entry for 23 May 1951.

Tibet will be like a turtle climbing up a mountain, Mao replied with a joke, "*Even a turtle climbing a mountain is too fast.*"[30] On another occasion, Mao's suggested to General Zhang that when he reached Lhasa and presented his gifts to the Dalai Lama, he should follow Tibetan custom and prostrate. When Zhang hesitated to reply, Mao said, "Comrade Guohua, you have risked your life for the revolution many times, so what is so hard about doing a prostration for the revolution?"[31]

This policy was disseminated to troops and officials at all levels. In July 1950, Deng Xiaoping, one of the two heads of the Southwest Bureau, conveyed it to the officers of the Eighteenth Army Corps who would soon be going to Tibet.[32]

In the past there was deep hatred between minorities and Han, so the situation is very complicated. With minority nationalities we should not now use outside force to implement class struggle or divide society into classes or to make reforms. It is not okay to do any kind of revolution [socialist reforms] using outside force. If we do not do reforms, the minority nationalities cannot overcome their poverty and they will remain backward; *however, we should wait until the conditions of the people are completely appropriate to do this.* Now our main responsibility is to make harmonious relations and to eliminate hatred between nationalities. If we can achieve this, that will be a great accomplishment.[33]

And on still another occasion, just as the Eighteenth Army Corps was leaving for Tibet, Deng Xiaoping told its officers: "If the soldiers go to Tibet with the idea of class struggle in their heads, when they get to Tibet and see the exploitation of the landlords they will become very anxious to intervene so will do something against our policy. Therefore, in order for that not to happen, go to Tibet with one eye open and one eye closed."[34]

Detailed instructions for the PLA troops going to Tibet were elaborated in the thirty-four-point *Handbook for the Military Advance (into Tibet)*, issued by the Eighteenth Army Corps's political department in January 1951. Its aim was to ensure that Chinese troops did not act as victors and superiors

30. Zhao 1998: 50 (emphasis added).

31. Phünwang, interview, 2000, Beijing. He said that Li Weihan personally told him about this incident.

32. At this time the three top leaders of the Southwest Bureau were Deng Xiaoping, Lui Bocheng, and He Long, the first, second, and third party secretaries, respectively. He Long also was the commander of the Southwest Military Area Headquarters, while Deng was the political commissar, and Lui was commander-in-chief of the Second Field Army and the chairman of the Southwest Military-Administrative Committee. The entire Second Field Army consisted of approximately 160,000 troops and personnel (Zhongguo zangxue yanjiu zhongxin keyan chu zhuban 1993: 2).

33. Yin 1992: 6 (emphasis added).

34. Yin 1992: 8.

but at all times showed respect for Tibetan customs, especially religion. It said, in part,

> Officers and the military troops are strictly forbidden to use taxes and corvée labor. In the Kham and Tibet areas you are allowed to propagandize only under the conditions described by the Party Committee; you are not allowed to propagandize about land reform and class struggle. You must protect monasteries and cannot touch the ritual equipment [of monks and monasteries]. You are not allowed to propagandize against superstition and spread rumors that contain untrue words about religion. Do not reside inside monasteries or temples. If a monk wants to join the army, do not allow him to join and persuade him to return to the monastery. Usually when visiting monasteries, you should first make contact. And when you go on a visit, you are not allowed to touch the images. Also you should not spit or fart in the vicinity of the monastery, and you should not hunt or fish or slaughter animals around a monastery. You must respect the customs and habits of the Tibetan people and work for amicable relations with them. When they put a ceremonial scarf over your neck you should return it. All government officials that held positions in the past will continue to hold their positions. If they run away or leave, you should try and convince them to return.[35]

However, after only a few weeks in Lhasa, Zhang Jingwu could see for himself that "winning over" the Tibetan elite in Lhasa would not be easy, so he sent the Central Committee an interesting set of ideas about what the troops on their way to Tibet should be taught.

1. All the soldiers and officers of the troops marching (to Tibet) should study the "spirit of the agreement" carefully. And the army should be a political propaganda troop and a model for propagandizing and implementing the agreement. The troops should continually promote the principle that our policies and our discipline are much more important than even one's life, and they should promote the traditional practice of working hard and bearing hardship. The troops should stress propagandizing the facts about the imperialists' invasion and exploitation [in Tibet] and the importance of the reinforcement of national defense.

2. Propagandizing about the equality and unity of nationalities should be stressed. Especially Tibetan religious beliefs should be respected, and [the troops] should get more information about religion. Do not argue with believers.

3. When propagandizing, the troops should use more examples and stories and should not use political terms [jargon], for it is difficult for Tibetans to understand them.

---

35. *Zhonggong xizang zizhiqu dangshi ziliao zhengji weiyuanhui* 1990, entry of January 1951.

4. Initially, do not stress local poverty. We will not implement reforms soon, so if we stress poverty, we will be trapped in passivity [doing nothing about it] and promote unnecessary doubts and fears among the Tibetan government officials.

5. When entering Lhasa, the troops should look good and be well-organized and should carry the national flag and military flags. When meeting with the welcoming committee, the troops can exchange ceremonial scarves. It is unnecessary to shake hands, because Tibetan people do not have this custom.

6. The army should know about the local situation when purchasing supplies and materials. The army has to contact the authorized big merchants first and then go ahead.

7. When going out, the soldiers should be divided into groups of three members each. This is to prevent assassination and conflicts by rascals who are being taken advantage of by spies and bandits.

8. If you want to do any sort of investigation, the troops should consult the lamas to show their respect for religion.

9. The troop should take advantage of all kinds of methods to approach the Tibetan army and create fellowship with them. If we do this, we can get more information. Do not look down on them, but unify and cooperate with them to reinforce the national defense together.

10. The aristocratic officials under the feudal structure are very proud and even arrogant. They care about etiquette. So our cadres should be very patient and inventive when carrying out united front work with the upper class. Most things should be done in a legal fashion via the Tibetan local government.[36]

The Southwest Bureau agreed with his ideas and added, "The Tibet issue is extremely complicated. We have to take each step very carefully to prevent creating big troubles. Therefore, in our work, above all, we should obviate the 'impetuosity fault.' All cadres must realize this point."[37]

Consequently, although Tibet was hopelessly "feudal," Mao and the CCP leadership had concluded that China's long-term national interests required integrating Tibet in a positive and cooperative fashion rather than through force and fear. To accomplish this optimally, winning over the Dalai Lama and the elite was required. Reforms would come only in a gradual and deliberate way (ch. shen zhong wen jing) when conditions were completely appropriate and Tibetans themselves were ready to accept them. The cadres in Tibet, therefore, were ordered not to attempt to stir up class conscious-

36. Zhao 1995: 34–35.
37. Zhao 1995: 35.

ness and class hatred among the Tibetan masses. The Chinese officials were also instructed to treat Tibetans with respect and to emphasize that they were a "new" breed of Han (Chinese) who would not exploit or oppress the Tibetans, as had the Qing dynasty and Guomindang governments. They were to stress that Han Chinese were not Tibet's enemies and did not want to harm Tibetans. Rather, they respected Tibetan culture and religion and the Dalai Lama and wanted to work with Tibetans to improve conditions in Tibet. And they had to reflect this in their behavior and demeanor.

Mao, therefore, was willing to permit the exploitive feudal system to continue to rule Tibetan internally for an open-ended period of time. Feudal lords would be free to command and punish their serfs, and the Dalai Lama's government would continue to operate its own legal and economic system. Life in Tibet would be virtually the same as it had been before the arrival of the Chinese. This obviously was not meant to be permanent, but there was no fixed timetable, since it was not at all clear how long it would take to win over the Dalai Lama and the elite to agree voluntarily to reform Tibet. At this point in time, Mao was in no rush and was willing to let this extend for three, four, five, or even ten or more years. Even a turtle going uphill was too fast! By leaving the enemies of the CCP in control of an army, a currency, and a government, Mao was taking a gamble that he did not have to, since the PLA had overwhelming military force and could have quickly eliminated the old system by brute force and intimidation. But Mao had something more important in mind and believed his gradualist strategy was the way to achieve it. China's long-term national interests were served best not by quickly destroying the old Tibet but rather by slowly winning over Tibetans to become loyal citizens of a new Tibet.

Mao's laissez-faire gradualist approach, however, had limits. The Chinese side was committed to implementing the agreement and especially to establishing their position in Tibet firmly with respect to supplies, communications, and transportation. As we shall see in later chapters, the PLA from the start made a major effort to secure stable control over these sectors. Also, it was obvious to Mao that implementation of the agreement and the incorporation of Tibet into the PRC would not be straightforward, as it had been in the Han parts of China, and would require shrewd, ongoing assessment of the conditions in Tibet. The framework for achieving this was the Seventeen-Point Agreement, but how exactly to implement its various provisos, some of which were somewhat contradictory, was not precisely specified by Beijing and was initially left up to the judgment of the Chinese officials in Tibet. That would turn out to be a mistake.

TIBET'S INITIAL STRATEGY

In comparison with the Chinese side's clearly defined approach, the Tibetan government's strategy and tactics were less cohesive—in essence almost inchoate. In the first weeks after the Dalai Lama's arrival, not only did no consensus emerge regarding China, but policy meetings of top officials were not even held in an attempt to establish such a consensus. Part of the reason for this was the lack of any tradition of formal strategic planning, for example, of having staff outline multiple strategic options and their expected consequences so that a final unified course of action could be selected. However, specifically in 1951, an additional problem was created by the peculiar administrative anomaly that occurred in the Tibetan government when the traveling Kashag returned to Lhasa from Yadong and found itself subordinate to the sitsab.

The two sitsab had been appointed almost by accident just a few months earlier in December 1950, when the Kashag, worried about the safety of the Dalai Lama in Lhasa, had moved him and most other top officials to the border town of Yadong. As mentioned earlier, stand-in officials were needed in Lhasa to replace those who left with the Dalai Lama, and in accordance with a precedent begun earlier in 1904 when the 13th Dalai Lama fled to Outer Mongolia, the Tibetan government decided to appoint two high officials to serve jointly as temporary rulers in place of the Dalai Lama. They were called the sitsab, or "acting" chief ministers. Since the two Kashag ministers then in Lhasa (Ramba and Surkhang) wanted to accompany the Dalai Lama to Yadong, they could not serve, so the Kashag submitted the names of five lower officials to the Dalai Lama. After divination, one of the Dalai Lama's personal staff, the monk official Lobsang Tashi, was appointed sitsab together with the lay official Lukhangwa.[38]

Structurally, the authority of the two new sitsab superseded that of the Kashag ministers, but given their lower prior positions, the role of the sitsab at this time was to look after the routine affairs of the government while the full Kashag ministers in Yadong handled all major political decisions. For the Yadong Kashag, the new sitsab were caretakers—officials responsible for looking after the day-to-day affairs of the country while they, the ministers, dealt with the key foreign policy decisions in Yadong. But the sitsab in Lhasa had strong ideas about Sino-Tibetan affairs and critically came not only to disagree with the Kashag's decisions in Yadong but also to consider themselves more than simply temporary caretakers. Consequently, when the Yadong Kashag returned to Lhasa, the two sitsab now ranked structurally above them. Lhalu, one of the Kashag ministers at that time, explained how the ministers were unable to push the sitsab aside and continue to control the government.

---

38. Shan kha ba (Shenkawa) 1999: 307–8. Lobsang Tashi had held the high monk official rank of khenche, and Lukhangwa had been one of four tsipön who headed the Revenue Office (Tsigang). Shenkawa was one of the two new acting Kashag ministers appointed to remain in Lhasa at this time.

When the Dalai Lama came back, there was no easy way to get them [the sitsab] to resign.

Q. Couldn't you have told them, "You have done well, thank you; now your duty is over"?

Oh. The Kashag didn't dare to tell the sitsab, who were higher in authority, to resign. And the Dalai Lama was young and didn't understand things like this. So that's why things got complicated, since the Kashag couldn't dismiss the sitsab. . . .

Q. Couldn't the Kashag go around the sitsab and directly approach the Dalai Lama?

No. The custom was for us to send requests through the sitsab.

Q. Could you have done it secretly without the sitsab knowing?

If the sitsab had found out [we were doing that], there would have been real trouble. When there were sitsab present, we had to go through them. If, for example, the Kashag prepared a document for the Dalai Lama to approve, [it had to be sent to the sitsab, and] they would make changes to the document before sending it to the Dalai Lama. So everything was under them; they were like a throat—all the food, et cetera, had to go through it. If there had been no sitsab, then the Kashag could have dealt directly with the Dalai Lama, and the power of the Kashag would have increased a lot. In the past there was no custom of having a sitsab when there was a Dalai Lama [present in Lhasa]. But they were appointed when the Dalai Lama was going to Yadong, so when the Dalai Lama returned, he didn't want to say immediately that we didn't want them. So they stayed on.[39]

Thus, the Kashag, the dominant political force in Tibet in December 1950, found itself relegated eight months later to a vastly diminished position vis-à-vis the two lower officials whom they had somewhat casually and hastily appointed to the "temporary" higher position of sitsab. All of this would not have mattered much had the sitsab shared the views of the Kashag or had the sitsab worked closely with them, but they did not. The sitsab did not trust the Kashag, whose ministers they felt had mishandled the negotiations and now were, in their view, too friendly toward the Chinese, so they unilaterally pursued their own highly confrontational, hard-line approach.

As mentioned earlier, the sitsab objected to most of the Seventeen-Point Agreement. They thought everything in Tibet was already excellent and did not want to have thousands of occupying Chinese troops and officials forcing changes, particularly to religion, the Tibetan government, and the Dalai Lama's status. They saw no need for reform. What they wanted instead of new institutions, such as the Military-Administrative Committee, was to go back to something like the loose protectorate status that Tibet had enjoyed during the last century of Qing dynasty rule: Tibet would acknowledge Chi-

39. Lhalu, interview, 1992, Lhasa.

nese superordination, but the Chinese would maintain only a token garrison in Lhasa together with an ambanlike representative or two. Internally, Tibet would remain virtually unchanged, ruled as a theocratic bureaucracy headed by the Dalai Lama in a matrix of large-scale monasticism supported by serfs and manorial estates.

The sitsab's looking back to the Qing as a model for the future was seen in their use of protocol from that period for welcoming and meeting Zhang Jingwu and was seen even more clearly in a comment Lukhangwa made to Zhang Guohua at one of their early meetings, in which he referred to a popular Qing amban named Zhang Yintang. Zhang Guohua's biography reported what Lukhangwa said.

> In the past, there was an amban from the Qing dynasty whose last name was also Zhang. While in Lhasa, he set up an office, but he didn't bring an army. Everybody called him "Great person Zhang" (ch. Zhang daren). Now another Zhang daren has come, but why have you brought so many soldiers? Ngabö was not authorized to talk about military affairs in Beijing. The Seventeen-Point Agreement was done suddenly and really should be revised.[40]

Amban Zhang Yintang had been sent by Beijing in 1906 to investigate the situation in Tibet and was known as the "overseas amban" because he initially came to Tibet via India. He favored training Tibetan soldiers rather than stationing Qing troops and had a good reputation when he left Tibet in 1907 to negotiate trade regulations in India and then returned to Beijing. So Lukhangwa's allusion refers to this.[41]

To the sitsab, a Qing-like relationship is what *would* have been formalized in the Seventeen-Point Agreement, had they, rather than Ngabö and the Yadong Kashag, been overseeing the negotiations. To be sure, all Tibetans in the elite would have preferred this to the Seventeen-Point Agreement, but the Chinese Communist Party was not the Qing dynasty, and it was both arrogant and naive for the sitsab to think that they could have achieved this if they had been left in charge. But naive or not, the Seventeen-Point Agreement was signed, the Chinese Communists were now in Lhasa, and the Tibetan government had to develop a strategy for interacting with them.

An obvious course of action would have been to strive to win the friendship and trust of the Chinese leaders and to use that to control the rate and magnitude of change. This, however, as we have already seen, was not at all what the sitsab had in mind. From the start, they refused to respond positively to the Chinese and, in their face-to-face meetings, challenged and confronted them in an angry and adversarial manner, which grew worse as the

40. Zhao 1998: 68–69.
41. Ya 1991: 226–39.

main Chinese army force arrived and very serious matters had to be discussed. The sitsab's confrontational behavior was so unusual that it was commented on by S. Sinha, the head of Indian Mission in Lhasa, in one of his monthly reports from Lhasa to Delhi: "The Prime Ministers [sitsab] habitually oppose and resent all advice and suggestions that come from the Chinese irrespective of their merits."[42]

The anger and hostility conveyed by the sitsab are, perhaps, not that surprising if one views the Chinese as an army of occupation, as they did. In fact, their use of confrontation and their venting of anger were widely admired by many Tibetans who similarly resented the occupation of their country and capital by Chinese troops and deeply feared that the Chinese, if left unchecked, would soon destroy all that they loved and valued. Lukhangwa's outbursts of anger, therefore, in a sense reflected the nationalistic and anti-Chinese feelings that were widespread in Lhasa, but more important, they also emboldened Tibetans to express their anger and hostility similarly in a public manner. It should be recalled that Tibet had been a polity in which political criticism was illegal; even the street songs cited earlier were not officially permitted. Consequently, as word of Lukhangwa's encounters spread through the Lhasa elite and middle class, not only did they make many Tibetans feel proud that their government's leaders were standing up to the Chinese, but also they sent Tibetans a message that it is acceptable to also oppose and resist the Chinese.

The sitsab's behavior, however, while popular with the people, was not part of a larger government plan aimed at persuading or pressuring the Chinese to modify the agreement. As the heads of the government, they were the ones primarily responsible for fashioning a strategy to deal with the Chinese, but they did not. The Dalai Lama commented on this in an interview, saying that Lukhangwa was just "acting out of emotion [and was] not [employing] some subtle form of strategic thinking."[43] And the sitsab, as the following incident illustrates, were not even interested in trying to coordinate with the Kashag before joint meetings with the Chinese, let alone develop an overall strategy with them for Tibet.

Lhalu recalled that in late 1951 or early 1952 a major meeting took place that included the sitsab, the Kashag ministers, and the Chinese leadership. It did not go well and ended with a very nasty verbal exchange between Lukhangwa and the Chinese. This exchange placed the Kashag ministers in an awkward position, since they did not agree with Lukhangwa's comments but also did not want to undercut the sitsab in front of the Chinese. Lhalu, who was at the meeting, recalled the Kashag ministers' frustration.

42. British Foreign Office Records, FO371/99659, monthly report of Indian Mission in Lhasa for the month ending 15 April 1952.
43. Dalai Lama, interview, 1995, Dharamsala.

After this [meeting] we [the Kashag ministers] held our own separate meeting at which Shasur said, "On the one hand we cannot support the sitsab's arguments, but on the other, not supporting what they say is also not acceptable, since it means we are not showing solidarity in front of the Chinese. It would be as if we are handing them over to the Chinese. So what should we do to solve this dilemma? I was the youngest of the ministers [then age thirty-seven], and I said frankly, "What we should do is suggest to the sitsab that they change their style a bit. Whatever they are going to say to the Chinese, they should first discuss it with us, and then after we all settle what to do internally, we can say it to the Chinese with a unified front. If we meet beforehand in this manner, if there are things the Kashag is doing wrong, the sitsab can criticize us, and if they are doing things we feel are wrong, then we will give them our suggestions." The Kashag ministers agreed that this should be done, and when the question arose as to who would tell this to them, I volunteered, because I used to work together with Lukhangwa as one of the heads of the Revenue Office.

So I went to him and said that in the future he should not suddenly say all kinds of things but should first discuss a strategy with the Kashag. I told him, "If you suddenly say things like you just did, it is hard for us to support you." When I said this he got really angry. He said, "I am [like] an Amdo. Whatever it is, I say straight off what I think and feel [without thought of future ramifications]." So from this time on Lukhangwa disliked me. I said this to help him, but he didn't listen and said, "I am an Amdo so won't do it." So later there were no discussions between the sitsab and the Kashag about strategy. Lukhangwa was someone who did stupid things without first thinking them through.[44]

In contrast to the sitsab, the Kashag pursued a more conciliatory strategic outlook. In general, they too preferred a minimalist Chinese presence in Tibet, but they considered the sitsab's behavior counterproductive and out-of-touch with the military and political realities of the situation. They believed that it was important for the Tibetan leadership to maintain cordial relations with the Chinese, although within the Kashag there were different views about change and reforms. Lhalu explained the dominant viewpoint.

We fought and lost at Chamdo, so we [ministers] thought that if we had disturbances and fought here again, we would lose again. . . . [Acting Council ministers] Shasur and Thubden Ramyang were easygoing and wanted to have friendly relations with the Chinese. Shasur used to say that if we act nicely to the Chinese, then they will reciprocate and act nicely to us in turn. If we act only so-so to them, then they will also act only so-so back to us. If we act hostile to them, then they will reciprocate. He always used to say this. *However, to be honest, I do not know what my colleagues on the Kashag were really thinking deep down, since we never spoke much about such things. . . .* But for myself, when I was in Chamdo I saw the military strength of the PLA, so I was very much in favor of trying to have good relations with the Chinese.[45]

As Lhalu's comments indicate, the Kashag also had not sat down to hold discussions about strategy and had not tried to hammer out a consensus decision on policy. Policy was created by the cumulative effect of ad hoc decisions on specific issues that arose.[46]

Nevertheless, although the Kashag ministers believed that Tibet could no longer remain unchanged, the dominant attitude was that they should try to slow the process of change, for example, by implementing changes slowly over a long period of time. As Lhalu frankly put it, "I didn't think that the old society could continue. But I also didn't think that it would vanish at once. I thought that the reforms would occur slowly, over time. For example, I thought that if there were five points, we should implement one each year, not all at once. I didn't think we should implement all the points at once. If we did it very slowly, I thought all would be fine."[47] Most ministers felt like Lhalu; however, some, such as Ngabö and Shasur, were in favor of working more closely with the Chinese and quickly undertaking reforms. Consequently, no consensus strategy was developed.

Because of this lack of a single agreed-on policy, the government was working at cross-purposes. The sitsab pursued a hard-line approach, and the Kashag pursued a more conciliatory approach—each independent of the other. This was not a subtle Tibetan version of the "good cop–bad cop" routine. There simply was no tactical or strategic planning at the top of the Tibetan government.

In addition to the views and approaches of the Kashag and the sitsab, the elite itself was not homogeneous. Many, such as the lay aristocratic official Gyegyepa, agreed with Lukhangwa that traditional Tibet was great.

The agreement said . . . many points, such as there would be a military-administrative committee, so I thought there would be big changes in Tibet. However, my own thoughts were that the old system and government were excellent. For example, we thought the government was great. We didn't see that at the county level things weren't being implemented so well. So while I thought that this was a time when we would have to compare the old system and the

45. Lhalu, interview, 1992 (emphasis added).
46. The comments of Phündra, a Tibetan from Amdo who was Zhang Jingwu's translator, echo this: "The Tibetan government officials all had suspicions about each other. So they didn't dare come to us often. The Shapes didn't even go to visit each other because of these suspicions [what others would think]. If they had visited each other, it would have become widespread [known] right away. So they didn't come to us often" (Phündra, interview, 1993).
47. Lhalu, interview, 1992.

new ideas, at this time I didn't have any enthusiasm for changing the old system, even though I could see that the time to compare and evaluate it had come.[48]

Gyegyepa also recalled that most aristocrats believed that the sitsab's actions were correct, whether or not they said this openly. In his own case, he said, "I also thought that they were correct in their views."[49]

But there were a few others who had very modern and progressive ideas. In particular, a small number of elite Tibetans genuinely favored working closely with the Chinese to implement the agreement and modernize Tibet. They were intellectually committed to change regardless of whether the Chinese were there and saw the coming of the Chinese as a way to accomplish this.[50] Well-known officials and figures in this camp included Shölkang Jedrung, Ngabö, Tsögo, Kumbela, Samling, Sursur Dzasa, Tshatru Rimpoche, Gyentsen Phüntso, Horkhang, Thangbe, Jija (Tashi Dorje), and Canglocen. They were, in a sense, a continuation of a movement for reform and change that began in the period after the failed Simla Convention in 1914, when a group of young aristocratic officers led by Tsarong realized that some day Tibet would have to face a serious Chinese threat so sought to create a modern and effective army. They had been thwarted by clerics and conservative aristocrats who (in the middle 1920s) persuaded the 13th Dalai Lama that they were a threat to his rule and to religion, since they were too enamored with British secular ideas. The 13th Dalai Lama dismissed or demoted them all.[51]

One of the most famous Tibetans in favor of reforms was the ex-monk Gendün Chompel. His thinking influenced a number of young monk officials, as Ngawang Thondrup recalled.

> I was influenced by Gendün Chompel. He gave us advice. At that time, we were saying that the way the Tibetan government was ruling should be reformed. Gendün Chompel especially was saying that the system of people owning other people (tib. dagpo gyab) should be reformed.
>
> Q. What do you mean "people owning people"?
>
> I mean the aristocrats had serfs (tib. miser) and estates, and they owned the people. For example, the serfs of the Tsarong family had to seek permission when they wanted to leave, right? . . . And they did not own the land. So we were saying that the feudal system should be reformed. . . . Gendün Chompel was a monk who had left the monastery, and he was saying monasteries didn't need to have their manorial estates at all.

48. Gyegyepa, interview, 1992, Lhasa.
49. Gyegyepa, interview, 1992.
50. Dalai Lama, interview, 1994, Ann Arbor, MI.
51. This is discussed in Goldstein 1989: 89–139.

I joined the service of the Tibetan government in 1948 [as a monk official].
At the time of the Second World War, we had an organization, and we took an
internal oath not to reveal anything about our group to others.

Q. What year was that?

That was in 1946, just after the Second World War had ended and [just be-
fore] India gained the independence [in 1947]. At that time, we were not allowed to say that Gendün Chompel told us about that.

We took an oath to be fair and not oppress the people and not take bribes
after we entered the service of the Tibetan government. We had many plans
for reforming [Tibet].

Gendün Chompel also suggested public toilets should be built everywhere,
and we should impose taxes on the rich households, making them spend the
same amount for building public toilets on their land as they spent for their
own houses. . . .

At that time, the newspaper called the *Tibet Mirror,* which was published by
Tharchin Babu [in Kalimpong], was very useful for us. Before that, we didn't
know about the outside world. But that newspaper wrote all about the Second
World War and also had maps in it. After that, I knew about the independence
of India, and I got the idea that we should do something outside. After reading the newspaper, I met Gendün Chompel.

We didn't give ourselves a name like the Youth Association, but the purpose of the association was to make reforms in Tibet. At that time, we used the
term *to repair* (tib. sopjö) to convey the idea of reforms. The current terms [for
reforms], such as *jögyur* and *legjö,* were coined only later. We were saying that
we have to change the estate system of the aristocrats and the monasteries and
that the workers and the farmers should have their rights and should have their
livelihood improved.[52]

These idealistic young monk officials were also excited by the new opportunities the Chinese offered (e.g., going to school in Beijing) and were willing to see the Chinese as harbingers of long-needed modernizing change in
Tibet. Thubden Wangpo, a young monk official who was one of the first Tibetan students in the new Society School (tib. jitso lapdra), which started in
Lhasa in 1952, put it this way:

There were only two thoughts [in Lhasa in 1951–52]. One, that revolution (tib.
sarje) was good. The poor would rise, and everyone would be equal in standard of living. The other said it would be terrible if there was revolution. . . .
Youths like change, and so I thought it was good to join the Youth Association.
Some thought that if I didn't join, I would be left behind, so [I] joined [for
this reason]. My thought was that if I go to China, it will be fun. They'll give
food, and I'll go to school. I didn't have any great long-term profound plans.
I thought it would be fun and useful, since unless you knew spoken and written Chinese, later it would be hard to find good work. . . .

52. Ngawang Thondrup, interview, 1992, Dharamsala.

We thought that now things were changing, and the Chinese were going to be in power, and there would be a change in society, so I thought it would be good to go to China.[53]

Others also became excited at the general prospects of change and modernization. Takla (Phüntso Tashi), the Dalai Lama's brother-in-law (who then was twenty-nine years of age and spoke and read Chinese),[54] recalled,

I met quite often with the Chinese. For example, a youth organization was formed after they arrived, and so sometimes I used to go there. Also a football team was formed. Whatever organization they formed, I was there. The reason was that at that time we were sort of quite "attracted" to the Communists' ideas. That's how young people think, isn't it? . . .

Q. Did some see the Chinese coming as something positive?

. . . If something new is to be done, it is always the youth. Anything that is new, the youth take it up. Take myself, for example. Among us youth, when something new came up, we thought it was good. The youth have a lot of heart. For example, whether it is the Chinese or the West, the youth are always enlisting in the army. The reason is that their minds are yet unclouded, ever ready to jump in and fight, full of bravado. But as time goes by, one begins to think why and learns to have better judgment. So the message that the Communists brought was that of a modern system and that it was great to do these new things, these new reforms. And so the youth thought that it must be really true. What the Communists had going for them was their great emphasis on the modern message and reforms.[55]

Moreover, a number of elite officials supported the need for reforms in Tibet, not because of a long-held desire for modernization, but mainly because the circumstances—the Chinese Communists being in control of Tibet—led them to conclude that now Tibet had to change. The Dalai Lama explained this.

I think that among the group of people who want some change, there . . . can be two categories. One is most probably like Shölkang Jedrung. He felt that whether the Chinese are there or not, we need change and some kind of modernization. That is the genuine one. The other one is whether we like it or not, the Chinese have already come. So we have to do some change. . . . Perhaps Ngabö belongs, most probably, I think, in the first one. He saw the need for change. . . . Kumbela, Tsarong, and, even to some extent, the 13th Dalai Lama also thought that some changes are needed. He started a little bit of Westernization mainly in the sense of mechanization.[56]

53. Thubden Wangpo, interview, 1992, Lhasa.
54. He had grown up in Qinchai Province and gone to Chinese medium schools as a child.
55. Takla (Phüntso Tashi), interview, 1992, Dharamsala.
56. Dalai Lama, interview, 1994.

Among the top leaders in the Tibetan government, the key progressive figure was the Kashag minister Ngabö. He had headed the negotiating delegation in Beijing and was on his way back to Lhasa with the Advance Unit of the Eighteenth Army Corps (see chapter 8). He would arrive back in Lhasa on 9 September. In marked contrast to Lukhangwa, Ngabö felt that the Seventeen-Point Agreement, given the circumstances, was an excellent agreement that gave Tibet a unique status in China: no other local government in China had such a formal written agreement with the central government. Consequently, he believed that the best strategy for Tibet was to strive to preserve that special status within China by maintaining friendly relations with the Chinese and quickly showing them a willingness to implement the agreement and reform Tibet. Ngabö was convinced that Tibet could not stay unchanged, but it could tailor the reform process so as to maintain the essence of Tibet culture, religion, and political autonomy under the leadership of the Dalai Lama. The feudal system would gradually end, to the benefit of the Tibetan people, but the role of Dalai Lama would continue, and the elite would be compensated for the loss of their feudal estates.[57] But Tibet had to commit to create a new, modern Tibet that was an integral part of China and had to accept the friendship that the Chinese Communist Party was offering to Tibet. A real partnership with the new Chinese, he felt, had to be developed.

The Dalai Lama's recollection of his first meeting with Ngabö supports this. He recalled that Ngabö said:

> We didn't get all we desired [in the agreement], but it stopped the Chinese army invading Tibet. Now it's difficult, and under these difficult circumstances you have to think carefully what to do. The most important thing is that, unlike other nationalities in China, for Tibet there was an agreement made between the government of Tibet and China. This is unlike all other nationalities. We have to work hard to actualize this [special] right.[58]

Within the Kashag, Ngabö, supported by Shasur, was far more progressive and pro-reform than other ministers. Not surprisingly, Ngabö, from the start, was also the Chinese side's closest ally and the person to whom they continually went for advice and help. Because of this, some Tibetans believed Ngabo had sold out to the Chinese, and rumors to this effect were common in Lhasa. Lukhangwa himself was critical of Ngabö, whom he felt had exceeded his instructions; at one meeting when Ngabö made a comment about the need for reforms, Lukhangwa is said to have told him: "You brought light to the other's country and darkness to your own country."[59]

57. Chabtsom, interview, 1992, Lhasa.
58. Dalai Lama, interview, 1994.
59. In Tibetan, "mi yul 'od kyis rgyang rang yul mun pa sgrib" (Tashi Tsering, interview, 1992, Lhasa). Lukhangwa's daughter-in-law (Mrs. Lukhangwa, interview, 1993) had the Tibetan

On the other hand, many Tibetan officials respected Ngabö's straight-forward style, including the most important figure in Tibet, the Dalai Lama. Ironically, Ngabö, the official most closely assisting the Chinese, immediately became a trusted adviser to the Dalai Lama, who explained, "At that time, regarding matters relating to the Chinese, I consulted and sought advice and recommendations from Ngabö. Even regarding other matters, poor fellow, I was very familiar with [close to] him. He was a bit revolutionary minded (tib. sarje) [and someone] who openly and frankly said what he thought and felt (tib. khasey dingsey), so I relied more on him even on matters that did not relate with the Chinese."[60]

Further complicating this situation in Lhasa were two other important factors—the age and personality of the ruler and the legacy of the Reting-Taktra conflict. In November 1950, the Dalai Lama had assumed political authority at the age of fifteen, three years earlier than this assumption usually occurred, because of the need to create internal unity in Tibet in the face of the Chinese conquest of Eastern Tibet. Taktra, the regent for the past nine years, had been a polarizing figure because of the Reting incident and corruption in his administration.[61] Elevating the young Dalai Lama to the rulership was a way to bring all sides together to confront the Chinese Communists. But the Dalai Lama was young and poorly prepared to assume the role of ruler at this very difficult juncture. He knew almost nothing about China, communism, or world history.[62] And why should he? Those in charge of his education had not given him any training in modern secular subjects such as history and politics and science. His education was completely religious, concentrating on the traditional curriculum of Buddhist logics and metaphysics. This education was meant to make him a great scholar monk (tib. geshe), not a great political ruler.

His knowledge of ordinary life in Tibet was also virtually nil. He was not allowed to go outside his palace and talk to people on the street, nor did visitors come to see him except in the most formal setting of an audience. He interacted almost entirely with a small number of monks (his tutors and attendants) and informally with a similarly small number of common laborers ("sweepers") who worked in his palaces. Until he was twelve, he was able

---

syllables slightly different: "rang yul 'di, sa rub pa 'dra bo bzos mi yul 'di nam langs pa 'dra po bzos" (You have brought sunset to your own country while bringing dawn to the country of another). I am not certain whether this was actually said to Ngabö's face or behind his back.

60. Dalai Lama, interview, 1993, Dharamsala.

61. See Goldstein 1989: 427–521) for a detailed exposition of the Reting conspiracy.

62. The Dalai Lama has said of his knowledge in 1950, "I knew nothing about the world and had no experience of politics" (Dalai Lama 1962: 83), and in his later book, "I had almost no knowledge of the Chinese. And of Communists, I was almost entirely ignorant, although I was aware that they had been causing terrible hardship for the people of Mongolia" (Dalai Lama 1990: 54).

Figure 6. High officials at a meeting, left to right: Ngabö, Shasur, unknown, and Sambo, in Lhasa. Source: Chen Zonglie

to visit regularly and spend time with his family at their house in Lhasa (once every month or six weeks),[63] but after 1947, his isolation was exacerbated when the regent both forbade him to make these home visits and curtailed visits by his family members to his palace.[64]

The extent of his isolation from the life of Tibetans, and thus his dependence on a small group of attendants, teachers, and officials for knowledge of the outside "reality," is reflected in the Dalai Lama's own recollection of what he saw as a unique opportunity he once had to meet and talk to common people. It occurred when he was moving from Lhasa to Yadong in December 1950. He was traveling disguised in laymen's clothing to preclude Tibetans' trying to stop him from leaving Lhasa, and for the first two days this went well. However, the monks at Jang, the famous winter debating camp, saw this large caravan with high officials and suspected the Dalai Lama must

63. Dalai Lama 1962: 52.
64. See Dalai Lama 1990: 37 regarding the forbidding of home visits.

be with them, so they stopped his senior tutor, Ling Rimpoche, and began imploring him to turn back. The Dalai Lama, however, was riding ahead of Ling Rimpoche at the front of the caravan, so he continued on his way while Ling Rimpoche tried to calm the monks. The Dalai Lama recalled the special opportunity this afforded him.

> I was able to make the most of the situation by going on ahead, still in disguise, and using every occasion I could to stop and talk with people. I realised that I now had a valuable opportunity to find out what life was really like for my fellow countrymen and women and managed to have a number of conversations during which I kept my identity secret. From these, I learned something of the petty injustices of life suffered by my people and resolved as soon as I could to set about making changes to help them.[65]

Consequently, it took unusual circumstances like this one, in which he was fleeing from the capital in disguise, to allow the Dalai Lama to go outside his palaces and interact with regular Tibetans. The Dalai Lama mostly had to be content to look at life outside his Potala Palace through a telescope on its roof.

Notwithstanding this structured isolation, the Dalai Lama developed a lively curiosity about the world, science, machinery, and, as the above quote reveals, the hardships and injustices the traditional manorial system imposed on his people. In his autobiographies he mentions this.

> I was always fascinated by mechanical things . . . but I was never content to play with them for long—I always had to take them to pieces to see how they worked. . . . One of the minor pleasures of the Norbulingka [Palace] was that it had a motor generator for electric light, which often broke down, so that I had every excuse to take it to pieces. From that machine, I discovered how internal combustion engines work. . . .
>
> I was curious also about the affairs of the world outside Tibet, but naturally much of that curiosity had to go unsatisfied. I had an atlas, and I poured over maps of distant countries and wondered what life was like in them but I did not know anyone who had ever seen them. I started to teach myself English out of books. . . . My tutor read in a Tibetan newspaper, which was published in Kalimpong in India, of the progress of the Second World War . . . and they told me about it. Before the end of the war, I was able to read such accounts myself.[66]

The Dalai Lama's horizons were expanded after 1948 by the accidental presence of Heinrich Harrer, an Austrian mountaineer who had fled internment in India and managed to reach Lhasa, where he was given permission to reside.[67] For about a year and a half beginning in 1948, he met with the Dalai

---

65. Dalai Lama 1990: 59.
66. Dalai Lama 1962: 55 and 57.
67. Harrer spent seven years in Tibet and became an unofficial tutor of the Dalai Lama. The story of his time in Lhasa is found in Harrer 1954.

Lama roughly once a week and, as the Dalai Lama put it, "From him I was able to learn something about the outside world and especially about Europe and the recent war."[68] At this time a few books on the Second World War were translated for the Dalai Lama by Tsarong Rimshi, an aristocratic official who was fluent in English, and the Dalai Lama also had access to magazines in which some of the captions were translated, such as *Life* and *National Geographic.*[69]

But this very exceptionality of his access to nonreligious education reveals how ill-prepared the young Dalai Lama was educationally to rule Tibet at this difficult and dangerous point in its history, when the dominant issues to contend with were international, political, and military in nature. One should recall that in the Tibet of 1949–50, no newspapers, magazines, or translations of modern books were published there,[70] and no modern schools existed yet. With the exception of a few aristocrats, Tibetans at this time were living in self-imposed ignorance of the modern world, in which they now had no choice but to compete.

The Dalai Lama himself, looking back at Tibet in 1951–52, recalled an incident that illustrates the low level of secular knowledge in Tibet. He recalled that when he first met Zhang Jingwu in Yadong, his eighteen-year-old brother, Lobsang Samden, was with him and was secretly peeking in at the meeting from the next room. Neither had previously seen a Chinese "Communist." After the visit ended, Lobsang Samden ran into the Dalai Lama's room and said with amazement to his brother, " 'Oh, these people are also human beings.' That was his first expression after he saw the Communist Chinese."[71] Lobsang Samden was not an illiterate Tibetan villager. He was a member of the elite who had been educated in Tibetan and who would be appointed jigyab khembo, the highest position in the monk official segment of the government, the very next year. That someone of his background and stature could have such thoughts gives a sense of the general level of knowledge among the religious elite and much of the secular elite.

The Dalai Lama's life was governed by his tutors and personal staff, all of whom, as mentioned above, were monks and incarnate lamas who were far more interested in developing his religious knowledge and stature than his political control of the government. His trip back to Lhasa, for example, is interesting because it was not characterized by great urgency. Although the Chinese had invaded Eastern Tibet, a treaty had been signed in Beijing with-

---

68. Dalai Lama 1990: 38.

69. Personal communication from his son, Tsarong (Paljor), 2004.

70. Some in the elite did, however, subscribe to the Kalimpong-published Tibetan newspaper called the *Tibetan Mirror,* and a few who had gone to school in India and knew English had shortwave radios and listened to the BBC.

71. Dalai Lama, interview, 2004.

out his knowledge, a Chinese Communist official was in Tibet, and thousands of PLA troops were about to arrive there. Strangely this was not seen by the Dalai Lama's tutors as a crisis requiring his immediate presence in Lhasa, for example, to oversee the planning process on how to deal with the situation. Instead, his staff and tutors were focused more on enhancing the young Dalai Lama's religious stature among Tibetans and took his return trip as an opportunity for what we might call the traditional religious equivalent of public relations—having the Dalai Lama stop along the way to give religious teachings and audiences. In Gyantse, as mentioned earlier, the Dalai Lama performed the multiday Kalachakra religious teaching at the Pegaw Chöde Monastery.[72] This orientation continued even after his arrival in Lhasa, as was noted by Sinha, the head of the Indian government mission in Lhasa in one of his monthly reports to Delhi: "The Dalai Lama is having many receptions and religious meetings, apparently attempting to draw the people closer to him in devotion and worship. He has borrowed public address equipment from the Indians for this purpose."[73]

At this time, the Dalai Lama was the only one who could have stepped in and molded the disparate views of the elite into a single strategy, but he was clearly not focused on political affairs, nor did those around him think that this was what he should be doing.[74] And in regard to his personality, the Dalai Lama himself was not oriented toward exercising his power and overriding the bureaucracy who operated the government.

The most recent model for a Dalai Lama was the 13th Dalai Lama. He was famous for being a hard-headed, tough, hands-on ruler who took control of the bureaucracy and ruled it with a strong hand. He was much feared, and he punished officials as he saw fit. The 14th Dalai Lama, however, did not adopt that model and conveyed to me that he does not feel his personality was appropriate for that. He explained this in response to a question about whether he ever thought of ruling like the 13th Dalai Lama.

> But my nature. What comes naturally, I do that. It is spontaneous. I never sort of calculate. [My tutor] Trijang Rimpoche [once] told me, today there is a new set of circumstances, not only because of the Chinese, but there is sort of a new era, and your personality is very suitable for this [new era]. In this new era the 13 Dalai Lama's personality would not fit, but during his period his personal-

72. Phündra, interview, 1993.

73. U.S. National Archives, 793B.00/1–2552, 25 January 1952, copy of report of the Indian Mission in Lhasa for 16 September–15 October 1951.

74. I suspect that this was related to challenges made to the authenticity of the Dalai Lama by some supporters of Taktra in 1947 at the end of the Reting coup attempt (this will be discussed later in this chapter). For those around the Dalai Lama, this challenge made it a priority to enhance his stature and sanctity through public teachings and audiences, despite his young age and despite the overwhelming political crisis.

ity was useful. Once he [Trijang Rimpoche] told me like that. And even if I felt I wanted to act like the 13th Dalai Lama, I couldn't have done it at all. [The Dalai Lama asks,] "Tarala [head of his private secretariat], could I have done it? Tarala, the previous Dalai Lama was serious (tib. sgam po), not frank (tib. sbug pu), etc., could I have done like?" . . . A person's personality is important. Without such a personality, one can't act like that.[75]

So via experience, training, advice, and personality, the young Dalai Lama was not inclined to step in and actively manage governmental affairs. Phündra, Zhang Jingwu's translator, recalled his lack of assertiveness during the early 1950s: "When Zhang Jingwu would directly report something to the Dalai Lama, sometimes he would say, 'Yes, I understand, and I will tell the Kashag ministers. They will discuss and give you the answer.' He didn't say anything definitely [himself]."[76] In addition, as was explained in the introduction, the Kashag (and sitsab) traditionally tried to control decision making by limiting the information going to the Dalai Lama on any issue, so it took a strong and proactive Dalai Lama to overcome that and exercise substantial control. Unlike his predecessor the 13th Dalai Lama, the 14th Dalai Lama had a very different personality and approach, deferring the initiative to older government officials, at least in these early years. He was the ruler in name in 1951–52 but in fact was not deeply involved in day-to-day political affairs and was not interested in asserting himself to become so.

Finally, another important factor that complicated relations among the elite and added to the lack of unity in the government was the bitter residue left by the Reting-Taktra conflict, in particular, the bad feeling between the Yabshi family (the name used for the family of any dalai lama, in this case in reference to the family of the 14th Dalai Lama) and Taktra and his supporters. These feelings operated under the surface but were real, at least for members of the 14th Dalai Lama's immediate family.

THE YABSHI FAMILY AND TAKTRA

When a new dalai lama is selected, his family is brought to Lhasa, ennobled, and given wealth commensurate with their new lofty status—a grand house and a number of manorial estates with their bound serfs. Such grants were substantial, and the Yabshi families, as they are called, become members of the top aristocracy. The family of the 14th Dalai Lama, called Taktse (or now usually Takla), was no exception.[77]

---

75. Dalai Lama, interview, 2004. The Dalai Lama answered in English, and this is presented without editing for English grammar. Tarala agreed with the Dalai Lama's comment.

76. Phündra, interview, 1993.

77. The Yabshi Takla family received grants of six estates: Drongtse, Chayü, Jora, Seshin, Niu, and Gyatso (Stag lha [Takla] 1995: 164).

The relationship between the Takla family and the Tibetan government, however, became complicated and strained by the family's close relations with and loyalty to Reting Rimpoche, one of the most divisive figures in modern Tibetan history. The background of this is relevant.

When the 13th Dalai Lama died in 1933, a regent had to be selected to rule while the search for a new dalai lama occurred. That regent would normally have continued to rule until the new dalai lama reached majority age, usually age eighteen. In this instance, a coregency was initially established, with a young twenty-three-year-old incarnate lama, Reting Rimpoche, assuming the dominant role. Reting took the lead in the search process for the new dalai lama and, on the basis of a vision he had in a holy lake, overrode some opposition and decided that a young boy from Amdo was the true 14th Dalai Lama. He oversaw this boy's transfer to Lhasa in 1939 and his enthronement the following year.

Reting, however, turned out to be petulant, corrupt, and, critically, not celibate.[78] Consequently, when it came time for the Dalai Lama to officially take his monk's vows, a silent crisis arose. Custom had it that the Dalai Lama's vows had to be given by the incarnate lama who was regent, that is, Reting. Tibetans consider that such vows have passed unbroken from ancient times, from one celibate monk to another. Consequently, a secretly uncelibate monk would not really be transmitting the vows, since he himself no longer had any, so no matter what Reting said at the Dalai Lama's ceremony, the Dalai Lama would end up having no vows. And since the Dalai Lama would himself give vows to thousands of monks during his lifetime, they too would not have vows. This was unacceptable, and pressure was placed on Reting not to transmit sham vows to the young Dalai Lama. But how to do this without admitting the heterosexual problem? Reting turned to mysticism. He created a story about a dream in which he learned that his life was in danger and said that because of this he had to resign the Regency and go into a three-year retreat. So at the height of his power, in 1941, Reting resigned and selected an old and not well-known lama, Taktra Rimpoche, to succeed him and administer the vows to the Dalai Lama. Reting apparently believed that after the three years in retreat, Taktra would step aside and allow him to reassume the Regency. He was wrong.

Taktra Rimpoche had been appalled by the dissolute and corrupt behavior of Reting and his staff and set about to reverse this. He appointed senior officials such as Lhalu and Surkhang, who were hostile to Reting for personal reasons, and also set about restraining and punishing aristocratic families and monk officials who had been core supporters of Reting. One of the

---

78. This is discussed in detail in Goldstein 1989: 310ff., and the reader is referred there for more information.

most important families he went after was that of the 14th Dalai Lama, specifically, the head of that family, the father of the 14th Dalai Lama, who was very close to Reting.

The Dalai Lama's father had let his new status go to his head and had begun to act unilaterally, reversing court decisions and fining individuals when it suited him. He also refused to pay taxes on his estates and began requisitioning free transport from other serfs without going through the government. And he demanded unheard of deference when traveling in Lhasa; for example, all mounted persons, regardless of rank, had to dismount and pay respects to him or risk being beaten by one of his servants. On one occasion when a sick person en route to the British Mission for treatment did not dismount, he immediately confiscated the man's horse.[79] His son Gyalo Thondup acknowledges his excessive behavior, saying,

> People in Lhasa had shown a great deal of respect to our family because we were the Dalai Lama's family. They treated us with great kindness—and my father often took advantage of them. If he saw a horse he fancied in the street, he would make the owner sell it to him then and there. He would bargain and force the price right down. The people he treated like this naturally got very upset and began to have second thoughts about the Dalai Lama's father.[80]

While Reting was in power, he was free to do as he liked, but once Taktra acceded to power, the new regent set out to clamp down on his excesses. From the beginning of the Taktra regime, therefore, relations between the Yabshi Takla family and the regent Taktra were bad. They became so strained that in late 1942 the regent promulgated a humiliating national edict chastising the Dalai Lama's father.[81]

Meanwhile, after Reting finished his three-year "retreat" in his monastery, he returned to Lhasa in 1944–45 to try to reassume the regency. Taktra refused to resign, and Reting had no choice but to return to his monastery. Reting and his aides then plotted a coup against Taktra. In 1947, after discovery of a bomb plot and an appeal by Reting to the Guomindang for support, Reting was arrested and apparently murdered by poison in prison. A few months before the bomb plot was uncovered, in January 1947, one of his closest supporters, the Dalai Lama's father, died mysteriously. As the following excerpts illustrate, the Dalai Lama's mother and her second oldest son believed he was poisoned and that Taktra was behind this.

The following is Dalai Lama's mother's view of this period:

79. India Office Records, L/PS/12/4179, letter from Norbhu Döndup, assistant political officer in Sikkim (who was then in Lhasa), to the political officer in Sikkim, dated 2 January 1942.

80. Gyalo Thondup, interview with Mary Craig, as cited in Craig 1997: 106.

81. See Goldstein 1989: 370–73.

Our family was close to Reting. Before his arrest the Kashag tried to recall my son and son-in-law [Gyalo Thondup and Takla (Phüntso Tashi)] from China. They told me that I should send someone to fetch them back to Lhasa. The Kashag wanted to place all my male children and my son-in-law in prison, but they could not do anything because none of them was in Lhasa.[82] I had also heard that the Kashag wanted to send my daughter and me back to Tsongkha [Amdo]. Thus, they would have been able to disperse my family and eliminate all opposition to their power. . . .

Reting Rimpoche and my husband had been very close friends. They had shared a love for horses. The arrest and assassination of Reting would not have been so simple if my husband had been alive, since he had more resources at his disposal than I had and would at least have prevented the arrest and imprisonment from occurring so smoothly. This is why people are convinced that my husband was poisoned.

At about this time word started to spread that His Holiness was not the real Dalai Lama, that a mistake had been made. It was said that my son was Ditru Rinpoche, while Ditru Rinpoche was the real Dalai Lama. Ditru was the child of a relative of the thirteenth Dalai Lama.[83] Finally it was decided to place both names in a vessel and, before the image of Je Rinpoche, to shake it and see which name fell out. This was done three times. My son's name leaped out three times, and the regent Taktra and the Kashag had nothing more to say for themselves.[84]

The Dalai Lama's older brother Gyalo Thondup has explained this period almost identically.

I am certain my father was murdered. He was a simple farmer who knew nothing about politics, especially about the complicated saga of the two Regencies. We were close as a family to Reting, who was especially close to my father. I was told that the Taktra clique wanted to depose His Holiness because he had been brought to Lhasa by Reting. They had plans to dispose of Reting, and they feared that if His Holiness took over the political power later he might punish

---

82. Actually, the son-in-law, Takla (Phüntso Tashi), who was in China, returned to Lhasa in 1947 and experienced no negative consequences.

83. Another name mentioned was Tashi Rapgye, an incarnation who was Taktra's nephew.

84. Tsering 2000: 124–25. Another former government official heard a similar account. Kapshöba (Chögye Nyima) told some people after the fall of Reting that the Kashag had a discussion, and it was said, "If the condition of the one who recognized him is no better than this, then the lama who was recognized also is not definite" (tib. ngos 'dzin zhu mkhan gyi kha dog 'di las med par ngos 'dzin zhus pa'i bla ma de yang tan tan yod pa ma red). So the other ministers said that the reincarnation of the Dalai Lama may not be the true one. Kapshöba then said that if this is the case, we should make sure whether this reincarnation is the true one or not by doing a divine lottery in front of the statue of Avaloketisvara (tib. 'phags pa lo ka'i sha ra) in the Potala Palace. After that the ministers went to the Potala and did the divine lottery, which said he is the correct reincarnation. The ministers then decided not to tell anybody about this (anon., interview, 2000).

them. So they wanted to remove him [the Dalai Lama] while there was still time and replace him with a candidate of their own, a young lama called Ditru Rinpoche. Then there was my father, if he remained alive, he would get in the way of their plans for Reting. So they poisoned him.[85]

While some of these charges are clearly fanciful (for example, that the Tibetan government wanted to put one of the Dalai Lama's brothers and his brother-in-law in prison), these accounts reveal the Yabshi family's deep distrust (at least that of Gyalo Thondup and his mother) toward the Taktra regime and the continuing animosity between the supporters of Reting and those of Taktra. This is important, because in 1951 four top officials who had been close supporters of Taktra held very powerful positions in the governmental hierarchy—the jigyab khembo Ngawang Namgye, the lord chamberlain Phala, and the two Kashag ministers who had gone to arrest Reting at his monastery north of Lhasa in 1947, Lhalu and Surkhang. At lower ranks there were many others as well. Consequently, while the accession of the Dalai Lama to power in 1950 had partly assuaged the anti-Taktra elements and forged unity on the surface, an undercurrent of animosity still permeated elite attitudes and politics, and considerable bitterness remained in the Yabshi family toward key supporters of Taktra. It is not surprising that by mid-1952, the Dalai Lama had retired Lhalu and replaced Ngawang Namgye with his twenty-year-old brother, Lobsang Samden. And while Surkhang remained an important Kashag minister, the Dalai Lama says he did not have rapport with him. As will be seen in subsequent chapters and the next volume, the estrangement and distrust of the Dalai Lama's relatives for the Tibetan governmental elite is an important component of the history of the 1950s.

If all this were not enough, there was still another schism within the Tibetan side that deeply affected political affairs in the 1950s—the bitter conflict between the Dalai Lama and the Panchen Lama (and their respective officials). This will be discussed in detail in chapter 10.

In sum, in the period after the Dalai Lama arrived in Lhasa in August 1951, the Tibetan government faced major decisions about what strategy to em-

---

85. Gyalo Thondup, as quoted from an interview (Craig 1997: 120). Another former government official, Shelling (Tsewang Namgye) (interview, 2003, Cleveland, OH), said that while he was in prison in the 1960s and '70s, he heard that Kala, a manager of Niu, one of the estates of the Dalai Lama's family, had confessed that he had poisoned the Dalai Lama's father. This is interesting because Kala originally was a serf of the pro–Taktra Phala family and had been the manager of Phala's valuable Drongtse estate. He became a serf of the Dalai Lama's family when Reting confiscated the Drongtse estate and gave it (and its serfs) to the Dalai Lama's family. The Dalai Lama's father died the first day of the Tibetan New Year in 1947 (late February).

ploy vis-à-vis the Chinese. Various viewpoints existed among the top elite, but no meetings were held to establish a unified course of action or even discuss the costs and benefits of alternatives. Rather, adherents of each perspective pursued their own approach on an individual and ad hoc basis. Lhalu's earlier comment about his colleagues on the Kashag is worth repeating here: "To be honest, I do not know what my colleagues on the Kashag were really thinking deep down, since *we never spoke much about such things.*" This was possible because the Tibetan government was reactive rather than proactive at this time. Issues were addressed individually as they were raised by the Chinese side, rather than addressed proactively according to some unified Tibetan plan. The only political figure who could have imposed a unified strategy on the government was the Dalai Lama, but he was only sixteen years of age, intellectually unsure of international and secular politics, and under pressure from his entourage to concentrate on religion, not secular governmental affairs. The end result was that the two sitsab were able to pursue their own views without restraint, and Tibet began its new relations with China under a hard-line, anti-Chinese, anti-agreement policy that utilized confrontation and obstructionism. In a sense, Tibet began the new era even more disunified than it had been before the Chinese came.

Chapter 8

The Advance PLA Force
Arrives in Lhasa

On 9 September, approximately six hundred troops of the Eighteenth Army Corps's Advance Force, under the command of Wang Qimei, arrived in Lhasa accompanied by Ngabö.[1] These were the first PLA troops to enter Lhasa, so the Chinese wanted to make their entry impressive. Phünwang, who accompanied Wang, recalled their entry.

> We entered Lhasa in a grand way. Carrying pictures of Mao and Zhu De, Wang Qimei and I marched around the Barkor at the front of the troops. . . . There were thousands of Tibetans watching us and I recall being surprised to hear one lady say, "These are the communist soldiers we heard so much about, but they are nothing special—they are still Chinese." They had heard that the communist soldiers were different from the Nationalist troops, and thought they would look physically different.[2]

One Tibetan who was thirteen years old recalled his own reaction: "I was very afraid. I ran away when I saw the Chinese [troops], because people were saying that the ones who were wearing gauze face masks were human-flesh eaters. There were those kinds of rumors, so we were extremely scared."[3]

For the first weeks after their arrival, the new Chinese military officials paid courtesy visits to Tibet's top officials, just as Zhang Jingwu had done. During these visits, the Tibetan officials continued to be polite, albeit noncommittal about accepting the Seventeen-Point Agreement, except for Lukhangwa, who showed increased hostility and anger now that PLA troops

---

1. For a firsthand description of their six-week journey, see Goldstein, Sherap, and Siebenschuh, 2004: 154–63.

2. Goldstein, Sherap, and Siebenschuh 2004: 160.

3. Lobsang Phüntso, interview, 2002, Lhasa.

Figure 7. PLA troops marching around the Bakor after entering Lhasa, 1951.
Source: Chen Zonglie

were actually in Lhasa. For example, when Wang Qimei initially met the two sitsab on the afternoon of 18 September, Lukhangwa lashed out at the Chinese, interrupting them often and angrily saying things such as, "Only a small number of [PLA] soldiers should come to Tibet, and these should be sent to the borders to defend there [not kept in Lhasa]." At the same time, he was totally dismissive of their comments that they were "new Chinese" and repeatedly referred to China and Tibet as "the large nation and the small nation," rather than one as a part of the other. He also said that some of the points of the agreement needed to be discussed again, and he commented that "Tibet, as a Buddhist country, is neutral (stays in the middle). Because of this, from the past, we have had no desire to take Chinese lands so whoever has thoughts of taking Tibet's lands will be unsuccessful."[4]

Phünwang was present at that visit and recalled that, for a Tibetan aristocrat, Lukhangwa was incredibly rude.

> When Wang Qimei, a few other officials and I visited Sitsab Lukhangwa, we got a real surprise. Wang Qimei first said something innocuous like, "The Seventeen-Point Agreement between the Central Government and the Tibet local government has been signed, and today we have come to visit you. We would like to present you with these gifts." He immediately responded with an angry tirade, the gist of which was that because China and Tibet in the past had been in a priest-patron relationship, there were now two governments, one Tibetan and one Chinese. "You Chinese seized our territory in the Tartsedo [Tachienlu] area in the past, and now you have brazenly attacked us by force and, under the name of 'liberation,' seized our territory in Chamdo.[5] Wang Qimei," he said pointing at him, "during the Chamdo war you were one of the military officials. People called you 'Vice Political Commissar Wang.' Now, after you have defeated our troops, you have arrived in Lhasa promoted to 'Commander Wang.' But we here will not be easy to suppress. Leaving everything else aside, the grain for your soldiers will not last." Lukhangwa was highly emotional.
>
> I was shocked. This outburst went completely beyond any norm of acceptable Tibetan aristocratic behavior. The Lhasa elite did not confront one another directly in this manner. Even bitter enemies would talk politely, as if they were old friends.

4. Le 1985: 245, entry for 18 September 1951.

5. After the defeat of the Tibetan army in Chamdo in October 1950, the entire Chamdo region was reorganized under the administrative control of a liberation committee that was established on 19 October 1950 directly under the State Council in Beijing. After the signing of the Seventeen-Point Agreement, Chamdo was not returned to the Tibetan government and remained administratively separate until 1956, when it became part of the Preparatory Committee for the Tibet Autonomous Region. The loss of Chamdo was no small matter. A Chinese document on Tibet's population in 1958 reports a population total of about 1.26 million people in Tibet (in the areas that had been political Tibet before the liberation). Of this, Chamdo contained 315,742 persons (25 percent), while Labrang, the Panchen Lama's administrative unit, contained 93,861 (7.5 percent) (Dui xizang gongzuo de zhongyao zhishi [wei chuban de shouji], n.d).

Ironically, Wang never understood the full impact of what was said because our interpreter, Tarchin, took it upon himself to mistranslate so as not to provoke Wang. Consequently, he translated Lukhangwa's use of the terms "China" and "Tibet" as the Central Government and Local Government, and toned down his verbal attacks. Later, when we returned home, I told Tarchin that in the future he should not change what people said; he had to translate exactly. Tarchin said he knew that he should do that but feared that if he had translated correctly, both of them might have gotten very angry and it might have created a serious incident. . . .

Even though Wang Qimei did not know exactly what Lukhangwa had said, he realized by his expression that it was a criticism. I recall that Wang's face became red as he listened. It was a tense moment for this first visit, but it would have been much worse had Tarchin done his job correctly.

Afterward Wang asked me what Lukhangwa said, and I told him without softening the message. He responded, "That man is really a reactionary. However, at least he is honest and says what he thinks. Those other aristocrats always say good things to your face, but you never know what they are really thinking." I had to admit he was right.[6]

As mentioned earlier, news of each of the sitsab's outbursts spread everywhere by word of mouth, and the arrival of the PLA troops now gave hostile Tibetans a concrete object at which to express their anger. On the streets of Lhasa some Tibetans, particularly Tibetan soldiers and the dobdo ("punk" or "fighting") monks,[7] started to heckle and hassle the Chinese troops when they encountered them, occasionally even spitting and throwing rocks at them. One Tibetan from Kham who was then a thirteen-year-old member of the PLA's dance troop recalled such incidents.

At first we lived in Dosenge (in tents for one year).[8] It was right beside the Ngadang magar [the Gyantse Regiment]. We had many females in the dance troupe, but otherwise the [PLA's] Tibet Military Area Headquarters had very few women. The Tibetan soldiers really were terrible and behaved very badly. We in the dance troupe had to get up early in the morning and practice singing musical scales. I didn't have to do this, but the girl singers did. The Tibetan soldiers would stand on the roofs of their barracks and pick up their dresses (tib. chuba) and urinate facing the girls. When the girls would turn away, the soldiers would go on the other side and also urinate in front of them to embarrass them. . . .

Q. Did you as a Tibetan go and say hello to the Tibetan soldiers?

6. Goldstein, Sherap, and Siebenschuh 2004: 162.

7. See Goldstein 1964 and Richardson 1986 for detailed examinations of this type of monk. Goldstein 1964 can be accessed at www.cwru.edu/affil/tibet/booksAndPapers/Study%20of%20Ldab%20Ldob.pdf.

8. They actually also were in what is the adjacent area called Magar sarpa. The two were connected by a small bridge.

No, we were afraid they would beat the hell out of us. And we didn't go much to Lhasa, as we had no money, . . . [but] when we did go to the market, the Gyantse Regiment troops would push us and spit at us, and they would throw stones at us from the roofs.

. . . At this time the Lhasa people weren't too bad to us; the worst were the dobdo monks and the Tibetan soldiers. The dobdos would push us and spit at us in the market. At this time we had a rule that if anyone hit you, you could not hit them back. If anyone said something bad to you, you could not reply badly (in kind). At that time the PLA soldiers were very angry but could do nothing about it.[9]

As a result of this, the Chinese tried to keep all troops in their quarters as much as possible, but some harassing still occurred, and Wang Qimei's advance troops felt threatened by this. They were billeted in a militarily precarious position in the southern part of Lhasa, their backs up against the Kyichu River and their flank boxed in by a Tibetan army garrison. And people in Lhasa were making inflammatory statements, such as "When the flame is low one should put it out," meaning that when the Chinese have only a few troops they should be annihilated. More ominously, the Tibetan troops in Lhasa were bragging that they could easily wipe out these Chinese in a matter of a few days' time.[10] And they probably could have.

At one point a few days after he arrived, Wang Qimei became so worried by this hassling and heckling that he contacted the commander in chief of the Eighteenth Army Corps, who was en route with the main force, and asked him to quickly send an additional company (ch. lian), because there was danger of an uprising. Zhang Guohua, however, thought this was an overreaction and declined the request. In a response dated 16 September, he expressly instructed Wang to use restraint and caution, saying: "If one looks at the entire situation carefully, there is no possibility of an uprising. In particular, if we base our actions on doing things very carefully and cautiously, we will be able to settle matters. We should not use military force."[11]

In addition to courtesy visits to the Tibetan governmental elite, the new Chinese officials also made a major effort to ease the fears of Tibet's religious sector by visiting incarnate lamas and abbots and giving them assurances that they would not constrain or harm religion or monasteries. To demonstrate the sincerity of their comments, they actually gave alms to all twenty thousand monks

9. Jambey Gyatso, interview, 1993, Beijing.
10. Dangdai zhongguo congshu bianjibu 1991: 57. At this time, the Tibetan army in Lhasa still outnumbered the PLA troops.
11. Le 1985: 243–44, entry for 17 September 1951. Zhang Guohua may have known that Wang Qimei was an exceptionally suspicious person. Phünwang, the Tibetan cadre who traveled with Wang to Lhasa, spoke at length about Wang's suspicious nature (Goldstein, Sherap, and Siebenschuh 2004: 154–63).

Figure 8. PLA camped in tents near the Lhasa River. Source: Chen Zonglie

in Lhasa's three great monastic seats, as well as to all the monks at the annual Mönlam Chemmo (Great Prayer Festival) in Lhasa (in early 1952). A government official, Chabtsom, recalled what Lukhangwa had told him one day: "They are very clever in how they act, giving the monks and monasteries many dayan in alms. They are giving out dayan coins like giving gifts to children."[12]

This was shrewd and effective, since the Tibetans' fear of the Chinese was focused more on the danger to religion than on the abstract political notion of the total independence of the Tibetan government. As one monk official explicitly explained,

> The [Tibetan] people were hard-headed. What they thought was that the Chinese were going to destroy religion or that religion was going to lose its glory. They did not think much about whether the political power of the government was being taken away. They didn't quite understand political power. They thought that having come to our country, they [the Chinese] would ultimately destroy our religion and make the country completely black. So the main reason why they did not like the Chinese was from the religious perspective.[13]

The Chinese also sought to turn their rhetoric about coming to help Tibetans into something concrete by immediately starting a free medical clinic. The

12. Chabtsom, interview, 1992, Lhasa.
13. Drakten, interview, 1992, Dharamsala.

Figure 9. Zhang Jingwu giving alms to the monks in a Lhasa monastery, October 1951.
Source: Chen Zonglie

Indian Mission in Lhasa reported that it instantly became very popular. "A free medical dispensary, staffed by very courteous personnel, has been opened in Lhasa by the Chinese. In the first five days of operation, it deprived the Indian hospital of half of its patients."[14] Nevertheless, paying courtesy calls and giving monks alms could go only so far. With all of Tibet's key officials now back in Lhasa and thousands more PLA troops on the way, the maneuvering between the sitsab-led Tibetan government and the Chinese side began over how to operationalize the Seventeen-Point Agreement.

THE FIRST ITEMS OF BUSINESS

The Chinese side initially had a number of issues that they wanted to pursue—some small, some major. One of the easy ones concerned finalizing a date

14. U.S. National Archives, 793B.00/1–2552, copy of the Lhasa Mission of the Government of India's report for the month from 16 September to 15 October 1951.

and plans for a ceremony at which Zhang Jingwu would formally present the Central Committee's gifts to the Dalai Lama. Two other similar issues concerned organizing a joint celebration in Lhasa for China's second National Day (1 October 1951) and having the Tibetan government send a high-level delegation to Beijing to attend the upcoming meeting of the Chinese People's Political Consultative Conference (CPPCC),[15] including possibly the Dalai Lama.

In addition to these, there were several more substantial issues to be addressed. One was the formal affirmation of the Seventeen-Point Agreement by the Dalai Lama. A second was finalizing the arrangements for the Panchen Lama's return to Tibet. And a third was the critical issue of getting the Tibetan government to make plans to meet the food needs of the main PLA force (roughly six thousand troops), which was expected to arrive in a month.

In all this, the Chinese viewed Ngabö as their key ally in the Tibetan government and tried to handle much of their business through him, for example, by asking him informally to bring their concerns to the attention of the Kashag and by asking his advice on how to proceed on issues. He had been physically with them for a year (since his capture in Chamdo), and they considered him not only frank and progressive in his thinking but also committed to the Seventeen-Point Agreement and to the smooth incorporation of Tibet into the PRC. He helped them enormously, but as we shall see, this did not solve their problems, because the sitsab were in charge and they were not going to make anything easy for the Chinese.

Arranging the gift-giving ceremony was an immediate priority, and Le Yuhong went to discuss it with the Kashag on 23 September 1951, two weeks after the Advance Unit had arrived. He described the meeting in his diary.

> 23 September—I went to the Kashag to discuss the issue of the gift ceremony. . . . I said that from the view of politics it should show respect for the People's Government of China, and from the view of local religion it should show respect for the head of the religion. . . . They said they will discuss it tomorrow and send a reply the day after tomorrow.[16]

Two days later, the Kashag replied:

> 25 September—In the evening, Kheme and Liushar [the two liaison officers] came to me to convey several Kashag responses. Concerning the gift ceremony, they agreed that the Chinese government should be shown respect and that the Dalai Lama and Tibetan religious customs should also be shown respect.

15. The CPPCC is a united front organization that is composed of the CCP, other political parties, mass organizations, and representative public personages (old elite) from all walks of life. It held its first meeting in 1949. It is an important organ of multiparty cooperation under the leadership of the CCP.

16. Le 1985: 251–52, entry for 25 September 1951.

They then explained their ideas in detail. The Dalai Lama will be sitting on a chair in front of his throne when the ceremony begins. As soon as Zhang Jingwu enters the hall, the Dalai Lama will rise to receive the gifts. Then he will sit on his throne, and Zhang will sit to the left of the Dalai Lama on a throne higher than all the other officials [but not the Dalai Lama]. They thought it would be better if Zhang offered the Dalai Lama a ceremonial scarf (or a mendredensum) himself.[17] After the ceremony is finished, the Dalai Lama's attendants will escort Zhang to the Dalai Lama's living quarters, where they will have a discussion.

As soon as Zhang Jingwu agreed, I said that the place opposite Zhang's throne should be empty and that Zhang's throne should be higher than that of the sitsab, and that when Mao's picture is carried into the hall the Dalai Lama should clasp his palms together [in the gesture of religious respect] and should bow his head in respect. Mao's picture should be placed higher than the Dalai Lama's throne. I also asked that the Kashag ministers send us a detailed written statement of their plan for the ceremony.[18]

At the same time, the Chinese side proposed that Chinese National Day be a joint celebration of the PLA and Tibetans and that the Chinese national flag be flown that day on the Potala and the Tibetan government's military headquarters.[19] This was poorly received by the sitsab, who were adamant about not losing any of the symbolic trappings of Tibet's de facto independent status (for example, its own army and currency) and not accepting any—or as few as possible—new symbolic accoutrements of its being part of Communist China. The sitsab, therefore, instructed the Kashag, first, that the celebration should be solely a *Chinese* celebration and, second, that no Chinese flags should be flown on any Tibetan buildings. The Tibetan and Chinese versions of these discussions agree on the outcome but not in their tone. One account of this is found in Le Yuhong's diary.

> Regarding . . . the 1 October celebration—the Kashag felt it is best not to have it [joint], because they were afraid that it will precipitate trouble. Their opinion is that the PLA should hold a separate celebration to which the Kashag would send representatives [to attend]. Also, the Kashag said it would arrange for all the people of Lhasa to dress up in good clothes, play majong, drink beer, dance, and have parties [act as if it is a holiday]. They also said that the Tibetan army will do a circumambulation of the Barkor Road.
>
> I then said that the national flag must be flown on the holiday. They [the liaison officials who brought the Kashag's reply] said, "You should not do many

17. The mendredensum, a type of religious offering given to lamas, represents the body (via a statue), the speech (via a text/scripture), and the mind (via a stupa).

18. Le 1985: 254–57, entry for 25 September 1951.

19. Le 1985: 254–57, entry for 25 September 1951; Drakten, interview, 1992. The Tibetan government's military headquarters was located in the walled town of Shöl, immediately below the Potala Palace.

weird [unprecedented] acts in Tibet. If you do things slowly, things will be okay."
They also said that the Tibetan people are backward, and from long ago only
the Tibetan army has carried the Tibetan flag. They said this many times, over
and over [i.e., there was no custom of flags being flown on Tibetan government buildings]. I didn't push this but asked, "Well then, what about hoisting
the flag first on the Tibetan army's headquarters?" Kheme objected to this also,
saying we should act in accordance with what is in the agreement, and it says
there that the Tibetan army should be incorporated into the PLA only gradually. Since Zhang Jingwu had already said [to me] that whether it is hoisted
earlier or later isn't a big issue, I didn't say anything again.[20]

Zhang Jingwu's biography adds that the Chinese side also asked that Lhasa
residents put up small national flags on the National Day holiday.[21]

Eventually, a meeting was held between the Chinese leaders and the two
sitsab in Norbulingka to discuss flying the Chinese flag on National Day and
having Tibetan soldiers wear PLA uniforms. The Chinese had been irritated
by the fact that the troops and officers of the Dalai Lama's Bodyguard Regiment wore British uniforms and played British songs such as "God Save the
Queen," and the officers of the other Tibetan regiments also wore English
uniforms (although their troops wore Tibetan uniforms).[22]

Lukhangwa responded angrily to the request to fly the Chinese national
flag, saying that that this could never take place. "How can this be possible?"
he said. "It just cannot be. How can you put two flags on one house? What
kind of a custom is that? How can two people sit on one chair? This is not
possible, and it will never be possible."[23]

The depth of the sitsab's feelings about this issue can be seen by the measures they took to ensure that the Kashag did not try to go around them to
mollify the Chinese. Soon after this meeting, they summoned the Kashag
minister Dombor to their office and warned him not to make a mistake about
this: "'The Chinese want to hoist flags temporarily on the Potala and the Tibet Military Area Headquarters, but this is not at all permissible. Since you

20. Le 1985: 254, entry for 25 September 1951.

21. Zhao 1995: 38.

22. Phünwang, interview, 2000, Beijing. During the time of the 13th Dalai Lama, it was decided to make the uniforms of the Bodyguard Regiment distinctive, so the uniforms of different countries were examined and compared, and it was finally decided that British uniforms
would be used, along with British drills, commands, and songs. It was also decided that the commanders-in-chief and other commanders (tib. depön) would wear British-style officer's uniforms (Drakten, interview, 1992). This was what the Chinese found in existence in Tibet in
1951. The Bodyguard Regiment continued to wear British uniforms until the Dalai Lama returned from Beijing in 1955, when they switched to Chinese uniforms. The other Tibetan regiments, however, continued to wear Tibetan uniforms until 1959 (Takla [Phüntso Tashi], interview, 1994, London). Takla was one of the commanders of the Bodyguard Regiment.

23. Drakten, interview, 1992.

are the head [of the celebration preparations],[24] if the Chinese try to trick you by saying they have already spoken to us about this, let it be known that this is what we have said. It will not be tolerated for you to say something different later [for example, that they had misunderstood].' So this is what Dombor said when he returned [from meeting the sitsab]."[25]

In keeping with the sitsab's hard-line attitude, the Tibetan government also declined to send representatives to Beijing to attend the meeting of the Chinese People's Political Consultative Conference, which was scheduled to start on 15 October. Le Yuhong's diary comments on this.

> 24 September—In the morning, I went to meet the Kashag minister Ramba to discuss the Central Committee's inviting delegates to the . . . meeting. I told them that the Chinese People's Political Consultative Conference has great concern for Tibetans and wants to invite the Dalai Lama and delegates from the local government to attend. I explained about this in detail and said that provisions had been made for special delegates from Tibet. After they are finalized, I explained, we will make travel arrangements via India through our ambassador there.
>
> When Ramba asked what rank the delegates should come from, I replied that they should be from the rank of Kashag minister or above.[26]

The very next day the Kashag's liaison officers brought the following negative reply:

> They finally said that the Kashag had discussed the upcoming Chinese People's Political Consultative Conference in Beijing and could not send a delegation. To select officials for this required requesting names from the various ranks of the government, and since the meeting starts [soon], on 15 October, the Kashag said they do not think they can make the decisions in time. I said, "The conference will last half a month to a month, so it would be good if you could send people to arrive [at least] before the meeting adjourns. Please consider this well." They [the liaison officers] said they will tell the Kashag about this.[27]

The Tibetan government, however, held fast and did not send a delegation to Beijing.

Regarding the gift-presentation ceremony, on 25 September the Kashag sent a detailed plan for holding the ceremony, and three days later, on 28 September, the ceremony took place.[28] The team of Chinese presenting the

---

24. Kashag minister Dombor, Commander-in-Chief Kheme, and General Tashi Bera were the ones who had been sent by the government to help the PLA prepare for the celebration.

25. Drakten, interview, 1992.

26. Le 1985: 252–53, entry for 24 September 1951.

27. Le 1985: 254–55, entry for 25 September 1951.

28. The gifts included: Mao's picture, a souvenir book of the first session of the national Political Consultative Conference, a slide projector with nine sets of slides, a set of pictures of

gifts was led by a PLA army band followed by a team of waist-drummers. Thousands of people stood on either side of the street watching this procession. The ceremony itself went well; Ngabö later reported to the Chinese that the respect shown to the Dalai Lama and Tibetan customs made a positive impression on Tibetan officials.[29] However, in point of fact, the Chinese had to settle for only part of what they had wanted, because the Dalai Lama did not clasp his hands together or bow in respect to the picture of Mao.

Zhang Jingwu's biography indicates that after the formal gift-giving ceremony, the Dalai Lama invited Zhang into his private apartment and that Zhang took that occasion to raise an issue the Chinese were extremely concerned about: the Dalai Lama's acceptance of the Seventeen-Point Agreement. Zhang Jingwu said,

> The second anniversary of the People's Republic of China is coming soon. It will be a very precious day. On that day there will be a spectacular naval, land, and air force show. The agreement was signed months ago, and I have been here for over one month. I hope the Dalai Lama will send a telegram to the Central Committee before the National Day [1 October] and explain your opinions about the agreement.[30]

As we shall see, that also did not happen.

The Chinese National Day celebration (on 1 October) occurred and was described glowingly by the Chinese.

> In the very early morning, Zhang Jingwu and the others were separately gathered around the radios, listening to the ceremony of inspecting the troops in Tiananmen Square in the capital and to the orders of Commander-in-Chief Zhu De. Zhang Jingwu solemnly sat upright and looked straight ahead. His thoughts surged emotionally. He was listening respectfully to the radio broadcast and thinking about the immediately coming celebration on the Tibetan plateau.
>
> Because of the time difference, it was one hour and a half earlier in Beijing than in Lhasa, so 8:30 A.M. in Beijing was 7:00 A.M. in Lhasa. At that time, many residents in Lhasa were listening to the voices from the capital of the motherland. Many groups of men and women dressed in rich attire began to throng to the square in front of the Potala Palace. Some noble women also held the colorful umbrellas and went up to the square.
>
> At the meeting spot [where they were camped alongside the Kyichu River], a five-star red flag was flying in the wind. Under the sunshine, the flag and the

China, many carved ivory objects, many green jade and porcelain containers, embroidery, silk brocades, a pair of cloisonné vases, and other valuable gifts. In the end the Tibetan government seated Zhang on the same level as the sitsab (Zhao 1995: 45).

29. Zhonggong xizang zizhiqu dangshi ziliao zhengji weiyuanhui 1995, entry for 28 September 1951.

30. Zhao 1995: 45.

golden top of Potala [in the distance] were reflecting each other brilliantly. It was a magnificent scene. Four huge slogans in both Chinese and Tibetan were hung around the meeting spot. They said, "Implement absolutely the Seventeen-Point Agreement for the Peaceful Liberation of Tibet," "Build up Tibet and reinforce the national defense," "All Tibetans should be unified and determinedly drive the imperialist invasion forces out of Tibet," and "Long live Chairman Mao, the greatest leader of all the nationalities of China." Soon, five thousand or six thousand monks and laymen thronged to the meeting to join the PLA troops and cadres who were in Tibet. So this became a grand celebration meeting of thousands of people from all groups, including both the military and the civil branches in Lhasa.

At 11:00 A.M., the president of the gathering stated that the meeting had started. Then the Central Committee's representative, Zhang Jingwu, stepped to the podium and the microphone and in high spirits immediately disseminated his powerful voice to Lhasa and the plateau.

Zhang Jingwu first stated, "We are here in Lhasa to celebrate the second anniversary of the founding of the People's Republic of China. Today is historically significant and is a good start for the unity and equality of nationalities in Tibet." He said this was a significant celebratory meeting accomplished by the Tibetan people, who overcame all kinds of obstacles and have come back to the great family of the motherland. Then Zhang reported all the accomplishments of the mother country in the past year regarding all kinds of construction projects and its support of Korea against America. Finally, he reiterated the nationality policy of the Central Committee and the spirit of the Agreement of Peaceful Liberation on Tibet. He called on all the PLA troops and cadres and the Tibetan monks and laymen to unify closely and strive to build up Tibet.

The representative of the Tibetan local government, Rimshi [fourth-rank official] Tsesum Phunkhang also gave a speech. He said, "It is very good that Tibetan monks and laymen can join this meeting with the PLA today." He praised the Agreement of Peaceful Liberation of Tibet for completely ironing out the differences between Tibetans and Chinese that had been created by reactionary rulers in history. Even though his speech was not sincere, it was really good that he could give such a speech at this meeting.

Wang Qimei, the commander of the advance troop, stressed that the PLA entering Tibet was a troop for the Tibetan people and would serve the Tibetan people loyally forever. They would respect the customs of the Tibetan people, protect religious freedom, and were determined to drive the imperialist invasion force out of Tibet and reinforce the national defense. . . .

At 3:00 P.M. in the afternoon, Zhang Jingwu presided over the National Festival banquet in the Tsidrunglingka Park. He invited the Kashag ministers and Tibetan local government officials above the third rank, as well as famous incarnate lamas and great abbots to this, and over sixty people gathered together. Zhang Jingwu went to their tables to toast them and celebrate the festival. Before the banquet, there was a photographic exhibit in which pictures of the negotiations [in Beijing] and the picture of Chairman Mao toasting with the Panchen and Ngabö to celebrate the agreement were displayed.

> During the whole afternoon, thousands of Tibetan people brought butter, tea, and food to the park's lawns around the meeting spot. They set up tents and rugs and had picnics there, dancing and singing until the late evening. Under the sunset, the five-star red flag was still flying overhead.[31]

The day went well, to be sure, but not quite as well as the Chinese had hoped for. The sitsab once again did not yield to their urgings and, as mentioned above, forced the Chinese to accept this as a *Chinese* celebration that the Tibetan government attended rather than a joint celebration of the PLA and the local government of Tibet. Symbolically, they were still unwilling to act as if China was also their nation.

The sitsab and others were pleased with their ability to thwart Chinese initiatives and to ignore requests, but they had no understanding that the reason for their successes was Mao's gradualist policy. No matter how angry and frustrated Zhang Jingwu and the other leaders were over the sitsab's attitude and actions, they were not free to secure their ends by threatening Tibetans. As we shall see, occasionally they would lose their temper at a meeting and yell and scream at the sitsab, but they could not take the next obvious step and secure their ends by force. Thus, at this period in time, the gradualist policy was inadvertently emboldening the sitsab, who found they could insult and obstruct the Chinese with no negative consequences—at least immediately.

Chinese "deference" to the Tibetan government's wishes, however, did not carry over to the formal acceptance by the Dalai Lama of the Seventeen-Point Agreement. The Chinese side was angry and embarrassed that months had passed since the signing of the agreement without an acceptance statement from the Dalai Lama or the Tibetan government. On this issue, there was no room for compromise.

Ngabö played a pivotal role in settling this. As indicated earlier, Ngabö considered the agreement good for Tibet (given the military and international realities). The other Kashag ministers knew this made sense but were not eager to take the lead personally, since the sitsab were opposed to affirming the agreement as it then stood. Ngabö, however, was being pressed by the Chinese to get the Tibetan government to act and was frustrated by the delays and the procrastination on the Tibetan side. He believed that the Seventeen-Point Agreement gave Tibet a powerful legal framework in which to maneuver within the People's Republic of China, so it should be quickly accepted. Eventually the National Assembly was convened to discuss the issue. Lhalu, a Kashag minister, recalled how this came about.

> The Kashag ministers didn't say anything special about the Seventeen-Point Agreement, as they were clever. And (Sitsab) Lobsang Tashi also said nothing.

---

31. Zhao 1995: 39–40.

Lukhangwa didn't quite say he opposed it, but he didn't say anything definite [such as he accepts it]. He kind of implied that [Ngabö's] not sending telegrams [from Beijing] to the sitsab was bad and was a mistake. . . .

Basically, everybody kept quiet and did not say yes or no. Ngabö said that we have to accept the agreement, but the [other] Kashag ministers said if we accept it will not be good, so it was decided that it was best to call an Assembly meeting to discuss this issue. Consequently, the Kashag sent a report to the sitsab, saying we have to indicate our attitude [to the Chinese] about the agreement, so our recommendation is to call an Assembly meeting to discuss this.[32]

For two days during the last week of September, a large Abbreviated Assembly was convened in the Shabden lhagang room in Norbulingka. It was attended by about sixty representatives selected from each of the different ranks in the government, as well as monastic representatives (abbots and ex-abbots).[33]

Ngabö was worried about what would occur at this gathering and thought it would be best if he and the others who had gone to Beijing came in person and explained what had happened and why it was essential for Tibet to affirm this publicly.[34] Chabtsom recalled this meeting.

At this time in Lhasa there were many rumors regarding Ngabö, the most serious of which was that the Chinese had bribed him to sign the agreement. Ngabö therefore broke with the Tibetan custom that Kashag ministers should not attend Assembly meetings, and on this occasion he and the other four negotiators attended the Assembly's meeting [to explain their actions].

Ngabö spoke for a long time. [He said,] "When I was captured I thought my life was in danger, but leave alone my life being in danger, the Chinese didn't even say any harsh words to me. The same held true for the officials with me." . . .

He started with a historical discussion, saying that in the past there was a close historical relationship between Tibet and China, but this was broken during the 13th Dalai Lama's time. He emphasized that he had wanted to avoid the *military* liberation of Tibet, so negotiated the Seventeen-Point Agreement and thus achieved *peaceful* liberation. Then he explained each of the seventeen points in the agreement.

He said that the most important thing for Tibet now is to be able to continue Tibet's joint religious and secular government (tib. chösi nyiden). For this, the Dalai Lama has to be the head of the political system, and it is also imperative that Tibet maintain its own customs and not adopt Chinese ones. And the most important of the important aspects is that religion not be changed. All of these necessary things, he said, are guaranteed in the Seventeen-Point Agreement. If we put this agreement into practice, Tibet's economy and po-

32. Lhalu, interview, 1993, Lhasa. Nga phod (Ngabö) (1989), however, says that it was the sitsab who said the Assembly had to be convened to discuss whether this should be done.

33. Le 1985: 259–62, entry for 28 September 1951.

34. Nga phod (Ngabö) 1989.

litical system will be guaranteed to continue. The feudal system will change little by little but not the position of Dalai Lama. We feudal lords will lose our serfs, but our livelihood will increase, not decrease. . . . [35]

After this, Kheme spoke, and then Lhautara, each making similar comments. The other two more junior negotiators, Sambo and Thubden Lengmön, did not speak.[36]

The Assembly then broke out into small groups to discuss the agreement. After each of these reported back to the assembly, a final report was written that thanked the negotiators for their work in negotiating the Seventeen-Point Agreement and basically said that the agreement was acceptable. It particularly mentioned that points 4, 7, and 12 in the agreement were good. But it also mentioned they [the Assembly members] did not like some issues, chief among which was the presence in Tibet of a large number of Chinese soldiers. The Assembly's report said that it would be better if many Chinese soldiers do not come and that the soldiers who do come be kept in border areas rather than in Lhasa. For example, it suggested that those soldiers going to Yadong should go straight to the border via the south road without passing through Lhasa.

A second (problem) issue it commented on concerned the authority of the Military-Administrative Committee. The Assembly said that since this is the office of the representative of the Central Committee [i.e., a Chinese government office], it should enforce strict discipline over the Chinese soldiers. Similarly, implementing development in Tibet and the issue of the defense of the international border should be done in ways that are compatible with Tibetan customs (e.g., with regard to not starting mining in Tibet). And it said that if the Chinese do things that are not in accordance with the agreement, the Tibetan government should be allowed to interfere.

A third worry the Assembly expressed was that while it is okay to improve the livelihood of the people and to develop education quickly, this should be done carefully so that there are no [negative] effects, for example, causing the number of monks to decline [as a result of the opportunity to go to school].[37]

A Tibetan attending this meeting summed up the elite's feelings well, "The sixty or so delegates to the Assembly pretty much didn't like the agreement in their hearts, but at the meeting no one opposed it."[38] The head of India's Lhasa mission also commented on this in his monthly report to Delhi, adding important elements not mentioned by Lhalu.

[Ngabö] stated that he received verbal assurances that the Chinese would not interfere in the internal affairs of Tibet. Their Military-Administrative office

---

35. Ngabö believed the statement about estates and serfs, but it seems unlikely that he would have raised such a sensitive issue in his Assembly comments, since implementing reforms was not an issue then.

36. Chabtsom, interview, 1992 (emphasis added).

37. Lhalu, interview, 1993.

38. Chabtsom, interview, 1992.

in Lhasa would exercise control over the Chinese troops and supervise Chinese interests. After hearing Ngabö, the Tibetan authorities decided not to ask the Chinese that the talks be reopened, but instead to request official assurances that the Chinese Communists' understanding of what was agreed upon corresponded to Ngabö's statement. If the Chinese reply was satisfactory the Tibetans would notify the Chinese of their acceptance of the Peiping agreement.[39]

The report on the Assembly meeting contained in Le Yuhong's diary closely parallels that made by Lhalu.

1. The 4th, 7th, and 12th points [in the agreement] were very good.

2. It is better if many soldiers do not come, and all the soldiers (our PLA) who come should not be kept in Lhasa. For example, those soldiers going to Yadong shouldn't come through Lhasa but should go straight via the south road.

3. When implementing the agreement, if there are issues that are unacceptable, they can be taken out [not implemented] [this referred to the military].

4. As for the authority/responsibility of the Military-Administrative Committee, it should enforce strict discipline over Chinese soldiers and not let them violate policies. It should also be involved with development in Tibet. National defense and development should be done in a manner that is compatible with Tibetan customs (for example, mining). If there are violations of the agreement, the Tibetan government can interfere when it implements the agreement.

5. Some supporters of Lhalu said that the reason for Chamdo being liberated is that some superiors [Ngabö] did not carry out their responsibility and were careless and that some Tibetan generals had wanted to fight but Ngabö surrendered. (At this time Ngabö immediately replied that a committee should be started to investigate this charge.) Another person said this should be decided well (whether or not Ngabö is to blame).

6. Education should be implemented as soon as possible, but starting schools should be done carefully so that there are no negative effects (i.e., so that the number of monks doesn't decline).

7. We should send a telegram saying we agree to the agreement in time for the 1 October holiday.

8. The delegates who went to Beijing worked hard, and we say thanks.[40]

---

39. British Foreign Office Records, FO371/92998, Monthly Report of the Lhasa Mission of the Government of India, from 16 September to 15 October 1951.

40. Le 1985: 259–62, entry for 28 September 1951. He said that Ngabö came and told him about the results of the Assembly meeting.

This acceptance by the National Assembly, however, did not result in a speedy public affirmation of the agreement, but it did get the Tibetan government moving. On 30 September, the Kashag gave the Chinese a draft telegram regarding the agreement, which said the sitsab had approved. The Chinese made some changes and returned it the same evening. Then, for almost a week, there was no further word from the Kashag. Chinese National Day (1 October) came and went with no comment.

On 5 October, Zhang Jingwu went to Ngabö's house and discussed the agreement issue with him for two hours, learning for the first time that the Tibetan government had decided not to send an acceptance telegram until Zhang answered some questions in writing. Ngabö explained to Zhang that when the sitsab looked at the Kashag's draft telegram, they wanted the Chinese to clarify three issues. The first concerned the responsibility and power of the Military-Administrative Committee (vis-à-vis the Dalai Lama). The second concerned limiting the number of PLA troops coming to Tibet. And the third concerned the return of administrative control of Chamdo to the Tibet government. Ngabö told Zhang that these were the opinion of the National Assembly and had been approved by the Dalai Lama.[41] The Chinese side did not want mention of troop numbers in the formal acceptance telegram and suggested placing it in a separate telegram. Two days later, on 7 October, Kashag minister Shasur informed the Chinese that the Kashag had agreed to this.[42]

However, the sitsab still did not approve the final acceptance telegram, and on 10 October, Lhalu came to ask the Chinese how many PLA soldiers were coming. When Zhang Jingwu replied between twelve thousand and eighteen thousand, the Chinese reported that Lhalu was glad to learn this and said he thought the other ministers would also be pleased. Lhalu, the Chinese said, asked again and again about the Military-Administrative Committee. Zhang Jingwu answered all his questions. After that, the Chinese asked the Tibetan government to arrange for supplies in grain and firewood and for additional quarters as early as possible.[43]

The next day, the Kashag gave Zhang Jingwu a letter in Chinese, which again stated that before a telegram could be sent, Zhang should reply to three questions, but now a new question had been added:

(1) What are the responsibilities and power of the Military-Administrative Committee and the command post (tib. gagö bu) of the (Chinese) military headquarters?

41. Le 1985: 271, entry for 5 October 1951. Zhang Jingwu's biography, however, did not mention anything about Chamdo (Zhao 1995: 45).

42. Le 1985: 275, entry for 7 October 1951.

43. Le 1985: 277, entry for 10 October 1951.

(2) What about Tibetan unity after Tibet develops its politics, economy, cul-
     ture, and so forth; that is, what about returning control over Chamdo?

(3) What about the return to Tibet of the ethnic Tibetan areas east of the Up-
     per Yangtse River (Xikang Province)?[44]

The third point appears to have been a completely new issue.

On 14 October, Zhang Jingwu, Le Yuhong, and Phünwang went to meet
with the Kashag to answer its questions and discuss related issues concerning the agreement and the number of PLA troops that would be stationed
in Tibet. Zhang Jingwu's biography says he told them about twenty thousand
troops would be involved and that they would stay to do border defense at
places such as Gyantse, Shigatse, Ngari (ch. Ali), and Kongpo. He said only
about five thousand personnel would be stationed in Lhasa.[45] The Chinese
side also proposed that a joint office be established with the Tibetan government to oversee the purchase of grains and that the army set up a bank.[46]
Zhang also commented on the Military-Administrative Committee and the
Tibet Military Area Headquarters, saying, "The Military-Administrative Committee is the office of the representative of the Central Committee. The Tibetan Military Area Headquarters is an office solely for military affairs. It will
be in contact with the Tibetan local government frequently. The Military-
Administrative Committee will *manage/administer* (ch. guan li; tib. dagnyer)
both the Tibetan local government and the PLA. Our plan is to appoint the
Dalai Lama as the chairman of the Military-Administrative Committee and
the Panchen Lama and Zhang Guohua as its vice-chairmen."[47]

The Kashag ministers asked Zhang many specific and pointed questions,
and there was a lively discussion. For example, they asked what the Dalai
Lama's authority and responsibilities would be as the chairman of the Military-Administrative Committee. They also asked how the committee would
be convened, how the Dalai Lama's seat would be set up, and whether the
committee would settle issues in accordance with Tibetan traditional customs,
that is, whether each issue would be submitted through the Kashag to the
sitsab to the Dalai Lama for final approval. They also asked whether the Dalai
Lama would be able to send a representative to participate on his behalf in
the Military-Administrative Committee. Some on the Tibetan side also said

44. Le 1985: 279, entry for 11 October 1985.

45. Zhao 1995: 46. There are two accounts of this meeting, both from the diary of Le
Yuhong, one in Chinese and one in Tibetan. The material in Zhang Jingwu's biography cited
in this footnote is based on the Chinese-language version, which contains a few additional items
not mentioned in the Tibetan version, but otherwise the two accounts are the same.

46. Le 1985: 280–81, entry for 14 October.

47. Zhao 1995: 46 (emphasis added).

that the Dalai Lama was not ready to be chairman of the Military-Administrative Committee, since he was yet to take his Geshe degree (the advanced monastic degree). He was, they said, like a flower that had bloomed, but the fruit was still to ripen, so we should wait for that. A disagreement also arose about whether the acceptance telegram to Mao had to include the statement "The Tibetan people shall unite and drive out imperialist aggressor forces from Tibet." Some Kashag ministers thought this sentence was offensive and should not be included in the telegram. After quite a long discussion, the meeting ended with no agreement.[48]

On 18 and 19 October, while Zhang Jingwu went to Sera and Drepung monasteries and gave alms to each of the monks,[49] the acceptance telegram issue continued. On 18 October, Ngabö visited the Chinese side and said that he had discussed mentioning "expelling imperialists" with all the Kashag ministers as well as another issue involving the Tibetan government sending an edict to all counties (tib. dzong) in Tibet about adhering to the agreement, but then he gave them the bad news: the Tibetan ninth (lunar) month, which was about to start, was an astrologically inauspicious month (tib. danag), and it was considered bad to do things during that time, so the acceptance telegram would have to wait until the Tibetan tenth month.

Ngabö also had unfavorable news about the Chinese side's suggestion to create a joint Tibetan-Chinese grain purchasing office. The Kashag, he said, felt that it would be better to let them, the Kashag, handle this.[50] Three days later, when the main Eighteenth Army Corps force was less than a week away from Lhasa, Le Yuhong went to meet with the Kashag ministers and urged them to make a plan to purchase grain. He also informed them that the Chinese would like to give additional alms to monastic "scholar monks" (tib. pechawa)[51] as well as to Lhasa's beggars and the students in Tibet's monastic medical school. And he once again asked about the status of the acceptance telegram. Interestingly, the Kashag seemingly took a step backward and said that only after Zhang Jingwu responded in writing to the Kashag's previous three questions would the ministers discuss this issue.[52]

It is not clear whether Zhang ever gave the Tibetan government any written response, but on the 22 October, notwithstanding the date falling in an "inauspicious" month, Ngabö came to the Chinese and said the Tibetan gov-

---

48. Le 1985: 280–81, entry for 14 October; Le 1991: 14–32.

49. He gave twenty ngüsang to each common monk and, in accordance with tradition, more to the monk officeholders. This was a very generous amount.

50. Le 1985: 285–86, entry for 18 October 1951.

51. These were the monks who were actively engaged in studying Buddhism and thus generally were poor, since they were not engaged in income-generating activities.

52. Le 1985: 289, entry for 21 October 1951.

ernment had finally agreed to send the telegram on 24 October.[53] Consequently, five months after the agreement had been signed in Beijing, the formal acceptance Beijing wanted, including the controversial phrase about driving out the imperialists, was sent by telegram in the Dalai Lama's name.[54] Despite all the initial talk of renegotiating parts of the agreement, Tibet had developed no clear strategy or policy and held no formal discussions with the Chinese about this.

This telegram from the Dalai Lama formally validated the agreement and finalized Tibetan acceptance of China's sovereignty over Tibet.

> Chairman Mao Zedung. At the end of April 1951 there arrived in Peking a special delegate, Kashag Minister Ngabö and four other plenipotentiary representatives sent by the local Tibet government. They held peaceful negotiations with the plenipotentiary delegates appointed by the Central People's Government. The representatives of both sides, on May 23, 1951, signed on a friendly basis an agreement relating to the measures for the peaceful liberation of Tibet. The local government of Tibet, the monks, and the entire Tibetan people express their unanimous support for this agreement. Under the leadership of Chairman Mao Zedung and the Central People's Government they are actively helping units of the People's Liberation Army which entered Tibet for strengthening the national defenses, driving out of imperialist forces from Tibet and guaranteeing of sovereignty of the entire territory of the motherland.[55]

On the same day, Zhang Jingwu gave alms to the beggars of Lhasa, and the troops of the main Eighteenth Army Corps reached the banks of the Kyichu River in Lhasa.[56]

While these major events were transpiring in Lhasa, the United States made yet another attempt to induce the Dalai Lama to renounce the agreement and flee into exile.

ANOTHER AMERICAN INITIATIVE

Despite the news in late July that the Dalai Lama had left for Lhasa, the U.S. Embassy in Delhi still felt there was a chance to persuade him to reverse his decision. Basing their evaluation on the misleading comments of sources such as Taktse Rimpoche, Shakabpa, Heinrich Harrer, and George Patterson, the embassy officials came to the conclusion that the failure of their

---

53. Le 1985: 290–92, entry for 22 October 1951.
54. The Panchen Lama had responded to Mao almost immediately (on 28 May and 1 June 1951), expressing the importance of respecting the agreement (Zhonggong xizang zizhiqu dangshi ziliao zhengji weiyuanhui 1990).
55. British Foreign Office Records, FO371/92998.
56. Le 1985: 292, entry for 24 October 1951.

Figure 10. Chinese and Tibetan government officials at a banquet celebrating the "peaceful liberation" of Tibet. Left to right, front row: Ngabö, Langdün, Zhang Guohua, Ramba, Lhalu, Ragasha; middle row: unknown, Shasur, unknown, Jigyab Khembo Ngawang Namgyal, Taktra Dzasa, Dombor, Kheme Dzasa, Horsur Dzasa, unknown; top row: unknown, Kapshöba, Sambo, Dzasa Gyethakpa, Liushar, Lobsang Samden, Tsarong, unknown. Source: Chen Zonglie

previous attempts had been primarily a result of "unreliable intermediaries."[57] The State Department agreed that it had made a mistake in trying to send messages only to the Dalai Lama, ignoring the other influential officials, such as the Kashag ministers, who, they suspected, were unaware of the United States' offers.[58] The United States, therefore, took a number of additional steps in early August 1951, when the Dalai Lama was on his way to Lhasa.

On 4 August, Secretary of State Dean Acheson approved the following verbal message for transmittal to the Tibetans:

US Govt understands and sympathizes with reasons and circumstances which might lead to ur [your] remaining Tibet at this time. However, US Govt de-

57. U.S. Department of State 1983: 1769, 793B.00/8–151, telegram no. 295, from the U.S. secretary of state to the U.S. Embassy in India, dated 4 August 1951.
58. U.S. National Archives, 793B.00/8–1351, telegram no. 114, from the U.S. consul general in Calcutta to the U.S. secretary of state, dated 13 August 1951.

sires repeat its belief that you can best serve ur people and country by evading Communist control at earliest opportunity and by denouncing agreement with Communist China after you will have reached safe asylum. Taktser is well and safe in US and hopes that you will consider favorably US Govt pledge of assistance previously made you and [a] limited entourage in asylum.[59]

Two days later, the U.S. Embassy in Delhi asked permission to translate this into Tibetan for transmission to Yadong by courier, albeit with all references to the United States removed. The embassy also suggested that the phrase "in India or Ceylon" be added to the end of the message. On 9 August, Washington agreed.[60]

The United States' unwillingness to state anything officially in writing, however, created doubts among Tibetans about America's sincerity and greatly weakened the impact of the U.S. offers. Even before this new letter, this issue had already arisen in late July, when an unsigned message was delivered by the Sikkimese princess Coocoola to her uncle, the Kashag minister Ragasha. Coocoola informed the United States that Ragasha had expressed "incredulity as he could not believe if US willing assist, US unwilling make formal pledge. He told [name redacted] unsigned message would not convince Kashag if, as he believes, opportunity should arise in Lhasa to make effective use US offer assistance in bringing about DL's departure."[61] Ragasha also said that it did not matter exactly who signed the letter, so long as it was signed and was a formal statement on U.S. government letterhead. However, he also indicated that "the Dalai Lama might still come to India but that he [Ragasha] could not convince the Cabinet [Kashag] that the United States was really interested without a signed letter."[62]

In mid-August, the very week that the Dalai Lama arrived in Lhasa, Wilson, the U.S. consul general in Calcutta, urged the State Department in Washington to approve a formal statement quickly, because the final negotiations regarding the Seventeen-Point Agreement would begin shortly in Lhasa. He told Washington that the Dalai Lama *still desired to go to India*

59. U.S. National Archives, 793B.00/8–15, telegram no. 295, from the U.S. secretary of state to the Embassy in Washington, D.C., dated 4 August 1951.

60. U.S. National Archives, 793B.00/8–1351, telegram no. 114, from the U.S. consul general in Calcutta to the U.S. secretary of state, dated 13 August 1951.

61. Ibid. Another Tibetan who carried a message to the Dalai Lama in Yadong in July (who apparently was Takla [Phūntso Tashi]) later told E. M. Wilson in Calcutta in mid-August that the Dalai Lama had commented that the message was unsigned (U.S. National Archives, 793B.00/8–1851, enclosure to dispatch 68, from the U.S. consul general in Calcutta to the U.S. secretary of state, dated 18 August 1951).

62. Cited in U.S. National Archives, 793B.00/11–157, 15, "U.S. policy concerning the legal status of Tibet 1942–1956."

and that Tibet might still disavow the agreement. Therefore, he said, "in such circumstances, [a] formal statement of our attitude might be [the] deciding factor."[63]

However, at this time, Loy Henderson, the activist ambassador, was not in India, and Horace Holmes, the embassy's chief agricultural officer, was temporarily acting in his place. Holmes was much less of a "Cold War warrior" and opposed sending a signed letter. In a long cable to Washington, he crafted a cogent argument opposing Wilson's advice.

> *Ref Contel 114, rptd New Delhi 110, August 13 from Calcutta,*
> Emb appreciated opportunity which exists in possible transmittal letter on US letterhead signed by American official to Tib Defense Min . . . for purpose persuading Tib officials to disavow Sino-Tib agreement and to advise Dalai Lama to leave Tibet.
>
> Emb believes, however, risks involved in transmittal proposed letter are far greater than advantages which may result for US and Tibet. If such a document fell into Commie Chi hands, it might be used as evidence US endeavor imperialistically to interfere in internal affairs of Tibet and to disrupt ostensibly friendly relations between China and Tibet. It might even be possible, if Tibs were hard pressed in further negots with Commie Chi, that Tibs might use such document to reinforce their position.
>
> Emb questions, in any event, whether additional communication from US, even on US letterhead and signed by Amer official, would increase Tibet knowledge and belief in US position. As Dept and ConGen aware, all previous msgs re US position were transmitted to DL through two and in some cases three channels of communications. These channels included Shakabpa, Taktse and Harrer.
>
> Important Tib officials surrounding DL were probably informed substance these msgs in transmission to DL by DL for receipt. Harrer has informed Emb DL sent him two ltrs in which DL acknowledged receipt all US communications and indicated he would have preferred to leave Tibet but decided return Lhasa in accordance with "wishes and opinion of the majority of Tibet."
>
> On balance, therefore, Emb believes DL and Tib officials are well informed re US position and that the proposed letter to Tib Defense Min would not sufficiently add to such knowledge to justify risks involved. Furthermore, Dept msg quoted in Deptel 295, Aug 4 as amended in Embtel 507, Aug 6, which [name redacted] will carry to Lhasa when he leaves Calcutta . . . should provide further evidence to DL and Tib officials of continuing US interest.
>
> At later stage, when some definite indication of developments at Lhasa is recd, Emb envisages that a further message of encouragement might be sent. In such message Emb believes it might be helpful to suggest that DL send personal rep in whom he and Tib officials had confidence to India for informal

---

63. U.S. Department of State 1983: 1776–78, 793B.00/8–1351, telegram 114, from the U.S. consul general in Calcutta to the U.S. secretary of state, dated 13 August 1951.

discussion with Amer officials. Such rep would be able return Tib and make report which would confirm substance US position and wld be more likely serve as basis for such further actions as DL prepared to take. In addition, Taktse might write DL at that time observing that Taktse's own ltrs may not be reaching him and recommending rep be sent India for informal discussion with Amer officials re possible future courses of action.

Suggestions advanced in foregoing para are based on belief Tibs in Lhasa will continue to "stall" in their negots with Commie Chi and have merit of avoiding dispatch official US documents to Tibet where they may reach unfriendly hands.

Holmes[64]

The State Department concurred. Not only were its officials worried that a signed letter might fall into Chinese hands, but also they admitted internally that "to be of use to the Kashag, U.S. Govt wld have appear commit itself to courses of action such as financial and arms aid, which it is not in position explicitly to do."[65]

Nevertheless, given what it was hearing from its sources in India, the United States still sought to persuade the Dalai Lama to flee Tibet. On 15 August, Wilson prepared another *unsigned* letter on untraceable paper with the message approved by Acheson on 4 August (cited above). It was sent to the Dalai Lama through an unnamed English-speaking Tibetan who was going to Lhasa and who promised to hand it directly to the Dalai Lama.[66]

A little less than a month later, on 10 September, the day after the Advance Unit of Wang Qimei arrived in Lhasa, the issue of a signed U.S. letter again surfaced when Heinrich Harrer told Wilson in Calcutta that Yuthok Dzasa, a high Tibetan official, was anxious to return to Lhasa to persuade the Tibetan government that the Dalai Lama should leave Tibet. Yuthok believed, he said, that in presenting arguments to the Kashag and important lay aristocratic officials, he must be able to swear he had seen a signed letter from the U.S. government promising aid.[67] Harrer suggested that the Americans prepare such a letter and show this to Yuthok but not give him a

64. U.S. Department of State 1983: 1786–87, 793B.00/8–14511, telegram no. 613, from the U.S. chargé d'affaires in India to the U.S. secretary of state, dated 14 August 1951 (emphasis added).

65. U.S. Department of State 1983: 1790, 793B.00/8–1351, telegram no. 81, from the acting secretary of state to the U.S. consul general in Calcutta, dated 15 August 1951.

66. U.S. Department of State 1983: 1791, 793B.00/8–1651, telegram no. 121, from the U.S. consul general in Calcutta to the U.S. secretary of state, dated 16 August 1951.

67. Yuthok was a well thought of and influential official who had been the governor of Chamdo before Lhalu. Not only was his wife from the Surkhang family and Surkhang's wife from his family, but also his son Rinzin was married to Coola, one of the two princesses of Sikkim. He was thus someone whose comments would be taken seriously.

copy. Harrer played on U.S. hopes by exaggerating what they wanted to hear, namely, that the Dalai Lama was still *extremely* eager to leave Tibet but lacked sufficient support among his lay officials to overcome the continuing opposition from the monks (and monk officials). Although the Chinese armies were closing in on Lhasa, Harrer estimated that they would not arrive for two months. Therefore, Yuthok could make a significant impact if he were able to take an oath that the United States had made such an offer.[68] Ambassador Henderson, back at station in New Delhi, supported the plan and requested permission from the State Department to implement it.[69]

Secretary of State Acheson approved this venture on 14 September, provided that the letter never leave the possession of U.S. officials and that the Tibetans see it only in the presence of U.S. officials. Acheson suggested that a letter similar to the earlier letters sent to the Dalai Lama would be suitable, with one important exception—*the section dealing with aid to resistance groups must be limited to only a general statement that aid would be furnished as was feasible under existing political and physical conditions.* In other words, there would be little if anything. The final text and implementation were left to the discretion of Henderson, who composed a very strong letter, although again it offered support only for Tibetan autonomy, not independence.[70]

A few weeks later, on the evening of 30 September, a top secret meeting took place at the Calcutta Consulate. Present were the CIA station chief Linn, Yuthok, and Harrer (translating for Yuthok). Yuthok was shown a letter addressed to the Dalai Lama that had been signed by Ambassador Henderson. He studied it thoroughly and took notes on it in Tibetan. After he was finished, the letter was replaced in the consulate's safe. The letter said,

AMERICAN EMBASSY New Delhi, September 17th, 1951

Your Holiness:

The Government of the United States has observed with deep sympathy your efforts over a long period to prevent Chinese Communist aggression from destroying the *autonomy* of Tibet. My Government also fully understands that Your Holiness has hoped that by remaining in Tibet you might be able to be of some service in protecting the Tibetan people from subjugation. It is convinced, how-

---

68. U.S. National Archives, 793B.00/9–1051, telegram from the U.S. consul general in Calcutta to the U.S. secretary of state, dated 10 September 1951; and U.S. National Archives, 793B.00/9–1251, report of conversation with Harrer in an enclosure to dispatch no. 117, from the U.S. consul general in Calcutta to the U.S. secretary of state, dated 12 September 1951.

69. U.S. Department of State 1983: 1803–4, 793B.00/9–1251, telegram from the U.S. ambassador in India to the U.S. secretary of state, dated 12 September 1951.

70. U.S. Department of State 1983: 1807–8, 793B.00/9–1251, telegram no. 128, from the U.S. secretary of state to the U.S. consul general in Calcutta, dated 14 September 1951; U.S. Department of State 1983: 1815–16, 793B.00/10–151, telegram no. 185, from the U.S. consul general in Calcutta to the U.S. secretary of state, dated 1 October 1951.

ever, that if you remain in Tibet you will either be [redacted] or compelled to become a servant of the Communists. It believes that if you remain in Tibet you will not be able to be of aid to your people.

It is the opinion of the United States Government that if you could arrange to leave Tibet and to seek asylum in some country such as Ceylon, you might be able to continue your struggle to preserve the *autonomy* of Tibet and the liberty of the Tibetan people. Since my Government believes that Tibet should not be compelled under duress to accept the violation of its *autonomy*, it wishes to do all that is possible and proper to prevent this violation from taking place. If, therefore, Your Holiness would like to seek asylum in Ceylon, or in some other country, my Government would be prepared, in case you should desire, to endeavor to assist you in making arrangements for such an asylum and for obtaining permission to pass through various countries in transit. *Furthermore, my Government would be prepared to arrange for the payment of the travel expenses of Your Holiness and for those of your family and retinue. It would also be prepared, so long as mutually satisfactory purposes are being served, and to the extent required, to enter into arrangements which would provide for appropriate financial support for Your Holiness, your family, and a retinue of approximately one hundred persons.*

My Government ventures to express the hope that in case you decide to leave Tibet, Your Holiness gives consideration to the factors of political effectiveness and influence in selecting persons to accompany you. My Government is also prepared to make arrangements that you and some of your retinue may find asylum in the United States in case it should seem impracticable to take refuge elsewhere.

It is the belief of my Government that resistance to Communist encroachment in Tibet must be regarded as a long range problem, the solution of which is necessarily limited by political and physical conditions in Tibet and in adjoining areas. The United States has, of course, no control over such conditions, but it is prepared to support resistance now and in the future against Communist aggression in Tibet, and to provide such material aid as may be feasible.

Your Holiness will understand, of course, that the readiness of the United States to render you the assistance and support outlined above *is conditional upon your departure from Tibet, upon your public disavowal of agreements concluded under duress between the representatives of Tibet and those of the Chinese Communists, and upon your continued willingness to cooperate in opposing Communist aggression.*

An essential part of our cooperation would be *a public announcement by the United States that it supports the position of Your Holiness as the head of an autonomous Tibet. The United States would also support your return to Tibet at the earliest practicable moment as the head of an autonomous, and non-Communist, country.* The position of the United States in this regard is fundamental and will not be affected by developments in Korea or by Chinese Communist intervention in that area.

It is suggested that Your Holiness may care to approach the Government of India informally in order to obtain a clarification of the attitude of that Government with regard to your departure from Tibet and related problems. It is the understanding of my Government that the Indian Government would be prepared to permit Your Holiness either to pass through or to reside in India.

In case you should so desire, the Government of the United States would be
prepared to discuss the matter with the Government of India.

(signed) Loy W. Henderson
Loy W. Henderson
American Ambassador[71]

After reading the letter and taking notes, Yuthok seemed satisfied and told
Linn that he would see Ngabö, Ragasha, and three or four other ranking
officials, including the two sitsab and the Dalai Lama's brother, Lobsang
Samden.[72] However, the next day Yuthok apparently had second thoughts
about all this. He was worried that key people in Lhasa would demand proof
that the American consul general would not alter the letter or even go so
far as to rescind it after he left Calcutta, so Yuthok suggested that the letter
be "locked in a strong box and placed in the safe deposit vault of a local
bank to which only a duly designated representative of the Dalai Lama would
have access." Linn, who apparently felt that this bizarre U.S. scheme was perfectly reasonable, behaved as if insulted by this suggestion. He testily answered, "If [Yuthok] was so suspicious of the motives of the American Government that he believed there was a danger of our going to the length of
changing the wording of the Ambassador's letter after he had seen it, he
had a wholly mistaken impression of the way in which the American Government did business."[73]

Yuthok then let that matter drop but did raise two other issues. First, he
asked whether the United States would also provide financial support for
the families of the Dalai Lama's retinue. He said that if they were left behind
they would provide the Communists with a very effective means of applying
pressure. He said that the total number of people, including families, would
be between 150 and 300 persons, and he emphasized that this was a very
important issue for the Tibetans. Second, Yuthok asked what the U.S. attitude would be if the Dalai Lama stayed in Lhasa but sent a small group of
trusted officials to organize resistance from outside Tibet. Wilson said he
did not know the answers to these questions and would ask Washington, but
he indicated that all previous discussions had been predicated on the Dalai
Lama's leaving Tibet.[74] Wilson, of course, was correct. The United States was

71. U.S. National Archives, 793B.00/9–1851, enclosure no. 1 in letter to the Dalai Lama,
in dispatch no. 662, from the U.S. Embassy in India to the U.S. secretary of state, dated 18 September 1951 (emphasis added).

72. U.S. National Archives, 793B.00/10–551, dispatch no. 157, from the U.S. consul general in Calcutta to the U.S. secretary of state, dated 5 October 1951.

73. Ibid.

74. Acheson responded on 6 October, saying that the support of the Dalai Lama's entourage
was primarily the responsibility of Buddhists and that the American pledge for financial aid

primarily seeking to secure a propaganda coup, not sponsoring a clandestine guerrilla movement in Tibet.

Yuthok left Calcutta for Kalimpong on 3 October but then did not leave immediately for Lhasa.[75] This led the Americans to decide that Yuthok was unreliable, so on 11 November 1951 the U.S. gave the same message to the Dalai Lama's mother who was then living in Darjeeling.[76] In the meantime, the Dalai Lama's second oldest brother, Gyalo Thondup, arrived in the United States to visit Taktse Rimpoche.

GYALO THONDUP IN CHINA AND THE UNITED STATES

The Dalai Lama was discovered in Qinghai Province in western China and brought to Lhasa in 1939 together with his family. They came from Amdo, one of the Tibetan ethnic subareas, which was centered in Qinghai Province. However, within Amdo, they came from a relatively Sinicized area, and many Tibetans in their village spoke Chinese primarily as their first language. The Dalai Lama's mother explained this: "Because we came from Tsongkha, we spoke the Tsongkha dialect, but my parents were also acquainted with the Amdo dialect. There is a great difference between the two. In Tsongkha, since there were many Chinese, the younger generation conversed in Chinese and often forgot their native Amdo. In Guyahu [her home area] the older people used Amdo; the younger people spoke Chinese."[77]

It is, therefore, perhaps understandable, but still surprising, to learn that in 1943, when it came time for the Dalai Lama's parents to put their son Gyalo Thondup in school in Lhasa, he and his brother-in-law, Takla (Phüntso Tashi) (who was an Amdowa married to the Dalai Lama's sister, Tsering Dolma), were sent to study written Chinese with a native Chinese teacher named Ma rather than studying written Tibetan at one of the Lhasa private

---

would be limited to 150 persons. On the second point, the State Department did not agree to support unless the Dalai Lama fled and repudiated the agreement (U.S. National Archives, 793B.00/10–651, telegram from the U.S. secretary of state to the U.S. consul general in Calcutta, dated 6 October, 1951). This response does not seem to have been passed along to Yuthok.

75. U.S. National Archives, 793B.001/11–451, telegram from the U.S. consul general in Calcutta to the U.S. secretary of state, dated 4 November 1951. According to Coocoola, Yuthok was closely watched by the Chinese and unable to pass the U.S. message to the two prime ministers until April 1952 (U.S. National Archives, 793B.00/7–252, telegram from Consulate General in Calcutta to Department of State, dated 1 July 1952.). The Chinese, in fact, did suspect Yuthok was an imperialist spy and were watching him carefully (Phünwang, interview, 2000).

76. U.S. National Archives, 793B.00/11–157, "U.S. policy concerning the legal status of Tibet 1942–1956."

77. Tsering 2000: 30. See also Stag Lha (Takla) 1995: 1:109 for a comment on language difficulty when they first arrived in Lhasa.

schools. They continued to study Chinese with Ma (at Reting's monastery in Lhasa) for about a year, until Ma gave this up because of ill health.[78] At this point, Gyalo Thondup (and his younger brother Lobsang Samden) were sent to a private Tibetan school called Tarkhang.[79] But the idea of Gyalo Thondup studying Chinese did not disappear, and it appears that by the middle of 1945 the Dalai Lama's father had decided to send him and Takla to China to study. Gyalo Thondup was then seventeen years of age, and Takla was twenty-two. It is probable that the Dalai Lama's father discussed this with Reting when that lama made a two-month visit to Lhasa in December 1944 to try to regain the Regency,[80] and in September 1945 he specially sent Gyalo Thondup and Takla to visit Reting at this monastery in northern Tibet, presumably to say good-bye before they embarked on their adventure to China.[81] Private arrangements were made with the head of the Goumindang's Bureau Office in Lhasa,[82] and then the two youths were sent to India at the end of 1945, ostensibly on a trading venture but actually to go to China. Their trip to Nanjing, China's capital, was organized by the Chinese Consulate in Calcutta. On 7 April 1946, they arrived in Nanjing, where both youths were enrolled as students in Chiang Kai-shek's Political Academy.[83]

At this time, sending one's children to China to attend school was unheard of in the aristocracy. Those families who chose to send their children for a modern education (which was not possible to obtain in Tibet) all sent them to India, so the Yabshi family's decision set them far apart from the norm. The Dalai Lama's mother, Gyalo Thondup, and Phüntso Tashi have made interesting comments on the events surrounding this decision. The Dalai Lama's mother said that her husband thought it would be a good experience for Gyalo to study in China, which, it should be noted, was ostensibly Tibet's enemy.

> We had sent my son Gyalo Thondup to China at the age of sixteen. I did not want to let him go, for China was so far away, and I was led by a mother's sentiments. But my husband thought it would be a good experience for him. My

78. Stag lha (Takla) 1995: 1:164. A recent book explained further: "Gyalo Thondup now desperately wanted to go and study in China. The Kung [Dalai Lama's father] at first objected, but his friend, ex-Regent Reting, talked him around," and Gyalo and Takla began taking private lessons in Chinese (Craig 1997: 116).

79. This was the school run by the monk official whose formal household name was Rong Phelung. However, he was known unofficially as Tarkhang, meaning telegraph office, since he had been in charge of that office at one time (Stag lha [Takla] 1995: 1:167).

80. See Goldstein 1989: 433–37 for a discussion of this visit.

81. Stag lha (Takla) 1995: 1:195–247.

82. Stag lha (Takla) 1995: 1:195–96.

83. Gyalo was then age nineteen, seven years older than the Dalai Lama. Takla (Phüntso Tashi) was then age twenty-four.

son was also very keen to go, and as a result there were many household arguments between us. Finally it was decided Gyalo Thondup would leave for China.[84]

She did not elaborate on why sending him to China for education would be a good experience. Gyalo Thondup, however, explained (in uncorrected English) that there were political ramifications involving the former Regent Reting.

> At that time the *Reting Regent* [ex-regent] *and my father* thought China was very important for me to go and to study, [and] to learn, and maybe eventually it can be useful for the Tibetan population and for the government of Tibet, and in particular for the Dalai Lama. . . .
> We [Gyalo and Reting] talked all about Taktra and all the politics, everything. He trusted me very much. And my going to China, I tried to balance the understanding with him, and hoping eventually he can recapture power, like that. These things also we discussed.[85]

The Dalai Lama's father and Reting, as mentioned earlier, were very close. Both saw China as a potential supporter of Reting against Taktra, so it is not surprising that the Dalai Lama's father wanted his son to study in the capital of China and thereby inevitably develop ties and friendships with important Chinese officials. This, of course, is what happened. For the Tibetan government, which was not consulted at all about this, the situation became sensitive and complicated, because Gyalo not only was embraced by Chiang Kai-shek and the Guomindang elite but also quickly became engaged to Zhu Dan, a schoolmate who was the daughter of Chu Shikuei, a Guomindang general. They were married in 1948.

As mentioned above, before sending their son to China, the Dalai Lama's family members had not discussed their decision with the Kashag (only with the ex-regent Reting), and, not surprisingly, the Tibetan government was not pleased that Gyalo Thondup was studying at a Guomindang school and engaged to a Guomindang general's daughter. When the Dalai Lama's father died in early 1947, Gyalo was now the head of the Yabshi family, and his presence in China with a Chinese fiancée had obvious potential political ramifications. The family worried about him being used and/or controlled by the Chinese. Consequently, the Kashag sent instructions to its Bureau Office in Nanjing, telling the office heads to do everything they could to persuade Gyalo Thondup to return to Lhasa. Gyalo, however, accidentally saw

84. Tsering 2000: 135.

85. In fact, as mentioned earlier, Gyalo Thondup and Takla (Phüntso Tashi) were sent by the Dalai Lama's father to visit Reting Rimpoche in October 1945, just before they left for China (Gyalo Thondup, interview, 1995 [emphasis added]; Stag lha [Takla] 1995: 1:185–94).

the Kashag's instructions one day while visiting the Bureau Office and was furious to learn of them. Knowing of the instructions, he confronted the office heads, who were playing majong.

> I walked up to their majong table, and all of them suddenly were getting up, saying, "Oh, Mr. Thondup, you have come. . . . Very good. We have something very important to talk to you about." I told them, "Don't worry, and let's talk about it slowly, so you play your majong." They said, "No, no, no, we're not going to play any more majong," and they discontinued their majong, and they asked me to go to their office. So I went to their office, and they sat down there, and they were saying that they are very worried about my future. They never mentioned anything about the cable. They told me they are very worried and anxiety about my future and my welfare if I stayed too long in China. I said, "Why?" They said because the civil war and all the disturbances in China. And then they said my father passed away, and then my father is Kung, duke of Tibet, and that has to be replaced. His title had to be taken over, and no one else can take it except myself. They say, since my mother is alone, I should go back now and take that title. And then I said, "Any other concerns?" And they said, "No, nothing else." And then—I was so naughty—I picked the cable out of my pocket and said, "You know, the Kashag is quoting like that. They say that Gyalo Thondup, the Dalai Lama's brother, if he remains too long it is going to be very very complicated. It is not suitable for the interests of Tibet and the Tibetan government and the Tibetan people. So therefore [use] whatever tactful methods, including whatever money can be spent, to persuade him to return to Tibet." You know, that kind of language. Because I read my own Tibetan language.
>
> So I said, "You people are lying to me." They are all shocked that I already saw it. So they were very much embarrassed. So they saying yes, but it is not because of a bad intention of Kashag and the government of Tibet. It was good intentions that they wanted me to return because things are now very bad in this area. Nothing else. I was very angry and told them to tell Kashag to go to hell. I'm in China to study. I'm a student. I have nothing to do with the politics. Why does Kashag suspect me? Kashag should do something that is good for Tibet and for the country and for the interest of Tibet and for the welfare of the people of Tibet. And don't fight among themselves and don't suspect me in China. I'm doing studying in Chinese. I have nothing to do with the politics. . . . You know that cable is still with myself.[86]

Gyalo Thondup flatly refused to leave China and instead insisted that his brother-in-law, Phüntso Tashi, return to assist his mother in Lhasa. Phüntso Tashi agreed and returned to Lhasa in 1947.

Gyalo Thondup, however, was not able to remain for long in China because of the impending victory of the Chinese Communist Party in the civil war. He

---

86. Gyalo Thondup, interview, 1995 (in English, uncorrected).

left mainland China for Hong Kong in 1949 and then went to India with his wife. In India, he found himself extremely short of cash and wrote to his family (to Takla [Phüntso Tashi]) in Lhasa asking for money.[87] At this time, the Yabshi family had two Tibetan government–appointed "guardians" who oversaw their finances,[88] and Gyalo soon found that the Tibetan government was still trying to force him to return, because they still considered him (and his Chinese wife) a potential danger or embarrassment. Consequently, after sending no response to his request for money for a month or so, the Yabshi guardians finally said they did not have any money to send and told him to return to Lhasa. If he needed money for the return trip, they told him, he should borrow some in India and come quickly. Moreover, they told him that if he continued to stay in India, it would be difficult for them to send him money in the future from Lhasa.[89] Gyalo was furious and again refused to listen to the Tibetan government. Instead, he borrowed money from Reting Labrang's (the ex-regent's) business office in Kalimpong, where he was staying, and went to New Delhi on 29 July 1949, accepting an invitation from Prime Minister Nehru. From Delhi he went to Calcutta, where he again tried to get money, this time from two important aristocratic officials who happened to be in Calcutta, Shakabpa and Pandatsang. They also refused. Lhamo Tsering, Gyalo's secretary, says that this was the saddest period in Gyalo's life, since he had to borrow to live.[90] From Gyalo's point of view, this was the Tibetan government again trying to control and manipulate him. As the titular head of the Yabshi family, Gyalo was entitled to decide how to use its money, not the Tibetan government's appointed guardians. This manipulation further fueled the suspicion and animosity Gyalo and the Yabshi family already felt because of the whole Reting conflict and the death of the Dalai Lama's father.

Gyalo Thondup then decided to go again to Hong Kong, where his wife's relatives were living, and from their go to the United States for further education. Gyalo also thought that from Hong Kong he would directly contact Communist leaders in China.[91] However, he was unable to secure a visa for Hong Kong, so he again changed his plan and now went to the Philippines, hoping from there to be able to get to Hong Kong. He left for Manila on 21 April 1950. Gyalo, however, once more changed his mind and from Manila went to Taipei instead of Hong Kong. There, he found himself trapped when the Guomindang government refused to grant him an exit visa to visit his

87. Lha mo Tshe ring (Lhamo Tsering) 1992: 57–58.
88. Because the Yabshi family quickly acquired considerable debt, in approximately 1945 the Tibetan government appointed two government officials (Shasur and Dombor) as guardian-advisers (tib. tsondzin) for the family (Stag lha [Takla] 1995: 1:183).
89. Lha mo Tshe ring (Lhamo Tsering) 1992: 58.
90. Lha mo Tshe ring (Lhamo Tsering) 1992: 58.
91. Lha mo Tshe ring (Lhamo Tsering) 1992: 69.

brother Taktse in the United States—or anywhere else.[92] Like the Tibetan government, the Guomindang government preferred him on its own territory. There he had to stay for over a year until the fall of 1951, when, under pressure from the U.S. government, Taiwan finally issued him an exit permit to go to America.

While Gyalo was in the United States, he met with State Department officials several times, although it is clear that his older brother, Taktse Rimpoche, remained the United States' main source of information and liaison. On 26 September 1951, Gyalo had a meeting with William O. Anderson of the State Department's Office of Chinese Affairs, at which the United States frankly conveyed to Gyalo the parameters of U.S. support for Tibet, saying, "The United States recognized both the claim of the Republic of China to suzerainty over Tibet and Tibet's claim to de facto autonomy." In the same conversation, Gyalo Thondup was also told that American consideration of events in Tibet would be qualified by the consequences of the continued U.S. recognition of the Chinese National government.[93]

Despite such caveats, as we have seen, the United States was still very interested in Tibet and continued to hold some hope that the Dalai Lama wanted to flee into exile. New discussions arose concerning sending yet another message to the Dalai Lama, again raising the ante slightly. The new one was to be similar to the letter shown to Yuthok in Calcutta in September 1951 but would have an added comment that the United States had recently learned from the Indian government that it was willing to grant asylum or transit privilege if the Dalai Lama requested it.[94] The embassy in New Delhi thought this additional enticement was so important that it didn't feel the United States should wait for final confirmation from the Government of India before informing the Dalai Lama. Interestingly, the embassy telegraphed Washington on 3 November urging officials there to take action and advising them to discount the Dalai Lama's telegram to Mao accepting the Seventeen-Point Agreement: "In Emb view, it is unnecessary await further word from Bajpai before sending contemplated msg to Dalai Lama. Tibetans probably ratified Sino-Tibetan agreement under pressure. If that shld be case, then wld provide valuable info to Tibetans."[95]

On 4 November, the Consulate in Calcutta similarly urged action, arguing that, since Yuthok had still not left for Lhasa, "this delay unfortunate and

92. Lha mo Tshe ring (Lhamo Tsering) 1992: 67–70.

93. U.S. National Archives, 793B.00/11–157, "U.S. policy concerning the legal status of Tibet 1942–1956."

94. U.S. National Archives, 793B.00/11–1451, telegram from Consul General Wilson in Calcutta to secretary of state, 14 November 1951.

95. U.S. National Archives, 793B.00/11–351, telegram from Bowles, Delhi, to secretary of state, 3 November 1951.

re-emphasizes advisability that favorable GOI attitude re asylum be delivered DL soonest."[96]

At the same time, in Washington, Gyalo Thondup again met with Anderson of the State Department on 2 November 1951 and further confused the United States' understanding of what was going on in Tibet by giving officials a wildly incorrect assessment of recent events there. The American report of this conversation reads as follows:

> Having called at his own request, he and his wife discussed with me today (1) recent information which they have received from Tibet, and (2) the possibility of [his] receiving educational assistance from the US Government.
>
> Gyalo said that he received, approximately the middle of October [1951], a letter from Lhasa reporting that opposition among Tibetans to the Chinese communists is increasing very rapidly and may break out into open fighting at any time. He said that the monks at the leading monasteries possess arms and know how to use them. These monks have refused to surrender the arms to the Chinese. I inquired whether Gyalo had translated for him recent news reports alleging that the Dalai Lama has accepted the May 23 agreement. *Gyalo replied that both he and Taktse agree that their private letters from Tibet led them to believe that the Peiping report is a fabrication of propaganda. Their relatives advise that the wave of opposition to Chinese aggression is comparable to that which existed in Tibet in 1911. At that time the Tibetans successfully drove the Chinese from the country. Under those circumstances Gyalo and Taktse believe that acceptance would be impossible.* Gyalo repeated his previous opinion that there are not more than 500 or 600 troops in Lhasa,[97] that the Dalai Lama can still escape although with some difficulty, and that he will probably escape before the passes are closed by winter.[98]

Such misinformation about events in Tibet was to become a constant component of the history of the 1950s. At this time, it should be noted that the CIA had no officers who spoke Tibetan and had no agents in Tibet, so they had no independent sources of information. In fact, as late as 1957 when the CIA began air-dropping Tibetans into Tibet, the coded messages they sent back were translated by a Mongolian monk (Geshe Wangye) who knew Tibetan because he had lived in Lhasa in a monastery. This monk operated a dharma center in New Jersey and would travel to Washington, D.C., by train to read and translate the messages.[99]

---

96. U.S. National Archives, 793B.001/11-451, telegram from Soulen in Calcutta to secretary of state, 4 November 1951.

97. Actually, by the time of this meeting, the main Eighteenth Army Corps (about six thousand troops) had arrived in Lhasa.

98. U.S. National Archives, 793B.001/11-251, Department of State, portion of memorandum of conversation between W. Anderson and Gyalo Thondup, 2 November 1951.

99. Frank Holober, interview, 1995, Washington, D.C.; Taktse Rimpoche, interview, 1993, Bloomington. Taktse said he also sometimes helped.

The extent of America's confusion about what was going on in Lhasa can be seen in a proposal made by Wilson in Calcutta two weeks later, on 14 November. Sent to the secretary of state, this plan included the possibility of the United States sending planes to the vicinity of Lhasa to fly the Dalai Lama to exile. As bizarre as all this now seems, the Calcutta Consulate strongly supported it as "probably the last chance to get DL out."

> [Names redacted] plan to proceed Lhasa in about 2 weeks with msg and will attempt persuade DL leave Tib. Both seem confident DL's willingness come but foresee great difficulties and while realizing this is primarily DL's problem feel he may be unable escape without assistance. They asked if US could send one or more planes to vicinity Lhasa. They believe exit by horse impossible in view length of journey and presence Chi Commie troops along route in some strength. However, if plane operation not feasible (and ConGen aware of serious difficulties involved) they believe possibly DL can enlist support of monks who, if armed, could perhaps overcome Chi in Lhasa (reported numbering 3,000) and permit DL withdraw to point where planes could evacuate him and retinue. Latter alternative would require arms, supplies and possibly leadership from USA. [Names redacted] hope that before departing to receive from ConGen some detailed info re possibility our assistance in flight from Lhasa as well as more info our plans for assisting DL after leaving Tibet. . . . Gibson emphasized implementation any plans would require assurance DL's intention leave Tibet denounce Sino-Tib agreement and continue fight against Commies and would also require precise communications, planning and timing. ConGen believes if DL is persuaded leave Tibet considerable US advice and aid will be required.
>
> Would appreciate indication Dept's and Emb's views. We realize foregoing raises great many problems but this is probably last chance to get DL out. Today's press states Chi troops have reached Gyantse. Dept may however wish at least take advantage this opportunity get ltr from Taktser to Dalai Lama. . . .
> Wilson[100]

The new ambassador in Delhi, Chester Bowles, also believed the Dalai Lama wanted to flee Tibet, but Bowles was far more realistic about the overall situation and especially felt Wilson's suggestions went too far. He suggested sending photographic equipment and color film instead of a plane, as the following telegram to the secretary of state illustrates:

> Emb has no doubt DL remains personally willing leave Tib in spite his return Lhasa from Yatung last July. Emb also believes DL personally still opposed provisions Sino-Tib agreement although recent reports re Tib ratification have been confirmed by GOI. . . . We have no reason believe DL has changed his

---

100. U.S. Department of State 1983: 1847–48, 793B.00/11–1451, telegram from Consul General Wilson, Calcutta, to secretary of state, dated 14 November 1951.

mind in either respect and interpret both developments, particularly latter, as indicating DL and his govt are no longer free agents and are gradually succumbing pressure created by presence Chi Commie troops in Lhasa and elsewhere in Tib. Under such circumstance it is understandable [names redacted] who have . . . fears for his safety wld dream of ways in which he cld achieve freedom.

Emb believes, however, their suggestions for overt US provision of planes, arms, supplies and leadership are practically impossible and politically undesirable at this time. Overt US aid wld be considered by Commie Chi as US intervention in Tib affairs; it wld provide Commie Chi with ready-made excuses for further extension their control Tib; and it wld also subject US to renewed propaganda charges imperialism in Asia. Furthermore, provision US aid wld require full coop on part India because of Tib geographic position. It is highly unlikely GOI wld be willing permit US aid to transit Ind or itself to supply Tib for fear effect on Ind relations with Commie Chi. It is also likely Ind wld resent any US effort provide covert assistance to Tib at this time.

Although . . . US assistance felt practically and politically undesirable at this time Emb believes US shld make at least one final effort by letter or oral message to encourage DL to resist in ways best known to Tib Govmt. Emb believes new letter from Taktse who carries document from DL as latter's authorized rep wld be best means.[101] It might reiterate previous US statements in simple terms and include practical suggestions by Taktse whose knowledge sit [situation] in Lhasa shld assist him in recommending steps to be taken in immediate future. Although it may not be feasible, DL might for example make pilgrimage to Buddhist shrines in Tib from one of which he might escape southward to India.

Dept might also . . . send DL small gifts such as newest photographic equipment and colored film in which DL greatly interested. On basis previous experience Emb believes latter although small wld rep tangible evidence to DL of US friendship and wld have effect far out of proportion to their monetary value. . . .

Bowles[102]

Based on such comments from U.S. diplomats in India, eventually a new message was sent in the form of a letter in Tibetan from Taktse that affirmed "our original position—full aid and assistance when you come out." It also stated that while it was not possible to fly into Lhasa to get the Dalai Lama, should he need help in his flight from Tibet, the United States would give

101. Actually, the United States should have known from its own documents that the Dalai Lama had instructed Taktse in July 1951 to return from Calcutta to Yadong; thus, he was clearly not an authorized representative. U.S. National Archives, 793B.00/7–351, telegram no. 13, from the U.S. consul general in Calcutta to the U.S. secretary of state, dated 3 July 1951.

102. U.S. Department of State 1983: 1848–49, 793B.00/11–1551, telegram from Ambassador Bowles, in India, to the secretary of state, 15 November 1951.

aid if it was feasible. On 26 November 1951, the letter from Taktse was forwarded to the Consulate in Calcutta and from there to Tibet.[103] The U.S.
government, accepting as accurate what it was hearing from Taktse and Gyalo
in the United States and from Western sources in India such as Harrer and
Patterson, believed that the Dalai Lama still really wanted to flee to exile and
hoped this new message would tilt the scales in U.S. favor. It now would wait
for an answer.

In the meantime, the Chinese presence in Lhasa had changed significantly, because the main Chinese army force arrived in Lhasa on 26 October 1951. It consisted of roughly six thousand troops from the Eighteenth
Army Corps (ch. shiba jun), under the command of General Zhang Guohua. A little over a month later, on 1 December, another twelve hundred
troops from the Northwest Bureau's First Field Army, under the command
of Fan Ming, joined them in Lhasa, bringing the total number of PLA troops
and officials in Lhasa and Central Tibet to roughly eight thousand. The PLA
now far outnumbered the Tibetan army. However, while the presence of this
large influx of troops provided military security for the Chinese side, it further strained relations with the sitsab and, as will be examined in the next
chapter, placed the Chinese in a precarious situation with regard to food.

103. U.S. Department of State 1983: 1849, footnote to telegram from Ambassador Bowles,
in India, to the secretary of state, 15 November 1951.

Chapter 9

The Food Crisis

Lhasa's population at the end of 1951 was small—approximately thirty thousand people[1]—so the influx of over eight thousand Chinese troops and officials in the three months from September to December represented a dramatic increase of roughly 27 percent. In regard to housing, this created no major problems, because the Tibetan government gave the Chinese several large park areas in the south of the city beside the Lhasa (Kyichu) River, where they could set up tent camps.[2]

Housing for the officials and offices also posed no great problem. As was mentioned, when Zhang Jingwu first arrived in Lhasa, the Tibetan government gave him the old Trimön house (which it owned), and this was more than adequate. When Wang Qimei and Zhang Guohua arrived in succeeding months, the Chinese rented and purchased houses to meet their new space needs, as Phünwang explained.

> With the influx of all these officials, we realized we had to have more space, so I was assigned the task of renting one or more houses. Since all the good property in the center of Lhasa was owned by aristocrats and the monasteries, it wasn't easy to find quarters that were suitable. Fortunately, I was able to arrange to rent my old friend Yuthok's house. It was centrally located and large enough to accommodate Zhang Guohua, myself, and most other newly arrived

---

1. Larsen and Sinding-Larsen 2001: 15; also reported in a Xinhua News Agency release from 23 February 1999. This figure excludes the roughly fifteen thousand monks residing in Sera and Drepung monasteries (respectively, three and five miles outside the city).

2. The Tibetan government gave the Chinese space in two main areas, "the New Regimental Headquarters" (tib. magar sarpa) and Dosenge, which was adjacent to Yamön, where the Tibetan Ngadang Regiment was stationed.

officials with enough room left over to store some of our grain. Zhang Jingwu remained in the Trimön House.

Not long after this, we decided we needed even more space and concluded that it would be better for us to buy rather than rent a house, so I again spent a lot of time visiting and negotiating with the families who owned suitable buildings. I didn't have to search long before I was able to purchase a handsome house that was owned by Sandutsang, the big Khamba trading family. . . . It became the formal office building for the Tibet Work Committee. (Since the building was a private house, we did not need to get the Tibetan government's permission to buy it. We simply paid the owner the selling price and he gave us a certificate of ownership.) In all our dealings we paid in Chinese silver dayan coins since Tibetans did not accept Chinese paper currency.[3]

Securing food for the now thousands of Chinese soldiers, however, was a problem of a different magnitude and did not go well.

FINDING FOOD

The PLA calculated each soldier's food requirements at 2 jin (2.2 pounds) of grain per day, so for the roughly 8,000 troops in Lhasa the army needed about 16,000 jin per day, 480,000 jin per month, and 5.7 million jin per year. In addition, the Chinese had 1,200 horses and mules, each of which required 3 jin of fodder per day, so they also needed an additional 1.3 million jin per year for this.[4] In addition, they also needed a variety of goods such as meat, butter, tea, firewood, and vegetables. And they needed all of these immediately, because the main army arrived in Lhasa with virtually no surplus stores of food.

Not surprisingly, Beijing had been worried about this from the beginning. Although the Chinese Communists possessed overwhelming military superiority, their fundamental political strategy of "peaceful" liberation precluded them from simply taking whatever they needed by force. They understood, therefore, that handling this issue could be difficult and were pursuing several avenues to deal with it.

Beijing's long-term answer was to develop a secure motor road network between western China and Tibet. Until this was completed, Beijing rightly felt that the PLA's stay in Tibet would be insecure, so the Chinese immediately launched a crash program to complete two roads to Lhasa. One of these would run roughly one thousand kilometers from Chamdo to Lhasa via Giamda (the southern road); the other would start in Qinghai and run via Nagchuka to Lhasa (the northern road).

---

3. Quoted in Goldstein, Sherap, and Siebenschuh 2004: 167–68. Lhalu, however, says that the Kashag negotiated with the house owners (Lha klu [Lhalu] 1993: 252).

4. Le 1985: 294–95, entry for 29 October 1951.

Work on the southern route started on 6 May 1951, when the PLA began extending the road from Xikang Province toward the Tibet frontier with the intent of extending it to Chamdo once that area was liberated. More than thirty-one thousand military personnel from the Fifty-third and Fifty-fourth divisions of the Eighteenth Army Corps, as well as over nine thousand technicians and workers, were allocated to build what the Chinese now call the Sichuan-Tibet Road.[5]

Initially, the PLA engineers thought this road could be completed by the end of 1952, but the altitude and rugged terrain made progress much slower than expected.[6] The lowest point on the road was 11,500 feet and the highest was 17,500 feet above sea level, and the road crossed six mountain passes that were over 16,500 feet high.[7] Thus, even before Zhang Guohua's army reached Lhasa, it was obvious the initial completion estimate was completely unrealistic. This prompted Mao to order a major change in tactics on 13 September 1951, when he instructed the Southwest Bureau to make food production an equal priority with road construction.

Comrade Deng Xiaoping: Our advance troops have arrived in Lhasa, and the troops headed by Zhang Guohua will soon arrive along the route via Kongpo to Lhasa. Is the main task of these troops in 1951 [to be] road construction or grain production?

Zhang Guohua told me when he was in Beijing [in 1951] that if we do road construction, we will not do production. Zhang thought that the road from Ganzi to Lhasa could be completed during the next year. However, according to the information I received lately, it is impossible to complete the road next year [in 1952]. It may take two or three years. If this is the case, our troops will have serious problems regarding supplies if they obtain no grain from their own production. It is not good for the Tibetans if we rely on the Tibetan government for supplies or get supplies by purchasing them. Thus, could you please consider making a change so that the [Eighteenth Army Corps] will engage in production and road construction at the same time? This means giving the order to the troops along the route from Ganzi to Lhasa that part of them will be responsible for production and part of them will be responsible for road construction. During busy production seasons, use more of them in production, and during the other seasons, put all your manpower into constructing the road. This arrangement needs to be decided now, so they can make preparations during this winter.[8]

5. Zhao 1998: 55–57; Zhonggong xizang zizhiqu dangshi ziliao zhengji weiyuanhui 1990, entry for May 1951.

6. Just the section to Chamdo, for example, was not completed until late November 1952.

7. Zhao 1998: 55–57; Zhonggong xizang zizhiqu dangshi ziliao zhengji weiyuanhui 1990, entry for May 1951.

8. Dui xizang gongzuo de zhongyao zhishi (wei chuban de shouji), n.d.; Mao's orders are also mentioned in Zhonggong xizang zizhiqu dangshi ziliao zhengji weiyuanhui 1995, entry for 13 September 1951.

Figure 11. Building the road from Chamdo to Lhasa. Source: Chen Zonglie

As I shall discuss later in this chapter, growing food became a major priority in Lhasa and the other areas where the PLA was stationed.

Mao also instructed the Eighteenth Army Corps to disperse troops quickly
from Lhasa to other areas in order to reduce the demand for food there. In
the same telegram as above, Mao explained this.

Another question is the deployment of the troops. Specifically, during September, some of the troops should be sent to stay in Shigatse as well as places between Shigatse and Lhasa. They should be engaged in production in these places so the Panchen can return to Back Tibet [Tsang]. This arrangement will also help our work in Tibet. The original plan of not stationing them [the Southwest Bureau's troops] in the above place [Back Tibet] should be changed. The time of such movement can be after Zhang Guohua's arrival in Lhasa and after he has set up a relationship with the Tibetan government. It will probably be in three or four months. Please reply.[9]

Growing their own food, however, would not solve the troops' immediate problem of securing food in Lhasa for 1951 and 1952. One obvious option—transporting food by yak caravan from inland Chinese areas (tib. nang sa; ch. neidi), such as Sichuan or Qinghai[10]—was not immediately feasible. Shipping a one-month supply of grain from inland China to Lhasa would have required at least five thousand transport yaks and taken about two to three months round-trip over difficult trails, which often were not passable in winter. The Chinese, therefore, understood that in the short term food and fuel would have to be purchased in Tibet, and to this end they brought with them hundreds of yaks laden with boxes of silver dayan coins. However, notwithstanding an almost endless supply of coinage, securing food proved extremely difficult.

Tibet was a subsistence agricultural economy with no national network of commercial trade in foodstuffs. Excess grain was mostly in the hands of a relatively small number of feudal aristocratic and monastic landlords (and the government), who generally stored their annual surplus for later use, since grain could be kept for years (even decades) without spoiling in Tibet's dry climate. Lhasa residents who did not have their own manorial estates (i.e., craftsmen, laborers, traders, small businessmen, and monk officials) bought grain either directly from these lords or from a small number of shops that purchased barley from the surrounding village areas and processed it into tsamba for sale. These shops, however, were in no position to meet the enormous food needs created by the thousands of new Chinese troops and officials.

Consequently, the Chinese side initially required the assistance of the Tibetan government and had raised this issue many times in September and October (before the main army arrived), suggesting the creation of a joint committee to oversee procurement. The Tibetan government, however,

---

9. Dui xizang gongzuo de zhongyao zhishi (wei chuban de shouji), n.d. This change had unintended consequences for intraparty conflict, as will be examined in later chapters.

10. Once Tibet became an integral part of China, calling the Han areas of China "China" implied that Tibet was not part of China, so the term *neidi*, which normally means "inland areas," came into use for all of China beyond Tibet.

would not move forward on this. The Chinese were able to secure their food needs during September and October, because at this time only six hundred soldiers and officials were in Lhasa and because a few large aristocratic families such as Lhalu, Ngabö, and Tsarong stepped forward and sold them grain from their private granaries.[11] But once the troops of the main Eighteenth Army Corps reached Lhasa, a crisis quickly emerged, because the sitsab-led Tibetan government continued to drag its feet in assisting the PLA. This, of course, is not surprising given the sitsab's attitude. The last thing they wanted to do was to facilitate the stay of the Chinese army in Lhasa.

Using food (and fuel) to pressure an invader such as the Chinese to keep only a small number of troops in Tibet was predictable and a tactic previously employed in historical eras. The Chinese knew this well and had specifically added points 2 and 16 to the Seventeen-Point Agreement to preclude this. Point 2 stated, "The local government shall actively assist the People's Liberation Army to enter Tibet." Point 16 more explicitly stated, "The local government of Tibet will assist the People's Liberation Army in the purchase and transport of food, fodder, and other daily necessities." Nevertheless, the sitsab were unwilling to make a concerted effort, although they were careful not to overtly refuse to help or to order government offices not to cooperate. However, they repeatedly complained to the Chinese that grain production in Tibet was not adequate to supply such a large number of troops and, as mentioned above, stalled on developing a plan to stabilize a secure source of grain. One Tibetan official recalled, "No one openly said you can't sell to the Chinese, but private people saw the government's policy of not wanting to sell [grains] and followed that lead."[12] Another Tibetan official commented, "The big aristocrats . . . had lots of grain, but they sold the Chinese only small amounts at a time."[13]

For the thousands of PLA troops who arrived on 26 October, the immediate consequence was hunger, because the Tibetan government continued to stall and the Chinese supplies on hand dwindled. Three days after the main Eighteenth Army Corps arrived in Lhasa, on 29 October, the Kashag told the Chinese that it had devised a plan in which the richest religious estate holders (such as Drepung, Sera, and Ganden monasteries and the three incarnate lamas, Kundeling, Taktra, and Reting) would soon provide them grain, but that never materialized.

Two days later, on 31 October, the Chinese went to Ngabö to discuss their food emergency. Ngabö had some good news. The Kashag, he said, had just

11. The Tibetan government had provided only about five thousand jin of grain between the time the Advance Unit arrived and when the main PLA force arrived (Le 1985: 294–95, entry for 29 October 1951).

12. Shatra, interview, 1992, Lhasa.

13. Chabtsom, interview, 1992, Lhasa.

ordered each of the thirteen districts near Lhasa to provide the Chinese with 10,000 khe of grain (about 280,000 jin—or roughly a twenty-one-day supply of grain).[14] It is not clear whether the Chinese eventually received this, but Ngabö also told them the government would immediately sell them 5,000 khe (about 140,000 jin) of grain from a granary below the Potala Palace. The bad news was that this grain had been in storage there for *fifty years.* Ngabö, however, reassured them that probably half of this grain was still edible. The Chinese, desperate, immediately went and tested a sample of this grain and told Ngabö the next day that the grain was totally inedible and that *their own supply of grain would only last for three more days.* Ngabö disagreed and responded that while the grain on the top might be inedible, they should go back and check the grain underneath, since he had been informed that it was usable. Ngabö also said that he had called in monastic officials and asked them to lend the Chinese grain until the matter was sorted out, guaranteeing repayment for these loans personally.[15]

At the same time, the Kashag again said there was not enough grain to supply a large force in Lhasa, so strongly suggested that the Chinese disperse their troops to border areas as soon as possible. When told this, Le Yuhong could not restrain himself from conveying his incredulity at the Tibetan's "lack of grain" argument, saying, "You have left grain in storage granaries for fifty years, allowing a lot of it to be wasted through spoilage, and some of the aristocratic landlords have millions of pounds of grain in storage, so how can you say there is a scarcity of grain?"[16] However, as indicated above, Mao had already ordered the PLA to disperse, so on 2 November, they informed the Kashag they were moving four thousand to five thousand troops to areas outside Lhasa. The Kashag immediately agreed to allow those troops to buy whatever grain was stored in the government granaries in these places and now agreed that there would be enough grain to meet the Chinese needs in Lhasa for one year if the number of troops and personnel did not exceed four thousand.[17] With food extremely short in Lhasa, the Chinese dispersement of troops went quickly, and by 11 November, the 154th Regiment had already arrived in Gyantse.[18]

In addition to pressuring the Tibetan government, the Chinese took the

14. Khe was the standard unit of measure used in traditional Tibet. It was a volume measure, so differed in weight for different items, but for barley one khe was equivalent to about thirty-one pounds.

15. Le 1985: 296–300, entries for 31 October and 1 November 1951.

16. Le 1985: 300–301, entry for 2 November 1951.

17. Le 1985: 300–301, entry for 2 November 1951. After the redeployment, there would have been about two thousand troops in Lhasa, but when the Northwest Bureau's army contingent arrived, the number in Lhasa would have increased to about four thousand.

18. Zhonggong xizang zizhiqu dangshi ziliao zhengji weiyuanhui 1990, entry for 11 November 1951.

drastic step of restricting their dietary intake to less than one jin per day, that is, half of what they had originally planned. One young Tibetan member of the Eighteenth Army Corps's dance troupe recalled how the acute food shortages impacted common soldiers like himself.

> When we PLA soldiers first arrived, we didn't have much grain and no rice or barley to eat. At this time Ngabö . . . and Tsarong sold us black beans (tib. trema), and that is what we ate. We had no fuel to roast these and no mills to grind them even if we could have roasted the grain, so we ate boiled beans for half a year [for Tibetans, trema is a very low-quality food]. It was not good, but surprisingly the voices of the singers in our troupe seemed to improve on this terrible diet. Because of this we all started to call them "Trema gyaling" ("the bean clarinet")—because while eating the boiled trema their voices sounded like a beautiful Tibetan clarinet.[19]

The dietary intake became so low that some Chinese took to supplementing their diet by eating wild foods.[20] Yang Yizheng, for example, recalled, "We were all starving. . . . Once we dug up a kind of plant with a round root, like a potato, and since we were hungry, ate it. But it was poison, so some people had to be immediately sent to the hospital."[21] This infuriated the Chinese officials, who, it should be noted, were all battle-hardened PLA army officers accustomed to using force to solve problems and certainly not used to being insulted by defeated aristocrats and monk officials. But in Tibet, they, of course, could not use force.

Liushar, the Tibetan foreign minister and one of the Tibetan liaison officers to the Chinese, recalled an example of such Chinese restraint.

> After a while, all of the [Chinese side's] fuel ran out. At that time, there were very dense trees in Nortölinga uncultivated. If the Chinese had been like other people, they would have cut the trees right away [for fuel]. But the Chinese soldiers were educated people, so they didn't touch even a single tree and remained for two to three days without any hot drinks. At the beginning, they were like this.[22]

The already bad relations between the Chinese and the sitsab quickly worsened, and a series of very nasty verbal fights occurred. For example, at one meeting between them, Lukhangwa responded to Zhang Guohua's request for help with grain by asking him why he had brought so many troops to Tibet when it is a poor country without enough grain to feed its own people, let alone thousands of Chinese. As the discussion heated up, Lukhangwa sar-

19. Jambey Gyatso, interview, 1993, Beijing.
20. Dangdai zhongguo congshu bianjibu 1991: 202–9.
21. Ji 1993a: 395–96.
22. Interview with Liushar, 29 October 1981, by the International and Information Office of the Tibetan Government in Exile, Dharamsala.

castically asked at one point, "Commander Zhang, is it not harder to go hungry than to be defeated in battle?"[23] Consequently, despite Mao's commitment to a moderate, gradualist strategy, in the months following the main army's arrival, relations between the sitsab and the Chinese administration worsened, not improved.

One of the most interesting questions about the food crisis was whether the Chinese food needs were really beyond the capacity of the Tibetan government, as the sitsab argued. The Chinese requirement of roughly 500,000 jin of grain a month seems enormous, but there appears little doubt that it could have been met without too much difficulty, at least for the first two or three years, by requiring aristocratic and religious landlords to sell their *stored* grain to the Chinese. For example, Shelling, a middle-sized aristocratic family with four estates, had an annual grain yield of about 150,000 jin of barley, most of which was sold. His family also kept about 42,000 jin in storage in their granary.[24] The largest aristocratic families such as Lhalu had annual incomes from their estates roughly in the range of 550,000–850,000 jin and proportionately larger private granaries. Lhalu himself privately sold the PLA about 420,000 jin from his stores in late 1951.[25] A number of other aristocrats such as Ngabö did likewise, but, as Lhalu says, as mentioned before, there was pressure not to do too much: "Private individuals sold grain to Chinese, but they didn't dare sell much to the Chinese because of Lukhangwa's attitude."[26]

In addition to the aristocracy, some large monasteries and the eight or nine huge religious corporations (labrang) of incarnate lamas such as Kundeling and Reting had vast grain holdings, and all could have easily sold much more than Lhalu. And this, of course, does not take into account either the annual yield from the Tibetan government's own estates or the government's scattered grain reserves (granaries), which Lhalu estimated at that time to be about 2.8 million jin but probably contained even more.[27] Consequently, in Tibet as a whole, the available surplus grain appears to have been sufficient to meet the Chinese short-term needs, and the acute grain shortage that ensued in late 1951 and into 1952 was clearly artificial. Had the sitsab allowed creation of a joint procurement office to organize the purchasing and transporting of grains from other parts of Tibet before the mass of troops arrived, there would have been few, if any, problems.

The dire food problems of the Chinese led Ngabö to push successfully for one interesting innovation in Lhasa—the creation of a subcommittee of the Kashag whose mission was to deal effectively with matters concerning

---

23. Zhang 1983: 212. This comment is well-known and is also reported by Tibetan officials.
24. Shelling (Tsewang Namgye), interview, 2000, Cleveland, OH.
25. Lhalu, interview, 1993, Lhasa.
26. Lhalu, interview, 1993.
27. Lhalu, interview, 1993.

the arrangements and accommodations of the Chinese, including food for the PLA. If any new order or regulation was needed, this office drafted it and sent it to the Kashag to affix the official seal. It was created soon after the Dalai Lama formally accepted the Seventeen-Point Agreement in late October, and it came to be called the Surjong Kashag, because it met separately from the Kashag in the Surjong room in the Tsuglagang.[28] It consisted of three Kashag ministers—Ngabö, Shasur, and Dombor, with Ngabö as its director. It was also the brainchild of Ngabö, who was frustrated by the inability of the Tibetan government to cooperative effectively with the Chinese.[29] This office gave him a mechanism for dealing quickly with Chinese needs, so long as these were more or less routine, as with food.[30]

The Surjong Kashag took a number of steps to find grain for the Chinese troops and officials, such as launching an investigation of the status of government granaries in different parts of Tibet as well as the reserves of the richer monasteries and the upper strata of the aristocracy.

Changkyim, a Tibetan monk official (and the brother of Tsipön Shakabpa), collected grain in 1952 under orders from the Surjong Kashag and recalled his own experience of finding far more grain in the government granaries than was listed.

> In 1951, when I was in Phari, I was told that the Panchen Lama was coming from China and would be going to Tashilhunpo Monastery . . . and there would also be some . . . soldiers coming to Shigatse, so we had to supply them with a large amount of grain for their tsamba and for their horses' fodder.
>
> At that time, there were fourteen counties and estates under my authority. We [he and his co-governor] were told to go to these and check how much grain was stored in their granaries, and we were to use this grain to supply Labrang [referring here to the Panchen Lama's administration] the amounts it needed. At that time we supplied about 100,000 khe of grain (2.8 million jin) to Labrang. We were also told to supply the Chinese as much grain as they wanted. The Chinese said that they would pay for it, and at that time we took receipts from the Chinese. I don't know whether they later paid or not.
>
> . . . I was told that the main office [for preparing the grain] should be set

28. Ji 1993a: 267. Le Yuhong's diary (1985: 297) mentions it in his entry for 31 October 1951. However, some others say it was not started until after the Panchen Lama arrived in Lhasa in April 1952. Le appears to be correct. The Tsuglagang is the huge main temple in Lhasa. It contains numerous chapels and the Jokhang, the chapel where Tibet's most famous statue of the Buddha resides. The famous Barkor Road circles the Tsuglagang. In addition to its religious activities, the Tsuglagang also housed a number of government offices such as the Kashag in the past.

29. Shan kha ba (Shenkawa; Shasur) 1990: 344–45. The mini-Kashag also included two aristocratic staff officers from the Kashag, the Kashag kadrung Tsögo and the Kashag kandrön Samling. Both of these had been with Ngabö in Chamdo and were committed to change and working with the Chinese.

30. Shan kha ba (Shenkawa; Shasur) 1990: 344–45.

up in Shigatse. At that time, I talked with the Kashag through a wireless set, for which I was given a secret code. . . . I was told that if the grain [in the government's granaries] was insufficient, I was to buy grain from the local areas at the going price. But there was a lot of grain in storage, and it was enough to supply them. In some counties there was grain in storage that was not included on the accounting lists. We checked all of the accounts and found there was a large amount of grain still remaining.[31]

The Surjong Kashag, therefore, was able to identify and sell the PLA a large amount of grain over the next year.

Not only was the food crisis a dietary disaster, but it was also a public relations disaster for the Chinese side, because the inflation it created tarnished the image the Chinese were trying to project and angered the residents of Lhasa. The Chinese side had worried from the start that their coming would create high inflation, but, as seen above, they were unable to persuade the Tibetan government to take steps to prevent this. So at the same time that the PLA was telling Tibetans that they had come to help them, it was obvious to all that the PLA's presence was causing the price of grain in Lhasa to skyrocket and their cost of living to increase. The speed and extent of this inflation was dramatic. For example, when the Chinese first arrived in August 1951, the price of one khe of grain in Lhasa was about fifteen or sixteen ngüsang.[32] By November 1951, this had more than doubled to thirty ngüsang, and then it almost doubled again to about sixty ngüsang by April 1952.[33] The impact of this inflation was mentioned in one of the monthly reports the Indian Mission in Lhasa sent to New Delhi in late 1951: "The arrival of large numbers of Chinese troops has shaken the local economy. This inflation affected not just grain but also butter, meat and firewood."[34]

It also was commented on in two satiric Lhasa street songs that appeared at this time.

The price of barley is fifty ngüsang,
butter and beef are priceless.
Dear Chairman Mao,
what can we poor men do?[35]

31. Changkyim, interview, 1992, Dharamsala.
32. Tibetans had their own currency, which they continued to use until the uprising in 1959.
33. Lhalu, interview, 1993. The March-April 1952 monthly report from the Indian Mission in Lhasa to New Delhi said similarly that the price increased from sixteen to as much as sixty ngüsang (per khe) (U.S. National Archives 793B.00/6-2752).
34. U.S. National Archives, 793B.00/2-652, copy of monthly report from India Mission in Lhasa, 16 November to 15 December 1951.
35. Ji 1993a: 385. Ji did not provide the original Tibetan words for this song.

Figure 12. A meeting of a few aristocrats to discuss grain procurement for the PLA, left to right: unknown Chinese cadre, Phünwang, Ngabö (standing), unknown, Canglocen, Ramba Theiji, unknown. Source: Canglojen family

Mao has liberated (us),
(and) butter has become a hundred ngüsang (in price)
Shamelessly,
all material goods have increased (in price).[36]

The Chinese side took several actions to lessen inflation but without much success. One step was to implement a unified shopping rule for its troops, requiring that all purchases for the army be done centrally. Another was to prohibit its personnel from buying things for themselves in the market.[37] Yu Dehua, a female member of the Eighteenth Army Corps's dance troupe, recalled how she experienced this firsthand.

36. Maogi jingdrö dangne / marla gyalor chasong / hamba tshando kabo / ngörig gangga pharsong. Lhatsün Labrang Chandöz, interview, 1992, Dharamsala.
37. Zhao 1998: 42.

At the time, the Kashag did not sell us any grain, and we could not find any wild vegetables in Lhasa once winter came. We were very hungry. After we arrived in Lhasa, each of us women soldiers received two silver dollars for our special needs. There was no cash for anything else. We saw that the Tibetans sold flat breads in the street, so I saved my money in the hope that I could use it to buy food. Our military discipline, however, was very strict—no one was allowed to purchase any food from the street. However, I could not stand my hunger, so one day I sneaked out and bought a bag of flat bread. Carrying my bag of flat bread, I ran home to where we were quartered. I could smell the bread; it smelled so delicious. I wanted to eat the bread right there in the street but dared not for fear that I would be found out by our leaders. When I got back, I started to divide the bread among my mates, but just then our political commissar walked in. He asked who bought the bread, and I admitted that I had. He confiscated all of it. (I heard that he returned it to the seller.) I was disciplined for this.[38]

The Chinese, however, did make a major effort to start producing food for themselves. And they developed an effective plan to transport as much grain as they could from outside Tibet, particularly from India.

THE PLA OPENS NEW FARMLAND

At the same time that Zhang Guohua was dispersing troops from Lhasa to reduce pressure on food, he secured approval from the Tibetan government to convert Nortölinga, a large uncultivated area west of Lhasa that had been used as a source of fodder for the stables at Norbulingka Palace, into fields to grow food for themselves. It was already late in the year when the Kashag agreed to give them this land, but the Chinese side did not want to wait until the following spring, fearing that if they waited they would miss getting a crop in 1952. So on 25 November 1951, the PLA launched a crash effort to prepare that swampland for sowing the following spring. About 70 percent of all the PLA troops and cadres worked on this, despite their own frequent hunger.[39]

Jambey Gyatso, the young Tibetan PLA dance troupe member mentioned earlier, recalled that work: "At the end of 1951, we first had to turn over the frozen land, take out the thorn bushes, and bring in fertilizer. We brought manure from the bathrooms in Lhasa and also collected bones from the roads and burned these to make fertilizer. We collected lots of manure."[40] However, some of what the PLA did shocked Tibetans, for example, their use of dog and human excrement collected from the streets. The smoke from the

bones also led to complaints from Tibetans that this was polluting and offending Lhasa's protector deities.[41] One Tibetan put it this way:

> They were doing some things that we normally do not do. The characters [of
> Tibetans and Chinese] were incompatible. They were saying that they had come
> to serve the Tibetan people, but in the streets and alleys of Lhasa they were
> collecting [human] feces and putting the feces on their vegetable gardens and
> said they were doing development. So whatever they did we only saw fault with
> them and did not see it as education for us.[42]

These activities of the Chinese prompted much derisive talk and jokes, such
as the following sarcastic street songs:

> Having good firewood
> we don't need [have time] to burn dog shit.
> Having the Dalai Lama,
> There is no need [no time] for liberation.[43]

> When there are yellow mushrooms on the meadows
> There is no one who picks up white mushrooms.
> When we have the Dalai Lama,
> There is no need [no time] for liberation.[44]

Within a period of seventeen days the Chinese troops and cadres opened
over 2,300 mu (153 hectares) of new fields, often working three shifts, day
and night, to do this.[45] The following March, most of the troops again worked
to open further fields as well as to plant those opened the previous year, and
as a result they were able to plant grain and vegetables on over 3,000 mu
(200 hectares) of land in 1952.[46] One Chinese source says that in 1952 Chinese troops planted 14,000 mu of land (934 hectares) and harvested
380,000 kilograms of barley and about 1 million kilograms of vegetables over
all of Tibet.[47] This was estimated to have provided all of their vegetable needs
and 30 percent of their grain needs.[48]

At the same time, the Chinese took steps to import food. Since the traditional east-west animal trails from Sichuan and Qinghai were long and

41. Tashi Tsering, interview, 1993, Lhasa.

42. Phu Gyagpa, intverview, 1991, Dharamsala.

43. In Tibetan, meshing shagpa shane / kyigya bülong mindu / dale lama shane / jingdrü
donglong mindu.

44. In Tibetan, bangle sersha shane / garsha gognyen mindu / dale lama shane / jingdrü
donglong mindu. Drakten, interview, 1992; Jambey Gyatso, interview, 1993.

45. One mu is equal to 0.01 acre.

46. Zhonggong Xizang zizhiqu dangshi ziliao zhengji weiyuanhui 1990, entry for 26 November 1951.

47. Dangdai zhongguo congshu bianjibu 1991: 194–202.

48. Zhao 1998: 70.

Figure 13. PLA opening new fields in Lhasa, 1952. Source: Chen Zonglie

difficult, the amount the Chinese could ship to Lhasa in the short term, for example, 1952, would be limited. The Chinese, therefore, decided to try to ship food to Tibet from China via India, which not only was nearer to Lhasa than Sichuan or Qinghai but also had a well-established mule-based caravan trade, since most Tibetan wool was exported to Kalimpong, in India.

IMPORTING RICE

In late 1951, the Chinese requested permission from the Government of India to transship rice through India to Tibet. The Chinese initially proposed shipping twenty-eight million pounds of rice from Guangdong Province in southeast China to West Bengal and then from there to Tibet via Kalimpong and Sikkim.[49] One U.S. report says that when the Tibetan government learned of this they requested that the Indian government refuse permission on the grounds that Tibet still hoped to force China to keep its troop numbers to a minimum, but it is implausible to believe that an official re-

49. Li 1991: 45.

Figure 14. The first yield of trial Chinese radishes, summer 1952.
Source: Chen Zonglie

quest was ever made, since doing so would have been a serious breech of the
Seventeen-Point Agreement, and there is no mention of this in the Indian
Mission's monthly report or in any Chinese sources.[50] The Indian government itself clearly did not want large numbers of Chinese troops in Tibet
but did want to maintain good relations with the Chinese, so it ultimately
agreed to assist Beijing, so long as China helped with one of its own
problems—a shortage of rice. The Chinese agreed, and the Indian government permitted the Chinese to ship a portion of the Guangdong rice to Tibet, buying the rest for its own people.

An Indian official explained the deal to the U.S. Consulate General in
Calcutta in July 1952, saying: "[The] recent arrival of rice in Calcutta from
China had been divided two ways, with 1,000 tons (one million pounds) [the
figure was actually more like 3,500 tons] going to Tibet and 6,000 tons having been sold to the Government of India for use in West Bengal."[51] The rice

50. U.S. National Archives, 793B.00/7-252, memorandum of conversation between
Princess Coocoola of Sikkim and Consul Garrett H. Soulen, dated 24 June 1952.

51. U.S. National Archives, 793B.00/7-2952, memorandum of conversation with J. K. Sen,
Sikkim Durbar Liaison Office at Calcutta, dated 29 July 1952.

for Tibet came already specially bagged in roughly one-maund bags to facilitate its loading onto mules.[52] It was dispatched by rail from Calcutta to
Siliguri, near Kalimpong, and from there by animal to Tibet.

The Chinese understood the political importance of this rice, that is, that
it would significantly lessen their dependence on Tibetan grains and thus
stabilize their position in Tibet, but it would be most effective if it could reach
Lhasa quickly. Beginning in April 1952, they worked out a system for transporting this rice, making the town of Phari, in southern Tibet, the transfer
point for the rice coming from Kalimpong.[53] From India to Phari the rice
was shipped on mules (or in some parts, porters), from Phari to Gyantse it
was shipped on horse carts (using a crude road the PLA had quickly built),
from Gyantse it went to Nanggartse on yak, and from there to Chushul, and
finally on to Lhasa.[54] At the request of the Chinese, the Kashag agreed to
help the Chinese to secure transportation (i.e., animals).[55]

In June 1952, the Chinese sent two officials to India to receive the shipments. One of those, Li Jue, recalled this work.

> The [Tibet] Work Committee and [Tibet] Military Area Headquarters dis-
> patched me to carry out this mission. On 18 June 1952, Comrade Luo Jiagao
> and I started from Lhasa, passed through Gangtok, the capital of Sikkim, and
> finally arrived at Calcutta, in India. Together with the comrades from the em-
> bassy and with the cooperation of the friendly Indian government, we spent
> over forty days there on this task. In addition, we purchased quantities of fat,
> cloth, medicine, shoes, etc. Plus, we bought stud oxen, stud pigs, stud chickens,
> and breeding stock for apple trees. We began to open the border trade between
> China and India.[56]

Shipping one thousand to thirty-five hundred tons of rice over the Himalayas
to Lhasa was an enormous challenge. One Indian official estimated that, since
each mule could carry about 166 pounds, 150 mules could carry 24,700
pounds of rice a day northward from Gangtok. But the trip took roughly sixteen days one way to Lhasa,[57] so using the traditional system, the turn-around
time for each team of 150 mules was about one month. To move the rice in
the fastest way, therefore, would require a constant stream of mules—30
teams of 150 mules (6,000 mules), staggered, so that each day new goods

52. One maund was roughly equivalent to 82.3 pounds. Normally rice came in larger units,
double that size.
53. Ji 1993a: 414.
54. Ji 1993a: 414.
55. Ji 1993a: 414.
56. Li 1991: 45.
57. Gangtok to the Nathula Pass took two days, Nathula to Phari took four days, Phari to
Gyantse took four days, Gyantse to Lhasa took eight days. Today by truck, the trip from Gyantse
to Lhasa takes about six to seven hours.

were sent off until the shipment was completed. Normally, transport on the Gangtok-Yadong trail was done in winter, because the area is plagued by heavy rains and malaria in summer. However, because the Chinese needed the rice to be shipped at once, they had to pay higher wages for labor and freight. A U.S. report says the laborers were "practically fed quinine."[58]

Since shipments from Gangtok had not even started at the end of July 1952, the earliest this rice could have reached Lhasa was in the early fall of that year. A British report written in 1953 says that two thousand tons had been moved into Tibet by February 1953, with the remainder shipped in the summer of 1953.[59] Zhang Jingwu commented on the incredible cost of this: "The cost of the food plus the transportation fee . . . is extremely expensive. One jin of food is more expensive than one jin of silver. We are eating 'silver' to live!"[60]

The Chinese also organized a large land transportation program from Sichuan in 1952. According to statistics compiled by the Tibet Work Committee in Lhasa, from 1952 to May 1954, twenty-eight million pounds of goods and materials were transported by animals from Chamdo. Statistics from the Chamdo area indicate that seventy-one million pounds of goods were transported from 1951 to 1954. More than 66,900 animals and over 15,600 laborers were used in this effort.[61]

Goods were also transported from Qinghai. In the winter of 1952, the Central Committee ordered the Northwest Bureau to organize a transportation company to ship food to Lhasa. It bought more than twenty-six thousand camels from Inner Mongolia, Ningxia, and Qinghai provinces in the summer of 1953 and transported millions of jin of food from Golmud (in Qinghai Province) to Lhasa. More than half of the camels died or were injured on the way to Lhasa.[62]

However, despite all these efforts, the Chinese troops initially in Tibet during the winter of 1951 and the spring and summer of 1952 were almost totally dependent on Tibetan grain. They had no choice but to tighten their belts as much as they could and wait until more grain could be brought in from outside Tibet.

TIBETAN TRADERS

In addition to this massive undertaking of grain shipment, the Chinese made a concerted effort to enroll Tibetan traders to purchase and transport other

58. U.S. National Archives, Amconsul desp 89, 31 July 1953.

59. U.S. National Archives, 793B.00/12–253, report from Consulate General in Calcutta.

60. Zhao 1995: 85.

61. Dangdai zhongguo congshu bianjibu 1991: 202.

62. Zhonggong xizang zizhiqu dangshi ziliao zhengji weiyuanhui 1990, entry for November 1953.

needed equipment and materials. A Tibetan official, Drakten, recalled this activity.

> The Chinese needed a lot of construction materials from India, such as steel, hammers, shovels, pick axes and other steel products, and metal basins that were like wash basins, the one the coolies carry on their heads.
>
> The Chinese ordered things, and the traders took the money from the Calcutta Bank and brought the items back. So there was a section of those traders who probably did quite well. Then for the students, they needed things like pens and books. Anyway, all the necessary items that the Chinese needed were ordered through traders, and they brought it [to Lhasa].[63]

To facilitate this, the Chinese set up a procurement bureau, and then a Lhasa branch of the Bank of China was opened in January 1952. Contracts worth millions of dayan were awarded to aristocrats and Khamba trading families, and the entire operation was made simple because the Tibetans were able to get drafts from the Bank of China in Lhasa and then cash these in India for rupees, either in Kalimpong or at the Hong Kong and Shanghai Bank in Calcutta.[64] Many Khambas, such as Alo Chöndze, ironically would later become part of the anti-Chinese resistance force, but at this time profits were huge and fortunes were made.

An Indian Mission report also commented on this trade: "Large profits were being made off of the Chinese who paid for everything in sliver dollars. . . . The Kutras [aristocrats] are doing well through the services which they provide for the Chinese. The Chinese officials have been incredibly over generous . . . in order to obtain lodgings, food, etc. [and] in a short time they have spent prodigal sums."[65]

A Chinese source commented on the trade and its political implications in Communist Party jargon, saying, "Through such trade relations, we not only purchased part of the materials we needed but also helped link the economic benefits of the upper-strata personages with the interests of the motherland, and this helped the upper-strata personages realize the great strength of the motherland and expand their trade relationships with those trade organizations [of the CCP]."[66]

Two Lhasa street songs from that time criticized the alacrity with which Tibetan traders, labrang, and aristocrats took to helping the Chinese:

63. Drakten, interview, 1992.

64. Dangdai zhongguo congshu bianjibu 1991: 210. If a check was under twenty thousand rupees, it could be cashed in Kalimpong by a Mr. Wang (Shingsar Lobsang Gelek, interview, 1993, Toronto).

65. British Foreign Office Records, FO371/99659, monthly report of the Indian Mission in Lhasa for the period ending 15 December 1951.

66. Dangdai zhongguo congshu bianjibu 1991: 210–11.

When the Chinese came from China,
They were called "communists, communists."
When the Chinese gave out dayan coins,
They were called "honorable lord, honorable lord."[67]

The Chinese Communists are our parents to whom we are grateful.
They throw dayan coins like stones and earth
(or, dayan coins are coming down like rain).[68]

On the negative side, Tibet's incorporation into China devastated its massive wool export trade by inadvertently closing its main export destination—the United States. The size of this Tibet–U.S. wool trade was surprisingly large. In 1950, for example, Tibet exported 4,333,612 pounds of wool to the United States, which were worth 8,050,218 Indian rupees ($1,690,545 U.S. dollars). Another 553,937 pounds of wool were exported to other countries, such as Britain, Italy, and Japan, worth $116,000 U.S. dollars.[69] In 1951, this trade was terminated because the U.S. Treasury Department had regulations prohibiting trade with Communist China, and Tibet had now become part of China. Liushar, the Tibetan foreign minister, raised this issue with the Americans in Kalimpong in mid-May 1951 but to no avail.[70] Despite Liushar's protests and pleas, one week after the Seventeen-Point Agreement was signed, the U.S. Treasury Department banned the import of Tibetan wool unless it was accompanied by an affidavit that the wool did not come from an area under Chinese Communist control.[71] When Liushar was told that the embassy could not help them on this matter, the U.S. consular official commented, "They feel embittered with India, the US and the UK."[72] Within two weeks of this announcement, the absence of demand from America resulted in a drop in the price of Tibetan wool by 60 percent and the suspension of

---

67. gyami gyane yongdü / kungdren kungdren sigi / gyami dayan dredü / bombola bombola sigi.

68. gya kungdren drinjen phamare / ngü dayan sayu rdoyu re. This initially was composed in Kham, where the Chinese spent huge numbers of dayan on transportation and road construction, but it also came to be used in Lhasa in 1951–52.

69. U.S. National Archives, 893B.24222/2–1651, American consul, Calcutta, to U.S. State Department, 16 February 1951. It should be noted, however, that Tibet did not receive these dollars. India refused to allow Tibetans to receive payment in dollars, which they kept and paid the Tibetans in Indian rupees (U.S. National Archives, 893B.24222/5–1751, Embassy, New Delhi, to secretary of state, 17 May 1951).

70. U.S. National Archives, 893B.24222/5–1751, Embassy, New Delhi, to U.S. State Department, 17 May 1951.

71. U.S. National Archives, 893B.24222/5–2251, Clubb, China Desk to McDiarmid, Monetary Affairs, 22 May 1951.

72. U.S. National Archives, 893B.24222/5–2251, Embassy, New Delhi, to U.S. State Department, 17 May 1951.

Tibetan wool transactions in Kalimpong.[73] Interestingly, this was used by anti-Chinese activists in Lhasa, who blamed the Chinese rather than the United States for the harm to Tibet's wool trade, and the Chinese actually stepped in and purchased the Tibetan traders' wool at a high price. One Chinese source says that by 1953 China had bought four million dayan worth of Tibetan wool.[74]

In sum, the PLA's first few months were made extremely difficult by the shortage of food. The combination of the Tibetan government's unwillingness to use its authority to secure supplies for the PLA and the unwillingness of the Chinese to use their real power to force compliance hindered a steady flow of foodstuffs. The Chinese were forced to buy as much grain as they could from the "sympathetic" large estate holders and from the Lhasa market, which, as everyone on both sides initially predicted, created sky-high inflation and partly undermined the Chinese side's hope of moving quickly to create a good impression as "new Chinese" among the people of Lhasa.

Another thorny problem still outstanding in these early months was the return of the Panchen Lama. It will be discussed in the next chapter.

73. U.S. National Archives, 893B.24222/5–2851, consul, Calcutta, to U.S. State Department, 28 June 1951.
74. Dandai zhongguo congshu bianjibu 1991: 210.

Chapter 10

The Panchen Lama and the People's Liberation Army

In addition to the lack of a unified strategy within the Tibetan government, there was also a long-term divisive conflict between Tibet's two greatest lamas, the Panchen Lama and the Dalai Lama. Throughout the 1950s, this conflict was like a dangerous riptide pulling all sorts of issues into its midst, not only on the Tibetan side, but also on the Chinese side, where it created a deep split between the leaders of the Northwest and Southwest Bureaus in Tibet.

THE 9TH AND 10TH PANCHEN LAMAS IN CHINA

The Panchen Lama was based at Tashilhunpo Monastery, in Shigatse, and owned vast territories with thousands of agricultural and pastoral serfs. To administer his people and resources, he maintained a government-like administration called Labrang gyentsen thombo, or in common parlance simply "Labrang."[1] Like the Tibetan government in Lhasa, it included both aristocratic and monk officials and was headed by an administrative council,

---

1. *Labrang* has two meanings. The general referent of the term is the property-owning legal entity of a successive line of lamas. In a manner analogous to a Western corporation, such labrang had property, internal leadership, and an identity that continued across generations. They differed, however, in that the head of the labrang was a lama selected as a young child through incarnation. The second meaning of *labrang* in Central Tibet refers specifically the labrang of the Panchen Lama. In other words, if a peasant belonging to the Panchen Lama was asked, "Who is your lord?" he would normally answer, "labrang," and everyone would understand that that refers not to any lama's labrang but rather to the Panchen Lama's. Similarly, when Tibetans talk about Labrang and Shung, or Lashung, they are referring to Panchen Lama's government and the Tibetan (Lhasa) government (which was officially called shung ganden phodrang choley namgye).

called Nangmagang,[2] which was usually composed of two or more officials called dzasa. At the apex of the government was the Panchen Lama.

The modern conflict between the Panchen Lama and Dalai Lama can be traced back at least to 1879, when the Tibetan government executed the Panchen Lama's head minister (Kyabying Sengchen Trulku) and severely punished others associated with him for helping what turned out to be a spy sent by the colonial Government of India.[3] Animosity toward the Panchen Lama increased in the early 1900s when the Dalai Lama was in exile and Tibetan officials in Lhasa felt that the Panchen Lama was consorting with their enemies (the British and the Chinese) to enhance his status. Their perceptions were not wrong, for the Panchen Lama and his officials were, in fact, trying to operate autonomously from Lhasa.

For example, in 1906, the Qing court sent Zhang Yintang to Lhasa as the new Imperial amban to restore Qing stature in Tibet following the British invasion and capture of Lhasa in 1904.[4] When he arrived in Gyantse, a town near Shigatse, the head of the Panchen Lama's council went to greet and lobby him about the Panchen Lama's conflict with Lhasa. According to Zhang, the Panchen's official "hinted that the Panchen might challenge the Dalai's position."[5]

Not long after this, the Panchen Lama sent Zhang a letter asking him to separate Tibet into "Back" and "Front" Tibet (ch. hou zang and qian zang), the former incorporating the area of Tsang, which the Panchen would rule, and the latter the area of Ü, to be ruled by the Dalai Lama.

Use of these terms began in the early eighteenth century during the reign of Emperor Shizong (1722–35) as part of a policy aimed at reducing the size (and thus the power) of the Lhasa government. At this time the Qing offered the 5th Panchen Lama control over a vast territory that comprised all the districts west and south of Shigatse, that is, virtually all of Tsang. The Panchen Lama refused this enormous offer, but when the Qing government again offered him six districts in Tsang (Lhatse, Ngamring, Phüntsoling, Jedrung, Tsongkha, and Ngari), this time he accepted three of them (Lhatse, Ngamring, and Phüntsoling).[6] From then on, the Qing dynasty used the terms *Front* and *Back Tibet* on their maps.

Zhang, however, was not favorably inclined toward the Panchen Lama and berated him both for seeking such a division and for his machinations with the British, saying bluntly to him,

2. Chinese-language sources usually refer to this as the Kanting or Kampo Council.
3. Zhwa sgab pa (Shakabpa) 1976: 2:65.
4. This is the same Zhang that Lukhangwa referred to in chapter 7.
5. Ya 1991: 238.
6. Ya 1991: 52.

You should know that Ü and Tsang can not be split into two independent regions as the one can not exist without the other. . . . Foreigners now keep coming to Tsang to collect information as part of their schemes to swallow up Tsang so that they may have easy access to Afghanistan and Kashmir. The threat to Tsang comes from these scheming, crafty foreigners, not from Ü. At a time like this when even the concerted effort of all Tibetans would not be enough to ward off foreign aggression, quarrels between brothers, which would gladden only the foreigners, must by all means be avoided. . . . I now reiterate the previous instructions that the matter will be discussed peacefully with the Dalai Lama when he returns to Tibet.[7]

The Dalai Lama at this time was in self-imposed exile in Outer Mongolia.

Relations further deteriorated after the 13th Dalai Lama returned to Lhasa from a second stint of exile in India in 1913. When the Dalai Lama imposed a new military tax on all estate holders including the Panchen Lama, the Panchen refused to pay, insisting that since his estates and territories had been given by the Qing emperors of China, the Lhasa government had no authority to levy new taxes on him. In essence, he was contending that he and his officials were not subordinate to Lhasa.

In Lhasa, the idea of a separate Front and Back Tibet had never been accepted, and, in fact, the separation was never a reality, even at the height of the Qing hegemony over Tibet. In Lhasa's view, the Panchen Lama had authority over his estates and districts in a manner no different from all the other feudal manorial lords. He did not rule the estates and subjects of other lords in the Tsang area, and, in fact, even in the Panchen Lama's home town of Shigatse, the head of the district was appointed by the Kashag from among its Lhasa officials. Lhasa, therefore, was adamant that it could unilaterally change rules and levy additional taxes that were binding for all feudal lords and their entities in Tibet, bar none. And since the Dalai Lama had an army and the Panchen Lama did not, once the Chinese were expelled from Tibet in 1913, there was no question whose view would prevail. Relations continued to deteriorate in the early 1920s, until finally the Panchen Lama decided to flee into exile in China in November 1923.[8] The Dalai Lama's government tried to capture him before he reached the Chinese border, but when that failed, it assumed total control of his estates and subjects, appointing two of its own officials as its administrators. Consequently, at the start of 1924, the 9th Panchen Lama and his officials found themselves in exile in China. They would remain there until 1952.

The 13th Dalai Lama's government was intent on compelling the 9th Panchen Lama's government to concede its subordination, and the Panchen

7. Ya 1991: 237–38.
8. See Goldstein 1989 and Mehra 1976 for more detailed discussions of these events.

Lama was equally intent on never again placing himself in such a weak and vulnerable position vis-à-vis Lhasa. With all the property and wealth of the Panchen and his officials controlled by Lhasa, it was obvious that their best hope for returning on their own terms was to secure the support of the Chinese government, and in the years following 1924, the Panchen Lama's officials worked energetically to develop close ties, first, with the new republican government and, then after 1928, with the Guomindang government of Chiang Kai-shek. As early as 1929, the Panchen Lama set up a bureau office in Nanjing, the capital of China, and the Guomindang, for its part, supported the Panchen Lama, covering most of his and his officials' expenses.[9]

The Guomindang Chinese, not surprisingly, were interested in reestablishing their own political hegemony in Tibet and saw the Panchen Lama as a valuable vehicle to help achieve that. Attempts to forge an agreement between the two great lamas almost succeeded in the mid-1930s, but in the end the Panchen Lama's insistence on bringing a Chinese military force with him derailed the tentative agreement, and the 9th Panchen Lama never returned to Tibet. In 1937, he fell ill and died in Qinghai Province.[10]

The death of the 9th Panchen Lama began the traditional discovery process for his reincarnation. That process parallels the process utilized for a Dalai Lama and in 1941 culminated in the late Panchen Lama's officials' discovery of a four-year-old boy in Xunhua County, Qinghai, by the name of Tseden Gompo.[11] He was recognized by the Panchen Lama's officials and followers as the new panchen lama and taken to Kumbum Monastery (ch. Ta'er), in Qinghai, for training. However, while this was ensuing, the Lhasa government had launched its own search process for the new panchen lama and had identified two other "candidates" in Tibet. It refused to recognize Tseden Gompo and instructed the Panchen Lama's officials to send Tseden Gompo to Lhasa for a final comparative evaluation with its two candidates. Given the animosity and distrust, it is not surprising that the Panchen Lama's administration refused. They believed they had already correctly identified the late Panchen's true incarnation and undoubtedly feared that Lhasa would choose one of the other "incorrect" boys for political reasons. The end result of this was that the Panchen Lama's government recognized Tseden Gompo as the 10th Panchen Lama, but the Lhasa government kept that decision in abeyance and recognized no one.

While these events were playing out, the Panchen Lama's officials asked the Chinese Nationalist government to recognize their selection as the true

---

9. Jiangbian Jiacuo (Jambey Gyatso) 1989: 11.
10. This period is discussed in detail in Goldstein 1989: 252–99.
11. Xunhua was an area inhabited by a number of different ethnic groups, such as the Salar, Hui, Tibetan, Han, Dongxiang, Baoan, Mongolian, Tu, and Manchu.

10th Panchen Lama. Since 1798, the Qing dynasty had claimed that it had the final right to select the panchen and dalai lamas by means of a golden urn lottery, so asking this was congruent with Chinese views of Tibetan history. However, the Chinese government did not immediately agree. Despite its close relations with the Panchen's officials, it stalled, seeing this as a possible bargaining chip in its separate dealings with the Tibetan government, a chip it did not want to give up—at least just then.[12] Consequently, when the Second World War ended, relations between the Tibetan government and the Panchen Lama in China were completely estranged with regard to political and economic issues as well as the very identity of the Panchen Lama.

This standoff with Lhasa continued until the Chinese civil war was winding down and the issue of the Panchen Lama's recognition became entangled in China's internal politics.[13] At this juncture, the Panchen Lama's administration was headed by two dzasa: Trendong (Che Jigme) and Lhamön (Yeshe Tsultrim).[14] Che Jigme, the dominant political decision maker, had lived in inland China for years and was fluent in Chinese language and politics.[15] He earlier served as head of the Panchen's Bureau Office in Nanjing and was once a representative to the Guomindang Party Assembly. He also had been a member of the Guomindang Party's constitution committee.[16] In April 1949, when the PLA forces crossed the Yangtze River and were about to capture Nanjing, he moved the Panchen's Bureau Office south to Guangzhou Province together with the fleeing Guomindang government and then moved, together with it, to Chongqing, in Sichuan Province.[17]

However, as it became obvious that the Chinese civil war was drawing to a close and the Guomindang was on the brink of defeat, the issue for Che Jigme and the Panchen Lama quickly changed to whether they should throw in their lot with the Chinese Communist Party or remain loyal to the Guomindang.

THE 10TH PANCHEN LAMA ALLIES HIMSELF WITH THE CCP

Once Chiang Kai-shek and his government decided to flee to Taiwan, ostensibly to regroup to retake the mainland, they sought to persuade important Tibetans to accompany them. At the top of their list was the 10th Panchen Lama. Persuading him to flee with them would have been a major

---

12. Jiangbian Jiacuo (Jambey Gyatso) 1989: 10.

13. For a more detailed explication of the Dalai Lama and Panchen Lama conflict, see Goldstein 1989: 252–99; and Jiangbian Jiacuo (Jambey Gyatso) 1989.

14. Madrong Mingyula, interview, 1992, Tibet. (Madrong was a former Labrang official.)

15. It is interesting to note that despite being very verbal in spoken Chinese, Che Jigme could not read Chinese (Phünwang, interview, 1999, Beijing).

16. Jiangbian Jiacuo (Jambey Gyatso) 1989: 11.

17. Jiangbian Jiacuo (Jambey Gyatso): 11.

symbolic victory, and Chiang Kai-shek instructed Gao Changzhu, the head of the Nationalist government's Mongolian and Tibetan Affairs Commission, to use all means to persuade the Panchen Lama to move with them. Gao, in turn, sent Lobsang Tashi, a Tibetan intelligence officer in the Nationalist government, to urge the officials in the Panchen Lama's Bureau Office in Chongqing to shift to Taiwan as soon as possible.[18]

With the Guomindang exerting pressure on the Panchen Lama to flee, Che Jigme flew to Qinghai in roughly April or May 1949 to discuss this with the Panchen Lama's parents and tutor, who were then in Kumbum Monastery near Xining. He left Senge Palden, the only college graduate among his staff, as the acting director of their Chongqing Office and instructed him to find out as much as possible from his Chinese college friends about the views and policies of the Chinese Communist Party, especially regarding nationality rights and Buddhism. He instructed Senge to stall the Guomindang and wire him anything Senge learned, using a secret code they had developed.[19]

At the same time, Gao Changzhu pressured Senge Palden, telling him that Chiang Kai-shek had always been very concerned about the future of the Panchen Lama and assuring him that Chiang Kai-shek genuinely wanted to help restore the Panchen's power and prestige in Tibet. Gao told Senge that the Guomindang was prepared to build a small airstrip in Qinghai to take the Panchen and his main officials directly from there to Taiwan.[20] Gao also tried to persuade Senge himself to go to Taiwan to make advance preparations for the Panchen's arrival, promising him that he would be appointed as the head of the Tibetan Affairs Department within the Mongolian and Tibetan Affairs Commission.

To try to influence the thinking of the Panchen Lama's officials, Chiang Kai-shek's Nationalist government now agreed to recognize Tseden Gompo formally. Skipping the casting process of the formal golden urn lottery, created by the Qing dynasty, Li Zongreb, the acting president of the Chinese Nationalist government, formally recognized Tseden Gompo as the 10th Panchen Lama on 3 June 1949. (His new name as Panchen Lama was Cöki Gyentsen.) A few months later, on 10 August, Gao Changzhu attended the Lama's formal enthronement ceremony that was held in Kumbum Monastery as the representative of the Guomindang Nationalist government.[21]

---

18. Ji 1993a: 42.

19. Jiangbian Jiacuo (Jambey Gyatso) 1989: 11.

20. Ji 1993a: 42–44.

21. In *The Snow Lion and the Dragon* (Goldstein 1997: 104), I incorrectly wrote that no officials from the Tibetan government were at the enthronement. In fact, although none was sent from Lhasa, the Panchen's retinue had invited the head of the Dalai Lama's Bureau Office in Nanjing to attend, and he did (and was photographed at the ceremony). Fan Ming (interview, 1993, Xi'an) said that Che Jigme provided the CCP the official GMD documents and photographs from the ceremonies at the time of the Seventeen-Point Agreement talks.

Despite this, because the Panchen Lama's officials were still not ready to agree to Taiwan, pressure from both the Guomindang and the governor of Qinghai Province (Ma Bufang) intensified to the extent that Che Jigme worried about what they might do unilaterally, so he moved the Panchen Lama out of Kumbum Monastery to Xiangride, a more remote monastery in central Qinghai Province.

The Guomindang, however, were not the only Chinese interested in the Panchen Lama. As we have seen, the Chinese Communist Party also was seeking to win the allegiance of influential Tibetans outside Tibet, and the Panchen Lama was at the top of their list also. Fan Ming, the PLA officer in charge of ethnic issues in Qinghai and Gansu for the Northwest Bureau, recalled this period from the perspective of the CCP.

> In 1949, at the start of August, just before Lanzhou was liberated, I was the director of the Liaison Office (ch. lianluo bu) of the Political Department of the Northwest's Field Army. We were based in Gansu, in a village in Yuzhong County. Around 19 August 1949, I got an order from Peng Dehuai, the commander in chief of the First Field Army, instructing me to come for a meeting at our military headquarters. When I got there, I found a number of important officials had already arrived. . . .
>
> Peng Dehuai showed us a telegram Mao Zedong had recently sent him discussing the strategy we should employ in the liberation of the Northwest area [of which Gansu and Qinghai were part]. Mao's telegram emphasized that when we fought to liberate Lanzhou from the Nationalist government, great care must be taken with Tibetans, especially the Panchen Lama, because it would have implications for settling the Tibet issue correctly.[22] Peng Dehuai said that this was the number one directive of Chairman Mao regarding the resolution of the Tibetan issue.[23]

After Lanzhou was liberated on 26 August 1949, Peng Dehuai again instructed Fan Ming about urgent tasks he had to complete. Reiterating Mao's guidelines, he said,

> First, we should establish good relations with the Panchen Lama . . . and win him over. Second, we should also work closely with Huang Zhengqing [Aba Alo], the commander of the Tibetan military forces in the south of Gansu [in the area of the monastery town called Labrang]. Third, we must do nationality work well throughout the area. Fourth we should establish good relations and win over and educate the Tibetan intelligentsia as well as select and nurture good minority officials, for example, he suggested we should establish a

22. Mao's telegram was dated 6 August 1949 and said: "The Banchan is in Lanzhou [he actually was in Qinghai] now. When you attack Lanzhou, please pay close attention to Panchen and the Tibetans in Gansu and Qinghai provinces. Protect and respect them so as to lay the groundwork for solving the Tibet problem" (Zhonggong zhongyang wenxian yanjiu shi 2001: 1).

23. Fan Ming 1987: 4; Fan Ming, interview, 1993.

training class [for Tibetans]. At this meeting, [Peng] took out the telegram of Chairman Mao and asked us to discuss it.[24]

Fan Ming immediately began to implement this policy, sending several officials from Gansu to work with the new Qinghai provincial government and the Panchen Lama's officials residing in Kumbum Monastery.[25] However, long before the telegram to Peng Dehuai was sent, Mao had instructed the CCP's underground party organization in Chongqing to watch the Panchen's Bureau Office and look for opportunities to influence it. The organization arranged for a party member, Liu Tongzuo, to work in this office, and he was able to develop a close association with Senge Palden. Through his efforts, Senge Palden became impressed with the Communists and reported favorably about them to Che Jigme.[26]

Meanwhile, in Qinghai, Che Jigme met often with the Panchen Lama's parents and senior tutor (Gyaya Rimpoche) to discuss what to do. Meeting secretly in the parents' bedroom, they were careful not to allow anyone to enter the room during their talks, which sometimes went on until late at night. They did not even let servants in, so when they wanted to drink tea they went out themselves to get it. The Panchen Lama, then only twelve years old, noticed this and grew curious about these mysterious meetings. Jambey Gyatso writes that he was mature for his age, strong-willed, and never liked to be controlled by anyone. Unlike the Dalai Lama (who was then fourteen years old), he wanted to exert his authority, which the following incident about these meetings illustrates. Jambey Gyatso says that one day the Panchen Lama's curiosity overwhelmed him, and he suddenly burst into the room during one of these discussions.

> Che Jigme and the others dared not say anything and remained silent. The Panchen's father, however, felt the child had interrupted their serious discussions and waved to tell him to leave. But the Panchen did not go. He sat down beside his father and asked Che Jigme, "What are you discussing?" Che Jigme did not lie and said, "Chairman Chiang [Kai-shek], Acting President Li, and Chairman Ma [Bufang] asked us to go to Taiwan with Chairman Ma. We are discussing if we should go or not."
>
> The Panchen Lama then responded, asking, "Who do they want to go with Chairman Ma?" "Us, mainly you," Che Jigme replied casually, raising his silver tea cup to drink tea. The Panchen Lama suddenly stood up from his seat, pointed directly at Che Jigme's nose, and said, "Then why don't you discuss this with me when it is my business? What right do you have to make decisions for me?"
>
> Che Jigme was so shocked he spilled some tea on his clothes and the car-

24. Fan Ming 1987: 5.
25. Fan Ming 1987: 5.
26. Ji 1993a: 42.

pet. For a moment, he did not know how to answer. He was loyal to the Panchen Lama but felt the Panchen was too young to understand such government affairs. He had always acted as the boy's guardian and never thought of discussing important things with this child.

The Panchen Lama continued, "In the future, when it comes to my business, you must discuss things with me; otherwise I will not listen to you!" The Panchen Lama was getting angrier as he spoke. He had a little stammer, so when he got angry, it became even more difficult for him to express himself. He stammered and threatened the adults in the room: "If you decide to go with Chairman Ma without [first] discussing it with me, I will remain in the monastery; and if you decide to stay here, I will leave with Chairman Ma."

The Panchen Lama's father then criticized him. "Tseden, sit down. Don't be rude to the director." And he pulled the Panchen down to sit beside him.[27]

After this, they included the Panchen Lama but worried about him and repeatedly urged him not to say a word to anyone about what was being discussed.[28]

Their decision was not long in coming. Having languished in exile in China for twenty-seven years, the leaders of the Panchen's administration had the overriding goal of returning to Tibet and reassuming control of their territory according to what they considered their historical rights. However, their hatred and distrust of the Tibetan government motivated them never to place themselves at Lhasa's mercy again. Rapprochement with the Tibetan government, therefore, was remote at best, because Lhasa would not even recognize Tseden Gompo as the true Panchen Lama, let alone compromise on other issues. And while the Guomindang Chinese said they would assist the Panchen's administration, they had not done so over the past twenty years and were no longer in any position to help vis-à-vis Lhasa. The new power in China was the CCP, so joining forces with them made the most sense, because they alone had the military power to help the Panchen and his administrators realize their goal of returning to Tibet. However, members of the CCP were known to be atheists, and many felt they would destroy Buddhism. Nevertheless, the CCP's unequivocal and repeated assertions that it would respect Tibetan religion and allow autonomy in minority areas, as well as the positive reports from Chongqing and Xining, helped to convince the Panchen Lama's side that it could work with the Communists to achieve its ends.

Consequently, in late August or early September 1949, the Panchen Lama sent Che Jigme to meet with the PLA. He found its officers reasonable and linked his and the Panchen Lama's future with them. Soon after, a group headed by Zhou Renshan, chief of the United Front Work Department in Qinghai, went to Xiangride to assist the Panchen Lama with financial and

27. Jiangbian Jiacuo (Jambey Gyatso) 1989: 13–14.
28. Jiangbian Jiacuo (Jambey Gyatso) 1989: 14.

other problems that needed immediate attention.[29] The Panchen Lama had now come under the wing of the Northwest Bureau of the CCP. Winning him over was one of Northwest Bureau's important achievements in the CCP's liberation of Tibet.

The Panchen Lama himself recalled this difficult period.

In April 1949 the People's Liberation Army broke through the natural barrier of the Changjiang (Yangtze) River and took Nanjing, the seat of the KMT [GMD] government. By autumn, the KMT [GMD] army was losing ground in the Northwest. Rumors circulated describing the Communists and the People's Liberation Army as demons with blue faces and protruding teeth. On the eve of the liberation of Qinghai province, I and my Kampo [Administrative] Council withdrew from Xining to Xiangride in central Qinghai province.

In Xiangride there was a monastery which was given to the 6th Panchen Lama by Emperor Qian Long of the Qing dynasty in 1780. We gathered there to discuss our future and that of Tibet. We couldn't reach an agreement. Xinjiang had not yet been liberated, and some suggested we go there and then to Taiwan by KMT [GMD] plane. Some wanted to go back to Tibet, while others proposed that we contact the Communists.

The decision was finally made to reject the first two proposals, but we hesitated about the third. The Kashag (the Tibetan local government in Lhasa) had not recognized me as Panchen, so I couldn't go to Tibet. There were many rumors about the Communists and I had not seen them for myself. I decided to send someone to contact the People's Liberation Army and find out what they were really like.

When the messenger came back, he told us that the Communist Party and the People's Liberation Army stood for the unification of the country and the unity of different nationalities. Although I was only 12, I knew that the 9th Panchen had gone to Qinghai from Tibet to try and achieve the same end. I was his successor and should follow in his footsteps. Therefore on October 1, 1949, the founding day of the People's Republic, I sent the telegram to Beijing.[30]

The Panchen Lama's telegrams to Mao, Zhu De, and Peng Dehuai reveal the extent to which Che Jigme and the others had decided to link their fate with the CCP, including their goal of liberating Tibet. The telegram to Mao said,

Chairman Mao of Central People's Government and Commander-in-Chief Chu [Zhu] of Chinese People's Liberation Army, Peking:

With superior wisdom and courage Your Excellencies have completed the grand salvation of the country and the people. The success of your army has brought joy to the whole country. For generations in the past I have received kindness and favor from the country. During the past twenty years and more

29. Ji 1993a: 42–44.
30. Panchen Lama 1988: 10–11.

I have ceaselessly struggled for the territorial and sovereign integrity of Tibet [in China]. It is to be deeply regretted that I have had no success. I am now lingering in Chinghai [Qinghai] waiting for an order to return to Tibet. Fortunately, under the leadership of Your Excellencies, the Northwest has now been liberated and the Central People's Government has been established. All those who are conscientious applaud with one accord. From now on, the realization of the democratic happiness of the people and revival of the country are only questions of time and it will not be long before Tibet is liberated. I sincerely present to Your Excellencies on behalf of all the people in Tibet [our] respects and our heartfelt support.

> Panchen 'O-erh-te-ni' [Erdini]
> 1st October 1949[31]

Eager to establish a strong relationship with the leaders of the Northwest Bureau, the Panchen Lama also sent a congratulatory telegram to General Peng Dehuai, expressing even more strongly his support for the liberation of Tibet.

Fortunately under the leadership of Your Excellency, the Northwest has been liberated and all the people on the border are united in their joy. From now on the realization of the happiness of the people and revival of the country are only questions of time. Even the people in Tibet who have for a long time been neglected are holding out great hopes and anticipate a quick opportunity of resurrection. *We sincerely beseech that you will lead your righteous troops to liberate Tibet, eradicate the traitorous elements, and rescue the people of Tibet.*[32]

Tibet's two greatest lamas, therefore, had now adopted very different agendas regarding how to respond to the victory of the CCP in China. As we shall soon see, at the same time key CCP officials also had very different agendas regarding how to respond to the two lamas.

The rapid development of close ties between the Panchen Lama and the Northwest Bureau was an enormous success for the CCP, but it also raised a sensitive new issue regarding how the CCP should position itself in the conflict between the Panchen Lama and the Dalai Lama. The Panchen Lama's agenda placed the CCP in clear opposition to the Tibetan government in Lhasa, and since the liberation of Tibet was yet to come, how the Communist Party managed the conflict could affect the relations of the CCP with the Dalai Lama and the Tibetan government.

The Chinese government took a first step toward developing such a strat-

31. British Foreign Office Records, FO371/83325, enclosure in Nanjing dispatch to the British Foreign Office, dated 27 December 1949. The enclosure was taken from the *New China Daily News*, Nanking, 25 November 1949.

32. British Foreign Office Records, FO371/83325, quoted from *New China Daily News*, Nanking, 25 November 1949 (emphasis added).

egy in October 1949, when Li Weihan (then the minister of the United Front Work Department) instructed the Intelligence Department of central government to send Yuan Xinhu and Yu Kai to set up the Qinghai Liaison Office in Xining with a mandate to investigate the history of the conflict between the Panchen Lama and the Dalai Lama and report their findings directly to the central government.[33] While they were investigating this issue, the first direct communication from Mao Zedong to the Panchen Lama occurred on 23 November 1949. On that day, Mao and Zhu jointly responded to the Panchen Lama's telegram:

> We were very happy to receive your telegram of October 1. The Tibetan people are patriotic and [are] opposed to foreign aggression. They are dissatisfied with the policies of the GMD reactionary government and wish to become a member of the big family of a united, strong and new China where all races cooperate on the basis of equality. The Central People's Government and the Chinese People's Liberation Army will undoubtedly satisfy this desire of the Tibetan people. We hope that the Master (ch. xian sheng) [the Panchen Lama] and other patriotic Tibetans all over Tibet will work together and strive for the liberation of Tibet and for the unity of the Han and Tibetan people. It is hoped that you and all patriots in Tibet will in unity exert all your efforts in the struggle for the liberation of Tibet and [the] unity between the Chinese and Tibetan peoples.[34]

Two months later, on 31 January 1950, the Panchen Lama sent another telegram to Mao calling for the prompt liberation of Tibet by the PLA and expressing his opposition to the Lhasa government's plan to send missions to Britain, the United States, and other countries to request assistance. The telegram left no doubts about the commitment of the Panchen Lama.

> It is recognized by the whole world that Tibet is the territory of China, and all the Tibetans think that they are one of the nationalities of China. The act of the Lhasa authorities today undermines the integrity of the national territory and sovereignty and runs against the will of the Tibetan people. We, on behalf of the Tibetan people, beseech you to rapidly send righteous troops to liberate Tibet, cleanse the reactionary elements, drive out the imperialist forces in Tibet, solidify the national defense in the Southwest, and liberate the Tibetan people.[35]

33. Fan Ming 1987: 5; Fan Ming, interview, 1993.

34. British Foreign Office records, FO371/83325, quoted from *New China Daily News*, Nanking, 25 November 1949; Jiangbian Jiacuo (Jambey Gyatso) 1989: 9–10; Zhonggong zhongyang wenxian yanjiu shi 2001: 1.

35. Fan Ming 1987: 8–19. At the same time other pro-Chinese Tibetans, such as Sangye Yeshe (Tian Bao), who was a member of the National People's Political Consultative Conference, Sherup Gyatso, who was vice chairman of the People's Government of Qinghai Province, Huang Zhengqing and Yang Fuxing, who were members of the People's Government of Gansu,

By early 1950, therefore, the Panchen Lama and his officials had bet their future on the CCP liberating Tibet. The CCP, they believed, could and would return them to Tibet. However, what their status would be vis-à-vis the Dalai Lama's government was still not clear. Having spent decades in exile, they now sought nothing less than equal political status with Lhasa, but attaining this would require them to secure the backing of the leaders of the Northwest Bureau and, through them, the Beijing leadership. Consequently, in the spring of 1950, Che Jigme asked the Communist officials with whom he was dealing in Xining (in Qinghai) to arrange a direct meeting between himself and Fan Ming, who was then in Lanzhou.

Fan Ming was receptive to Che Jigme's views, since his own study of Tibetan history (from Chinese sources) had convinced him of the historical correctness of Che Jigme's position. He quickly became the Panchen's leading supporter within the party, advocating strongly the Front and Back approach:

> In history, there was Front and Back Tibet. The Dalai's government was called Kashag, and the Panchen's government was called Kanting. Those two did not have a relationship in which one belonged to the other. They were parallel structures. When Tibetans met they would say just as the sun and the moon are in the sky, the Dalai and Panchen are on earth. . . . They were people under different rulers. . . .
>
> In the maps of China at the time [Qing Dynasty], you will see Front and Back Tibet; Tibet was not called Xizang [then]. The term *Xizang* was used after liberation. In the past, Front Tibet belonged to the Dalai, and Back Tibet belonged to the Panchen.[36]

Fan Ming also was convinced that, unlike the Dalai Lama's line, the line of panchen lamas historically were friends of China and strong supporters of the view that Tibet is part of China. He explained: "The Panchen's group always endorsed the unification of China. In history, the 5th Panchen Lama [Lobsang Yeshe, 1663–1737] endorsed the idea. . . . The 10th Panchen [1938–89] also insisted on the unification of the motherland. Under any circumstances, the Panchen's group always insisted on unification and opposed the separation of Tibet from China."[37]

Similarly, on the modern political relationship between the Panchen and Dalai lamas, Fan Ming said,

> After the Dalai's group drove the 9th Panchen away [in 1923], of course, they controlled both Front and Back Tibet. But legally and on the maps [Chinese]

---

and Reting's söpön, Yeshe Tsultrim, made speeches calling for liberation and attacking the attempt of the Tibetan government to "split" the motherland (Fan Ming 1987: 19).

36. Fan Ming, interview, 1993.

37. Fan Ming, interview, 1993.

of the times, the central government [Chinese] did not acknowledge it. At this time, Chinese maps designated a Front and Back Tibet. . . . The Panchen's group, of course, when they were trying to restore their power in Tibet, were thinking of controlling Back Tibet. At that time, without question, the Panchen's group was thinking of controlling Back Tibet.[38]

Che Jigme met with Fan Ming on 26 April 1950 and told him, among other things, that he would like to go on behalf of the Panchen Lama to pay his respects to leaders of the Northwest Bureau in Xi'an. Fan Ming arranged that, and in mid-May, Che went and met top Northwest Bureau officials there. Then, with Fan Ming's help, he asked Peng Dehuai for his support in forwarding a written proposal on the future of Tibet to Mao Zedong.[39]

The proposal was titled "A Plan concerning the Liberation of Tibet and the Organization of the Government." It began by recommending that the PLA forces simultaneously enter Tibet from four provinces—Yunnan, Xikang, Qinghai, and Xinjiang, but then it focused on the essential concern of the Panchen and his officials by requesting that the Chinese government support the position that the Panchen Lama had always been autonomous from Lhasa and called for the CCP to divide Tibet into Back and Front sections. It said, "Because Tibet is territorially large with only one minority [living there], it has the conditions that make it suitable for regional autonomy. [Thus, it will be appropriate to] Organize one administrative region and then separate it into Front Tibet and Back Tibet."[40]

In addition, the proposal also put forward a number of concrete, but far-reaching, requests that will be discussed below. Peng Dehuai agreed to it, and consequently, by May 1950, the Northwest Bureau, especially Fan Ming, had become the supporter and advocate of the Panchen Lama's claims and plans.

The next step in this relationship took place in early September 1950, when Mao met with Che Jigme in Beijing and accepted the requests made in his proposal. On 23 September, two weeks before the PLA forces attacked Chamdo, Mao sent instructions to all units involved in the liberation of Tibet, setting out the Central Committee's support for the Panchen Lama. It was titled, "Guidance regarding the Issues and Requests Put Forward by the Panchen's Delegation." It said,

The [Panchen Lama's] opinions about the political and religious organization of Tibet are very good. They are in the spirit of patriotism and unification (ch. suo ti zhengjiao zuzhi fang'an de yijian heng hao, shi hehu aiguo yu tuanjie de jinsheng). It's very good and very important that the Panchen's group is will-

38. Fan Ming, interview, 1993.

39. Fan Ming 1987: 6.

40. Quoted in Fan Ming 1987: 6. The Chinese is: Xizang you zhengkuai de tudi, tongyi de minzu, shihe quyu zhizhi de tiaojian, zuzhi yi xingzhengqu er jiang qian hou zang fenbie zhizhi.

ing to cooperate with us. No matter what form the liberation of Tibet will take and how the Dalai's group will change, we must actively win over the Panchen's group and win over people who are influenced by them to cooperate with us.[41]

At the same time, Mao made clear responses to the Panchen Lama's specific questions and requests (which are not available but can be inferred from Mao's answers):

(1) Determine the timing about the title [recognition] of the Panchen and make the decision according to the circumstances after the Tibetan delegation comes to Beijing and negotiates.

(2) It is determined that the Panchen will return to Tibet. The timing of his return to Tibet will be determined later according to the circumstances.

(3) It is agreed that the Panchen can organize an ethnic [Tibetan] army unit of from three thousand to five thousand people, including in that a bodyguard unit for the Panchen. The PLA will send people who are capable and can build good relations between nationalities to help them with organizing and training.

(4) In order to help them train personnel and cadres, it is agreed to establish a subinstitute of the institute for nationalities or an independent training class near Kumbum Monastery.

(5) It is agreed to establish a propaganda team.

(6) It is agreed to provide a medical clinic.

(7) The central government will help them establish an official consumers' cooperative.

(8) It is agreed to give them a transmitter-receiver unit and provide a telegraph operator and decoder.

(9) It is agree to give them a truck.

(10) It is agreed to establish four bureau offices [of the Panchen Lama] in Beijing, Chongqing, Xi'an, and Xining.

(11) Allocate fifteen hundred silver dollars per month for the personal expenses of the Panchen. The Panchen has 412 personnel and relatives, and they will be given a total of 2,468 bags of wheat flour per month (each bag holds 44 jin).

(12) Return the Xiangride pastureland [in Qinghai] to him. If, in the future, land reforms are instituted, deal with the pastureland in accordance with the government laws and regulations.

(13) It is agreed that the government will send liaison officers to join the field headquarters of Panchen.[42]

41. Quoted in Fan Ming 1987: 4.
42. Quoted in Fan Ming 1987: 6–8.

The Chinese central government, therefore, gave the Panchen Lama much of what he wanted, including its assent to his return to Tibet, the establishment of his own military force to protect himself against the Dalai Lama, and permission for him to operate his own bureau offices in key cities in inland China. It also implied that it agreed with his proposal for a new Front and Back Tibet. However, at the same time, the response did not publicly comment on his status or recognition, instructing that this should wait until representatives of the Dalai Lama reached Beijing. It also did not specify when he should return to Tibet, again saying this would be determined in accordance with conditions.

The reason for this is clear. As mentioned above, Mao had to walk a fine line between supporting the "progressive" Panchen Lama and having this support negatively impact the larger political goal of persuading the Dalai Lama to accept the peaceful liberation of Tibet. In particular, he did not want to do anything that might prompt the Dalai Lama and his officials to think that China's real plan was to use the Panchen Lama against him. Zhang Guohua, the commander of the Eighteenth Army Corps, later expressed this clearly: "We have to postpone the Panchen Lama's reentry into Tibet for a while. If we don't delay it, the reactionaries will have an excuse to criticize us. So we will have discussions with the Dalai Lama regarding when the Panchen Lama should return."[43]

At about this time, Li Weihan's investigatory team in Qinghai finished its research and reported favorably for the Panchen Lama, concluding that Front and Back Tibet were historically valid categories that were equivalent to the political entities of the Dalai and Panchen lamas. And significantly, it also recommended that the Eighteenth Army Corps (of the Southwest Bureau) should manage Front Tibet (the Dalai Lama's realm) and the Northwest Bureau army should take care of Back Tibet. If necessary, it suggested, two military regions (ch. junju) could be established in Tibet.[44]

Consequently, by the time Chamdo was invaded in October 1950, China was strategically making plans for a Front and Back Tibet with the Panchen's supporters, the Northwest Bureau taking control of Back Tibet. Fan Ming recalled the strange way he was ordered to take the lead in this.

Peng Dehuai, Jia Tuofu, and Xu Liqing returned to Lanzhou from Xinjiang in late September 1950, and I went to meet them at the airport. Jia Tuofu told me, "Commander-in-Chief Peng has decided that you will be the secretary and mayor of Urumuqi [capital of Xinjiang]. You should get there within a week." So I immediately made plans to leave for Urumuqi. But after a few days, Peng told me, "Don't go to Xinjiang. Be prepared to go to Tibet." He pointed at a

43. Zhao 1998: 46.
44. Jambey Gyatso, interview, 1993, Beijing.

map of Tibet and said, "Go to Tsang via Xining and Nagchu and take control of the Gampala Pass.[45] Cut the traffic between Ü and Tsang, and then go straight to Shigatse and liberate Tsang." He told me to speak with the deputy commander of the Northwest Military Command, Zhang Zongxun, for details.

So I prepared to go to Tibet. Then in late October 1950, the director of the Northwest Bureau's Political Department, Gan Siqi, told me, "You are not going to Tibet. Go with Commander-in-Chief Peng to 'Resist America and Aid Korea.'" So I began to prepare to do this. A few days later, Deputy Commander Zhang Zongxun told me, "You won't be going to 'Resist America and Aid Korea.' Instead you will be in charge of leading the army into Tibet." They were sending me there, because earlier I had done some nationality work.[46]

The Central Committee of the Communist Party of China issued an important directive about Back Tibet on 9 November 1950.

> Because the Northwest People's Liberation Army will undertake the task of entering Back Tibet and the Ali area [far Western Tibet] during the entire battle to liberate Tibet, [and because] the Panchen's group has the deepest historical relationships in Back Tibet and still has great influence there, and [because] the work related to the Panchen belongs to the Northwest Bureau, Liu Bocheng [of the Southwest Bureau] suggested that the Northwest undertake the political task of taking over Back Tibet and the Ali area simultaneously. Therefore, the Northwest Bureau should immediately start the preparatory work.[47]

As a result of this, the Northwest Bureau made preparations to send a cavalry division to Back Tibet with Sun Gong as its commander. Fan Ming would be the secretary of the Northwest Bureau's Tibet Work Committee (ch. xizang gongwei), and his Liaison Office would be in charge of the preparatory work.[48]

The strategic plan of the Panchen Lama's administration, therefore, had worked brilliantly. A year after its decision to link its future with that of the Chinese Communist Party, it had won the strong support of the powerful Northwest Bureau and, through that, Mao Zedong. Beijing had recognized the validity of the Panchen Lama and agreed to return him to his realm.

---

45. This is the mountain pass located just south of the Tsangpo River that traditionally separated the Tibetan provinces of Ü and Tsang (Front and Back Tibet).

46. Fan Ming 1987: 3.

47. Cited in Fan Ming 1987: 24. See also Zhonggong xizang zizhiqu dangshi ziliao zhengji weiyuanhui 1990, entry for 9 November 1950.

48. Fan Ming 1987: 24. The Work Committee (ch. gongwei) was the main administrative unit. Under it were a variety of offices, such as the Organizational Department, Propaganda Department, United Front Department, Democratic Movement Department, Secretarial Office, General Office, Research Office, Youth Affairs Committee, and Women's Committee. Also under the Work Committee were various work teams such as the Xinhua News Agency, newspaper, Cultural Work Team, Photography Team, Movie Team, Healthcare Office, Social Affairs Office, and Liaison Office.

And significantly, they also accepted the Panchen's view that there would be two autonomous political entities, one under the Dalai Lama and one under the Panchen Lama, with each occupied by troops from a different bureau and army, the first under the Southwest Bureau and the other under the Northwest Bureau. As Fan Ming recalled, "At first, [the task of liberating Tibet] was divided. Everything was divided into Front and Back Tibet. [It was] After the two troops joined forces [that] confrontation started."[49]

But as Fan Ming alluded to above, not everyone in the PLA agreed with this. When the 9 November telegram was sent to the Southwest Bureau, Zhang Guohua and Tan Guansan, the two leaders of the Eighteenth Army Corps, disagreed with its thrust, and by 14 December 1950, the Southwest Bureau's own Tibet Work Committee held a joint meeting with the Eighteenth Army Corps's Party Committee in Ganzi (in Xikang/Kham), at which, among other topics, the issue of dividing Tibet into Front and Back Tibet was discussed. This meeting concluded that the division would be a bad idea. The following are some of the reasons they put forward:

1. The [Tibetan] people will not like this, and the reactionaries will use this separating into two units as a pretext to stir up trouble. The reason for this separation in the past was the different political power of the Dalai and Panchen lamas, but the religion is the same, so it is not good to separate the two.

2. The current economic dependency between Front and Back Tibet is great. Front Tibet depends on Shigatse for its grain supply, and the nomads in the North export their goods though Yadong [via Back Tibet], so there will be great problems if we separate Tibet into two parts.

3. From the standpoint of having diplomatic relations with India, Nepal, and Bhutan, it is also not feasible to have two parts.[50]

The Southwest Bureau had done its own research on the relationship between the two Tibetan lamas and also had the firsthand knowledge of Phünwang, their high-level Tibetan cadre, who had lived in Lhasa twice in the 1940s.[51] This revealed to them that Tibet had never really been divided into distinct front and back parts. The Dalai Lama's government ruled all of Tibet including Back Tibet, and any attempt to separate the two would be unprecedented and thus would create tremendous anger and hostility in the Tibetan government and likely would compromise the entire gradualist approach. Consequently, when this meeting dispersed on 24 December (1950), it concluded that the front and back parts of Tibet should remain as one.

<hr/>

49. Fan Ming, interview, 1993.

50. Zhao 1998: 46; Zhonggong xizang zizhiqu dangshi ziliao zheng ji weiyuanhui 1990, entry for 14 December 1950.

51. For an account of his life and times, see Goldstein, Sherap, and Siebenschuh 2004.

The conclusions and criticisms from the meeting were sent as a report to the Southwest Bureau and the Central Committee.[52]

Nevertheless, Beijing continued to move toward dividing Tibet into two political entities. In December 1950, the central government sent a telegram to the Northwest Bureau inquiring about its preparatory work, and in mid-December, Fan Ming was sent to Xi'an to make a report. Xi Zhongxun, deputy chairman of the Northwest Bureau, then sent a group of officials, including Fan Ming, to Beijing to make a report to the central government. They arrived in Beijing on 31 December 1950. Li Weihan met them on 3 January 1951 at the Beijing Hotel, where they were staying, and told Fan Ming to prepare an outline to report to the central government. This was done, and on 30 January 1951, Li Weihan met with Fan Ming, Wang Zheng, and Ya Hanzhang and reaffirmed the Front and Back Tibet policy: "The Northwest's military task will be to cooperate with the Southwest, which will be the main force. It should be prepared to take over Back Tibet (Wang Zheng will send people into Ali from Xinjiang.)."[53]

In addition, on 13 February 1951, the Central Military Commission in Beijing sent the Northwest Bureau instructions on its work in liberating Tibet.

1. All of Tibet must be liberated this year. The Northwest must complete all the preparatory work for the entrance into Tibet before the end of March. No delay is allowed.

2. It is decided that fifteen hundred people (including the guard troops) for the Northwest's Work Committee, one thousand relatives (who will go to Tibet next year), and fifteen hundred people from the Panchen's group (including his guards), totaling four thousand people and eight thousand mules and horses, will enter Tibet in batches within two years.

All the conditions that the central government has promised the Panchen's group must be rapidly and completely realized. The Northwest Military Command is put in charge of equipping the Panchen's bodyguard troops with cadres, a hospital, and a radio broadcast station.[54]

So at this point in late January and early February, the central government clearly was still proceeding with the plan for the Northwest Bureau to take control of Back Tibet.

Fan Ming returned to Xi'an from Beijing in mid-February (1951) and reported to the Northwest Bureau. It was decided that the Tibet Work Committee of the Northwest Bureau would consist of Fan Ming, Ya Hanzhang,

---

52. Zhao 1998: 46; Zhonggong xizang zizhiqu dangshi ziliao zhengji weiyuanhui 1990, entry for 14 December 1950.

53. Fan Ming 1987: 33.

54. Fan Ming 1987: 36; Zhonggong xizang zizhiqu dangshi ziliao zhengji weiyuanhui 1990, entry for 13 February 1951.

Figure 15. Left to right: Fan Ming, 10th Panchen Lama, Tashi (party secretary, Qinghai Province), in Xining, February 1951. Source: Chen Zonglie.

Zhang Jun, Wu Kaizhang, Sun Diancai, and Sun Yijun. Fan Ming would be the first secretary. Later, Zhang Jun could not go to Tibet, so Mu Shenzhong replaced him. A few weeks later, on 27 February, on instructions from the Central Committee, Fan Ming was appointed as the "representative" of the Northwest Bureau to the Panchen Lama. He was responsible for escorting the Panchen Lama to Tibet.[55]

55. Zhonggong xizang zizhiqu dangshi ziliao zhengji weiyuanhui 1990, entry for 27 February 1951. Ya Hanzhang was appointed as the deputy representative.

THE PANCHEN LAMA IN BEIJING

For Fan Ming, everything had gone so well that he decided the time was right to further solidify the situation by having the Panchen Lama travel to Beijing to meet Mao and the other leaders of China in person. On 27 March 1951, the Panchen Lama (through Fan Ming) sent a telegram to Mao, asking for a meeting, and two weeks later, on 7 April, Lin Poqu, the general secretary of the Central Committee, replied affirmatively. Two days later Fan Ming went to Kumbum Monastery to discuss the details for this trip with the Panchen Lama's top officials. They were, he found, extremely concerned about the protocol for the meeting. They feared that that if the current panchen lama was treated less respectfully than his predecessors, it would send the wrong message to the Dalai Lama's people and have negative consequences for the future. Consequently, on 12 April, Fan Ming sent a telegram to the Northwest Bureau and the Central Committee raising this concern. The Central Committee quickly agreed that everything would be done the same as it was done for the previous (9th) Panchen Lama.

A week later, on 19 April, Fan Ming, the Panchen Lama, and the Panchen's entourage left Kumbum Monastery for Lanzhou. From there they flew to Xi'an and then Beijing. As he had promised, Fan Ming organized the journey precisely according to the etiquette done for previous panchen lamas.[56]

While these events were unfolding, the deadlock over negotiations with the Tibetan government broke, and as discussed earlier, at the end of January 1951, Tibetan government representatives met with Ambassador Yuan in New Delhi and agreed to send a delegation to Beijing for negotiations. This delegation left Yadong in late March.[57] Beijing now had in its grasp the peaceful liberation agreement it had so vigorously sought, and it turned to a serious assessment of how to maximize the likelihood of success in the upcoming negotiations. As a result of this, the Panchen-Dalai conflict was reassessed, and at some point in March or April, Mao and his main adviser on Tibet, Li Weihan, moved closer to the Southwest Bureau's view: that creating a distinct Front and Back Tibet was not historically accurate and that it would be a strategic mistake for the CCP to create that division now. Mao believed that the Dalai Lama was the most important figure in Tibet and was the key to incorporating Tibet successfully, so he decided to be careful not to inadvertently let support for the Panchen Lama negatively influence winning over the Dalai Lama.

56. Fan Ming 1987: 37.
57. The head of the delegation, Ngabö, actually arrived in Beijing only on 22 April 1951, a few days before the Panchen Lama.

Fan Ming wrote that he learned of this only when the Panchen Lama met Mao in Beijing.

> One thing planned at the time was to get the Panchen to present a Tibetan ceremonial scarf (tib. khata) to Chairman Mao at Tiananmen on 1 May, Labor Day, so that the whole world could see that the Panchen Lama was the first Tibetan to present such a scarf to Chairman Mao. It was very meaningful. The person who accepted the scarf for Chairman Mao was Li Weihan, and I was right beside Chairman Mao. . . . I escorted the Panchen when he met with Chairman Mao. . . . After Mao inspected the troops at Tiananmen, he had his first conversation with the Panchen. Premier Zhou, Li Weihan, myself, Che Jigme, and the Panchen Lama were present. During the conversation, Chairman Mao praised the Panchen's group. At the same time . . . he made a key point that all nationalities in China should be united and *all nationalities should be united internally.* We were unlike the GMD, who tried to win over one group and in the meantime tried to hit another group. *So at that time we asked the Panchen to cooperate with the Central Committee in winning over the Dalai Lama.* . . .
>
> This was when the Central Committee decided that Tibet should be a unified Tibet, not an entity divided into Front and Back Tibet. This was the first time such a decision was made. Tibetans should unite together internally and the Dalai and Panchen should unite together. The Central Committee would provide unified leadership to the whole Tibet.[58]

Consequently, by the time negotiations began in Beijing, Mao and the Central Committee had shifted to a strategy in which the interests of Dalai Lama were more important than those of the Panchen Lama. Mao and the Chinese central government, to be sure, were still committed to the Panchen Lama. Mao had personally accepted the Qinghai boy as the authentic Panchen Lama and was committed to assist him to return to Tibet and resume his territories and authority, although now there was no policy for what a settlement of the conflict should look like—only that a settlement should occur and the two lamas should cooperate in a unified Tibet.

The Chinese side got its first glimpse of how difficult this would be when the Tibetan negotiators refused to participate in a welcoming ceremony for the Panchen Lama, saying they did not recognize Tseden Gompo as the genuine incarnation of the previous Panchen Lama. Takla, the Chinese-language translator for Tibetan delegation (and the Dalai Lama's brother-in-law), recalled what happened when the Panchen Rinpoche arrived in Beijing on 27 April.

> The day after we arrived at Beijing, we were told that the Panchen Lama would arrive the next day and that all of us had to go to welcome him at the railway station.

---

58. Fan Ming 1987: 36 (emphasis added).

At that time, Ngabö and all of us discussed this, saying, "We [the Tibetan government] haven't recognized the Panchen Lama. According to the policy of the Tibetan government, there are three candidates—two in Tibet and one in Amdo, and this candidate [the Amdo one] cannot be recognized until he goes to Tibet [for examination]."

But, the Chinese insisted, saying that we had to go to welcome him. So Nagbö and we discussed this and decided that Ngabö and Kheme, the [chief] representatives, would not go to welcome the Panchen Lama, but the three of us, Sambo, Sandutsang (Rinchen), and I [one junior official and the two translators], would go to welcome him. This was to show that we did not accept the Panchen Lama.[59]

Sambo also recalled that day.

The Chinese told us to go and receive him at the railway station, but at that time we had yet to accept and recognize him as the real reincarnation of the Panchen Rinpoche. We discussed this among ourselves, and we decided that only I should go to receive him.[60]

Q: Did Ngabö give you instructions about how to receive him and how to behave toward him?

There were no instructions, but I acted as if I were meeting an old friend. I did not offer him a scarf. We also did not shake hands. The Chinese actually wanted me to go in full official dress, but Ngabö didn't say anything about doing this, so I went wearing an ordinary gown. Most probably the Panchen Lama thought that I was just an ordinary Tibetan.[61]

With the negotiations about to begin, the Chinese felt this situation was impossible and set out to pressure the Tibetan government to recognize the legitimacy of this Panchen Lama. Sambo recalled,

A few days later, when the talks began on 2 May, the Chinese side raised this issue when Li Weihan asked Ngabö what special instructions he had received regarding the Panchen Lama. When Ngabö told him that he had none, Li said, "How is that possible, because it is one of the most important concerns and events for Tibetans?" Ngabö agreed but told him again that he didn't have any instructions. Then Li asked him: "Would you accept him as the real Panchen Rinpoche?" Ngabö said that he could not accept anyone as the reincarnation of the Panchen Lama and explained how at present there were two or three candidates for the position of Panchen Lama in Lhasa. He went on to explain that ultimately a divination (tib. thukdam) would be done to select the correct person. To this Li replied that the central government had already accepted this one as the true incarnation, meaning that Ngabö had to support them in this.

59. Takla (Phüntso Tashi), interview, 1994, London. Also see Stag lha (Takla) 1995: 2:40.
60. He means that he was the only full member of the negotiating team to go; the other two (Takla [Phüntso Tashi] and Sandutsang [Rinchen]) were the delegation's translators.
61. Sambo, interview, 1981, Rajpur.

Ngabö then told them, "If you have accepted him that is good, but we have not accepted him." The Chinese were polite and diplomatic, and discussions on this went on for about six or seven days. The Chinese would put forward new arguments, trying to convince the Tibetans to accept the Qinghai boy Tseden Gompo as the Panchen Rinpoche, but the Tibetan side absolutely refused.[62] Finally the Chinese asked Ngabö to please accept him to save the "face" of Mao and the central government. The Chinese side simply would not go on with the negotiations, and ultimately the Tibetan team sent a telegram to the Dalai Lama in Yadong, asking for instructions. Ngabö said in the telegram, "If you don't recognize the Qinghai boy as the Panchen Lama, it will harm the negotiations." A response came quickly from the Dalai Lama, saying, "After doing divination it has been determined that the Panchen Lama in Beijing is the true incarnation of the 9th Panchen Lama."[63]

This response was welcomed by the Tibetan delegation, since it was beginning to look as if the negotiations would end before they started. In accordance with Tibetan customs, the next day the delegation went to visit the Panchen Lama and showed him the proper respect, prostrating three times and giving him the mendredensum offering.[64]

For the Chinese and the Panchen Lama, of course, recognition was only one issue to be resolved. Equally critical was the Tibetan government's acceptance of the return of the Panchen Lama to Tibet and the restoration of his control over his territories. In turn, that acceptance and restoration required the resolution of the dispute over the relative authority between the two. This provoked a terrible argument, as Ngabö recalled.

After it was decided to sign the Seventeen-Point Agreement and the seven-point [secret] codicil to the agreement, a new matter was put forward. They said, "Although the matter between the Central Committee and the local Tibetan government has been settled, now we have to settle an internal matter in Tibet. The 9th Panchen Lama and the 13th Dalai Lama didn't get along well, so the 9th Panchen Lama had to go to China. He passed away in Jyekundo, and the present 10th Panchen Lama was recognized. If we do not settle the important issues between the Panchen's Administrative Council and the local [Tibetan] government, it will not be okay, even if the matter between the central government and the local Tibetan government would be settled."

We were not given orders to settle this matter, and the contradiction between the local Tibetan government and the Panchen's Administrative Council is not so small an issue, so we were not in a position [to be involved in this

62. These arguments were being developed by Fan Ming and Che Jigme; for example, they showed Ngabö the photo of the Dalai Lama's Chongqing Bureau chief attending the Panchen Lama's inauguration ceremony.

63. Sambo, interview, 1981. Takla (Phüntso Tashi), who was present, also reports this in Takla (Phüntso Tashi), interview, 1992, Dharamsala; and in Stag lha (Takla) 1995: 2:40–44.

64. Takla (Phüntso Tashi), interview, 1994; Sambo, interview, 1981.

matter.] Therefore, we insisted that we could not accept this. We were ordered to negotiate with the central government for a peaceful agreement; we were not given the order to settle the matter between the local government and the Panchen's Administrative Council. Please do not talk to us about this matter. You can talk about this separately later on. All of us insisted on saying that.

The delegation of the Central Committee, however, kept insisting, saying, "That will not be okay. You people have to settle this matter." So we told them, "We will definitely not accept this, because we do not have orders concerning this; and we are not in a position to interfere in this matter."

At that moment, the head of the central government's delegation, Li Wei-han, said, "If you do not settle this internal matter, we will not be able to sign the agreement between the central government and the local government." We responded, "If this is the case, it does not make any difference to us (tib. khyebar mindu). We can leave the agreement. We do not need to sign the agreement. We are not going to meddle in this matter. If the [central] government insists on saying that we have to settle the matter between the local government and the Panchen's Administrative Council, we cannot do that, because we were not ordered to deal with it. If you continue to insist on that, we don't need to sign the agreement; we can tear it up."

[Ngabö then added,] "The central government should take responsibility for Kheme, Sambo, and the other delegates and send them back to Tibet safely. I have been appointed as a leader in the Chamdo Liberation Committee, so I kind of belong to Chamdo, and I can stay in Chamdo. I don't need to go back to Tibet. I can stay in Beijing temporarily if you say so." I told the four delegation members, "You people should go back to Tibet. I will stay in Beijing or in Chamdo. You were sent purposely [to negotiate] so the central government will take the responsibility to send you safely to Tibet." So the agreement, . . . on which we had been negotiating for days, was [figuratively] torn up.

After two or three days, Song Zhiyuan, a member of the central government's delegation, said that he wanted to see me. I told him okay. At that time, the interpreter was Phünwang. We were staying in the Beijing Hotel, so we met in the hotel at about 9 A.M. The other delegates were not present; only the two of us negotiated.

At that time, the Panchen Lama was about twelve or thirteen years old, so probably this was a request made by his attendants or the Panchen Lama's Administrative Council, or perhaps it was the idea of the central government. But anyway, they were talking about separating Ü and Tsang, saying the territories beyond [south of] the Gambala Pass should belong to the Panchen Lama's Administrative Council, and the territories beyond it [north], to the local [Tibetan] government.

I told them, "That will not be okay. No matter how many times you tell me about it, I will not accept it. This is a custom confirmed from ancient times, so it will not be okay for you to put forward some kind of new policies and new conditions."

We were talking to each other like this until noon, when we had our lunch and took a rest. We started talking again at 2–3 P.M. At that time, we did not accept their views, and they also did not accept ours. So we had a disagreement, and we were supposed to meet the next day. However, at about 7 P.M., Song Zhiyuan said, "I have an idea about how to write this in the agreement. [We should write] that we will not interfere with the rank and power held respectively when the 13th Dalai Lama and the 9th Panchen Lama were getting along well." I told him " . . . It is proper to say that, . . . so I will accept this. But, if you put forward some new policies that say more than that, I will not accept it." Then he [Song Zhiyuan] said, "That will be okay. I [Song] was sent by the delegation of the Central Committee as their representative." Now, the two of us had agreed on this, so we could continue the negotiations.[65]

So in the end, the Chinese side was able to induce the Tibetan government to recognize the 10th Panchen Lama, accept his return, and agree to vague language in the Seventeen-Point Agreement that specified that the Panchen Lama and his followers could assume his previous rights and powers. The two points dealing with this in the agreement said,

> Point 5: The established status, functions and powers of the Panchen Erdini shall be maintained.
> Point 6: By established status, functions, and powers of the Dalai Lama and of the Panchen Erdini are meant the status, functions and powers of the Thirteenth Dalai Lama and the Ninth Panchen Erdini when they were in friendly and amicable relations with each other.[66]

Fan Ming, who was there advising the Chinese delegation, did not get everything he had sought, but it was still a major victory for the Panchen Lama's side. The new Panchen Lama was now recognized by the Dalai Lama and would be able to return on what, to him and his officials, seemed like their own terms, since they would be returning for the first time with their own troops, the Bodyguard Regiment.

However, the negotiations were unable to clarify any of the issues that had caused the 9th Panchen Lama to flee, and both sides had to accept putting off discussions on these issues until a future time. It would be years before all the details of those rights would be mutually accepted.

MERGING THE TWO ARMIES IN LHASA

Mao's decision to create a "unified" Tibet meant that no longer would two work committees administer different parts of Tibet, one from the Northwest Bureau and one from the Southwest Bureau. Instead, Mao instructed the Northwest's Tibet Work Committee to merge with the Southwest's, and the Southwest's now became the major part of the new unified Tibet Work Committee.[67]

65. Ngabö 1989.
66. See chapter 4.
67. Ji 1993a: 45.

Chinese records reveal that the Southwest Bureau and the Central Committee were already discussing this at the end of March, when the Southwest Bureau sent a plan to the Central Committee regarding how to create such a new unified work committee.

> The Tibet Work Committee [of the Southwest Bureau] was previously under the leadership of Zhang Guohua and included seven others such as Tan Guansan, Wang Qimei, Chang Pingjia, Chen Mengyi, Li Zhai, and Liu Zhengguo (are all military cadres), and Phünwang. Zhang is the secretary, and Tan is deputy secretary. For the purpose of [creating] collective leadership, the Northwest Bureau's Tibet Work Committee members deserve to be included in the new committee organization. There are two alternative plans for doing this:
>
> The first one is that the members of the Northwest Party's [Tibet] Work Committee can all take part in being added to the cadres of the Eighteenth Army Corps. However, this plan involves a few too many people, and it would be difficult for all these people to work together.
>
> The second plan is that in addition to the previously mentioned eight people [from the Southwest Bureau], some of the Northwest's [Tibet] Work Committee members, such as Fan Ming, Mu Shengzhong, and Ya Hanzhang, could take part.
>
> We have concluded that this plan is better than the first one. It would be easier for fewer people to get together and discuss problems. However, before the two organizations become one, the two party organizations will be left unchanged.[68]

Two months later, after the signing of the Seventeen-Point Agreement in late May, Fan Ming was ordered to meet with the Southwest Bureau's Zhang Guohua and Deng Xiaoping in Chongqing to discuss the integration of the two army forces. They agreed that the Northwest Cavalry, which was entering Tibet and accompanying the Panchen Lama, was to be classified as an "independent detachment" (ch. douzi) of the Eighteenth Army Corps but would march into Tibet *separately* under the force's existing structure and remain under the leadership of the Northwest Bureau and Northwest Military Headquarters until it actually *arrived* in Lhasa. Only then would that cavalry force be unified into the single Tibet Military Area Headquarters. This decision was made on 25 May 1951.[69] On 11 June 1951, the Central Committee accepted the Southwest Bureau's second alternative and sent reply telegrams indicating this acceptance to both the Southwest and Northwest bureaus.[70] As both armies were preparing to march into Tibet, the issue of the

68. Zhonggong xizang zizhiqu dangshi ziliao zhengji weiyuanhui 1990, entry for 31 March 1951.

69. Fan Ming, interview, 1993.

70. Zhonggong xizang zizhiqu dangshi ziliao zhengji weiyuanhui 1990, entry for 11 June 1951.

Panchen Lama again arose, for it was still to be decided when he and his entourage (and troops) should return. Originally they were scheduled to return with Fan Ming and the Northwest Bureau's troops, but in late June the Central Committee decided that it would be better if the Panchen Lama left later than Fan Ming and the troops so that he would be arriving after the Dalai Lama arrived in Lhasa from Yadong.

> The telegram also gave information about the Panchen's departure and wanted him to postpone leaving until the Dalai Lama arrived. Once this occurred, the Panchen's arrival will be all the more fruitful. After Fan Ming's departure, Ya Hanzhang should continue to work at the Panchen's base. The Panchen's party can send a few people to accompany Fan Ming to Tibet [in advance of the Panchen].[71]

Fan Ming and his force left for Tibet on 22 August 1951. On 4 November they reached Nagchuka, where they stayed for ten days. They arrived in Lhasa on 1 December.

DISCORD WITHIN THE PLA

The Central Committee's decision to have a unified administration in Tibet sounded reasonable on paper, but serious problems lurked beneath the surface. Tensions involving the Northwest and Southwest armies arose even before Fan Ming reached Lhasa. These differences went beyond the divergent positions regarding the Panchen Lama and the issue of Front and Back Tibet; they also included the victorious Chamdo military campaign of 1950, for which the Northwest army people believed they had not received proper credit.

The main attack force in the Chamdo campaign was the Southwest's Eighteenth Army Corps, but troops from the Northwest were involved through their cavalry unit of five hundred troops, under the immediate command of Sun Gong and, above him, Fan Ming. They were well equipped with new bren guns and given the critical task of defeating the defending Tibetan forces on Chamdo's northwest border (at Riwoche) and then rushing south to the key crossroads juncture at Enda to cut the single road to Lhasa. This would then trap the entire Tibetan army, which by then would be retreating from Chamdo, where the main attack would occur. Sun's troops marched without stop for the last four days and nights and arrived at Enda only shortly before the retreating force of Ngabö. As mentioned earlier, when Ngabö learned of the presence of Sun's troops, he retreated rather than attempt to fight his way through and camped at a nearby monastery, waiting to sur-

---

71. Zhonggong xizang zizhiqu dangshi ziliao zhengji weiyuanhui 1990, entry for 25 June 1951.

render. Thus, the troops who actually captured Ngabö and the rest of the top Tibetan officials with him were the Northwest's cavalry unit. This was one of the campaign's most critical engagements, since the entire Chinese battle plan was predicated on cutting off the escape route of the Tibetan army and disabling it as a fighting force.

The Northwest Cavalry took Ngabö and the others back to Chamdo, where the main force of the Eighteenth Army Corps was now headquartered. At this juncture, friction arose between the Northwest and Southwest troops, the crux of which was that the Northwest troops felt they had played a crucial role in the campaign and this warranted recognition and honor that the Southwest leaders were not affording them. Gyentsen Phüntso, one of Ngabö's officials, recalled this clearly.

> Then Ngabö and . . . the rest were returned to Chamdo. The troops that captured them were cavalry from Qinghai. They were Fan Ming's troops and came from Riwoche. The ones who took Chamdo were the Eighteenth Army Corps. Then there was a meeting right after this of the two forces, and there was a big argument. The Eighteenth Army Corps said, "We liberated Chamdo," and Fan Ming's army said, "We captured Ngabö." This argument went on for half a day.[72]

Fan Ming also commented on this.

> The Northwest troops, my cavalry detachment, moved from Xiangride to Dingqing [Dengchen] to move around behind Ngabö and Lhalu. It was the cavalry detachment of the First Field Army [of the Northwest Bureau], and I was its division commander. . . . Ngabö was captured by my troops.
>
> After we captured Ngabö, there were some disputes among our troops [the PLA]. From this point on, we had some problems with the Southwest. When we captured Ngabö, his horse had a gold saddle, and there were other things of his, weapons, that we captured. The other side came [the Eighteenth Army Corps] and asked for these things. So they took the captives and all his things, including the gold saddle.[73] The troops of Peng Dehuai always gave consideration to the whole situation. So we gave them these things. They [the southwest force] did not get such orders from a higher level, just the division level officer, Wu Zhong. We handed over all the captives and their stuff to the Eighteenth Army Corps.
>
> [If Ngabo had escaped from this route and we had not outflanked him] we could not have won the opportunity to liberate Tibet peacefully. Ngabö's surrender to us really helped the peaceful liberation of Tibet. . . . Ngabö was captured by us, and through our work he changed his attitude toward us. . . . From

72. Gyentsen Phüntso, interview, 1992, Lhasa.
73. Phünwang (interview, 2000, Beijing) claims there was no gold saddle but agreed there was conflict.

this point of view, without the battles [of his troops] at this time, there would be no peaceful liberation of Tibet.[74]

In fact, to this day, according to Fan Ming and others, the former leaders of the Southwest Bureau do not adequately acknowledge the crucial role played by the Northwest troops. Consequently, the Northwest Cavalry troops felt slighted and returned to Qinghai somewhat bitter.[75] This resentment remained below the surface but was real and was an added factor complicating the relations between the two armies after they reached Tibet.

The lingering bad feelings between the two armies came to the surface as soon as Fan Ming's troops reached Nagchuka near Tibet's northeastern border. Le Yuhong recalled this in his diary.

> Zhang Jingwu and I went to the army headquarters to talk with Zhang Guo-hua and Tan Guansan [on 27 November 1951]. I said that I heard from the troops that Fan Ming's force has arrived at Nagchuka. We have an army station there, and Fan Ming's troops asked them for a lot of grain and fodder and food. They [the Southwest army station] thought they were asking for too much so gave them less. Fan Ming's troops were angry. The troops stationed in Nagchuka say that Fan Ming's troops were asking for too much, and later when Fan's troops reach Lhasa, if they demand lots of grain, etc., things will not work out well. [I said that] If there are not good and friendly relations between the two forces, it will be bad, and I am worried about this. Zhang Guohua said since this [news] came from the troops [i.e., was an unofficial rumor], we don't know if this is true or not. However, we have to be big-hearted and establish friendly relations [not be angry about small things]. . . .
>
> Three days later when Fan Ming reached the outskirts of Lhasa, he raised four points with the Southwest generals. On the basis of this, Le Yuhong wrote in his diary, "Because the demands he put forward for his troops when they arrived in Lhasa were too high, I think Comrade Fan Ming will have difficulties."[76]

Fan Ming, in an interview, conveys how differently he saw the two army units and how superior he felt his soldiers and officials were.

> When we first got to Tibet, the Tibetans viewed us as two military units. They called me Commander Pan [they pronounced Fan as Pan], and called Zhang Guohua, Commander Zhang [i.e., Fan was equal in status with Zhang]. My troops all wore khaki uniforms and were equipped with submachine guns. Our troops also had carbines from the Korean War. The troops of the Southwest were not equipped with good weapons. They knew our troops were Peng De-

---

74. Fan Ming, interview, 1993.
75. Fan Ming, interview, 1993.
76. Le 1985: 308–9, entry for 27 November 1951 to 30 December.

huai's troops.[77] . . . My troops all supported the Panchen. The Southwest's troops all supported the Dalai Lama.[78]

Phünwang, the only Tibetan cadre in the Southwest Bureau's Tibet Work Committee, was present at Fan Ming's arrival in Lhasa on 1 December 1952. His recollections parallel those of Le Yuhong.

Some tension arose between the two Bureau's forces even before the Northwest's troops arrived in Lhasa. As Fan Ming neared Lhasa, he sent one of his officials, Bai Yufeng, ahead to meet with Zhang Jingwu and Zhang Guohua regarding arrangements. Fan Ming had definite ideas about his arrival; he wanted his troops to march in a grand procession around the Barkor street. When Bai told us this, Zhang Guohua immediately said that this would be a bad idea. "On the one hand," he said, "your animals and soldiers will be tired after their long journey and therefore they will not make a good impression. On the other hand, when our main force entered Lhasa, there was an elaborate ceremony in which the Council Ministers and the Tibetan army participated, so it is really not appropriate to do this again." Then Zhang introduced me to him, saying, "This is Phünwang. He is the top official among Tibetans and a committee member of the Southwest Bureau. We should ask his opinion."

I was put on the spot, but I expressed my feelings honestly. "I agree with Comrade Zhang's reservations," I said. "And in addition to his concerns, I think that if you bring your troops into the city, it will be difficult to find enough grass to feed the hundreds of horses and camels you have." I also added that having another grand procession of troops would be an unnecessary flaunting of Chinese military power. "We are trying hard," I said, "to give Tibetans the impression that we are friends, not conquerors." So Zhang told Bai Yufeng to tell Fan Ming not to risk offending the Tibetans by marching around the Barkor. Fan Ming, however, ignored Zhang Guohua's instructions and did exactly what he wanted. Looking back, this kind of incident was a precursor to a serious conflict of views that emerged in Tibet within the party leadership throughout the 1950s.

Fan Ming's arrival in Lhasa also created problems with the Tibetan government because Fan was angry about his reception by the Tibetan government. We had told the Council of Ministers [Kashag] that they should send officials to receive Fan outside of the city in accordance with Tibetan custom. They agreed. However, they sent a delegation headed by only a middle-level fourth rank official. *From our side also, our top leaders, Zhang Jingwu and Zhang Guohua, did not attend. Rather we sent lower officials—Alo Putrang [Le Yuhong], Xu Danlu, Chen Jingbo and myself.*

None of these decisions was lost on Fan Ming. He was so furious with the Tibetans that when the head of the Tibetan welcoming delegation stepped to-

---

77. At this time Peng Dehuai was a major force in China, for he was the commander-in-chief of the PLA's army fighting in Korea.

78. Fan Ming, interview, 1993.

ward him to present him with a ceremonial scarf, he angrily pushed it away, treating the gesture with contempt. We were all shocked by his behavior. I overheard the Tibetan officials expressing disbelief at what they were seeing, and I had to admit that I agreed with them. I could not imagine what Fan was thinking. He should have been treating the representatives of the Tibetan government with respect, not disdain. His behavior made a powerful negative impression on me, and certainly on the Tibetan officials.[79]

Fan Ming's anger at his reception outside Lhasa was matched by that of the Panchen Lama's chief official, Che Jigme. He had come with Fan Ming's force to meet with the Tibetan government and work out the arrangements for the Panchen Lama's return to Tibet. Like Fan, he was insulted by the Tibetan government's relatively junior delegation. Le Yuhong recorded in his diary his meeting with Che Jigme just after he arrived in Lhasa.

> Then I went to Che Jigme to talk with him. . . . [He] was wearing Chinese clothes rather than Tibetan dress and said that he had no plans to wear Tibetan clothes. He said that we [the PLA] should be more assertive with the Council of Ministers [Kashag]. He also said that it isn't possible to say whether the Dalai Lama and Panchen Lama are higher or lower. There are reasons on both sides. No one but the Buddha can say who is higher.
>
> I thought that having harmonious relations between the two lamas was not a small thing and that this is rather a big issue.[80]

From the start, therefore, Fan Ming thought the Southwest Bureau's officials were not compelling the Dalai Lama's government to show respect to him and to Che Jigme, the Panchen Lama's top official. Bad relations between the Southwest and Northwest bureaus' officials would continue and actually worsen in the coming years, because Fan Ming also did not agree with Mao's gradualist policy and favored quickly implementing reforms.

THE NEW TIBET WORK COMMITTEE

The first task for the two armies was to disband each separate Tibet Work Committee and establish the new integrated Tibet Work Committee. As Phünwang put it,

> Although incidents like this [with Fan Ming at the welcome ceremony] were regrettable, our mandate from Beijing was to forge a good working relationship between the Southwest and Northwest Bureau units. Since each had their

79. Quoted in Goldstein, Sherap, and Siebenschuh 2004: 167 (emphasis added).

80. Le 1985: 309–10, entry for 29 November 1951. Zhang Guohua would later (in 1954) make a self-confession in which he said that it was his mistake and shortcoming not to apply more pressure on Ngabö to have a council, or Kashag, minister go to welcome Che Jigme (Zhao 1998: 86)

Figure 16. Joint celebration of the arrival of the Northwest army's troops in Lhasa, December 1951, left to right: Mu Shengzhong, Fan Ming, Zhang Jingwu, Zhang Guohua, Tan Guansan, 1 December 1951. Source: Fan Ming

own Tibet Work Committee, we set out to merge the two sets of officials into a new unified Tibet Work Committee which would be the group of our people who discussed and decided on all important issues on Tibetan affairs for the Chinese side.[81]

In keeping with previous plans, the new Tibet Work Committee was to include officials from both armies, with the first secretary and the majority of members coming from the Southwest Bureau. It would be like a party committee in a province of inland China. On 5 December 1951, Zhang Guohua reported the formation of the new unified Tibet Work Committee to the Southwest Bureau, which forwarded his report to the Central Committee on 12 December. A week later, on 19 December, Beijing gave its approval. A few weeks later, on 10 January 1952, a formal meeting marking the establishment of the new unified Tibet Work Committee was held in Lhasa, at which Zhang Jingwu announced the appointments approved by the Central Committee. The first party secretary was Zhang Guohua (SWB); the deputy secretaries were Tan Guansan (SWB) and Fan Ming (NWB). The other members were Ya Hanzhang (NWB), Mu Shengzhong (NWB), Chang Binggui (SWB), Wang Qimei (SWB), Cheng Mingyi (SWB), Li Jue (SWB),

81. Goldstein, Sherap, and Siebenschuh 2004: 167.

Liu Zhengguo (SWB), and Phünwang (SWB).[82] Zhang Jingwu was not included in the new Tibet Work Committee, since he had come as the representative of the Central Committee and was scheduled to return to his
position in Beijing.

From the outside, therefore, all seemed well. The Tibetan side had no
idea about the tensions between the two forces, but they were there and
quickly made themselves felt, because not only did Fan Ming and Zhang Guohua differ in opinion about the Panchen Lama and how to deal with the two
hostile sitsab, but also Fan Ming had issues concerning his own status vis-à-
vis Zhang Guohua. Fan thought of himself as the "representative" (ch. dia-
biao) to the Panchen Lama in a manner analogous to that of Zhang Jingwu,
even though he was the representative from only the Northwest Bureau, while
Zhang Jingwu was the representative to the Dalai Lama from the Central
Committee. Nevertheless, he took this issue seriously and considered that it
gave him a status more equivalent to Zhang Jingwu and more elevated than
that of Zhang Guohua and Tan Guansan, who were just military commanders. In his own words,

> Zhang Jingwu was the representative to Lhasa in Front Tibet, and I was the
> representative to the Panchen's administration. These two representatives were
> both under the direct leadership of the Central Committee, just like Dalai and
> Panchen were parallel and both under the leadership of Beijing. As the rep-
> resentative to the Panchen's administration, I was also under the leadership
> of the Central Committee. Zhang Jingwu, the representative to Dalai's gov-
> ernment (Kashag), was the same as I was. The Central Committee had direct
> leadership of the Dalai's group and the Panchen's group as well. It was just like
> this. It was not like a small representative being under the leadership of a big
> representative. Many people do not understand this. . . . So as the represen-
> tative to the Panchen's administration, I was appointed by the Central Com-
> mittee and was under the leadership of the Central Committee.[83]

A Tibetan scholar who was in the Eighteenth Army Corps at that time explains further.

> Zhang Guohua was a general and was not very verbal. He just answered things
> directly. Fan Ming was educated and literate and was very verbal. Zhang Guo-
> hua acted like a military officer in his demeanor, whereas Fan Ming had a lot
> of elegance, like a Guomindang official. For example, when he gave lectures
> he would be very casual and would keep one hand in his pocket. Fan Ming
> was previously a Guomindang soldier but was also a secret spy for the CCP. So
> at this time everyone called Fan Ming "Da zhang wei" (Great Political Com-

82. Zhonggong xizang zizhiqu dangshi ziliao zhengji weiyuanhui 1990, entry for 20 December 1951; Ji 1993a.

83. Fan Ming, interview, 1993.

missar). In the regiment, when Fan Ming spoke, the solders didn't like it, but
the intellectuals liked him. He would speak in a way that highlighted his knowledge and learning. And his calligraphy was the best in Tibet. Over the past
forty years, Fan Ming was the best in Chinese writing and poetics. [In addition, Fan Ming] had strong backing from Peng Dehuai and Xi Zhongxun [the
leaders of the First Field Army and Northwest Bureau].[84]

Fan Ming thought that he should have the lead role in the Tibet Work Com-
mittee, while Zhang Guohua should focus his work on being head of the
Military Headquarters, that is, on army matters, not civil and political affairs.
This would have meant that Fan Ming would have had all the power.[85]

The internal discord between Fan and the Southwest Bureau that quickly
bubbled to the surface became so significant that Mao was alerted (probably by Zhang Jingwu), and two months later, on 7 March, the Central Committee reversed itself and instructed Zhang Jingwu to remain in Tibet and
serve as first party secretary (while also retaining his position in Beijing as
director of the General Office of the Central Military Commission). Zhang
Guohua now became first deputy secretary, and Tan Guansan and Fan Ming
became second and third deputy secretaries. This, of course, meant that now
it was a central government official rather that a Southwest Bureau official
who was the head secretary in Tibet. Zhang Guohua remained head of the
PLA forces in Tibet. In addition to this, a deliberate attempt was made to
placate Fan Ming and the Northwest by giving them important positions. As
Phünwang recalled, "The Northwest Bureau officials were given important
posts and ended up having substantial power in the day-to-day work activities. Fan Ming, for example, was appointed director of the United Front Work
Department, a critical office because it was responsible for managing relations with Tibetans. Mu Shengzhong and Ya Hanzhang, the other two senior Northwest officers, were given important positions as well."[86] Fan Ming
confirmed this: "Before 1958, I was in charge of the work in Tibet. Zhang
Guohua was in charge of the army in Tibet. . . . Zhang Jingwu was the party
secretary, but I was in the Tibet Work Committee, which had the political
power. In fact, I was like a deputy secretary for day-to-day work."[87] As will be
discussed in a later chapter, Fan Ming subsequently pursued a more hard-
line leftist, pro–Panchen Lama agenda than Zhang Jingwu and Zhang Guohua, creating bitter conflict within the party in Tibet.

Jambey Gyatso commented on the extraordinary nature of this reversal.

84. Jambey Gyatso, interview, 1993.
85. Jambey Gyatso, interview, 1993.
86. Goldstein, Sherap, and Siebenschuh 2004: 167. Ya Hanzhang was general secretary of
the TWC.
87. Fan Ming, interview, 1993.

So Zhang Guohua and Fan Ming were opposed on the way of looking at all things such as democratic reforms, people, and seating arrangements. Basically on everything. . . . The way of seeing things was different. This different way of seeing things is also (present) now.

And because these two were not friendly, Mao told Zhang Jingwu to stay in Tibet. He became the senior secretary, and Zhang Guohua and Fan Ming were deputy secretaries, as was Tan Guansan. This was the only place where there was one secretary and three deputy secretaries. At the time I didn't realize there were these fights, but later I read it in documents. There are twenty-odd provinces in China, and in all of these there is only one senior secretary and one deputy. Tibet's having four secretaries is unique. . . . So Zhang Jingwu was told to stay in Lhasa.[88]

Unique though this solution was, it was a shrewd move on the part of Beijing, diffusing one aspect of the discord within the party in Tibet. But serious strategic and tactical differences remained, and Fan Ming had no intention of deferring to the views of the Southwest Bureau personnel.

88. Jambey Gyatso, interview, 1993.

Chapter 11

First Steps toward Implementing the Seventeen-Point Agreement

By the end of October 1951, the Dalai Lama had formally accepted the Seventeen-Point Agreement, and the main PLA force had arrived. This set the stage for the Tibet Work Committee to initiate serious discussions on starting to implement the agreement. The committee's problem, however, was deciding which items to push and how hard. The Chinese leaders in Lhasa clearly understood they should avoid volatile issues such as land reforms and class struggle campaigns, but beyond that, things were murkier.

In November and December 1951, the Tibetan and Chinese sides still had completely separate administrative structures, so one of the first issues the Chinese raised was setting up two new joint administrative structures that would be directly under the central government and would include Chinese and Tibetan government officials working side by side.

THE TIBET MILITARY AREA HEADQUARTERS

One of these "new" offices was a Tibet Military Area Headquarters, which would ultimately oversee both Tibetan and Chinese troops. It had been specifically mentioned in point 15 of the Seventeen-Point Agreement.

> In order to ensure the implementation of this agreement, the Central People's Government shall set up a military and administrative committee[1] and a military area headquarters in Tibet.

In addition, point 8 of the agreement called for the gradual integration of the Tibetan army into the PLA and the Tibet Military Area Headquarters.

---

1. This name is sometimes translated as "committee" and sometimes as "bureau." I will use "committee" in this book except in quotations that use "bureau."

Tibetan troops shall be gradually reorganized by stages into the People's Liberation Army, and become a part of the national defense forces of the People's Republic of China.[2]

As mentioned in earlier chapters, the Tibetan army was a sensitive issue for the sitsab and many other Tibetan officials who saw the continuation of a separate army as an important symbol of Tibet's unique political status. At this time, the Tibetan government had its own military headquarters, which was located in the Shöl area below the Potala Palace. It oversaw—recruited, paid, disciplined—its own troops without consultation or interference from the Chinese side. When the Chinese raised this issue, the sitsab totally opposed all steps that would in any way begin *merging* the Tibetan army into the PLA. Even discussions about changing the Tibetan army's uniforms and its flag, therefore, precipitated heated arguments, not only between the Tibetan and Chinese, but also within the Chinese side, with Fan Ming and the Northwest cadre taking a much tougher line on this than did Zhang Guohua and the Southwest Bureau cadre. The Tibetan cadre Phünwang recalled this.

We noticed that the Tibetan army carried a "snow lion" flag in its drills and ceremonial appearances and did not carry the national flag of China. (They also continued to wear their own uniforms.) Some of our leaders, especially Fan Ming, believed this was not appropriate; it made it seem that Tibet was still not part of China. This led to heated arguments at the time the Tibet Military Area Headquarters was established in February 1952.

The Tibet Military Area Headquarters was the new office that would be in charge of all PLA troops in Tibet, including, in the future, the Tibetan troops. The Tibetan army was slated for eventual integration into the PLA, but in 1951 and 1952 it continued to function independently under its traditional leadership. Many of our cadre, like Fan Ming, disapproved, but this had been agreed upon in the Beijing negotiations. However, the Central Government also thought it was important symbolically to show that the new Military Headquarters was for both Chinese and Tibetan troops and had stipulated (in the secret codicil) that two senior Tibetan officials would serve as its Vice-Commanders. The Tibetan government complied and selected Ragasha and Ngabö for this. Both wore PLA uniforms at the inauguration ceremony, as did the commander-in-chief of the Tibetan army. However, the Tibetan army troops who participated in the ceremony continued to carry their own "snow lion" flag. This infuriated Fan Ming and others in the PLA who insisted that since Tibet was not a country it could not have its own national flag. Fan felt that we should force the Tibetan government to stop what he considered blatantly reactionary and "separatist" activities.

Serious arguments occurred over the use of this flag, but Acting Prime Minister [Sitsab] Lukhangwa refused to yield. His position was that this was not a "national" flag at all but rather the flag of the Tibetan military. As evidence for

2. See chapter 4.

this, he stated that this flag had never been flown on any Tibetan government buildings, and technically he was correct. I wasn't involved in this issue so I don't have a clear recollection of the whole chain of events and the many arguments, but to be honest, I could understand how seeing the Tibetan army carrying their snow lion flag made many PLA troops and commanders unhappy.

Zhang Guohua and Zhang Jingwu opposed Fan Ming on this issue. The 18th Army Corps' basic instructions from Chairman Mao and the Central Government clearly said we must go slowly and make every effort to win over the Dalai Lama and the elite. Holding this as the prime directive, Zhang Jingwu and Zhang Guohua believed that forcing the Tibetans to stop using their "military" flag would be counterproductive. They felt it was a minor symbolic issue that was not worth an acrimonious fight. I supported their view at the Tibet Work Committee leaders' meetings since I knew better than the others that it was essential for our side to advance cautiously and focus on our long-term goals. We needed to convince the Tibetan elite that we were not their lords or enemies if we were to eventually persuade them to begin making changes themselves. Of course, Fan Ming strongly disagreed. For him, I thought, the flag was not the real issue. He wanted to end the independence of the Tibetan army and government altogether, regardless of the consequences for Tibetan-Chinese relations. So he insisted that we should not let such behavior go unpunished. I used to joke with some of my Tibetan colleagues that Fan Ming's personality was like that of a brash Khampa who was aggressive and always ready to fight, whereas the Southwest Bureau's officials were more like the cautious and calculating Lhasans.

Fortunately, the views of Zhang Jingwu and Zhang Guohua carried the day and the Tibet Work Committee did not push on this issue. Actually, as late as 1958, when I last left Lhasa, the Tibetan army was still carrying their military flag, although by then they were carrying the national flag as well. This flag issue was the first big difference of opinion that occurred within the Tibet Work Committee. It would not be the last.[3]

The emotions this issue provoked are illustrated by one wild meeting at which Fan Ming told the sitsab, "If you don't do fly national flags, we [the Chinese side] will put it up on your Military Area Headquarters," and so on. Lukhangwa responded angrily, "Even if you put up flags one hundred times, we will tear them down one hundred times." Fan Ming in turn yelled back that Lukhangwa and Lobsang Tashi were creating problems between the Chinese and Tibetans and that he (Fan Ming) was going to tell the Dalai Lama that he should dismiss them. Lukhangwa, however, did not back down, telling Fan Ming, "If you Chinese order us to resign we will not obey, but if the Dalai Lama tells us to jump into the fire, we will kill ourselves by doing that, and if he says jump into the water, we will jump."[4]

3. Quoted in Goldstein, Sherap, and Siebenschuh 2004: 174–76.
4. Shan kha ba (Shasur) 1999: 361–62.

Figure 17. Tibetan army troops with regimental flag, 1950s.
Source: Phünwang Collection

The Chinese side, however, knew from their many discussions with Kashag ministers that opposition to this went far beyond the sitsab and was deep and widespread. Consequently, they backed off, and Tibetan troops were not merged, nor were uniforms changed, nor the Tibetan flag discontinued. However, the Tibetan side gave the Chinese a small victory by appointing the two Kashag ministers as vice commanders of the Tibet Military Area Headquarters, which opened on 10 February 1952.[5] This was a step forward for the Chinese but a tiny and mainly symbolic step, since the two ministers did no work in the Military Area Headquarters and the headquarters had no authority over any Tibetan troops. Moreover, the Chinese paid a price for this success, because the bitter arguments it precipitated exacerbated tensions

5. Yang 1987: 58–60.

and anger in Lhasa. This was not how Mao Zedong had envisioned the implementation of his gradualist strategy.

TIBET MILITARY-ADMINISTRATIVE COMMITTEE

The other new administrative entity was the Tibet Military-Administrative Committee. It also had been clearly mentioned in the agreement, and, as explained earlier, in other parts of China the Military-Administrative Committee was an interim administration operated by the military until "people's governments" could be organized. In Tibet, however, the Military-Administrative Committee would have a slightly different role, since it would not replace the traditional government but would coexist with it, at least for some unspecified period of time. The Military-Administrative Committee in Tibet was also very different because the Tibet Work Committee was unwilling to create it unilaterally without the approval of the Dalai Lama and his government.

The idea of creating a military-administrative committee in Tibet had been strongly opposed by Tibetans right from the start at the negotiations in Beijing and, like the Panchen Lama issue, almost resulted in the breakup of the negotiations in Beijing, as Phünwang recalled.

> Before raising the issue [of a military and administrative committee] at the formal meetings, Li Weihan invited Ngabö and me to his quarters. Li Weihan's thinking was that it would be useful to give Ngabö some time to think about and discuss the issue of the bureau with his delegation. That night, Li Weihan began very smoothly. "Things are going well," he said. "We have been working very hard. Although we have had some disagreements, for the most part the problems have been solved and agreement reached. However, there is one last item we need to discuss." He paused. "There is a need for us to establish a Military and Administrative Bureau in Tibet. It will be an administrative office of the Central Government, but the Dalai Lama will serve as its head and a Chinese representative and the Panchen Lama will serve as vice directors." When he finished explaining this, Ngabö, who had listened in silence, politely excused himself. He and I walked back to our hotel. He did not say anything at all about Li's proposal, and so what happened next surprised us all.
>
> Three days later, feeling he had given the Tibetan delegation plenty of time to digest the news, Li Weihan called a meeting. He began by discussing the proposal to establish a Military and Administrative Bureau in Tibet. When the Tibetan delegation heard the details, they erupted in surprise and anger.
>
> The Tibetan delegation had liked the fact that the agreement as they understood it allowed the traditional government of the Dalai Lama to continue to function internally in Tibet. When they heard about the new condition, they were angry because the idea of a Military and Administrative Bureau operating in Tibet seemed to undermine the traditional government's supremacy. It seemed to them as if what the Chinese side was giving them with one hand

they were taking away with another. While Li was explaining the details, I could hear Kheme whispering things like, "That's bizarre. These talks are never finished. This is not good."

It was obvious that it was the first time he or any of the others had heard about the idea. And things went from bad to worse. I think Li was about to say something like, "I'm sure Ngabö and you all have discussed this," but he was interrupted by Lhautara, a monk official, who was livid. He rolled up his sleeves and shook his fist in anger. "What is the matter with you people? Every day there is something new coming down from the Central Government. For months we have been arguing about a variety of topics, and now, when we thought things were just about finished, you propose something new like this!" Ngabö didn't say anything. He sat there, silent. The other Tibetans were shocked by Li's proposal. After more angry comments from the Tibetan side, Li Weihan got angry and said, "If that's the way you feel, then you can all pack up your bedding and go home." The implication, of course, was that the PLA would liberate Tibet militarily.

Things seemed to be spinning out of control and I decided to try to calm the situation. I rose and said, "Today at the meeting everyone has gotten angry. There have been lot of comments made and many misunderstandings. Li Weihan has said let us all return to the Beijing Hotel. So let's stop here for today. Later we can think and discuss the matter more calmly." I said this on my own to soften Li's ultimatum, making it sound as though he had meant for them to return to the *hotel*, not *Tibet*.

The Chinese delegation was caught off guard. It had not thought this was going to be a difficult issue, not only because it was presumed that Ngabö had already prepared the way but also because there were Military and Administrative Bureaus like this all over China. It was not something special we were going to impose in Tibet. . . .

Since we had heard nothing from the Tibetans about this after Li Weihan told Ngabö, we thought they had agreed. When we got back to the hotel, I went directly to the Tibetan delegation and tried to explain to them what the Chinese proposal actually meant. Kheme said to me, "Phünwang-la, this Bureau makes no sense. It is just like adding a rider on the neck of a rider already on horseback." He was very upset and angry. I tried to provide a different interpretation. The first thing I emphasized was that the Military and Administrative Bureau was standard Chinese policy; it wasn't something invented just for Tibet. I explained that the Central Government had set up such committees in four or five large areas in the new People's Republic of China. In every case, they were intended to be temporary administrative structures that would represent the Central Government until more representative permanent structures could be established. The committee in Tibet would be just one of these temporary administrative structures and would not be above the Tibetan government. And, I reminded them, the Dalai Lama was to be the rider of the horse, i.e., he would be the head of this committee and would therefore be in charge. So they didn't have to fear this.

I also indirectly told Kheme and Lhautara that this issue didn't come out of the blue, but that Li Weihan had raised it with their side earlier. I didn't mention Ngabö specifically, though, as I thought that this would have been obvious to them. After we talked awhile like this, Kheme and the monk official, Lhautara, said, "Oh, I see. Now we understand." Then I asked Kheme if he thought it would be acceptable to continue the meeting on this subject the next day. He said, "Yes. If it is like this, there is no problem."

While I was working hard to calm the fears of the Tibetan delegation, the Chinese government representatives were preparing for the worst. They genuinely believed that the Tibetan delegation would probably go home because of this issue, which would have been an enormous embarrassment. It would have meant war.

I immediately called Li Weihan and said I needed to meet him. The first thing he asked was, "Are your people going to pack up their things and go back to Tibet?" I was glad to be able to tell him that they weren't. "Things are back on track," I said, "because I explained what the Military and Administrative Bureau really represented, and I convinced them that it would be temporary and would not negate the authority of the Dalai Lama's government." Li Weihan was surprised and a bit incredulous at first. "Really?" he asked. "Are you sure?" I told him it was true, and the next thing I knew he picked up the phone, called Mao, and said, "Phünwang has just told me that the problem has been solved. We can talk with the Tibetan delegation tomorrow." It was quiet in the room and I could hear Mao's voice clearly. He was extremely pleased and so, obviously, was Li Weihan, who began to shake my hand enthusiastically. The next morning, with tempers cooled, both sides continued the discussion.

I never found out for sure why Ngabö did not tell the Tibetan delegation about the proposal ahead of time. I never discussed it with him, but I told Li Weihan my thinking when Li asked why they had been so startled when I raised this issue. I said I thought Ngabö kept the information to himself because he had been captured and there were many rumors that he had been bought off by the Chinese. So he may have felt that if he indicated he was meeting separately with the Chinese side about an issue as volatile as this, it could add further fuel to these suspicions. After this last crisis, the talks were quickly concluded.[6]

Now, back in Lhasa, the idea for such an office was, if anything, even more unpopular, especially with the sitsab, who asked repeatedly about it in the discussions leading up to the Dalai Lama's approval of the agreement. Now the Chinese side patiently tried to persuade the Tibetan government to accept it by explaining that the Military-Administrative Committee's sphere of activities would be limited only to "new activities" involving the implementation process of the agreement or to other modernization efforts, for example, schools, roads, and so forth. Tibetan governmental administrative tasks would, therefore, be divided into a traditional sphere of activities operated by the Dalai Lama's government and the new sphere administrated by the Military-Administrative Committee, of which the Dalai Lama would

6. Quoted in Goldstein, Sherap, and Siebenschuh 2004: 148–51.

also be the head—the chairman. In addition, the Chinese also offered to return administrative control over the Chamdo region to the new Military-Administrative Committee (but not to the Tibet local government).

But the sitsab strongly opposed this, as did virtually the entire governmental elite. The use of the term *military* linked to political administration conjured up the image of the Chinese military running civil affairs, including ultimately Buddhism. And this raised the fear that the Dalai Lama would lose his power and authority, and the Tibetan government would then become superfluous.[7] The Tibetans, therefore, argued using point 4 of the agreement, which stated, "The central authorities will make no change with regards to the existing political system in Tibet. The central authorities also will not alter the established status, functions, and powers of the Dalai Lama. Officials of various ranks shall hold office as usual."[8]

The Chinese, however, continued pushing, arguing that since the Military-Administrative Committee was specifically agreed to in the Seventeen-Point Agreement, it should be implemented. And at first they began to make inroads. On 20 November 1950, the three Kashag ministers in charge of the Surjong Kashag came to visit Zhang Jingwu and were told by him to think about providing him with a list of candidates from the Tibetan government for the Military-Administrative Committee. Three days later, Le Yuhong recorded in his diary that he had been called to the Kashag, where they had talked about nominees for the Military-Administrative Committee.[9] But there was no way the Kashag could move forward in the face of such widespread opposition, including that of the sitsab, so on 25–26 November the Kashag opted to shift responsibility by bringing this issue to the Assembly for discussion. Not unexpectedly, the Assembly recommended that the Dalai Lama should not agree to become chairman of the Military-Administrative Committee.[10] In December, January, and February, the Chinese side continued to pressure the Tibetan government to agree, but the Tibetans stalled, refusing to take any steps to move forward.

At the same time that these issues were being pushed without much success, the Chinese side proposed the creation of new schools. Point 9 of the Seventeen-Point Agreement had said, "The spoken and written language and school education of the Tibetan nationality shall be developed step by step in accordance with the actual conditions in Tibet."[11]

7. Chabtsom, interview, 1992, Lhasa. He was a kadrung until the end of 1951, when he became the county head in Shigatse.

8. See chapter 4.

9. Le 1985: 306–7, entries for 20 and 23 November 1951.

10. British Foreign Office Records, report of the Indian Mission in Lhasa for 16 November—15 December, contained in U.S. National Archives, 793B.00/2–652.

11. Goldstein 1989: 767.

THE LHASA PRIMARY SCHOOL AND THE PLA CADRE SCHOOL

In 1923 and again in 1944, the Tibetan government had hired a British head-master and set out to open a modern school in Tibet. These attempts failed because of opposition from the monks and conservatives, so in 1951 there were no modern schools anywhere in the Tibet, although a small number of private schools existed in Lhasa and other towns. These private schools basically taught students only how to read and write the different scripts of the written Tibetan language.[12] Members of the elite who wanted their children to obtain a modern education sent them to Darjeeling and Kalimpong, in India.

The Chinese were committed to changing this by creating a new education system for Tibetans. This was considered politically important, since giving Tibetans an opportunity to obtain a modern education would, they hoped, create a group of educated youth who would be favorably inclined toward modernization, socialism, and the Chinese.

Similarly, Zhang Jingwu and Tan Guansan felt education for their own cadres in the Tibetan language was also important for successfully implementing Mao's gradualist policy, and one of the first things they did was to set up a Tibetan-language school for the PLA. There was some opposition to this within the Tibet Work Committee, because some of the Chinese cadres, especially those from the Northwest Bureau, felt studying Tibetan was a waste of time, arguing that Tibetan as a language wasn't as complete as Chinese or English, but the majority criticized this as a kind of Han nationality chauvinism.[13] In the end, the Tibet Work Committee opened a Tibetan-language school for its younger men and women soldiers and cadres, especially Tibetan members of the PLA, since they were seen as a potential backbone for the future development of socialism in Tibet.[14]

The school, headed by Tan Guansan, secured permission from the Kashag to use Trungjilingka, a large park adjacent to the Chinese military base along the Lhasa's Kyichu River. More than forty teachers were selected from the Tibetans who had come with the army and from Lhasa intellectuals, monk officials, and aristocrats.[15] The Cadre School started classes on 12 January 1952 with over eight hundred students.[16] Mrs. T. D. Taring, an

---

12. For a discussion of these attempts to start modern schools, see Goldstein 1989: 121, 419–26. Note should be taken that in the 1940s the Guomindang operated a small "modern" school that taught Chinese and served mostly Chinese Muslims in Lhasa. It closed in 1949 when all Guomindang personnel were expelled from Tibet.

13. Le 1986: 303–5, entry for 12 January 1952.

14. Jiangbian Jiacuo (Jambey Gyatso) 2001: 116.

15. The school was called either the Cadre School (tib. leje labdra) or the Tibetan Language School (tib. pögi geyik jongdar dzindra).

16. From those with the rank of "company" (ch. lian) and "platoon" (ch. pai) head.

Figure 18. Teaching PLA troops Tibetan before going to Tibet. The sentences say: "We are the army of the people." "After arriving in Tibet, we will help the people." Source: Chen Zonglie

aristocrat who was one of those Tibetan teachers, discussed her involvement and feelings.

> The Chinese leaders wanted all their soldiers to know Tibetan, so in 1952 an Army school was organized. For a school building, the invaders requisitioned the Trungji Trokhang, the summer house of the lay-officials by the riverside. . . . Eight hundred Chinese Army students slept on the floors.[17]
> At that time the Chinese came many times and said we should teach Tibetan to their young soldiers. They told the Tibet government that they needed some wives of high-ranking officials to be teachers for the male and female soldiers. So five of us [women] were sent to be teachers.[18] . . . I taught in the Chinese school for about two years. I did my best. Those children were not responsible for the situation [in Tibet]. I liked them, and those children also liked me.[19]

17. Taring 1986: 206.
18. These five were Tangme (Kunchok Pemo), Taring (Rinchen Dolma), Janglocen (Yangjen), Samling (Söpal), and Tsögo (Deyang). They were all from the more "progressive" Tibetan aristocracy. They asked for and received permission from the Kashag to do this.
19. Taring (Rinchen Dolma), interview, 1992, Rajpur.

The Chinese organized the classes very efficiently. Teaching began at 8 A.M. and ended at 5 P.M., five days a week, with an hour's break at midday. All classes were held in the open air and during early spring it was cold, yet the students had to sit on the bare ground. Most of them picked up Tibetan fast, learning a hundred words a day and at the end of every month they had to do a test, reading and writing a hundred sentences. As soon as the students knew enough to make themselves understood, they were replaced by others, but those who were very clever were kept on to study fully and many of them became official interpreters in place of the men from Ba [Batang] who did not have a good Tibetan education.

. . . During the ten-minute breaks between classes they brought me a mug of hot water, to which I added little packets of coffee, sugar and milk powder. My students were girls of sixteen to eighteen who used to say, "You look like my mother." Some of them had not seen their parents for three or four years and the first batch, especially, had a lonely time as the motorable roads from Chamdo to Lhasa and from Sining [Xining] to Lhasa were only made within the next two years.

I taught my students sincerely, patiently repeating the sentences many times, which the girls appreciated. It gave me a funny feeling to be always amongst the Chinese; we were so frightened of them, yet now we were teaching them. But I carefully remembered that they were human beings and should not be hated. Poor little things, what could they do? They also were very frightened. . . . I taught about 700 male and female students who were soldiers in the school.[20]

Even more important than this Cadre School, however, was the plan to start Tibet's first primary school for Tibetans.

THE LHASA PRIMARY SCHOOL

Phünwang, one of the officials charged with organizing the new primary school, recalled his and the Tibet Work Committee's thinking: "One of the things that I felt strongly about was the need for modern education in Lhasa. . . . From early on we in the Tibet Work Committee discussed the need to start providing public education. . . . I believed the school would be the foundation for educating progressive young Tibetans. This was the first step toward creating a new and modern Tibet."[21]

The emphasis in the new school was to be on the Tibetan language, but teaching would also include modern subjects such as math and geography. Chinese would not be formally taught but would be introduced informally through songs.[22]

20. Taring 1986: 206–8.
21. Quoted in Goldstein, Sherap, and Siebenschuh 2004: 178.
22. Le 1986: 308–9, entry for 16 February 1952.

Operationally, the Chinese side thought it was important to make this not just the Tibetan Work Committee's school but a joint Chinese-Tibetan school, so they involved important Tibetans at all levels.[23] The first thing they did was to convene a large meeting with about fifty important Tibetans, such as Ngabö, Tsarong, Kapshöba, Sambo, Surkhang Khenjung, Takla (Phüntso Tashi), Tsadrü Rimpoche, Kheme Dzasa, and Janglocen to discuss this idea. Everyone at the meeting was enthusiastic, so at the end of this meeting Le Yuhong and Ngabö put together a list of people to compose a preparatory committee for the school.[24] After these were agreed to, real work began immediately.[25] Tasks were divided up; for example, Tsarong and Kapshöba were responsible for buying the notebooks, and others for making desks and chairs. There was talk of actually opening the school that April (1952).[26]

In February 1952, a perfect house in the heart of the city was found when the Dalai Lama's family agreed to sell their Seshin house for eight thousand dotse.[27] Work also started on preparing the teaching materials, which was a more sensitive task, since a basic rule for the Tibet Work Committee was that their content must be compatible with the party's political line. Textbooks, in fact, could not be altered without permission from the central government.[28]

However, the issue of curriculum content raised second thoughts, and quickly the whole idea of a school ran into problems in the Kashag. Ngabö informally explained to the Chinese that while all the Kashag ministers were giving indications that they were in favor of having a primary school, some were saying that the teaching should be controlled by the Tibetan government and that it was necessary to include some supplemental religious teachings in the curriculum. Ngabö was opposed to this and thought that it would create serious problems, so he advised the Chinese that they should not discuss this again with the Kashag, in other words, they should go ahead on their own.

In the next weeks, the Chinese side worked on the political education content of the textbooks and did not push for Kashag approval. The Chinese also settled the question of funding by having the central government pay for the school's expenses. However, as knowledge of the planned school became more widely known, opposition in Lhasa grew markedly. On 27 March,

23. Goldstein, Sherap, and Siebenschuh 2004: 178.

24. They were nine from the Tibetan side (Surkhang Khenjung, Kapshöba, Sambo, Tsarong Dzasa, Takla [Phüntso Tashi], Pandatsang, Tsadrü Rimpoche, Janglocen, and Ngabö) and four from the Chinese side (Ling Liang, Li Anjie, Phünwang, and Le Yuhong).

25. Le 1986: 310, entry for 18 February 1952.

26. Le 1986: 313–15, entry for 18 February 1952.

27. Le 1986: 323, entry for 6 March 1952.

28. Le 1986: 315–16, entry for 22 February 1952.

Le Yuhong recorded in his diary that the Chinese side had heard that people in Lhasa were signing a petition against the primary school and that Surkhang, one of the more senior of the Kashag ministers who had just recently returned from India, was among them.[29] While this is unlikely since Surkhang was very much in favor of modern education and all of his children were in school in India, there was growing opposition from monk officials as well as from a new political group that called itself the People's Association. Coming on top of the anger caused by the arguments over the army, the Military-Administrative Committee, and the high inflation, the push to start a primary school further enflamed Tibetan anger at Chinese attempts to change Tibetan society, and it created an extremely dangerous and unstable situation in Lhasa. The story of this tide of unrest and how the Chinese dealt with it is the subject of the next chapter.

29. Le 1986: 339, entry for 27 March 1952. Gyalo Thondup, the Dalai Lama's older brother, commented in an interview with me (1995, Hong Kong) that the Chinese told him at this time that Surkhang was helping them by coming at night and telling them what was going on in the Kashag. Many top officials visited the Chinese, but it seems clear from Le's diary that Gyalo was mistaken and that the Chinese side considered Surkhang one of their key enemies. A number of other Chinese telegrams that are presented in chapter 12 also reveal the same opinion of Surkhang. In reality, what is surprising is the extent to which Ngabö was privately informing the Chinese about what was being argued in the Kashag.

Chapter 12

The Tibetan People's Association

Tibetan politics traditionally was the prerogative of a tiny elite of lay (aristocratic) and monk officials.[1] There was no notion of popular democracy— no political parties and no freedom of political expression. Public opposition to the government or its policies was not permitted. Tibet's traditional political ideology was simple and straightforward: the work of governing was not the concern of its subjects. However, the signing of the Seventeen-Point Agreement and the arrival of thousands of Chinese officials and troops led to the emergence—for the first time in Tibetan history—of an organization of nonelite Lhasa residents whose aim was to influence political affairs independently of the government. Called the Mimang Tsondu (People's Association/Assembly),[2] not only was it anti-Chinese and anti-communist, but also it was critical of the Tibetan government, which it felt was weak and ineffectual in dealing with the Chinese. The association's activities almost precipitated an outbreak of Sino-Tibetan fighting in the spring of 1952.

The idea of the common people becoming active in Tibetan politics, however, had been in the air for some years and derived in part from a seed sown decades earlier by the 13th Dalai Lama, who, in 1932, the year before he died, wrote an essay usually called his "political statement" or "last testament."

---

1. On major issues, the abbots (and ex-abbots) of the three great monasteries around Lhasa (Drepung, Sera, and Ganden) were also involved by virtue of their participation in the meetings that were convened occasionally to deliberate on difficult or serious issues (see the introduction for a discussion of the Assembly).

2. It has been called a number of related names in Tibetan, such as "mimang tsondu," "mimang tsogpa," "mimang thrötsog," or "Chundru mimang thrötso." All of these basically mean People's Association or Assembly, or in the case of the last name, the People's Association of the Water-Dragon year (1952).

In it he warned of a future communist threat to Tibet and called on all Tibetans to work together for the common good, as the following section illustrates:

> This present era is rampant with the five forms of degeneration, in particular the red ideology. In Outer Mongolia, the search for a reincarnation of Jetsun Dampa (the Grand Lama of Urga [later renamed Ulan Bator]) was banned; the monastic properties and endowments were confiscated; the lamas and the monks were forced into the army; and the Buddhist religion destroyed, leaving no trace of identity. . . .
>
> In the future, this system will certainly be forced either from within or without on this land that cherishes the joint spiritual and temporal [political] system. If, in such an event, we fail to defend our land, the holy lamas, including "the triumphant father and son" [the Dalai Lama and the Panchen Lama] will be eliminated without a trace of their names remaining; the properties of the incarnate lamas and of the monasteries along with the endowments for religious services will all be seized. Moreover, our political system, originated by the three ancient kings, will be reduced to an empty name; my officials, deprived of their patrimony and property, will be subjected to fear and miseries, will be unable to endure day or night. Such an era will certainly come! . . .
>
> It is the . . . duty and responsibility of all my subjects, the religious and lay members of the various orders, to think and work unerringly in unity and cooperation for the promotion of the common welfare and of peace. . . .
>
> It is evident that if you do not devote yourselves to the service of the state but consistently indulge in seeking to benefit yourselves and act with prejudice and nepotism, the long-term common objectives will not be realized, and then nothing will help and regrets will be useless.[3]

The previous Dalai Lama, therefore, warned not only about external threats but also about the dangerous consequences of self-serving behavior on the part of the elite. In Lhasa in 1950–51, many felt his warning had come to pass.

The period following the death of the 13th Dalai Lama in 1933 had been marked by precisely the kind of internal degeneration that the 13th Dalai Lama had alluded to. As mentioned previously, graft, corruption, and immorality under the regent Reting (1933–43) were rampant, and internal disunity reached crisis proportions when a major conflict over power erupted after Reting had resigned but then tried to regain the regency. When the new regent, Taktra (1943–50), also an incarnate lama, resisted, the monks of the Che College of Lhasa's Sera Monastery rebelled in support of Reting in 1947. The Kashag, led by Surkhang and Lhalu, arrested Reting Rimpoche after it received information that he was seeking help from Guomindang China (Chiang Kai-shek) and ordered the Tibetan army to attack his rebel-

3. Alo Chöndze 1958. Based on the translation by Lobsang Lhalungpa with slight changes.

lious monk followers in Sera. The army easily defeated the monks and ended the uprising, but when Reting Rimpoche mysteriously died in prison in the Potala Palace, his supporters and many other Tibetans believed that he had been murdered.[4] The events of this sordid affair—one high incarnate lama (Taktra) fighting another high incarnate lama (Reting), the monks of a great monastery fighting against the Tibetan government, and the current lama regent probably assassinating the ex-regent—deeply troubled many Tibetans.

The 13th Dalai Lama's political testament, in saying that it was the duty of *all* Tibetans to think and work on behalf of the nation, also provided an opening for nonelite Tibetans to partake in politics. Alo Chöndze, a prominent people's leader in Lhasa in the mid-1950s, in fact, said he had this in mind when during the Reting incident he and some other lay Tibetans intervened and tried to persuade both sides to reach a peaceful settlement.

> I was a trader and had nothing to do with politics, but in 1947, at the time of the civil war with Sera Monastery, the masses were very sad so we . . . started a traders group to act as mediators. . . . The monks had taken possession of the hill on top of Sera, and the government made all kinds of preparations. The government had a plan to destroy the monastery, and the Sera monks had the idea to fight against the government, so we requested that the abbot of Ganden Monastery (the Ganden tripa) ask the government not to go to war. At the same time, we summoned some monk leaders [from Sera's Che College] to the sand dunes below Sera Monastery for talks. We advised them not to fight against the government, because it has many troops and they would lose. We told them to please listen to us, "the people," . . . but the monks refused. . . . [They said] that Tsenya truku had consulted Nyare gyejen, their protector deity, and he had told them not to be timid and they would definitely win.[5]
>
> So we left and went to the Tibetan army garrison at Trapchi and met with Kapshöba, the Kashag minister in charge of the army there. We told him that if he had to go to war (against the monks), please not to destroy the monastic college [the edifice].[6]

Mediation in disputes was a time-honored tradition in Tibet, but for political conflicts like this, not by "common folk." So even though these Tibetans had no political ideology or identity and by even loose standards certainly were not an organization, their initiative brought the prophecy of the 13th Dalai Lama into the public arena through their explicit use of it as justification for their efforts.

The failure of the Reting coup and the Sera revolt, however, did not bring stability or unity to Tibet. The supporters of Reting were incensed at what

---

4. See Goldstein 1989:486–91 for a detailed discussion of this.

5. Deities in Tibet were consulted though mediums (oracles), who went into a trance and were possessed by the deity, who would then answer questions posed to him or her.

6. Alo Chöndze, interview, 1993, Cleveland, OH.

they considered his murder, and as the Taktra regime became increasingly debased by bribery and corruption, it became very unpopular. Moreover, it was unable to prevent the Chinese Communists from entering Tibet by either diplomatic or military means. As Alo Chöndze put it, "The Tibetan government was very aggressive against their own people [then], but [later] against the Chinese they were useless."[7] A second precursor people's activity occurred in August 1951, when, as we saw in chapter 2, Alo Chöndze felt the people needed to express their feelings by organizing a welcome committee for the Dalai Lama when he returned to Lhasa from Yadong.

These beginnings coalesced in November-December 1951, when an organized association of common people was created and explicitly chose to use the term *the people* in its name and for its identity. The Tibetan term for "the people," *mimang*, is actually a neologism that had been coined by the Chinese Communists to translate the Chinese term *ren min*. Like the Chinese term, *mimang* joined two traditional Tibetan terms—"mang," meaning "ordinary" or "common" with regard to people,[8] and "mi," meaning "person" or "people." Such a term was needed, because Tibetan had no exact term for "the people" as a collectivity. Once coined, it became widely known in Lhasa, because it was prominently mentioned in the Seventeen-Point Agreement and was part of the name of the People's Liberation Army and the People's Republic of China. A member of this association explained the thinking behind the choice of this term for their organization. Although his comments on Chinese excesses are highly exaggerated, they reflect what many Tibetans at that time felt.

> The Chinese army . . . came, and no matter what they said [in their propaganda], they had already shown their true character at Chamdo. So the Chinese came from everywhere, and a month or so after they came they acted worse and worse. . . . They started saying such things as they wanted to put a flag on the Potala and a flag on the Tsuglagang. Then they said, " . . . one country can't have two military camps, so the Tibetan military regiments have to join with the Chinese ones and wear Chinese uniforms." So like this, [the people thought] that even the power of the Dalai Lama [was now in doubt], even though it may have been written in the agreement [that he would remain in power]. . . . So the very fact that even now [at the beginning] they were doing such things [made us think that] later on the country would have nothing. So while it is true that the [Tibetan] government had discussed this with them, they [the Chinese] did all kinds of things that weren't really in the agreement, and this would not be good in the future for the country and the people. So the people felt that they should do something, since they [the Chinese] were

7. Alo Chöndze, interview, 1993.
8. For example, the term *gendün mang* means the "common monks" in a monastery as opposed to the "leaders."

not listening to what the government was saying. At that time the two sitsab were there, and they were advising them [the Chinese] a lot, but the Chinese were not listening.[9]

Another Tibetan who was part of this movement reflected similarly on the thinking in those days.

A few [Tibetans] were acting very close to the Chinese . . . [but] from the perspective of the people, if one were to think in terms of an enemy, then the Chinese were it. The people had great fears that the Chinese would destroy Buddhism and that, from whichever angle one looked, the power of His Holiness would be wrecked and the Chinese would forcefully rule Tibet. So because of this, the people never looked to the Chinese, nor did they ever like the Chinese at all. So from this perspective the people were criticizing the [Tibetan] government officials and saying, "If you [officials] don't work properly, then it will be like oil absorbed by paper." They also said that when the Chinese first came, the government did not take proper steps, so now we have landed in such a situation, and . . . they said that even now the Tibetan government is listening to what the Chinese are saying and that if this continues it is not right and so on. So this kind of talk was present everywhere. . . .

[On the other hand the government felt that it] had to be extremely careful. Likewise, the Dalai Lama was very careful and doing his best to work within the terms of Seventeen-Point Agreement. But the Chinese made the Seventeen-Point Agreement a tool to trick us. When they first came they showed themselves to be well-disciplined and good. Then gradually they got worse and worse and more and more powerful, and finally things became unworkable. So in such a situation, if our government became very forceful and broke relations, then the Chinese were already here with a lot of soldiers. So fearing suppression, our government tried their best to be very diplomatic. . . . Anyway, this was the opinion of the government, but the people did not agree with that.

The people wanted to see the Chinese practice what they were preaching. They said that they came to help and improve Tibet, and they said that the Seventeen-Point Agreement said that if the people do not agree with things that were being done, the Chinese will stop doing them. So the people thought that the Chinese would adhere to this and do what they preached. Therefore, although the Tibetan government and the people did not disagree on basic issues, there was a great difference in how they approached the problem. The government always wanted to make good relations with the Chinese, but the people felt that something had to be done and that they couldn't just sit around doing nothing while time moved on and the Chinese got stronger and stronger.[10]

A former Tibetan aristocratic official recalled the situation more incisively.

9. Lhatsün Labrang Chandzö, interview, 1992, Dharamsala.
10. Namgye Wangdü, interview, 1993, Dharamsala.

It had come to the point where one had no choice but to think politically. As I look [back] at it . . . if the Chinese did not give any lectures [on political ideas], then that's it, right? [People would not be so conscious of the term *the people*.] But whenever they gave a lecture, they always had the word "the people" on the tip of their tongues. It was almost a case where if the people said, "Jump into the river," then the Communist Party might jump. That's how much they thought of the people. . . . So when we needed to challenge the Chinese, if we didn't use this word, then no other word would do. It is definite that this is how the name "the people" was used. That's for sure. The Chinese considered the people a most precious thing, saying that they have come to serve the people, and this and that about the people, so if the people revolted against them, then [laughs]—if the thing that they considered so precious revolted against them, then what's going to happen? What are they going to say?

If, on the other hand, the upper classes did it [criticized them], there are many labels they [the Chinese] could give them. Likewise, if religious figures and monks revolted, there are many labels they could give. But since they always had "the people" on the tip of their tongues, when the very thing that they said was so good revolted against them, then the thinking was that maybe this is the best strategy. It was definitely something thought about and put into action and was not something that just arose by itself. It is exactly . . . because the Chinese used the word *people*, not because of a conception [to start] democratic processes.[11]

Chinese sources date the start of this organization to late November 1952,[12] precisely the period when high inflation and the sitsab's emotional opposition to the Chinese attempts to change the Tibetan army and create the new Military-Administration Committee was creating a climate of widespread anger against the Chinese.

However, despite the prominent use of the name "People's" for this association, its founders and leaders were not really common folk. They were, to be sure, of the people in the sense that they did not belong to the aristocratic and monk official government elite, but they were also not proletarian folk in the communist sense. Tibet in 1951 had no well-defined hierarchy of social strata. At the apex of the social hierarchy was an elite upper stratum consisting of several hundred aristocratic government officials (and their families) and an equal number of monk government officials (and their households). There were also a few—less than a score—major incarnate lamas with vast property and their own monasteries in Lhasa, for example,

11. Maya, interview, 1991, Dharamsala.

12. Dangdai zhongguo congshu bianjibu 1991: 61. The Tibetan name of the party commonly includes "Water-Dragon Year" in it, and that year began in late February 1952. This discrepancy relates to the earlier date's reference to the time when the idea and preliminary discussions first arose; and the latter date, to when actual membership was solicited and its petition was delivered.

Kundeling, Tshecoling, and Tshomöling. Together, this elite category probably numbered no more than a few thousand people.

As explained in the introduction, beneath them almost all of the remainder of the population hereditarily belonged to estates owned by aristocratic and monastic lords or by the government itself. And while there were significant differences within this vast social category—for example, some had land and others did not—they all shared the characteristic that they were hereditarily bound to their lord and could not change that status unilaterally.

Between the elite and the "masses" was a numerically small category sometimes referred to in Tibetan as "those in the middle" (tib. badzalaga). This middle stratum was primarily made up of administrators and managers who worked privately for the elite—for monasteries, for the labrang of incarnate lamas, for aristocratic families,[13] and even sometimes for government offices. The vast majority of these administrators and managers were worldly monks or ex-monks who had learned writing and managing skills while living as monks. The great monasteries in Tibet were major economic enterprises with vast landholdings and extensive grain and money-lending operations, so at any given time they required hundreds of monks to administer their resources. The simpler of these monastic "economic" jobs rotated among monks as a kind of "new monk tax" obligation that all young monks were required to perform for some period of time. The higher-level managerial tasks, however, were typically carried out by monks who were interested in such work and who had special aptitude, in particular, monks who were bright and knew how to write well and keep accounts. A number of such monks became, in essence, literate, "worldly" monks. They were still monks in the sense of having vows of celibacy, but they no longer lived in a monastery or participated in the cycle of monastic prayer sessions and so on. Some, along the way, actually lost their celibacy and married, but all of them held great affection for and loyalty to their monasteries and the traditional institutions of Tibetan Buddhism in general.

The job market for such manager-administrators was excellent, because the elite government officials disliked leaving Lhasa to collect taxes or loans or to conduct other trading activities and because there was no general education system to produce large numbers of other lay people with equivalent skills. Many of these manager types, therefore, came to work for the elite and were well-connected with powerful figures in the society, particularly among the monk official segment. Consequently, among the nonelite in

13. Most larger aristocratic, estate-holding families conscripted some youths from their estate serfs, bringing them to Lhasa and educating them for later use as estate managers. One of the earlier Kashag ministers in exile, Wangdor, was such a servant-manager from the Surkhang family.

Lhasa, there was a small stratum of individuals who were especially conscious of government activities and personages and had important personal relationships with the elite.[14]

The founders of the People's Association were from this segment of society. They knew well the tough anti-Chinese attitude of the two sitsab, whose verbal rebuffs to the Chinese generals had spread widely by word of mouth, and about the importance of the people to the Communists. In their eyes, someone in the government was finally standing up for Tibetans and their religion and was confronting the Chinese. Thus, at the end of 1951, a few of these types decided that the time had come for the Tibetan people to help support the sitsab by conveying the people's feelings to the Chinese.[15] In doing so, they created the first large-scale involvement of a heretofore unpoliticized segment of Lhasa society. And although political dissidence was not traditionally permitted in Tibet, the sitsab's open opposition to the Chinese had provided an ideological green light for this kind of political protest.

The acknowledged leader of this group was Thamjö Sonam, a literate ex-monk who, while still a monk, had served as one of the managers of Sera Monastery's Mey College. The other top leaders included Jayan Dawa from Drepung's Loseling College, Tsha Trunyila, a monk who had served as the secretary of Tshawa Khamtsen in Sera's Mey College, Kamika Chöndze, and Drubthola from Gomang College.[16] All were from the monk/ex-monk managerial segment. Their specific goal was to present a formal petition to the Chinese authorities in the name of the people, a petition that, on the one hand, would tell the Chinese clearly that the Tibetan people did not want thousands of Chinese troops and officials residing in Lhasa and, on the other hand, would offer an alternative less than independence, namely, a return to the relationship between Tibet and China that resembled the one existing under the Qing dynasty. This, of course, was also the general view of the sitsab.

Since this petition was to represent the voice of the Tibetan people, not the government, the organizers needed to recruit large numbers of com-

14. In addition to these badzalaga monks and ex-monks, in the urban setting the middle stratum also included a small category of laymen who had learned writing in one of the three or four small private schools in Lhasa. These individuals were typically the children of the above-mentioned ex-monk managers, or the relatives of government monk officials, or the sons of successful craftsmen and clerks in Lhasa. Some were even the sons of rich suburban village families. This stratum also included a small group of clerks working in government offices, small shopkeepers, large and small traders, and noncommissioned officers in the Tibetan army and police.

15. Namgye Wangdü, interview, 1993.

16. Tsha Trunyila was also known as Chagdrung Lodrö Phüntso. Kamika Chöndze got his nickname because he was Samye karme, that is, the monk in charge of the collection of the butter tax for butter lamps at Samye. He was also known as Kargang Phüntso Tashi.

mon people as members of their association. Their idea was to have an inner circle of about twenty to thirty top members, who would do the planning and make the decisions, and then another much larger outer organization, which would meet less frequently to discuss the proposals created by the inner circle. By spring of 1952, sixty to one hundred Lhasa residents had formally signed up as members and were attending the People's Association meetings in Lhasa, which, it should be noted, were not secret, because Thamjö Sonam and the other leaders were intent on representing these gatherings as meetings to assess and convey the views of the Tibetan people to the Chinese and Tibetan governments, not to organize an anti-Chinese insurgency.

A former member explained how the sweet tea shops in Lhasa served as recruitment vehicles.[17]

> Normally there was a lot of conversation in the sweet tea shops. For example, if four or five people were there, they would [talk about the Chinese situation and] suggest various ways to deal with the situation, but they were unanimous in wanting to challenge the Chinese. And so in the sweet tea shops one might say to someone you could trust, "Come to my house when you're free sometime, please come." So one person meets and then two, then three, et cetera. We would gather at Thamjö Sonam's place or at Jayang Dawa's place. The house of our teacher, Chagdrung Lodrö Phüntso, was another place we met, as was Kamika Chandzö's house.[18]

One person who was asked to join was Setrong Wangye, a Tibetan from a rich family in an area adjacent to Lhasa. He and his family were actually serfs of the government (tib. shungyupa), but they had large landholdings and serfs of their own. He and his brothers had been educated in a private school in Lhasa and were serving as government-appointed tax collectors for the upper part of their district. Because of this, Wangye lived in Lhasa for much of the year. He recalled the attempt to recruit him there.

> I didn't like the old society, because we weren't aristocrats and the government officials didn't enforce the law honestly. Many people felt this way. But I also didn't believe in the new society that the Chinese were talking about, so I didn't join up with them. However, when the People's Association started, one of its members, Lobsang Trinley, an ex-manager from Sera Monastery who was an old friend from childhood, tried to get me to join.
>
> I asked him what kind of people were in the association, and he answered, "People like you," that is, people who knew how to read and write and who had

17. As a result of British Indian influence, Lhasans had become fond of drinking black tea mixed with milk and sugar. It was served premixed in glasses and was called cha ngamo (sweet tea). Many tea shops specialized in serving this kind of tea (and they still do in today's Lhasa).

18. Chandzö Ngawang Temba, interview, 1993, Dharamsala.

good relations with the people of lower status and yet also knew the high government officials. That was the kind of people they were after. When I asked him who was in the group, he named people who were well known in society, such as Thamjö Sonam. . . . Lobsang Trinley urged me to join, saying, "We want people like you who are experienced and capable and can tell the difference between good and bad."

I asked him quietly who is providing the expenses for this initiative, and he said it was the Lower Tantric College in Lhasa.[19] Then when I asked him the main reason for starting this organization, he told me a lot of things about how the Chinese were doing terrible things in Tibet and how the 13th Dalai Lama's last testament had said the Communists are bad and should be stopped. So the main reason he gave me was to expel the Chinese from Tibet. We leaders, he said, are going to stir up and mobilize the people, and then together with them we will be able to expel the Chinese. . . .

That night I went home and discussed this with my two brothers, . . . and kidding around, I told them I planned to join. My older brother immediately got agitated and said that was impossible. He said that later all kinds of trouble would come from that. He also said that I should know this, because I had had some direct experience with the Communists [really Chinese] and knew their strength.

He was referring to a trading trip I had taken to Sadam in Yunnan just before liberation [of China in 1949]. There was a district there called Lijiang, where the Guomindang had headquarters. And I happened to be there at the time of a Guomindang holiday, so all the soldiers were out marching on parade. I was deeply impressed by this spectacle and thought at the time that just those Guomindang soldiers from that one area were stronger than all of Tibet's army. They carried weapons and cannons, all of which were American. Their rifles were German, but all the bullets were American. I bought some guns . . . from them, but I thought there was no comparing the strength of Tibet's army with just that one Guomindang unit. So if the Communists could destroy the Guomindang, how could Tibet cope? After that, my brothers always used to tell me that the CCP was too powerful, and no one could handle them. So my older brother was adamant that there would be no advantage to joining a group like this [the People's Association]. In 1949, he said, we easily threw out the Chinese, but now there is no way. He also didn't think the association could mobilize the masses, since most of the common people were very poor, and the CCP was telling them that they would make their livelihood good. So if the Chinese did that, the organization would not be able to mobilize them.[20]

19. tib. gyümed tratsang. Another member added that "the association's leaders would announce often at the meetings that So-and-So Lama agreed to make a contribution and that such and such aristocratic household also provided things. . . . Many people came forward to be patrons of the association, so at first things were developing very well" (Namgye Wangdü, interview, 1993).

20. Setrong Wangye, interview, 1993, Lhasa.

The People's Association also included members from the Tibetan army. One soldier from the Gyantse Regiment (which was stationed in Lhasa as the police force) explained his involvement.

> Since the association was opposed to having close relations between Tibet and China, the military did not come out openly in support of it. However, secretly, various regiments gave their support and were involved in the organization.
> My joining was a case in point. I had not specifically heard that the people were organizing. Rather, my regiment's officers seem to have been secretly in touch with the People's Association's leaders and decided to send a representative from the regiment. Since it would be too conspicuous to send one of the [higher officers such as] captains (rupön) or lieutenants (gyagpön), a sergeant (sheyngo) called Wangden Lhakpa Gojey was sent. I was ordered to accompany and assist him. I was quite young [about eighteen years old], so that's how I got there. So I went to Shide [where the association's headquarters were] and stayed there for over a month [until the petition was handed in]. In the morning I did things like copy letters, and I also took messages and put up posters throughout Lhasa.[21]

Another soldier also explained his involvement.

> In the military it was thought that the "people" had done so much, so we also must try to do something. However, we couldn't openly come out and do it, but it was thought that unless we supported them [the association] we would not be satisfied. So with this thinking they [the military representatives] went there [to the meeting] and told them, "We support you in every way." . . .
> I did not go to the meetings, but they came back to the military camp and brought letters saying that we were taking pledges [to join the association]. So we said, "We agree with you and we support you." . . . Each person came out and said now we had to do something; now we just couldn't stay like this.[22]

Since the raison d'être of the association leaders was to present a strong statement from the people to the Chinese, the leaders decided to have members not just from Lhasa but from all over Tibet. Consequently, they wrote to friends and sent members to other districts in Tibet where they had connections, in order to compile a long list of members supporting the petition. The local district officials would be told that a petition is being made to the Tibetan and Chinese authorities and that all the people of the district must support this. In this manner they were able to collect thousands of names relatively quickly.[23] One Tibetan explained,

> Around this time I had been working as an official in far Western Tibet (tib. Tö ngari), . . . so I had many connections there. Consequently, I sent people

21. Namgye Wangdü, interview, 1993.
22. Gyagpön Kedram, interview, 1992, Dharamsala.
23. Namgye Wangdü, interview, 1993.

to this area to collect names for the association. . . . People in these areas were [traditionally] organized into groups (tib. shoga), each with its own leader, so the people we sent worked through these leaders, who in turn sent out people with a letter asking how many households and household members there were in each area. They returned with the household names and seals.[24]

Using this technique to expedite recruitment, the People's Association was able to rapidly expand their membership list to thousands, although most of these people were neither active members nor had they even seen the petition. They were mainly names taken from district records. At most they knew only that a people's association was forming that wanted to preserve religion and oppose the Chinese Communists.

Interestingly, the monastery leadership was missing from the membership. Although the manager-type monks and ex-monks dominated the association, and although many regular monks were involved, there were no official representatives from the Three Monastic Seats: Sera, Drepung, and Ganden. In fact, these monasteries had decided not to support the association's plan to present a petition to the Chinese. From their perspective, the Chinese were not interfering either in monastic life or in the monastery's estates and loan operations. Furthermore, the Chinese had assured monastic leaders that they were not hostile to Buddhism and had concretely demonstrated this by giving alms to all the monks. So the monasteries declined to associate themselves with the association; for example, Drepung Monastery would not even accept the petition and returned it.[25]

By the time the leaders had finished drafting their petition, it was the end of the Tibetan lunar year (late February 1952), and the important annual Great Prayer Festival (Mönlam Chemmo) was due to start, so the association leaders postponed submitting their petition until the festival was finished. However, they let everyone in Lhasa know their intentions by putting up traditional "wall-posters" (tib. yiggyur) in the city that said,

> We Tibetans have concerns to express regarding the welfare of Tibet.[26] However, this matter cannot be expressed now, since the twelfth month is almost over, and the New Year is on us with the Great Prayer Festival of the first month about to begin. It would not be appropriate for us to engage in political action that would conflict with the Prayer Festival. Therefore, we will submit our petition between the end of the Mönlam Prayer Festival and the start of the Tsongjö Prayer Festival [in mid-April].[27]

24. Lhatsün Labrang Chandzö, interview, 1992.

25. Lhatsün Labrang Chandzö, interview, 1992.

26. In Tibetan, rgya bod zung 'brel thog la bod yongs kyi bde sdug cig zhu yag yod.

27. The period of the Tsongjö prayer festivals went from the 19th to the 30th of the second Tibetan month. In the Western calendar, it would have started about 14 April. Lhatsün Labrang Chandzö, interview, 1992. Lhalu, the Kashag minister, recalled the incident similarly:

The Chinese claimed then (and they do now) that this organization was really the work of the two sitsab rather than the spontaneous and genuine voice of the people and therefore always referred to it as the "fake" people's party. While it is difficult to prove that the sitsab organized this, the idea that "the people" should play a role in pressuring the Chinese not to station a large army in Tibet clearly seems part of their thinking. The Dalai Lama explained this.

> The two sitsab were thinking and saying that the final agreement should be done at Lhasa. They did not at all wish to have the agreement signed at Beijing. They were saying, "One can't finalize an agreement in Beijing," which was an enemy's territory. "The final agreement should be done at Lhasa." So this was in their petition, but the agreement was already done. They said that it was a big mistake to have the agreement made in Beijing. It should have been done at Lhasa. *"At Lhasa, while the negotiations are in process, the Tibetan people, the old folks, not with guns but with prayer wheels in hand, should say that ours is a small country and that if a lot of Chinese come up, then there would be famine and stuff."* So I remember this so vividly, what Lukhangwa and Lobsang Tashi said. So, beneath the Dalai Lama, the two of them were there, right? So they never wished the agreement to be done at Beijing.[28]

Many Tibetans also believe there was a connection between the People's Association and the sitsab. For example, Setrong Wangye said,

> The leaders like Thamjö Sonam . . . all had good relations with government officials. Their main supporters were the two sitsab. . . . If the sitsab hadn't backed the People's Association, it wouldn't have continued. The sitsab's idea was to keep the old customs and oppose the new. This was the same view as that of the People's Association, so that is why Lukhangwa didn't eliminate it.
>
> Actually, Lukhangwa was the "guardian" of the Lower Tantric College in Lhasa, so whatever economic activities that monastery did, they consulted him first.[29] After Lukhangwa became sitsab, for example, the Lower Tantric College became rich. All eighteen of their estates built new manor houses. So they listened to whatever he advised. One day he told the Lower Tantric College that the Communists are people who will eliminate religion, so if you, who are the foundation of religion in Tibet, would help the People's Association a lit-

---

"In 1952, just before the Great Prayer Festival, a protest poster was put up on the Tsuglagang's main door (tib. Shingra shunggo). The Lhasa Nyertsang office tore it down and gave it to the Kashag. The message said: 'When the Monlam and Tsongjö are finished we have some news to say'" (Lha klu [Lhalu] 1981: 351).

28. Dalai Lama, interview, 1993, Dharamsala (emphasis added).

29. In the role of guardian (tib. gtso 'dzin), Lukhangwa would have helped the monastery whenever something important arose, such as a dispute.

tle financially, that would be good. As a result of this, the Lower Tantric College covertly gave the People's Association the money equivalent of two thousand khe of barley. If they had given actual grain, it would have been too conspicuous, and people would have known, so instead they gave money—it was all very secret. . . . I was told this by Lobsang Trinley.[30]

Lhatsun Labrang Chandzö similarly believed there was a linkage between the People's Association and the sitsab. He said, "Later it was said that the two sitsab were inciting the people, and the Chinese insisted that they resign. At that time we had a head and a tail, and whatever the top people (the "lama-pombo") said to do, we did. So speaking frankly, there was something [a connection]."[31]

Maya, the Tibetan aristocratic official whose steward was a member of the People's Association, expressed a similar opinion.

The statement that the people did it on their own and that the two sitsab were not involved was a statement made for politics. There was no choice but to say that. . . . However, unless there was someone to show the road and give the orders to the people, it would not have been possible for the people to gather. This is my opinion. Even if they all did gather together, some would say east and some west—it would be disunified [without guidance from on top]. . . . There was definitely someone to show the way.[32]

The sitsab, therefore, were almost certainly the ideological stimulus for this association, although there is no concrete evidence that they directly told these manager types to organize it. But much in Tibet happened informally through friendships and patron networks, and this may be the case here. A word to a monk official from the monk sitsab saying that something should be done by the Tibetan people and then another word to Thamjö Sonam about the need for the people to get involved could easily have set this in motion and then quietly nurtured it along. But whether this is what transpired or whether Thamjö Sonam and the others decided this on their own, the end result closely conformed to the sitsab's idea that the voice of the Tibetan people should be used to pressure the Chinese to make concessions about the size and nature of their presence in Tibet.

The leaders of the new association also appear to have been encouraged to pursue their ideas and assisted by important Tibetan officials such as Namseling, one of the leaders of a secret group of anti-Chinese Tibetan government officials that we can loosely call the Namseling clique.

30. Setrong Wangye, interview, 1993.
31. Lhatsün Labrang Chandzö, interview, 1992.
32. Maya, interview, 1991.

THE NAMSELING CLIQUE

Just as the manager types distrusted the Chinese and felt compelled to do something about the increasing presence and power of Chinese officials and troops, so did many government officials see the Chinese as an army of occupation who, despite their current gentle talk, were really intent on destroying Tibet. A few of these officials started talking informally about this and gradually decided to make a life-or-death commitment to do something about the situation.

On 12 November 1951, seventeen days after the main Eighteenth Army Corps's troops arrived in Lhasa, a small group of lay and monk government officials formally took an oath to oppose the Chinese occupation however they could. There was no immediate aim other than to seize or create opportunities to oppose the Chinese in peaceful or militant means, whichever was more appropriate.[33] In the simplest sense, their goal was to motivate the populace to oppose the Chinese and prevent Tibetans at all levels from being taken in, or won over, by what they considered the deceptive rhetoric and financial enticements of the Chinese. They dedicated themselves to trying to make a difference, because they understood that if the government itself (the Kashag) tried to do something like this, the relations between it and the Chinese would be destroyed, and the losers would be Tibetans.[34]

This group initially was composed of a monk official, Khenjung Lobsang Gyentsen, and two lay aristocratic officials, Tashi Bera (commander of the Trapchi Regiment in Lhasa) and Namseling (one of the four members of the Revenue Office), with Namseling acting as the leader for the day-to-day activities.[35] An important political figure who was closely associated with them was the Dalai Lama's lord chamberlain, Phala. He was from an important aristocratic family that is related to Namseling and had been strongly in favor of the Dalai Lama going into exile, since he, too, did not trust the intentions of the Communists.[36] Drakten, a former monk official, explained the motives of these officials on the basis of what Phala had told him after they all were in exile.

So what they had decided was to be united and to sacrifice even their lives if need be. They wanted to come up with an alternative way of thinking. They

---

33. Rnam gling (Namseling) 1988: 70.

34. Drakten, interview, 1992, Dharamsala.

35. Rnam gling (Namseling) 1988: 70–71. Others say it also included Tsendrön Kesang Ngawang, Tseja Gyentsenla, and Tsendrön Lodrö Kesang, but they may not have been involved at the start, since Namseling did not mention them in his book.

36. Namseling and Phala were first cousins (Namseling's mother and Phala's father were siblings). Drakten, interview, 1992; Phala, interview, 1983, Library of Tibetan Works and Archives, Dharamsala.

would let the Kashag continue to work with the Chinese, for to have the government itself openly fight the Chinese would lead to the destruction of Tibet. But they took an oath to operate in secret, independent of the Kashag. Their thinking was that if this did not work, then later, although they might lose their lives, it would be just them, and the government would not be implicated.

This group was extremely secret. Namseling's wife told me that Namseling and Phala had good relations, and it seemed as if these two were handling the inner matters of the group. She recalled that later when the guerrilla leader Andrutsang consulted Phala and Namseling [in the period 1956–58], she always stood guard near the door [to the room where they were meeting in her house], and no one was allowed in. She would serve the tea and herself go back and forth to get things. The servants were not confided in. No one knew. That is how secretive it was.[37]

This group was involved behind the scenes with the 1952 People's Association and probably played an important role in the association's strategy and in the preparation of its petition. Namseling's wife explained, "Yes, it seems that my husband was also in that group. Thamjö Sonam used to come often to our house, and my husband often went to see the sitsab, as well as to see Phala."[38] Setrong Wangye similarly recalled contacts between them: "One day [in 1952] when I was standing in front of my house [in Lhasa] giving my horse fodder, Lobsang Trinley came by. I asked him where he was coming from, and he said he had gone to see Namseling, who was one of the supporters of the People's Association. Then he pulled out a document from his pocket and said, 'I went to show this to Namseling.'"[39]

The emergence of the People's Association helped further to fan the flames of the anti-Chinese resentment in Lhasa and led to increasing incidents—posters, street songs, pushing and shoving Chinese, and spreading negative rumors about the Chinese during the months of November 1951 through March 1952. An entry in the history of the Chinese Communist Party in Tibet from late November 1951 commented on this. "After the entrance [of the PLA] into Lhasa, the upper-strata reactionaries were centered around Lukhangwa. The masses were instructed to create troubles and shouted slogans such as, 'PLA, don't just go home, starve first and then leave hungry.'"[40] Some of the rumors being spread in Lhasa according to Chinese sources were bizarre and fanciful, for example, that Mao Zedong and Zhu De had been

37. Drakten, interview, 1992. Mrs. Namseling confirmed this in a separate interview (1994, Dharamsala).

38. Mrs. Namseling, interview, 1994.

39. Setram Wangye, interview, 1993. The document presumably was a draft of the petition they were planning to deliver to the Chinese.

40. Zhonggong xizang zizhiqu dangshi ziliao zhengji weiyuanhui 1990, entry for 25 November 1951.

captured by the Americans in the Korean War, and that the Communist Party was going to fall soon, and that American troops had already landed in India in preparation for invading Tibet to expel the Communists.[41]

However, the increasing frequency and severity of these anti-Chinese activities led the Chinese to visit the Dalai Lama in person to try to persuade him to put an end to them. The Dalai Lama recalled this in his autobiography.

> The eventual result was an extremely amusing incident with General Zhang. One day he came to see me and demanded that I issue a proclamation banning any criticism of the Chinese, whether in songs or on posters, since these were "reactionary" activities. However, despite new laws prohibiting opposition to China, notices began to appear in the streets denouncing the presence of the Chinese forces. A popular resistance movement was formed.[42]

The Tibetan government, however, made no attempt to rein in the People's Association and the protests they sponsored. By mid-March, the Chinese were angry and nervous and began fortifying their positions in Lhasa. The 11 March 1952 entry in the history of the Chinese Communist Party in Tibet reports the following:

> Under the guise of a people's meeting, an anti-revolutionary organization aroused riots in Lhasa. Upper-strata reactionary elements including two representatives of the Tibet local government of the Dalai Lama—Lukhangwa and Lobsang Tashi—took advantage of our military, as they were not on very solid ground yet. On the one hand they boycotted grain in an attempt to starve us, and on the other hand they picked up all kinds of social dirt and formed an anti-revolutionary organization with the intent of inciting riots and disturbances. This organization was headed by some merchants and hooligans, and the first of the fake people's meetings was held in November 1951. On 11 March 1952, this anti-revolutionary organization drafted a petition calling for the withdrawal of the PLA and the cancellation of the peace agreement [the Seventeen-Point agreement]. At the same time there were demonstrations, and many shops were closed, as order was disturbed. There was chaos in the city.[43]

Another account from a Chinese official who was in Lhasa at that time describes the situation similarly.

> Lukhangwa, Lobsang Tashi, and the People's Association incited people to cut the Lhasa phone lines, shoot at PLA quarters at night, to hit PLA soldiers going outside, to yell at and hit the PLA guards [standing outside their buildings], to tease the PLA in the market and push, spit, and block their way for no reason. They also teased the PLA female troops and stole things from the

41. Ji 1993a: 400.

42. Dalai Lama 1990: 73.

43. Zhonggong xizang zizhiqu dangshi ziliao zhengji weiyuanhui 1990, entry for 11 March 1952.

PLA. Such things were done every day. During March and April, there were over a hundred such incidents.[44]

A Tibetan soldier from the Gyantse Regiment who was also a member of the People's Association had a similar recollection of those times.

> So when this People's Association was organized, there was a great surge from the Big Three monasteries and everywhere. Monks put on laymen's clothes and trickled into Lhasa carrying guns and knives. So at that time there were many groups of people gathered here and there. It was even said that we had to go to Zhang Jingwu's residence.
>
> Since so many people were arriving, the Chinese were very suspicious and alarmed, and wherever they were living, they set up bunkers as if any day a war might break out. So when this happened, the various Tibetan army regiments could not just stay still; they also had to make preparations. For a few days in Lhasa it was as if there were no shopkeepers in the city [as the stores closed], and since so many people had come, the feeling was that war might break out any day.[45]

The situation became so dangerous that the Chinese felt compelled to close their Tibetan cadre school temporarily, as one of its students recalled.

> The [Tibetan] teachers in the Cadre School were people loyal to the state, so they were sent letters to scare them. These letters said that you teachers are devils (tib. dü), and we will kill you one day. Moreover, when these teachers went to the market, some people threw stones and spit at them and told them to stop teaching at the school immediately. I recall seeing one of our teachers crying under a tree. He told the students that from today on I cannot come to teach you, because my safety is at risk and there is a danger to my life. So for the time being I can't come. . . . Because of this we had to stop the school for a while. I was a student, and I returned to the . . . Tibet Military Headquarters.[46]

A young Tibetan in the PLA also said that when they closed the school he returned to the Chinese military base and worked at preparing fortifications. He said that he and his colleagues slept in their clothing so they would be ready in case of an attack.[47]

Both sides also made military adjustments. On the Tibetan side, the government ordered its Artillery Regiment in Shigatse to recall its troops, who had all been sent to their homes the previous year.[48] The Chinese misunderstood this and thought that the sitsab had ordered the Artillery Regiment

44. Yang 1987: 75.
45. Namgye Wangdü, interview, 1993.
46. Yang 1987: 75–76.
47. Jambey Gyatso, interview, 1993, Beijing.
48. Lhalu, interview, 1992, Lhasa.

to come to Lhasa from Shigatse.[49] They took this as extremely threatening and responded by recalling the First Battalion of the 155th Regiment from Lhuntse, in southern Tibet, ordering them to travel day and night to reach Lhasa quickly. At the same time, the Chinese not only fortified their positions but also built underground tunnels between the commander-in-chief's offices, the political headquarters, and the payroll office and forbade its troops to leave their bases, in order to minimize the risk of fights and incidents occurring.[50] In addition to this, the continuing shortage of food and firewood weighed heavy on the Chinese side. As one Chinese source put it, "Between February and March 1952, the troops in Lhasa really had only enough grain to last about three days, and at best it could last only about seven or eight days. Sometimes they had to ration the supply of firewood, and sometimes the firewood was just enough to boil water to drink but not to wash their faces and use for other purposes."[51]

Then, on 30 March 1952, after the Great Prayer Festival had ended, the leaders of the People's Association finally took the step of presenting their petition to the Tibetan government, choosing a day when the Kashag was having discussions with the sitsab, since the association hoped to meet with them both.[52] The association delegates addressed the petition to both the Tibetan and the Chinese governments, because they did not want the Tibetan government to think it was deliberately being bypassed and because they felt this would increase the likelihood that the Chinese would take it seriously.[53] Their delegation was made up of about twenty people, including the main leaders.

When this delegation arrived at the Kashag's office, the ministers were immediately given the document. Lhalu recalled the event and the Kashag's fear of dealing with them.

> [When] the Kashag was meeting in the Potala, we received a petition written in Tibetan scroll format that was called the "Tibetan people's petition." Its main point was that the PLA troops in Lhasa should follow the custom of the Qing emperor's troops [i.e., not stay long in Tibet and leave only a token garrison].
>
> We were a little afraid about the petition. We had lost the liberation war in Chamdo and disturbances and trouble could break out here in Lhasa. Because of this, we concluded that if we accepted the letter [from the representatives] serious difficulties would occur. We wanted to maintain good relations with the Chinese, so we gave the petition back to the people's representatives and told them we cannot accept it.

49. Dangdai zhongguo congshu bianjibu 1991: 66. This was the Chadang Regiment.
50. Yang 1987: 76.
51. Dangdai zhongguo congshu bianjibu 1991: 199.
52. Namgye Wangdü, interview, 1993.
53. Lhatsün Labrang Chandzö, interview, 1992.

When we did this, they surprised us by saying, "We have already shown the petition to the two sitsab, and they said to ask the Kashag to take it." We told them that we did not know whether the sitsab had really seen this, so we would look into the matter and give them an answer after reporting this to the sitsab.

We then looked at the petition and took it to the two sitsab, who did not say whether they had seen the petition before. Lukhangwa simply informed us that this petition is genuinely the opinion of the Tibetan people, so the Kashag should accept it and give it to Zhang Jingwu. Actually the Dalai Lama should have been consulted, but he wasn't. Lukhangwa settled it on the spot, telling us to accept the petition.[54]

The Kashag ministers then returned and accepted the petition. The representatives of the People's Association, not surprisingly, felt their idea to meet first with the sitsab had been correct.

When they [the representatives] went to the Potala Palace, it seems that the Kashag ministers and the sitsab said that the petition was very good. Lukhangwa especially said, "It is very good that you are doing these things," and told them that they must pursue the matter to completion. Besides this, there were others who said that this was very good, and the monks of the Namgye Tratsang [the Dalai Lama's monastery housed in the Potala] served them a meal of rice and sweet potatoes. . . . So when they returned they were very pleased, saying that the higher-ups are of the same mind as we are.[55]

On the next day, the Kashag sent Zhang Jingwu a copy of the petition and arranged to meet with the People's Association representatives at the Chinese Tibet Work Committee headquarters in the old Sandutsang house (which also served as Zhang Jingwu's residence). The Chinese reported that there was a mob of armed people outside shouting at the Chinese: "Fully armed Tibetans were everywhere in the street. They shouted in front of Zhang Jingwu's gate, demanding that Zhang 'immediately withdraw the PLA from Tibet,' that the Tibetan governing system should not change, 'that the agreement should be revised.' They demanded an immediate response from Zhang."[56]

Kashag minister Lhalu continued his narration of the event.

The next day we [the Kashag ministers] went to Zhang Jingwu's residence. The representatives of the People's Association had already arrived. . . .

When the petition was given to Zhang Jingwu, the People's Party representatives said only, "Our content is in the document, so look at it." Zhang Jingwu handed it to me and asked me to read it. So in the presence of Zhang

54. Lhalu, interview, 1992. Lhalu also discussed this event in Lha klu (Lhalu) 1981: 351–52.
55. Namgye Wangdü, interview, 1993.
56. Ji 1993a: 401.

and the other Kashag ministers, I read it once. At this point Zhang called the "fake" people's representatives up and photographed them, and they left.[57]

One of the association members also recalled this meeting.

So we went there at around 4 P.M. For a while, when the Kashag ministers and the Chinese discussed this, no one paid any attention to us. We were about sixteen people. [Then they looked] to see what identifying marks we had, such as scars on the face, or whether we had gold teeth or not or any wounds. All these were written down. Then they took photos from the front and from the side and from a distance when we moved about. By the time we had delivered the petition, it was already sunset.[58]

The people's representatives apparently were quite pleased with themselves and, when the photographs were being taken, lined up posing stylishly with their rosaries hanging down from their hands.[59]

The Chinese side presents this historic meeting as follows:

The People's Association elected three representatives headed by Jayan Dawa to enter Zhang Jingwu's residence to petition to him. Zhang asked them to sit down first. He immediately sent someone to invite the Kashag ministers over to meet with the three representatives of the People's Association together with him. In front of the Kashag ministers, Zhang seriously pointed out that this riot was encouraged by someone behind the scenes. The masses who participated in the riot were being used by others. They were not responsible for it. Zhang Jingwu demanded that the Kashag should handle the incident at once in an appropriate way or would be responsible for any severe consequences. Afterwards, Zhang patiently explained the seventeen points of the agreement one by one [to the representatives]. He explained the religious and ethnic policies of the Communist Party to them and then he asked them to leave their petition to him and wait for a reply.

Though the representatives bringing the petition did not want to hear anything Zhang tried to explain, they all pretended they understood Zhang's comments, since they did not want to make the Kashag ministers and the Tibetan local government look awkward. They asked the masses that surrounded Zhang's residence to leave in the afternoon, but they still kept a few armed people to watch the residence closely.[60]

The petition itself is an impressive document that consisted of six points. It was diplomatically crafted so as not to convey either hostility or hatred toward the Chinese. Using a heading typical of the Qing dynasty period, it tried

57. Lhalu, interview, 1992.

58. Lhatsun Labrang Chandzö, interview, 1992.

59. Shingsar Lobsang Gelek, interview, 1993, Toronto. He recalled seeing the photos of them, since he was on the Judicial Investigation Committee that later interrogated them.

60. Ji 1993a: 401–2.

to convey to the Chinese that the new relationship between Chinese and Tibetans could be successful if both sides went back to the Qing model, and it actually thanked the Chinese for many things. Interestingly, it also chose to show social "progressiveness" by criticizing the Tibetan government and the abuses of the traditional feudal system and stating that the association would submit a plan on how to fix it. And critically, it did not *demand* anything. Rather it "asked" the Chinese to *please help* "the people," and it asked this using an honorific term, *gyamju*, which is normally used by persons of lower status to officials, lamas, and others from whom they want a favor or loan. This petition was so well-crafted that it seems probable that the leaders had help from more knowledgeable and sophisticated government officials, for example, perhaps from Namseling and other officials in his clique.

The actual petition begins with an introductory heading composed in the style of that used during the days of the Qing dynasty:[61] "From the lay and religious people of Tibet with a single voice, to the feet of both the emperor, priest and patron, and the lamas and lords of Tibet and China."[62] It then goes on to make six points.

Point One

Buddhism is the source of all benefit and happiness. In the past, the Buddha prophesied the Dalai Lama would be the holder of Buddhism and especially assigned him as the deity of Tibet. He became the precious stone placed on the heads of all sentient beings. He is the pillar on which the present and the future lives of the monks and laymen of Tibet depend. As for the essence of the friendship between Chinese and Tibetans, it is what was said [in the agreement], namely, that "our customs will not be changed." In order to serve the Tibetan government so that the activities of the government will flourish like a rising moon, all matters, regardless of whether they are civil or military, are decided through submitting a plan to His Holiness the Dalai Lama and seeking his approval. We are definitely following this.

Furthermore, the PRC has thought about creating friendship and sent officials and soldiers to Tibet. It was written [in the Seventeen-Point Agreement] that the title and power of the Dalai Lama will not be changed. So it is independent as before. Therefore, we, the Tibetan people, monks and laymen, are very satisfied and glad, and we say "thank you" for this.

Point Two

The foundation of Tibetan Buddhism is mainly the three great monasteries [around Lhasa] and the other major and minor monastic institutions. These are the places where all sentient beings accumulate their merit. Consequently, in order to develop and restore these monasteries, patrons have donated es-

61. The language in the petition was flowery, and the translation that follows has been kept literal so may seem stilted in places.

62. In Tibetan, gong ma mchod yon gyi mnga' bdag rgya bod lha dpon lhan rgyas mchog gi zhabs pad mngon mtho'i drung du gus 'bangs bod ljongs mi dmangs ser skya spyi mgrin nas.

tates, animals, fields, houses, and people to them. And money and barley were also donated as religious trust funds to continue the timely religious offerings of rituals. The Central Committee (ch. Zhongyang) has said that it will protect the monasteries and that their income will not be changed. Therefore, we request that this continue forever.

Point Three

There is no denying that, like the source of water, the management of the Tibetan government is important to both religion and politics. Because of the lack of merit of sentient beings, the Great 13th Dalai Lama, to whom we have incomparable gratitude, passed away at the age of fifty-eight in the Water-Bird year [1933]. His subjects were left like a blind man in the middle of a plain. His Holiness the 14th Dalai Lama came into existence as the savior of sentient beings in Tibet. But he was unable to take the religious and temporal power until the Iron-Tiger year [1950]. During these nineteen years, the work to improve the political system of the Tibetan government was not carried out well. Therefore, the government and the subjects have had a very hard time. The government officials and the subjects know the cause of this situation, which resulted in the people being left like a doctor abandoning a patient.

The Central Committee has made it clear that in the future it will not change the political system of Tibet, so there is no other choice but to heal the disease [in the Tibetan political system] by ourselves. There is no need for us to find a good medicine from somewhere else to heal it. Therefore, all people should think about developing the political system of the Tibetan government so that it would be beneficial for the subjects. In order for the Tibetan government to become well-organized and flourish as soon as possible, we are [later] going to submit a petition with a plan.

Point Four

Regarding the overall good livelihood under the leadership of the Tibetan government, Tibetans have been happy and peaceful through the kindness of all the dalai lamas who have reigned. For instance, even beggars have had full freedom and no worries. They enjoyed absolute freedom until the Chinese came. Now, probably because of the negative merit [karma] of the people in general, there have been crop failures, war, lawlessness between the Chinese and the Tibetans and the arrival of quite a large number of people, which has caused the price of food and clothing to increase day by day. Some of the rich subjects placed their own desires [first] and stirred up discord, which caused the fundamental welfare of subjects in general to be completely destroyed, so they could not manage their livelihood and faced unbearable hardships. But nobody was investigating the matter, and they were able to do whatever bad practices they wanted. Therefore, it is out of the question for the Tibetan government to make any progress. The people's living conditions are getting worse day by day. This is because the Central Committee [permitted] evil people to escape through the upper (tib. tö) and lower parts (tib. me) [of Tibet] and gang up and kill and rob [the people] continuously. [This last sentence is unclear.]

When the people said [to the Chinese] that you should correct these problems, they said that they will consult with the leaders of Tibet and make a decision to take action. If you cannot put into practice actions that make the people free from the suffering of poverty, the disgrace between the Chinese and the Tibetan will spread all over the world.. Therefore, we request that you please help us (tib. gyamju).

We have no choice but to agree to pay the major and minor government taxes according to the land that we have. However, we request [that the Tibetan government] exempt payments in kind and corvée labor for civil and military taxes like the horse and pack animal corvée tax and the human corvée labor, which have exceeded or are disproportionate to the amount of land that we have. There are also high-interest loans for which the interest has been added on top of interest, and those [lenders] who are pursuing the loans have done so in an unbearably harsh manner, taking away by force the lands, houses, and possessions, as well as the things that were left as collateral, according to their own wishes. Therefore, the poor and humble people have no basis for subsisting, so they have had to run away abroad. The people were unable to serve those who own the people and land, and they have had to go through unbearable torture and suffering. Regarding this matter, in order to advance the good and prevent the bad, we are going to submit petitions from the people living in the upper and the lower parts [of Tibet]. We request (tib. gyamju) that you settle the matters appropriately according to the customs of the country.

Point Five

Concerning the defense forces in Tibet, in the past, at the time of the priest and patron relationship between the Chinese and the Tibetans [during the Qing dynasty], there was a small military force. During the 13th Dalai Lama's reign, we started training an army to protect our territories in the upper and lower areas and had just enough weapons to protect our own land. We bought some rifles according to our own economic condition. Our aim was never to fight with outsiders. Our country, Tibet, is known as a place of religion. Tibetans think of nothing but religion and religious offerings. We Tibetans didn't have any power, technology, wealth, or knowledge like other countries. We are simple people who are very friendly with everybody. We got along like this.

But now, if you are planning to reform the rules of the Tibetan military as well as their army uniforms and the conduct [of the soldiers], this would cause severe disappointment among the people. The Central Committee has said that the [Tibetans] shall have the power to preserve or reform the local customs and the religious faith. We request permission that the local customs remain as before.

We have no choice but to protect our own territories in the upper and lower areas. The customs of a big country do not suit a small country. They will cause harm instead of being beneficial. So in order for the people to live happily, *according to the previous custom, with the exception of a few Chinese officials and troops [in Tibet], the rest should withdraw.*[63] We request you to think about this and re-

---

63. In Tibetan, sngar lam dpon dmag phran bu tsam las de byings 'phral du phyir 'then yod pa.

quest to [your] superiors in order to make a clear response and help us with our request.

Point Six

After using our natural resources [for ourselves], everyone knows that Tibet's surplus products such as wool, yak's tail, musk, deer horns, and medicinal herbs were exported in exchange for iron, gold, and silver from foreign countries such as India, Britain, and America. This kind of trade was done according to the religious faith and trust and loyalty. Actually . . . several trade agreements have been signed to transport the goods by land, sea, and air, and the Chinese and Tibetans have respectively collected custom taxes.

But this year, on the pretext of the friendship between China and Tibet, the wool trade was stopped. If we have to remain like this, the wool that has been transported to India will be mixed with earth and stone [will rot], and the wool we have in Tibet will also become scattered, and the traders will not be able to recover from having fallen down. We request as a favor to us to continue to do the wool trade as before. Otherwise, the money of the Tibetan government, the three great monasteries, the religious funds for doing offerings, and the welfare of the rich and the subjects/serfs (tib. miser) will be damaged. So we request you to please help us. The Central Committee said that they would develop agriculture, animal husbandry, handicrafts, and trade according to the situation in Tibet to improve the livelihood of the people. Actually, the ban on the wool trade has really affected the welfare of the Tibetan government, the religious offerings in the monasteries, and the people. Everybody can see this clearly. So therefore the Chinese should lift the trade ban.[64]

The petition, therefore, tried to situate the Seventeen-Point Agreement within the priest-patron ideology that was associated with the Qing dynasty (and before that with the Mongol emperors) and tried to give the impression that under the right conditions—the Qing dynasty arrangement—Tibetans could have cordial relations with China. The petition was polite, in thanking the Chinese for leaving the Dalai Lama in power and for promising to protect the monasteries and their sources of income and in indicating that the association was in favor of reforming aspects of the traditional feudal estate system. But it asked the Chinese to change their strategy in Tibet by leaving the Tibetan military as it then was, by retaining only a small force of Chinese officials and soldiers in Lhasa, by allowing Tibetans to reform their social and tax systems, and by resuming the wool export trade. In the end, if the Chinese side had accepted these requests, a "protectorate" relationship somewhat analogous to Tibet before 1913 would have been created. Tibet would have been part of China, but it would have functioned with its own governmental system and institutions, with only a handful of Chinese soldiers and officials overseeing things in Lhasa. This was precisely what the sitsab had in mind.

---

64. People's Association petition 1952 (emphasis added). The ban on wool was actually a U.S. ban on buying goods from communist countries.

The Kashag ministers took the petition from the representatives and told them that they would be contacted later and should not cause trouble while they waited for a reply. The Chinese, in the meantime, had placed all their troops on alert and fortified their positions with sandbags and the like. One Tibetan recalled, "So at this time, the Chinese bought everything the Nepalese and others who were selling cotton cloth had. They made an astounding number of bags and filled them with sand and barricaded their doors and windows and rooftops. So the Nepalese and the Muslims had a prosperous business."[65] However, at the same time, the Chinese troops were strictly instructed absolutely not to fire the first shot. The Chinese had plans for a powerful counterattack, not a preemptive strike.[66]

The leaders in the People's Association were not sure what to expect when they sent their representatives to see Zhang Jingwu so had taken the precaution of devising a plan to free them should the Chinese have placed them under arrest. The rescue plan would have involved an attack on the Chinese building, so individual members had been given arms and told to congregate outside the main Chinese headquarters.[67] Chinese accounts of that day confirm that a large number of Tibetans milled around in front of Zhang's residence and other places: "At this time more than two thousand [armed] reactionary elements encircled the residence of Zhang Jingwu, the People's Bank, and the Foreign Affairs Bureau. Lukhangwa and Lobsang Tashi directed the Tibetan army and monks of the three great monasteries to create uprisings against us."[68]

It was already past sunset when the people's representatives left Zhang's residence. The Kashag ministers and the Chinese officials then discussed the situation for a while. To the Chinese, the reports they were getting made it sound as if the situation might turn violent at any moment, so when the Kashag ministers also said they were going home, Zhang Jingwu expressed great concern over the large number of demonstrators still milling around outside his residence and said he suspected that they were planning to start trouble later that evening.[69] Phünwang recalled that Zhang Guohua warned the Kashag ministers, saying, "We will not fire the first shot, but when we fire the second shot, we will not let them easily get away." The ministers responded

65. Lhatsün Labrang Chandzö, interview, 1992.

66. Dangdai zhongguo congshu bianjibu 1991: 194.

67. Amdo Samdrup, interview, 1994, Dharamsala; Chandzö Ngawang Temba, interview, 1993.

68. Zhonggong xizang zizhiqu dangshi ziliao zhengji weiyuanhui 1990, entry for 31 March—1 April 1952.

69. Fan Ming (interview, 1993, Xi'an) said that the Chinese side had received information about plans for a disturbance: "Ngabö gave us some information we needed; we also had our own intelligence system."

simply that the situation would not become that bad.[70] Nevertheless, Zhang Jingwu asked the Kashag ministers to remain in his headquarters overnight to calm the situation in case trouble flared up, and they agreed.[71] Lhalu recalled the evening: "It was Ngabo and I who stayed. Zhang Jingwu said we two should stay. I thought there might be trouble, and we didn't sleep all night. We just sat there all night. If the people came, we were going to go out and tell them to disperse and go home. But nothing happened, and the next day we left."[72] Phünwang, who also was there, remembered that they played majong to pass the time but also recalled that Surkhang was there too.[73]

But while nothing happened at Zhang's house, there was trouble elsewhere; for example, the Chinese believed that shots were fired at Ngabö's house. So with tension at a heightened level, the Chinese, as we shall see in the next chapter, now decided to bypass the sitsab and turn directly to the Dalai Lama for assistance in restoring order.

70. Phünwang, interview, 2000, Beijing.
71. Lhalu, interview, 1992; Lha klu (Lhalu) 1981: 353; Ji 1993a: 401.
72. Lhalu, interview, 1992.
73. Phünwang, interview, 2000, Beijing. Zhao (1995: 71–72) and Ji (1993a: 401) also state that Surkhang was present too.

Chapter 13

Turning to the Dalai Lama and Removing the Sitsab

Upset by what they saw as a deteriorating situation, orchestrated, in their view, by the sitsab, the Chinese turned directly to the Dalai Lama, hoping he would intervene. Between 31 March and 4 April (1952), Zhang Jingwu sent three letters to the Dalai Lama (via the Kashag) about this. The first, sent on 31 March, made two points.

1. For the past one or two days we witnessed that there are a lot of improper monks in Lhasa from Sera and Drepung monasteries who have disguised themselves as common people and have come bringing weapons. They organized some officers and soldiers from the Tibetan army and other scoundrels and held meetings at which they took an oath and carried out reactionary activities aimed at creating disturbances against the PLA, robbing the crowd (ch. qunzhong) and creating a disturbance in the city of Lhasa.

2. Today the Kashag's secretary (tib. kadrung) brought a formal note from the Kashag saying that the so-called People's Representatives will give a petition to both the PLA and to the Tibet local government and [they] asked me to attend. Our investigation showed that those false people's representatives who pretend to represent the people's will are supported by some people behind the scenes. They are trying to use the method of making a petition and rioting (ch. sao huan) to accomplish a conspiracy of sabotaging the agreement for the peaceful liberation of Tibet and the unity between nationalities. [Therefore] You (ch. nin: respectful term) should immediately give an order to effectively stop this [their actions].[1]

1. Dangdai zhongguo congshu bianjibu 1991: 196. See also Zhao 1995: 70–71.

That same evening, the Dalai Lama's brother, Lobsang Samden, came to the Tibet Work Committee and told them that the Dalai Lama would meet with the two sitsab the following day to discuss the situation.[2]

On the next day, Zhang Jingwu sent a second, much more specific, letter, asking the Dalai Lama to abolish the People's Association and quell the disturbances. It said,

> To all the Kashag ministers, and, via them, pass it on to the honorable Dalai Lama:
>
> . . . Regarding the reactionary organization and its actions in Lhasa, after investigations and discussions with the leaders in Lhasa, including the head of the Nangtsesha Office,[3] we learned that among today's reactionaries were monks disguised as laymen and Lhasa hooligans, as well as Tibetan soldiers and officers with their weapons. They organized the reactionary so-called Lhasa liberation force, and they secretly went to our residence at the Sandutsang house and massed on the left and right sides, planning to launch an armed rebellion. At this time, our PLA troops followed our excellent political policy and showed great restraint using only a defensive military strategy. With the help of the Kashag ministers, we avoided bloodshed. This is very good.
>
> However, I have something I must say. The reactionary group and their activities were not a sudden (spontaneous) affair. Important people from behind the scenes secretly supported them in accordance with a plan. These secret bad activities are in conflict with the Dalai Lama's thoughts. They are also opposed to nationality harmony and to the ideology of developing Tibet. And they are destroying the peaceful agreement and are committing the crime of opposing the unity of the motherland. If they do not cease showing their strength, the Tibetan people will definitely experience a very bad result. Consequently, as explained below, use your power and give orders as soon as possible to solve the issue.
>
> 1. Immediately send an order to all Tibetan troops (including the Bodyguard Regiment) that from today on they should return to their regimental barracks. You should exercise strict discipline over them and not allow them to go outside anywhere and do any illegal acts. You should put into practice the Seventeen-Point Agreement immediately and should educate people on nationality harmony and prohibit instigation. And you should decree that the Tibetan people cannot consider the PLA as an enemy and cannot outwardly show a friendly attitude but inwardly cause trouble.
>
> 2. Immediately send an order to the Three Monastic Seats (and other monasteries) stating that from today all the monks should return to their monasteries. The abbots, moreover, should exercise strict discipline over the monks and prevent them from going outside the monastery and committing bad acts. You should order the monasteries to give guarantees that they accept this.

2. Zhao 1995: 71.
3. This was the office of the Lhasa city government.

3. Immediately issue an order abolishing the Fake People's Association. All those who were members will not be investigated in the future if they return to their respective homes (and areas). However, the representatives of the association may stay in the Kashag and wait for the meeting. We plan to meet with the Kashag ministers to listen to all their opinions and then discuss them. Then we will answer [the representatives] formally.

4. Order the Kashag at once to have discussions with the Tibet Military Area Headquarters and immediately issue a joint announcement that all those who are destroying nationality harmony and the Seventeen-Point Agreement must stop their activities completely. All illegal acts should be forcefully stopped. Together with this, you should guarantee the security of Lhasa. The shopkeepers and so forth should continue to work as usual, and you should protect them. If you do this the people will feel at ease.[4]

Xu Danlu, the Chinese head of security, went with two guards to take this letter to the Kashag, which was meeting in the Potala. A Chinese report on this said,

Xu sat down in front of the Kashag ministers, took out Zhang Jingwu's letter, and gave it to Surkhang, asking him to give it to the Dalai. Then he told the ministers that the destructive activities of the "people's association" were still going on and that without a powerful force behind them, they would not be so daring. He insinuated that if the ministers did not completely stop having relations with those doing reckless things, the consequences would be unimaginable.

The senior Kashag minister, Ramba, expressed doubts about the accuracy of the Communists' information. He said that he believed that things were not as bad as they claimed and that the best thing to do was to take the whole thing less seriously. Ramba acted as if this was not very serious. Xu then seriously and easily listed a series of facts and firmly asked the Kashag to take immediate measures or they would be responsible for all the consequences. The Kashag ministers agreed and said they would investigate and report back to Zhang Jingwu.[5]

On the same day, 1 April, the Central Committee sent the Tibet Work Committee a revealing telegram, telling its members to be alert to dangers but also giving them a lecture on the realities of nationality loyalty and how they should be conducting themselves. The telegram represents the beginning of Mao's loss of confidence in the independent judgment of the leaders of the Tibet Work Committee. It said,

Your telegrams of 3 March and 18 March [1952] were received. In the past, for a long time, the Tibetan local government took a position that opposed

4. Dui xizang gongzuo de zhongyao zhishi (wei chuban de shouji), n.d., 14–16. See also Ji 1993a: 404.
5. Ji 1993a: 404.

the motherland. The relationship between Tibetans and Han has just begun to improve. However, the imperialists have not yet given up [plans of] invasion and the conspiracy to stir up a war in Tibet. The conspiracy may have a new development recently with Gyalo Thondup, Surkhang, and the Dalai's mother returning to Tibet.[6] You need to pay very close attention and be alert all the time.

On the other hand, even though the Tibetan people are not satisfied with the Tibetan local government, it is still the contemporary local government of the Tibetan nationality. And because it is the administrator in Tibet, it still holds nationality feelings together. So the Tibetan people will have negative feelings if we fail to treat the Kashag properly, even though there is the Agreement for the Peaceful Liberation of Tibet and they recognize that Tibet is a part of the People's Republic of China.

Your work in the Tibet area not only should insist on implementing the agreed-upon agreement but also should involve collecting all kinds of information in order to work on a case-by-case basis. You may experience many twists and turns in order to achieve the goal of carrying out the agreement. You need to do so in a scientific and systematic way so that you support those who are inclined to be close to the Central Committee (such as Ngabö, etc.), win over those in the middle, and isolate those stubborn ones (such the two sitsab).

You have paid attention to the above policies, but the Central Committee hopes that every step you take you will be still more consciously aware of them, especially because we currently still do not have complete control over the Tibetan area either politically or militarily. The prices in Lhasa are rising fast, the road from Kham cannot be completed in a short time, the troops cannot support themselves this year, and we cannot improve the material lives and welfare of the Tibetan people for a while. All in all, our standing in Tibet will not be stable for the next couple of years. Hence, we have to take an extremely cautious attitude on politics and progress steadily. Do not do any relatively drastic reforms until the road is completed, we are self-sufficient in production, and the material interests of the Tibetan people are improved.

Currently, if you need anything to be done by the Tibetan local government, you may ask Jingwu to propose to the Kashag that it handle it. However, you should negotiate things with the Kashag ministers in advance and fully explain the issues in order to get support from the majority. Also you should negotiate it with the sitsab. If it is necessary and beneficial, you could let Jingwu (as the representative of the Central Government) and Guohua (as the commander of the Tibetan Military Area) attend informal meetings (ch. zuo tan hui, "sit and chat"). But it is not appropriate for Jingwu and Guohua to attend meetings of the Kashag directly. It would be especially awkward if at such a meeting both sides get stuck in a deadlock. Jingwu, as the representative of the Central Committee, should be well prepared when making contacts with all kinds of people. If you want to make a proposal at a meeting such as a "chat and talk" meeting, you have to anticipate that it will get the support of the majority. Un-

6. They had returned to Lhasa in mid-February.

der those circumstances, the minority will not openly oppose or confront your proposal. Otherwise, it would be better to talk with individuals, explaining and convincing them before you make a formal proposal. In addition, it is necessary to maintain direct contact with the Dalai.

Hope you will pay attention to collecting information and report to the Southwest Bureau and the Central Committee consistently.

Central Committee
1 April 1952[7]

The next day, a number of Kashag ministers, including Surkhang and Ramba, went to the Chinese side to discuss security issues and jointly agreed to placing a curfew in Lhasa. The Lhasa "mayor" (the Nangtsesha mipön) immediately issued orders imposing a curfew from 8 P.M. until 5 A.M. People were also prohibited from spreading rumors or instigating others to do bad things, and all secret meetings and other illegal activities were banned.[8]

However, the Dalai Lama again did not take action regarding the bigger issues raised by Zhang Jingwu, and on the streets nothing changed. In the view of the Chinese, members of the People's Association, together with some monks and soldiers, continued actively to harass them. And on 2 April, the Chinese reported that they held a public meeting in front of the Shöl Parkhang (in front of the Potala Palace), which over a hundred people attended. At the meeting they decided to continue their activities until their goals were met, and they organized some people to continue to hang around Zhang Jingwu's residence.[9]

Then, on 4 April, Zhang Jingwu sent yet another letter to the Dalai Lama, this time requesting that he convene a meeting with the sitsab and Kashag ministers to discuss measures to prevent further disturbances. This meeting was held but went badly, because the sitsab supported the People's Association, as the following account relates:

> The two sitsab said, "Our government has its own organizational rules. The petition of the people concerning their own situation was done according to tradition. They are making a petition humbly [literally, with scarves in their hand and their cheeks touching the ground, i.e., prostrating]. Our subjects are stating the difficulties in their lives and saying that they are having such and such difficulties. So they are saying, "Please do such and such things regarding these difficulties." So when the people are speaking like this, we have to listen to all of it. Then after listening, if there are genuine grievances and if there is room for governmental consideration, then we will say to them, "You have petitioned regarding this and that matter, and the government will do

7. Dui xizang gongzuo de zhongyao zhishi (wei chuban de shouji), n.d.
8. Yang 1987: 72–73; Ji 1993a: 404. Chinese sources say that the curfew was not obeyed.
9. Yang 1987: 72–73.

such and such things. And regarding this matter, it is all right, but regarding that matter, although you have asked for such and such things, because of our government policy, they are not possible." So in this way we have to give replies. Just giving orders and saying to arrest people who have come to petition humbly is not at all acceptable.

When Lukhangwa said this, [the Chinese] did not reply directly but rather said, "Behind the curtain there are people hiding, behind the curtain there are people hiding."[10] Then they suddenly got up and said there is no use talking and left the meeting. . . . [Their saying,] "Behind the curtain there are people hiding," meant that behind those people are the sitsab.[11]

In the meantime, with the Tibetan government doing next to nothing to address the Chinese demands for action against the People's Association, Beijing responded on 6 April 1952 with important new instructions to the Tibet Work Committee, which showed even more caution and restraint than the 1 April telegram. Beijing now instructed them to stop pushing to reform the army and start the Military-Administrative Committee. In essence, it instructed them to back off implementing the agreement in these sensitive areas.

We basically agree with the instructions that the Southwest Bureau and the Southwest Military Region Headquarters telegraphed to the Tibet Work Committee and the Tibetan Military Area Headquarters on 2 April [1952].[12] With the exception of reorganizing the Tibetan army, we believe the basic policy and a lot of the specific steps mentioned in this telegram are correct. You should keep moving in this direction so that we will never be defeated in Tibet.

The situation in Tibet is different from that in Xinjiang. Politically and economically, Tibet is a lot more backward. Wang Zeng's troops [in Xinjiang] can supply themselves now. They worked hard to calculate carefully and became self-sufficient in production. Now they have a firm standing and receive good support from the nationality groups. Currently they have done work reducing the rents and interest rates. They will start land reforms this winter and then people will support us more. There is also convenient truck transportation between Xinjiang and the inland areas, and [Xinjiang also has] close economic ties with the USSR. We have helped the ethnic nationalities a lot with respect to material things and welfare.

[In Tibet for] At least a couple of years [two or three], there should be no reductions [in rents and interest] and no withdrawals [in tenancies]. There are hundreds of thousands of Hans in Xinjiang, but there are no Han in Tibet at all. Our army now is residing in a totally different ethnic region, and we rely on two basic policies to win over people and not to be defeated.

10. In Tibetan, yöle gyabla mi du.
11. Drakten, interview, 1992, Dharamsala. He said his source was Shatsela, a very close intimate of the sitsab Lobsang Tashi. Shatsela had told him that Lobsang Tashi himself had related this to him.
12. This telegram was not available to me.

First—to calculate carefully and become self-reliant in production in order to influence people through this. This is the most basic thing. Even after the road is completed, we cannot depend on it to transport large quantities of food supplies. India may agree to transport food into Tibet through bartering, but our standpoint should be that our troops can still survive in case India stops supplying food someday in the future.

Our troops should make all efforts and appropriate approaches to win over the Dalai and the majority of his upper-class group, to isolate the minority bad ones, *and to achieve the goal of gradually reforming Tibet politically and economically over a period of many years without shedding blood.* However, we should also be ready to deal with a situation in which the bad ones may lead the Tibetan troops to rebel and attack us. Even under such circumstances, our troops should still be able to survive in Tibet and not fall down. All the above things must depend on careful calculation [of our resources] and self-sufficiency in production, which is the primary policy to be accomplished.

Second—what may be done and what must be done now is to open trading relationships between India and the inland [the rest of China], to balance the exports and imports of Tibet, to prevent the living standards of Tibetans from being slightly lowered because our army came into Tibet, and to strive to improve their living standards. If we fail to solve the two issues of production and trade, we will lose our material foundation, and the bad ones will have an excuse to stir up the backward people and Tibetan troops [to oppose us]. Our policy of unifying the majority and isolating the minority will be weakened and cannot be realized.

Of all the Southwest Bureau's opinions on 2 April, only one is worth reconsideration—that is the issue of the possibility and appropriateness of reorganizing the Tibetan local army and establishing a military-administrative committee within a short period of time. *Our opinion is that we should not reorganize the Tibetan army at present, and we (also) should not establish a [unified] military area, and we should not organize a military-administrative committee.* Keep everything as usual. Delay and wait for one or two years until our troops can support themselves and our army has won the support of the masses. Then we will raise these things again.

During the next one or two years there are two possible situations. One is that our united front policy with the upper class to unify the majority and isolate the minority will work. The Tibetan people will gradually come close to us, so the bad ones and Tibetan troops will not dare to revolt.

The other will be that the bad ones will think we are weak and easily bullied, and this will lead the Tibetan army to launch an uprising. We will defend ourselves and fight back. Either of the above situations will benefit us.

From the Tibetans' point of view, currently there are not enough reasons to carry out all the terms of the agreement and to reorganize the Tibetan army. It will be different in a few years. [Then] they may feel they have to agree to implement the agreement completely and reorganize the Tibetan army. If the Tibetan army starts an uprising once or even several times, they all will be defeated by us, and we will then have more reasons to reorganize the Tibetan army. It seems that currently not only the two lönchen [sitsab] but also the

Dalai and his group feel reluctant to accept the agreement and do not want it to be carried out.

For the time being we don't have the material foundation to implement the agreement completely, nor do we have the foundation in people to implement the agreement completely, nor do we have the upper-class foundation to implement the agreement completely. *More harm than gain will be gotten from pushing the implementation. It is okay if they are not willing to carry it out. We will not carry it out now and will delay it. The longer we delay, the more reasons we will have and the fewer reasons they will have. It will not do much harm to us if we delay, but perhaps it will do much good.* Let them do all the bad and unreasonable things to people. We will do only good things for people, such as production, trading, road construction, building buildings, united front [unifying the majority, patient education] to win over people. *We will wait until conditions are ready and raise the question of carrying out all those terms again. If they think it is inappropriate to establish elementary schools, we will stop founding elementary schools. We shouldn't take this as an expression of only the two sitsab and bad ones, etc.* [who are doing this], *but also as the opinion of the majority of the Tibetan government. The content of their petition is tactically very skillful. They did not say they will just break with us but asked us only to back up [compromise] a little bit. They did not actually mean it when they implied we should return to the ways of the Ming-Qing era regarding not stationing the PLA [in Tibet]. They obviously know this is impossible. They intended to use this issue for bargaining for other things.* They criticized the 14th Dalai in their petition [this refers to the comments on corvée taxes and loans] in order to let him escape political responsibility for the demonstrations. They represent themselves as protecting the interests of the Tibetan people, because they know they are weaker than we are in military capability but stronger in the social situation [power]. *We should substantially accept the petition [not formally] and meanwhile delay the overall implementation of the agreement.*

They have considered and chosen a time before the Panchen's arrival for this demonstration. When the Panchen arrives in Lhasa, they may make all sorts of efforts to persuade the Panchen to join them. If we can do a good job and the Panchen isn't deceived by them and arrives in Shigatse safely, the situation will become more advantageous to us at that time.

However, for a short time, our deficiency in material foundation cannot be changed. So the Dalai's group is not willing to carry out the agreement fully, and this will not change soon either. *So at present, in appearance, we should take an attacking attitude toward the demonstrations and petition, saying that they are unreasonable and they are destroying the agreement, but in reality we should be prepared to compromise. Wait until conditions are ready and prepare for the future attack.* What are your opinions about this? I hope you will think about this.

Central Committee
6 April 1952[13]

13. Dui xizang gongzuo de zhongyao zhishi (wei chuban de shouji), n.d. (emphasis added).

Notwithstanding this amazing telegram, the Tibet Work Committee in Lhasa feared that the situation was spinning out of control and felt they had to do something to quell the unrest and keep the situation in Lhasa under control, so after lengthy discussions, they concluded that nothing could be done to relieve the tension in Lhasa so long as the two sitsab were in power. This required more than an "attacking attitude" in appearance; it required the removal of the sitsab. To achieve this, the Chinese set out to persuade or pressure the Dalai Lama to dismiss Lukhangwa and Lobsang Tashi. This was the kind of intrusive tactic that they had heretofore tried to avoid, but now they decided that the time had come to force a change.

First, however, the Tibet Work Committee sent a telegram on 7 April to the Central Committee in which they laid out their plan to ask the Dalai Lama to dismiss the sitsab and asked for instructions. The Central Committee responded the next day, but not to the telegram of the 7th, which they had not received. Instead they sent another amazing telegram that criticized the Tibet Work Committee for acting precipitously and made a major break with the existing chain of command by taking direct control of all decisions regarding Tibetans. Mao, still totally committed to his gradualist strategy, had concluded that the situation in Lhasa was so complicated and sensitive that he had to exercise more direct control over the actions of the cadres in the Tibet Work Committee. Lhasa now had to seek permission for everything, not from the Southwest Bureau as before, but directly from Beijing. This telegram from Mao was sent on 8 April 1952.

[To the] Southwest Bureau together with the Tibet Work Committee:

We have received a telegram from the Southwest Bureau at 11 P.M. on 7 April. We agree with the suggestions of the Southwest Bureau that the incident of the uprising in Lhasa will be directly handled by the Central Committee. *The Central Committee has also decided that in the future the Central Committee will directly settle all dealings, discussions, and negotiations between us and the Tibetan side regarding political, military, foreign affairs, trade, religion, and cultural issues. The Tibet Work Committee will directly report to the Central Committee,* and at the same time it should inform the Southwest Bureau. The Southwest Bureau will provide its opinions to the Central Committee regarding those issues.

The Southwest Bureau and the Southwest Military Area will still take charge of internal issues of the Tibetan Party and Military Area, including organizational structure, arrangements, training, production, construction, mutual support, etc. The Tibet Work Committee should not handle any issues involving the Tibet side and foreign affairs with India, Nepal, etc., until it reports each of them [to us] and asks for instructions.

It is not right that recently you did not report and seek instructions regarding establishing an elementary school in Lhasa. In addition, it seems there are some other things you didn't report in advance and seek instructions. The Tibet Work Committee must pay serious attention to this point. The extreme seriousness of the issues involving the Tibetan nationality must be realized and must be dealt with properly. It cannot be treated like ordinary relationships.

The Central Committee
9:00 P.M. 8 April
Printed according to the handwriting of Mao Zedong[14]

Not receiving any instructions on the sitsab issue, on 10 April,[15] the Tibet Work Committee sent another telegram to Beijing, proposing a specific course of action for securing the two sitsab's dismissal.

Tibet Work Committee to the Central Committee and the Southwest Bureau about the plan on how to deal with the Lhasa reactionaries [10 April, 9 P.M.]

Regarding the specific arrangements about how to deal with the Lhasa riots, it is decided it should take the form of a political struggle [rather than a military struggle], and we should openly propose to the Dalai that he dismiss the two sitsab. We will insist on realizing the four points proposed by us on 1 April [see above]. If we do this, we anticipate three possible outcomes.

First, the Dalai and the Kashag may agree to dismiss them easily.

Second, the two sitsab may stake everything on a single throw and do whatever they can to fight militarily. [If this occurs] we absolutely will fight back militarily and contend for victory in both the military and the political sphere according to the principle "reasonable, moderate, and beneficial to us" (ch. youli youli youjie).[16]

Third, the two sitsab may hide in the Potala and manipulate the Dalai, delaying to try to bargain with us or maybe plotting to continue to organize a force to fight back. If so, we will insist that the Kashag ask the Dalai to resolve this quickly and dismiss them and deal with this.

Specific work:

First, on the 11th, we will call a meeting of the abbots of the Big Three Monastic Seats. We will use the chaos in Lhasa as an excuse to insist that they cancel the 14 April Tsongjö Prayer Festival [in Lhasa's Tsuglagang Temple] and change it so that it is done in each of their monasteries. Then we will go to each of the monasteries to give alms and do propaganda work properly. We will inform the Kashag to record this [alms].

Second, on the 13th, Zhang Jingwu, as representative of Central Committee, will ask [the Dalai Lama] to dismiss those two people. He will give this decision in written form to the Dalai. He will request (ch. yao qiu) that the Dalai

14. In Chinese: genju mao zedong shougao kanying. Zhonggong zhongyang wenxian yanjiu shi; zhonggong xizang zizhiqu weiyuanhui; zhongquo zangxue yanjiu zhongxin 2001: 65 (emphasis added).

15. Dangdai zhongguo congshu bianjibu 1991: 196 says that on 8 April, Zhang Jingwu had a talk with the Dalai Lama and requested that he issue an announcement that he dismissed the People's Association, but this seems incorrect.

16. This is Zhou Enlai's famous axiom.

issue this order before noon on the 14th. Also he should make an announcement about this.

Third, we will call a meeting with the Kashag and explain the Central Committee's policies and attitudes. Also we will separately try to win over the monks and lay nobles and the Tibetan representatives to the negotiations. On the same day, we will call a meeting with the aristocratic military officers to explain the policies.

Fourth, (our) military preparations should be ready before the 12th.[17]

On 11 April, the Central Committee responded to an earlier telegram sent on 7 April, which was received late.

[To the] Tibet Work Committee together with the Southwest Bureau:

After we received and replied to the 10 April, 9 P.M., telegraph from you, we received the telegraph you sent on 7 April that described Comrade Zhang Jingwu's participation in a meeting with the Kashag. From these reports, we can clearly see that not only do the middle factions, such as Dalai's faction, but also the reactionary factions, such as two sitsab's faction, dare not admit that the rebellion and the so-called people's conference are legal.

Hence, the policy in the telegraph you sent at 9 P.M. on 10 April, in which you mentioned the plan to dismiss the two sitsab, dismiss the "People's Association," and punish the chief instigators (those instigators are the so-called imperialist invasion elements, namely, Lukhangwa, Lobsang Tashi, and Surkhang, etc.) is absolutely correct and necessary. At the Kashag's meeting, Jingwu pointed out the three reasons why the "people's conference" was illegal (it was instigating rebellion, sabotaging unity, and opposing the Dalai). He also pointed out that in order to settle down [calm] the majority, we will punish only those imperialist invasionist elements and Guomindang spies who instigated this incident, not the others. All these measures are correct. The number of so-called imperialistic invasionist elements such as Lukhangwa, Lobsang Tashi, and Surkhang, who are the chief figures in the reactionary faction and who were chief elements of the Taktra reactionaries in the past, should be determined after the matter is gradually made clear. Don't restrain yourself.

The Central Committee
11 April
Printed according to the handwriting of Mao Zedong[18]

The very next day, the Central Committee clarified its prior advice on the Seventeen-Point Agreement, ordering the Tibet Work Committee not to

17. Quoted in fn. 2 to the 11 April telegram from Central Committee to TWC, in Zhonggong zhongyang wenxian yanjiu shi; zhonggong xizang zizhiqu weiyuanhui; zhongquo zangxue yanjiu zhongxin 2001: 67–68.

18. Telegram from Central Committee to TWC and Southwest Bureau on 11 April 1952, in Zhonggong zhongyang wenxian yanjiu shi; zhonggong xizang zizhiqu weiyuanhui; zhongquo zangxue yanjiu zhongxin 2001: 69–70.

mention compromise until after this crisis was resolved, since Tibetans might mistake that for weakness. It now instructed,

[To the] Tibet Work Committee together with the Southwest Bureau:

We received the telegraph on 11 April. At present, do not mention the compromise policy that was mentioned in the telegraph from the Central Committee on 6 April. We should decide these after we ensure the victory of the current political struggle. Right now you should carry out political struggle only. Do not mention [compromising on] matters such as reorganization of Tibetan army, establishment of military subarea, or establishment of Military-Administrative Committee. Otherwise, the reactionaries will think that we are showing weakness.

Central Committee
3:00 P.M. on 12 April
Printed according to the handwriting of Mao Zedong[19]

On the same day, the Tibet Work Committee sent Beijing a draft of a letter it planned to send to the Dalai Lama, stating that Lukhangwa and Lobsang Tashi were sabotaging the Seventeen-Point Agreement and should be dismissed.[20] At the same time, the Chinese in Lhasa were making military plans to respond to an attack and issued precombat orders to its troops, which presented the situation as follows:

Tibetan Military Area Headquarters' precombat order (Lhasa, 11 April 1952):

A. Situation
  1. Since 31 March, imperialist invaders, Guomindang spies, and a minority of the Tibetan upper hierarchy, together with Tibetan army soldiers, hoodlums, traders, and a monk-organized reactionary "people's association," [formed a] "Lhasa liberation team." They petitioned and attempted to destroy the agreement through riots. Such a scheme is still being carried out.
  2. There are altogether 2,150 Tibetan soldiers in Lhasa. A specific deployment plan can be found in Bulletin No. 3.
B. Situation
  In order to defend ourselves and to hit strongly at the unrest organized by the imperialists and Guomindang spies and to guarantee the realization of the peaceful agreement, our operational policy is: *first, let them attack us; let them fire the first shot. Our troops should not fire first. Thus, they become politically unreasonable, and we are politically reasonable.* When enemies come and attack us, our defense

---

19. Telegram from Central Committee to TWC and Southwest Bureau on 11 April 1952, in Zhonggong zhongyang wenxian yanjiu shi; zhonggong xizang zizhiqu weiyuanhui; zhongquo zangxue yanjiu zhongxin 2001: 71.

20. Footnote to telegram from Central Committee to TWC and Southwest Bureau, 13 April 1952, in Zhonggong zhongyang wenxian yanjiu shi; zhonggong xizang zizhiqu weiyuanhui; zhongquo zangxue yanjiu zhongxin 2001: 73.

troops must hold on to their places and must not take one step backward. They must cause casualties among the enemy. Then our attack troops should launch severe counterattacks against the enemy.

First, quickly eliminate the enemies' organized armed forces, then occupy their ammunition warehouse and grain warehouse, their communication equipment, and the Jagpori Hill and other key points. *Make sure to protect the Dalai Lama and strictly observe our discipline and policies in the city. Observe our policies of protecting monasteries and our policies of how to treat captured enemy soldiers. Troops are forbidden to take any property of merchants or people, to destroy monasteries, to kill any captured enemies or civilians. Anyone who breaks those rules will be severely punished.*

> Order from
> Commander Zhang Guohua
> Political Commissar Tan Guansan
> Vice Political Commissar Fan Ming
> Second Vice Political Commissar Wang Qimei
> Chief of Staff Li Jue.[21]

On 13 April, Zhang Jingwu met with the Kashag ministers, the trungtsigye and abbots, and representatives of the Three Monastic Seats. Zhang Jingwu reviewed the situation of the past four to five months, and then he explicitly said for the first time that the Tibet Work Committee would be asking the Dalai Lama to dismiss the two sitsab. However, by then it was getting late, so it was agreed that the Kashag ministers would respond to this and convey their thinking to Zhang Jingwu the following day.

On the same day (13 April), the Central Committee sent Zhang Jingwu a set of interesting instructions, toning down his proposed draft letter to the Dalai Lama and explaining how to criticize the sitsab in a way that would *indicate a willingness to compromise.*

[To the] Tibet Work Committee together with the Southwest Bureau:

(1) We have received the telegram at 9 P.M. on 12 April about the notice to the Dalai from the Central Committee's representative [Zhang Jingwu]. This notice is basically right. If it has already been sent out, just let it be. If it has not yet [been sent], please correct it a little bit.

Among the three entries describing the criminal acts of the two sitsab, the second entry, which said that the two sitsab protested against forming the military area office and reorganizing the Tibetan army and spoke about the PLA beating the Tibetan army and making it bloody, etc., this should be deleted and changed to "not implement the agreement. They took the opposing attitude toward several important stipulations in the agreement such as reorganizing the Tibetan army, etc. They did not at all understand that all the terms

21. Ji 1993a: 409–11 (emphasis added).

in the agreement are beneficial to the prosperity and happiness of both the Tibetan nationality and the Tibetan people. *Also, they did not give constructive comments on steps and approaches for implementing certain terms [in the agreement],* but protested against implementing the agreement completely." This way of writing it can win over the majority and *also give a hint that we might accept reasonable suggestions about the steps and approaches of implementing the agreement.*

(2) When comrade Zhang Jingwu meets with the Dalai or when you talk with Ngabö or other people, for the time being do not mention the compromise policy. At present, only carry out the political struggle [struggle politically, not militarily] and prepare a military counterattack. In the future, whether or not we should mention the compromise policy, when we should propose it and how we should propose it should wait until the results of this political struggle are seen clearly. Then you should report to the Central Committee about making specific decisions. However, at present, do not stress that either the army or the Military-Administrative Committee will be established immediately. *If they ask what are "constructive opinions on the steps and methods of implementation," you may tell the people that all opinions that are beneficial to the unity of Han and Tibetans and to the proper implementation of the agreement are constructive opinions. If [they] have these sort of opinions, we would like to listen and also would like to negotiate. However, you should not give out your specific opinions easily [impetuously] so that you will not be trapped in a passive position [without options in negotiating].*

(3) Regarding the Tibetan army in Lhasa, we definitely have to reform them step by step. The Tibetan army in other places may be reorganized slowly, step by step, not all at the same time. As to how the reforms should be carried out—after the patriots such as Ngabö take over power, you should gradually remove some of the most reactionary officers and arrange for the rest of the military officers to get training by batches in order to gradually have some officers in the Tibetan army be close to us. Using this approach, we can achieve the goal of reorganizing the Tibetan army gradually.

Central Committee,
13 April
Printed according to the handwriting of Mao Zedong[22]

The next day, the Central Committee responded to the Kashag's comments on the 13th, sending the Tibet Work Committee instructions that clearly emphasized that the sitsab's removal had to be done in a manner that would make this appear a Tibetan government decision, *not a forced imposition by the Chinese side.*

[To the] Tibet Work Committee together with the Southwest Bureau:

We received the telegraph you sent at 12:00 P.M. on 14 April

---

22. Telegram from Central Committee to TWC and Southwest Bureau, 13 April 1952, in Zhonggong zhongyang wenxian yanjiu shi; zhonggong xizang zizhiqu weiyuanhui; zhongquo zangxue yanjiu zhongxin 2001: 72–73 (emphasis added).

(1) It is very appropriate that you still have not submitted the written letter from the representative of the Central Committee to the Dalai but rather have let Jingwu notify the Dalai and Kashag orally in advance, elaborating the reasons for dismissing and investigating the two sitsab and about our intentions.

(2) The Dalai is still hesitating about this. He has not yet made up his mind to dismiss the two sitsab, and the Kashag will hold a meeting about this matter. Therefore, we should wait for the results of that meeting and then decide whether we should send the official [written] notice to the Dalai. If they [the Kashag] decide to take the path of letting the two sitsab resign, we should not send out the notice requesting their dismissal. The public edict for dismissing the two sitsab becomes unnecessary too.

(3) It is very necessary to make the Kashag, the other civilian and military officials, and the monks in the Big Three Monastic Seats understand completely that the sitsab are heinous criminals and also that the armed rebellion and the illegal "People's Association" are not allowed. We should influence the Dalai via the Kashag ministers in order that the Dalai can make his own determination to dismiss the two sitsab, [but] if the two sitsab will not resign, we will dismiss them. All this is very necessary. We need [to wait] several days or longer. Anyway we have concentrated our army forces, so no matter how the reactionaries may struggle against us, whether by civil or military methods, we will defeat them. Therefore, the two documents, the written notice and the edict, temporarily should not be presented.

If, in the future, the edict is to be made public, it would be better to let the Dalai himself do it. If we let the Kashag ministers make the draft, and then we revise it and persuade the Dalai to give his permission, and then if we send it out, it will be relatively normal. [Doing it this way] *The Dalai and those elements of the middle faction in the Tibetan local government will not feel humiliation. This point is very important. Please pay attention to it.*

The Central Committee
4:00 A.M. 15 April
Printed according to the handwriting of Mao Zedong[23]

At the same time, in Lhasa, the Kashag met with the Chinese on the 15th and agreed to ban the People's Association but also argued that the Chinese side should withdraw its request to dismiss the sitsab because of the widespread support for the sitsab in society. The Kashag assured the Chinese that the sitsab were not behind the group. They may have made some mistakes in what they said, but their style of speaking was the same with Tibetans and Chinese. In other words, they proposed a compromise: dismiss the People's Association but retain the sitsab. Their comments derive from the minutes of the meeting kept by the Tibetan side.

---

23. Zhonggong zhongyang wenxian yanjiu shi; zhonggong xizang zizhiqu weiyuanhui; zhongguo zangxue yanjiu zhongxin 2001: 74–75 (emphasis added).

The People's Association has previously given a letter to both the Chinese and Tibetans. You recall the series of detailed discussions between the Chinese and Tibetans that occurred in between. However, concerning this, the Kashag and the trungtsi now will discuss this in detail.

The People's Association is the cause of unneeded disturbances between Chinese and Tibetans. It is a small cause that has produced a large harm. At the same time, under the pretext of a people's association, a few evil people have spread many rumors with the hope of making a commotion and deceiving others. Because of this, the people have not been able to live in a happy and relaxed manner. This is a bad thing, so in the future we will not allow the People's Association to meet.

To leave no doubt in the minds of all people, and to give them strict and accurate instructions, and to answer their petition, in which they have gone on the wrong path and made mistakes, we have decided to issue an official government edict (tib. bugdam dzatsig). We will give you a copy to look at after we make a copy of it. Then we will tell the representatives [of the People's Association] that we are issuing the edict. We think this is a good thing. We will also explain our views in detail to the [people's] representatives, persuade them of the benefits and the dangers, and forcefully tell them that we have decided that in the future they cannot meet. So regarding this, would you please give us your suggestions from the Chinese side.

In accordance with our detailed discussion about eliminating the People's Association, which is the cause of unneeded suspicion between Chinese and Tibetans, and as we have uprooted the People's Association like the roots of a tree, you now do not have to have suspicions concerning their supporters, whoever they are. In particular, the two sitsab are not backing the People's Association. We have collectively and privately assured you that they are not behind it. When the sitsab and the Kashag ministers have met together, the sitsab have made it clear about that. Therefore, you don't need to have any suspicions, but if your doubts are not cleared up, all of us will guarantee that [this is true, i.e., guarantee their good behavior in the future].

Similarly, you mentioned five violations of the agreement made by the sitsab when they met with Chinese officials formally or privately. Regarding this, [we want to say that] the two sitsab have been very concerned about settling all kinds of government affairs [not just these with you], and, regardless of whether to internal people or to outsiders, they have been and they still do say everything straightforwardly, so there might have been some kind of slightly inappropriate way of talking. But we Chinese and Tibetans have signed an agreement, so, as with relatives, it is possible for small mistakes to happen. Therefore, [when this happens] you should give us your instructions internally. So we all ask you to cast aside your fury and not be intensely angry. In the future, in accordance with the agreement, there is no reason for there to be violations against the friendship between Chinese and Tibetans, and we should work harmoniously and have discussions on this. . . .

Minutes (tib. nyeljang shogle) [from the Tibetan side of the Kashag ministers' comments at the meeting][24]

24. CHMC 1986b: 282–84 (emphasis added).

Thus began a very interesting and illustrative give-and-take over how to deal
with the sitsab, with Mao himself directing Chinese tactics from Beijing. The
next step occurred at 5 P.M. on the 15th, when the Tibet Work Committee
sent a telegram to Beijing, explaining how it wanted to deal with the members of the People's Association and the others the committee members believed were behind them. The Tibet Work Committee adopted a very moderate position and recommended that, with the exception of the two sitsab,
who were to be eliminated from the political scene, no punishments would
be meted out.

> According to the situation in Tibet, we decided to deal with the so-called
> People's Association using "the policy of supporting the progressive power of
> the patriots, uniting and winning over the middle elements (including stabi-
> lizing those wavering elements), and totally isolating the reactionary ele-
> ments." In this political struggle we will firmly attack the two reactionary sitsab
> and drive them from the political stage. Regarding the other chief separatists,
> such as Surkhang, etc., we will temporarily paralyze/blunt them.
>
> As to the so-called people's representatives, in general, we should be lenient.
> We should totally settle accounts regarding all the reactionary speeches and
> actions of those pro-imperialist separatists who made armed rebellion and op-
> posed the agreement and the unity between the Han and Tibetan peoples. Also,
> we will take advantage of this to let them register with the Tibet local govern-
> ment and the PLA and write letters of repentance [that indicate they are] turn-
> ing over a new leaf. If they repent, we will not punish them.
>
> Regarding the important leaders and representatives like the ex–jigyab
> khembo, the government will keep close watch on them so that we can settle
> issues whenever they occur and so that we can find out clues about imperial-
> ist spies and the inside story of the reactionary organizations. We will treat it
> [the People's Association, etc.] as an important reactionary case. We will an-
> nounce that we will not investigate all the other people who were hoodwinked
> to become involved.[25]

Meanwhile, on the same day, senior Tibetan government officials met to
discuss the decision to abolish the People's Association. A telegram from the
Tibet Work Committee to the Central Committee on 15 April discussed
the Tibetan side's decision at that meeting to go en masse to Zhang Jingwu
to try to persuade him to allow the sitsab to remain in office.

> Today, all the Tibetan senior officials gathered to hold an emergency meeting
> in the Potala Palace. The Kashag ministers first met the two sitsab and told them
> the two final opinions from the Kashag ministers' meeting on the 14th [sic,
> 15th, see above] [namely] "that the Han and Tibetan people should be

25. Cited in fn. 2 to the 16 April 1952 telegram from the Central Committee to the Tibet
Work Committee and the Southwest Bureau, in Zhonggong zhongyang wenxian yanjiu shi;
zhonggong xizang zizhiqu weiyuanhui; zhongquo zangxue yanjiu zhongxin 2001: 76–77.

unified; the agreement should be implemented; and the 'people's association is illegal and should be dismissed." The Kashag decided to issue a proclamation in the name of the Dalai to dismiss the people's conference. In the report it was also mentioned, "all the officials unanimously agreed on this, and tomorrow morning all the officials will come to our residence to say that the 'people's association may be dismissed and to intercede [on their behalf] (ch. jiang qing) asking [us] not to dismiss the two sitsab."[26]

Since the Tibetan side was still trying to avoid dismissing the sitsab, on 15 April Zhang Jingwu finally sent the letter to the Dalai Lama requesting that he immediately give the order to dismiss Lukhangwa and Lobsang Tashi. In this letter, Zhang Jingwu escalated the pressure on the Dalai Lama by stating that from that day forward he would no longer recognize the position of Lukhangwa and Lobsang Tashi and therefore would no longer discuss any issues with them. Zhang requested that the Dalai Lama give the Kashag an order that henceforth the Kashag would be immediately under the Dalai Lama (rather than under the sitsab) and should deal with Zhang directly. The letter listed the faults, with much hyperbole, of the sitsab:

1. They adhered to the position of splitting for the purpose of securing the independence of Tibet.

2. They opposed and did not carry out the regulations and stipulations of the agreement with regard to some important stipulations in the agreement, such as the adaptation of the Tibetan army.

3. They falsely represented the will of the people and presided over the unlawful people's congress.

4. These two sitsab recalled the general who was originally stationed in Shigatse, a very important place of national defense, without the approval of the military headquarters of the military area of Tibet. They did this in order to plot a military armed rebellion.

5. They did not respect the power of the Dalai Lama, who had already come to power, and on several occasions disobeyed the orders of the Dalai Lama and sabotaged the political and religious prestige of the Dalai Lama.[27]

The next day (16 April), at 6 A.M., Mao telegraphed his agreement with the Tibet Work Committee's proposed action against the members of the People's Association and, interestingly, once again reminded the committee members that they had to clear all important decisions with Beijing.

---

26. Cited in fn. 2 of the 16 April 1952 telegram to the TWC and the Southwest Bureau from the Central Committee, in Zhonggong zhongyang wenxian yanjiu shi; zhonggong xizang zizhiqu weiyuanhui; zhongquo zangxue yanjiu zhongxin 2001: 79.

27. Dangdai zhongguo congshu bianjibu, 1991: 197–98; Zhonggong xizang zizhiqu dangshi ziliao zhengji weiyuanhui 1990, entry for 15 April 1952.

[To the] Tibet Work Committee together with the Southwest Bureau:

(1) We received the telegraph sent 5:00 P.M. on 15 April. We think your measures for dealing with the so-called people's congress are correct.

(2) In dealing with the "people's congress," there will definitely be many new situations. Please report to us any time you take a specific step. When dealing with important issues like this, you must get permission from the Central Committee before carrying them out. Since you already have the confirmed general policy, when you take specific measures you have to be both determined and cautious so that you can strike the vital part of the enemy accurately to win over the broad masses. Thus, it is better to spend more time exchanging ideas with the Central Committee and then take action.

> Central Committee
> 6:00 A.M., 16 April
> Printed according to the handwriting of Mao Zedong[28]

Two hours later, Mao sent a second telegram, in which he conveyed a major tactical decision he had just made, instructing the Tibet Work Committee to consider reciprocating the concessions of the Tibetan government by agreeing to let the sitsab *resign* rather than be *dismissed*.

[To the]: Tibet Work Committee together with the Southwest Bureau:

We received the telegraph sent at midnight on 15 April

(1) On the 15th, the meeting at the Potala decided to disband the "People's Congress" and to have the Dalai issue an edict about this. If this comes true, it will be a great victory. Before the Dalai issues the edict, you and the Kashag should expose the reactionary crimes conducted by the two sitsab and the imperialist spies to the majority of the "people's representatives" and to all civil and military and monk and lay officials in order that you can win over the majority when the edict is issued rather than [waiting] and doing it all of a sudden. The edict should be signed by the Dalai himself. Do not put Zhang Jingwu's name on it.

(2) When the Kashag officials come to your residence to ask to let the sitsab resign instead of being dismissed, we agree with your opinion "to patiently expose the crimes conducted by the two sitsab and persuade them to agree unanimously to request the Dalai to give the order to dismiss them." This is because the written letter by the representative of the Central Committee [Zhang Jingwu] has just been sent out [on the 15th], and we cannot change it immediately; it is also because dismissal is a more serious punishment than resignation. It is more powerful to punish reactionaries and influence the masses.

However, you should pay attention to the attitudes of the Dalai and the majority of the Kashag ministers. *If they ask again and again to let the sitsab resign*

---

28. Zhonggong zhongyang wenxian yanjiu shi; zhonggong xizang zizhiqu weiyuanhui; zhongguo zangxue yanjiu zhongxin, 2001: 76–77 (emphasis added).

and cannot accept dismissal, you should be prepared to accept resignation. That is because regarding the issue of the "People's Congress," they have agreed with our opinion and have made a big concession. If we insist on dismissing the two sitsab, it may cause the Dalai and the middle faction to feel dissatisfied and feel that we are making the two sitsab suffer too much (ch. zheng ren).

Regarding this, please have detailed discussions with Ngabö, Che Jigme, and Phüntso Wangye [Phünwang] to see which way is more appropriate. We are looking forward to your notifying us of your decisions.

Central Committee
8:00 A.M. 16 April
Printed according to the handwriting of Mao Zedong[29]

As predicted, on 16 April, a group of twenty senior Tibetan officials came to Zhang Jingwu to intercede on behalf of the sitsab, asking that they be allowed to continue in office. The meeting lasted until 10:00 in the evening, but the Chinese side did not yield and continued to insist that the Dalai Lama should dismiss the sitsab.[30] This visit was reported in a telegram sent that same evening to the Central Committee, and Mao responded the next day (17 April) with very clear instructions, reiterating his previous instructions that they could not agree to let the two sitsab remain, but they could accept their resignation if the Tibetans insisted on this rather than dismissal.

[To the] Tibet Work Committee together with the Southwest Bureau:

We received the telegram sent at midnight of 16 April. Those people who came to intercede did not say that the two sitsab would resign. They still talked about retaining the two sitsab. They meant to exchange dismissing the "People's Congress" with the sitsab not [having to] resign their position. You should not relent for a couple of days and should insist, first, on dismissing the People's Congress and, second, the two sitsab. When the Dalai's edict has been issued and the People's Congress dismissed, then you should see whether these interceding people are still proposing to exchange/trade resignation for dismissal. If they do not ask for resignation, you should insist on dismissal. If they propose resignation, *you will accept resignation according to the situation. The Tibetan aristocrats are very good at political struggle, and you should learn from them. Maybe they will issue the edict after they confirm the exchange conditions (keep the two sitsab or let them resign). You should insist on disbanding [the People's Congress] and dismissing [the two sitsab] at the same time. Or you can suggest disbanding the People's Congress first and then dismissing the two sitsab. If they insist on exchanging disbanding the People's Congress with the two sitsab's position, you should firmly reject it. If they propose exchang-*

---

29. Zhonggong zhongyang wenxian yanjiu shi; zhonggong xizang zizhiqu weiyuanhui; zhongquo zangxue yanjiu zhongxin 2001: 78–79 (emphasis added).

30. Discussed in fn. 3 to the 17 April telegram from Central Committee to the Tibet Work Committee and the Southwest Bureau, in Zhonggong zhongyang wenxian yanjiu shi; zhonggong xizang zizhiqu weiyuanhui; zhongquo zangxue yanjiu zhongxin 2001: 81. See also Le 1986: 355.

ing disbanding the People's Congress with the two sitsab resigning, you can make some compromise and agree to let the sitsab resign. I hope you will act according to the situation.

Central Committee
12:00 P.M. 17 April
Printed according to the handwriting of Mao Zedong[31]

However, to the consternation of the Chinese, nothing concrete from the Tibetan side happened on 17 and 18 April with respect to either the People's Association or the sitsab. In fact, on the 18th, Le Yuhong recalled hearing about talk that a disturbance would occur that evening and was so nervous that he was unable to sleep and stayed up reading a book until midnight.[32]

The Tibet Work Committee, therefore, concluded that Zhang Jingwu, as the representative of the Central Committee, should try to cut through the impasse by meeting the Dalai Lama in person. Many in the Tibet Work Committee were dubious about doing this, because they feared that the Tibetans would kill him, but Zhang Jingwu thought this was unlikely and decided to go. The Tibet Work Committee concluded that one of three outcomes was likely and developed plans for how to respond.

1. Lukhangwa and Lobsang Tashi would kill Zhang Jingwu. If this occurred, the PLA would use this opportunity to destroy the power of the upper-level reactionary Tibetan group and the illegal activists in the People's Association in one fell swoop.[33]

2. Lukhangwa and Lobsang Tashi would detain Zhang Jingwu in the Potala Palace and, in conjunction with the People's Association, launch an attack on the PLA stationed in Lhasa. If this happened, the PLA could attack in self-defense and achieve the same final goal listed under situation 1. . . .

3. Dalai Lama will follow Zhang's request and demote Lukhangwa and Lobsang Tashi, thus peacefully ending the disturbance of the People's Association.[34]

One Chinese official who was involved recalled the morning Zhang left for the Potala Palace.

31. Zhonggong zhongyang wenxian yanjiu shi; zhonggong xizang zizhiqu weiyuanhui; zhongquo zangxue yanjiu zhongxin 2001: 80 (emphasis added).

32. Le 1986: 355–56.

33. Interestingly, the Chinese looked back in history and found only one case in which a Chinese Amban was killed by Tibetans, and that was in 1750, when the amban didn't have their own military force in Lhasa. The TWC, therefore, thought that while there was a danger to Zhang, it might be okay (Yang 1987: 79–80).

34. Ji 1993a: 408; and Yang 1987: 79–81. Shakya (1999: 104–5) mistakenly writes of this apprehension with regard to Zhang Guohua attending a meeting with the Kashag and sitsab on 31 March. The source he cites (Yang 1987: 80), however, clearly says it is Zhang Jingwu who said this about an anticipated visit to the Dalai Lama on 19 April 1952.

Zhang Jingwu went to the Potala on 19 April 1952.[35] . . . Commander-in-Chief Zhang Guohua and others, such as Commissars Tan Guansan, Wang Qimei, and Li Jue, were staying in the newly built bunkers in the Military Area Headquarters waiting. At this time they suddenly received a phone call saying that Zhang Jingwu, together with a translator, two security officials, and one squad of ten bodyguard troops, had left [his quarters] for the Potala Palace.

Then Li Jue called me and said, "Zhang Jingwu has left for the Potala, so I am giving you an important task. Take a pair of binoculars and a flare gun and stay by the south side of the Military Area Headquarters beside the river. From there secretly observe what is going on in the Potala. We have discussed with Zhang Jingwu in advance, and he will either wave a flag from a window on the south side of the Potala or fire three shots from there if he is in trouble. If this happens, you should at once fire three flares into the air. As soon as we see this, we will attack. So this is important work and do it carefully." So I stayed watching the Potala without any break. When Zhang Jingwu appeared at the east edge of the mountain, he left the army squad at the bottom of the Potala Hill, and he and the translator and two security officers went up [to the palace].[36]

There is no definitive description of Zhang's meeting with the Dalai Lama, but Chinese sources all say he eventually was persuaded to remove the sitsab. The Chinese cadre told to watch the Potala recalled his feelings when Zhang left.

[At 2 P.M.] from the east door, first one person came out, then three people, and then I knew it was Zhang and the other three, and I was very happy. So I ran and yelled to those in the bunker that Zhang Jingwu has left the Potala safely. Everyone was very happy about this. . . . Zhang Guohua said, "It is great that Zhang is coming, but we don't know yet what was settled about the problem in Lhasa, so we should continue the military alert." After one hour, Zhang Jingwu called the Tibet Military Area Headquarters from Sandutsang house and said, "The Dalai Lama and I had a verbal struggle, but in the end the Dalai Lama agreed to demote the two."[37]

The Dalai Lama's accounts of the incident do not mention the face-to-face meeting with Zhang Jingwu at all (which certainly occurred). He wrote only,

Soon afterwards, I received a written report from the Chinese stating that it was clear that Lukhangwa was an imperialist reactionary who did not want to improve relations between China and Tibet and asking that he be removed from office. I also received a verbal suggestion from the Council [Kashag] say-

---

35. Shakya 1999: 110, mistakenly gives the date of 25 April and says erroneously that it was Zhang Guohua rather than Zhang Jingwu who went to the Potala. Some Chinese sources such as Zhao 1995 give a date of 8 April for this historic meeting, but this is certainly incorrect.
36. Ji 1993a: 409; see also Yang 1987: 58.
37. Ji 1993a: 409; see also Dangdai zhongguo congshu bianjibu 1991: 66ff.

ing that it would probably be for the best if I asked both Prime Ministers [sitsab] to resign. This saddened me greatly. They had both shown such loyalty and conviction, such honesty and sincerity, such love for the people they served.[38]

And in an interview he said,

> Finally, the Chinese wanted [their dismissal], and the Kashag also recommended to me that maybe it was best if the two sitsab resigned, since we could not have good relations with the Chinese with them [in place]. So I told the two sitsab, "As far as we are concerned we have no complaints from our side, but such a situation exists." Poor them. It was difficult for them to speak. They said that what is important is that the Dalai Lama is not put in "embarrassing situations" and that they have no regrets whatsoever. Poor fellows.[39]

The Dalai Lama explained further in the interview how the Kashag came to him and recommended he dismiss the sitsab.

> The entire Kashag came. I think mainly, I can't remember clearly, but logically I think the main speaker was Ngabö. Then perhaps Shasur also commented that it would no longer be useful to have them, although they appreciated their determination and loyalty.
> Q. Did they give any specific reasons?
> They were clashing with the Chinese. And if we do that we can't handle the Chinese.[40]

Lhalu recalled attending the same meeting.

> All the Kashag ministers had an audience with the Dalai Lama and reported in detail the situation [about Zhang Jingwu asking that the Dalai Lama dismiss the sitsab]. The Dalai Lama replied, "Concerning the disagreement between the Chinese PLA officers and the sitsab, it is like a crack on a porcelain cup. [Once it has appeared] It is difficult to fix. Consequently, the sitsab have to give up their work responsibilities, but their title and salary should be continued as before."
> The Dalai Lama then ordered us to go together and tell this to the Sitsab, so we all went, and Minister Surkhang, speaking in a respectful way, told them the [Dalai Lama's] order in detail. Sitsab Lobsang Tashi said in response, "Okay, okay" (tib. la les la les). And then Lukhangwa said, "The PLA have surrounded us, haven't they? For example, they have pitched their tents and are staying in the empty areas on the mountains in Trib. In the future we will talk about this with you, but now we two, in accordance with the order, will give up our responsibilities. However, as for our seal [of office], we two will give it back to the Dalai Lama [in person].[41]

38. Dalai Lama 1990: 73ff.
39. Dalai Lama, interview, 1995, Dharamsala.
40. Dalai Lama, interview, 1995.
41. Lha Klu 1981: 353–54.

However, it is clear that the Dalai Lama, in fact, already knew that the sitsab were too hard-line and were creating bad relations with the Chinese.

> Ngabö told me on a few occasions that the two sitsab were slightly too hard-headed (tib. trag tra). Finally, the Chinese formally asked me and then the whole Kashag collectively advised me that it was better if the two sitsab resign. Anyway, that's true. . . . I trusted and depended on the sitsab 100 percent. Occasionally I also noticed that they were a bit too hard-headed, but I didn't tell them that. I didn't have the motivation to tell them. I trusted them so much, and they respected and loved me so much. So that's how it went.[42]

> Poor fellows [the sitsab]. They were 100 percent reliable people. Amazing; they had totally sacrificed themselves. They were sort of a bit too hard-headed and too uncompromising (tib. gyongdrag).
> Ngabö and Shasur . . . did not necessarily disagree inherently with the sitsab, but the circumstances were such that they felt this way. They may have had sympathy with the sitsab, but they realized that the position of the sitsab would lead nowhere—that it had no future. The Chinese were already there—this just confrontation, it was no use. So now they, even Shasur, said the position of the two sitsab was too extreme and would not benefit us. We had to make closer relations with the Chinese. Ngabö also felt this, but this was not necessarily some kind of sympathy with the Chinese at that time.[43]

> By then the situation was such that we were already in their hands. So now all there was to do was to be diplomatic and friendly. There was no possibility to be obstinate. At that time the two sitsab were being very stubborn. That I remember clearly. At times the two sitsab, the Kashag, and the Chinese met together. At times only the Kashag [met with the Chinese]. When the two sitsab, the Kashag, and the Chinese met, they almost always sort of ended up in a fight. So in this manner, in 1952, Zhang Jingwu said that the two sitsab must resign.[44]

The Dalai Lama's refusal to intervene with the sitsab earlier, even though he knew their shortcomings firsthand and had heard about them from Ngabö, reflects again his lack of involvement in the critical political events going on around him. He was the ruler but chose to play a passive role, leaving the affairs of state to the government. In one interview with me, he, in part, explained his role then.

> When the two sitsab were there, now I was also brand new, right? Isn't it? The sitsab took the main responsibility until 1952. . . . So when the two sitsab were there, I totally relied on them.
> Regarding relations with the Chinese as well as other matters, the Kashag

---

42. Dalai Lama, interview, 1994, Ann Arbor, MI.
43. Dalai Lama, interview, 1995.
44. Dalai Lama, interview, 1993, Dharamsala.

makes the plan, which is handed to the sitsab and then to me. If they can decide on a matter, then they will do it. Important matters that they cannot decide, they will discuss with me. They would advise me, saying, "We think it is best to do it this way." And so I decide on that.[45]

However, following Zhang Jingwu's meeting with the Dalai Lama on 19 April and the visit of the Kashag, the Tibetan side still did not act immediately. It wasn't until a week later, on the afternoon of 25 April, that the Kashag ministers went to Zhang Jingwu's office to discuss the terms of the sitsab's dismissal. They informed Zhang that the Dalai Lama was willing to dismiss the two sitsab with several provisos: (1) that there should be no punishment, (2) that they should still receive a salary from the Tibetan government, and (3) that they would retain their ceremonial position. For the Tibetans, this was equivalent to their resigning or retiring. Zhang Jingwu, in accordance with Mao's previous instructions, now agreed.[46] Consequently, on 27 April, the Dalai Lama issued the order ending Lukhangwa and Lobsang Tashi's active positions as sitsab.

Lukhangwa's daughter-in-law confirmed that Lukhangwa, though no longer sitsab, still retained his ceremonial status and seat position.

> Ever since he was relieved of his work, he just stayed at home and said his prayers. He never went anywhere, and he really stayed at home. He never went anywhere, like picnics et cetera. During important ceremonies, he attended and wore whatever dress his rank entitled him to. After he was relieved of his work, he continued to receive his salary, because as far as the Tibetan government was concerned, he did not deserve any punishment.[47]

With the sitsab gone, the Kashag and Chinese now turned to deal with the leaders of the People's Association. Three days before the Tsongjö Prayer Festival was to end, on the 27th of the second Tibetan month (the end of April), a joint investigation committee met.[48] The heads of the investigation committee from the Tibetan side were Sambo Dzasa and Trendong Khenjung. Under them were two secretaries, one lay and one monk—Tsögo Sey and Shingsar (Lobsang Gelek). On the Chinese side, the main official was Lin Lai. Shingsar recalled the hearings.

> The investigation was held on the east side of the Tsuglagang Temple, above the Revenue Office. . . . When we met and discussed who should be asked to appear, the Chinese had a list. We then called those people to appear. . . . It

45. Dalai Lama, interview, 1995.
46. Ji 1993a: 416.
47. Mrs. Lukhangwa, interview, 1993, Dharamsala.
48. Lhatsün Labrang Chandzö, interview, 1992, Dharamsala; Shingsar Lobsang Gelek, interview, 1993, Toronto.

was easy. In Lhasa, the government sends a messenger saying come to such and such a place, and they will come. The first person was Jayan Dawa.

He was a calm person and made a satisfactory reply. We did not interrogate in our Tibetan fashion. The Chinese had written some questions such as, Who first brought you (into the association)? Who was there when you went? Did you affix your seal? Who was the one who wrote the petition? And who put their seals on the document? et cetera. So Jayan Dawa gave an appropriate reply. He said that nobody told him to join, that they all joined voluntarily. He also said that famine was coming to our country, and everybody was facing difficulties, so "I joined on my own. . . . There was talk like this, and I heard that some 'people' were meeting, and I went to look for this meeting and found it."

The Chinese sort of accepted his reply, and at the end of the first round of questioning, Lin gave Jayan Dawa some advice, saying that this kind of activity was illegal and unprecedented. However, he said this in a very mild way, so the Tibetan side immediately understood that this was not going to be difficult, and the Chinese were not going to demand harsh punishments—which the Tibetans would have strongly opposed.

After Jayan Dawa, the rest of the members were brought in one by one. However, the investigation was not done strictly according to Tibetan judicial norms, because the defendants were allowed to stand just outside the door, so they could hear what was asked and answered by the previous defendants. Normally, Tibetan investigations function by means of detailed comparisons of the different testimonies [of people who have been interrogated separately]. In this case, however, everyone followed Jayan Dawa's testimony, and all the answers were very similar.

. . . [They] said things like, "After the Chinese came, commodities became scarce, and the people suffered. . . . In our country we have to express our concerns so we don't die from starvation. Even in the Seventeen-Point Agreement, it seems there is a place for the people to have a voice, so I said it."[49]

After several days of interrogations and discussions, the Kashag and Tibet Work Committee met on 1 May 1952 to issue sentences. All the "defendants" appeared, as did the top Chinese officials and the Kashag ministers. The Kashag instructed the defendants that their organization went against all established customs and traditions and henceforth was banned. It decreed that the leaders would be freed if they each gave a written pledge guaranteeing that he would not engage in such activities in the future. They all did this, so the incident was over. Neither the Tibetan government nor the Chinese wanted to inflame passions further by leveling harsh punishments, so it was sufficient simply to abolish the "association" and secure the defendants' pledge not to organize again.[50]

49. Shingsar Lobsang Gelek, interview, 1993.
50. Shingsar Lobsang Gelek, interview, 1993.

On that same day, 1 May 1952, the Kashag sent an official edict to counties all over Tibet abolishing the People's Association.

Order to the counties (tib. dzong) regarding abolishing the Fake People's Association

Last year in Beijing the People's Government of China and the representatives specially sent by the Tibetan local government signed the Seventeen-Point Agreement for the Peaceful Liberation of Tibet and announced to the world that in the future both will maintain this policy. After that, the representative of China, Zhang Jingwu, came [to Tibet] via India, while the PLA officers and soldiers and military and civil officials came to Lhasa via the overland route. They met the Dalai Lama and gave him gifts from the Chinese government and so forth and made good relations with the Tibetan people. All the Tibetan people know and praise this.

All the PLA soldiers from the lowest and both the civil and military officials respected and adhered to the Seventeen-Point Agreement. Consequently, neither the poor classes nor the bourgeois class nor the high and low people ever saw any instance of the PLA doing acts in violation of the agreement. Although all the terms of the agreement have to be put into practice, the central government followed a policy of not doing things by force or urgently and instead did them in accordance with the local conditions and in accordance with the thoughts of the local people.

However, some people in Lhasa who are possessed by ghosts acted as leaders, inciting traders who had gone bankrupt, people who weren't able to repay their debts, people who ate and dressed well but didn't work diligently, and those who didn't pay taxes and didn't abide by the law [i.e., riff-raff]. In sum, wherever there were such kinds of people, they called them together and said to them that [they had to work] on behalf of Buddhism and the [Tibetan] political system and for the happiness of the people. Wearing such a mask, their external policy was to compose a letter with six points. Their inner strategy was to look and see whether peaceful or military means were best, and they took an oath to this effect. They also expanded the size of the organization, moving into the various villages of the Lhasa [municipality] [to recruit members]. So via untrue rumors, they created the foundation for destroying the harmony between Chinese and Tibetans.

Because of this situation, the honest and law-abiding people of Lhasa worried a lot and couldn't sleep at night or get good nutrition from their food. And because the price of grain in Lhasa suddenly increased, the aristocrats and subjects were not happy. The sitsab were unable to implement the Dalai Lama's thinking, which was to quickly eliminate the People's Association, which was doing illegal acts, and to stop all illegal activities and make things safe and secure for Lhasa. And in particular, they were working in opposition to the agreement at all times. So great harm was caused to the friendly relations between Chinese and Tibetans. Because of this, the Dalai Lama was placed in a situation in which there was no choice, and it was absolutely necessary and important to withdraw their responsibilities.

The heads of this illegal organization were investigated. There has never been an illegal association such as this, so they should be punished harshly. However, if in the future such bad actions do not recur, we will treat this as a one time occurrence. Those people in the association who were tricked by the people who were involved with foreign imperialists and those who were ignorant of what was going on will receive only light punishment. The ones who were the representatives of the People's Association will be given education about their mistakes, from both the Tibetan government and the central government. Together with this, all their agreements will be burned and torn up, and they will be made to agree that they will not partake in such activities in the future.

We have sent out a Kashag edict (tib. gadam dzadzi) with our seal to the people of Lhasa and Shöl, and moreover, before this, the Dalai Lama himself issued an edict (tib. bugdam dzadzi rimpoche) to Lhasa and Shöl.[51] By the kindness of the Dalai Lama, it is not possible for such a bad association to occur again; however, it is not certain whether some of the bad people in this association may go to village areas and say they were defending religion. *The Dalai Lama is thinking and doing this for Buddhism and the welfare of the subjects who are like his two eyes, and together with this, he is also thinking and talking clearly about the terms of the agreement. He is planning to put it into practice slowly. So all the people, regardless of whether they are monks or laymen, have complete trust that all the religious and secular deeds will come out well by the kindness of the Dalai Lama.* It is unnecessary to mention that they are enjoying the happy result.

However, a few people do not understand the external and internal policies and are unable to handle their own livelihood from the beginning to the end. It is absolutely inappropriate for these people to meddle in the affairs of the state and the government. All the people can see that the harm of these actions is more than the benefit. It is unlikely that they will follow them, like jumping into a chasm even though they have eyes. However, if people join a bad association like this, they will be given a very harsh punishment by the national law.

So you [the county heads] should give effective orders and instructions to the subjects so that they make a correct choice between right and wrong and between benefit and harm. And you should consistently investigate and supervise using all means—internally, outwardly, and secretly.

Later, in case there are any irresponsible actions against the benefit of religion and politics that may cause the recurrence of the evil gatherings, not only the persons who do that but also you, the heads of the counties and the landlords, will be severely punished.

This decision is not just words but will be implemented. So all people should keep it in their minds and be careful not to violate this edict. This edict should be kept with the records of the county.

The date, month of the Water-Dragon year [1952].[52]

---

51. "Gadam dzadzi" is name of the seal the Kashag used on its edicts. "Bugdam dzadzi rimpoche" is the name of the seal the Dalai Lama used on his edicts.

52. Translated from the Tibetan in CHMC 1986b: 285–89 (emphasis added).

And so a difficult interlude ended quietly without even a slap on the wrist of the demonstrators and leaders. However, the incident and petition had impacts. On the one hand, they heightened anger and hostility toward the Chinese and put them on the defensive for seven months. On the other hand, they persuaded the Chinese to stop pushing to implement reforms regarding the army and the Military-Administrative Committee.

This incident also illustrates the extent to which Mao was personally overseeing the situation in Tibet and was committed to his pragmatic, gradualist Tibet policy. Mao believed strongly that major reforms should not be done without first building consensus among the Tibetans, so as this incident unfolded he came to realize that his officials in Lhasa could not be trusted to make correct judgments on how to proceed. He then intervened and ordered that all decisions regarding Tibet first be cleared with him and the Central Committee. He also directly intervened and instructed his officials in Lhasa to compromise on the sitsab's "resignation," not to punish or jail any of the People's Association leaders, and, of course, to drop, for the time being, the military reform issues. The Chinese, under Mao Zedong's guidance, played their hand with finesse and restraint and managed to end the disturbance without inflaming the feelings of Tibetans any further than they already had.

The disbandment of the People's Association and the resignation of the sitsab were effective moves, and calm was quickly restored to Lhasa. A new iteration of the People's Association would emerge in 1955–56 under new leadership, but for the time being no attempt was made by its members to continue to oppose the Chinese. Its leaders seemed to be satisfied with having succeeded in giving the Chinese their petition.

On the Tibetan side, the resignation of the sitsab restored control of the government to the Kashag and eliminated the internal disjunction within Tibet's top leadership. From then on, the more moderate and realistic views of the Kashag would set a tone of cooperation and cordiality in Sino-Tibetan interactions, allowing the process of implementing the Seventeen-Point Agreement to move forward slowly. This, of course, was made easier because the petition and demonstrations had led Mao, unbeknownst to the Tibetan side, to take the contentious issues of the army and the Military-Administrative Committee off the table.

The incident, however, also reinforced Fan Ming's more hard-line and confrontational views regarding the Tibetan government and the Dalai Lama. And despite Mao's moderation, Fan would soon launch an initiative to change the CCP's Tibet policy.

By May 1952, therefore, the threat of fighting and bloodshed had passed, and calm had been restored. Tibet had gained another chance to try to fashion a comfortable place for itself within the PRC.

THE DALAI LAMA, THE UNITED STATES,
AND THE DALAI LAMA'S BROTHERS

As this process was unfolding in Lhasa, another page in U.S.-Tibetan relations occurred, again raising questions about whether those closest to the Dalai Lama, especially his older brothers, were dealing with the United States in his name but without his knowledge or approval.

In February 1952, Taktse Rimpoche, then living in the United States, told the State Department that he just received a letter for the U.S. government from the Dalai Lama. This was presumably in response to the various messages the United States had sent to the Dalai Lama in late 1951, imploring him to flee. A copy of this letter, which the State Department said was undated and unsigned, is not available, but a portion of it was quoted in a State Department memorandum of 12 February 1952, which began by stating, "With reference to [the] most recent secret letter from Dalai Lama to Tak Tser."[53]

This letter painted a relatively sanguine picture of the situation in Lhasa, presumably as an explanation of why the Dalai Lama did not flee to exile. "The Chinese," it said, "had given no open indication that they wanted to suddenly change matters in Tibet or injure the Tibetans. Under the circumstances, since the Chinese were being correct and careful, it seemed best to treat them in the same way."[54]

However, the letter was also carefully crafted to try to sustain U.S. interest in Tibet, saying that Tibet's "official friends" in the United States should not feel "vexed" because of this, since Tibet's policy remained and would remain the same, presumably meaning anti-communist. The letter also was said to have instructed Taktse to maintain contact with the Americans and not to allow misunderstanding or lack of confidence to develop between the United States and Tibet.[55] The implication was that the Chinese "correctness" would not continue, and Tibet would need its friend America again in the future.

John Allison, assistant secretary of state for Far Eastern Affairs, must have been surprised by this positive assessment of the Chinese, given the more negative information the United States was being told, but he responded to Taktse sympathetically, saying,

> The US fully understands difficult situation in which Dalai Lama finds himself, is not vexed at Dalai Lama's decision to adjust temporarily to superior force and wishes to reassure Dalai Lama that US sympathy will continue. He said that US has not changed the position which was stated by his predecessor, Mr. Rusk.

53. The letter is discussed in U.S. Department of State 1985: 9, in a footnote to a 13 February 1952 memorandum of conversation by Anderson (Office of China Affairs) that cited CA files, lot 59 D 228, folder 7p.

54. U.S. Department of State 1985: 9.

55. U.S. Department of State 1985: 9.

Mr. Allison stressed necessity for approaching present difficulties with courage and patience. He pointed out US sincerely sympathetic with Tibetan people for their loss of traditional religious and political freedom. Mr. Allison asked Tak Tser convey these thoughts to his brother, the Dalai Lama. . . . [Mr. Allison] Assured Tak Tser that US friendship and sympathy will continue. He explained his hope that fall of Tibet to Communists will resemble tactics of Japanese judo experts who fall in order to rise and gain the final victory.[56]

At the end of this meeting, when Allison asked Taktse for suggestions on how the United States could be helpful to Tibet, Taktse replied that the United States should continue contacts with the Dalai Lama through him and should not do anything to "invite undue attention to Tibet at this time through public statements." He also assured Allison that the Tibetan people were clinging to the hope that something could be done later and that the continued friendship of the United States was critical in continuing that hope.[57]

Although we do not know what the entire letter said, from the few excerpts cited, it seems a reasonable response. However, there is another less reasonable dimension to this event, namely, the real source of the letter. The Dalai Lama emphatically denies sending Taktse the February letter.[58] To be sure, his memory could be incorrect, or he could be worried about the impact of admitting this for his current political dealings with China, but if the Dalai Lama is correct, someone (or more than one) was clearly using the Dalai Lama's name to pursue relations with the United States independent of him and the Tibetan government. As we shall see later in this chapter, this was not an isolated incident.

At the exact same time that this letter arrived, another strange event concerning Taktse occurred. Taktse, for some time, had been working closely with the CIA to have the U.S. government launch a major publicity campaign on behalf of Tibet that would have included a statement by either the president or the secretary of state. However, Taktse now suddenly had a change of heart and told the United States to scrap the campaign. An excerpt of a State Department internal memorandum explained his puzzling overnight shift as follows:

This somewhat embarrassing situation arose because Tak Tser reversed his position between the afternoon of Feb. 11 and the afternoon of Feb. 12.

First he and CIA [had] strongly requested a double barreled approach to news for Tibetans: 1. a private statement for Tak Tser from Allison 2. a public

56. U.S. Department of State 1985: 9, fn. to 13 February 1952 memorandum of conversation between Anderson (Office of China Affairs) and Taktser (611.93 B/2–1352).
57. U.S. Department of State 1985: 9.
58. Dalai Lama, interview, 1995.

statement from either the Secretary [of State] or the President. Since CA [Office of China Affairs] has long since agreed that both would be necessary, we found no objection to meeting the original request. Apparently Connors reversed his prior opinion *after* learning that Allison's views were reinforced by Tak Tser's reversal. Tak Tser, in turn, was well pleased by Allison's private talk and *increasingly apprehensive about the possibility that a public statement would increase the risk to his mother who returns to Lhasa soon.* To me it makes no great difference.[59]

This sudden decision is surprising, to say the least, given that until then Taktse's main effort in the United States had specifically been to muster U.S. support for Tibet against China. After he had finally succeeded in securing this support at the highest levels of the U.S. government, canceling it suddenly like that is difficult to fathom. The reason Taktse gave, fear that such a campaign would increase the risk to his mother, is not credible. First, if this was important for Tibet, she could have delayed her return for several months. And if he was really worried about the impact on his family, what about his brother Lobsang Samden and the Dalai Lama, who were in Lhasa. Why would the U.S. campaign be more of a risk to his mother than to them? Moreover, the Dalai Lama's mother and her other children had been living in Kalimpong/Darjeeling since 1951, not in the United States, so there is no reason that she would be implicated by anything the United States did. And since the Chinese had been urging her to return to Lhasa, it seems obvious that they would have been overjoyed if she came, regardless of what the United States said or did. Thus, what the risk to his mother would have been from such a campaign is not at all clear, even if Taktse himself played a role in interviews and speeches. However, it may have been a risk to someone and something else.

The Dalai Lama's mother was returning to Lhasa in mid-February, together with her other children, including her twenty-four-year-old son, Gyalo Thondup.[60] Gyalo had been in the United States for the past five months and was planning to go to college when he too suddenly changed his mind and abruptly left the country in early February 1952 to return to Tibet with his mother. This was a dramatic reversal, since, at his specific request, the United States had just arranged for him to start college at Stanford.[61] His actions appear to have stemmed from his decision to get involved in politics in Tibet and try to influence the course of Tibetan history at this

---

59. U.S. National Archives, F810001–1885, no title, no date (probably February 1952) (emphasis added).

60. Her daughter, Tsering Dolma, and youngest son, Ngari Rimpoche, were also part of this group.

61. U.S. Department of State 1983: 1849, fn. to telegram from Ambassador Bowles, in India, to the secretary of state, 15 November 1951.

sensitive time. A major U.S. government pro-Tibet campaign beginning immediately after he left the United States could well have negatively impacted *his* credibility and *his* stature with the Chinese Communists, since it would be natural for them to assume that he had had a hand in it. Thus, an alternative explanation is that he and Taktse decided it was better to stop the U.S. publicity campaign in order to give Gyalo a better chance to influence affairs in Tibet.[62] Whatever the real reason for Taktse's reversal, an opportunity for a major U.S. government campaign on behalf of Tibet was lost.

Though young, Gyalo felt he understood the situation better than the less worldly leaders of the Tibetan government and had strong opinions about how Tibet should respond to the Chinese. From when he was studying in Nanjing in the late 1940s, he believed that Tibet needed political and social change. He was, for example, convinced Tibet must immediately end the feudal system in order to improve the lives of the peasants and win their loyalty. He feared that if Tibet was not proactive in reforming itself, the Chinese would win the loyalty of the peasants by themselves implementing reforms.[63] In Lhasa he met the important political figures on both sides. He recalled explaining to the sitsab.

> On the basis of my experience abroad, the situation in China, [and] the way the Communists thought, I told them [the sitsab] that we, the Tibetan government, under the leadership of the Dalai Lama, the two sitsab, and the Kashag, must take the initiative for land reforms. Our land system in Tibet was very ancient, and nothing had really changed. Not only for the betterment of the living conditions of the Tibetans, but I saw a great danger that the Chinese would use the land reform issue to meddle in our affairs if we didn't take the initiative. If land reforms and land redistribution were done [by us], the Chinese would not have much of an excuse to interfere in our affairs. I told the two sitsab that they must reform the land system. They said that what I had said was very important and that they would give it due consideration.[64]

The ultraconservative sitsab, however, were not interested in reforms, let alone major land reforms, and, since the Chinese were pursuing their gradualist policy, were not under pressure to do so. From their point of view, the masses were already behind them in the form of the People's Association,

---

62. This whole event did not leave a good impression on the U.S. government, as can be seen by what happened to Taktse. Shortly after this, Taktse went to Japan to attend the Buddhist World Fellowship but, while there, found that his Indian identification papers and his sponsorship by the Committee for a Free Asia had expired. When he applied for readmission to the United States, amazingly, he was rejected and was then stranded in Tokyo for the next three years (Conboy and Morrison 2002: 19)

63. Lhamo Tsering, interview, 1992, Dharamsala; Gyalo Thondup, interview, 1992, Dharamsala.

64. Gyalo Thondup, interview, 1992.

so they did not take Gyalo's suggestions seriously. It must have seemed impossible to them that the Tibetan people would turn against religion and the Dalai Lama for communism. And they were right. Mao and the sitsab at least agreed on that. The sitsab, therefore, ignored Gyalo's urgings.

Gyalo also met with the Dalai Lama, passing on the notes that Yuthok had taken in Calcutta the previous year from Ambassador Henderson's letter to the Dalai Lama. He says he tried to persuade the Dalai Lama to go into exile on the basis of the U.S. offer, but here, too, he was rebuffed. In a letter he sent later that year from India, he explained the situation to the U.S. secretary of state.

> I explained and discussed with His Holiness about the important issues you [the secretary of state] and I examined in the United States, and informed him that he should once more plan to leave and go abroad. I did my best to persuade him, but under the prevailing situation it is most dangerous, and he cannot take hurried and careless steps, because there is a large Communist force in Lhasa and they are very cautious and alert. If any signs of such a plan leaked out, there would be great danger to His Holiness's life and great sufferings would fall on the people. So if we want to accomplish this objective [having the Dalai Lama leave for exile], we should think of a way wherein we will definitely win entirely and not suffer even a small loss. Consequently, it will be very difficult to plan such an action.[65]

Gyalo also quickly found that the Chinese were ignoring his advice on the sitsab and the People's Association. Consequently, after a few months' stay in Lhasa, Gyalo was frustrated and unhappy with both the Chinese and the Tibetan leaders, neither of whom were paying attention to his opinions and plans. In an interview, he explained (in uncorrected English), albeit with considerable hyperbole, his thinking about the Chinese and the Tibetan governments.

> My purpose coming out from Lhasa in 1952 to India was mainly because I was very much disappointed with the behavior and the policies of the Chinese leadership in Lhasa. The general Zhang Jingwu and the Zhang Guohua . . . it was shocking . . . I returned from the United States anticipating maybe that the Communist government would be treating the Tibetans in a reasonable manner. But during my stay in those months I was really shocked and disappointed. . . . The Chinese troops were treating the Tibetans like their enemies. . . .
>
> All the Tibetan government officials except the Dalai Lama and maybe one or two regents, I mean regencies, they didn't accept Chinese payrolls. And the rest, everyone, in '52 was under the payroll. Even my sister and my sister's husband were on the payroll. Tibetan government officials were very busy collecting the silver dollars. Many of them were getting one hundred or two hun-

---

65. Translated from the Tibetan, in Lha mo Tshe ring (Lhamo Tsering) 1992: 153–59.

dred or three hundred or six hundred each month. So the Chinese were more or less bribing. So that was a terrible situation, and I never anticipated that the Chinese government would do such things, particularly the Communist government. And so they had a big gap between the nobility. The government officials were collaborating, completely drowned with money, with the Chinese silver dollars. And the parties going on like that. And then the people were shouting and complaining.[66]

Reciprocally, Gyalo was not well received in Lhasa, where many Tibetans were suspicious of his motives and loyalties. His long-time secretary-aide, Lhamo Tsering, has written about that: "There were some [Tibetan] government officials who were deeply suspicious of Gyalo Thondup because he had studied in China, and although justice was on his side and he had enthusiasm, there were only a few people supporting him. And leave alone his efforts having any result, some people were saying that Gyalo Thondup was more red than the Red Chinese themselves."[67]

Frustrated by being ignored by both sides, the twenty-four-year-old Gyalo quickly decided to return secretly to India and try to impact the situation in Tibet by pursuing anti-Chinese activities from there. He explained his thinking (in uncorrected English) in the same interview.

I discussed this with my other brother Lobsang Samden. He was the jigyab khembo in the [Tibetan] government. So my mother, myself, and Lobsang Samden discussed this and decided it was very vital for us to have some kind of contact with the outside world so they would know what the Chinese are doing and how the Tibetans are suffering. So my main purpose in going to India was to organize some kind of Tibet group and try to mobilize international opinion. . . . I thought that maybe through the Indian government I could persuade the Chinese to slow down some of their activities and behavior. So without informing anybody else except my mother and my brother, I made a plan to leave. . . .

I made up my mind that it was useless for me to stay in Tibet. I can't help the Tibetan government, I can't help my brother, I can't help the Tibetan people, on the one side. If I help and I speak the truth, I speak the correct things, the Chinese won't listen. The Chinese will suspect me.[68]

In another interview he said (in uncorrected English),

In 1952 when I was in Lhasa, some of my family members decided I should go to India secretly to try to establish some kind of contact with the India government. . . . The main reason at that time was that the situation in Tibet was very serious, because the majority of the population are very much against the

66. Gyalo Thondup, interview, 1995, Hong Kong.
67. Lha mo Tshe ring (Lhamo Tsering) 1992: 122.
68. Gyalo Thondup, interview, 1995.

Chinese occupation forces. You know the mimang [people's] movement. By that time the government of Tibet and the Tibetan people are completely cut off, isolated. No contact with the outside world and, particularly, nobody knows what is going on with Tibet. So we realized that it was very important that one of us should go to India and establish contact with the Indian government to try to promote some kind of understanding and try to inform the Government of India and other countries what is going on in Tibet. What the Chinese are doing. So my main purpose was to go and do that kind of a job.[69]

Gyalo's mother (the Dalai Lama's mother) has also commented on this.

When Gyalo Thondup returned with us to Lhasa [in 1952], he had already decided that Tibet was no longer a safe place and was making plans to leave again. No one knew of this at this time except me. He did not see eye to eye with the Communists, and in some anger, some Chinese said he had to be reeducated. This was an indirect threat, and my son told me that the time would come when the Chinese communists would try to "persuade" him to reform his ideas. He pleaded with me to let him go back to India. I reluctantly agreed. . . . Three months after he had come [he left for India]. The only people who knew of his departure were my son Lobsang Samten and me. *We did not inform His Holiness; Lobsang Samten said that if the Chinese asked His Holiness if he knew the whereabouts of his brother, he would reveal himself by a guilty flush on his face because he was yet tender in age.*[70]

As with the February letter to Taktse, the Dalai Lama has said that at this time he knew nothing about Gyalo's plan to leave Tibet secretly.

Later only after 1956, did Samden tell me that Gyalo Thondup had a discussion with him that Gyalo Thondup can no longer remain in Lhasa and will go to India on pretext of visiting Jayul [in southern Tibet]. And in their discussions they mentioned that this should not be said to Dalai Lama because if Dalai Lama knows, when the Chinese ask directly, Dalai Lama may not protect [the secret], so they deliberately kept it a secret to me.[71]

Lobsang Samden kept secrets from me on some matters. Later, he told me, "At that time, such and such things happened, but I didn't dare to tell you."[72]

Thus, the Dalai Lama's family made a conscious choice to exclude him from this decision as a result of their assessment that he might not be able to keep Gyalo's flight a secret in face-to-face interaction with the Chinese. Interestingly, in an interview given to me in 2004, the Dalai Lama himself said that

69. Gyalo Thondup, telephone interview, 1994.
70. Tsering 2000: 135–36 (emphasis added). It is important to note that the interviews with the Dalai Lama's mother were done in 1979–80, when the current political pressures were not present.
71. Dalai Lama, interview, 1995, Dharamsala (in English, uncorrected).
72. Dalai Lama, interview, 1994 (in English, uncorrected).

by nature he was more spontaneous than calculating and controlled, so perhaps his family understood this aspect of his personality.[73] But, in truth, the fear that the Chinese would read the Dalai Lama's facial expression is far-fetched, since the Dalai Lama rarely ever met with Tibetan officials, let alone Chinese officials. And even more surprising is why there was a need for such extreme secrecy.

Gyalo gives the impression that the Chinese would not let him leave Tibet, but that seems improbable. The Chinese were not restricting the travel of Tibetans to and from India, and since Gyalo's wife was in Darjeeling, it would have been easy for him to say she was sick and he had to return to assist her. Given Mao's gradualist policy, the Chinese could not have refused him. So why the need to lie to the Dalai Lama in the name of secrecy?

The real answer, I believe, is that Gyalo Thondup and Lobsang Samden were plotting to start a secret anti-Chinese organization in exile without the knowledge of the Tibetan government or the Dalai Lama. A key to the success of this organization was for Gyalo to secure the cooperation of Shakabpa, the most prominent anti-Chinese government official in India. As mentioned earlier, Shakabpa had adamantly opposed the Dalai Lama's returning from Yadong to Lhasa in 1951, and when he did return, Shakabpa remained in Kalimpong.

Gyalo, however, did not know Shakabpa well, so Lobsang Samden wrote an extremely dangerous letter to Shakabpa, telling him to remain in India and work with Gyalo to make relations secretly with the U.S. and Indian governments. It also asks the Shakabpa and Gyalo to send their advice secretly on how to oppose the Chinese and on what to do with the Tibetan government's gold; for example, should it be moved into an American bank? Since Gyalo would be carrying this letter, the decision to flee secretly was apparently made to avoid even the remote possibility that he might be stopped at the normal border checkpoints and searched. Gyalo and Lobsang were playing a dangerous game, for if this letter had ever fallen into the hands of the Chinese, it could well have brought down the Dalai Lama and the traditional government and ended the Chinese policy of moderation. The translation of the handwritten letter (cited in the original Tibetan in appendix A) follows:

> To the venerable golden ear of the gods,
>
> I am reporting to you that my brother Gyalo Thondup has purposely left [Tibet] temporarily. He will discuss this with you in detail, so it would be better for [you] Kungo Tsipön [Shakabpa] to stay there [India] temporarily.
>
> Now, I swear by the Three Jewels that the Red Chinese are using tactful means to suppress the Tibetan government, the Dalai Lama, and the monk

73. Dalai Lama, interview, 2004.

and lay Tibetan people. For the present, the Tibetan government has no choice but to be friendly with the Chinese, and the government indeed will do it.

The Tibetan people are showing their severe dislike of the Chinese officials and the Chinese soldiers. *In the future, if the Red Chinese remain in Tibet as now, the Buddhism of the religious country Tibet, the Dalai Lama, and the monk and lay people will have to suffer so severely that they will not be able to pass the days and nights.*

Therefore, I think it would be good if my brother Gyalo La and you would think carefully and then report on time [not late] your opinions secretly through telegrams (if that is convenient) regarding what would be best to do. Anyway, you have to have good unity over there, and please think about what should be done in the future.

Regarding the gold and the silver that was transported from Tibet last year,[74] please send your opinion regarding whether it would be good to leave it as it is, or to transport it back to Tibet, or to deposit it secretly in the American bank, if there is an American bank in India.

For the present you must secretly make internal friendly relations with the American government and the Indian government.[75] You should show great concern in serving the [Tibetan] government. I will inform you more through telegrams.

With auspicious flowers, from Lhasa, from me,
the personal attendant [of the Dalai Lama] acting jigyab khembo (Khentsab) Lobsam [abbreviation of Lobsang Samden].
On the 5th day of the fourth [Tibetan] month of the Water-Dragon year [mid-June 1952].[76]

This letter was not an official letter from the Kashag, but because it came on behalf of a brother of the Dalai Lama and from one of the highest officials in Tibet, the jigyab khembo, who was also the brother closest to the Dalai Lama, and was signed with Lobsang's official title, Shakabpa would have assumed it was sent with the Dalai Lama's knowledge. He would never have taken this as just a personal letter from the nineteen-year-old Lobsang Samden. Had this fallen into Chinese hands, they would also have assumed this, or, even if they could have been convinced that the Dalai Lama knew nothing of it, they would have known that the Dalai Lama's own family was secretly plotting from India to oppose them. Fan Ming, of course, would have jumped on this as validation of his views that trying to win over the Dalai Lama and his elite was a futile strategy.

74. The gold and silver came from both the Tibetan government's treasuries and the Dalai Lama's personal treasury and were left with the Maharaja of Sikkim. The Chinese knew these metals had been taken out of Tibet and were trying to persuade the Tibetan government to bring them back to Lhasa.

75. In Tibetan: snga 'phros a ri gzhung dang rgya gar gzhung so sor gsang ba'i thog nas nang don mthun lam chen po zhig nges par tu thugs zab thog.

76. Translation is of the original Tibetan letter from Shakabpa's personal effects (emphasis added).

For Gyalo Thondup and Lobsang Samden, however, giving the impression this had the approval of the Dalai Lama, directly or indirectly, was critical, since, without it, few would have taken seriously the views of a nineteen- and a twenty-four-year-old on grave matters such as this. We see this clearly when Gyalo Thondup went to see the head of the Indian Mission in Lhasa seeking India's permission for him to stay in India. He explained to me what transpired.

[First] I approached the Indian government through the Indian Consulate General in Lhasa and asked whether it was possible for me to come and stay in India, because it was impossible for me to remain in Tibet. . . . So Sinha [the head of the mission] sent a secret cable in code to Mr. Nehru. After a few days, a reply arrived by cable saying that I would be welcomed. . . . After that I began actively planning to leave. I discussed this with my mother and my brother, Lobsang Samden. No one else.[77]

However, in his official Monthly Report for June 1952, Mr. Sinha gives a significantly different account, reporting to Delhi that Gyalo had said that the Dalai Lama had approved his departure.

He [Gyalo] felt that it would be advisable for him to escape. He fully realizes the risks involved but *has carefully laid his plans with the active help and support of the Dalai Lama.* . . . *If and when the Chinese get to know of his escape, the Dalai Lama would express surprise and say that his brother Gyalo Dondup has always been an irresponsible nomad.*[78]

After the Government of India agreed to this request, Gyalo got to India without arousing suspicion by telling the Chinese that he had to visit his family's six estates on business. Since two of these estates were in remote areas in southern Tibet near the Indian border, once there, it was simple to cross over into India in Arunachal Pradesh (east of Bhutan).[79]

When I asked the Dalai Lama about this, as with previous issues, he categorically denied any knowledge whatsoever of the letter to Shakabpa until I read it to him. He was very convincing.[80] If we assume this is true, and I do, is it conceivable that these two young men did this entirely on their own? Would they, on their own, have dared risk bringing the wrath of the PLA down on the Tibetan government and the Dalai Lama by carrying a letter signed by the brother closest to the Dalai Lama (using his full government title) that instructed a senior anti-Chinese Tibetan official in India to work with the Dalai Lama's other brother to start anti-Chinese activities in India?

77. Gyalo Thondup, interview, 1995.
78. British Foreign Office Records, FO371/99659, monthly report for the period ending 15 June 1951, from officer in charge of Indian Mission in Lhasa, to the political officer in Sikkim (emphasis added).
79. Lha mo Tshe ring (Lhamo Tsering) 1992: 123; Gyalo Thondup, interview, 1995.
80. Dalai Lama, interview, 2004.

Lobsang Samden was known for being fun loving and was not someone interested in political issues, so he could easily have been influenced by his older brother Gyalo, who was, as we have seen, deeply committed to being a player in Sino-Tibetan politics. The exuberance of youth and the arrogance of being the Dalai Lama's family could have made them think they had the right to do whatever they thought best for the good of Tibet. I asked Gyalo Thondup about this. After expressing surprise that I knew about the hereto-fore secret letter to Shakabpa, he declined to answer clearly whether others were involved. When I pressed him, he cryptically said that it would be best for me just to write in my history what it looks like at face value, that is, that Lobsang Samden and he were involved. In the future, he said, when he writes his own book, he will explain what happened in detail.[81]

However, if there were others involved, who might they be? Since Gyalo did not trust the Kashag, he certainly did not discuss this plan with it. And the sitsab were already dismissed. And since he did not discuss it with the Dalai Lama, that eliminated the other major source of official authority. The only parties left to consider are those whom we can think of as the officials and attendants immediately around the Dalai Lama, what one official called the simjung gi thakor ("those around the Dalai Lama's living quarters"). Of these, the most likely figure is Phala, the lord chamberlain, or Trijang Rim-poche, the Dalai Lama's junior tutor, or both. I do not know if Lobsang Sam-den and Gyalo discussed this with them or with any others around the Dalai Lama, but in fact, in the summer of 1952, the Dalai Lama's brothers were planning to start an anti-Chinese opposition movement in India indepen-dently of the Tibetan government and the Dalai Lama.

In early May 1952, at about the same time that the sitsab–People's Asso-ciation affair was ending and Gyalo Thondup was planning to flee to India, in Washington, the eldest brother of the Dalai Lama, Taktse, again met with the State Department and the CIA, filling them in on recent communica-tions he said he had just received. Unlike the February information, this time he painted a bizarre anti-Chinese portrait, explicitly telling the Americans not only that the Dalai Lama himself was pursuing a secret anti-Chinese re-sistance strategy but also that the Panchen Lama, a major Chinese supporter, was about to defect from the Communist's side and secretly join hands with the Dalai Lama in resisting them. The U.S. memorandum of this meeting states the following:

The report, received May 13, conveyed the following information, based on mmunications recently received by Tak Tser.

. Thondrup, interview (phone), 8 December 2005. It should also be mentioned
  lo nor Lobsang Samden was skilled in the government style of writing, so they
  ɔ receive help in composing and writing the letter.

1. Tak Tser has no doubt that the Dalai Lama is developing the *long-range plan allegedly agreed on prior to Tak Tser's departure from Tibet; i.e., the Dalai Lama is quietly organizing resistance to the Chinese Communists while appearing to cooperate with them.*

2. Tibetans in Lhasa, encouraged by the monks, recently have sworn secret new oaths of allegiance to the Dalai Lama and to the three leading monasteries and, simultaneously, have renounced their allegiance to the present lay Cabinet [Kashag] and affirmed undying opposition to the Chinese.

3. The Panchen Lama secretly has indicated his intention to defect from the Communists while appearing to serve as their puppet, and to make common cause with the Dalai Lama in organizing a resistance movement.[82]

The source of Taktse's information is not indicated; however, point 1 appears to come from Taktse's own firsthand knowledge. It unambiguously says that the Dalai Lama had a strategy of overtly trying to maintain friendly and cooperative relations with the Chinese while he was secretly working to organize resistance to them. Given what we know of the Dalai Lama's lack of direct involvement in political affairs at this time and his own family's decision to lie to him about something as trivial as Gyalo's return to India, it does not seem credible to suggest he was really organizing a secret resistance movement in Tibet.

The United States explicitly realized that it had no way to evaluate Taktse's new information independently but decided nevertheless to take it to mean that Tibet, under the leadership of the Dalai Lama, was starting to organize a resistance movement.

> While evaluation of available information is extremely difficult, CA [Office of China Affairs] perceives no reason why Tak Tser's report should not be accepted as "probably true." Since CA believes that (1) the Chinese Communists in Tibet are doing an excellent job of creating their own troubles, (2) developments in Tibet are producing the desired effect on the Government of India, and (3) Tak Tser is on firm ground in believing that a public expression of US interest in Tibet would, at this time, have an undesirable effect on both the Government of India and on the incipient Tibetan resistance movement, CA recommends that the Department continue to avoid public statements concerning Tibet and refrain from any attempts at this time to communicate with persons in Tibet who are believed to be taking their first step toward organizing an anti-Communist resistance movement.[83]

A month later, on 24 June 1952, the U.S. consul general at Calcutta received another communication, purportedly from the Dalai Lama. This message

---

82. U.S. Department of State 1985: 51–52, memorandum by the acting director of the Office of Chinese Affairs (Perkins) to the assistant secretary for Far Eastern Affairs (Allison), 14 M 1952 (611.93B/5–1452) (emphasis added).

83. U.S. Department of State 1985: 51–52.

was oral and came through the Dalai Lama's brother-in-law, Takla (Phüntso Tashi), who passed it on to Princess Coocoola, of Sikkim (probably while Gyalo Thondup was still in Lhasa). She, in turn, passed it on to the consul general in Calcutta, who reported it as follows:

a) The Dalai Lama appreciates greatly the U.S. Government's feelings and attitudes toward him personally and toward his Tibetan subjects.

b) He sincerely hopes that when the time is propitious for the real liberation of Tibet from the Chinese, the United States will find it feasible and possible to lend *material aid and moral support* to the Tibetan Government.

c) The Tibetan people have not changed; they are not pro-Chinese; they are Tibetans first and last.

d) He hopes to be able to get a written message "down" soon.[84]

This message again suggests that the Dalai Lama was secretly biding his time to try to throw out the Chinese. No longer was the Dalai Lama talking about the Chinese being correct and proper, as in the February letter; now he was looking to America to help in *liberating* Tibet from the Chinese.

The Dalai Lama, however, again emphatically denied that he ever instructed Phüntso Tashi to convey those points to the United States.[85] When I asked Phüntso Tashi about this message, he carefully avoided saying whether the Dalai Lama knew but did say explicitly say that the Dalai Lama's lord chamberlain, Phala, knew about it.

Q. I am interested in learning about the answer [you passed on to the United States]. Did the Dalai Lama himself say, "Say it like this"? Or did he tell it via the Kashag?

It was not given through the Kashag.

Q. Did Phala know about that?

Probably he knew about that. [pauses] He knew. If it would have been given through the Kashag, it is not known what would have happened. [This implies the Kashag ministers were not reliable.][86]

Was Lobsang Samden or Lord Chamberlain Phala or both the source of this message in the Dalai Lama's name? I do not know. But the Dalai Lama's fam-

---

84. U.S. National Archives, from Calcutta, dispatch no. 5, 2 July 1952, enclosure 1 (em-
's added).

Dalai Lama, interview, 2004.

ˉakla (Phüntso Tashi), interview, 1997, London. (In Tibetan: Q. yid bzhin nor bu rang
'dra gsung rogs gnang" ser 'di 'dra bzo 'dra cig red yang min na bka' shag brgyud
bshad pa red? A. bka' shag brgyud nas rtsa ba nas yog ma red. Q. dper na, pha
' yod red pas? A. pha lha shes kyi yod kyi red/ pha lha shes kyi red/ bka' shag de
ˉang la gnas tshul ga 'dra yin min shes kyi ma red).

ily, perhaps with others close to the Dalai Lama, were clearly *using his name* to try to keep the United States interested in the Tibetan cause and to organize opposition to China in exile. And they were doing this *apparently independently of the Dalai Lama and certainly independently of the Kashag.* More will be said of this in later chapters.

· · · · ·

The sitsab's pattern of dealing with the Chinese was poorly conceived. If their goal was simply to vent their anger at the Chinese invasion and occupation of Tibet, they certainly succeeded, but if they had any inkling of inducing the Chinese to send home most of their troops and officials, then their behavior was counterproductive. The sitsab's outbursts made many in Lhasa feel good by opposing and resisting the Chinese, but they failed to compel the Chinese to renegotiate key aspects of the agreement. In fact, were it not for Mao's determined adherence to his gradualist strategy, the sitsab's actions might have led cadres such as Fan Ming to succeed in dismantling the old system quickly.

The Dalai Lama's late brother-in-law, Takla (Phüntso Tashi), astutely analyzed the sitsab's brief reign: "The two sitsab were good, honest, and straightforward, and as far as the [Tibetan] government and the people were concerned, the two of them were heroes (tib. pawo). My personal opinion is that there is no question as to their bravery, but it did not fit in with the reality of the situation. They were forcing their way with something that could not be done."[87]

The sitsab–People's Association incident revealed the lack of cohesion within the Tibetan government. The two most important offices, the sitsab and the Kashag, were pursuing different strategies and tactics, and the paramount rule, the Dalai Lama, was playing a very passive role, letting this situation continue without imposing order from the top. So while the sitsab chose to show the Chinese an angry and confrontational face, the Kashag tried to show them a friendly and cooperative face. No attempt was made to develop a unified government policy, so decisions were made ad hoc in response to issues that arose. And within the Kashag, while Ngabö and Shasur were more progressive and were trying to adhere to the agreement and assist the Chinese side, other ministers were less forthcoming for change. Thus, when something serious arose, such as the People's Association, the different views extant paralyzed the government until the Dalai Lama was forced to pay attention and act.

However, the People's Association's activities did have an important impact. While the Chinese were unwilling to go back to the Qing model, the

87. Takla (Phüntso Tashi), interview, 1992, London.

association's petition pushed the Chinese to compromise on several issues that Tibetans opposed, namely, incorporating the Tibetan army into the PLA and starting the Military-Administrative Committee.

The period of the sitsab and the People's Association also reveals how difficult it was for the Chinese officials in Lhasa to operationalize and implement Mao's gradualist policy effectively. In the end, as we saw, in April 1952 Mao and the Central Committee took immediate oversight away from the Southwest Bureau and henceforth took direct administrative control over Tibet. From then on, the Tibet Work Committee in Lhasa was required to get approval from the Central Committee (Mao) before it made decisions that affected Tibetan society and culture. Control of change in Tibet was now directly in Beijing's hands. It has remained there up to the present.

1. Tak Tser has no doubt that the Dalai Lama is developing the *long-range plan allegedly agreed on prior to Tak Tser's departure from Tibet; i.e., the Dalai Lama is quietly organizing resistance to the Chinese Communists while appearing to cooperate with them.*

2. Tibetans in Lhasa, encouraged by the monks, recently have sworn secret new oaths of allegiance to the Dalai Lama and to the three leading monasteries and, simultaneously, have renounced their allegiance to the present lay Cabinet [Kashag] and affirmed undying opposition to the Chinese.

3. The Panchen Lama secretly has indicated his intention to defect from the Communists while appearing to serve as their puppet, and to make common cause with the Dalai Lama in organizing a resistance movement.[82]

The source of Taktse's information is not indicated; however, point 1 appears to come from Taktse's own firsthand knowledge. It unambiguously says that the Dalai Lama had a strategy of overtly trying to maintain friendly and cooperative relations with the Chinese while he was secretly working to organize resistance to them. Given what we know of the Dalai Lama's lack of direct involvement in political affairs at this time and his own family's decision to lie to him about something as trivial as Gyalo's return to India, it does not seem credible to suggest he was really organizing a secret resistance movement in Tibet.

The United States explicitly realized that it had no way to evaluate Taktse's new information independently but decided nevertheless to take it to mean that Tibet, under the leadership of the Dalai Lama, was starting to organize a resistance movement.

> While evaluation of available information is extremely difficult, CA [Office of China Affairs] perceives no reason why Tak Tser's report should not be accepted as "probably true." Since CA believes that (1) the Chinese Communists in Tibet are doing an excellent job of creating their own troubles, (2) developments in Tibet are producing the desired effect on the Government of India, and (3) Tak Tser is on firm ground in believing that a public expression of US interest in Tibet would, at this time, have an undesirable effect on both the Government of India and on the incipient Tibetan resistance movement, CA recommends that the Department continue to avoid public statements concerning Tibet and refrain from any attempts at this time to communicate with persons in Tibet who are believed to be taking their first step toward organizing an anti-Communist resistance movement.[83]

A month later, on 24 June 1952, the U.S. consul general at Calcutta received another communication, purportedly from the Dalai Lama. This message

---

82. U.S. Department of State 1985: 51–52, memorandum by the acting director of the Office of Chinese Affairs (Perkins) to the assistant secretary for Far Eastern Affairs (Allison), 14 May 1952 (611.93B/5-1452) (emphasis added).

83. U.S. Department of State 1985: 51–52.

was oral and came through the Dalai Lama's brother-in-law, Takla (Phüntso Tashi), who passed it on to Princess Coocoola, of Sikkim (probably while Gyalo Thondup was still in Lhasa). She, in turn, passed it on to the consul general in Calcutta, who reported it as follows:

a) The Dalai Lama appreciates greatly the U.S. Government's feelings and attitudes toward him personally and toward his Tibetan subjects.

b) He sincerely hopes that when the time is propitious for the real liberation of Tibet from the Chinese, the United States will find it feasible and possible to lend *material aid and moral support* to the Tibetan Government.

c) The Tibetan people have not changed; they are not pro-Chinese; they are Tibetans first and last.

d) He hopes to be able to get a written message "down" soon.[84]

This message again suggests that the Dalai Lama was secretly biding his time to try to throw out the Chinese. No longer was the Dalai Lama talking about the Chinese being correct and proper, as in the February letter; now he was looking to America to help in *liberating* Tibet from the Chinese.

The Dalai Lama, however, again emphatically denied that he ever instructed Phüntso Tashi to convey those points to the United States.[85] When I asked Phüntso Tashi about this message, he carefully avoided saying whether the Dalai Lama knew but did say explicitly say that the Dalai Lama's lord chamberlain, Phala, knew about it.

Q. I am interested in learning about the answer [you passed on to the United States]. Did the Dalai Lama himself say, "Say it like this"? Or did he tell it via the Kashag?

It was not given through the Kashag.

Q. Did Phala know about that?

Probably he knew about that. [pauses] He knew. If it would have been given through the Kashag, it is not known what would have happened. [This implies the Kashag ministers were not reliable.][86]

Was Lobsang Samden or Lord Chamberlain Phala or both the source of this message in the Dalai Lama's name? I do not know. But the Dalai Lama's fam-

84. U.S. National Archives, from Calcutta, dispatch no. 5, 2 July 1952, enclosure 1 (emphasis added).

85. Dalai Lama, interview, 2004.

86. Takla (Phüntso Tashi), interview, 1997, London. (In Tibetan: Q. yid bzhin nor bu rang gis "o'o 'di 'dra gsung rogs gnang" ser 'di 'dra bzo 'dra cig red yang min na bka' shag brgyud nas skad cha bshad pa red? A. bka' shag brgyud nas rtsa ba nas yog ma red. Q. dper na, pha lha mkhyen gyi yod red pas? A. pha lha shes kyi yod kyi red/ pha lha shes kyi red/ bka' shag de tshos byas pa'i sgang la gnas tshul ga 'dra yin min shes kyi ma red).

For Gyalo Thondup and Lobsang Samden, however, giving the impression this had the approval of the Dalai Lama, directly or indirectly, was critical, since, without it, few would have taken seriously the views of a nineteen- and a twenty-four-year-old on grave matters such as this. We see this clearly when Gyalo Thondup went to see the head of the Indian Mission in Lhasa seeking India's permission for him to stay in India. He explained to me what transpired.

> [First] I approached the Indian government through the Indian Consulate General in Lhasa and asked whether it was possible for me to come and stay in India, because it was impossible for me to remain in Tibet. . . . So Sinha [the head of the mission] sent a secret cable in code to Mr. Nehru. After a few days, a reply arrived by cable saying that I would be welcomed. . . . After that I began actively planning to leave. I discussed this with my mother and my brother, Lobsang Samden. No one else.[77]

However, in his official Monthly Report for June 1952, Mr. Sinha gives a significantly different account, reporting to Delhi that Gyalo had said that the Dalai Lama had approved his departure.

> He [Gyalo] felt that it would be advisable for him to escape. He fully realizes the risks involved but *has carefully laid his plans with the active help and support of the Dalai Lama. . . . If and when the Chinese get to know of his escape, the Dalai Lama would express surprise and say that his brother Gyalo Dondup has always been an irresponsible nomad.*[78]

After the Government of India agreed to this request, Gyalo got to India without arousing suspicion by telling the Chinese that he had to visit his family's six estates on business. Since two of these estates were in remote areas in southern Tibet near the Indian border, once there, it was simple to cross over into India in Arunachal Pradesh (east of Bhutan).[79]

When I asked the Dalai Lama about this, as with previous issues, he categorically denied any knowledge whatsoever of the letter to Shakabpa until I read it to him. He was very convincing.[80] If we assume this is true, and I do, is it conceivable that these two young men did this entirely on their own? Would they, on their own, have dared risk bringing the wrath of the PLA down on the Tibetan government and the Dalai Lama by carrying a letter signed by the brother closest to the Dalai Lama (using his full government title) that instructed a senior anti-Chinese Tibetan official in India to work with the Dalai Lama's other brother to start anti-Chinese activities in India?

77. Gyalo Thondup, interview, 1995.

78. British Foreign Office Records, FO371/99659, monthly report for the period ending 15 June 1951, from officer in charge of Indian Mission in Lhasa, to the political officer in Sikkim (emphasis added).

79. Lha mo Tshe ring (Lhamo Tsering) 1992: 123; Gyalo Thondup, interview, 1995.

80. Dalai Lama, interview, 2004.

Lobsang Samden was known for being fun loving and was not someone interested in political issues, so he could easily have been influenced by his older brother Gyalo, who was, as we have seen, deeply committed to being a player in Sino-Tibetan politics. The exuberance of youth and the arrogance of being the Dalai Lama's family could have made them think they had the right to do whatever they thought best for the good of Tibet. I asked Gyalo Thondup about this. After expressing surprise that I knew about the heretofore secret letter to Shakabpa, he declined to answer clearly whether others were involved. When I pressed him, he cryptically said that it would be best for me just to write in my history what it looks like at face value, that is, that Lobsang Samden and he were involved. In the future, he said, when he writes his own book, he will explain what happened in detail.[81]

However, if there were others involved, who might they be? Since Gyalo did not trust the Kashag, he certainly did not discuss this plan with it. And the sitsab were already dismissed. And since he did not discuss it with the Dalai Lama, that eliminated the other major source of official authority. The only parties left to consider are those whom we can think of as the officials and attendants immediately around the Dalai Lama, what one official called the simjung gi thakor ("those around the Dalai Lama's living quarters"). Of these, the most likely figure is Phala, the lord chamberlain, or Trijang Rimpoche, the Dalai Lama's junior tutor, or both. I do not know if Lobsang Samden and Gyalo discussed this with them or with any others around the Dalai Lama, but in fact, in the summer of 1952, the Dalai Lama's brothers were planning to start an anti-Chinese opposition movement in India independently of the Tibetan government and the Dalai Lama.

In early May 1952, at about the same time that the sitsab–People's Association affair was ending and Gyalo Thondup was planning to flee to India, in Washington, the eldest brother of the Dalai Lama, Taktse, again met with the State Department and the CIA, filling them in on recent communications he said he had just received. Unlike the February information, this time he painted a bizarre anti-Chinese portrait, explicitly telling the Americans not only that the Dalai Lama himself was pursuing a secret anti-Chinese resistance strategy but also that the Panchen Lama, a major Chinese supporter, was about to defect from the Communist's side and secretly join hands with the Dalai Lama in resisting them. The U.S. memorandum of this meeting states the following:

> The report, received May 13, conveyed the following information, based on communications recently received by Tak Tser.

---

81. Gyalo Thondrup, interview (phone), 8 December 2005. It should also be mentioned that neither Gyalo nor Lobsang Samden was skilled in the government style of writing, so they would have had to receive help in composing and writing the letter.

Chapter 14

The Return of the Panchen Lama

With the Dalai Lama back in Lhasa, a key issue for the Chinese was ensuring that the Panchen Lama returned to Tibet with his rights and powers restored. As we have seen, it was at their insistence that this issue had been included as part of the Seventeen-Point Agreement. Despite this inclusion, Mao and the Central Committee had decided to treat Tibet as a unified entity, with the Dalai Lama as the head. In keeping with this, Mao had rejected the Back and Front Tibet model advocated by the Panchen Lama and Fan Ming and was concerned lest the Panchen-Dalai conflict inadvertently interfere with his gradualist strategy, which was focused on winning over the Dalai Lama. Mao, therefore, from the start, saw the promotion of unity between the Panchen Lama and the Dalai Lama as being in China's interests.

One dimension of this was Mao Zedong's decision that it would be best if the Panchen Lama returned to Tibet only after the Dalai Lama was there and could extend a formal welcome to the Panchen. This, he believed, would preclude any chance that the Dalai Lama's side would mistakenly think the Chinese were trying to replace the Dalai Lama with the Panchen Lama. It would also send all Tibetans a clear message that the Dalai Lama welcomed the Panchen Lama back to Tibet.[1] Consequently, the Panchen Lama did not leave Qinghai Province until mid-December 1951, four months after the Dalai Lama had arrived in Tibet.

Direct contact between the Panchen and Dalai lamas actually first occurred immediately after the signing of the Seventeen-Point Agreement, when the Panchen Lama sent the Dalai Lama the following cordial telegram from Beijing on 30 May 1951.

1. Fan Ming 1987: 45.

When you assumed temporal power . . . you sent representatives to negotiate with the Central People's Government and achieved the Agreement on Measures for the Peaceful Liberation of Tibet. This was a great victory of the Tibetan people, lay and monk. I will do my part for our unity and, under the wise leadership of the Central People's Government and Chairman Mao, will help you and the local government of Tibet to carry out the Agreement for the cause of the peaceful liberation of Tibet. I tender my congratulations and best wishes to you.[2]

A few weeks later, the Dalai Lama responded by telegram, clearly conveying his recognition of the Panchen Lama's legitimacy and welcoming his return to Tibet.

I was very glad to receive your telegram of May 30. . . . According to the favorable omens of the divine oracles that I have consulted, you are indeed the true reincarnation of the previous Panchen. I have informed Tashilhunpo Monastery and Kashag Minister Ngabö, the Tibetan delegate in Beijing, about this. I am looking forward to your early return to Tashilhunpo Monastery. Please inform us by wire which route you will take.[3]

On the 5th of the ninth Tibetan month (early November 1951), the Dalai Lama informed the Panchen Lama by telegram that he was sending two government officials with representatives of the Three Monastic Seats to meet him in Qinghai and welcome him back to Tibet.[4] He also ordered an armed escort of one hundred Tibetan troops to meet the Panchen Lama in Nagchuka and instructed Tibetans along the return route to provide the Panchen Lama corvée animals and labor.

The Panchen Lama immediately responded with a telegram expressing his thanks and informing the Dalai Lama that he was leaving Qinghai on the 17th of the tenth month (19 December) to return.[5] The Panchen Lama said in this telegram,

Your telegram was received. For the construction of a new Tibet, you urged me to return to Tibet early and are preparing everything for me, including ordering the Fifth [Regiment's] general to provide protection for me. I am very grateful for all these things that you have done. . . . I sincerely guarantee that after I return to Tibet we will, under the leadership of Chairman Mao, the Communist Party, and the central government, further strengthen the unity among Tibetans, closely cooperate with other brother nationalities within China, work

2. Cited in Ya 1994: 349–50. It is also quoted in Jianbian Jiacuo (Jambey Gyatso) 1989: 32.

3. Cited in Ya 1994: 350. It is also quoted in Jianbian Jiacuo (Jambey Gyatso) 1989: 32.

4. The monk official was Metok Jangse, and the lay official was Rimshi Kharna.

5. Jianbian Jiacuo (Jambey Gyatso) 1989: 32–33; Ya 1994: 350.

together very hard to carry out quickly and thoroughly the Agreement for the Peaceful Liberation of Tibet and build a prosperous and happy new Tibet.[6]

On 18 December, the day before the Panchen Lama and his group left for Tibet, Xi Zhongxun (vice chairman of the Northwest Military-Administrative Bureau), went to see off the Panchen Lama and convey the best wishes of Chairman Mao and the Central Committee. He was accompanied by Ya Hanzhang, who, in Fan Ming's absence, was accompanying the Panchen Lama on his journey to Tibet as vice "representative" of the Northwest Bureau.[7] The Panchen Lama held a big welcome meeting for Xi Zhongxun, at which he made a speech that reflected his close dependence on the CCP.

> Without the correct leadership of the Chinese Communist Party and Chairman Mao and without the truthful help of different brother nationalities in China, the peaceful liberation of Tibet would be impossible, and *our return to Tibet would also be impossible.* Thus, we say the Chinese Communist Party and Chairman Mao are the big emancipators of Tibetans, and they are our big benefactors. We Tibetans can become thoroughly liberated only if we follow the Communist Party and Chairman Mao and only if we closely unite with different brother nationalities. There is no other road.[8]

In accordance with Mao's strategy, Xi Zhongxun advised the Panchen Lama, "When you get back to Tibet, do not hurry to push various things. Please take account of the whole picture in Tibet. The priority is unity among Tibetans. Only when Tibetans unite can our work in Tibet really make progress." Xi especially emphasized that "everything in Tibet should follow the principle of cautious and steady progress. If conditions are not ripe for something, do not do it; if the upper-hierarchy patriotic public and leadership figures do not agree with it, do not do it. Work in Tibet should concentrate on the united front of patriotism and anti-imperialism."[9]

The Panchen Lama arrived in Nagchuka in March 1952, at the height of the People's Association incident. Zhang Jingwu was concerned that the Panchen's arrival in Lhasa might further enflame the disturbances as well as pose a risk for his safety, so Zhang asked him to stay in Nagchuka until the situation was resolved. Under the pretext of taking a rest, the Panchen Lama and his group stayed in Nagchuka for more than a month. While there, the Panchen Lama sent a telegram to the Dalai Lama in which he strongly criticized the actions of the People's Association and advised the Dalai Lama,

---

6. Cited in Jianbian Jiacuo (Jambey Gyatso) 1989: 32–33.

7. Zhonggong xizang zizhiqu dangshi ziliao zhengji weiyuanhui 1990, entry for 19 December 1951.

8. Cited in Jianbian Jiacuo (Jambey Gyatso) 1989: 33–34 (emphasis added).

9. Jianbian Jiacuo (Jambey Gyatso) 1989: 34.

saying, "In the spirit of bravery and with the Buddha's light of boundless benevolence, get rid of these acts and disturbances and treat this event properly and stabilize the feelings of the people."[10] The Dalai Lama didn't reply.

By mid-April, the danger of the sitsab and the People's Association had dissipated, and life in Lhasa was returning to normal, so Zhang Jingwu sent a telegram telling the Panchen Lama and his group to continue their journey. They arrived in Lhasa on 28 April 1952 and were welcomed at a large ceremony in the eastern suburbs, which was attended by a large number of government officials headed by the Kashag ministers and all the main officials from the Chinese side. After the ceremony, the Panchen Lama went to the Tsuglagang Temple, where he traditionally stayed while in Lhasa.[11]

RESPITE IN LHASA

For the Tibetan government, the return of the Panchen Lama after an absence of twenty-nine years was an extremely sensitive event. Not only was there the deep-seated animosity between the two lamas' retinues, but since the Panchen Lama's side was pro-Chinese, politically progressive, in support of fully implementing the agreement, and committed to a view of Tibetan history in which Back Tibet was not under the Tibetan government, there was a danger that the Panchen's retinue would try to manipulate the Chinese to gain advantages vis-à-vis the Dalai Lama. It was, therefore, obvious to the Dalai Lama and the Kashag that starting off the new relationship on a positive note of trust and solidarity was clearly in their and Tibet's interests. The Dalai Lama recalled his thinking then.

> When the young Panchen Lama was coming, we were saying that it would be good to have a fresh start in relations. We were fellow Amdowas [ethnic Tibetans from Amdo/Qinghai], and so we said that we must do our best to have good relations. All the elders were saying this, and so were many officials. Many were telling me this, and from my own perspective, this is also what I thought. . . .
>
> When the Panchen Lama first came to Lhasa, he was very innocent, very good. I told him, "The old days are gone, and now we are at a critical time, so we must have good relations." So it was very good. . . .
>
> [First,] the Panchen Lama was young, and second, we were fellow Amdowas. In this way we all hoped that relations would be good. Everyone hoped there would be good relations between the Dalai and Panchen lamas. Whatever ill feelings there were at the time of the previous Panchen Lama was regretted by everyone. Nobody was saying that it was good.[12]

10. Dangdai zhongguo congshu bianjibu 1991: 198.
11. Ya 1994: 356–57.
12. Dalai Lama, interview, 1993, Dharamsala.

However, getting off to a new positive relationship did not turn out to be easy. Not only did substantive issues concerning taxes and authority have to be reconciled, but also different perceptions of the two lamas' relative status made such a reconciliation difficult. This quickly came to a head over how to organize the formal ceremonial meeting between the two great lamas. This would set the tone for future relations, and for weeks there were discussions and arguments about how it should be done. Not surprisingly, this ended poorly.

Fan Ming felt the Tibetan government was trying to use this ceremony to diminish the status and authority of the Panchen Lama. His version of the events surrounding the meeting, though obviously biased against the Tibetan government, conveys the thinking of the Northwest Bureau's officials in Lhasa.

When the Panchen arrived in Tibet, there was a disagreement regarding the ceremony at which the Panchen would meet the Dalai. It turned into an important political issue. The disagreements involved the matter of prostrating, the height of their thrones, and the giving of gifts.

In truth, this disagreement was about whether we [the Chinese side, should] support the Panchen's original status or damage and decrease his original position. The Dalai's side was trying to find any pretext to decrease the Panchen's status and his influence. They proposed that the Panchen should prostrate before the Dalai, that the Panchen's seat should be lower than the Dalai's seat by two-cushions' height, the Panchen should present tribute to the Dalai, and the Panchen should not reside in the Jokang [Tsuglagang] temple.

When these suggestions were sent to the Panchen, his officials were very angry and said they would rather return straight to Shigatse than enter Lhasa under such conditions. Thus, both sides could not come to an agreement.

At this time, the Tibet Work Committee convened a meeting to discuss the impasse, but there were also disagreements there. One opinion [Zhang Jingwu and Zhang Guohua] thought that because the Panchen Lama was under the Kashag's leadership in the past and because our purpose was to win over the Dalai Lama, the Panchen Lama should prostrate before the Dalai Lama. The other opinion [Fan Ming] considered that historically both the Dalai and Panchen lamas were under the direct leadership of the [Chinese] central government. They both were, therefore, in the same position, so there was no relationship such that one controlled the other. . . . In religion, one was considered the sun, and the other the moon. They had a senior and junior apprentice relationship only when they had a teacher and student relationship. If the Dalai Lama had been the Panchen Lama's teacher or the Panchen Lama had been the Dalai Lama's teacher, then there would have been prostration at the ceremony. When there was no teacher and student relationship, they greeted each other by touching their foreheads together, but did not do prostration.[13] Therefore, in the meeting this time, neither one should be favored at the expense of the other.

13. Touching foreheads (tib. udu) was a custom between lamas of roughly equal status and replaced the need for one to prostrate before the other.

In the end, the Tibet Work Committee decided that it was not appropriate for us to interfere in so big an issue, so we thought that both the Dalai and Panchen Lamas' sides should send representatives to negotiate with each other. At the same time, the two different opinions within the Tibet Work Committee were reported to the Central Committee.

The Central Committee replied that the officials of the Dalai Lama and Panchen Lama should have direct negotiations but added that the Tibet Work Committee should be careful to keep this situation well in hand. On the one hand, the Tibet Work Committee should convince the Panchen to make some concessions. On the other hand, the Tibet Work Committee should safeguard the Panchen's original status and should not unify the Panchen *under* the Dalai's side.[14]

According to the spirit of the Central Committee's instructions, the Tibet Work Committee convinced both sides to have direct negotiations. The Kashag sent Ngabö and Liushar as representatives, and the Panchen's office sent Che Jigme and others as its representatives. Both sides went through several negotiation sessions, but still they could not reach an agreement. The negotiations were deadlocked.

The Tibet Work Committee again had meetings to discuss this issue and proposed a compromise. Since the Panchen Lama was younger than the Dalai Lama by several years, even though they did not have the teacher and student relationship, the Panchen Lama should prostrate to the Dalai Lama during their first meeting. From then on, they would both have equal status in etiquette and greet by only touching each other's forehead. . . . Regarding the seating arrangements, in history, when the Dalai Lama was the teacher, his seat would be one cushion higher than the Panchen's. This time it would be appropriate if both had equal seats at their meeting. The term presenting *tribute* to the Dalai would be changed to exchanging *gifts* between them.

After several discussions, the Tibet Work Committee made preliminary resolutions: the Dalai Lama would stand in front of his throne; the Panchen Lama would prostrate to the Dalai Lama; the Panchen Lama and the Dalai Lama would exchange ceremonial scarves; the Panchen and the Dalai lamas would touch each other's forehead; their thrones would be the same height.

The Tibet Work Committee then sent Zhang Guohua to persuade Ngabö to accept these terms, and I went to persuade the Panchen Lama and his staff. After a whole night of persuasion, the Panchen Lama's side reluctantly agreed to the resolution, but they asked us to guarantee that no changes would be made. I gave them my firm word and guarantee. Then I found Zhang Guohua and told him the opinions of the Panchen Lama's office. Zhang said that Ngabö also agreed to guarantee that no changes would be made.[15]

However, there are a number of variants on what was agreed on. The Dalai Lama recalled these events:

14. In Chinese: buneng ba banchen tongyi dao dalai fangmian qu.
15. Fan Ming 1987: 133–34.

Probably from the Tashilhunpo side they were saying that the seats should be of equal height. It was said from our side that this was not possible. Then another possibility was raised, namely, that the Dalai Lama should stand on his throne [on the platform on which the throne sits]. For example, when the Sakya Dakchen [the head of Sakya Sect] comes to Lhasa, the Dalai Lama stands on his throne, because the Sakya Dakchen is considered very high in stature. So it was said at this time . . . when Panchen Lama comes, maybe I should stand on my throne. This I remember very clearly.

At the Potala Palace there is a meeting room in the east side and another in the west. The one on the west had a low ceiling, so if I stood on my throne I would have to bend over. It was said that if I stood on my throne bending down when Panchen Lama comes it would not look nice. So instead of this, because the ceiling in the East Room is high, it was said that the meeting should take place there. This I remember clearly.

Now regarding the arrangement of the seats, the usual place for the Dalai Lama's throne is on a platform (tib. ding ja). Since this was the usual place for the throne, it was situated there. Below [the platform] the Panchen Lama's throne was set up in the place where the regents' throne is placed. So above was the platform, and below, on the right side, was the throne for the regents. So this was the place where the Panchen Lama's throne was placed.

When the Panchen Lama actually came, I did not sit on my throne, but I got down and stood in front of it. The Panchen Lama came, and later there was talk of whether he did or did not prostrate. But he did. So I stood in front of the throne, and the Panchen Lama came and prostrated. Then when the scarves were exchanged, each of us took our seat. This is what I remember.[16]

Fan Ming, however, recalled a very different set of circumstances.

On the afternoon of 28 April, the Dalai met the Panchen in the Potala Palace. However, when the Panchen prostrated to the Dalai, the Dalai did not stand. What should have been the exchanging of ceremonial scarves became the Panchen presenting the khata scarf and the Dalai receiving it. The Panchen's throne was not only set very low and was small but also was situated on the side. Thus, the Panchen's side was very angry. Ngawang Jimpa almost raised his iron staff, and the Panchen's bodyguards were so angry that they almost fired their guns. Fortunately, comrade Liu Xiuchu was there and averted a possible tragedy from happening. Afterward, the Panchen's side wept bitterly and said that we [the Chinese side] had duped them.[17]

It is not possible to definitively assess what happened at the ceremony, but some aspects are clear. The Chinese filmed the initial ceremony and a subsequent movie shows parts of it. That film shows the Panchen Lama approaching a platform, roughly four feet tall, on which the Dalai Lama's

16. Dalai Lama, interview, 1993.
17. Fan Ming 1987: 134–36.

throne was situated. The Dalai Lama was standing at the front edge of this platform as the Panchen Lama approached, so the Panchen Lama was dramatically lower than the Dalai Lama when he reached the throne platform. Consequently, he had to reach up to present his symbolic gift (e.g., the mendredensum) to the Dalai Lama and to touch foreheads, and the Dalai Lama had to bend over almost double at the waist so that his forehead would reach that of the Panchen Lama. This part of the interaction was clearly as Fan Ming described above—the Panchen Lama was giving the things to the Dalai Lama, who was accepting them; there was no mutual exchange (see figure 20). The placement of the Panchen Lama's throne is not shown, and it is not clear whether he ever sat on it, or for that matter whether the Dalai Lama first sat on his throne and then stood up or whether he was standing when the Panchen Lama entered the room. Other accounts indicate that the Panchen Lama prostrated when he entered the hall, but the film only shows him approaching the Dalai Lama's throne. Nevertheless, it is clear that the "plan" was not precisely followed, and the Dalai Lama's standing on this very high platform made the Panchen Lama appear vastly inferior. It is easy to understand why the Panchen Lama's people were furious.

The Dalai Lama also recalled that there was disagreement over the seating arrangements but clarified the role of the Ecclesiastic Office, saying: "The Ecclesiastic Office has no business in this. The lord chamberlain and the jigyab khembo are concerned with these matters. They and Ngabö and others discussed this. It was Ngabö who had relations with the Panchen Lama's Council, not the lord chamberlain and jigyab khembo. Ngabö [then] discussed this with the lord chamberlain and jigyab khembo. The fact that there were problems—that I remember clearly."[18] So either the lord chamberlain and jigyab khembo deceived Ngabö, or Ngabö knew and did not want to warn the Panchen Lama's people beforehand and take the risk of their canceling the historic meeting. But whatever the reason for what transpired, it is clear that the Panchen Lama's officials felt they had been duped, and an important opportunity to start the new relationship on a positive note was lost.

NEGOTIATIONS IN LHASA

While the Panchen Lama was in Lhasa, negotiations between the officials of the two lamas took place to resolve the many knotty issues regarding land and taxes that were outstanding from the era of the previous Panchen Lama.

18. Dalai Lama, interview, 1993.

Figure 19. Panchen Lama at his first ceremonial meeting with the Dalai Lama. Above, Dalai Lama bending down from his throne's platform; below, Panchen Lama about to reach up, in 1952. Source unknown.

Figure 20. Dalai Lama (left) meets with the Panchen Lama (right) in Lhasa, in February 1952. Source: Chen Zonglie

In theory the Seventeen-Point Agreement was the framework for this, but in reality, the agreement was vague and not easy to operationalize. It said,

Point 5. The established status, functions and powers of the Panchen Erdini shall be maintained.
Point 6. By the established status, functions, and powers of the Dalai Lama

and of the Panchen Erdini are meant the status, functions and powers of the Thirteenth Dalai Lama and of the Ninth Panchen Erdini when they were in friendly and amicable relations with each other.

The first issue discussed in Lhasa was the point in history that should be used as the baseline year for when the two lamas were friendly. Fan Ming described these meetings between the Kashag and the Panchen's officials.

> The Tibet Work Committee . . . asked them to respect and compromise with each other and told them they should look into the archives and find evidence to make sure of the year when the 13th Dalai and 9th Panchen had peaceful relations. After doing this research, both sides took 1897 as the year of good relations.[19] After establishing this date, both sides examined the archives to determine the power and authority of the Panchen at that time.[20]

On the basis of the customs in place in 1897, the negotiations resolved some of the outstanding issues that involved human corvée taxes (tib. ula), the horse corvée taxes (tib. tawu), and judicial authority fines. It was decided that all of the Tibetan government's edicts that subsequently made changes to the taxes and rules in place in 1897 would no longer have to be honored by the subjects of the Panchen Lama, thus dismissing them from the taxes specified by those edicts.[21]

However, the crucial military grain tax was a different story. Although it was a new tax imposed by the Tibetan government after the 13th Dalai Lama's return from exile in 1913, the Tibetan government insisted it had to be paid by everyone, contending that these costs were incurred in Tibet's protection against foreigners (specifically during the Anglo-Tibetan wars of 1888 and 1903–4 and the Chinese war of 1912–13), so the Panchen Lama had to pay his share.[22] The Panchen's side simply refused, using the same arguments that the 9th Panchen Lama had made in 1923 before he fled to China. The negotiations again reached a total impasse, but this time the Chinese side intervened. Sensing that failure to reach an agreement was imminent and that this would be a terrible defeat, the Tibet Work Committee persuaded the Chinese central government to pay these "military" costs itself.[23] A major hurdle was passed, and though many other issues still remained, these

---

19. This was the first month of the twenty-third year of Emperor Guangxu of the Qing dynasty; in the Tibetan calendar it was the 15th of the first month of Fire-Bird year (1897). The 13th Dalai Lama was twenty-one years of age, and the 9th Panchen Lama was fourteen.

20. Fan Ming 1987: 138–39.

21. The edicts referred to are the Fire-Snake year edict (1917) and the Water-Pig year edict (1923).

22. See Goldstein 1989: 110ff.

23. Fan Ming 1987: 138–39; Ya 1994: 358.

were left for later negotiations. The two sides signed an initial memorandum on 16 June 1952.

In the meantime, the 10th Panchen Lama ended his stay in Lhasa on 9 June and set off for Shigatse, where his monastic seat, Tashilhunpo, was located. He arrived there on 23 June, accompanied by Ya Hanzhang, a company of PLA troops, and Ramba, the monk Kashag minister representing the Tibetan government. Twenty-nine years after the 9th Panchen Lama had secretly fled to China, the 10th Panchen Lama now publicly arrived, receiving a tremendous welcome by many thousands of Tibetans.[24] As Ya Hanzhang described, the atmosphere in Shigatse, the heart of Back Tibet, was markedly different from that of Lhasa.

> [The Panchen Lama] arrived at the Tashilhunpo [Monastery] on June 23 to the enthusiastic welcome of tens of thousands of lay and monastic Tibetans. In Shigatse, people sang and danced and performed the waist-drum dance, *while the five-star red flags fluttered on top of all buildings in the city and portraits of Mao Zedong were hung in almost all the rooms in Tashilhunpo Monastery*—this being the way that the lay and monastic residents of the city expressed their love of and gratitude to the People's Republic of China, the Chinese Communist Party and Chairman Mao [for returning the Panchen Lama].[25]

. . . . .

The Panchen Lama's return to Lhasa, therefore, was a fiasco for the Tibetan government. Just what the Dalai Lama said they wanted to avoid occurred. Once again, the Tibetan government was unable to agree on and implement a single strategy. The meeting arrangement it used was not historically unreasonable, but it was strategically short-sighted if their aim was, as the Dalai Lama said, to start relations with the Panchen Lama on a positive note. Whoever suggested and approved this arrangement was more concerned with traditional issues of symbolically demonstrating the inferiority of the Panchen Lama than with taking a new step toward creating a cordial atmosphere in which the two great lamas might cooperate. Having opened relations with the Chinese on a confrontational note, the Lhasa officials now replicated that with the Panchen Lama's top officials, exacerbating the existing enmity and hatred and fixing them as implacable foes of the Lhasa government. There would be no chance of Tibet's two greatest lamas developing a common front to deal with future threats from the Chinese side. It was the second major strategic error in less than a year and another major occasion when the young Dalai Lama did not take an active role in molding tactical decisions.

24. Zhonggong xizang zizhiqu dangshi ziliao zhengji weiyuanhui 1990, entry for 23 June 1952; Ya 1994: 358.

25. Ya 1994: 358 (emphasis added).

The events surrounding the Panchen Lama's arrival also greatly exacerbated the split within the Tibet Work Committee. Fan Ming and his Northwest Bureau colleagues disagreed strongly with Zhang Guohua and Zhang Jingwu over this issue and within a few months would launch a strategy to try to split Tibet in half. The initial problems encountered when merging the two sets of Communist officials into a new unified Tibet Work Committee were now significantly worsened.

PART THREE

Cooperation and Change

Chapter 15

Winds of Change

With the Kashag now in charge on the Tibetan side and Mao directly controlling and moderating operational decisions in Tibet on the Chinese side, a new era of cordiality and cooperation began. The dire predictions of the Chinese destroying religious and social institutions had not transpired, and with the exception of the inflation fiasco, by and large life was continuing just as it had before the PLA arrived. The Chinese were respectful of Tibetan customs and institutions and were not trying to incite class hatred among the masses. And critically, Mao Zedong had ordered the Tibet Work Committee not to pursue the contentious issues of creating a military-administrative committee and of merging the Tibetan army into the PLA. The future for Tibet, therefore, looked somewhat more promising than it had just a few months before, although many Tibetans still considered the PLA an army of occupation and opposed reforms. But for many of the elite, there was a feeling of cautious optimism; a feeling that perhaps their way of life indeed could continue without drastic upheaval. And for those in the elite who had for years wanted Tibet to be a modern country, these were exciting times when new ideas and activities abounded. For them, the coming of the Chinese had created an opportunity to break the old mold. With the sitsab gone, both sides now moved cautiously forward to create new institutions and organizations in Tibet. One of the first of these new ventures was the opening of Tibet's first modern primary school in Lhasa.

THE "SESHIN SCHOOL"

The plan to begin a primary school was one of the issues that the Tibetan People's Association and many others had objected to and was specifically mentioned by Mao Zedong when he criticized the Tibet Work Committee for acting too hastily in implementing changes. Nevertheless, in the new improved atmosphere, the Tibet Work Committee—with the cooperation of the Kashag—quickly moved ahead with the plan, and the school actually opened its doors on 15 August 1952.[1]

The school was organized as a joint Tibetan government–Tibet Work Committee enterprise, although the curriculum was controlled by the Chinese. It had a twenty-eight-member Board of Directors, most of whom were from the Tibetan upper classes, and was nominally headed by Zhang Guohua. Dorje Tseden, a Tibetan cadre from Qinghai, was involved in organizing the opening of the school (and was then also a teacher). He recalled his involvement.

I arrived back in Lhasa on the 4th or 5th of May 1952 [from a stint at giving out interest-free loans to farmers around Lhasa] and met Zhang Guohua the next day. He told me he was starting a primary school in Lhasa and asked whether he could borrow me for one year to work on this, as he had heard that I had experience in the teacher's college [in Qinghai]. I said, "If you are starting a Tibetan school, as a Tibetan, I think that is great. So if it is all right with my superiors, I will stay." I then asked the State Nationalities Commission, and they sent a letter saying I could stay a year and a half working for the school, so on 1 June, I went to Seshin and started making preparations. . . .

After the school was approved, we settled on a plan for who would be the heads of the school. There were three senior leaders—the first was Trijang Rimpoche, the second was the Kashag minister Ragasha, and the third Lhautara. I was a deputy leader. . . . We secured seven or eight Tibetan teachers from the Tibetan government's monk official segment, and from the lay officials' side, we got Maya and Kharna Depön. . . .

The main subject was written Tibetan, but for some youths who had returned from India . . . we created a special class. The next most important subject we taught was arithmetic, and then natural sciences and geography.

The three Tibetan heads said that it is customary in Tibet to start school each day with a prayer, so we did the "Gyamdro" prayer for twenty minutes at the start of each day.

Q. Did you teach about communism in the school?

We taught a brief introduction to the ideas of Mao and Zhu De. If we tried to teach too much politics, the young kids wouldn't understand.

Q. Did the school teach Chinese?

No, but for some of the students who had gone to the Kyitöpa School [the Guomindang school in Lhasa] and knew some Chinese, we had a special class in Chinese, otherwise not. . . .

Q. At first, how many students were there?

About 340. And there were about ten orphans. We gave the orphans food, housing, clothing, and everything. After the school was started, we sent two

1. Zhao 1998: 76.

Chinese teachers to each student's house to find out about their situation [economic, etc.]. . . . On this basis, we decided what kind of financial support to give. Some students got seven or eight dayan per month, some got twelve or thirteen, some got eighteen to twenty per month.

Q. How many of the three hundred or so students got money?

About a third. [Because of this] at this time the dobdo monks and Tibetan soldiers used to call the school the "dayan school."[2] . . .

Q. How many grades or classes were there?

There were seven classes (years). The first was just for learning the alphabet (tib. ka kha). . . . We put kids in classes in accordance to their level of Tibetan.

Q. How did you teach Tibetan?

We used the jangshing (wooden slate board), as in the old society. From the fourth grade, we also taught Tibetan grammar (tib. sumtag). Traditional Tibetan [private] schools didn't teach this. In the seventh grade, poetics (tib. nyengag) was also taught.

Q. What about poorest kids? Were you successful in recruiting them?

If their parents brought them to us, we admitted them, but we didn't try to recruit them specially. . . . At this time many kids switched from the Tibetan private schools to the Chinese school.

Q. Why?

The Tibetan schools didn't teach grammar and math, and they beat kids a lot. So many students switched to the Chinese school. There were also music and singing in our Seshin School. At first we heard that people were saying there would be competition between the new government school (Seshin) and the private ones, and later we increased in numbers and the private ones decreased. If you look now among the higher officials, those with good Tibetan and Chinese are mostly from the Seshin School.[3]

The Seshin School was a great success. Its students liked the modern format, and it became a vivid symbol of modernization in action. It was the first step toward creating a group of youth knowledgeable about and, for many, sympathetic with the ideology of socialism. Not long after this, toward the end of 1952, a second school for youths and adults was started; this one was called the Society School (tib. jitso lapdra), its name conveying that it was started for the society at large, not just young children. It began in the Trungjilingka Park, where Tibet University is located today, and taught various topics, including beginning Chinese language. It, like the Seshin School, opened new horizons for some young Tibetans.

One such Tibetan youth was then a student in the Tibetan government's school for prospective monk officials (tib. the Tselabdra). He later went to Beijing, where he continued his studies and became a well-known professor of Tibetan language. His recollection of that time follows:

2. It was also derogatorily called the "doley lapdra," or school of the greedy.
3. Dorje Tseden, interview, 1993, Beijing.

I was one of the first three who joined the Society School in 1952. At first the school wasn't called the Society School, and it met for only two hours in a tent, in a spot next to the Tibet Cadre School. There was a good Chinese teacher who taught us the Chinese language. Later, when there were many people, it was called the Society School. . . . We thought that now things were changing, and the Chinese were going to be in power, and there would be a change in society, so I thought it would be good to [learn Chinese and] go to China. . . .

Q. Did the Tibetan government's Ecclesiastic Office send you to the school?

No. If you went to the Chinese school it was considered terrible. They would never send you. I did it on my own. When I went to China, I did it secretly. At this time I had no home. My parents had died, and I was living with a relative. I joined the Youth Association and, through this, secretly went to China. I sent a letter from Medrogonggar [a county seat northeast of Lhasa] to my uncle [in Lhasa] saying I had gone to China. My uncle didn't treat me well. If my parents had been alive and we had been okay in income, I doubt I would have gone. . . .

Q. How did you know about the school?

I had a friend from the Lhalung Surje family called Lodola. He said, "There is a Chinese teacher who speaks good Tibetan and is teaching Chinese. I'm going, so if you want to learn Chinese, why don't you also go?" So I went with him. No one told us to go there, nor did the Chinese invite people to go. I went quietly on my own.

Q. Was there salary?

Not when I was going. Later there must have been. I had no thought of being a monk official and getting a high post and staying with the old government. I thought it was best to join the "revolution" (tib. sarje), so I did this right from the start. So I went to China through the Youth Association tour. . . . [At the end of this trip] they said if I wanted to return I may go, or if I want to go to school [in China] I could stay.[4]

The success of these two schools quickly led to the start of a middle school in Lhasa.

All of these schools were begun with the agreement of the Kashag and were successful because they met a need that the traditional government had failed to address. They gave not only the elite but also the middle class and some of the lower class new ideas and new opportunities.

YOUTH AND WOMEN'S ORGANIZATIONS

A similar activity aimed at broadening the horizons of the elite and the middle class and engendering sympathy and support for the CCP was the creation of two "mass organizations" in Lhasa: the Youth Association and the Women's Federation.[5] In China, these functioned to foster patriotism and

4. Thubden Wangpo, interview, 1992, Lhasa.
5. Respectively, shünu tshogpa and pöme tshogpa.

to enlist broad popular support and involvement and were affiliated directly and indirectly with the Communist Party. In Tibet, however, both of these groups were organized mainly as places where Tibetans could socialize and have fun in a new way, not as a vehicle for transmitting socialist teachings. The Youth Association brought elite and middle-class youths, both male and female, together for evening mixers, at which there was singing and dancing (both the Western-style foxtrot and Tibetan-style dancing). This was the first time they had been able to interact in a social setting like this, and they enjoyed it.

The experience of T. N. Shelling, then a young aristocratic male, illustrates the complex and often contradictory feelings that elite Tibetans had about these changes. On the one hand, the mixers were new and exciting and fun, and on the other, they went against tradition, supported the Chinese, and were frowned on by many.

> Probably, in 1951–52, the Chinese established the Tibetan Youth Association. . . . I remember the main leaders were Shölkang Jedrung and a Chinese Muslim called Ma Boje. At that time, I was about fifteen years old, and I liked to go there just because they were teaching new songs and singing them, and sometimes there was also dancing.
>
> I wasn't interested in the communist system, because I didn't have any clear idea about that. And the Chinese also didn't make much propaganda regarding politics. They were just trying to gather people in the Youth Association using the method of teaching songs with new words, such as "The sky is blue and clear; the white clouds look beautiful; [and] the Tibetan people have gotten liberated."[6]
>
> I probably went there several evenings for a few weeks. One night, I was there very late, until midnight. At that time, my older brother, Sonam Tobgye, was at home. After my mother passed away, he had become the head of the family [he was thirty-four years of age at the time]. That night he got very angry with me and said things that I will never forget. "We [our family] have been living by the kindness of the Tibetan government for generation after generation, so it is very bad for you to go against the Tibetan government and join the Communist Youth Association." So after that I stopped going there. Later, when the Society School was set up, my brother was not in Lhasa [he had left for Western Tibet], so I went there for a few weeks, but then I remembered his advice and also stopped going to that school.[7]

The great success of the new "social life" caused problems even within the Communist Party. Tibetan cadre Phünwang recalled an incident in which Tan Guansan became infuriated because the Tibetans attending the Cadre

6. In Tibetan, was nam mkha' sngo la dwangs shing / sprin dkar lang long kha dog mdzes / bod ljong mi dmang bcing bkrol thob.

7. Shelling (Tsewang Namgye), interview, 2004, Cleveland, OH.

School, which he headed, were cutting classes so that they could attend the popular functions run by the Youth Association and Women's Federation.

Sports was another very popular activity the Communists developed, and a mini–soccer craze occurred in Lhasa. Traditionally, no Western sports were played in Tibet, with the exception of soccer, which was introduced by the British at the time of their conquest of Lhasa in 1904. Soccer was popular in 1923 at the short-lived Gyantse English School and again after 1936, when the British Mission (popularly called Dekyilingka) was started in Lhasa. In 1936, the British Mission started soccer matches between its staff and Lhasa residents, several of whom were Tibetan government officials. The Lhasans were called the Lhasa United (and had their own jerseys), and the British staff were called the Mission Marmots. Ultimately, this grew to include fourteen teams, which continued competition until the religious establishment induced the regent to ban soccer in 1944 on the grounds that kicking a football was as bad as kicking the head of the Lord Buddha.[8]

In 1952, soccer again became popular. It started when Tan Guansan wanted to make the Cadre School more exciting to young soldiers so decided to add sports to the curriculum. Tan's biography explains his thinking.

> In Lhasa, some aristocratic youth liked playing soccer, and this inspired Tan Guansan. . . . However, there were also no soccer balls available. All the soccer balls [in Lhasa] had been brought from India by the aristocrats' children themselves. Tan Guansan heard that Shölkang Jedrung loved to play football, so Tan persuaded him to get a soccer ball for the Cadre School.
>
> At that time, there was no soccer field in Lhasa, and few people had ever played soccer, so Tan Guansan invited Shölkang to coach and teach the students to play soccer. Later, they selected some students and formed a school team. Shölkang proudly claimed, "We are the absolute champions, having no match on the plateau"—because there were no other competitors. Tan Guansan also asked Shölkang to organize the aristocratic youth to form a Lhasa team so that they could have friendly matches with the Cadre School team.[9]

The Tibetan Lhasa team included both aristocratic and monk officials, most of whom were also in the Youth Association. The sons of the aristocratic families, such as Ragasha and Shelling, played with their official hair knots (tib. pachog), and monk officials such as Ngawang Senge and Yeshe Yönden also were on the team. The Lhasa youth met to practice at least once or twice a month and played matches roughly once a month. They thought a lot about what name to call themselves and finally agreed on the name All Kinsmen (tib. günche), to convey that they were all like brothers. The matches they

---

8. See Harris and Shakya 2003: 58–59 for photos of the Lhasa United and Mission Marmots, and McKay 2001 for a description of soccer in Tibet before 1950.

9. Jiangbian Jiacuo (Jambey Gyatso) 2001: 117.

played drew as many as one hundred to two hundred spectators, who watched and cheered the players on.[10] For many young elite Tibetans in Lhasa, these were exciting times.

At about the same time that the Youth Association began, the preparatory Women's Federation was started in Lhasa. Mrs. Taring, who would soon become one of its top officers, recalled the events surrounding its creation.

> Then the policy began to change and the Women's Federation was established. All of the wives of high-ranking officials, such as the elder sister of His Holiness and the wives of Tsarong, Sambo, Ngabö, Surkhang, and Shasur, together with their daughters, were invited to a huge dinner at which we were encouraged to establish a women's Federation. . . . We responded that such an organization had not existed before, so we needed to get permission from the Dalai Lama and the [Tibetan] government. "If they agree," we said, "we will establish one, but right now we really cannot agree to establish it." At that time, Zhang Jingwu's wife [Yang Kang] and some other wives of their [the Chinese] leaders were at the meeting. They said it was a good idea to ask the Dalai Lama, and we could meet another time about this.
>
> Some of the women who were wives of Kashag ministers [Ngabö and Shasur] then visited the Kashag and reported this. The Kashag said it was okay, so we had another meeting at Tsipön Shakabpa's summer house. . . . The elder sister of the Dalai Lama [Tsering Dolma] was appointed as the chairman, and about five wives were appointed as vice chairmen, including the wives of Sambo, Ngabö, Ragasha, and so on. . . . At that time I was appointed as a vice chairman. In addition, Tangme and I were appointed as secretaries of the association. From then on, the Tibetan Women's Federation was established, and I worked for it.[11]

Mrs. Taring, who later was a famous figure in exile in India, spoke again about the new organization.

> The Chinese treated people so cleverly. They gave dinners and parties, and many people thought it might be possible for us to keep things the way they were laid out in the Seventeen-Point Agreement. I guess many people thought the Chinese would continue to treat us well. The Women's Federation and the Youth Association were pretty similar. . . . [Initially] Everybody did not trust the Chinese, but that changed slowly. . . . In our Women's Federation, some women really hoped that if we set aside our old customs, the Chinese would treat us well. Some members liked the Chinese ways a lot. For example, Mrs. Tangme was that kind of woman. Later they completely changed their attitude toward the Chinese . . . because the Chinese had changed their policy. Of

10. Shelling (Tsewang Namgye), interview, 2004. Shelling recalled that after 1959 when he was in prison, the Chinese were very interested in learning whether this organization had taken on a political agenda. There is no evidence at all that it had.

11. Taring (Rinchen Dolma), interview, 1991, Rajpur.

course, some women in the Women's Federation, such as Samling, did not
change their attitudes toward the Chinese, and they kept a good attitude toward the Chinese.[12]

Mrs. Taring's comments reflect what was, among a segment of the younger
elite in these early years, a surge of enthusiasm for modern changes. New
things were happening, but these were not threatening the existing way of
life. Phünwang's recollections parallel this: "Most aristocratic wives were very
progressive. They gave parties and danced and put on makeup. They were
very lively."[13]

Another member of the group, Mrs. Surkhang, the wife of Kashag minister Surkhang, also recalled the politically progressive attitudes of some of the
aristocratic wives who were enthusiastic about the social changes going on.

[Mrs.] Samling and Tsögo and their type were very much against our old society. They said it was all rotten. . . . They would say that today we women have a
lot to be appreciative about. The Communist Party has given women equality,
and it is just great that we can meet in an office. . . . They were talking like this.
They wanted women to be respected. Equal rights for women; they called meetings and did things in the meetings. They were bold. . . . They said that in the
old days we Tibetan women were hopeless. Even regarding school, it was felt
women didn't need education. They were just kept at home. So today women
are on par with the men and can be educated. So they showed off a lot.[14]

But these views, while popular among a sizable segment of the aristocratic
elite, were the exception, and most Tibetans resented and opposed these
changes, considering the "progressive" Tibetans as communists and Chinese
sympathizers. One Tibetan soldier explained,

The women's organization and the like—I don't know whether they actually
liked the Chinese or not, but most of the "people" saw them as the running
dogs of the Chinese. Since that was the case, the monks caught some of them
and beat them up.
Q: Did the monks also say anything to the students and members of the
Women's Federation and Youth Association?
Yes. Once at the Trungjilingka, there was a meeting at which it seems Mrs.
Thangme said a lot of things, so the monks waited in "ambush" and beat her
with a stick quite a lot. And likewise, there were people like Shölkang Jedrung.
He did not fall into their hands, but if he had, they had thoughts of really tak-
ing care of him. Though one can't say that these people sincerely liked the
Chinese, but from their behavior, we, "the people," did not like them at all.[15]

12. Taring (Rinchen Dolma), interview, 1991.
13. Phünwang, interview, 2000, Beijing.
14. Mrs. Surkhang, interview, 1992, Dharamsala.
15. Gyagpön Kedramla, interview, 1992, Dharamsala.

However, despite such attitudes, for a sizable segment of the younger elite, the new organizations were exciting and popular and were a great success for the Chinese side. The strategy of gradually winning over the elite was finally having success among a key element of the Tibetan elite.

THE GRAIN PROCUREMENT BUREAU

Grain was still a major problem in mid-1952, and, as discussed in earlier chapters, the Chinese pursued several tactics to stabilize it. One new step taken after the fall of the sitsab was to raise again the idea of starting a formal joint grain procurement bureau (tib. drurig dagnyer legung).[16] The newly empowered Kashag quickly agreed to this, and during the fall of 1952 this new office took over from the Surjong Kashag. Phünwang was active in setting up this new office and recalled,

> One of the most important of these [new initiatives] was an initiative to stabilize the supply and price of grain and end the spiraling inflation. We decided that the key was to create a system in which grain stored in other parts of Tibet could be systematically obtained. To accomplish this we proposed to the Tibet government that we establish a new joint grain authority. The head of the board of directors for the grain authority was my old friend Surkhang, the most powerful of the Kashag ministers. Ngabö, Langdün and I were the vice directors.[17]
>
> We held many meetings to work out the details. I knew the customs of the Tibetan upper class, so I made sure that during the meetings we served sweet tea and biscuits. Our meetings became popular, and most of government officials associated with the enterprise actually attended them. People in Lhasa started joking that now the Tibetan government's offices were empty since most officials were attending the grain authority's meetings.
>
> We bought grain from distant estates of aristocrats and monasteries and then used the Tibetan government's corvée transportation network to move it to Lhasa to be stored and sold. The Central Government provided 100,000 dayan to us as capital for this. I was glad to be given this important responsibility from our side, and with the Tibetan government's help, we were able to quickly accomplish our goal.[18]

However, Phünwang's assessment is too rosy. In fact, shortages continued to occur, although they were not as great as earlier, and inflation continued to harm the economic situation of the poor and the middle class. This situa-

16. Although this bureau was initially called "shungdru jidzökhang," as indicated in chapter 9, it was ultimately known as "drurig dagnyer legung."

17. Four Tibetans were staff officials: Kapshöba, Canglocen, Kumbela, and Pandatsang Surpa.

18. Goldstein, Sherap, and Siebenschuh 2004: 177.

tion would not be controlled until after the two motor roads from China proper were opened at the end of 1954.

VISITING DELEGATIONS TO INLAND CHINA

The Chinese were also keen to invite Tibetans to see China, either to attend meetings in Beijing or simply to take tours of eastern China. This was, in a sense, another side of the strategy of trying to influence Tibetans through education. The Chinese felt that letting Tibetans see with their own eyes the disparity in development and modernization between Tibet and inland China would create a positive impression and enthusiasm for beginning to implement modernization in Tibet.

From 1952 to 1954, the Tibet Work Committee organized hundreds of people from various social circles for meetings and tours, and a string of delegations were organized and sent. Some were official government delegations, going to participate in a special event, while others were tours of youth, Buddhist monks and lamas, and so forth. Altogether, nearly a thousand people visited China this way during this period.[19] One progressive Tibetan who participated in the second such tour commented succinctly, "The point was to show how good things were in China so the youth would go back and tell others how great China was."[20]

One of the most important of these groups was the official Tibetan government delegation headed by Liushar, the co-head of the Tibetan government's Foreign Affairs Bureau. It was sent in 1952 to participate in the (1 October) National Day celebration and to present a ceremonial scarf to Mao Zedong.[21] This delegation included members from the Tibetan government, the Panchen Lama's administration, and the Chamdo government, and it stayed in inland China for almost a year.

The visit this delegation made was important, because Liushar had a meeting with Mao Zedong and was genuinely very impressed by what he saw and heard. He gave a radio speech at the end of the visit (which was broadcast in Lhasa and reprinted as a pamphlet), in which he talked about his trip and Mao's comments on religion, land reform, economic assistance, and the Military-Administrative Committee. Mao took this opportunity to reiterate that, while the Seventeen-Point Agreement had to be completely implemented, how and when this would occur depended on Tibetans. Liushar reported that Mao said to him:

19. Dangdai zhongguo congshu bianjibu 1991.
20. Thubden Wangpo, interview, 1992.
21. Because of this it was called the "gift offering group" (tib. denbul tshogpa).

1. "The CCP adopts the policy of protecting religion. Protection is given to all, whether one believes in religion or not, whether one believes in this religion or that religion; one's belief is respected; the policy of protecting religion is adopted today as it will be in the future."

2. "The problem of the division of land is different from that of religion. Land has been divided in the Han nationality areas, but religion is still given protection. Whether land should be divided in minority nationality districts is a matter for the minority nationalities to decide. In the Tibet region, the problem of the division of the land doesn't exist now. Whether or not land should be redistributed in the future the Tibetans will have to decide themselves; we cannot do it for you."

3. "The establishment of a military and administrative [political] committee and the reorganization of the Tibetan army have been stipulated in the Agreement. But since you are afraid, I have notified those comrades working in Tibet telling them to go slowly. However, the Agreement must be implemented, although it will be postponed because you are afraid. We can push it back to next year if you are afraid this year; we can put it back until the year after next, if you are still afraid the next year."

4. "Tibet covers a large area but is thinly populated. Its population should be increased from the present two or three million to five or six million, and then to over ten million. Then economy and culture should also be developed. Culture embraces schools, newspaper, cinemas, and also religion. In the past, the reactionary rulers, from the emperors of the Qing Dynasty to Chiang Kai-shek have oppressed and exploited you. Imperialism has done the same to you. As a result, you are weak economically, backward culturally, and your population is small. The Chinese Communists, standing for national equality, do not want to oppress and exploit you. We want to help you achieve development in population, economy, and culture. The entry of the PLA into Tibet is aimed at giving you such assistance. Not much assistance can be expected in the beginning, but in three years, much help can be given to you; if not, the Chinese Communist Party will be of no use."[22]

Shingsar (Lobsang Gelek), another Tibetan official who was a member of that first delegation, recalled,

There were about eighteen or nineteen officials. Our leader was Liushar. . . . If I tell you in brief, we just toured all over, to schools and factories and all over. Every day we had to go quite a few times [to different places], and it was not easy. When we got to a factory, the leader would give a lecture about how bad

22. Liushar's speech as quoted in *Renmin ribao*, 22 November 1952, as cited in Union Research Institute 1968: 42–46.

things were during the time of the Guomindang, and now after the Commu-nist revolution how things have improved and production has increased and such and such. Things like that. So it seems that they wanted us to say when we returned (to Tibet) that under the Guomindang things were bad and now they are good. So if I were to tell you in short, that was it. They say they have such and such, and we don't know what they had or did not have, right? So, it seems that they wanted us to disseminate information when we returned to Ti-bet. . . . The Chinese told us all the good things, and when the visit ended, they asked us what we thought. We basically repeated what they had told us, since we did not know what the situation was like in the past and what the present development projects were and what the production figures were. What we said ended up in a report.[23]

But this tactic was effective and impressed the Tibetans, as Shingsar also re-called: "So there was the feeling that all this was good. That the Chinese were doing something good. Even Liushar told one of our members one evening, 'There is freedom of religion, et cetera, and so isn't that good?'"[24]

However, these visits also sometimes raised doubts. One of the members of the second government tour in 1953 recalled how he discovered that their visits to a religious site had been staged just for their benefit.

Generally, as far as the development of the country [China] was concerned . . . there was a feeling that later in Tibet this also would be possible. It's hard to say what others thought, but my own thought was that it could later develop with factories, et cetera.

However, on the question of religious freedom, it was nothing but a mask. There was no way this could happen. . . . Let me give you an example. In Shang-hai, I was sick with intestinal problems, and they had to operate on me. Be-cause of this, I wasn't able to go on with the tour to Guangdong, so I went to Hamru before the others did. Up to that point, when I saw monasteries, I thought that they were good. At Hamru, the tour had not yet arrived, and I had some Chinese companions appointed to look after me. They said, "Let's go for a walk." So I said, "Sure." . . . We reached a big temple with an image of the Düsum Sanggye [the Buddha of the past, present, and future], but, oh, it was in a terrible state, with bird droppings on it. Outside there were remains of a fireplace used by an animal herder. Some kids were playing in front, and it did not resemble a temple at all.

Later, when the whole tour group arrived, they took us . . . to the same tem-ple. The temple had been made so beautiful. The statues were so clean and shining. All the walls had brocade hangings. In front, candles were lit and of-ferings were in place. There were four monks, and they were holding incense. I thought it was a very beautiful temple. However, going around a bit farther, I got the feeling that I had been there before. Then I remembered that below

23. Shingsar (Lobsang Gelek), interview, 1993, Toronto.
24. Shingsar (Lobsang Gelek), interview, 1993.

the temple were two stone lions, where we had previously stopped and eaten fruit. I had put the peels of my fruit in between the lion statues, so I looked and found that they were still there. So then it dawned on me that this is a tour created just for when we were taken there. . . . So I began to wonder if all the places were like this, and it really seemed that that is how it was. So these things [religious freedom] I thought could never be.[25]

In addition to tours, the Chinese also endeavored to bring Tibetans to Beijing to study at the Nationalities Institute, since in the long run educated people like this would likely become the leaders of a new socialist Tibet. The first group of students who arrived in 1952 included a number of young monk and aristocratic officials, several of whom had been part of the small group influenced by Gendün Chompel that was mentioned in chapter 7.

> In the beginning, Gendün Chompel's plan for us was to go to India [and see what was going on], but before it [the plan] was confirmed, the Chinese came to Tibet, and Gendün Chompel told me to go to China and learn the Chinese language. He said, "You shouldn't stay in your own house; you should know the situation of the enemy."
>
> On the other hand, Chinese propaganda was also saying that they would develop [Tibet], which we also wanted, and they were also saying that they had no thoughts of "eating" Tibet and were going to return to China.
>
> So in the beginning, when the Chinese came, they looked really good. They were just living in the New Regiment area . . . and didn't come to the Barkor Market street and act reckless. So I also had a kind of hope, and several others and I volunteered to go to China to study.
>
> Among us was Sursur Jigme. His father, Surkhang Dzasa, knew Gendün Chompel. He also told us to go to China and said that we should make changes [in Tibet].[26]
>
> There were also three monk officials, [one of whom was] Ngawang Senge. . . . We had been schoolmates, and I knew him from way back. . . . At that time, the Surjong Kashag had been set up for talking with the Chinese . . . so we told the Dalai Lama through this office that we want to volunteer to go to China because nobody was going. . . . His Holiness told them to send us to China, and he gave twenty-five dotse to each of us.[27]

The Chinese side was concerned with creating a positive impression, so the Tibet students had a number of special privileges. For example, the Tibetans did not have to sleep on bunk beds, because according to Tibetan custom

25. Lhautara Tsendrön, interview, 1992.

26. Surkhang Dzasa had been was one of the leading progressive army officers who was with Tsarong in the 1920s. He later became one of the Tibetan government's two foreign affairs ministers and was Kashag minister Surkhang's father, although he had separated from the Surkhang family decades earlier and started his own branch family, called Sursur.

27. Ngawang Thondrup, interview, 1992, Dharamsala.

dirty things should not be put on top of the talismans they wore on their bodies; therefore, they didn't want anyone sleeping above them. Also, they also had a special Tibetan canteen where the Tibetan students ate separately.[28] In the ensuing years, the Chinese recruited Tibetans from Shigatse and from nonelite backgrounds also to study in Beijing and then at a special minority institute for Tibetans that they opened in Xianyang, near Xi'an.

MERGING OF FOREIGN AFFAIRS

One important structural change that now went forward was the merging of the Tibetan government's Foreign Affairs Bureau into the Chinese Foreign Affairs Office in Lhasa. The new "joint" Chinese-Tibetan office was called the Tibet Foreign Affairs Department (ch. xizang waishichu). Unlike the Tibet Military Area Headquarters, the Tibetans assigned to it actually did work, although they remained officials of the Tibetan government. The Tibetan Foreign Affairs minister, Liushar, explained:

> It was written in the Seventeen-Point Agreement that the Foreign Office of the Tibetan government shall be merged with the Chinese Foreign Office. When I went to China [in 1952], the Kashag had already decided to merge the two foreign offices. After I came back from China, the Kashag told me, "We have merged our Foreign Office with the Chinese Foreign Office. There is a Chinese official called Yang Gongsi, so the two of you should make the decision about how to set up the [new] Foreign Office.
>
> When I consulted with Yang, he said they had already prepared to locate the office in the Sombö house, and we were kind of ready to start work. After that, the Kashag and all the Chinese officials came and celebrated the opening of the office. We didn't have much work to do. In Lhasa there was an Indian Consulate and a Nepalese Consulate. When they had to talk about border issues, sometimes they came to us and sometimes they invited us to their offices.[29]

Another Tibetan official who worked there added the following:

> Once they were joined together . . . the Chinese made three units: first, second, and third. In each unit there was one Chinese and one Tibetan. Under them there were mostly Chinese workers but some Tibetans also. The first unit dealt with relations with India. . . . The second unit dealt with Nepalese relations, and the third unit looked after the internal affairs, for example, procuring and looking after things, documents, et cetera. . . .
>
> These areas are concerned with Tibet, and so the documents are in Tibetan and had to be translated. For example, I was in the first unit, dealing with In-

28. Ngawang Thondrup, interview, 1992.
29. Liushar, interview, 29 October 1981 (interview and transcript made by the International and Information Office in Dharamsala).

dia, so whatever documents were needed, we Tibetans looked for them, examined them, and then they were translated into Chinese. Regarding relations with the Indian Mission, Tibetans knew how it had been done previously, so they would say, "That's how it was and how it should be handled now."[30]

Nevertheless, the merging of the Foreign Affairs Bureau was not without its problems, as the case of Sandutsang (Rinchen) reveals. He was one of the handful of Tibetan officials who had been educated in India and spoke perfect English. His family originally were Khamba traders who had been "ennobled," and he was allowed to serve as an aristocratic government official, although his family did not have manorial estates like traditional aristocrats. He was the English translator for the negotiating team in Beijing in 1951 and worked in the Tibet Foreign Affairs Bureau. His narration of the troubles he encountered after the new joint Tibet Foreign Affairs Department was established illustrates the suspicions the Chinese had about these Indian-educated Tibetans.

[At the Tibet Foreign Affairs Department] At first, the Chinese were very nice, but then they started to show a negative attitude toward me. I was educated abroad and knew [English], and it's obvious that we [people like me] were going to have some relations with Dekyilingka [the Indian Consulate] and the Nepalese, isn't it? Especially at Dekyilingka, where there were Sikkimese and Indians. Sometimes contacts were made, because they had the facilities to send telegrams, right? Then there were people we knew earlier from India. So when we had contact with them, the Chinese did not like this at all. So they were always telling us their opinion about this. Sometimes they used to call the workers together and start giving advice about how to make relations with foreign countries and what the procedures were. Actually what they were pointing out was that it is not permissible to have contacts with the Nepalese and Dekyilingka. They were saying this. So things went on like that, and then one day they criticized me. They did not tell me directly, but they told Liushar, "Sandutsang (Rinchen) is having contacts with Dekyilingka and the Nepalese, and this is not all right. If he does that, he cannot work in the Foreign Affairs Department."

So one day Liushar told me to come to his house, and I did. He said, "Now the Chinese are saying such things, and so it seems that something is not quite right." I said, "I am not having contacts with them regarding government matters. That is done by the office itself. I have friends and acquaintances there from a long time ago, and I have the freedom to continue those relationships. It is my wish. There is no reason for them to prevent me from doing so. . . . If the Chinese are saying such things, then I don't want to work there anymore. Besides, regarding my work at the Foreign Affairs Department, I am a person appointed by the Tibetan government. I am not paid and ordered by the Chinese to be a staff member there. I am not such an appointee, and so I don't

30. Lhautara Tsendrön, interview, 1992.

want to work there at all. . . . So you, Sir, please put my case before the Kashag, saying that such a situation has developed. . . . I have been appointed a government servant, so I will serve the Tibetan government in whatever office I am appointed, and if there are no appointments, then so be it. I will just stay home and do trading, but I never want to do this Chinese work again." So he (Liushar) requested this of the Kashag, and they appointed me to a new office in charge of communications.[31]

The Chinese had no say in this, since Sandutsang (Rinchen) was an employee of the Tibetan government, and it still had the authority to do as it pleased with its own officials. For most internal issues, this would remain true right up to 1959.

ROAD BUILDING

As we saw in chapter 9, building motor capable roads from inland China to Lhasa was a priority from the start, and work on the 445-kilometer stretch of the road from Ganzi to Chamdo began on 6 May 1951. It was completed on 20 November 1952, a year after the PLA had captured Chamdo.[32] Chamdo, however, was still over a thousand kilometers from Lhasa, over difficult mountainous terrain. That phase of the road was approved by Mao on 1 January 1953 with a target date of 1954 for completion.[33] It is known as the southern road or the Kang-Tibet Road, because a second northern route was also approved that would run from Xining, in Qinghai Province, to Lhasa. As soon as Zhang Guohua and Zhang Jingwu received this approval, they immediately divided the work on the southern road into east and west sections and started construction from both ends. This was coordinated on the eastern side with the Eighteenth Army Corps's rear construction troops, which were based in Chamdo. Zhang Guohua and Zhang Jingwu conferred with the Tibetan government and set up a joint construction committee that would assume responsibility for the construction of the road starting from the western side (from Lhasa). Tan Guansan was named its director.

On 17 February (1953), work began from the Chamdo side. This sector used sixteen thousand civilian workers and technicians and about thirty-one thousand soldiers.[34] Almost all workers were Chinese. Tibetans were enrolled

---

31. Sandutsang (Rinchen), interview, 1989, Kalimpong, India.

32. Zhonggong xizang zizhiqu dangshi ziliao zhengji weiyuanhu 1990, entry for 20 November 1952. At this point, the rear headquarters of the Eighteenth Army moved to Chamdo.

33. Zhonggong xizang zizhiqu dangshi ziliao zhengji weiyuanhui 1990, entry for 1 January 1953.

34. Zhonggong xizang zizhiqu dangshi ziliao zhengji weiyuanhui 1990, entry for 17 February 1953.

mainly to provide carrying animals, as a result of which the elite who owned the large herds of yaks made enormous sums of money.

The western sector began work from Lhasa, two months later, on 20 April. In addition to the thousands of PLA troops, Chinese records state that, up to 1954, 8,061 Tibetans from forty-eight counties were hired and engaged in mainly manual labor (e.g., breaking stones and digging earth).[35]

This road work and construction jobs in Lhasa and other towns led to the creation of the first generation of a new Tibetan working class from among the poorer segments of society. Tibetan society still functioned on the basis of corvée tax labor, and the Tibetan government ordered areas to send laborers, but the Chinese were committed to not levying any new taxes on the people, so paid the workers good salaries in dayan coins.[36] Gao, one of the Chinese officials involved, said that on average each Tibetan worker could earn about eighty dayan a month.[37] For most of these poor peasants, this was the first time in their lives they actually had substantial cash.

The story of one young orphan girl from the Chamdo area illustrates one of the ways that poor Tibetans, independently of political or class ideology notions, were drawn into the orbit of the Chinese on material grounds. At age fourteen she ran away from her aunt and started to walk to Lhasa, which she had heard was a wondrous place.

> When I came from Kham [in 1951], I was just an orphan. . . . I came alone, begging for tsamba on the way.
>
> Q. Where did you first see the PLA?
>
> I saw the PLA at Bayi, in Nyingtri [in Kongpo]. There was an office of a big PLA brigade (ch. da dui bu) who were working on timber and cutting planks. There was an Bapa [a Khamba from Batang] interpreter who asked me what I was doing. I told him I had run away from Kham and was going to Lhasa. He asked me if I had any relatives in Lhasa. When I told him I didn't, he told me that I should go [work for] his regiment. I couldn't do any manual work, so they let me stay in the kitchen. They told me, "If you can clean the tables and wash the dishes, the soldiers will treat you well."
>
> The next day, the political commissar (ch. zhi dao yuan) came and interviewed me. I told him my history and that I was an orphan. He asked me if I had any relatives in Lhasa, and I told him I didn't have any relatives, but I had

---

35. Gao 2001: 126.

36. Since it was difficult to transport thousands of dayan to road sites, sometimes the Tibetan officials involved converted these into Tibetan paper currency and paid the workers with this (Phüntso Dorje, interview, 2000, Lhasa).

37. Gao 2001: 128. Interestingly, Gao writes that the Chinese soon found out that the money they were paying the Tibetans was being taken by some Tibetan upper-class people, who were using their power to get it from their peasants, so the Chinese then switched and either paid them in kind (clothing, tea, etc.) or paid them in dayan but had a trading store right there so the workers could buy things immediately.

heard people saying that Lhasa was a very happy place; therefore, I was going there. He asked me if I would be willing to stay with the regiment. When I said yes, he said, "We won't let you do kinds of work that you cannot do. You should get some knowledge." I think he meant to say that I should learn Chinese. Then, they gave me towels and soap, garments, trousers, and bedding. I was told to live in one bedroom with a woman from Kongpo, whose work was feeding pigs. They asked that woman to take care of me. I was told that whenever the soldiers had meals, I could eat with them.

Later, the years passed one by one. At that time, the soldiers got three dayan per month. I was also given the same. Being a child, I had never handled money; therefore, I was extremely glad.

Q. What did you do with that three dayan?

I just kept it. I didn't need to buy anything. I was given whatever I needed, such as washing utensils and food and so on.

Later, the political commissar and the interpreter told me, "We are going to Lhasa. If you want to go to Lhasa, we can take you. If you want to go to school, we will get you into a school. If you want to join the PLA there, you can join it. If you want to remain like this, you can remain like this. These are all your choices." I told them I wanted to go to Lhasa, so they told me that I could go with them. . . .

I didn't go to school; I am an unlucky person. I stayed in the military head-quarters . . . and was assigned as a caretaker in the reception office. There were two or three Chinese and Tibetans working with me. I remained like that for a couple of years. I didn't get much salary. Actually, the [Chinese] government raised me.

Later, I met some colleagues and friends, who told me, "You shouldn't re-main in the regiment like this. Although the regiment feeds you, if you go to cut planks in the wood-manufacturing place (ch. jia gong chang) located near the People's Hospital, they pay ten yuan for one cubic meter (ch. gong fang). You can earn twenty yuan (per day), so let's go to that place."

I asked for leave from the regiment. At that time the political commissar was not there, so I told the interpreter, "I am going to cut planks. People say that I can earn good money if I cut planks." He said that this was my choice. "We do not want you to go. The political commissar introduced you to this place, and he said a lot about you [to the leaders]. But if you want to go, we can't stop you. However, if you don't succeed over there, you can just come back."

Then I went to cut planks. My partners were fellow Khambas. At that time, being young and strong, I could cut a couple of cubic meters a day, so I could make a lot of dayan. Later, I stayed working in that manufacturing place.[38]

It was from the many Tibetans like this, who had worked for the Chinese on roads, in army bases, and on construction projects, that the thousands of lo-cal Tibetan cadres were recruited immediately after the 1959 uprising.

38. Pema Dikyi, interview, 2001, Lhasa.

To help organize the labor and arrange the compensation for land lost to the road itself, the Tibetan government sent officials to work with the Chinese. One of these, Maya, worked in Medrogonggar, a county immediately northeast of Lhasa. He explained in detail how this worked.

At this time Thönpa Khenjung and I were sent [by the Kashag] to begin the road construction. The plan involved all the various land areas under Medrogonggar district—the monastic, aristocratic, and government estates. So the various people who were appointed went to Medrogonggar and met with the county and estate heads. . . . So one day everyone met. . . . The Chinese soldiers and the two of us were there. Our main job was to collect the people [for work on the road]. . . .

Q: Whatever they required for road construction, for example, workers, et cetera, would the Chinese make the request to you two?

Yes, they informed us how many people they required, and we discussed with the village leaders the number of people to be sent from the various areas. Second, we discussed the salary to be paid and the compensation, either in cash [from the Chinese] or in new land [by the Tibetan government], to be paid for the loss of fields to the road.

At that time wages were paid in accordance with the going rates. . . . Workers were organized in groups of ten and were paid by the number of meters of road they completed. Payment, when possible, was every two weeks, or monthly, if not. . . .

All we had to do was to summon the people, because we didn't know how to do the measurements, and we didn't have the money to pay the wages. So there wasn't much to be done. But if we didn't talk to the Tibetans, then they were not going to listen, right? They really didn't listen to the Chinese. Even the poor serfs didn't listen to the Chinese. . . . Actually it was very strange. So they really needed us [Tibetan government officials], and they would assign guards and do many things for us.

. . . I had a large area to oversee including six or seven counties in Kongpo and Dakpo. The Kashag told us the number of workers to be recruited from each and had also sent orders to each of these areas about this. . . . If the people did not arrive [to work] by the instructed time, I had to go all the way to the area to get them. In some areas, such as Po, the population was low and workers were scarce, so they were very reluctant to send people. I had to tell them that they would be paid money so they would gain, not lose, by doing this. I also said that the road would be in their own area, so later this would benefit them, since it would make the animal transportation corvée tax unnecessary [since there would be motor roads]. So I had to go to the various places and do a lot of persuading. . . . This work began in 1953 and continued all through 1954. . . . In 1954 when the Dalai Lama went down to China, we were still working on the road. . . .

Q: And during these times, did they talk about politics and things like socialism?

At first they didn't. They concentrated just on building the road. They continually said that when the road was completed, clothing and food items were going to come from Beijing. Now, they had to fool the people right? They said this with the masses in mind. That they would get good clothing and an abundance of food. So at that time they spoke just about the work and nothing else. . . .

Q: Since the Tibetan workers were being paid by the meter, did they work diligently?

Yes. Since it was paid according to the work done, it was very easy to organize. You don't have to say things like, "Oh, you are not doing enough work" or "You are just sitting around." It was a situation where they may have even worked more than they had to! And then the Chinese encouraged competition and gave performance awards (tib. paysang). They generally chose women as exemplary workers. . . . So on a particular day there would be a meeting, and snacks would be handed out and tea and tables set with chairs, and they would say, "This girl named Yangki is so good and works so industriously." . . . So when they showered praise on women, the men became ashamed, and so they were compelled to work harder. The men would say, "Oh my, using women as examples like this is too much." So the Chinese were very skilled in getting work done. On the one hand they gave praise and made people compete with each other, and on the other they paid them on a piece-work basis. It was absolutely different from the way we organized work [laughs]. You do not have to say, "Do this!" or "You guys, stop sleeping." . . . So there was none of this. All the work was competition. Poor fellows—it takes its toll on the people. But they were experts at getting people to work.[39]

Not long after construction on the southern road began, Beijing authorized work to start also on a northern route from Qinghai Province. An office for the construction of the Qinghai-Tibet Road was set up in the summer of 1953, and in November 1953 that office sent surveyors in horse carts over the Kulun Mountains and the Tangola Pass to survey the route. On 23 January 1954, that survey team reached Nagchuka, and on 11 May 1954, construction began from Golmud.[40]

Ultimately, both roads were opened for vehicle transport on 25 December 1954. The total number of military and civilian laborers used for the construction of these two road projects was 111,000. In the four years of the project, over 3,000 people died.[41] The Xikang-Tibet Road involved construction of more than 597 large and small bridges and crossed 2,860 culverts.[42] However, in the rush to finish by Mao's stipulated date of 1954, the quality of some of the work was below even the lowest grade for roads in

39. Maya (Tsewang Gyurme), interview, Dharamsala.

40. Zhonggong xizang zizhiqu dangshi ziliao zhengji weiyuanhui 1990, entry for 11 May 1954.

41. Zhonggong xizang zizhiqu dangshi ziliao zhengji weiyuanhui 1990, entry for 25 December 1954.

42. Gao 2001: 136.

Figure 21. The road from Sichuan, which opened for traffic in December 1954.
Source: Chen Zonglie

China, and maintaining the Tibetan roads became a big problem.[43] Notwithstanding this, the opening of the roads finally solved the problem of dependable food supplies, and the Chinese secured the stability they sought in Tibet.

· · · · ·

Despite the greater unity of purpose in the Tibetan government after the fall of the sitsab, there were still important differences among the Kashag officials. Ngabö gained the most from the restoration of the Kashag's full authority, since he was the most committed to working closely with the Chinese and reforming Tibet. He believed that Tibet was now firmly a part of China and that the Tibetan government should work to create a niche for itself within the People's Republic of China, not try to resist the Chinese and dream of staying the same. He felt that the Seventeen-Point Agreement gave the Tibetan government a unique opportunity to take the initiative and begin to reform and modernize Tibet in partnership with the Chinese Com-

43. Gao 2001: 137.

munist Party. He was in a strong position, because he had the trust of the Dalai Lama, who liked his frankness, his desire for change and modernization, and his optimism that Tibet could have a good future as part of China.[44] And, of course, he had the complete support of the Chinese, who considered him their key ally in the Tibetan government. They constantly discussed matters with him, as we saw earlier with the plans to open a primary school. Ngabö quickly moved to initiate a Tibetan government reform program. This will be the subject of a later chapter. Closely associated with Ngabö was the acting Kashag minister Shasur and a number of progressive aristocratic families, such as Samling, Tsögo, Sambo, Horkhang, Shölkang, Trendong, Janglocen, Thangpön, Thangme, Nedö, Muja, Changöba, and Maya.

Kashag minister Surkhang's viewpoint, in one sense, was similar to Ngabö's, but in another sense very different. As mentioned earlier, he had reluctantly returned to Lhasa in mid-February 1952, just as the People's Association activities were unfolding. Like Ngabö, Surkhang was in favor of change and development for Tibet. However, unlike Ngabö, Surkhang did not believe the Communists would really leave Tibet as it was or that there was a long-term future for Tibet's elite way of life. Sooner or later, he felt they would destroy the religious and lay elites and the institutions that sustained them. But he was also deeply pragmatic and very diplomatic in his interpersonal relations. He was well-known for never revealing what he really thought in face-to-face interactions and for using the stylized honorific speech mode to deflect his real views. Having decided to return, he considered it important for the Kashag to maintain good relations with the Chinese and was willing to play the game and see what transpired over time. Consequently, like Ngabö, he was always friendly with the Chinese side in his personal and professional interactions and was in favor of modernization. Those on the Chinese side, however, understood that his sympathies did not lie with them and, as we saw, considered him a major supporter of the People's Association and their main enemy in the Kashag.[45]

The other Kashag ministers were ideologically closer to Surkhang than to Ngabö, in that they distrusted the Chinese and were deeply apprehensive of their motives. However, they realized that confrontation was counterproductive and that change had to come, but they wanted it to come as slowly as possible. They hoped to maintain good relations with the Chinese side but tried to manage change so that the core political and social institutions remained intact. A substantial portion of the government elite shared this view.

However, it should be remembered that almost all of the elite considered Tibet as having been conquered, not "liberated," and initially perceived the

---

44. Dalai Lama, interview, 1994, Dharamsala.

45. I could find no corroborating data to support the Chinese assertion about Surkhang, and doubt that he played any significant role with the People's Association.

PLA as an army of occupation. Despite this, by the end of 1952, many in the elite were surprised and perhaps even impressed by the respect and moderation shown by the PLA and were willing to cooperate and see whether this could be sustained in the future. However, there were also many who were implacably opposed to the Chinese in every way. They considered Ngabö pro-Chinese and distrusted him and therefore also distrusted the Kashag. They wanted the Chinese out of Tibet and were eager to find ways to oppose them.

The Dalai Lama, of course, was the ruler and could have implemented new policies if he had made it his priority. Instead, throughout this period, he continued to play a passive role in politics, responding to crises such as that of the sitsab only after enormous pressure. And although he was personally inclined toward reform and modernization and became a bit more involved in political affairs as Tibet moved into the post-sitsab era in 1952–53, he was still not motivated to play an active hands-on role.

Meanwhile, unbeknownst to the Tibetan government, the conflict between Fan Ming and the Southwest Bureau officials in Lhasa erupted openly in the second half of 1952.[46] It is the subject of the next chapter.

46. Dalai Lama, interview, 1994.

Chapter 16

Conflict within the Communist Party in Tibet

As the Chinese side's relationship with the Tibetan government and local Tibetans was improving, party unity was deteriorating within the Tibet Work Committee when fundamental differences between Northwest and Southwest bureau officials exploded over the status of the Panchen Lama and the overall strategy for reforming Tibet.

The debacle at the Panchen Lama's ceremony in Lhasa reinforced the decades of animus that the Panchen Lama's officials had held toward the Lhasa government. It also exacerbated the split between the Northwest and Southwest bureau officials within the Tibet Work Committee. Fan Ming and his Northwest colleagues felt the party should have insisted that the Dalai Lama treat the Panchen Lama as an equal, while Zhang Guohua, Tan Guansan, and Zhang Jingwu disagreed with this, interpreting the Central Committee's instructions to mean they should treat the Dalai Lama (and his government) as superior to the Panchen Lama. The Southwest's view prevailed, but Fan Ming and the Northwest officials thought this approach was ill conceived. As we shall see, the issue was not only about the Panchen Lama but also about how best to accelerate the start of democratic reforms in Tibet and the relative prestige and power of the key officials.

Fan Ming explained what happened after that from the perspective of the Northwest Bureau. In his comments, he scathingly criticizes the pro–Dalai Lama policy of the Southwest Bureau and blames it for the negative way that the situation in Tibet turned out.[1] He said:

---

1. He believes that if his strategy had been implemented, there would have been no 1959 uprising, no flight of the Dalai Lama to India, no reinternationalization of the Tibetan situation, and no ethnic conflict in the present.

At that time, the Panchen had already arrived back in Tibet [Shigatse]. In 1952, the Tibetan army and the Panchen's Bodyguard Regiment had a competition of arrow shooting from horseback[2] . . . and they had confrontations. Soon afterward, troops of the Eighteenth Army Corps that were stationed in Shigatse also had a confrontation with the Panchen's troops. This was due to different ideas about the position of the Panchen and Dalai within our party. One group tried to put down the Panchen. They tried to put the Panchen under the Kashag. There was a big policy problem in this. They put the Panchen's Bodyguard Regiment under the military command of Zhang Guohua's Eighteenth Army Corps and withdrew all the guards for the Panchen and Che Jigme.[3] This was an internal problem—I don't have to hide this—it was a problem between the Northwest and Southwest. The problem of unity within the party affected the troops; the Eighteenth Army Corps supported the Dalai, and the Northwest troops supported the Panchen.

The masses' problem was our problem, and we made a big mistake in Tibet. Because of this, the situation later has turned out like it has in Tibet, and it serves us right. From the very beginning, different opinions existed within the party. Later on they called it "factions," or opinions of a certain group—opinions of the Northwest and the Southwest, the Dalai and the Panchen. When the question of the Dalai and Panchen occurred within the party, the party was divided into Northwest and Southwest [factions]. At the time, I was still the representative to the Panchen's administration. When the same problem occurred among the masses [non–party members], the Northwest troops protected and supported the Panchen, and the Eighteenth Army Corps supported the Dalai. The divisions were like this among ourselves. I need to tell you this, because maybe you do not know where the real problem was.

The mistakes started from this time. The crucial factor in our internal problem was, in truth, a big mistake in the policy of the party. This was very typical. The policy of the Central Committee was very clear: to have a united front of patriotism and anti-imperialism and have the main task be to win over the Dalai's group and firmly unite with the Panchen's patriotic group. The policy of the Central Committee was very correct. The Central Committee insisted that we unify Tibet through peaceful means. These were the basic policies for Tibet.

The Central Committee was very clear in its Tibetan policy. It held that the Panchen was not under the leadership of the Kashag. He was still under the leadership of the Central Committee. The Central Committee treated the Dalai and Panchen in the same way. This was all decided by the Central Committee. When the Panchen wrote reports or other things, he did not go through the Tibet Work Committee or the Dalai; he passed his writings directly to the Central Committee. He was a small religious leader, and the Dalai was a big reli-

---

2. It was part of an important festival in Shigatse.

3. Initially, troops from the Northwest Bureau were slated to be stationed in Shigatse, but the food shortages forced the Chinese to disperse their troops before Fan Ming's troops arrived in Lhasa, so it was the Southwest Bureau troops that ended up stationed there.

gious leader. That was it [the difference between them]. At the time, big disputes and differences in opinions occurred within the party regarding the
peaceful unification of Tibet. They [the party] later said there were mistakes
in Tibet, and the mistakes started from here.

One group, the Northwest group, was headed by me. We had more experience in doing work with ethnic populations, many years of experience, but
they [the Southwest Bureau] had no experience in this area. Regarding the
policy of the peaceful unification of Tibet, *we believed we should use the two progressive and patriotic regions of Shigatse and Chamdo to influence the Dalai's group, to
urge them to be progressive and patriotic and to help the Dalai's group become a patriotic group instead of a pro-independence group that would go against our country.
Through the leadership of the Central Committee and the influence of the two progressive regions [Shigatse/Tsang and Chamdo], we thought we could change the Dalai's
group and change the Kashag into a patriotic group. In this way, we could unify the regions of Shigatse and Chamdo with the region of Lhasa and unify Tibet as a whole,
[making] a new Tibet. This was our idea.*

*The group headed by Zhang Guohua, however, listened to the opinions of Ngabö and
others and believed that in order to build a unified Tibet through peaceful means we had
to put the Panchen's group and the region of Chamdo under the Kashag, the Dalai's
group. That meant unifying the Panchen's group and Chamdo under the unpatriotic,
pro-independence Kashag, and sacrificing [the Panchen's group] in exchange for a
unified Tibet under the Dalai. This was the root of all the problems. Disputes occurred
within the party, and there was no solution for a while.*[4]

Fan Ming's view of unity, however, did not involve simply supporting the
Panchen Lama. It represented a different Tibet policy. Fan Ming thought the
Dalai Lama and his officials were hopelessly reactionary and would never agree
to implement socialist reforms. Since the Seventeen-Point Agreement said
there had to be consent and agreement from *both the masses and the leaders* to
start reforms, placing the Dalai Lama at the head of the unified Tibet meant
that nothing would change. On the other hand, the Panchen Lama and his
officials were "progressives," who he knew would favor quickly implementing
socialist reforms and overturning the old system. Fan Ming's strategy, therefore, was to work with the Panchen Lama's officials to implement reforms
in their territory. When the peasants under the Tibetan government of the
Dalai Lama saw the end of the feudal system in the Panchen Lama's area, they
would demand the same from the Dalai Lama's government, and it would
have no choice but to agree. Fan Ming, therefore, saw the issue of unity between the Dalai and Panchen lamas as really a conflict between two models
of how to integrate Tibet. In his model, China would use the Panchen Lama
to institute socialist reforms quickly within the guidelines of the Seventeen-
Point Agreement and create real unity. He framed this as directly opposite

4. Fan Ming, interview, 1993, Xi'an (emphasis added).

to the policy of the Southwest Bureau, which was arguing for slowly trying to win over the Dalai Lama to persuade him to agree to reforms.[5]

Fan Ming continued his narration of that period.

Just at this time, in December 1952 [actually it was in late August and September], the Dalai's Tibetan army had confrontations with the Panchen's bodyguards, and the PLA's Eighteenth Army Corps was also involved. Under such an emergency situation, the Central Committee and Chairman Mao sent me a telegram asking me to rush to Shigatse as soon as possible. It took me and a squad of soldiers six days to get to Shigatse. I resolved the confrontations, and things returned to normal. It was peaceful and quiet again. However, while I was in Shigatse, they—Zhang Guohua and Zhang Jingwu—using the name of the Tibet Work Committee, sent me a telegram. In the telegram, they asked me and the deputy representative, Ya Hanzhang [who had accompanied the Panchen Lama from Qinghai to Shigatse], to persuade the Panchen to surrender to the Kashag unconditionally. . . .

When we got to Shigatse, we had gathered the officials of the Panchen and talked with them about patriotism, unity [within China], internal unity among Tibetans, mutual respect with the Dalai's group, et cetera. We had resolved the confrontations, and everything was fine again. Then they sent me this telegram urging Ya Hanzhang and me to persuade the Panchen to surrender to the Kashag unconditionally in order to complete the unification of Tibet. There was this written document. *We believed that the Panchen could unify only with a patriotic Kashag, not a pro-independence Kashag. If we sent the two progressive regions [Chamdo and the Panchen Lama's territories] to this pro-separation Kashag, we were actually helping them [the separatists]. We would hurt our friends and help our enemies.* We did not agree with the telegram. We sent a telegram to the Central Committee with their telegram attached.[6]

The telegram they sent to Lhasa conveys their views well.

Telegram from the Shigatse Branch Work Committee to the Tibet Work Committee. Please send it to the Southwest Bureau:

On 10 September, we received the Tibet Work Committee's telegram [addressed] to Ya [Hanzhang], the Shigatse Branch Work Committee, and the Central Committee's Southwest Bureau regarding "making clarifications about the Panchen's ideas for reducing corvée taxes and separate rule." We have the following replies to each issue.

[The telegram first summarized two relatively trivial issues mentioned in the Tibet Work Committee's telegram and then raised a volatile third issue about unity and separate rule.]

. . . 3. The telegram sent by the Tibet Work Committee said that "the Panchen's group has returned to Back Tibet and holds deeply rooted ideas

5. Fan Ming, interview, 1993.
6. Fan Ming, interview, 1993 (emphasis added).

about restoring their former status and authority and demanding separate rule, and that these ideas are totally in contravention of the Central Committee's policy of a unified administration in Tibet (either the current Tibetan local government or the future Tibetan Autonomous Region government). Before the establishment of the Tibetan Military-Administrative Committee, which is an organ that represents the Central Committee, we hope you will pay more attention to the issue of unified politics and administration in Tibet. At the appropriate moment and when specific questions occur, you should give the cadres affiliated with the Panchen much more ideological education about strengthening unity to gradually overcome their ideas of separate rule. (This is, in fact, about separation [ch. fenlie].)"[7]

Charging the Panchen's group of trying to split the unity of Tibet was a serious accusation that infuriated Fan Ming and his associates in the Shigatse Branch Work Committee (which was controlled by cadres from the Northwest Bureau). The branch committee in its response, therefore, set out to rebut these charges and present its own version of the issue. This telegram, orchestrated by Fan Ming, questions the instructions about unity in Tibet by making the somewhat ingenious argument that since the Panchen Lama already *had* separate rule, he should not relinquish it until a new government, the Military-Administrative Committee, was created. In fact, it argues, if the CCP were to support the Panchen's autonomy now, it would actually facilitate overall unity when the Military-Administrative Committee started.

We do not clearly understand the meaning of the above instructions:
1. Referring to the specific issue of organizing a visiting delegation to Beijing,[8] we believe that there are questions about the Panchen's group becoming "unified" with "the current Tibetan local government" in terms of administration. It is currently impossible. Before the Panchen's visiting delegation started their trip, we talked individually with Che Jigme and Lhamön [the two heads of the Panchen Lama's Administrative Council], et cetera. Later, we held a meeting with all the delegation members. We suggested to them, "When you get to Lhasa, perhaps you will form one unified visiting delegation with the Dalai's group." They immediately replied they could not possibly agree to merge into the delegation of the Tibetan local government. They had no objection to forming a joint Tibetan visiting delegation [without using the name of the Tibetan local government]. However, they said that it would be the best if the delegation could have two leaders (one from Dalai's side, another from Panchen's side). If this could not be done, they said, at least one from the Panchen's side should be a deputy leader of the delegation. We delivered their request to the Tibet Work Committee (please check in the former telegram).

7. Dui xizang gongzuo de zhongyao zhishi (wei chuban de shouji), n.d.
8. This referred to the first Tibetan delegation to Beijing in 1952 and specifically to whether the Panchen Lama's people should be subsumed as part of the Dalai Lama's delegation or function as a separate delegation on a par with the Dalai Lama's.

2. If what was said [in the Tibet Work Committee's telegram to us] about "a unified Tibetan administration" conveys a more general meaning [than simply about this delegation], it deserves even more consideration.

Not only does the Panchen's group hold deeply rooted ideas of separate rule, but also they *have practiced separate rule* as a consequence of the reactionary policy of divide and control that the Qing ruling class employed on the Tibetan classes. In the fifty-second year of [Emperor] Kangxi, the "emperor's representative (ch. qinchai) went to Tibet to present the golden and silk [scroll]. Inside it specified that all monasteries and places under Tashilhunpo Monastery should be under the Panchen's management, and no one else should intrude." (General History of Wei Zang [Protect Tibet], vol. 5)

During the more than two hundred years from the fifty-second year of Kangxi until the twelfth year of the Republic of China, when the Panchen escaped to inland [China], the Dalai's group and the Panchen's group managed their own land and people respectively, and "separate rule" was established. During the nearly thirty years from the time when the Panchen escaped to inland [China], in the twelfth year of the republic until 1951, when the Agreement for the Peaceful Liberation of Tibet was signed, on the surface, the Dalai's group unified the whole of Tibet and got rid of the "separate rule" situation. However, in reality, the Panchen's group still existed. People who used to belong to the Panchen still preferred the Panchen. The gap between the Dalai's and Panchen's groups did not disappear but instead became stronger.

During the peaceful negotiations in Beijing, the Panchen's group raised the issue of restoring their former status and authority. Both the Central Committee and the Tibetan local government agreed to their request and made specific rules in points 5 and 6 [of the agreement]. The so-called restoration of the status and authority of the 13th Dalai and the 9th Panchen at the time when they had friendly relationships *actually meant a return to the "separate rule" situation during the Qing dynasty.*

This does not mean that our party also carried out the policy of "separate rule" as in the Qing dynasty, since [here] it is for the purpose of first solving the problem of unity within the Tibetan nationality. In order for the Dalai and Panchen to achieve reconciliation, we had to take this path to create good conditions for the internal unification of the administration of Tibet in the future.

After the question of the restoration of the prestige of the Panchen's group was basically solved at the negotiations in Lhasa, the Panchen's group raised the question of leadership last year. At that time, they said that if they were asked to be under the Tibetan local government, they could not accept this.

Later on, the Central Committee approved [a policy that said] that before the establishment of the Tibetan Military-Administrative Committee, the Panchen's group would be directly under the leadership of Representative Zhang [Jingwu] of the Central People's Government. At that time, the Central Committee did not give any instructions "to unify" the Panchen's group with "the current Tibetan local government" in "administration."

Tibet has been unified in its internal administration and ought to be unified (meaning true unification). However, achieving that unification will require a long process (since the situation of separate rule has had a history of over three hundred years). [Also we need] to create some favorable conditions for the unification. Specifically, we have to wait until after the establishment of the Tibetan Military-Administrative Committee, when the officials from both the Dalai's and Panchen's sides can participate in it [the committee]. Only then can they achieve unification in policy, in laws, in decrees, and in local administration. We think that it is too early to raise the question of "unified administration" now, especially with the requirement of asking the Panchen's group to "unify" with "the current Tibetan local government in administration." Not only is it too early, it may cause trouble. The Panchen's group is not going to accept it. They will think that we are showing favoritism toward the Dalai's group and are oppressing them to yield to the Dalai's group. As a consequence, it will destroy our relationship with the Panchen's group, and it will also deepen the gap between the Dalai's and Panchen's groups.

Thus, we implore the Tibet Work Committee and the Southwest Bureau of the Central Committee to provide a reasonable explanation of the Central Committee's policy regarding administrative unification in Tibet, [either regarding] the current Tibetan local government or the future Tibetan Autonomous [Region] government. In this way it will be easier for we subordinates to work. Otherwise, a whole series of mistakes in principle will be committed. Please instruct if this is appropriate.

Shigatse Branch Working Committee
15 September 1952.[9]

Fan Ming also sent a telegram in his name from Shigatse (on 27 September), asking to establish a separate autonomous region in Tsang under the Panchen Lama. A copy of this does not exist, but Phünwang, a Southwest Bureau cadre, recalled the incident and Fan's telegram. He also explained Fan Ming's larger motives in pushing the Panchen Lama's agenda. The hostile tone of his comments are as revealing as the details.

[The position that the Panchen had been politically separate from the Lhasa government] was not the view of Mao Zedong or Zhou Enlai or the cadres from the Southwest Bureau in Lhasa like Zhang Guohua. They considered Tibet had been ruled by the Dalai Lama and his government and agreed with the Central Committee's policy of giving priority to him. I agreed with Zhang Guohua and the Southwest Bureau. I knew that politically all of Tibet was (and had been) under the Tibetan government in Lhasa. There were many districts in Tsang (the so called "Back Tibet") that were under the Lhasa government, many others also had to pay taxes to Lhasa, and the entire area was under the authority of a governor appointed from Lhasa. The Manchu [Qing dynasty's] notion of a "Front" and "Back" Tibet was simply a myth. . . .

While Fan Ming was still in Shigatse (with the Panchen Lama), the Tibet Work Committee in Lhasa received a telegram from him, out of the blue, sug-

9. Dui xizang gongzuo de zhongyao zhishi (wei chuban de shouji), n.d. (emphasis added).

gesting that we establish an autonomous administration in the Tsang area under the Panchen Lama. Zhang Jingwu and Zhang Guohua were shocked by this proposal and immediately convened meetings of the Tibet Work Committee (in Lhasa) to discuss the telegram in detail. Most totally opposed the suggestion. The feeling was that it would exacerbate the existing conflict between the Dalai and Panchen Lamas, alienate the Tibetan government, and produce intense hatred of us among Tibetans in Lhasa. Most importantly, it would totally undermine Mao's gradualist strategy and make the long-term goal of winning over the Tibetan elite impossible.

As the only Tibetan cadre in the leadership group, I, of course, was asked my view. I felt strongly that giving the Panchen Lama a separate autonomous region was not only politically a terrible idea, but also was based on *bad* history. Historically, the Panchen Lama's government was clearly subordinate to the Dalai Lama. Moreover, creating two autonomous regions violated the Seventeen Point Agreement which stated that in the future we would establish *one* autonomous administration in Tibet. The Agreement did not say anything about *two* autonomous administrations in Tibet. The Tibet Work Committee in Lhasa, therefore, totally rejected Fan Ming's proposal.[10]

By this time, the issue of the Visiting Delegation to Beijing had been decided, with the Tibet Work Committee supporting the Tibetan government. There was to be one Tibetan delegation that included all of Tibet (excluding the Chamdo Liberation Committee's area), and it was to be headed by the Tibetan foreign minister Liushar. The best that the Panchen's side obtained was that the vice head would be from the Panchen Lama's administration.

But the dispute concerning the underlying issue of autonomy (and tactics to start reforms) could not be ignored, and the Tibet Work Committee, in Lhasa, next sent a second telegram to the Shigatse Branch Work Committee on 8 October 1952, clarifying its position.

About the issue of the Policy of Unification in Tibet

We received the Shigatse Branch Work Committee's telegram of 15 September as well as Comrade Fan Ming's telegram of 27 September. Since the policy of unification in Tibet is an important question of principle, we must form a clear notion so that when we carry out the agreement we can smoothly resolve the unity [problem] between the Dalai's and the Panchen's groups and solve many specific issues we encounter in work and so that we will not lose direction.

We think the policy of the Central Committee is a policy of peaceful unification in Tibet. The agreement signed between the Central Committee and the Tibetan local government includes the Panchen's group and has the goal of enabling the Dalai and Panchen [lamas] to move from separation (ch. fenlie) to unity (ch. tuanjie), from "separate rule" to unification, and from back-

10. Goldstein, Sherap, and Siebenschuh 2004: 181–82 (emphasis added).

wardness to progressiveness. It is not a policy of separation, separate rule, and conservatism. The goal of the peaceful liberation of Tibet has been realized. We must strengthen it and must realize that the core and key central issue in the peaceful unification of Tibet is to win over the Dalai's group and [create] internal unity between the Dalai's and Panchen's groups. Otherwise, the Tibet issue cannot be resolved well.

In principle, the Central Committee has agreed to put Chamdo under the administration of the Tibetan local government. This was for the purpose of winning over the Dalai's group, and it was also the Central Committee's recognition of the [facts of] history and nationality relationships [in which] the Tibetan local government had ruled the Chamdo area for nearly thirty years. It was for the goal of solving the problem of unification in Tibet when the conditions are ripe.

As to the issue of restoring the Panchen's former status and authority according to the agreement, we ought to guarantee to see that it is realized. However, that doesn't mean that we recognize the past regulations of the Qing dynasty so that the areas under Tashilhunpo Monastery in Back Tibet should enjoy high autonomy and that we will, therefore, treat the situation [now] as one in which the Panchen has a separate ruling government. That is incorrect.

According to the history of Tibet, areas under Tashilhunpo Monastery must still be responsible to the Kashag, and Tibet is still unified politically and administratively in form. Tibet became more unified during the 13th Dalai's reign. This is the objective truth.

As to the Panchen, after he returned to Tibet, he should get his inherent status and authority based on the old regulations, but he may not take the name of Back Tibet in order to rule the entire Back Tibet area. We must draw a clear line regarding this point. According to the guidelines of carrying out autonomous rule in ethnic regions, *there is no reason for Back Tibet to implement regional autonomy. Also, looking at the current situation of the Dalai's group, we cannot conceive of carrying out regional autonomy in the areas under the Panchen first in order to propel the Dalai's group to make progress.*

It is correct that under the Tibetan Military-Administrative Committee (which will be the Central Committee's representative organ), the unification of Tibet will be realized; they [the Panchen Lama's people] will be unified to carry out the agreement and unified to make progress. (It is also correct) that the current direct management by the Central Committee's representative [Zhang Jingwu] of the status and authority of the Panchen's group according to the old regulations is for the purpose of future unification.

However, you did not realize the importance of unity and unification within the Tibetan nationality (and you did not realize that) in the future there should be a Tibetan local government or a people's government of a Tibetan autonomous region. And to achieve this goal, we have to solve the problem of unity between the Dalai's group and the Panchen's group first. Right now the Dalai's group have doubts and are worried that the Central Committee will elevate the Panchen's position while lowering the Dalai's position. They have concerns about whether the Central Committee is carrying out a policy of breaking up the ethnic groups. Though there are pro-imperialists within

Dalai's group who could waver about carrying out the agreement, we must make sure to continue winning them over politically with greater effort. *We should not act like the Panchen's group and arbitrarily believe that the Dalai's group cannot be won over and that they cannot make progress.* We must recognize that after the Panchen's group returned to Back Tibet, they are patriotic and they support the Central Committee, which is their progressive aspect. They have returned to Tashilhunpo Monastery successfully. They are resuming unity with the Dalai's group, and we must strengthen these things and develop them further.

However, we must understand that the Panchen's group also belongs to the feudal aristocratic class. Though they support the Central Committee today, they still have their bad side of being selfish and backward. Especially, we need to prevent them from using the power of the Central Committee for their own purposes of grabbing more power for themselves and other things that are against the Central Committee's policy of peacefully achieving unity and unification in Tibet.

This means there is some distance between the Panchen's group and the Central Committee's policies. We can only require "largely identical with minor differences" (ch. da tong xiao yi). On major principles and issues they will follow the same stand, and on trivial things they can be different. We could make mistakes in our work if we evaluate the progress of the Panchen's group either too high or too low. For example, the Central Committee asked the Dalai to be the chairman of the Military-Administrative Committee, and the Panchen to be the vice chairman, but Che Jigme was not satisfied. He thought it would be better if the Central Committee could send someone [else] to be the chairman [above the two lamas]. Essentially, he wanted to treat the Dalai and Panchen equally. Even more, he said the Panchen should have a higher position because of the [Panchen's] thirty years of patriotic and revolutionary experience. They did not understand that the Central Committee was going to send someone to be the second vice chairman for the purpose of winning over the Dalai to solve the question of unification of the Tibetan nationality. When the Tibet Military Area Headquarters was established, Che Jigme asked to have someone from the Panchen's group for the position of deputy commander (ch. fu siling).

Regarding the issue of purchasing wool, Che Jigme wanted to send representatives under the name of Back Tibet. According to the reports of Luo Jiagao, when he discussed the above issue with the Panchen, he had already got permission from the Branch Working Committee. So Luo said yes to the Panchen, but the Kashag did not agree. This incident made us lose the initiative.

[The Panchen's group] was not willing to form a unified visiting delegation; they insisted on having the title of delegation leader and were not willing to have the title of only the deputy director. According to the religious and political relationship [between the Dalai and Panchen], the Panchen ought to have prostrated before the Dalai when he returned to Lhasa. After Che Jigme got the notice, he did not make any proposal [about the ceremony] to the Kashag for a long time, but suddenly he asked the representative from the Central Committee to act on their [the Panchen's group's] behalf. In the end, he still said that the representative of the Central Committee seemed to have oppressed them because of the difference in power [between the Dalai's and Panchen's sides].

In addition, they verbally agreed that the Panchen's Bodyguard Regiment (ch. jingwei ying) would be reorganized into the Tibet Military Area Headquarters and that they would report to the representative of Central Committee for approval when they appointed officers above the fourth level (ch. si pin). However, when it came to carrying this out, changes occurred.

This conservative and deeply held "separate rule" idea must be overcome gradually. If the Panchen's group insists on ruling separately and does not recognize the leading position of the Dalai, there will not be good unity between the Dalai and Panchen, and without such unity, Tibet cannot be truly unified. [Thus] we must give appropriate education and criticism to [the Panchen's group's] conservatism and backwardness and their idea of "separate rule" and their other bad sides that are against the policies of the Central Committee. So the Tibet Work Committee reminded the Shigatse Branch Work Committee in the telegram of 10 September to pay attention and seize appropriate opportunities to give the cadres of the Panchen's group more ideological education on unification and gradually overcome their idea of "separate rule." This, in our opinion, was correct.

Regarding the strategies and steps on how to strengthen and develop the unity between the Central Committee and the Panchen's group and about how to achieve good unity between the Dalai and Panchen in order to unify Tibet [we think]:

First, restore the Panchen's inherent status and authority honestly in accordance with the facts (ch. shi shi qiu shi). However, this issue is very complicated, because it involves a long history (for example, people in Back Tibet under the rule of the Panchen paid 30 percent of the tax, while people under the Dalai's and Sakya's rule had a heavier responsibility). In addition, many changes occurred during the thirty years while the Panchen was away from Tibet. [For instance] the Kashag added the wool and leather taxes, which did not exist before. Also, those Qing dynasty rules are not completely reasonable and need to be changed to apply to the current situation and to meet things in the future as well. For all the above reasons, the Central Committee did not make any strict rules and regulations toward either side but instead agreed to let both sides send small groups to negotiate the issues. If they have disputes, you should collect the detailed information and then report to the Central Committee for decisions, and the representative from the Central Committee will then mediate.

Second, you should unify and win over the Panchen's group to work with us in winning over the Dalai's group. You should understand the importance of winning over the Dalai. (Do not say that the Dalai is higher than the Panchen; only say that the two leaders of the Tibetan people ought to have good unity). You should recognize in your mind the leadership roles of the Dalai and Panchen in unifying the Tibetan nationality. You should strengthen and develop the Panchen's patriotic and progressive side, patiently educating and appropriately criticizing to overcome his conservative and backward side. You should influence and promote the Dalai's side to make progress with methods of unity and progress. Don't use the method of "separate rule" to [try to] stimulate the Dalai's group to make progress. This means that you must pay attention to the whole situation in Tibet with regard to all progressive and reform measures of the Panchen.

Recently, the Kashag decided to hold a meeting next year to discuss the reduction of debts and the reduction of corvée labor (tib. ula), and they decided to invite representatives from the Panchen's side to discuss questions about jointly doing the reforms, and [also] representatives from all counties (the Panchen's four counties will also send representatives to the meeting). We will provide you with detailed information of these things after the Kashag formally submits a written report to the representative of the Central Committee. We hope that the Panchen will send representatives to the meeting and that they will push forward progress in the whole of Tibet at the meeting.[11]

Regarding the unsettled questions for restoring the Panchen's inherent status and authority fairly and reasonably, we hope that after Comrade Fan Ming finishes his work inspection, he will invite Che Jigme, et cetera, to Lhasa together [with him] to continue discussions with the Kashag to seek further and better solutions to the question of unity between the Dalai and Panchen.

Whether the above opinions are correct or not, [we request that] the Southwest Bureau and Central Committee please instruct us so that we can obey and carry them out.

Tibet Work Committee
8 October 1952[12]

It is not clear if Fan Ming responded to this through the Shigatse Branch Work Committee or directly, but three weeks later, Mao and the Central Committee stepped in and decided in favor of the supremacy of the Dalai Lama. On 27 October, they sent the following telegram to Lhasa:

We agree with the Tibet Work Committee that Tibet should be united.

We received the telegram from the Tibet Work Committee on 8 October and the transmitted telegram from the Shigatse Branch on 15 September. *The Central Committee thinks that the position of the Tibet Work Committee is correct. We hope you will work according to this principle.*

The unity of the entire area under the united leadership of the Central People's Government (this refers to Front Tibet, Back Tibet, and the Ali area, and even includes the Chamdo area when conditions are ready), will help the development of Tibet. It will also be of benefit for the harmony of the entire Tibetan nationality. There will be difficulties in getting unified, so consequently we should advance stably and cautiously to realize this. You should not do things impetuously. It is good that the Shigatse Branch noticed this point [that there

11. This is a reference to the Reform Assembly and Reform Office. These will be discussed in chapter 17.

12. Dui xizang gongzuo de zhongyao zhishi (wei chuban de shouji), n.d. (emphasis added).

will be difficulties], *but you should never take the step of first divide and later unify (ch. xian fenzhi, hou tongyi). If such a step is taken, it will do harm in the present and future. Consequently, the position of a unified Tibet autonomous region will be the unshakable policy.*

The unity of Tibetans within Tibet will depend on the unity of the Dalai Lama and the Panchen Lama. This is not only a point of view but is proved by the actual experiences of the past two years. However, when we unify the Dalai and the Panchen we mean that we are trying to create unity inside Tibet peacefully. On the one hand, to some extent we have to consider the progressiveness of the Panchen's side and take advantage of this progressiveness, but on the other hand, we must fully understand and consider the fact that the Dalai's status and influence is higher than the Panchen's not only in the region of Tibet but also among all ethnic Tibetans.

So for all policies concerning peacefully liberating Tibet and peacefully unifying Tibet and for all kinds of work after peacefully liberating Tibet, *the chief task above all must be to win over the Dalai's group. We have to do absolutely everything that helps to accomplish that task* (in this there are two sides, unifying and struggling, in which the struggling is for unifying, taking the principle of youli youli youjie [reasonable, beneficial, and stable], for example, the struggle against the People's Association). *Anything that is not beneficial to realizing this task should be delayed or avoided (for example, temporarily not starting the Military-Administrative Committee and reorganizing the Tibetan army).* Our work on the Panchen's side also must be concerned with and obey this main task. So on the Panchen's side, we shouldn't only do the unifying thing and not do the necessary criticism and struggle.

Winning over the Dalai's group is a long-term and complicated job. However, after winning over and educating and doing the necessary struggling and dividing internally, we must be certain to accomplish that goal [winning over the Dalai Lama]. *Therefore, the principle of winning over the Dalai's group will be the unchangeable main task.*

According to all kinds of specific issues such as the argument between the Panchen and the Dalai, et cetera, you may report to the Central Committee any time and ask for instructions on dealing with them.

Central Committee
27 October 1952[13]

Although this decision seemed crystal clear, Fan Ming did not let the matter drop, and the conflict within the Tibet Work committee continued to deteriorate. After his return to Lhasa, Fan continued to push for treating the Panchen Lama's group as the equal of the Dalai Lama, now arguing that the Central Committee's call for a unified Tibet and emphasis on winning over the Dalai Lama did not preclude treating the Panchen and Dalai lamas equally. Since both were under the unified rule of the central government,

---

13. Dui xizang gongzuo de zhongyao zhishi (wei chuban de shouji), n.d. (emphasis added).

it did not explicitly mean that the Panchen Lama was subordinate to the Dalai Lama's government. He also chose to focus less on the above instructions than on Mao's criticism of some of Zhang Guohua's actions that were hostile to the Panchen Lama. As he explained in an interview,

> Chairman Mao seriously criticized Zhang Guohua for dismissing the Panchen's Bodyguard Regiment without the permission of Chairman Mao. The Panchen's Bodyguard Regiment was set up by the Central Committee, so how could Zhang simply dismiss them and absorb them into his own troops? It was wrong to do things like this in an undisciplined way. Chairman Mao criticized Zhang Guohua very severely, and *from then on, they [the Southwest officials] truly hated us.* Each time when it came to things like distributing weapons or recreational things, they would treat the Panchen's group as a part of Dalai's group, not a parallel group under the direct leadership of the Central Committee. The problem became more and more serious.[14]

THE TIBET WORK CONFERENCE IN BEIJING

The continuing conflict in Lhasa led the Central Committee to instruct the Tibet Work Committee in November 1952 to convene a meeting to resolve the internal disorder. When this failed, the Central Committee went one step further and, at the end of October 1953, summoned the main players to a major meeting in Beijing to be headed by Li Weihan, the director of the party's United Front Work Department. The participants summoned were Zhang Guohua and Wang Qimei from the Southwest Bureau and Fan Ming and Ya Hanzhang from the Northwest Bureau.[15] They met fifty-nine times over a period of more than three months.[16] From the beginning, the discussions were vitriolic, both sides expressing wildly divergent views about the problem of the relationship between the Dalai and Panchen lamas and how to treat their respective positions.

An important factor at the work conference was the view of Ya Hanzhang. He had been instructed by Li Weihan to investigate thoroughly the historical basis of the Panchen and Dalai lamas in Tibet, especially the relative authority of the Dalai Lama vis-à-vis the Panchen Lama.[17] Although from the Northwest, Ya ended up supporting the contention of the Dalai Lama's government and the Southwest Bureau. Ya reported that there is no difference in their status in the religious realm. However, with regard to political power,

14. Fan Ming, interview, 1993 (emphasis added).
15. Zhao 1998: 84–85. Mu Shengzhong (Northwest Bureau) initially attended but then left Beijing after only eight sessions.
16. Zhonggong xizang zizhiqu dangshi ziliao zhengji weiyuanhui 1995, entry for 10 February 1954.
17. Jambey Gyatso, interview, 1993, Beijing.

he said that the Dalai Lama had more of it, and China's repeated mention of a front and back Tibet was not historically correct. All the soldiers in Tibet and along the border were from the Tibetan government (Kashag). The Panchen Lama's Administrative Council had no soldiers.[18] Ya's report undercut Fan's arguments on history and incensed Fan, who referred to Ya as a nei jian, "a hidden traitor in one's ranks," and sarcastically called him Ya Hanjian ("Ya Han traitor") instead of Ya Hanzhang.[19]

The meetings of this small group became infamous in nationality circles in Beijing because of their acrimony and bitterness and because of the rigidity of the positions. One day Deng Xiaoping criticized the participants and then sarcastically compared their discussions to the vitriolic negotiations that ended the Korean War, saying, "You are making this meeting into the Panmunjom of Beijing."[20]

Ultimately, this dispute was settled as a result of pressures stemming from a larger conflict within the national CCP, the famous purge of Gao Gang in February 1954. Gao Gang was a powerful senior cadre who was then a member of the Politburo and chairman of the State Planning Commission. He was a leftist and a power player who was opposed to Liu Shaoqi's and Zhou Enlai's more moderate economic policies. After Gao Gang targeted Bo Yibo as a proxy for Liu Shaoqi at an economics conference held in Beijing in June 1953, Mao concluded that he was creating dangerous divisions within the party and, at a December Politburo meeting, wrote instructions about the need to strengthen unity within the party and about the dangers of individualism and pride that create disunity among comrades. These instructions were aimed at Gao Gang, although he was not specifically named. These instructions were then promulgated as a resolution called the "resolution on strengthening the unity of the Party" (ch. guanyu zengjiang dang de tuanjie de jueyi) at the Fourth Plenary Session of the Seventh Party Central Committee, which met in February 1954. Without mentioning names, it indicated that high-ranking cadres had violated party unity and were trying to seize control of the party. This was followed by an informal Central Committee meeting targeting Gao, who tried to commit suicide on its third day. He failed but tried again on 17 August 1954, this time succeeding.[21]

The Tibetan Work Conference delegates were aware of this, because Deng Xiaoping brought a draft of the resolution on unity to their meeting and

18. Zhao Fan, Li Weihan's secretary, attended the meetings and took notes. He later wrote a book about this meeting, whose publication the Chinese government has not yet permitted.

19. Phünwang, interview, 2000, Beijing.

20. Zhao 1998: 84–85. At that time, Deng Xiaoping (Southwest Bureau) had been transferred to Beijing to serve as the secretary-general of the Central Committee.

21. See Teiwes 1993b: 130–65.

told them to study it thoroughly and carefully grasp the views of the Central Committee.[22] The issue of individualism and disunity within the party had now become a highly dangerous one, which had a special impact on Fan Ming, since Gao was politically linked to Peng Dehuai and the Northwest Bureau. Fan now reassessed his intransigence and reluctantly accepted the policy that the Dalai Lama is superior and the Panchen Lama is subordinate.

The Tibet "Panmunjom" conference in Beijing issued a long report that summarized the dispute and its conclusions and clearly rejected the Panchen Lama's and Fan Ming's strategies and views. Phünwang recalled this.

> After several months of heated debate and argument (I was not present), Mao Zedong himself settled the issue by deciding that in Tibet the Dalai Lama was the superior and the Panchen Lama the subordinate. Mao demonstrated this visually by holding his forefinger and middle finger extended horizontally (with the remaining fingers in a fist) and saying the Dalai and Panchen are not like this. Then he turned the two fingers vertically and said, they are like this [one higher than the other]. In other words, the Dalai Lama is on top of the Panchen Lama. So Chairman Mao settled that there would be a unified Tibet, with the Dalai Lama at the head.[23]

The summary report also sharply criticized the Tibet Work Committee officials for personal failures and arrogance and for letting self-interest override the common good. It is a major, albeit long, statement of the conflict and what the policy should be moving forward. It provides a unique window into the extent of the discord that plagued the party in Tibet during its first two and a half years so warrants quotation in full.

The Concluding Report of the Tibetan Work Discussion Conference to the Central Committee

> After signing the "Peace Agreement" and after the PLA and the party and administrative workers entered Tibet, a lot of work has been done under the leadership of the Tibet Work Committee in the strange and tough minority region during the past two years. Our troops and staff members in Tibet have carried out the Central Committee's policy and principles for the Tibetan region. They have achieved good success in road construction, production, transportation, united front work, finance, trading, sanitary hygiene, cultural and educational work, diplomatic work, public security, information gathering, and gaining the support of the Tibetans. These successes are the main part [of what has oc-

22. Zhao 1998: 85.

23. Cited in Goldstein, Sherap, and Siebenschuh 2004: 182. Jambey Gyatso also commented on Mao's graphic depiction of the relations with his fingers (interview, 1993). Zhao (1998: 88) mentioned Mao's hand gesture but places it a month or so later, when final plans for how to treat the Dalai and Panchen lamas were finalized for their trip to Beijing. This trip will be discussed below.

curred]. These achievements are attributed first to the correct leadership of the Central Committee and Chairman Mao. They also cannot be separated from the correct leadership of the Southwest Bureau, the Northwest Bureau, and the Southwest and Northwest Military Area Headquarters.

The facts of the past two years prove that the instructions of the Central Committee about our work in Tibet are completely correct and timely.

However, there are mistakes and shortcomings in the work in Tibet. The mistakes mainly originate from the incompleteness of the party leadership and the collectivized leadership of the Tibet Work Committee and from a lack of unity within the Tibet Work Committee. There were fundamentally different opinions within the Tibet Work Committee regarding the analysis of the basic situation in Tibet, regarding what steps to take to unify Tibet and how to do united front work there, and regarding the reorganization of the Tibetan army. These different opinions were not resolved for a long time and affected the internal relationships within the Tibet Work Committee.

In November 1952, the Central Committee noticed the above problems and instructed the Tibet Work Committee to hold a conference of the [Tibet Work] committee members [in Lhasa] and put the problems on the table so they could work toward agreement and improvement of relationships among the comrades. The Tibet Work Committee meeting achieved agreement in certain issues but failed to resolve the major differences of opinion.

The Central Committee considered the severity of the above internal situation and designated the United Front Work Department to organize a conference [in Beijing] of the main comrades who are in charge of the Tibet Work Committee to discuss the work in Tibet. These included Comrades Zhang Guohua, Fan Ming, Mu Shengzhong, Wang Qimei, and Ya Hanzhang, et cetera. (Comrade Mu Shengzhong left Beijing for some reason and attended only eight discussion meetings.)

The discussions started by analyzing the basic situation and doing self-criticisms regarding our policies and principles in Tibet. Furthermore, the participants did self-criticisms on the question of unity within our party in order to make clear the right and the wrong and to know one another better and to achieve an agreement. The conference had a total of fifty-nine meetings.

Regarding the basic situation in Tibet and our party's comprehensive work in Tibet, they carried out heated debates/arguments, and they also criticized one another, which was very necessary. However, the situation of comrades within the Tibet Work Committee having abnormal relationships for a long time was also reflected at this meeting. (Also during the debates sometimes people were swayed by personal feelings and were not objective, and they lacked the spirit of mutual help. This is a shortcoming that was reflected in the meeting.)

The conference made great progress when it started to discuss the question of unity within the party. The instructions on strengthening party unity proposed by the Politburo to the Fourth Plenary Session of the Seventh Party Central Committee (draft) alerted the comrades so that they quickly overcame the elements of their personal feelings and the arguments about their different opinions and reached basic agreement. The relationships among comrades also improved satisfactorily after self-criticism. Regarding the entire conference, the final result is relatively satisfactory, although the process was full of twists and turns.

We have fundamentally reached agreement regarding the assessment of the current basic situation in Tibet as well as the anti-imperialist and patriotic united front work, the relations between the Dalai's and Panchen's groups, fiscal-economic work, and unity within the party. Now we will present the report below and request that the Central Committee examine it and instruct us.

(1) Assessment of the current basic situation in Tibet and our fundamental policy and tasks

Tibet and the motherland have had a close, inseparable relationship since a long time ago. Tibet is one part of the territory of our great motherland. However, after the Republican Revolution (1911), Tibet's rulers were controlled and manipulated by imperialists and abandoned the motherland, relying on the imperialists. To a great extent, imperialists controlled Tibet, signed unfair treaties, and gained great privilege in the spheres of politics, economics, and military. Also they took numerous pieces of territory from the border areas of Tibet. Because of the development of the anti-imperialist struggle of the entire Chinese people and the existence of an anti-imperialist force within the Tibetan nationality (among them, a part of the upper-class lamas and aristocrats), they failed to conquer the whole of Tibet. During this period of time, Tibet was semicolonial and mainly took an independent attitude toward us.

After the peace agreement was signed and the Communist Party and the People's Liberation Army entered Tibet, the situation in Tibet underwent an epic change. The semicolonial status ended (but the remnant power and influence of the imperialists still exist and should not be neglected). The Tibetan nationality returned to the embrace of the big family of our motherland, which realized the unification of Tibet with the motherland. The Tibetan local government became a local government under the leadership of the central government. Though the relationship between the Tibetan local government and the central government is not normal at present, it is in the process of gradual improvement.

Tibet has become part of the great motherland. For the past two years, the patriotic forces among Tibetans have been increasing under the nurturance of our party's organizations and the entering troops. These forces are gradually playing an important, or even a decisive, role in Tibetan politics. However, the roads are not completed, we are not self-sufficient in our production, the Tibetan upper class still has many worries and concerns about us, and the gap between Tibetans and Han is still very deep. So we still have not gained a solid standing in Tibet. We have not reached an unconquerable status. At the same time, the imperialists and the Goumindang have retained their concealed forces and considerable influence in Tibet. We cannot relax our alertness toward their attempts to undermine and destroy us. However, if the Tibet Work Committee can unremittingly carry out the Central Committee's policy and principles toward Tibet and make no major mistakes, we still will gradually assist the Tibetans in cleansing the influence of the concealed forces of the imperialists and the Guomindang, gradually reinforce the patriotic forces, and achieve a leading and decisive position.

When taking a broad view of our work in Tibet, several important issues regarding the Tibetan nationality deserve special attention:

(a) A serious gap exists between the Tibetan and Han nationalities. Plus, the imperialists are sowing discord, so they [the Tibetans] still have doubts and worries about the policy of today's new China and the Central Committee.

(b) Tibetan Buddhism (Lamaism) has caused severe damage to the Tibetan nationality, yet it encompasses deeply rooted beliefs among all Tibetans. The Central Committee pointed out very clearly in their 26 October 1952 telegram to the Tibet Work Committee, "You must fully consider the long history and profound influence of Buddhism among Tibetans and the religious faith that the Dalai and Panchen enjoy among Tibetans at all levels of society. Also you must fully understand the long-term international relations and the political significance of how to treat Buddhism in Tibet (the religious question will take a long time for us to deal with)."

(c) Tibetans today are still living in a feudal serf system. Though our socialist economic forces have entered Tibet, the serf system is basically untouched today. The theocracy of the monks and aristocrats forms the superstructure of the serf system, and not only do they rule, but also they are the representatives of the Tibetan nationality.

"The opinion on whether we should propagandize our party's fundamental policy in the transition period in the ethnic minority regions and how we should do it" was proposed by the Central Committee's United Front Work Department and the Central Committee's Nationalities Affairs Commission and was approved by the Central Committee.

This document points out that the party's fundamental task in dealing with ethnic questions during the transitional period is to "strengthen the unification of our motherland and the unity between all nationalities, build up our great motherland together, guarantee the equal rights of every ethnic group within our big family of the motherland, and implement nationality regional autonomy. During the development of the common goals of our motherland, we should develop the politics, economy, and culture of all ethnic groups . . . so as to get rid of the actual remaining historical inequality between ethnic groups and enable the backward ethnic groups to catch up with the advanced nationalities and together be transformed into a socialist society. This fundamental task of our party's nationality policy is part of the party's general policy during the transitional period." The above general policy and general tasks are absolutely applicable to the nationality work in Tibet.

In order to accomplish the historical task of gradually changing the Tibetan nationality into a socialist nationality, we must take the following steps according to conditions in Tibet:

From [the time of] peaceful liberation to some years still in the future, the chief task is to carry out the peace agreement. The Seventeen-Point Agreement contains the chief principles under which our party works to achieve the support of Tibetans in the Tibetan region. *The basic tasks of the Seventeen-Point Agreement include increasing patriotism and anti-imperialism, trying to gain support of the Dalai's group, working on the Dalai and Panchen, nurturing patriotic ideas and forces among Tibetans, and realizing the autonomous rule of the region. These are the first steps. When the time is ready, we will take the second step, which includes conducting land reform, getting rid of the feudal exploitation system, and moving Tibet from its serf system to that of a people's democracy. The land reform in Tibet must be carried out by Tibetans and has to take "winding, not straight, steps and moderate measures." . . .*

When land reforms are completed, the Tibetans will enter a period of building a

*planned economy, culture, and socialist reform and will gradually transform themselves
into a socialist society. We must point out that the key points in this period are educating Tibetans, raising their class consciousness, and making communist cadres among
Tibetans.*

(2) Anti-imperialism, patriotism, and the united front

Maintaining and expanding our united front of anti-imperialism and patriotism are among the chief tasks we have in Tibet at present. The Central
Committee pointed out in the telegram to the Tibet Work Committee on 18
August 1952, "Your work for a long period of time in the future centers around
gaining the support of the upper hierarchy, first the Dalai and the Panchen
and the majority of their groups. In doing this, we will gain time to solve our
problems of production, self-sufficiency, and transportation. Any other work
should follow this chief task." The united front of anti-imperialism and patriotism in Tibet for a certain period of time is a united front with the upper hierarchy. The principles of this united front for a certain period of time are the
Seventeen-Point Agreement. The leading forces of this united front are made
up of our party's organizations and the Liberation Army in Tibet. We cannot
require high standards for participants of the united front among Tibetans.
Except for the running dogs of imperialists and Guomindang spies, everyone
else will be acceptable. We should try to win over anyone to join the united
front—anyone who is against imperialism and loves our motherland, who accepts the seventeen points to some degree, and who is willing to cooperate with
us to a certain degree.

Within the united front, the participants can be divided into three categories
according to their attitudes toward anti-imperialism and patriotism: left, middle, right. The left are firm in anti-imperialism and patriotism. The middle have
doubts and may change their attitudes on these issues. The right have feelings
of resistance toward the agreement, and they even have pro-imperialist ideas or
ideas of separation from the motherland. Among them, some have not clearly
expressed their political ideas. However, it is not appropriate to divide the anti-imperialist united front into "the faction of patriots," "the faction of the middle," and "the faction of the stubborn." (The faction of the stubborn was divided into pro-imperialists, separatists, and symbols [ch. qizi?].) It is certain
that within the united front, there are concealed running dogs of the imperialists and Guomindang spies. We must remain alert all the time.

Within the anti-imperialist and patriotic united front, it is unquestionable
that we should support the left. However, at the same time, we must try our
best to win over the middle, because otherwise we and the left will be isolated.
If we can win over the middle, we can expand the left faction (so the left will
have their alliance [with the middle], and also part of the middle may turn to
the left). Then we can undermine and win over the right (the right are isolated). We should also patiently educate the right. Regarding those who have
a great influence among Tibetans, we must especially try everything possible
to help them. As to the concealed running dogs of the imperialists and Guomindang spies, when we deal with them we must provide very concrete proof
and also see if this is the proper time. If they didn't commit too much of a
crime and are not very dangerous, and if they have certain influence among

the upper-class Tibetans, we should not make haste to attack them. Regarding those elements who have escaped to a foreign country, we should not give up trying to win them over. No matter what their political attitudes were in the past, we should still welcome them back if they are willing to leave the imperialists and the Guomindang and return to our motherland.

In both the Dalai and Panchen groups, there are the left, the middle, the right factions. (Also both groups have concealed running dogs of imperialists and Guomindang spies.) It is not appropriate to see them as homogeneous. The Dalai and Panchen have no differences in terms of their class nature. According to their present political attitudes, the Dalai belongs to the middle but may possibly turn to the left, and the Panchen belongs to the left. It is not appropriate for us to consider that the Dalai belongs to "the stubborn group" within the left. [Also] it will not benefit us in terms of strategy. The Dalai belongs to the middle; the Panchen belongs to the left. This is the principle difference in their current political attitudes. It is also not right to deny such a difference.

The Dalai and Panchen are the two symbols of the Tibetan nationality, but they are both young now and are influenced and controlled by the power of certain factions. We must try all possible means to win them over, since this has significant meaning for the work of our party in Tibet.

(3) The issue of the relationship between the Dalai's and Panchen's groups

Regarding the issue of how to correctly handle the relationship between the Dalai's and Panchen's groups, earlier, on 27 October 1952, the Central Committee gave clear instructions in a telegram to the Tibet Work Committee [stating], "We must fully understand and consider the fact that the Dalai's status and influence are higher than the Panchen's, not only in the region of Tibet, but also among all ethnic Tibetans. So for all policies concerning our contending for peacefully liberating Tibet and peacefully unifying Tibet and for all kinds of work after peacefully liberating Tibet, the chief task above all must be to win over the Dalai's group. We have to do absolutely everything that helps to accomplish that task (in this there are two sides, unifying and struggling, in which the struggling is for unifying, taking the principle of youli youli youjie [reasonable, beneficial, and stable], for example, the struggle against the People's Association). Anything that is not beneficial to realizing this task should be delayed or avoided (for example, temporarily not starting the Military-Administrative Committee and reorganizing the Tibetan army). Our work on the Panchen's side also must be concerned with and obey this main task."

For the past two years, the Tibet Work Committee has basically followed the principles contained in the above instructions. However, some impetuosity has been present, which is shown by the Tibet Work Committee's eagerness to set up the Military-Administrative Committee and the branch of the Military Region and to reorganize the Tibetan army.

The Dalai's and Panchen's groups are the same in nature in terms of their class. They are both made up of [individuals of the] upper class of the feudal aristocracy and lamas. According to religion, the Tibetan people believe greatly in the Dalai and Panchen, and Tibetans metaphorically refer to them as "the sun and the moon." However, if we analyze this according to historical, political, and real power, the two groups are very different. The Dalai and his group have superior status in Tibet compared with the Panchen and his group. The area ruled by the Dalai is very big and has more population and stronger power. They occupy the political and religious center of Tibet. They play a decisive role in resolving the entire Tibetan problem. Therefore, the Dalai's group and the Tibetan local government represent the whole of Tibet. Thus, now we have to make it our chief task to win over the Dalai's group so that they are close to the Central Committee. This is the decisive and the key factor of our party's current work in Tibet. However, the Dalai cannot represent the Panchen. And the Panchen's Labrang is also not subject to the Kashag. In order to consider the unity between the Dalai's and Panchen's groups and to avoid the quarrels, we should try our best to use the names of both the Dalai and Panchen when we deal with the issue of the entire Tibet.

Facts from the past two years prove that the Dalai's group is getting closer to us instead of further away from us, which is a development in a good direction, not a bad direction. For the sake of stabilizing and winning over the Dalai and the majority of his group, the consideration of the establishment of a military-administrative committee and the reorganization of the Tibetan army should wait until the completion of the roads and transportation to Lhasa. This is good for us. Also you should utilize peaceful methods to reorganize the Tibetan army (except when a revolt of the Tibetan army occurs) instead of taking militant (forcing) measures.

In the Lamaist religion and within the Tibetan nationality, the Panchen enjoys almost the same prestige as the Dalai. Thus, historically, the Qing government, the Guomindang, and the British imperialists all intended to use the Panchen to counter the Dalai, to sow discord and divide the unity within the Tibetan nationality. As a consequence, the Dalai and Panchen split, and the Panchen fled. However, the Panchen's group turned not to the imperialists but to the rulers of the old China. Thus, they maintained the relationship with the motherland. After the peaceful liberation of Tibet, it is we who sent the Panchen back to Tibet and supported him basically to resume his previous status and authority. All of the above shaped the friendly attitude of the Panchen's group toward the Central Committee and their active attitude of anti-imperialism. Our party's policy to unify the Panchen's group is unshakable. On the other hand, the Panchen's group is not satisfied with their weak situation, and they want to expand their power. (For example, [they] previously asked to expand their Administrative Council [tib. Nangmagang] to eight bureaus [ch. jü] and have three chief ministers [tib. jigyab], etc.) They wanted to be equal with the Dalai's group. In order to get support from the Central Committee, they have to show a progressive attitude and act very progressively. All these are very natural.

The Dalai's group still has many anxieties and doubts regarding the Central Committee. Historically, the imperialists and the domestic reactionary ruling class tried to use the Panchen in place of the Dalai, so even today the Dalai's group fears that we will also adopt the policy of assisting and strengthening the Panchen's group to replace the Dalai. Henceforth, we must be very careful when we close ranks with and assist the Panchen's group and take advantage of the progressiveness within the Panchen's group. We should persuade the Panchen to give up those things that are not helpful for winning over the Dalai's group and for the future unification of Tibet. For example, the Panchen's group asked to set up three chief ministers and expand the Administrative Council into eight bureaus. We should persuade them to give up this kind of thing.

The policy of our party in Tibet is to unify Tibet gradually and set up a unified Tibetan autonomous region rather than first (setting up) separate regional autonomous [units] and next going into unification. It is not appropriate to think that "we may con-

sider carrying out regional autonomy for the Panchen's area in the future in order to stimulate the early realization of unified regional autonomy." This is not profitable either for winning over the Dalai's group or in taking steps toward the unification of Tibet in the future. However, it is also not appropriate to criticize such an opinion and some other opinions as "an idea for (creating) separate rule (ch. dang nei fen zhi) within the party" and "a matter of standpoint" (ch. lichang wenti). [This refers to the criticism of Fan Ming.]

More progressive methods are allowed in the Panchen's area; however, it is not appropriate to be too obvious so that this influences [negatively] winning over the Dalai.

You should pay attention and do more work with the Panchen's group. You should gradually persuade them to recognize the actual leading position of the Dalai's group in Tibet and should ask them to be good at compromising and waiting for the Dalai's group and, together with us, to win over the Dalai's group. At the same time you also should do more work on the Dalai's group to persuade them to respect the position of the Panchen.

Regarding the current situation, the Dalai's and Panchen's groups are two [entities]. They do not enjoy unity, and the gap between them is quite deep. Thus, it is correct that the Tibet Work Committee apologized (ch. jian tao) in the 5 February 1953 concluding report for [trying to] persuade the Panchen's group to be unified under the present Tibetan local government. The groups of the Dalai and Panchen lamas should wait until conditions are ready in the future and then unify under the Military-Administrative Committee and, after that, develop into a unified Tibet autonomous region. It is not appropriate that you criticized the approach of persuading the Panchen's group to be unified under the present Tibetan local government and other shortcomings as "winning the Dalai at the expense of the Panchen."

Regarding the Panchen's inherited status and authority, according to the information we have, they have been basically resumed. If some of these rights have still not been resumed, it is okay to leave them. It will harm the unity between the Dalai and Panchen if we force them to be resumed, so we may not resume them. If the two sides still have disputes over something, we should take the attitude of mediation and persuade both sides to respect each other and compromise to solve the problem by negotiation.

(4) The issue of finance and economics

The Central Committee has already given explicit instructions on the financial and economic issues in Tibet in the telegram of 6 April 1952: "The first thing is to try to influence the Tibetan people by planning and calculating carefully and achieving self-sufficiency through production. That is the fundamental issue. Even after completion of the roads, it will be impossible to transport grain in large quantities via them. India may agree to exchange grain to Tibet, but our basic standpoint should be that our army can still survive even if some day in the future India stops the grain. . . . Second, you may and you must set up trading relations between inland China (ch. neidi) and India in order to achieve a balance in the imports and exports of Tibet and improve the living standards rather than lower the living standard of Tibetans as a result of our troops entering Tibet." In the past two years, the Tibet Work Committee has basically carried out the above instructions, but there were shortcomings. *The main thing is that during the purchasing and transportation process, you didn't adjust the prices in time, and [also] a large numbers of yaks died during transportation. These harmed the current interests of the common Tibetan people. [Also] the problem of the prices has not been solved well so far. These two issues affect quite a large number of people.*

Tibet has a vast land, a small population, no good transportation, and backward production, and there is miserable and heavy exploitation, and so the people live a very tough life. So we would rather underevaluate the overall assets of Tibet and try hard not to take anything from it. Chairman Mao instructed in the past, "March into Tibet and take no supplies from it."

The spirit of the Central Committee's instruction of 6 April 1952 also asked us to gain self-sufficiency through production. In the last two years, however, because self-sufficiency is not yet achieved, and the grain from the inland transportation didn't meet our needs, we had to purchase part of the grain and yaks and sheep in the Tibetan areas, and this unavoidably affected inflation. [Also], because we have to purchase and transport our supplies through the upper class, in addition to our other weaknesses in work, we hurt the interest of ordinary Tibetans, which has caused widespread discontent (later we checked and compensated [for this], and [the bad] influence has been changed). However, we should not merely treat our shortcomings as a "simple financial and economic issue."

In order to change the above situation fundamentally, we can make efforts only in the following four ways: First, complete the roads to Lhasa quickly. Second, actively do production and try to achieve self-sufficiency. Third, build up new trade and transportation routes with inland China and foreign countries. Besides the Tibetan route, last winter we set up the northwest transportation route. At the same time we should strengthen our efforts to sell local products to India. *Fourth, we need to reduce expenses and simplify our bureaucratic structure. We have done these in the past, but still not enough. Except for the armed forces and staff members who are necessary, the rest of the people should return to inland China temporarily to study or to get other positions. In all aspects we should cling intensively to one principle—keep in mind the word* tight *[frugal] in all our work, and suffer this tightness for two or three years.*

The basic principle of the party's own finances and economy in Tibet is to guarantee supplies to the troops and at the same time take care of civilian needs. Thus, we should try our best not to take any grain and other supplies from the Tibetan people but do some good things for them and bring them some material benefits. Regarding the price of purchasing things and transportation, the Tibet Work Committee should negotiate with the Tibetan local government to solve it properly. Regarding the issue of setting up our own farms and ranches in Tibetan areas, we also need to negotiate with the Tibetan upper and lower classes. *It should be done under the principle of having no conflict with the interests of the Tibetan people.*

The markets in Tibet are small, and the resources are scarce, so it was necessary to adopt the "tight" policy about expenses in finances and economics. This should be continued in the future. We had some shortcomings on Tibetan finances and economic work. However, it is not "conservative shortcomings" on finance.

The issue of Tibetan currency is relevant to the issue of the relationship between the Tibetan local government and the Central Committee. It also is related to the immediate interests of the Tibetan people. From our past experience, it is appropriate to follow the policy of "neglect and care less" [don't ask, don't tell]. [However,] It will be profitable in the future if we can gain the agreement of the Tibetan local government and then use this to issue and print currency by adopting the method of subsidizing the administration of the Tibetan local government.

(5) The issue of unity within the party

The phenomenon of very severe internal disunity within the Tibet Work Committee existed. It was mainly illustrated by the imperfect party committee institution and the [fact that the] collective leadership was not well-formed. The disagreements on policies and opinions within the Tibet Work Committee were not resolved for a long time, and the relationships between the leading comrades were not normal. The existence of the above phenomenon had a bad effect on our party's work. Also, because the leading comrades in the Tibet Work Committee did not set a good example of unity, cadres working below were influenced negatively, and even non–party members had a lot of negative influences.

The major reasons for the unity problem within the Tibet Work Committee are the following:

First—It comes from [the fact that] comrades in the Tibet Work Committee did not fully realize the importance of unity in our party, the importance of collective leadership, and the very serious political responsibility that was on their shoulders. [You] should know that the Tibet area is an ethnic minority region where the working conditions are extremely complex and tough. The Tibet Work Committee had serious political responsibilities and the high expectations of the Central Committee and people in the whole of China. We have to admit that the political understanding and the depth of thinking of the Tibet Work Committee members are not high. Also, they do not have a profound mastery of Marxism. So [the Tibet Work Committee] will be competent for this task only if they are united and work conscientiously under the leadership of the Central Committee. However, the contrary happened, and within the Tibet Work Committee the disunity phenomenon came out. The Tibet Work Committee comrades spent part of their energy on their internal problems and exhausted their own strength and caused a certain unnecessary loss of the party's work. This is a very painful matter, and we should learn a lesson from this mistake.

Second—Comrades on the Tibet Work Committee have ideals of individualism, lack self-criticism, take self-interest very seriously, and are arrogant. They lack respect for other comrades, and there is not enough mutual help. Their emphasis is on the reputation of the individual and the self-esteem of the individual. They are too impatient to listen to different opinions and criticisms. When there was a debate, there were individualistic emotional elements and an emphasis on showing the correctness of one's own opinions. So with this relationship between the individual and the group, things came out very wrong. Since the individual was placed above the organization, he failed to fulfill his responsibility within the organization's responsibility. These are the ideological roots for the incompleteness of the collective leadership of the Party Committee, the abnormal relationships among leading Tibet Work Committee comrades, and the long unresolved policy issues under debate.

Regarding the issue of who is responsible for this, it is mainly the leading comrades within the Tibet Work Committee who are responsible for these problems. The [initial] meeting of the [two PLA] troops entering Tibet was not pleasant, and this affected party unity. The leading institutions of the Eighteenth Army Corps should take more responsibility [for this], because the entering troops from the Eighteenth Army Corps were the main force, enjoyed the lead position, and entered Tibet first.

According to the problems examined and revealed at this conference and the individual self-criticisms, we sense more deeply that the unity within the party in the Tibetan area is the key point for our success in Tibet. This is just as the "Resolution of Strengthening the Party's Unity," from the Fourth Plenary Session of the Seventh Party Central Committee, pointed out: "The unity of the party is the life of the party." In the future, party organizations in the Tibetan area, especially the party's leading institutions, must make all efforts to consolidate and strengthen the unity of the party under the leadership of the Central Committee and Chairman Mao and according to the Central Committee's instructions and self-experience. Make sure the following important lessons are learned and remembered:

First, one should keep in mind that party unity is above everything. One's standards of speech and actions are based on the principle of party unity. If it is good for the unity of the party, say it, or do it; otherwise, do not say it, do not do it. "Our party's unity must and can be only the kind of unity that is based on Marxism and Leninism and based on correct political principles and organizational principles." (This is the point of the Resolution of Strengthening the Party's Unity from the Fourth Plenary Session of the Seventh Party Central Committee.) The Tibet Work Committee in the future should carry out the above resolution from the Central Committee absolutely to strengthen the party's unity.

Second, one should protest absolutely against individualism and decentralism. In the future, when handling any questions and issues in the party, we have to have the right motivation, which means to have the right standpoint.

If we consider everything on the basis of the collective interests of the whole party without any element of individualism, unity can be achieved absolutely. The resolution of the Fourth Plenary Session of the Seventh Party Central Committee points out, "[We should] protest against things that treat a region and a department as if they were under one individual's leadership, like his own independent kingdom, and that consider oneself above the organization, and that emphasize the role of an individual inappropriately, and [that emphasize] arrogance and the worship of an individual." These words have special significance for the organization of our party in Tibet.

Third, strictly obey the rule of democratic centralization and the principle of collective leadership. "These are basic principles to guarantee the unity of our party" (from the Resolution of Strengthening the Party's Unity, i.e., from the Fourth Plenary Session of the Seventh Party Central Committee). In order to accomplish this, one must put oneself in a right position within a group and fulfill the required responsibilities to the group. If one can do this, one will not emphasize one's own role, and arrogance will not occur.

Fourth, regarding the different opinions and arguments within the Party Committee, one must seek truth from facts (ch. shi shi qiu shi), obey the truth, adopt an honest and frank and open attitude, and put one's problems on the table for mutual exchange and then try to resolve these problems. Truth can be discovered only with the strength and wisdom of the group. That is why we have to carry out the rule of democratic centralization and collective leadership. If this has been done and problems still cannot be resolved, we need to rely on the Central Committee, trust in the Central Committee, and ask for instructions from the Central Committee. Then the truth can be obtained. Debates about work are permissible within the Party Committee. However, regarding these kinds of debates, the Tibet Work Committee in the past did not take appropriate methods in time to get things resolved, and neither did it report to the Central Committee in time [about the problems]. Consequently, the unity within the Party was affected, and this caused certain harm to the work. This is very bad, and we must take this as a lesson to be remembered. Without the permission of the Tibet Work Committee, debates within Tibet Work Committee should not be spread to the lower cadres. If there are different opinions about the Central Committee's instructions, one should especially report these to the Central Committee in a timely fashion.

Fifth, developing democracy within the party and practicing criticism and self-criticism are good measures to strengthen unity within the party. Whenever there is a problem in a comrade's relationships, one should critique oneself. First examine oneself, and next try to help another comrade. One can help another well only when one has abandoned one's own mistakes.

For the unity within the Tibet Work Committee and the party's organizations in Tibet, an important issue also is how to pass down the message of this conference in the right way. The following methods should be adopted: First, within the Tibet Work Committee, you should pass it down according to the "Resolution of Strengthening the Party's Unity" from the Fourth Plenary Session of the Seventh Party Central Committee and the approval statement of the Central Committee regarding the conclusion report of the Tibetan Work Discussion Conference. Let the members of the Tibet Work Committee first grasp the spirit of the conference and achieve agreement in their understanding of the conference. Then call a meeting of senior cadres and pass the information on the conference to them. Leaders of Tibet Work Committee need to examine their mistakes and set good examples in working toward unity. People below will follow, and the unity of our party in Tibet will be guaranteed.

Comrades who attended this conference all worked for the benefit of the party. Everyone should study hard, correct one's mistakes and weaknesses, work hard and well, and accomplish the tasks the party gives us.

10 February 1954[24]

A month after this remarkable conference report, the Central Committee distributed it widely. The displeasure of the Central Committee was expressed clearly in the scathingly critical telegram that accompanied this distribution:

---

24. Dui xizang gongzuo de zhongyao zhishi (wei chuban de shouji), n.d. (emphasis added)

Approval Statement from the Central Committee on the Conclusion Report
of the Tibetan Work Discussion Conference

11 March 1954. Distributed to the Tibet Work Committee, the Southwest Bureau, the Northwest Bureau, together with other bureaus of the Central Committee and the party committees in all military headquarters.

The conclusion report of the Tibetan Work Discussion Conference has been discussed by the Politburo of the Central Committee, and the Central Committee has approved this report.

During the last few years, the Tibet Work Committee basically has carried out the Central Committee's principles and policies regarding work in Tibet. In a strange and difficult environment, our party members, soldiers, and our other staff members who entered Tibet have done a great deal of work and gained great success for the party's mission, the unity of all ethnic groups in our motherland, and the liberation and development of the Tibetan nationality.

However, there are mistakes and shortcomings in the work in Tibet. The most serious one is the nonunity phenomenon of several leading comrades in the Tibet Work Committee due to the growth of their individualism. It was absolutely necessary that such problems were exposed and criticized at this Tibetan Work Discussion Conference.

However, we must point out that in the past, the phenomenon of disunity among the main leaders of the Tibet Work Committee had developed to a very serious degree. They disputed for a long time over the unity issue within the Tibet Work Committee and had different opinions relative to the principle Tibetan issues. Also, they showed that they were not capable of solving these problems. The more serious thing is that they still have disputes over policies regarding Tibetan work issues, although the Central Committee gave them explicit instructions a long time ago. The Tibet Work Committee, however, could not itself eliminate the disagreements.

Disputes and different opinions are allowed within our party, but certain leading comrades within the Tibet Work Committee were proud and arrogant, calculating for their self-interest, and were swayed by personal feelings. This caused the debates and differences to remain unresolved for a long period. This is not right. The issue they kept debating in appearance looks like an issue of principle, but in essence they were arguing for personal interests and disguising this with the interests of our party. To insist on defending personal feelings, which are actually for one's self-interest, they destroyed another fundamental principle of Marxism—the principle of unity within our party. This is the main mistake of several of the leading comrades of the Tibet Work Committee. This made it impossible for them not to commit the big mistake of nonunity and not to do damage to the party. This is a very painful lesson that should be remembered forever and taken seriously.

The Tibet region is threatened directly by imperialism. Also, the underground forces of imperialism and reactionaries in Tibet have still not been totally destroyed. If our party is not unified, and individualism is developed, not only we will not be able to improve the situation in Tibet, defeat internal and external enemies, and further completely change the look of Tibet, but also our enemies will take advantage of our internal disunity and use it to destroy us. They will look for their agents among us, try to dissolve us, and our Tibetan work will end in failure. Regarding all of this, the Central Committee requires our comrades of the Tibet Work Committee to pay serious attention and be alert to all of this.

The Tibetan Work Discussion Conference was held at a time when the Fourth Plenary Session of the Seventh Party Central Committee was held. On the basis of Comrade Mao Zedong's proposal, the Fourth Plenary Session of the Seventh Party Central Committee passed a resolution regarding "Strengthening the Unity of the Party" and directly educated and warned the comrades of the Tibet Work Committee who attended the Tibetan Work Discussion Conference. The report to the Central Committee, which was agreed to unanimously by the discussion conference, was achieved after the criticism of individualism and the improvement in the consciousness of party unity. It shows that by relying on unity within the party and on the leadership of the Central Committee, we can correct any mistakes and overcome any difficulties. Those comrades of the Tibet Work Committee who attended the discussion conference, such as Zhang Guohua, Fan Ming, Ya Hanzhang, Wang Qimei, et cetera, have all guaranteed to the party that after going back to Tibet they will correct their mistakes and shortcomings, strengthen the unity of the party, and do a good job. They will absolutely carry out the party conference's resolution and the summary report of the Tibetan Work Discussion Conference. This is good. The Central Committee is anticipating they will realize their own guarantee. The Central Committee thought that all comrades of the Tibet Work Committee should make the decision to do so.

The Tibet Work Committee members and the senior leading comrades in the army should all act according to the spirit of the resolution from the Fourth Plenary Session of the Seventh Party Central Committee, help in passing the message of the Tibetan Work Discussion Conference, and be responsible for educating our party members about strengthening the unity of the party so as to ensure carrying out the resolution of the party's conference and ensure carrying out the decisions made in the report of the Tibetan Work Discussion Conference in order to unify all our party members and our soldiers in Tibet to do a good job there. Thus, we can we achieve unity with the Tibetan nationality, defeat any possible conspiracies by our internal and external enemies, and get ready to build a new Tibet in the long term. Let us contend to consolidate and develop the unity of the big family of the motherland and the great mission of building socialism.[25]

Back in Lhasa, the Tibet Work Committee convened an enlarged meeting of the Tibet Work Committee from 7 to 17 July 1954. Zhang Guohua conveyed the contents of the conference's "summary report" and the opinion of the Central Committee.[26] He, of course, expressed his support for the Cen-

---

25. Dui xizang gongzuo de zhongyao zhishi (wei chuban de shouji), n.d.

26. Zhang Jingwu and Fan Ming were not in Lhasa. They had left with the Dalai Lama on his trip to Beijing.

tral Committee's decision and pledged to implement it carefully in the future,[27] but interestingly, in keeping with the spirit of the Central Committee's decision, he made an illuminating self-criticism on 10 July in front of a large meeting. The self-criticism had three parts: the first part discussed the shortcomings and mistakes he made in his work, the second was his self-criticism about the dissension that had arisen within the party, and the third conveyed his criticism about his own personal thoughts and attitudes (ch. sixiang zoufeng). Although this comes from a report of his speech rather than the direct transcript, it is important for understanding the conflict between Zhang Guohua and Fan Ming.

> On the issue of unity within the party, he said, "Concerning the lack of unity within the Work Committee and the fact that the Northwest and Southwest troops did not get along well, in general, I should take the main responsibility, because the Eighteenth Army Corps was the main body entering Tibet, and it took the leading position. Also, at the time that the two troops met and after that, when I dealt with many specific tasks, I had shortcomings and I was not very considerate when distributing material things, plus I was not patient or democratic enough in my personal style, [all of which] undoubtedly harmed the normal running of the party committee and the unity within the party."
>
> And he said, "Regarding the issue that the meeting of the two armies was not good, I had shortcomings as follows: when welcoming the 'Independent Detachment' to Lhasa (which was the Independent Detachment of Eighteenth Army Corps, entering Tibet from the northwest [Fan Ming's troops]), although I asked Comrade Wang Qimei to visit Ngabö many times to try to persuade him that the Kashag ministers should to go to welcome Che Jigme for the sake of unity, the work was not done adequately, so it caused a misunderstanding between us and the comrades from the Independent Detachment. Therefore, we did not fulfill the responsibility that we had. . . . Concerning the distribution of supplies/materials, the organs of the Eighteenth Army that distributed supplies were not very considerate and did not take good care of every aspect of this work."
>
> [And] "Regarding the issue of unified purchasing, I implemented the policy of 'unified purchasing' and centralized the financial and economic materials rigidly (mechanically)." If we examine this from today's point of view, when we implemented unified purchasing, it would have been feasible to allow the Independent Detachment to have purchased things separately in order to take care of the difficulties they confronted at the beginning. [Similarly] If we examine things from today's point of view, when we carried out the unified distribution of financial and economic things, it would have been feasible to carry out a policy that would have allowed the Independent Detachment to be in charge [of some materials] and then be responsible to the Work Committee. However, I handled things very rigidly and distributed things in a unified fash-

27. Zhao 1998: 86.

ion so that most of the troubles happened [in this sphere], especially regarding the three billion in old money (ch. jiubi).[28] This did more harm to the unity within the party, so I should take more responsibility for it, since I was especially in charge of financial and economic work and was the main person in charge."

"The issue that the Party Committee of Tibet Work Committee was not complete and that there was disunity within it is illustrated mainly by the disunity between me and Comrade Fan Ming. We two had the most disagreements. Though many disagreements were about our different opinions on principles, there were still some disputes caused by personal feelings/prejudice (ch. geren yiqi). I thought Comrade Fan Ming was biased, and his standpoint was problematic with regard to issues that were relevant to the Panchen's group. Since sometimes I had some personal feelings like this, when I looked at the problems, it was certain that I did not have the patience to help comrades and did not have the attitude to humbly learn [from others], so the problems could not be solved. And the longer the time passed, the more the problems accumulated."

According to the self-confession about his personal thought and attitudes, he said, "More or less, mentally I have the conceited attitude of individualistic heroism (ch. geren yingxiong zhuyi) [meaning he is somebody unique and can do things all by himself and doesn't need to cooperate with other comrades], which was usually manifested by my often thinking that my own opinion was correct, by my not listening humbly and patiently to the opposite opinions, and by not knowing how to absorb the right things from the different opinions, so I obstructed the complete and true harmony of opinions inside the party, obstructed the normal running of democratic life inside the party, obstructed the carrying out of criticism and self-criticism within the party, and finally obstructed the unity of party."[29]

The attempt of Fan Ming and the Panchen Lama's officials to create an autonomous region for the Panchen Lama, therefore, failed. Mao and the Central Committee unambiguously affirmed that the guiding principle must be that the Dalai Lama and his government are the primary entity in Tibet, and the Panchen Lama is secondary. As we shall see in a subsequent chapter, this was finally made public later in 1954 with respect to the arrangements made for the Dalai Lama's visit to Beijing.

The Central Government also disparaged Fan Ming's arguments about the Panchen Lama by subtly questioning the "progressiveness" of the Panchen and his officials and suggesting that they are really part of the same feudal

28. The term *jiubi* refers to the Chinese currency used until 1955. Ten thousand of the old money was equal to one of the new currency, so one billion of the old currency was equal to three hundred thousand in the new currency. It is not clear what this refers to in Zhang's report.

29. Dui xizang gongzuo de zhongyao zhishi (wei chuban de shouji), n.d., report on the self-confession of Zhang Guohua in the enlarged meeting of the Tibet Work Committee of the CCP on 10 July 1954.

elite as the Lhasa elite but were acting progressively to secure their own political gains vis-à-vis Lhasa. However, while the bitter argument over policy and principles had been settled by Chairman Mao and were not raised again, the underlying difference in viewpoint concerning the tempo of reforms in Tibet continued, and less than two year later, Fan Ming would take the initiative and launch a major effort to begin socialist land reforms in Tibet.

This incident is also revealing, because, although Mao was already moving toward the left in China proper, his Tibet policy remained moderate and "rightist," in that he continued to pursue a strategy of winning over the Dalai Lama and the elite in Tibet, rather than pushing for speedy socialist reforms and change.

At the same time that the Chinese were trying to rectify their internal leadership problems in Tibet, the Tibetan government itself, independently of this, began to look inward and moved to start to reform some of the most oppressive aspects of its traditional feudal system. This will be discussed in the next chapter.

Chapter 17

Tibet's First Steps toward Socioeconomic Reform

The removal of the sitsab placed Ngabö in a powerful position, and he set out to use this to reform Tibet from the inside. As mentioned earlier, Ngabö believed that in the long run Tibet could not retain estates and serfs as a part of Communist China. But he was also convinced that it would be best for Tibet if Tibetans themselves took the lead in reforming the current system. One Tibetan official recalled hearing Ngabö express his views on this at a meeting called to discuss reforms after the fall of the sitsab.

> It would be very good if some reforms are done [by us]. If one has a hat that is custom made, it will fit well and be very comfortable. However, if you [don't do that and] have to take a hat that has been made for someone else, then it is too late to talk about whether it is comfortable or not. So it is better if we do some reforms. The conditions of our miser (serfs) are really difficult, so it is very important for us to look into the affairs of the miser. . . . And although it is mentioned in the Seventeen-Point Agreement [that reforms need the agreement of the elite and people], they [the Chinese] will never leave this issue alone. They will definitely do it [enact reforms]. So if we let others cut the pattern [for the hat], then later there will be nothing left for us to say [about the fit].[1]

Ngabö, therefore, argued that regardless of what individual Tibetan officials really felt about the ethical need to reform the serf system and improve the life of the peasantry, change was inevitable, and it was far better if Tibetans crafted their own reforms in a manner maximally compatible with Tibetan values and interests rather than wait for those on the Chinese side to impose their own version of reforms. Doing this, he felt, would also show the Chi-

---

1. Drakten, interview, 1992, Dharamsala.

nese that the Tibetan government was a good partner for bringing Tibet and Tibetans into the mainstream of the People's Republic of China.

Ngabö was able push these views forward after the fall of the sitsab, in part because of the more politically realistic views of his fellow Kashag ministers, but also because his views fit well with those of the Dalai Lama, who himself was favorably inclined toward reforming and modernizing Tibet. In his first autobiography, the Dalai Lama observed that Tibetans didn't think critically about their social system, because they believed that it had come about naturally (by itself without the hand of humans). Thus, in Tibet there was no tradition of comparing Tibet with systems and standards in the rest of the world. However, the Dalai Lama indicates that, despite this, he had understood since his youth that there were, as he put it, "mistakes" in the Tibetan system, such as the great disparities in wealth.[2] In an interview (in English, uncorrected), he expressed in more detail his early thinking:.

> The need for reforms, probably I remember when I was young. For example, perhaps on the one hand it probably had to do with the fact that since I was young I loved mechanical things. I used to look at a lot of Western books, like war albums. There were books from the time of the 13th [Dalai Lama] on the First World War. Later I took special interest and I ordered a whole set of Second World War books. There were about eight or nine books. So in this way I was very attuned to the West's progress and development. Ever since I was young, I thought about cars and better communications, although Western books like the French Revolution and things like that I did not take any notice.
>
> On the other hand, when I was young, my playmates were the sweepers [in the palace], and they used to tell me all sorts of things about what was being said in the city, et cetera. At that time the regent was there. When I was young it was Reting Rimpoche, and then it was Taktra Rimpoche. So at that time they used to say that the ruler was not fair, and the Kashag did dishonest things, as did the Ecclesiastic Office also. That so-and-so took bribes, took wealth and money, gold. They used to continuously tell me things like that.
>
> At times, the Shöl Office [below the Potala] used to sort of give beatings. And in the front of Shöl, the prisoners were kept, poor fellows. During winter when I was living at the Potala, I used to take binoculars and look at them. So they would look up and recognize me and prostrate. We did not meet at close quarters, but I recognized a few of the prisoners through the binoculars, poor fellows. Likewise, I used to hear quite a lot of things about taxes and corvée labor and loans. Poor fellows, these sweepers were all from the villages, and so

---

2. Ta la'i bla ma (Dalai Lama) 1963: 58. In Tibetan: nga lo na son mtshams chos kho na'i thog nas lta dus nor 'khrul ji 'dra yod spyi btang bod mi'i bsam par/ bod kyi spyi tshogs 'gro stang de ni rang bzhin gyi byung ba zhig yin par ngos 'dzin byed pa las/ gzhung gzhan dag gi 'gro lugs la bsam gzhigs gang yang mi byed pa rnams mthong gi 'dug/ rgyu nor dbul phyug ma snyoms pa chen po de ni sangs rgyas kyi chos dang mi mthun pa zhig yin.

during my young days I used to hear these things. So on the one hand, I took interest in modern technology and machines.

As far as machines are concerned, during the time of the 13th Dalai Lama, Tsarong had begun an electrical gold mint, and so things like that I used to hear. The same with Trapchi. And when my predecessor was living at the Norbulingka [summer] Palace, electricity was used in a number of rooms, and there were quite a few batteries. So I used to take interest in these things. So, the culmination of these two [sets of] reasons resulted in my wish to modernize since I was very young.[3]

As mentioned earlier, the Dalai Lama also respected and trusted Ngabö and regularly met with him, seeking his advice on a wide range of issues. On one such occasion, the Dalai Lama recalled that Ngabö had urged the creation of a modern school system: "As soon as he [Ngabö] returned from Beijing [in 1951] we started to discuss making some improvements mainly in the education field. I also had a strong feeling about this. One day in the Jokhang, the Tsuglagang, after some official briefing, we spent some more time just talking. [He said] That we need a more modern program of modernization and the first thing we need are modern schools."[4]

In the Kashag, Ngabö's views on reforms were supported by Surkhang, another more forward-thinking Kashag minister, who also believed that social and economic reforms were inevitable and favored starting them. Surkhang's father had been one of the pro-reform clique working with Tsarong in the 1920s during the reign of the 13th Dalai Lama,[5] and his own children were all in English medium schools in Kalimpong and Darjeeling. Shasur and Ragasha were also in favor of modernization so also supported Ngabö's ideas on reforms. The other Kashag ministers were more neutral but realized that change on some level was necessary so, in the new atmosphere after the fall of the sitsab, agreed to Ngabö's plan for Tibet to start its own reform program. Consequently, in September 1952, the Kashag, with the Dalai Lama's approval, announced that a large Assembly meeting of government officials and monastic leaders would be convened early the following year to discuss the issue of reforms. It came to be known as the Reform Assembly (tib. Legjö Tsondu).[6]

THE REFORM ASSEMBLY

Ngabö considered this initiative so important that he participated directly in the meeting as the representative of the Kashag, despite the tradition of

3. Dalai Lama, interview, 1993, Dharamsala.
4. Dalai Lama, interview, 1993.
5. See Goldstein 1989: chs. 3–6.
6. Kun bde gling (Kundeling) (2000, vol. 1), however, calls it the Legjö Jitso (Reform Conference). Both names seem to have been used.

Kashag ministers not attending Assembly meetings. Initially, around sixty to seventy representatives met in a kind of plenary session, but after a few days, a smaller group of about forty-five delegates began to meet regularly once or twice a week. In the following year, 1954, a "standing committee" headed by one monk and lay official from the Ecclesiastic and Revenue offices was created and met daily.[7] It was commonly called the Reform Office (tib. Legjö Leygung) and consisted of about thirty people (including staff), whose main duty was to draw up practical reform plans and deliver these to the larger Reform Assembly for approval and submission to the Kashag and the Dalai Lama.[8]

Although some Tibetans and Westerners have claimed that the Chinese side prevented the Tibetan government from making reforms in the 1950s, the evidence does not support this. The Chinese side was in favor of this reform process, and, as we saw in the last chapter, the Tibet Work Committee sent a telegram to its Shigatse Branch office on 7 October 1952 asking them to encourage the Panchen Lama's officials to send delegates to the coming Reform Assembly and support the Kashag's initiative.

The Reform Assembly started meeting in 1953 and had mixed success. Merely the ability to convene an Assembly to discuss reforms was a victory for Ngabö and those who favored change, but securing consensus to actually undertake major reforms did not come easy, given the conservative views of most of the elite, especially the abbots and monk officials.

As indicated in the introduction, aristocrats, lamas, and monasteries derived their income overwhelmingly from estates on which hereditarily bound peasants worked their fields without pay, as corvée tax obligations. Much like medieval Europe, this system provided the estate-owning class a permanent, always present, no-cost labor force, who worked their land, shepherded their animals, collected their firewood, and produced their wealth. Even most of the government monk officials who themselves did not own estates were strong supporters of the estate system, because they considered it essential for the economic foundation of the monastic system and thus for the very institution that Tibetans believed made their country great and unique. So when the issue of land reforms was raised, it met strong opposition.

Sambo and Takla (Phüntso Tashi), aristocratic officials who attended the Assembly, recalled that the abbots protested vigorously whenever land and tax reforms were proposed, saying that these changes couldn't be done because they would hurt religion and would be actively opposed by the mass

---

7. These two, Bumdang (Chömpe Thubden) and Tsipön Namseling, were called the trungtsinyi.

8. Kun bde gling (Kundeling) 2000: 1:128–37. Kundeling says that the Reform Office started in 1954, but that seems to be just the ceremonial opening. He lists all members in his book (131–35).

of common monks.[9] Bisu, a member of the People's Association, similarly recalled,

> The reform office wasn't very effective. There were a lot of objections and arguments. Even though the aristocrats had estates, they were more in favor of change than the monk officials, who actually didn't have any estates. The monk officials made the most obstructions to change and reform. The monk officials and the representatives of the Big Three Monastic Seats would say, "We absolutely cannot have such a reform."[10]

It became obvious early on, therefore, that there was too little support to reform the feudal estate system itself, so attention turned to less radical reforms. After a great deal of discussion, agreement was finally reached for starting modestly with an issue that was important for the well-being of the peasants: the enormous debt load that rural households were carrying. Kundeling, an Assembly member, recalled,

> For many in rural Tibet, loans were a recurring necessity. In addition to special one-time occasions such as deaths or weddings, bad harvests . . . frequently left farming households short of grain for food and seed for planting. . . . And as there were no banks in Tibet, peasant families borrowed grain from the lords of estates and particularly from monasteries and labrang, which functioned informally as Tibet's main lenders. Moneylending, moreover, was lucrative, since interest rates were not regulated in Tibet, and most lenders, including the monasteries, charged high interest—from 25 percent at the top to a minimum of 10 percent.[11]

But it was not just the high interest rates that were the problem. More devastating was the widespread presence of ancient loans, that is to say, loans that had been inherited by households from past generations through a process called "putting interest on top of interest" (tib. gyela gye gya).

Loans taken in spring came due the following fall when the new crop was harvested. Throughout rural Tibet, therefore, monasteries and other lenders sent loan collectors to the villages in the fall to collect their loans. Farmers who were unable to repay their loans would sometimes be allowed to pay just the interest, and sometimes the lender simply took an animal or a piece of land to plant for a period in lieu of payment, but frequently the farmer was allowed to add the interest on to the principal. Because this happened repeatedly over generations, the principal on many loans became so huge

9. Sambo, interview, 1981, Dharamsala; Takla (Phüntso Tashi), interview, 1992, Dharamsala.
10. Bisu, interview, 1991, Lhasa. Bisu also listed some of the main monastic representatives: the Sera's Töba Khembo, the Drepung's Ngagpa, Loseling, and Gyeba Khembo, and two representatives from Ganden, one named Lobsang Dawa and one nicknamed Abra (hamster). Kun bde gling (Kundeling) (2000: 1) discusses this in detail.
11. Kundeling, interview, 1992, Dehradun, India.

that the households could at best hope only to pay the interest due each year. Not surprisingly, once when I asked a loan-collector monk how villagers responded to his arrival, he laughed and said they ran away like mice running into mice holes.

Consequently, many families had enormous debts carried down from previous generations, sometimes from several sources and often so distant that they no longer knew who had originally taken the loan. And no matter how hard they worked, there was no way for them to get out from under this debt burden—the interest payments kept them perpetually poor. Such ancient loans were clearly one of the most impoverishing aspects of rural Tibetan life, so if the livelihood of the peasantry was to be improved, reforming this problem was clearly a priority. It was the first issue the Reform Assembly addressed.[12]

THE REFORM DECREE ON LOANS

The first edict promulgated by the Kashag in 1953 was a far-reaching law that reformed the system of loans and interest for middle-level and poor families, especially those who belonged to estates owned by the government. The Kashag at this time was still in control of internal affairs in Tibet so did not have to secure formal permission from the Chinese side to do this, but the Tibet Work Committee was apprised of this initiative and did not object. The introduction to the new edict set out in a straightforward fashion the Kashag's logic for the reform.

> According to the plan submitted previously by the Reform Assembly, loans were among the various kinds of reforms that should be put into practice. As a result of the obligation to send both taxes and soldiers [as a corvée tax] and, on top of that, failures in both their crops and animal husbandry, the poor serfs (tib. miser) had to take loans from the government, the aristocrats, and the monastic estates for their food and seed. They were [often] unable to repay the loans in autumn, which caused the interest to be added onto the interest for many years.
>
> One debtor had to pay loans to many lenders, so the loans and the borrower became imbalanced like the proverb "The sickle and mountain are imbalanced" [a sickle is too small to cut all the grass on a mountain].[13] So even if they paid [the interest] from generation to generation, it was impossible for them to repay the loans [the principal] and therefore they became extinct [ceased to exist as a household]. So the poor taxpayer households had a very hard time physically and mentally during their entire lifetime.

---

12. Actually, loan reform (tib. bünshib) had been tried previously on a smaller scale by the government and by individual lords for their subjects (Tsarong Rimshi, interview, 1991, Kalimpong).

13. In Tibetan, ri zor ga 'dzol.

Consequently, H.H. the Dalai Lama gave profound instructions that we should not let this continue and must implement a reform that gives relief to these poor people. So we don't have any choice but to adhere to these profound instructions and implement reforms as soon as possible.[14]

The edict dealt separately with the loans from monastic, aristocratic, and government sources and took into account the age and type of the loan, as well as the current economic status of the debtor. Two aspects of loans, the principal and the interest, were considered. As an example, let us look at the regulations for loans borrowed from the government, that is, from one or another government office or county government.

Within the category of middle-class peasant debtors, those who were better off and who had taken government loans before 1949 received a 10 percent reduction in the principal. The middle segment of the middle-class debtor category received a 12.1 percent reduction in principal, and the lowest of the middle-class debtor category obtained a 20 percent reduction in their principal. The remainder of the principal of these loans was to be paid at a rate of 10 percent interest per year.

The category of poor debtors were given a much better deal. They received a 50 percent reduction in principal and were required to pay interest on the remainder at rates ranging from only 1 to 10 percent, depending on the amount remaining on the principal. Relief was also given to holders of other types of loans in a series of complicated adjustments.[15] This edict goes on to discuss many different types of debtors and loans in detail but actually left much unoperationalized and vague, for example, how to determine the various economic categories. Nevertheless, it represented a major step forward.

A second difficult burden for the peasantry was the onerous "horse and transportation tax" known as tawu khema. Tibet had an extensive network of transportation stations (tib. satsig), among which goods were moved by peasants as a corvée obligation. Households responsible for this obligation were required, without payment, to move goods on demand from their area's transportation station to the next one in either direction. There, another group of serfs would be waiting to move the goods to the next station. However, because holders of government permits could arrive at any time, the villagers had to maintain transport animals always ready to work on demand.

The Reform Assembly recognized that this was a heavy burden on the peasants, but it was unable to abolish the burden completely, since the delegates feared that if this was made voluntary (market based), most of the peasants

14. Bka' shag 1953, translated from the original Tibetan woodblock edict housed at the Library for Tibetan Works and Archives, Dharamsala, India. The decree is cited in its entirety in appendix B.

15. Bka' shag 1953. See appendix B.

would simply choose not to participate, causing the transportation system to crash. Nevertheless, the Reform Assembly took a small step forward by requiring payment of a transportation fee to the villagers and by reducing the number of the horses and transport animals required. It also tightened up rules for who was eligible to obtain such permits, thereby presumably reducing the number of people who would be demanding transport.[16]

Putting both these reforms into practice had mixed results, but they clearly benefited some poor villagers, as the following example from Panam County illustrates.

[In 1955] . . . they made a loan investigation. I am not sure whether that was because of the [Chinese] revolution or it was done by the old government. At that time, they investigated the old loans [we had]. . . . Before that, these loans had interest rates of 20 percent and 14 percent They reduced the interest rates and rearranged the payment of the principal to the aristocrats and the monasteries. The elders were saying that the loan investigation was very good, because it lessened the burden on our children. Our loans were supposed to be paid off in four years, but before the loan was cleared up, the [1959] revolution took place.[17]

However, despite some successes like this, the Tibetan government wasn't able to implement this reform widely, because no mechanisms were set up to enforce the changes, particularly with respect to the serfs under monastic and aristocratic lords. It was a start but a modest one.

The Reform Assembly also crafted a third important reform that dealt with the administration of counties (tib. dzong). Tibet was divided into roughly two hundred contiguous counties, each normally headed jointly by a lay and monk official appointed by the government for three-year terms. These county heads collected taxes in their county from both the government's own estates and those of other lords who had tax obligations, as well as adjudicated disputes and collected payments on loans.

Counties generally provided lucrative income for their heads, since they were required to transmit only a specified amount of grain and other taxes to Lhasa. Anything they collected over the required amount they kept for themselves. This income was particularly important for monk officials, since they had no estates and were paid poor salaries. The situation gave them real incentive to squeeze peasants for extra payments and to try to force peasants to sell goods at submarket rates so that they, the monk officials, could resell these at higher prices, pocketing the profit. Excesses such as these were particularly egregious in cases in which the Tibetan government leased out the administration of a county to private individuals, that is, to nongovern-

16. Kundeling Dzasa, interview, 1992, Dehradun.
17. Doye, interview, 2002, Panam, Tibet Autonomous Region.

ment officials, since these lessee county heads had to recoup their lease fee before they started making profit. The Reform Office, therefore, set about to end this form of exploitation by developing a new law that (1) required the government to "nationalize" (repossess) all leased counties and send its own officials to administer them (this nationalization was called "shungdzin" or "shungzin phumpa silu"); and (2) required county heads to pass on to the government in Lhasa everything they collected from the peasants.

To compensate the county heads, the government now paid them better salaries and gave them adequate allowances for the servants who would accompany them. Drakten, a government official, explained,

> So . . . the two [county] officials . . . got a permanent salary. If the district was at quite a distance, they were entitled to take more servants, and for each servant they got [an allowance of] around seventy khe [of grain]. The officials themselves got anywhere from one hundred to two hundred khe [a year]. For distant districts, more servants were needed. Without that [allowance], one could not really manage. If one had to travel long distances on the Changdang [Northern Plain], you had to be armed and have companions with you. Even among the peasants, one person could not manage, since there are very dangerous persons there.[18]

Under this new system, much more grain now arrived in Lhasa than previously, so the Reform Office ended up with huge quantities of excess grain after it sent the amounts required to the various offices. It had made no provisions for this so was free to use the grain, butter, and so on, however it wanted.[19] Horkhang, another member of the Reform Office, recalled that the office began to use this new income to fund a number of the regular official picnics in Lhasa: "There were parties/picnics like the trunggo linga, the tsidrung gi yarkyi, the kashag gi thawdro, the tseja gi druchen, and the Lajen gi drochen. It used to be that two officials from [each of] these offices were required to provide the expenses for each of these celebrations each year [from their own income], but then the Reform Office funded them from its general funds."[20]

These achievements of the Reform Assembly were all genuinely aimed at improving the life of rural peasants and reducing corruption and exploitation, and they were an important beginning. However, as mentioned above, it readily became apparent that a consensus was lacking in regard to more major reforms to the hereditary estate system itself, because the monasteries and many aristocrats were unwilling to have their estates repossessed by the government in return for salaries. Moreover, the very success of the county

18. Drakten, interview, 1992, Dharamsala.
19. Drakten, interview, 1992.
20. Horkhang, interview, 1992, Lhasa.

reform created problems for it. As a result of the tremendous flow of excess grain to the Reform Office, its officials began to spend more and more time managing this grain and less time thinking of new reforms. By 1955, Ngabö had become so disillusioned with this turn of events that he became less active, feeling that the Reform Office was wasting its time.[21] The early momentum, therefore, was lost, and in the end the larger, more fundamental issues of serfdom, corvée taxes, and the rights of the peasantry were not addressed. As one Tibetan explained, using a Tibetan saying, "A wooden saw can't cut wood. Later, it [the Reform Office] was virtually useless."[22]

21. Dalai Lama, interview, 1994.
22. In Tibetan, shing gi sog le shing la 'gro gi ma red. Bisu, interview, 1991, Lhasa.

Chapter 18

Events in India

THE DEVELOPMENT OF A TIBETAN RESISTANCE GROUP IN EXILE

The Dalai Lama's twenty-four-year-old brother Gyalo Thondup arrived in India in late June 1952, rejoining his wife in Darjeeling, where she had stayed while he had gone to Lhasa. Ignored and frustrated in Tibet, as mentioned earlier, he had gone to India to publicize what he considered the "plight" of Tibet and, even more, to develop relations with India, the United States, and perhaps Taiwan to assist the cause of Tibet. At the same time he hoped to make contact with Shakabpa and other active figures outside Tibet, such as Coocoola, Thando Rimpoche, Lhalungpa, Dadang, and Phünkang Sey, and to organize a group to oppose Chinese activities in Tibet from exile.

This, however, was not going to be easy, since the Government of India did not allow exiles to engage in politics and kept close surveillance on the Tibetans in Kalimpong and Darjeeling. Gyalo actually knew that before he left Tibet, because he had had to promise the Indian Mission in Lhasa not to engage in anti-Chinese political activities and not to live in either Kalimpong or Darjeeling. Gyalo immediately broke that agreement by living in Darjeeling and also by writing letters to President Eisenhower, Chiang Kai-shek, and the U.S. secretary of state (see below).[1] The Government of India took notice of this and a few months later, in January 1953, discreetly warned him that since he was a guest in India, he should refrain from engaging in anti-Chinese activities and having relations with foreign countries such as the United States.[2] For Gyalo and the other Tibetan exiles living in Kalimpong or Darjeeling, therefore, organizing opposition to China from India, even at the level of pub-

---

1. Gyalo mentioned the letters in an interview (Gyalo Thondup, telephone interview, 1994).
2. Lha mo Tshe ring (Lhamo Tsering), 1992: 159–60.

licity, was risky, since the threat of expulsion from India hung over their heads. Shakabpa, in fact, commented specifically on this situation in a memo he wrote some years later, saying: "Because the Indian government had good relations with the Chinese government, we suspected that if we made even a small political move, all of us might get expelled from India. Therefore, we didn't have any plans to do any kind of [political] work."[3]

This policy is not surprising, since India was trying to maintain good relations with China and was in the process of negotiating a major treaty with that country. Nehru, therefore, opposed anything that might create friction with China or transform the two-thousand-mile frontier with China from a quiet one into a hostile one. Allowing anti-Chinese activities by Tibetan exiles from India was, therefore, seen as unwanted provocation.

However, at the same time, Nehru and his intelligence leaders also worried that the presence of the Chinese army in Tibet represented a potential threat to India. India held many areas on the Tibet border that China/Tibet claimed, and it was not unlikely that China might cause trouble along the border once its position in Tibet was solidified. Consequently, in March 1952, Nehru authorized Indian intelligence to begin to develop plans to collect intelligence from Tibet/China.[4] As this initiative developed, Indian intelligence would gradually work more actively with the Tibetan exiles, but this was still two years away.

Gyalo's initial attempts to connect with the United States also did not go well. His first face-to-face contact with a U.S. official in India occurred on 6 September 1952, when he met Gary Soulen, the Calcutta consul general. Soulen had been returning to Calcutta through Darjeeling from a visit to Sikkim, where he had gone to meet Princess Coocoola (who had been a source of information on Tibet for the United States).[5] Soulen's report of this meeting, however, is surprising in revealing that Gyalo had little of substance to report, given that he had just returned from Tibet a few months earlier. And much that he did say was inaccurate, for example, his comment on land reforms: "He . . . claims Dalai Lama's power [and] influence over people [is] increasing but many officials unreliable. Tib food situation poor, govt has distributed to people two-thirds its grain reserves and DL has reduced taxes and plans despite nobles resistance [to] distribute landlords large holdings to people beating Commies at own game."[6]

3. Handwritten draft letter in Tibetan, Shakabpa to Indian government, 1954, provided by the Shakabpa family.

4. Mullik 1971: 179–80. Mullik was the director of the Indian Intelligence Bureau from 1950 to 1965.

5. Conboy and Morrison 2002: 23. For a general description of the U.S.-Sikkim connection, see 21–24.

6. U.S. Department of State 1985: 96, consul at Calcutta (Soulen) to Department of State, 10 September 1952 (793B.11/9–1052).

By this time, the United States was no longer interested in actively pursuing a Tibet program, but it was still interested in accurate information on what was going on in Tibet, and Gyalo seemed a potentially useful source for this. Soulen's meeting with him, therefore, generated a discussion within the U.S. government about the utility of working with him as a source of such information. Ultimately, however, nothing came of this discussion, because the consensus was that it would be almost impossible to communicate with Gyalo regularly in India without arousing the attention of the Indian government.[7]

Receiving no follow-up from this meeting, Gyalo bypassed the U.S. officials in India and contacted the U.S. secretary of state directly, sending him a letter dated 12 November 1952, in which, among other things, he raised the idea of creating a guerrilla-type resistance group from Tibetans in exile. It gives a good idea of what Gyalo was thinking at the time.

> In the seven months since I left the States, I have hoped you are in good health and always remember you in my prayers. When I was in the States I always approached you for your advice, and you showed great interest and took great care of me, especially when you saw the danger to the Tibetan people. I always remember these, and the Tibetan people would like to thank you for your friendly love and sympathy. I regret that I lost the opportunity to study in the States, but it was because of my way of thinking and because of the changes in the status of the Tibetan people and my urgent responsibilities.
>
> I remained in India, meeting my family members for a short period of three or four weeks, after which I returned to Tibet. During my three-month stay in Lhasa, I met His Holiness after a long separation as well as my other family members and had full and leisurely discussions. I reported to His Holiness what you and the American government had said, and he said, "I would like to express my thanks to the U.S. government for taking great concern about the Tibetan people and extending friendly greetings. I understand that when I was in Yadong the U.S. government offered support and did as much as it could to help me leave and go abroad, but due to the situation, the difficulties, and the wrong course of action, etc., [we] could not make appropriate decision. Therefore, it [the U.S. help] became useless."[8] If I tell you something else about that time, it was very necessary for His Holiness to return to Lhasa to look after his people's hopes. He did not return to Lhasa because he agreed with the communist system.
>
> During the one year of Communist rule since his return, the Dalai Lama and, under his leadership, the Tibetan people have fully understood the policy of the Communist government and their aggression and terrorization of

---

7. U.S. Department of State 1985: 96 fn. 3, from consul general at Calcutta (Soulen) to Department of State, 10 September 1952 (793B.11/9–1052).

8. In Tibetan, skabs de'i gnas stang dang/ dka' tshegs byed phyogs nor 'khrul sogs thag gcod 'ol 'tshams ma byung ba'i rkyen gyis phan thog ma thub pa.

the people. They understood full well about their taking away the people's freedom by trickery and force. At present, His Holiness has taken the religious and political power because the people were under an extremely difficult situation, so he had no choice but to respond to this situation.

I explained about and discussed with His Holiness the important issues you [the secretary of state] and I examined in the United States and informed him that he should once more plan to leave and go abroad. I did my best to persuade him, but under the prevailing situation it is most dangerous, and he cannot take hurried and careless steps, because there is a large Communist force in Lhasa, and they are very cautious and alert. If any signs of such a plan leaked out, there would be great danger to His Holiness's life, and great sufferings would fall on the people. So if we want to accomplish this objective [having the Dalai Lama leave for exile], we should think of a way wherein we will definitely win entirely and not suffer even a small loss. Consequently, it will be very difficult to plan such an action.

At present, people are under the correct leadership of the Dalai Lama and are united firmly and love and respect him more than ever. We are confident enough to stop the Communists' invasion, but I think the reason why we didn't openly protest is that our policy was based on the situation at that time. Under the slogan of mobilizing our people to endeavor to do the liberation ourselves, we will try to improve the livelihood of the people and enhance the people's trust in the [Tibetan] government and their cooperation with it. We will establish a stable relationship between the Dalai Lama and the Tibetan people, and on this foundation *we have a plan to organize the people and launch an overall protest* [all over Tibet]. . . . From the time when the Communist Chinese invaded Tibet until now, they were unable to spread their doctrine among the people, and at the same time they were unable to dominate the Tibetan people forcefully. And they could not sow seeds of dissent and hatred among the people. These were the reasons that they could not establish their power firmly.

But even though the Red Chinese met such a strong opposition, they were still determined to carrying out their plans in Tibet. Their evil hope of corrupting the people has advanced. The Chinese are using the Tibetan people, but because of the people's enthusiasm, the Chinese were working hard for their own collapse. They plan to establish a military-administrative committee office at an early date. The Red Chinese are facing great difficulties in controlling affairs (in Tibet), which so far have been firmly organized under the leadership of the Dalai Lama.

My view is that, after the establishment of the Military-Administrative Committee, there is no doubt that the committee will rob the political power of the Tibetan government and the rights of the Tibetan people. This office is under the direct command of the Central People's Government of China. The head of this office will be the Dalai Lama, and the committee's members will be fifty-fifty from the Chinese and Tibetan government. The office will carry out whatever orders are directed to it. Under these circumstances, the Government of Tibet will be taken over. Under this office, reforms will be forcefully carried out to convert Tibet to communism. The Dalai Lama will be only a figurehead, and the country's future will end completely and be in darkness.

This is the evil plan of the Red Chinese toward the Tibetan government and its people.

My personal inspiration is that I hope to request that the U.S. government establish a special research office to study the Tibetan case. Since there is a very strong will to fight the Red Chinese aggression in both Outer and Inner Tibet [Tibet proper and the Tibetan areas of Qinghai, Gansu, and Xikang], it would be appropriate to establish an organization that would fight from the border areas from all sides. Tibetans would be selected from those who are outside Tibet and given training in secret service activities so that they could then go into Tibet to let the people know about the opposition and encourage them to support it. If our effort progresses well, then we could organize a proper military command center. These are my hopes. If there is any chance of your government favoring this, I will then present my plans in detail and discuss them with you and will then put them into action. As mentioned above, such action would not only greatly help the Tibetan people but also help to prevent the Chinese from secretly infiltrating India, Nepal, and Bhutan. I would like to request your views on this.[9]

This gave Washington an excellent opening, but the United States did not pursue this, and there is no mention of any response from the State Department. Gyalo Thondup's failure to get the attention of the United States would soon change, but during his first years in India, Washington had no interest in Gyalo or Tibet.

Gyalo received a more positive response from Taiwan. He said that Chiang Kai-shek was willing to give him serious assistance, but the Guomindang insisted that this be framed as part of the Guomindang's effort to regain the mainland (with Tibet part of Guomindang China). Gyalo said that he would not accept their aid under those conditions.

General Chiang Kai-shek is very sympathetic and sending many emissaries to come and see me, and they are always offering whatever assistance, training, and help. They are willing to extend whatever possible. But then our argument is always based on requesting them to change their publicity, and they must recognize it is a spontaneous movement of the Tibetan population. It has nothing to do with the Guomindang's leadership or instigation for the Tibetans to fight the Chinese Communists [or] because the expectations of the return of the Chinese Nationalists to China. So these things we argued all these years. Since that is not agreed, this is more or less all delayed and not reaching any agreement with the Chinese Nationalists. I think that is the main argument between them and us. So that is why we never accepted any assistance from the Chinese Nationalists.[10]

The possibilities in India, however, soon began to improve. Gyalo Thondup had been trying for some time to arrange a meeting with Mullik, the head

9. Cited in Tibetan in Lha mo Tshe ring (Lhamo Tsering) 1992: 153–59 (emphasis added). Lhamo Tsering was Gyalo's aide-secretary.

10. Gyalo Thondup, interview, 1995, Hong Kong (in English, uncorrected).

of Indian intelligence, so when Mullik was making a trip to Darjeeling in 1953, he asked Nehru whether he should meet with Gyalo. Nehru agreed, instructing Mullik "to keep in touch with the Dalai Lama's brother and all the other Tibetan refugees and help them in every way possible."[11] This help, however, did not include assisting them in organizing resistance to the Chinese, as Nehru further explained, "Such contacts would also indirectly help us to *prevent any machinations by them from the Indian soil against the Chinese.*"[12] Nevertheless, this approval set in motion direct relations among Indian intelligence, Gyalo Thondup, and Shakabpa.

On the Tibetan exile side, however, it was not until 1954 that real progress was made in creating a resistance organization in India. An important catalyst for this was the announcement of a new Chinese-India agreement at the end of April in that year.

THE SINO-INDIAN TREATY ON TRADE AND TRANSPORTATION BETWEEN TIBET AND INDIA

At the time of the Seventeen-Point Agreement, India still maintained the special privileges in Tibet that it had inherited from the British, who had obtained them as a result of their invasion of Tibet in 1903–4. These included trade offices in several towns, such as Gyantse and Yadong, the right to maintain escort troops at the specified trade marts, trade advantages, and extraterritoriality. In addition, in 1937, the British opened a mission office in Lhasa, which the Indians inherited. In 1951, after the Seventeen-Point Agreement, these immediately became anachronisms, and in late 1952, negotiations between the Indian and Chinese governments began with the aim of restructuring India's long-established trade, pilgrimage, and diplomatic relations with Tibet in line with the new realities. The result of these talks was an important agreement on trade and communications between India and the Tibet Region of China that was signed on 29 April 1954. It was followed on the next day by an exchange of a formal note spelling out issues India and China did not want placed in the agreement.

Politically, the new agreement's language reinforced India's acceptance of Chinese sovereignty over Tibet. The agreement talked about the "Tibet Region of China," and it stated that it was based on "Five Principles of Peaceful Coexistence," namely, mutual respect for territorial integrity and sovereignty, mutual nonaggression, noninterference in each other's internal

11. Mullik 1971: 180. Craig (1997: 172) quotes Gyalo as saying that this occurred in October 1952 and that Mullik had told him, "[I was] free to do whatever I wanted. So from October 1952 onwards I was in constant contact with Indian intelligence, and Nehru simply turned a blind eye." However, I think he is incorrect about the date.

12. Mullik 1971: 180–81 (emphasis added).

affairs, equality and mutual benefits, and peaceful coexistence. Also, since Tibet was now an internal and integral part of China, all relations concerning Tibet would be handled by the Chinese government. India, therefore, agreed to engage no longer in direct relations with Tibet. In keeping with this, no Tibetan government officials were involved in the negotiations, and none were signatories to the agreement. A half-century of Indo-Tibetan direct relations was over.

The agreement (and note) abolished all the unequal benefits India held in Tibet. The Indian government was allowed to continue "trade agent" offices in three areas, but, reciprocally, China for the first time would set up equivalent trade offices in Delhi, Calcutta, and Kalimpong. At the same time, India agreed to transfer to China all of the Indian government's rest houses as well as all its postal, telegram, and telephone offices and equipment in Tibet (with the understanding that China would compensate India "at a reasonable price"). In Lhasa, the Indian government's Mission Office was changed to the Consulate General of the Indian Government and would deal only with the Chinese government's new Foreign Affairs Office, not the Tibetan (local) government. Reciprocally, China would establish a consulate in Bombay.[13]

Gyalo Thondup was shocked by the news of the treaty and India's formal renouncement of its direct relationship with Tibet. On 30 April 1954, the day the treaty was announced publicly, he immediately took a taxi to Kalimpong and met with Shakabpa and Khenjung Lobsang Gyentsen, a new Tibetan monk official who had recently arrived in India, so that they could discuss what to do.

Lobsang Gyentsen had been sent by the Tibetan government to assume the position of trade agent in Kalimpong.[14] He had been one of the original members of the anti-Chinese Namseling clique (discussed in chapter 12),[15] so soon after reaching India he went to see Gyalo Thondup and Shakabpa to urge them to use their experience in dealing with foreign countries to help publicize the Chinese takeover of Tibet and try to organize resistance.

The three men agreed that the new treaty was terrible for Tibet and decided to try to improve their relations with the Indian government in order to influence Indian policy. The next month, therefore, on 17 May, Gyalo invited the political officer in Sikkim to tea at his house together with Shakabpa and Lobsang Gyentsen, and the three conveyed their views on the Tibet situation. Following this, under the pretext of having picnics, the three

13. For the full agreement and note, see Union Research Institute 1968: 63–73.

14. Lobsang Gyentsen said, in an interview recorded in 1983 by the Library of Tibetan Works and Archives, in Dharamsala, that he came to India in 1953. This would probably have been at the very end of that year.

15. Rnam gling (Namseling) 1988: 70.

started meeting discreetly to develop a strategy for organizing opposition to the Chinese from Indian soil.[16] These three came to be known by the acronym: Jenkhentsisum (meaning the three: the older brother, the khen-jung, and the tsipön).

Interestingly, the Dalai Lama's reaction to the treaty was very different. He recalled that he didn't think it was very significant given the reality of what had already happened to Tibet over the past four years. "We had already finished the Seventeen-Point Agreement, and we couldn't say that we signed in duress and had to abide by it [we had to say we accepted it]. So the agreement between India and China was not so big a deal."[17] Nevertheless, in international legal terms, the new treaty was, in fact, very significant, in that the only country that had special treaty relations with Tibet now agreed to relinquish these and did so without consulting the Dalai Lama or the Tibetan government.

The new treaty obviously had serious implications for the Tibetans living in Kalimpong and Darjeeling, particularly with regard to whether the Indian government would now want to expel all Tibetans. The Government of India understood the sensitivity of the treaty and sent Mullik to Kalimpong-Darjeeling in 1954 to assess local reactions to it. Mullik recalled his trip as follows:

In May, 1954, I again visited the Darjeeling-Kalimpong-Gangtok area to assess the reactions amongst the local Indians and Sikkimese and refugee Tibetans to the Sino-Indian Agreement of 1954. I found the Tibetans shocked and anguished. They felt that they had been let down badly by India though they had reposed their trust in her. . . . Though bitter, the Tibetans saw India's difficulty also and sought for some assurances from India which could help to keep up their morale. They desired that the Tibetan refugees should be allowed to enter India freely and would not be surrendered to the Chinese on the latter's demand. Secondly, that the Tibetans should be allowed to transfer their money and valuable property to India for safe deposit and that these should be exempted from the provisions of currency, customs and income tax rules. Thirdly, that responsible Indian leaders should issue statements stressing that the cultural relations and ties between India and Tibet were eternal and would not change due to the Chinese occupation of the country. The fourth point was that India should openly criticise the Chinese violation of the 17-Point Agreement with Tibet. The fifth point was that the Dalai Lama's purchasing mission [trade office] in Kalimpong should exist as a separate entity and should be given a status equal to that of the Chinese Agent. The Tibetans were also anxious to maintain their opposition to the Chinese. They knew that they could not get any material help from India but they felt that even moral support would sustain them in their fight. . . .

On my return to Delhi, I reported these reactions to the Government. The

16. Lha mo Tshe ring (Lhamo Tsering) 1992: 165–66.
17. Dalai Lama, interview, 1995, Dharamsala.

Prime Minister sent for me a few days later. . . . The Prime Minister then said that the Tibetans hated the Chinese and would never submit to them. The very nature of the country rendered the inhabitants tough and hardy, and it would be impossible for the Chinese to colonise that country. But it would be unwise for the Tibetans to carry on any armed resistance which the Chinese would be able to put down swiftly, effectively and ruthlessly. The Prime Minister then instructed that the Tibetan refugees of all classes should be given an assurance that they would not be handed over to the Chinese even if the latter demanded their surrender. As regards the property of the refugees, the Prime Minster held the view that these could be exempted from the customs, currency and income tax rules and they should be allowed to bring in gold, silver and money freely just as many moneyed people of Nepal were doing. *Regarding the spirit of resistance in Tibet, the Prime Minister was of the view that even if these refugees helped their brethren inside Tibet, the Government of India would not take any notice and, unless they compromised themselves too openly, no Chinese protest would be entertained. He, however, suggested that the best form of resistance would be through nonviolence and struggle for the protection of Tibetan culture and regional autonomy and not by taking arms which would give the Chinese an excuse to use their military might to suppress the poor Tibetans.* He referred to our military weakness due to which it was not possible to give any military assistance to Tibet.[18]

In the end, therefore, the new Sino-Indian Agreement did not produce any negative changes for the Tibetans in India, and, in fact, it was from this time in 1954 that Nehru agreed to turn a blind eye to anti-Chinese activities so long as the Tibetans were discreet. Consequently, relations between Jenkhentsisum and Indian intelligence now actually began to expand into active cooperation and funding.

In the midst of all this, on 17 July 1954, one of the worst floods in Tibetan history occurred in Gyantse, a rich agricultural area (and town) in Tsang, south of Lhasa. More than 170 villages were submerged, over 16,000 people were injured, and over 690 people drowned. The Tibet Work Committee, the Tibetan government, and the Panchen's Administrative Council established an aid office to carry out relief efforts, and the State Council in Beijing initially allocated over 180,000 dayan to the flood victims and Chinese personnel stationed in the area. Other offices gave relief grain and rice and cloth, and various military personnel donated more than one hundred thousand yuan. On 13 October 1954, the Central Committee agreed to allocate an additional three million dayan to construct roads from Gyantse to Yadong and from Gyantse to Shigatse, and more than four thousand Tibetans obtained income by participating in the construction work.[19]

18. Mullik 1971: 181–83 (emphasis added).

19. Zhonggong xizang zizhiqu dangshi ziliao zhengji weiyuanhui 1995, entry for 17 July 1954.

In India, Jenkhentsisum learned of this only on 29 July, because the Chinese government initially did not release the news. They immediately started to organize Tibetans in India to provide relief to the flood victims but also saw this as a perfect opportunity to launch the political organization they had been planning. On 5 August, they met in Kalimpong and openly started the Tibet Relief Committee (tib. pögyob tshogpa), whose aim was to raise relief funds for the flood victims. At the same time, they covertly started the Association for the Welfare of Tibet (tib. pö dedön tshogpa), a political organization that was to work for Tibetan independence.[20]

The members of the political organization took an oath in front of various protector deities, swearing to serve the cause of the organization for as long as it might take. That document began with a long historical introduction, listing all sorts of Chinese oppressions, but its most important points are the following:

1. Till we accomplish our independence, we would sacrifice our lives and our wealth without ever retreating from difficulty and loss of moral. We would continue our effort year by year, even it takes a lifetime.

2. Effort should be made for the speedy return of His Holiness to the capital of Tibet. [The Dalai Lama was then en route to China.]

4. All discussions should be kept secret, and they should not be permitted to reveal to outsiders. Shall undertake to bear all penalties should anyone be seen, heard and proofed.

10. Our main political aim is that His Holiness would retain his leadership of the duel Government, all people in U, Tsang, Dokham, Amdo and Golok will have equal power in the administration of the country, which consists of education, health, improvement of people's living condition, freedom of speech, defense, freedom of various sects of religion. Whatever the best should be taken up. Such activities that hampers the progress should avoided so that the people may not be disappointed. We must ban all the activities of Communists and the atheists.[21]

The manifesto is interesting in that it specifically calls not just for Tibetan independence under the old Tibetan political system but for an independent Tibet that would include Greater Tibet, that is, all the ethnic Tibetan areas in Sichuan, Qinghai, Gansu, and Yunnan, with *all having equal power.*

---

20. Lha mo Tshe ring (Lhamo Tsering) 1992: 173.

21. Mimeograph copy in English. (The original Tibetan document is not available.) None of the mistakes in grammar and so forth have been altered. This document was given by the Shakabpa family to Paljor Tsarong for this history project. It is cited in full in appendix C. The English mimeograph copy says the oath was taken two and a half weeks earlier on 14 July 1954, but I think that Lhamo Tsering's dating is probably correct.

It is also interesting to consider that, although Gyalo Thondup was the Dalai Lama's brother, this organization was started without the Dalai Lama's knowledge and was not in accordance with his views. As we have seen, at this time in Lhasa, relations between the Chinese and the Tibetan governments were cordial, and it looked as if Tibet was moving forward to carve itself a niche within the People's Republic of China. The resistance movement in India, modest though it was at this time, was interested in precisely the opposite—in driving the Chinese out of Tibet, not compromising and adapting to Chinese communism.

Shakabpa took this opportunity to contact the U.S. Consulate in Calcutta, urging them to provide flood relief for Tibet. He thought a U.S. offer of assistance would be good propaganda against the Communists, for Chinese acceptance of the aid would indicate they did not have the means to handle the disaster, and their refusal of it would show their intransigence.[22] The consul general recommended that the United States not respond to the Tibet Relief Committee's appeal, as did the U.S. Embassy in Delhi. The State Department ultimately agreed, arguing internally that the Chinese had twice rejected the International Red Cross's offer on the grounds that they were able to handle the situation themselves. The Chinese government also refused to accept any aid from the Tibet Relief Committee.

The new freedom to operate in India led to a big demonstration in Kalimpong a few months later, on 4 October 1954, when the Association for the Welfare of Tibet organized a ceremony to offer prayers for the safe return of the Dalai Lama from China. Over four thousand Tibetans met and, for the first time in India, publicly carried Tibetan flags.[23]

For Jenkhentsisum, however, it was the Government of India, not America, that was the main focus of its activities at this time. Jenkhentsisum's connections with the Indian government had developed substantially in 1954, which is illustrated in the following excerpt from a letter Shakabpa sent to the Government of India in late 1954 or early 1955:

> In short, the Chinese are torturing the Tibetan people like hell on earth. Therefore, all the monasteries led by the three great monasteries, Sera, Drepung, and Ganden, the thoughtful lay and monk government officials, and the people place their hope in us from the bottom of their hearts. And they are sending messages and letters requesting us to request the Indian government, and so on, to help us through whatever means are appropriate, military or peaceful, so that we can stand up from where we have fallen down. However, if the Indian government does not consider this, it [our work] will become like clapping with a single hand, and we will not be able to do anything and will have to remain quiet.

22. U.S. National Archives, American Consulate, Calcutta, dispatch no. 100, 20 August 1954.

23. Lha mo Tshe ring (Lhamo Tsering) 1992: 176–77.

Recently, the officials of the Indian Intelligence Bureau, such as Mr. Bose and B. Mullik, told us several times that Tibet should try to regain its freedom through peaceful means, and the Indian government also will support whatever is appropriate, whether military or peaceful.

Because the Indian government has good relations with the Chinese government, we were suspicious that if we made even a slight political move, all of us might get expelled from Indian territory, so therefore we didn't have any plan to do any kind of work. However, because Mr. Bose and Deputy Director Mr. Majumdar said this to us frequently, and furthermore, because we were told through the director in Delhi that the recent work that was done was in accordance with the ideas of Prime Minister Nehru, all of us have deep trust [for the Government of India] from the bottom of our hearts.

Since Tibet and China are completely incompatible in nationality, language, culture, religion, and ideology, we set up communications through messengers in order to make friendly relations with important people in Tibet. They go back and forth seven or eight times a month. . . . And we are trying our best through internal and external methods to gather all the Tibetans into one association. Gradually, we will make a big Tibetan association and try to help Tibet.

In order to mentally win over Tibetans to us, we will ask for donations for the victims of the flood damage in Gyantse and help Tibet with food and clothing. We have condemned the Chinese, and we will try to distribute a Tibetan-language newspaper to advise the Tibetan people. In order to revive Tibetan Buddhism if it comes to be damaged, we will set up a library on religion and history and a school for teaching Tibetan. All Tibetans, regardless of whether they are monks or laymen, will send telegrams and appeals to the Dalai Lama telling him to return to Tibet [from his trip to China] as soon as possible.

In order to know the news in Tibet quickly, we have set up a training program for the secret wireless equipment [tib. sangwe lungdrin] [from the Government of India]. Until now, we have done many activities. *In the future, we will try our best to regain Tibet's freedom through peaceful means, but ultimately [if this isn't successful] we will try to gain Tibet's freedom through military means. We have no other choice but to try ceaselessly and right to the end to gain complete independence (tib. rangtsen tsangma).*

This was followed by the heart of the letter, a list of specific requests for military and peaceful aid, which reveals just how far Jenkhentsisum's relationship with the Indian government's intelligence branch had developed over the past year.

We seek your support for the following points:

1. If the policy in Tibet changes, and if they [the Chinese] make changes concerning the power and work of the Dalai Lama, and if matters are decided by the people in between, and if they obstruct Buddhism, and if all of these occur either directly or indirectly, the people inside Tibet will consider this as their own cause and make a move [to do something]. At that time, we request that the Indian government publicize this all over the world and report it to the U.N.

2. Tashilhunpo Labrang [the Panchen Lama's government] and the Chinese are the same, like the proverb "Dogs and wolves have the same face."[24] So if they incite people such as Pomda Tobgye and Derge sey to make Ü, Tsang, and Kham separate and create civil war, how much help would the Indian government give us?[25]

3. As mentioned above, Kalimpong is a very important border area between India and Tibet, so we are trying to take action among the people and the monasteries in order to avoid any communist influence in this area. Therefore, we request the Indian officials, spies, and police officers to be unified and hold inner talks with us and consider methods to improve the situation.

4. We have already recruited people to study how to use wireless machines, and still there are some students who will gradually come from Tibet [for this]. So please sell us fifteen to twenty sets of simple and good-quality wireless equipment that is easy to operate and can use batteries.

5. We thank you for telling us that the Indian government will pay the wages of the wireless teachers and the rent [of the training place]. Please lend us monthly expenses of four thousand rupees on time. In the future, when Tibet again has its freedom, we will pay you the principal with interest.

6. As we requested before, please arrange training in the use of explosives, and for the time being sell us the equipment to blow up the Chinese weapons, and the places where they keep their supplies, and their roads and bridges.

7. So we will be reassured, please make an agreement in advance to help us with the expenses we will need when our work gets enlarged and, in the future, when we need military support. As mentioned above, we will pay the money back when Tibet gains its independence.

8. As we requested before, if the Red Chinese try forcibly to take the Tibetan government's gold and silver that is in Gangtok [Sikkim], we will never hand it over to the Chinese. We will transfer it to an appropriate Indian bank. So we request that you help us internally to get the gold and silver transferred.

9. We request that the Indian government agree not to stop private individuals when they bring their gold and silver, coins and valuable things, and relics to India and not to impose taxes on them.

10. Because the price of [Tibetan] food is high, many Tibetans are coming to India. We request that the Indian police and the passport office not stop them or cause them hindrances. When they come to India for road building, many of them get sick and die during the hot weather season. We can't bear this responsibility, so we request that the Indian government give them appropriate land, where they can farm and stay legally. We also request support by providing seed and money [for them].

11. As for the Tibetan schools and the library set up in Kalimpong, we re-

---

24. In Tibetan, khijang kharis jiggyur.
25. Pomda Tobgye and Derge sey were well-known Tibetan leaders in Kham who were working with the Chinese.

quest that the Indian government give us annual support so that these can develop and not decline.[26]

Indian intelligence agreed to most of these items but not to the training in explosives.

On 18 August 1955, Jenkhentsisum met and took the next step, deciding that it was time to establish a base in Tibet. Khenjung Lobsang Gyentsen was delegated to send secret agents to Lhasa and generally to be in charge of relations with Tibet.[27] By late 1955, India was regularly providing funds to Jenkhentsisum and working with them to create a secret identity card so that their people coming from Tibet would not be stopped at the border.[28]

At the same time that this anti-Chinese resistance organization was developing in India, a major political event occurred within Tibet—an invitation from the Central Committee for the Dalai Lama to visit China. This is the subject of the next chapter.

26. Unsigned and undated handwritten note in Tibetan in Shakabpa's handwriting (emphasis added). Given by the Shakabpa family for this project. (Dating was done from events mentioned in the letter.)

27. Lha mo Tshe ring (Lhamo Tsering) 1992: 184.

28. Shakabpa's diary (Tibetan ms.), book 1. (This document was given to Paljor Tsarong by the Shakabpa family for this history project.)

Chapter 19

The Dalai Lama Goes to Beijing

AN INVITATION

In the spring of 1954, the Central Committee set September as the date for the inaugural meeting of the National People's Congress. This was a milestone event in the history of the PRC, because the new National People's Congress would be adopting the PRC's first constitution and electing the leaders of the nation. The central government, therefore, decided to invite the Dalai and Panchen lamas to Beijing to participate, setting the stage for one of the most dramatic moments of the 1950s. With things going well in Tibet, this was to be China's first chance to gain direct access to the Dalai Lama and influence his attitudes and thinking.

At the start of June, a telegram signed by Deng Xiaoping informed the Tibet Work Committee about this decision and urged them to "strive to secure the attendance of the Dalai Lama and Panchen Lama."[1] In Lhasa, it was decided that Zhang Jingwu would consult with the Dalai Lama and the Tibetan government, while Liang Xiangxian, the head of the Tibet Work Committee's branch office in Shigatse, would inform the Panchen Lama.[2] The Panchen Lama quickly accepted the invitation, but the issue of whether the Dalai Lama should go precipitated a heated debate among his officials over the potential advantages and dangers.

The Kashag and the Dalai Lama's influential junior tutor, Trijang Rimpoche, felt that it was better for him to go, but many in the Tibetan elite objected, including the Ecclesiastic Office (Yigtsang), the abbots of Sera, Drepung, and Ganden monasteries, and the Dalai Lama's senior tutor, Ling

---

1. Li 1996: 3.
2. Li 1996: 4.

Rimpoche. Lobsang Samden, the Dalai Lama's brother and jigyab khembo, was also not enthusiastic. In the face of this lack of consensus, the Kashag convened the Assembly to discuss the invitation. Kundeling Dzasa, a participant, recalled the positions of the two sides at the meeting.

> Some were saying that it is possible that His Holiness might not be able to return, that they [the Chinese] might give him a grand title and insist that he stay there. . . . Yes, and if it should happen like that, then we will not be able to accept this. Others were saying that if His Holiness went down and met face to face with them [Chinese leaders] and if they made harsh statements, His Holiness would have to be meek, and then we would be at a loss. So instead of that, it is better for him to stay and talk from here. Then there were comments that if His Holiness went to attend the "National People's Congress," just by attending a Chinese national meeting as a people's representative, the status of the Dalai Lama would be degraded. So there was a lot of talk like that.[3]

Another important concern that Kundeling did not mention was the fear that a long visit with exposure to new things in Beijing might influence the Dalai Lama's attitudes and views in ways conservatives and traditionalists would not favor. As was discussed earlier, controlling what the Dalai Lama saw and experienced was an implicit part of the Tibetan political system.

However, Kundeling also recalled that others felt strongly that the Dalai Lama should go.

> Then there were those who said that [the Dalai Lama] should go. He should attend and participate in the discussions, listen to what they say, and tell them what we think. And he should take a look here and there. It was not only us, but many other leaders who were coming, and so it would be good to meet and get to know them and hold discussions with them. They thought that this is what we should do rather than stay in a corner and think that we are so great. We can't deal with them [the Chinese] like that.[4]

In the end, although a strong majority in the Assembly felt that the Dalai Lama should not visit China, the stakes were too high for the Kashag to quietly accept that view as final. Zhang Jingwu had been telling the Kashag and Ngabö that this was an extraordinary event in China's history, and it was extremely important for the Dalai Lama to attend and meet the top leaders of China. This made so much sense that the Kashag summoned all the Assembly's delegates and tried to persuade them to change their position. When this failed, the Kashag reported the impasse to the Dalai Lama.

Unlike the most of the religious establishment, the Dalai Lama was personally in favor of going, although he understood the fears of those against

3. Kundeling, interview, 1992, Dehra Dun, India.
4. Kundeling, interview, 1992.

the trip. He explained, in English, "As a young person, of course, [I was] always eager to see new places. [It was] more sort of a modern thing. But then the Three Monastic Seats at our Assembly [were] very very critical about the possibility of my visit to China, and also I think many senior Tibetan officials were very very concerned about it. On one side Ngabö and a few others feel very strongly I should go to China, I should take this opportunity."[5]

Kundeling also recalled that the Dalai Lama said, "When we first discussed things with the Chinese, they said that they were going to assist us greatly in the development of Tibet; however, at this moment we are just talking with some of the Chinese leaders in Tibet, and we have not met face to face with the people who shoulder the main responsibility, like the main leader Mao Zedong, so I think it's better to go than to stay."[6]

However, when neither side was willing to change its view and the Dalai Lama was unwilling to decide himself, the Tibetan government again turned to the gods for guidance and held a divine lottery (tib. senril) in Norbulingka before the deity Yeshe Gompo. It replied in favor of going to China, so on 10 June 1954 the Tibetan government informed the Tibet Work Committee that the Dalai Lama would go to Beijing but not without a number of conditions, meant to assuage the fears of those opposed to the trip. Chinese sources describe these as follows:

> At 5:00 P.M., many gaily dressed Tibetans came to the front of the Tibet Work Committee. They included of all the Kashag ministers, the trunyichemmo, the tsipön, the present and past abbots of the Three Monastic Seats, and the representatives of all the monk and lay government official ranks. They came here specially to notify Zhang Jingwu of the Dalai Lama's agreement to attend the National People's Congress. . . .
>
> After everyone sat down, [Minister] Surkhang spoke first. He said he represents all the monk and lay officials from the Kashag, the Ecclesiastic Office, and the Three Monastic Seats and wants to convey that they agree to the Dalai Lama's going to Beijing and have come to formally notify Representative Zhang of this.
>
> After Surkhang finished speaking, Zhang Jingwu warmly welcomed the news of the Dalai Lama's going to Beijing and expressed his appreciation for the support of all the officials. Zhang Jingwu also asked them to relax and not worry, because the central government has prepared everything for the [Dalai Lama's] accommodations, transportation, and health, and so forth.
>
> Then Zhang Jingwu noticed that the representatives were looking at one another, and it seemed as if they had something on their minds. Therefore, Zhang Jingwu said, "Please tell me whatever is on your mind. Do not be shy and think too much." In accordance with this, Surkhang said that he had three requests to make to Representative Zhang that they definitely want to be granted. . . .

5. Dalai Lama, interview, 1995, Dharamsala.
6. Kundeling, interview, 1992.

"The first request is to ask the Central Committee and Representative Zhang to guarantee absolutely the safety of the Dalai Lama."

When Zhang Jingwu heard this, he had no problem, because both the central government and all the local governments [en route] took the issue of Dalai Lama's safety as their first priority and had made very careful arrangements. So he said, "You can relax completely about this point. The Dalai Lama and Panchen Erdini are going . . . as honored guests invited by Chairman Mao and the Central People's Government. Not only are you concerned about the safety of Dalai Lama, but so too is the Central People's Government, which has paid much attention to it. The Central People's Government has sent telegrams to all the local governments and military regions along the trip [route], arranging preparations for the Dalai Lama's stay in these areas and particularly emphasizing the safety of Dalai Lama and Panchen Erdini. Just relax [about this]."

After this explanation, all the representatives were relieved and nodded their heads. . . . Then Ta Lama [the senior head of the Ecclesiastic Office] made the second request, namely, that it would be best if the period of the Dalai Lama's stay in Beijing would be less than ten months; and it must not be longer than one year.

Zhang Jingwu had no problem promising that the Dalai Lama would come back within one year. [However] Zhang Jingwu said, "I may promise that the Dalai will come back within one year, but as everyone knows, it is such a long distance from Lhasa to Beijing and transportation is still not that convenient, so who can predict what might happen during the trip? We cannot control all the factors such as the weather, transportation, and the health of Dalai Lama. What can we do if they are late by a couple of days? What are you going to do if they are late by a couple of days?!" . . .

An abbot responded, "Representative Zhang, this is our hope. If Representative Zhang promises this, only then will it be easy for us to go back and persuade the others. Certainly the situation will change if they really meet unexpected troubles and difficulties that they cannot overcome. We are just afraid that the Dalai Lama will stay in Beijing and inland China too long and will not come back. That would cause all kinds of doubts and worries among the monks and the Tibetan people, and it would not benefit the work of both Tibet and the Central Committee."

When Zhang Jingwu listened to their comments, he was thinking and calculating in his mind . . . [that] it was certain that the Dalai Lama could return to Lhasa within one year, so he said, "Okay, I promise that Dalai Lama will return to Lhasa within one year. As the representative of the Central Committee, my word is good. You should trust me." . . .

"Good, good," all the representatives said and were very happy and smiled.

"So what is your last request?" Zhang Jingwu asked.

Surkhang then said, "There are certain customs regarding the food and drink of the Dalai Lama. We hope he can still be taken care of according to Tibetan customs while in inland China."

[Zhang replied] "This is no problem. Since long ago the Central Committee has prepared for the Dalai Lama to live in inland China in accordance with his own life habits. The Central Committee asked me and other people to accompany the Dalai Lama and Panchen Erdini to Beijing so that we could take special care of them with regard to their life style and so on. Everyone, please be relaxed."

All the representatives nodded and said thanks. However, it seemed they still had something on their minds. Zhang Jingwu said, "Just be frank; don't have any worries."

With this encouragement from Zhang Jingwu, they said, "We request that the Dalai Lama should not take an airplane to Beijing this time."

"Why is this?"

"The airplane is neither linked to the heavens, nor does it touch the earth. It is very dangerous. In case of emergency, we cannot risk it."

. . . Zhang Jingwu laughed, "Has anyone taken an airplane before?"

All the representatives looked at one another again and shook their heads at Zhang Jingwu, saying, "No, we have not tried it before."

"How do you know it is unsafe if you have never taken an airplane?" Zhang Jingwu said mildly. "The airplane is the fastest, most convenient, and safest modern transportation tool. It takes less than one hour [to travel] several hundred li by airplane. A moment ago every one of you said that the Dalai Lama must come back within one year, but then you do not want him to take an airplane. This request is kind of unreasonable. If the Dalai Lama is going to take an airplane, I will take the same plane, so the safety of Dalai Lama is guaranteed with my life. You do not have to have any worries. On the other hand, after the Dalai Lama goes to inland China, if he really wants to take an airplane, how could you and I stop him? Among all of you, who can tell Dalai what to do and what not to do?"

However, all the representatives still insisted that Zhang Jingwu should pass on the message to the Central Committee about not letting the Dalai Lama take an airplane.

The two sides had come to a deadlock, so Zhang Jingwu answered with flexibility, "Let us come to the solution that at present I promise as you wish. After Dalai Lama goes to inland China, we will make the decision according to Dalai's opinion and the specific circumstances. Is this okay?"

What's done cannot be undone. Zhang Jingwu made the promise to the general requests, so all the representatives were satisfied and thanked him.[7]

The invitation to the Dalai Lama had another important consequence; it led to a revival of the People's Association. Alo Chöndze, one of its new leaders, recalled how he and others were deeply opposed to the Dalai Lama going to China and how the "people" began to get involved in politics again.

We in the People's Association had connections with Phala [the Dalai Lama's lord chamberlain], who said to us that the Dalai Lama is going to the National

7. Li 1996: 21.

People's Congress meeting. He has agreed to this. So you in the People's Association should try to stop this if you can. He said this [to us] secretly.[8]

Q: How did you meet Phala?

I had a personal relationship with him. He invited me to parties and I played majong with him.

A few days after this, we in the People's Association took a ceremonial scarf and went to Phala to request that he ask the Dalai Lama on behalf of all the Tibetan people not to go to China. Several representatives went to the Dalai Lama's secretariat office (tib. Tse ga) to see Phala. . . . There was no written letter; it was oral. We gave a ceremonial scarf and shog ja [money wrapped in a traditional paper-folded sheath]. . . . Phala told us he would give us an answer in a few days.

After a few days had passed, I went to see if there was an answer, and Phala told me that the Dalai Lama said that his visit to China is finalized and that he has to go for the benefit of fostering good Sino-Tibetan relations. So we left and again called a meeting, at which we decided to offer a Long Life Ritual (tib. denshu shabten) for the Dalai Lama.

Then we went to Ngabö.[9] He was on the Communist's side, but we thought he spoke truthfully. So three or four representatives went to him. . . . We told Ngabö to tell the Chinese not to take the Dalai Lama to China to attend the meeting. Ngabö responded, "The Dalai Lama's going to China is his own decision, not that of the Chinese, and the trip is already settled, so you, the People's Association, can have a Long Life Ritual, but the trip is finalized in accordance with the Dalai Lama's own wish."

The Long Life Ritual was done in Norbulingka. First there were prayers [by monks], and then we gave scarves [and a mendredensum] to the Dalai Lama, then gifts. Many people were there; lamas, monks, aristocrats, and People's Association members. The expenses for this were all from patrons in the People's Association. . . .

Before the ritual we had a meeting, and the Khambas within the People's Association said that we should prostrate at the Long Life Ritual and then yell, "Dalai Lama, please do not go to China." However, if we did this, we would be doing an illegal petition (tib. dongshu), and that was a very serious thing to do. The Khambas didn't understand the [Tibetan] government's customs, so others explained about this, and they didn't do it.[10]

8. The Dalai Lama, however, recalled that Phala was in favor of his going and said that he did not think Phala would tell him to go and then tell Alo Chöndze to try to block this. He said, "To tell me one thing and the mimang (the people) something else, probably he wouldn't say. But actually he is very capable [clever], and he is capable of doing some yugyu (trickiness), but to Dalai Lama to say like this, I don't think so" (interview, 2004, Dharamsala, English uncorrected). On the other hand, Phala, who was anti-Chinese, may simply have been trying to use this to stir up new opposition to the Chinese among the people.

9. In his book, Alo Chöndze says that Phala told him to go to the Kashag to try to stop the Dalai Lama's trip, so therefore they went to Ngabö (A lo chos mdzad [Alo Chöndze] 1983: 420–21).

10. *Dongshu* literally means an "appeal to the face" and refers to the custom of making a direct appeal to the Dalai Lama without first going through his lord chamberlain. It was done by

All the members of the People's Association in Lhasa attended the Long Life Ritual ceremony, at which the Dalai Lama said, "My going to this meeting in China is very important, because it is very important to have good relations with China. This was decided by divination. . . . Today the People's Association has given me a Long Life Ritual, and that is very good. You people are worried about me, and I can't blame you for that. I am going to China, but I will definitely return after no more than one year. Up to now you have done things carefully, and while I am gone you should not cause trouble." So he promised not too stay for more than one year (at most).[11]

The Chinese side was not pleased with this emergence of the new People's Association, which they thought had been permanently disbanded in 1952. Although it was still in a nascent form, they describe its reappearance as follows:

The Fake People's meeting organized the so-called Long Life Ritual gift-presenting conspiracy activity. After the announcement of the Dalai Lama's planned trip to Beijing to attend the first National People's Congress, Alo Chöndze and Ananla, and so on, and elements of the Fake People's meeting directed the Shigatse and Gyantse reactionary organizations and persistently attacked and slandered us in the name of offering the Dalai Lama a Long Life Ritual. In Lhasa these people, in the name of offering the Dalai gifts, instigated lamas [monks] of the three great monasteries to send a petition to the Dalai to try and stop him from going to Beijing.[12]

In the end, though, the Dalai Lama and the Kashag prevailed, and the Dalai Lama made his first visit to Beijing in the summer of 1954.

THE DALAI LAMA DEPARTS

For the people of Lhasa, the Dalai Lama's departure from Lhasa was an emotional time. One Tibetan government official recalled the atmosphere in the city that day.

When His Holiness was actually leaving for China, he went from the gate of the Norbulingka to Shöl, and then to Lhasa, and finally all the way to Kumbumthang,[13] where the journey was made in coracles (yak-skin boats) [across the Kyichu (Lhasa) River]. So the distance was great, from Norbulingka all the

---

someone coming forth while the Dalai Lama was in a procession or at a ritual and, without permission, prostrating before him and making an appeal. This was one way to get a case heard by him, but there was a heavy price to pay, since it was punished by one hundred lashes.

11. Alo Chöndze, interview, 1993, Cleveland, OH.

12. Zhonggong xizang zizhiqu dangshi ziliao zheng ji weiyuanhui 1990, entry for July 1954.

13. The actual boat site was called Lhadong shenka. Kumbumthang was the plain just before it.

way down [to the river, and people] were just sprawled out along the route, seeking [a visual] audience with the Dalai Lama. Everyone was prostrating, and then running farther down the line for a second [visual] audience, and then [getting up] again and going still farther along. From the gates of Norbulingka, people were spread out all along the route until finally, when he entered the boat, the [people] were like a huge forest; a sea of people were on this side of the river. One could not even see the white earth, since the riverbank was so full of people. The number of people who were crying was limitless.

When His Holiness's procession passed by, it was not like here [in India]. Then there were bodyguards who would whip people, and so there was a lot of apprehension. The older women were fainting and calling out, "Gyawa Rimpoche [Your Holiness]! Please don't stay for more than a year. Please come back immediately!" [Gyawa Rimpoche! Lo chik le mashu ro nang. Namgyang pheronang!] So even though it was dangerous to their lives, they were endlessly shouting their request. . . .

When [the Dalai Lama] reached the other shore, all the people on this side were in tears. Some elderly women fainted, and it was said that they had to be carried away. It was said that one even died, but I did not see it. So when His Holiness went down to China, the people just couldn't restrain themselves. They thought only that the Chinese would do something bad. No matter how good the Chinese said that they were going to act, in the minds of the Tibetan people there was not an inkling of hope that the Chinese would do something good.[14]

Another Tibetan official recalled similarly,

In the minds of the Lhasa people there was the worry that the Chinese may not do good things [to the Dalai Lama]. That was everybody's concern. A lot of people cried. . . . Radö Rimpoche and myself were there. Both the tutors [of the Dalai Lama] were there, and so I crossed over to the other side [of the river] to help the Dalai Lama. . . . Some of the older women were shouting, "Please don't go, its no good," and so forth, and among the people there was a lot of shouting. So everybody was concerned and thought that His Holiness should really not go and that "he" [the Chinese] might do something [to the Dalai Lama].[15]

The Dalai Lama himself said of that day, "When I was leaving Lhasa so many were crying. So many. I remember very clearly that at that time there was no bridge over the Kyichu River. . . . When we were crossing the river in coracles, on the side, on the rocks, there were so many people crying, and some it seemed might have even jumped into the water."[16]

The fact that both the Panchen Lama and the Dalai Lama were going to be in China together brought to the surface all of the difficult issues regarding how each side looked at its relative status and authority. This meant deci-

14. Drakten, interview, 1992, Dharamsala.
15. Radö Chantsö, interview, 1992, Dharamsala.
16. Dalai Lama, interview, 1995.

sions had to be made about their positions and then reflected correctly in the protocol arrangements. For the first part of the trip this would not be too complicated, since the Panchen Lama and his entourage were to travel separately up to Xi'an. The Dalai Lama (accompanied by Zhang Jingwu) left Lhasa on 15 July using the southwest route, while the Panchen Lama set out for Beijing the next day, accompanied by Fan Ming, using the northwest [the Qinghai] route.[17] However, for the last leg of the journey, the Central Committee insisted that all parts of the Tibet delegation travel together, so showing relative status was important.

The chance to start a new page in Panchen-Dalai relations had been lost in the fiasco of the 1952 ceremonial meeting in Lhasa, and, as we saw, the enmity of the Panchen Lama's officials at that time was great. The Dalai Lama said he noticed that the demeanor of the Panchen Lama in 1954 had become less friendly and more competitive.

> At the time [when] we were to go to China, the two of us met at Norbulingka. . . . When the Panchen Lama came to Lhasa, his attitude had changed somewhat, and now he had quite a bit of a sense of competition. Some people noticed that. We met briefly at Lhasa, and then he went via the northern route. We met at Xi'an, and when we first met there, he shook my hands in the Western style. My lord chamberlain [Phala] and my attendants said, "Oh, that was very strange" [Dalai Lama laughs]. . . . So such an impression was felt.[18]

The Central Committee, however, as indicted in a previous chapter, had already decided that the Dalai Lama was superior in status and authority, which meant he had to be treated as higher than the Panchen Lama in all aspects of etiquette on this trip. Phünwang, who was then in Beijing, recalled the importance of this issue.

> This would be the Dalai Lama's first visit to China, so the central government was extremely concerned that it go perfectly and that it would play a great role in winning over the Dalai Lama. But because the Panchen Lama was also coming, the entire issue of the autonomy of the Panchen Lama and so forth had to be dealt with. Since the recent decision of the Panmunjom meeting in Beijing [in February 1954] on this had ended with the central government's decision that the Dalai Lama was to be considered as the main one and the Panchen as the secondary one, it was decided that this opportunity would be used to demonstrate this clearly in action so that all officials in Tibet and China would see for themselves and help resolve the contradiction between the Northwest and Southwest bureau officials.[19]

17. Zhonggong xizang zizhiqu dangshi ziliao zheng ji weiyuanhui 1990, entry for July 1954.
18. Dalai Lama, interview, 1993, Dharamsala.
19. Craig (1997: 177–78) incorrectly wrote that since the Dalai and Panchen lamas were both going to Beijing, "the Chinese lost no opportunity of showing that the two most important Lamas of Tibet were equal in status." It was, of course, just the opposite.

Beijing carefully prepared each aspect of the visit. A document called the Solution of Reception (ch. jie dai zhang cheng) was drafted by Li Weihan, the minister of both the Nationalities Affairs Commission and the United Front Work Department, and approved by Mao. It stated that the Dalai and Panchen's reception was an important political event, and each component of their reception must follow this "Solution." It was also stated that wherever they went and whatever activities they participated in, the Dalai should be treated as chief (ch. zheng), and the Panchen should be treated as deputy chief (ch. fu).[20]

In fact, on 2 August, while the two lamas were en route, the Central Committee sent instructions to all provinces clearly laying out the background for the different statuses. This telegram urged officials to do what they could to improve relations between the two but also specified without qualification that the Dalai Lama was to be considered number one, and the Panchen Lama, number two.

Arrangements for Dalai and Panchen's Visit and Related Propaganda Work

The Dalai and Panchen are coming to Beijing to attend the National People's Congress. This is a sign that Tibet is getting closer to the motherland and the Central Committee; it has important political meaning. However, the gap between Han Chinese and Tibetans is very deep, because imperialists and the Guomindang are still trying to worsen the relationship between Tibet and the central government (one of their measures is to spread rumors that the central government supports the Panchen and oppresses the Dalai in an attempt to replace the Dalai with the Panchen). The Dalai and Panchen groups do not like each other, and both suspect that the central government secretly supports the other group. We need to be extremely careful when dealing with questions of the Dalai and Panchen. Try to work out appropriate ways to avoid irritating either of them or arousing the suspicions of one of them. Try to encourage harmony between them.

The Dalai and Panchen are two religious leaders of Tibetans. They enjoy very high prestige and popular influence among Tibetans. In history, they were teachers of each other. But their positions are different in Tibet. The Dalai's religious influence is greater than the Panchen's. The Dalai is number one, and the Panchen is number two. More important, in the whole of Tibet, the Panchen controls only a small part in Back Tibet, about 10 percent of the population. The Dalai controls Front Tibet, all of Ali, and most parts of Back Tibet, about 90 percent of the population. The Kashag is under the leadership of Dalai, and for a long time, it served as the ruling institution of Tibet. In other words, it is the Tibetan local government. It once controlled Tibet's military and diplomatic power and represented the whole of Tibet. This means that the Dalai and the Dalai's group occupy the leading position in Tibet.

As a result of the split between the 13th Dalai and 9th Panchen, both sides

20. Phünwang, interview, 1999, Beijing.

Figure 22. Left to right: Panchen Lama, Lia Hanshan, Fan Ming, May 1954, Xi'an. Source: Fan Ming

have deep hatred toward each other. Because of the Panchen's special posi-tion in religion, the Panchen's Administrative Council became the adminis-trative institution in areas controlled by the Panchen. Up to now, the Panchen's group has not recognized the Dalai's leading position. They try to increase their own power all the time and try to be equal with the Dalai. The Dalai's group does not want to recognize the power that the Panchen deserves and emphasizes that there can be only one leader in Tibet; the Dalai is the only leader, and only the Dalai can represent Tibet. *The policy of the Central Committee is to move Tibet to be a unified autonomous region under the principle that the Dalai is number one and the Panchen is number two.* It is to unite the patriotic forces of the Dalai's and Panchen's sides, as well as any other patriotic forces in Tibet, to build a unified Tibetan autonomous region. To realize the goal, we need to go through many years of complex and difficult work. We have already done something during the past few years, but there are severe difficulties, one of them being that both sides are suspicious about the central government.

Because of the above situation, while the Dalai and Panchen are in Beijing attending the National People's Congress, all institutions of the Central Committee, local party committees, and the local governments should follow the regulations below in arranging welcome meetings, entertainment, meetings with leaders, and news reporting.

Regulations omitted.

Central Committee
2 August 1954[21]

Phünwang saw the above instructions (and regulations) and said of them,

The two sides' response to the document revealed their different views. Zhang Jingwu responded that the solution [to treat the Dalai Lama as superior] was completely correct and in accordance with the situation in Tibet. He said he would follow the guidelines one hundred percent. Fan Ming's reply was more equivocal. His telegram said some comrades like Liang Xiangxian (the head of the Shigatse branch of the Tibet Work Committee and the secretary to the Panchen Lama) disagreed with the decision. I got to see these telegrams because I was working in the State Nationalities Affairs Commission in Beijing. I immediately knew it was really Fan Ming who disagreed because Liang Xiangxian was from the Northwest Bureau and would do whatever Fan Ming told him. I told Liu Geping and other leaders my opinion about Fan's telegram, and they agreed but said it didn't matter because Mao himself had authorized these guidelines. So we prepared the reception exactly according to the reception document.[22]

Phünwang further recalled that everything, even the size of the beds, was made different for the two lamas.

So important was this visit that every aspect of the arrangements was monitored carefully by top leaders. For example, both Xi Zhongxun and Deng Xiaoping personally came to inspect the arrangements for the two lamas' residences. Xi was from the Northwest Bureau and was close to the Panchen Lama's group.

---

21. Dui xizang gongzuo de zhongyao zhishi (wei chuban de shouji), n.d. (emphasis added). The actual regulations are not available.
22. Goldstein, Sherap, and Siebenschuh 2004: 187–88.

He shook his head when he saw the different level of arrangements for the Panchen Lama but did not say anything. On the other hand, Deng Xiaoping— from the Southwest Bureau—praised us and said everything had been arranged perfectly.[23]

As the time approached for the Dalai and Panchen lamas to arrive in Beijing, a disagreement arose regarding who should receive them at the train station, which is illustrative of how carefully all aspects of this trip were planned. Phünwang explained,

> Within the State Nationalities Affairs Commission, three of us were responsible for handling the reception [of the Tibetans]: Zhao Fan (personal secretary to Li Weihan, the Commission's director), Peng Sika, a Mongol who was vice director of the General Office of the Nationalities Affairs Commission, and me. We were informed that the higher authorities had decided that Zhou Enlai would receive them. I was unhappy with that plan and said in our subcommittee that this was not appropriate. When Ngabö came to Beijing in 1951 for the Seventeen Point Agreement negotiations, Zhou Enlai went to receive him, but in Tibetan society, Ngabö was only a council minister and was subordinate to the Dalai Lama. So if only Zhou Enlai now came to receive the Dalai Lama it would appear to Tibetan officials (who were highly attuned to etiquette) to be showing a lack of proper respect to the Dalai Lama. We all agreed and Zhao Fan reported this to our superior, Li Weihan. Li responded that Premier Zhou Enlai was the top leader in the State Council and was also one of the most senior figures in the party. If Zhou received the lamas, he said, it would be perfectly acceptable. But, he concluded, since our views differed, "I will tell Mao and Zhou and let them decide."
>
> The next morning, Li called us to his office and told us that the Central Government agreed with us and decided to also send Zhu De to the train station. Zhu De was commander-in-chief of the PLA and member of the Standing Committee of the Politburo. At that time his was one of the two pictures hanging on the walls of almost all offices—the other one was Mao's. This was perfect to show the Central Government's special respect for the Dalai and Panchen Lamas.[24]

The two lamas, therefore, were welcomed at the railway station in Beijing by Zhou Enlai, Zhu De, Li Weihan, and various other leaders of the Communist Party. So began a critically important visit that had the potential of changing Sino-Tibetan relations. It is the subject of the next chapter.

23. Goldstein, Sherap, and Siebenschuh 2004: 187–88.
24. Goldstein, Sherap, and Siebenschuh 2004: 188–89.

Chapter 20

The Dalai Lama in Beijing

The arrival of the Dalai Lama and his top officials in Beijing on 4 September 1954 opened a critical window of opportunity for the Chinese leadership. Winning over the Dalai Lama had been central to Mao's gradualist strategy, but until then direct access of the Chinese to the Dalai Lama had been extremely limited. The CCP now had a rare opportunity to create a favorable impression about China, the CCP, and socialism. It also afforded the Chinese an excellent opportunity to revisit a number of outstanding issues that had been left in abeyance in 1951 and 1952, such as the Military-Administrative Committee, the Tibetan army, Tibetan currency, and the Panchen-Dalai lama conflict.

. . . . .

The campaign to win over the Dalai Lama began at once. The day after the Dalai Lama arrived, Zhu De personally hosted a banquet in his and the Panchen Lama's honor.[1] This was followed on 11 September by a meeting with Mao Zedong at Zhongnanhai, the command compound for China's top political officials. Phünwang, the Tibetan cadre who was designated to accompany and translate for the Dalai Lama, recalled this first conversation of Mao and the Dalai Lama.

> Three or four days after the Dalai Lama arrived, a major meeting was arranged for the Dalai Lama and the Panchen Lama with the top leaders of China— Mao, Liu Shaoqi, Zhou Enlai, Zhu De, and Deng Xiaoping. I was to be the translator. It was the first time the Dalai Lama had met China's top leaders, and they him. Interestingly, only Mao spoke. Mao told the Dalai Lama that he and the

1. Dangdai zhongguo congshu bianjibu 1991: 209–17.

Central Government were very happy about the Dalai Lama's first visit to Beijing and they welcomed him. The relationship between Chinese and Tibetans, he said, was very important, and in the future the Central Government would expend great effort to support the development of Tibet.

The Dalai Lama in turn told Mao that he was happy to have come to Beijing. Previously, he said, he had not known the real situation in China, so he had gone to Yadong on the Indian border and had thought about seeking asylum abroad. But, he said, after Zhang Jingwu came, he gradually came to learn more about the overall situation, and now he was very happy to have an opportunity to meet Mao and the other leaders.

The Dalai Lama was impressive. He was only nineteen years old, but he spoke well without exhibiting any signs of nervousness. Mao was friendly and forthcoming. He did not act like the great ruler he was but spoke informally, like a friend. . . .

The conversation lasted about an hour. Mao and the other leaders then accompanied the Dalai Lama out of the house and Mao personally opened the car door for him. Mao seemed quite happy about the meeting. He shook the Dalai's hands and told him, "Your coming to Beijing was like coming back to your own home. Whenever you come to Beijing, you can call me. You can come to my place whenever you want to. Don't be shy. If you need anything, you just tell me directly." When the Dalai and I were seated in our car going back to our quarters, the Dalai Lama was also very happy. He was so exited he hugged me and said, "Phünwang-la, today things went very well. Mao is a great person who is unlike others." I was also very pleased that this critical first meeting went so well. My hopes for Tibet, in a sense, rested on this.[2]

This first meeting with Mao was also very well received by the Tibetan government delegation, many of whom had initially feared that the leaders of China would show disrespect to the Dalai Lama or be dismissive of Tibetan dress and customs. These fears were now put to rest. Zhu De, one of China's greatest leaders and heroes, had met them at the train station and hosted a grand welcome banquet, and Mao, the equivalent of the "emperor "of China in the eyes of the older Tibetan officials, had not only shown friendship and warmth during the meeting but had also made a grand gesture of respect by walking the Dalai Lama to his car and opening the door for him. For Tibetans, the gesture of a host walking his visitor to the "gate" conveys respect to the departing person. From the beginning, therefore, the Dalai Lama and his attendants were pleasantly surprised and favorably impressed by the respect with which they were treated and by the attitude of Mao and the other top leaders.

The first session of the National People's Congress began on 15 September, and for the next two weeks, the Dalai Lama (and the Panchen Lama)

2. Goldstein, Sherap, and Siebenschuh 2004: 189–91.

Figure 23. Dalai Lama (right) and Panchen Lama (left) voting in the National People's Congress, Beijing, September 1954. Source: Chen Zonglie

were involved in the meetings as delegates, primarily discussing China's constitution. On 16 September the Dalai Lama gave a speech to the National People's Congress, summing up the past four years and prominently mentioning the right of minority nationalities to autonomy but also commenting that there had been problems. He said,

Chairman Mao Tse-tung,

Fellow Deputies,

The first session of the First National People's Congress now being held in Peking, the capital of our motherland, will solemnly enact the Constitution of the People's Republic of China, an event that conforms with the interests of all nationalities in the country.

As regards minority nationalities, the Draft Constitution sums up the achievements and experiences in applying Chairman Mao Tse-tung's policy of equality and unity among the nationalities. It provides, in particular, that all nationalities may draw up their rules governing the exercise of autonomy and separate regulations in accordance with the special features of the development, so that they may exercise full autonomy.

Besides, the Draft Constitution lays down clearly that "in the course of economic and cultural development, the state will take care of the needs of the different nationalities and, in the matter of socialist transformation, it will give full attention to the special features in the development of the various nationalities."

All this is absolutely right, and the whole of the people in Tibet warmly support it.

For a long period in her history, Tibet suffered oppression undei domestic reactionary governments and, in particular, was for sometime more or less alienated from her motherland as a result of foreign imperialist provocation.

But since the signing of the Agreement on Measures for the Peaceful Liberation of Tibet in 1951, the delegates of the Central People's Government, the People's Liberation Army and working personnel have come to Tibet one after another, and carried out the Central People's Government's policy of unity among the nationalities, and have followed out and applied the 17 articles of the Agreement on Measures for the Peaceful Liberation of Tibet. The correctness of all these policies and other measures have been visible to everyone.

At the same time, during the past three years and more, many visiting groups and delegations carrying good wishes have gone from the Tibet Region to the interior areas of the motherland and on returning to Tibet have published and interpreted what they saw. In this way the apprehensions and misgivings of the Tibetan people had disappeared step by step.

Close unity is growing daily among the fraternal nationalities, in particular, between the Han and Tibetan peoples. The return of the Panchen Ngoerhtehni [Erdini] to Tibet and his meeting with me have further strengthened internal unity in Tibet. In accordance with Chairman Mao Tse-tung's policy of unity among the nationalities and within each nationality a new peaceful and friendly atmosphere now prevails in Tibet.

On the question of religion, one of the main fabrications of the enemy for sowing discord is that the Communist Party and the People's Government destroy religion. The Tibetan people are very earnest in their religious faith and these rumours caused apprehension and misgiving among them. But now these pernicious rumours that "the Communist Party and People's Government destroy religion" have been utterly exploded. The Tibetan people have learned from their own experience that they have freedom of religious belief.

As regards the economic and cultural development of Tibet, it was difficult formerly for Tibet to engage in economic and cultural development because of the inconvenience of communication. But with the tremendous assistance of the Central People's Government, much wasteland has been reclaimed, people's banks have been established and grant loans for agriculture, stock-raising and handicrafts, and wool which hitherto had difficulty in finding an outlet has been bought at good prices in the past three years and more. All this had helped forward Tibet's economic development.

Secondly, schools and hospitals have been established and Tibetan cadres trained to promote education and cultural development.

Worthy of special mention in economic construction is the fact that the Central People's Government has earmarked huge sums for the building of the Sikang-Tibet Highway. The road builders have carried on their diligent labour in the face of every danger along the steep mountains and across the fast-flowing rivers. This highway that is expected to reach Lhasa by the end of this year not only lays the foundation for the building of a prosperous new Tibet, but has tremendous significance in national defence.

Recently, part of Shigatze Area, Tibet, suffered flood. On learning the news, the Central People's Government immediately allocated eight thousand million yuan for the flood victims. The agreement that was signed between the People's Republic of China and the Republic of India on trade and intercourse between the Tibet Region of China and India, fully reflects the needs and desires of the people in Tibet Region, and has won their support. All this is a concrete demonstration of the profound concern of the Central People's Government for Tibet and the Tibetan people, and at the same time shows the great strength of our motherland.

In accordance with the Agreement on Measures for the Peaceful Liberation of Tibet, the Tibetan Local Government and the people, monks and laymen, are now doing their best to help the People's Liberation Army with food purchase and transport and communications. The 17 articles of the agreement are being carried out in order that Tibet may move forward to a richer political and economic development. *Some weaknesses have shown themselves in the work, because of the residue of estrangement between the nationalities caused by long years of national oppression under the former reactionary rulers, and because of insufficient understanding of the motherland among the Tibetan people, but these are being overcome. We Tibetans all fully understand that the disinterested measures undertaken by the members of the People's Liberation Army and the working personnel in Tibet are indeed in the interest of the Tibetan people. In some minor individual cases, there have been some misunderstandings, mainly because of language and a lack of understanding of customs and habits, but these were immediately corrected after explanation.*

Henceforth we shall unreservedly take part in criticism and discussion. With the help of the advanced Han nationality, under the leadership of Chairman Mao, the beloved and great leader of all the nationalities, we are strongly confident that, by following the Constitution and carrying out the 17 articles

Figure 24. At the National People's Congress meeting, Beijing, 1954; left to right, front row: Li Weihan, unknown, Zhang Lan, Song Qingding, Panchen Lama, Mao Zedong, Dalai Lama, Liu Xiaoqi, Li Jieshen, Guo Moro, unknown; back row: Phünwang, Tsering Tsomo (the Dalai Lama's mother), Ngabö, unknown, Fan Ming, Teijar, Zhang Jinsun, Ling Rimpoche, Wang Feng, unknown, Panchen Lama's father, Che Jigme, unknown, unknown. Source: Chen Zonglie

of the agreement, Tibet will gradually be built up into a place of happiness and prosperity both in the political and religious field.

Finally, allow me to wish Good health to all deputies and resounding success to the Congress.[3]

The following week, on 27 September, as the National People's Congress was winding down, the Dalai Lama was singled out for special honor; he was selected as a deputy chairman of the Standing Committee of the National People's Congress. Although this position did not have real political power, it gave the Dalai Lama high stature in the Chinese governmental hierarchy and clearly differentiated him from the Panchen Lama, who was selected as only a member of its Standing Committee.[4]

The Tibetan delegation then participated in the celebration of Chinese

3. New China News Agency as cited in British Foreign Office Records, FO371/110228 (emphasis added).

4. Later in December, the Panchen Lama was elected as the deputy chairman of the Political Consultative Conference organization.

National Day (1 October), but once this was finished, the Chinese turned to "business"—to revisiting and settling the issues mentioned above. Mao had actually raised the issue of the Military-Administrative Committee at his first meeting with the Dalai Lama.[5] He surprised the Dalai Lama by telling him both that it was still too early to implement all of the clauses of the Seventeen-Point Agreement and that it was no longer necessary to create a military-administrative committee. These "committees," he said, were meant to be transitional until people's governments could be started and had already been terminated in all large regions. He proposed, therefore, that Tibet skip this stage and go directly to creating the Tibet Autonomous Region, with the Dalai Lama as its chairman and the Panchen Lama as the deputy chairman. An autonomous region, Mao said, would be better for Tibetans, because it would be in accord with the new constitution, which specified that minority regions will exercise autonomous rule.

Actually, the Tibet Autonomous Region with the Dalai Lama as its head was legally problematic according to China's new constitution, since the head of an autonomous region should be elected, not appointed. Mao addressed this problem some months earlier in a speech to the first meeting of the Constitutional Draft Committee in Beijing, at which he clearly explained the strategic need to ignore the problem.

> *The actual form of the Tibet autonomous government should be decided*
> *by the majority people in Tibet.*

23 March 1954

In order to give special consideration to minority nationalities and the situation in Tibet, we created the third point of the sixty-first item in the draft [constitution]. It states, "The actual form of the autonomous government in the areas where minority nationalities live should be determined according to the will of the majority people of that nationality."

At present, the Dalai manages Tibet. If we follow the third point of the sixty-first item, we will have to hold a conference of the People's Congress to elect officials for the People's Government. If that is the case, the Dalai probably won't be happy. He could raise questions with us regarding the Seventeen-Point Agreement he signed with us. What shall we do? We should act according to the third point. [But] It is not feasible to set up a people's government; however, we can choose other forms. The Dalai is a living Buddha. He is a living god. He was not elected by the people. So we should let the majority of people decide what is the form of the new power. They believe in the Dalai and tusi [local chiefs] much more than they believe in us. It is impossible to shake his position. Therefore, let us act according to the will of majority of the people [who support the Dalai Lama as their leader].

5. Zhonggong xizang zizhiqu dangshi ziliao zhengji weiyuanhui 1995, entry for September 1954.

I once told a group of representatives from Tibet, "We will not force you to do anything. You will decide yourselves whether you want land reforms or elections." However, can we discard the Seventeen-Point Agreement? No. We must realize it. However, if they do not want to realize one of the points in the agreement right now, we could temporarily hold up doing that, because the agreement did not stipulate that the points must be realized before a certain date. We have delayed it by three years. *If necessary, we can wait three more years. After three years, we can wait for another three years.*

We cannot do things that other people dislike. We should wait for the day that the people gain the initiative. We believe that the people will understand this. We once published in an editorial, "The Han cadres should not do things that the Tibetan people dislike. They should act according to the will of majority people." In the third point of the sixty-first item, should we add the will of the leaders of minority nationalities besides the will of people? It is okay if we do not add this point. In a word, they absolutely support their own leader and believe that their leader is sacred and inviolable. However, in the constitution, if we were to add these words, it would look bad. So we did not.

Printed according to the recording of the speech of Chairman Mao kept in the Central Archives.[6]

Mao's pragmatic and gradualist strategy also led him to conclude that an autonomous region could not be done at once. It would require extensive planning and time to recruit and train personnel. The first step, therefore, should be to establish a "Preparatory Committee" for the establishment of the Tibet Autonomous Region.[7]

The Dalai Lama discussed Mao's recommendation to create the Tibet Autonomous Region in an interview, translated in part here.

So the main thing was that in the Seventeen-Point Agreement, it was said the Military-Administrative Committee should be established. So when I was in Beijing, Chairman Mao suggested to me that now the Tibet situation over the past few years has made much progress, there is no need to establish that Military-Administrative Committee. So instead of that, the autonomous region should be established. So for that there should be a preparatory committee.

To us, it seemed that the very name Tibet Autonomous Region [tib. pö rang-gyong jong, which in Tibetan literally means "Tibet, a region ruled by itself"] was much nicer than the Military-Administrative Committee, so we appreciated this and promptly agreed. . . .

Q: How did the Chinese explain it was going to function? The Tibetan government existed, and now there is going to be a Tibet autonomous region. How did they explain the difference between these two in terms of work?

6. Zhonggong zhongyang wenxian yanjiu shi; zhonggong xizang zizhiqu weiyuanhui; zhongquo zangxue yanjiu zhongxin 2001: 104–5.

7. Hereafter abbreviated PCTAR. Dui xizang gongzuo de zhongyao zhishi (wei chuban de shouji), n.d.; Dalai Lama 1990: 89.

I can't remember clearly anything about how to dissolve the Tibetan government. But for the PCTAR, they said that all the important people should be Tibetan. They used as an example Ulanfu as the chairman of the Mongolian Autonomous Region and [an important central government official]. . . . So when that started, I was to be the head, and the Panchen Rimpoche the deputy.[8]

The Kashag ministers in Beijing convened all the senior officials in Beijing as a mini-Assembly to discuss it.[9] As one would expect, there were different views. On the negative side, there was clearly anxiety about the future of the Tibetan government. Would the start of a Tibet autonomous region mean the end of the Tibetan government, or would both administrative entities be able to continue to function side by side in some ways, and, if so, what functions would each control? These kinds of questions were not specifically addressed by the Chinese, and the Tibetan side did not seek clarification, but clearly taking this step called into question the future of the Tibetan government as they knew it.

Another negative was the Chinese side's conception of the Tibet Autonomous Region as including three discrete Tibetan components: the Dalai Lama's government, the Chamdo Liberation Committee, and the Panchen Lama's government. These, however, had all been integral parts of the Tibetan government in 1950, so it was difficult now to agree to them being politically distinct units.

Ultimately, however, the Dalai Lama was eager to cooperate with Mao, and Ngabö was strongly in favor of change and cooperation, so it was difficult for the other officials not to agree.[10] Tibet had lost the war and accepted the Seventeen-Point Agreement, including accepting the creation of the Military-Administrative Committee. It had resisted implementing the Military-Administrative Committee, objecting to the concept of the military being involved in administering Tibet, but now that Mao had suggested creating an autonomous region instead, they had no obvious grounds to object. As the Dalai Lama said above, the term *autonomous region* made it appear that Tibetans would rule themselves. Since the Dalai Lama was to be the overall leader, an autonomous region government run by the Dalai Lama and Tibetans did not seem so ominous to the Tibetan way of life. Moreover, since

8. Dalai Lama, interview, 1995, Dharamsala.

9. Kun bde gling (Kundeling) 2000: 161. Kundeling lists the following as participating: Surkhang, Ngabö, Lobsang Samden, Ngawang Dondrub, Liushar, Kundeling Dzasa, Simkhen Chemmo, Phala, Tsipön Kusangtse, and Takla (Phüntso Tashi). Probably Trijang Rimpoche also was involved.

10. A draft of this convention of the ministers was wired to Lhasa, where the other Kashag ministers (Shasur, Gadrang, Ragasha) also discussed the situation with the Abbreviated Assembly (Kundeling, interview, 1992, Dehra Dun).

there was first to be a preparatory committee, nothing would change substantially for years. Consequently, in the atmosphere of friendship and cordiality, the Dalai Lama and his officials agreed to look to a new future rather than try to hold on to the past. But many were apprehensive.

Once this was accepted in principle by the Tibetan government, a subcommittee of representatives from the four constituent groups (the Tibetan government, the Panchen Lama's government, the Chamdo Liberation Committee, and the CCP) started focused discussions on how to operationalize the PCTAR.[11] Beginning in November, this group held many meetings and private talks and, on 30 December 1954, unanimously issued a work report that set out the concrete measures to be taken to form the Preparatory Committee. The State Council approved this on 9 March 1955.[12]

The preparatory committee would consist of fifty-one members, 90 percent of whom would be Tibetans. Of the fifty-one members, 29 percent (fifteen) would come from the Tibetan government, 20 percent (ten) from the Panchen Lama's government, 20 percent (ten) from the Chamdo Liberation Committee, and 10 percent (five) from the Chinese cadre in Tibet. The remaining 21 percent (eleven) would come from important individual Tibetans throughout the autonomous region. In terms of leadership, the Dalai Lama was to be the chairman, the Panchen Lama the first deputy chairman, and Zhang Guohua the second deputy chairman. Ngabö was to be the secretary general, and the deputy secretary generals were to be from the Chamdo Liberation Committee and the Panchen's administrative council.[13]

Administratively, the PCTAR was to be under the leadership of the State Council, which would also have the final say in its appointments of personnel. The PCTAR would consist of a range of offices, including an administrative office, a finance and economy commission, a religious affairs commission, a department of civil affairs, a department of health, a department of culture and education, a department of public security, a department of agriculture and forestry, a department of animal husbandry, a department of industry and commerce, and a department of communications.[14] These offices were gradually to be expanded in size and function so that at some point they could become the administrative structure of a Tibetan autonomous region.

While this plan was being finalized, discussions about the Tibetan govern-

---

11. Dangdai zhongguo congshu bianjibu 1991: 209–17.

12. The text of this resolution is cited in Liang Nai-min 1968: 141–43. The official Preparatory Committee for the Tibet Autonomous Region was actually inaugurated the following year in April 1956. The actual Tibet Autonomous Region was not inaugurated until 1966, long after the uprising of 1959.

13. Dangdai zhongguo congshu bianjibu 1991: 209–17.

14. Xizang zizhiqu dangshi bangongshi 1998: 39–42.

ment's currency and army occurred. As mentioned in earlier chapters, according to the Seventeen-Point Agreement, both of these were to be gradually ended, but the Tibetan government had resisted doing this in 1951–52.

The Tibetans themselves had anticipated that the army issue would be raised in Beijing and tried to forestall conflict by telling the Chinese just before the Dalai Lama left that they were planning to reduce their army to fifteen hundred troops. Ironically, this worried the Tibet Work Committee, which sent a telegram to the Central Military Committee (on 5 July 1954), stating their opposition to giving the appearance of reducing the Tibetan army behind the Dalai Lama's back (i.e., while he was in Beijing).[15] Mao agreed, and in the end, the Kashag was persuaded to postpone taking action until the Dalai Lama's trip was over.

But the military issue did come up in Beijing. The Chinese argued that since they were taking full responsibility for guarding the borders, there was no longer any need for a separate Tibetan army. The Kashag was already willing to reduce the size of the army, so it readily accepted further reductions, although it still resisted completely dismantling it or merging it into the PLA. The Tibetan side prevailed on this issue, and the Chinese settled for an agreement to decrease the total number of Tibetan troops to only one thousand. Of these, five hundred would constitute the Dalai Lama's Bodyguard Regiment, and the remaining five hundred would be a Lhasa police force. No Tibetan troops would be stationed outside Lhasa.[16] Moreover, the Chinese government agreed to pay the expenses and salaries of these troops as well as to help the soldiers who would be laid off. However, the Tibetan government would continue to be in charge of these one thousand remaining troops.

With regard to the issue of currency, the Tibetan officials in Beijing, at the urging of the Dalai Lama, agreed to a plan to discontinue the use of Tibetan currency. The Chinese central government would buy back all outstanding Tibetan currency and replace it with Chinese paper notes. Since the Tibetan government would no longer be printing its own currency, Beijing agreed to provide annual funds to the Dalai Lama's government.

Kundeling, who was in Beijing, recalled that he understood that these "decisions" were left to be finalized according to the opinion of the Tibetan people after the officials returned from Beijing.[17] The Chinese government's records are not clear, but one Central Committee document appears to confirm this, for it uses the word *tentative* for the army and currency agreements.[18]

15. Zhongguo zangxue yanjiu zhongxin keyan chu zhuban 1993.

16. Gyagpön Kedram, interview, 1992, Dharamsala.

17. Kundeling, interview, 1992.

18. Zhonggong xizang zizhiqu dangshi ziliao zheng ji weiyuanhui 1990, entry for 11 March 1955.

Most Tibetans were still reluctant to give up these symbols of their separate political identity, but with Tibet moving to become an autonomous region, more sophisticated leaders such as Ngabö and Surkhang felt it obvious that they were no longer very meaningful. Times had changed. Whether the Dalai Lama and the monastic system were going to continue to flourish and whether Tibetans were going to exercise real autonomy would depend on the strength of Tibet's relationship and friendship with China, not on whether Tibet had one thousand or two thousand of its own troops. In these leaders' view, Tibet was going to be an integrated part of the PRC, and it was now necessary to be active participants in constructing this.

Ironically, the most difficult issue to resolve in Beijing involved not Sino-Tibetan authority but the bitter dispute between the Tibetan government and the Panchen Lama. The Tibetan government was willing to accept greater subordination to the Central Committee and the CCP, but yielding to the Panchen Lama's view that his administration was equal to the Tibetan government's was unacceptable, despite urgings by Ngabö, who felt that all this would become irrelevant when the Tibet Autonomous Region started to function. At their meetings in Lhasa in 1952, a number of points of conflict had already been settled, but very significant issues still remained to be resolved.

As indicated earlier, Mao considered this intra-Tibetan enmity a significant issue. It had already spilled over to create serious discord within the Tibet Work Committee, and there was a risk that it would impede the smooth implementation (and operation) of the coming PCTAR and the Tibet Autonomous Region. However, Mao also understood that the CCP should not impose the terms of a settlement, because, whatever it imposed, the other side would resent it, and the conflict and hatred would continue. Beijing, therefore, insisted that both sides meet face-to-face and work to finalize a solution themselves.

The Chinese looked to Ngabö to finesse a solution. Mao, in fact, conveyed to Ngabö that it would be best if he focused on the present and did not dwell on history. Ngabö agreed and first informally met with Che Jigme to discuss the outstanding issues. Once these two reached a satisfactory level of understanding, each side selected a team of two officials to negotiate the specifics.[19]

The issues they fought over, in one sense, seem hard to believe, given that this was four years after Tibet's incorporation into the PRC. Some involved the right to collect corvée labor from serfs, a few involved the control of specific estates that had been confiscated by the Tibetan government, and one, amazingly, specified that the serfs of the Panchen Lama who had placed

---

19. The four were Ngabö, Liushar, and the two Labrang representatives, Trendong (Jigme Drakpa) and Denlhün (Tsering Paljor).

themselves under a new lord (such as the Agriculture Bureau or the Dalai Lama's treasury) would be returned to the Panchen Lama, their original lord. Since serfs like these were likely to have married serfs from other lords, the agreement specifies that the Panchen Lama's estates should try to avoid splitting up such families by giving the runaway serfs "human lease" status or by allowing the serf to send another person as his or her replacement.[20]

The Dalai Lama and the Central Committee wanted to settle these issues, so the Tibetan government conceded on a number of points, and an agreement was crafted and signed on 19 January 1955.

THE DALAI LAMA ON TOUR

After the National People's Congress adjourned, the Dalai Lama went on tour to other Chinese cities, such as Tianjin. The Chinese side sought to use this time not only to impress him with China's modernization and industrial development but also to educate him about the Chinese Communist Party and socialism. In Tibet, Chinese officials had had no way to secure this kind of personal access to the Dalai Lama, so two very sophisticated Communist cadres, Phünwang and Liu Geping, were assigned to go with him on his visits. Phünwang explained the Chinese hopes.

> Liu Geping and I accompanied the Dalai Lama. . . . Liu Geping was an important official who was a member of the Hui (Muslim) minority group. He also was an activist member of the CCP since the early days. We discussed the coming tour and both felt this was a great opportunity to influence the Dalai Lama about the history of the Chinese Communist Party and its policies. Since Liu Geping was an old party member, we decided he should talk to the Dalai Lama about the party's history. I would explain to him about the Soviet Union's nationality polices and Marxism-Leninism. The Dalai Lama was very eager to learn about all aspects of communism, and I think we had an effect on his thinking. Even now he sometimes says that he is half Buddhist and half Marxist. But he was also realistic and understood that in practice things are sometimes different from theory [in terms of socialism], just as not every Buddhist follows the Buddha's words in the same way [so too every Communist cadre is not the same in thinking].[21]

The trip and the discussions had a tremendous impact on the Dalai Lama. He has described his stay in China in a number of interviews and in his biography,[22] conveying in all these the great intellectual awakening he experienced in China and his excitement with what he was learning about so-

---

20. Bka' shag 1953.
21. Goldstein, Sherap, and Siebenschuh 2004: 195.
22. Dalai Lama 1990.

cialism. During these trips, the Dalai Lama came to realize clearly the depths of Tibet's backwardness and the real need for reform and modernization. He said,

> In 1954, I went down to China and met Mao Zedong many times; and when I went on tours, whichever place I got to it was easy to talk to Communist Party members. When they gave an opinion it seemed that they really gave meaningful ones. . . . From their mouth they used to say "comrade," and it really looked like they were really comrades; [it was] kind of strange [in a nice way]. When the non–party members spoke, it seemed like they were too polite and without substance.
>
> My nature since young had a strong urge to help the poor. So from this perspective, the Marxist philosophy of the proletariat used to seem very attractive and believable to me.
>
> I also liked their internationalism, which advocated the nonexistence of national boundaries or race but the equality of all mankind. The poor were to become a worldwide proletariat in an international movement. So from this perspective, I liked the ideas and the equality of all people under socialism. When the Communists called each other comrades, it seemed like they really trusted each other and were really dedicated persons. So I went down to China in 1954 and came up in 1955. At that time I liked [the socialist ways] quite a lot. I had great hopes that we could make progress in Tibet, sort of with the help of the Chinese.[23]

The impact of all this on the Dalai Lama was so great that he actually asked to join the Communist Party (the Dalai Lama's English is unedited).

> Q: You said a number of times, Your Holiness, that you would like to become a party member. Who did you say that to?
>
> Yes. Because there was an attraction. Not [for] power. Because [of] Phüntso Wangye and Liu Geping, and during, I think, [the] six to seven months' tour within China, every place I had talk[s] with leaders, so when I met a party member like the [party] secretary, . . . so those party members' discussions [were] always very useful; non–party member, too much polite and sometimes there is nothing to talk about; they are very polite and talking about the weather. Tibet, in winter it is windy and in summer rainy. Silly. Wasteful.
>
> The party member, hard work, lead people and change. I remember in Jiangsu, the Fu Shengzhang [deputy provincial governor], one member of the Long March who had been injured, his voice [was] very weak. I remember his voice and face very clearly. And we just casually discussed about New Years, and I mentioned some of the ceremonial in Tibet, in Lhasa. Long ceremony. Then he told me [that] to change old ceremony [at] once [is] impossible. Each time reduce [it] by one hour. Like that, always their side some commitment, how to change, how to improve. So I have very good impression. And then, of

course, there was Peng Dehuai. Very straightforward. Not much talk. Lobsang Samden gives him nickname Dobdo, also called him Guri [shaven head]. Also Chen Yi, Liu Shaoqi, Zhu De, Deng Xiaoping; all these party leaders, top party leaders, something, something, Then non–party member . . . all have very high position but already experienced that they are just a name, so accordingly they act like everything [is] very superficial.

So through that, [the] long lecture[s] from Liu Geping translated by Phüntso Wangye, I got genuine interest on Marxist revolution. So therefore I still describe myself as half Marxist and half Buddhist. So still I have some admiration, [and] agreement with Marxist theory. . . .

So that is my main motivation. I wanted to join the party. And Liu Geping told me it is not good. It is better to postpone. Phüntso Wangye and, I think, Liu Geping both told me you can participate in party meeting with the status of non–party member but can [still] meet. . . . So Phüntso Wangye [is] one Khamba revolutionary; I am one Amdo revolutionary, I think.[24]

The Dalai Lama returned to Beijing in late January 1955, where he celebrated the Tibetan New Year (Losar) by hosting a large banquet, to which he invited all the top leaders of the central government—Mao Zedong, Zhou Enlai, Zhu De, and Liu Shaoqi. All came, sending another very visible sign of respect that all the Tibetans noticed and appreciated.

Mao met with the Dalai and Panchen lamas that day and, interestingly, emphasized that when they returned to Tibet they should not try to rush reforms prematurely and risk alienating the more conservative elite.

Chairman Mao's Conversation with Dalai and Panchen
23 February 1955 (Tibetan calendar: First month, First day)

Chairman: Happy holiday. We are very happy that you can spend the Tibetan New Year in Beijing. People of the whole of China are happy for it. We Chinese have two New Years too. One, the lunar new year, is a custom that has been kept for a long time through history. Up to now, most people still celebrate this New Year. Another New Year is the solar New Year.

Dalai: We celebrated three New Years in inland China this year.

Panchen: We have visited the northeast, and soon we will go to the eastern part of China for a visit. During our visit to the northeast, we saw a lot of heavy industry construction. We feel that socialist industrialization will soon be achieved, and we are extremely happy about it.

Chairman: Our country is a backward country. Industry is not well developed. There are many machines that we cannot make. We do not have a lot of steel. But this does not matter. We can do our construction. In fifteen years, we will build our country into good shape. Our

24. Dalai Lama, interview, 2004, Dharamsala.

Figure 25. Tibetan New Year's celebration, Beijing, 1955, left to right, Zhou Enlai, Panchen Lama, Mao Zedong, Dalai Lama, Liu Shaoqi. Source: Chen Zonglie

country was often bullied by others; the one that treated us most high-handedly was the American imperialists. Our country has vast lands, rich resources, a big population, and good natural conditions and climate. But in the past, the leaders were bad and the politics were bad. That is why we are one hundred years behind the advanced countries in various aspects.

In our country, many places are still very backward, Tibet is very backward, and we should acknowledge it. It is better for us to acknowledge it. We can learn from the advanced countries, learn from the USSR. In this way, we are learning from advanced nations and countries, and the different nationalities learn from one another within our country. We must unite closely and do the construction of our country together. All of the nationalities in China are hopeful; the whole country is hopeful.

Dalai: During our visits to various places, we stopped for only a very short time at each place, but because of the fraternal relationships, we felt in harmony with everyone. Tibet is as Chairman Mao says. It is backward in various aspects, but we can guarantee the chairman that under your leadership and the leadership of the Chinese Communist Party, we will do a good job in various fields in Tibet and will constantly improve Tibet.

Chairman: Being backward does not matter. There are a lot of backward places in the Han regions. Like Tibet, these places will improve.

Panchen: As a result of the past oppression of the GMD reactionaries and imperialists, Tibet is very backward. However, under the leadership of Chairman Mao, [we] have confidence we will unite the Tibetan people, develop various kinds of construction, and make progress in Tibet.

Chairman: I have confidence that under the leadership of you two, things in Tibet will improve. *But do not hurry. Do things gradually and do things with the consent of a majority. In three to five years, there will still be opponents when you do try to do good things. These opponents will not be common people but the aristocrats, officials, tribal chiefs, and abbots of monasteries. You should teach them as if you are teachers, and try to unite with them patiently.*

If you do not make any progress at all, we do not agree. We will welcome your progress, but you should work together with others on the basis of the realistic conditions of Tibet. After seeing the development of construction in inland places, do not get very impatient. In the past, after some Communist members visited the USSR and saw the advanced conditions there, they somehow got impatient too. Without carefully thinking things out, they started many things at the same time. However, the conditions were not ripe for these, and their good intentions led to bad results.

When you do things, you should discuss them widely with everyone. For example, take the question of Tibetan currency. At first, the Kashag did not agree. Then you explained to them and asked for their opinions. This was very good. You are very good at getting things done. When we do things at the central government, we often get the opinions of the local people. We discuss these with you. So please relax; we will not force you to do anything.

Dalai: In terms of Tibetan currency and other questions, in the beginning some people did not understand the whole picture, so they disagreed. After we discussed this with them, many of these people changed their ideas.

It is the Tibetan New Year today, and we came specially to say Happy New Year to the chairman. Also, we are just back from our visits in other places, and we have come to learn things from the chairman. Just now the chairman gave us a lot of valuable instruction. We feel educated.[25]

On that same day Mao met privately with the Panchen Lama and skillfully conveyed that the Central Committee was interested and supportive of his government and at the same time strongly encouraged him to work with the Dalai Lama. He also expressed interest in whether the top Chinese cadres were learning Tibetan by directly asking Zhang Jingwu and Fan Ming, both of whom were at the meeting, about their personal progress in studying Tibetan. The following is a transcript of what he said in that conversation:

25. Zhonggong zhongyang wenxian yanjiu shi bian zhonggong xizang zizhiqu weiyuan hui 2005: 117–20.

Chairman Mao's Conversation with Panchen Erdini
23 February 1955 (Tibetan calendar: First month, First day)

Chairman: How is your health? I heard your health was not very good. How are you now?

Panchen: I am pretty good now.

Chairman: Do you plan to visit Shanghai?

Panchen: I plan to visit Shanghai and Hangzhou according to your instructions. I also want to go to Guangzhou.

Chairman: Very good. You must visit Humeng [in the south of Guangzhou; the place where the English opium was destroyed] when you visit Guangzhou. That place has historical meaning. You can ask them. They will tell you the story.

Panchen: Today, you came here specially to visit us. We feel very happy.

Chairman: You are leaving, so I wanted to come to see you.

Panchen: In the past, we [the Panchen Lama and his officials] could not return to Tibet for dozens of years. This time [1952], we got the opportunity to go back to Tibet. We really appreciate your leadership in achieving this.

Chairman: This is not my own accomplishment. It should be attributed to the leadership of the Communist Party, the help of the People's Liberation Army, and it is also due to your efforts and the welcoming attitude from the Tibetan people. Things need to be done step by step. There are problems between the Lhasa government and you. Have you solved the problems this time?

Panchen: When I went back to Tibet, the Dalai cared about me very much. Although we have had some trouble between each other, the problems have all been solved during this visit to Beijing.

Chairman: You have important work to do. You support them [Tibetan government]; they will support you. In this way, unity will be strengthened.

Panchen: Right. We will act according to your instructions.

Chairman: In the past, you were not sure. You were afraid that we would only take care of Front Tibet and leave you alone.

Chairman [continues commenting to Zhang Jingwu and Fan Ming, who were present at the meeting]: You should not only say Long Live Chairman Mao in Tibet. This is not good. Do not only hang portraits of Chairman Mao, but also hang the portraits of the Dalai and Panchen lamas, because this is a custom of Tibetans. Every nationality has its own leader. It is very good that Tibetans have leaders like the Dalai and Panchen. For example, Kim Richeng is the leader in Korea. When you try to do things in Korea, you have to respect him.

[to the Panchen Lama]: Your policy is good. It is good that you can take the initiative to endorse them.

To compromise, you let the Dalai be the chairman [of the future Tibet Autonomous Region], and you will be the deputy chairman. Je Jigme took the initiative to suggest that Ngabö should be the secretary general. All these are very good. It is better for you to do this than to have the CCP put forward such suggestions. In this way, things will be easier in the future.

There are many officials and many monasteries in Lhasa. Some of them may not fully agree with the Dalai Lama's suggestions on some questions. When you handle things, you should take account of their difficulties. Do not hurry. Take time. With anything you do, it is better to get the people's consent to it gradually.

You are afraid of the Lhasa government; the Lhasa government is afraid of the Han people. It is not strange that the small is always afraid of the big. In the past, because the reactionary Han class ruled you and suppressed you, you have a bad impression of the Han people. Thus, in the future, we should do a lot of good deeds so that the Tibetan people will believe that the Han people will help them instead of taking advantage of them.

In the past, I told Zhang Jingwu and Fan Ming to tell our cadres that we entered Tibet to help Tibetans, not to rule them. And when we help people, we would like to make sure that people feel comfortable with our help. I also told them to use these two standards to test our cadres. You need to help them [the cadres] too. Tell them your opinions. If they are wrong, they should correct their mistakes; if they don't, you can tell us so that we will transfer them.

[to Zhang Jingwu and Fan Ming]: In the past, there were problems in Shigatse. Did they voice their opinions?

Zhang: [answer redacted]

Chairman: Did you correct the mistakes?

Zhang: [answer redacted]

Chairman [to Je Jigme]: Is a regiment of bodyguards under your leadership?

Panchen: [answer redacted]

Chairman: How about the officers in the regiment? Are they all their officers?

Zhang, Fan Ming: [answer redacted]

Chairman: The number of Han cadres should gradually decrease. We should train their [Tibetan] cadres. The uniform of their Bodyguard Regiment does not have to be the uniform of the People's Liberation Army. They can wear their own uniform.

Panchen: [answer redacted]

Chairman *[to Panchen]:* The problem of the regiment is one example. You gave criticism and they listened. They had to correct their mistake.

Panchen: [answer redacted]

Chairman: That is true. There will still be problems in the future.

Panchen: [answer redacted]

Chairman: Didn't another thing happen?

Zhang, Fan Ming: [answer redacted]

Chairman: Has the problem been solved?

Zhang, Fan: Yes.

Chairman: We cannot only say that the Han helped minority nationalities. Minority nationalities also helped the Han. When you cooperated with us, you expended a huge amount of capital. Tibet is such a vast place with many resources. Now that the Tibetans are cooperating with the Han, our national defense line is not the Upper Yangtse (Jinsha) River but the Himalaya Mountains. That is why you have received welcome from all people in our motherland. Our People's Liberation Army has not done enough for the Tibetan people since they entered Tibet. They built two roads, set up two elementary schools [one in Lhasa and one in Shigatse], and inoculated some Tibetan children. They have helped you only a little. On the other hand, they brought three harmful things to you: rising prices, the death of yaks during transportation, and unfair prices in their purchasing for a period of time.

Panchen: In the past, there were some problems. The price of goods increased. However, you helped us a lot. For example, you opened a People's Hospital and granted us all kinds of loans. As to the transportation, you paid us for the usage of yaks. And if our yaks died during transportation, you compensated us. In our economy, our main product is wool. In the past, we shipped the wool from pastoral areas to farm areas and from there to India. We did not get reasonable purchase prices. Even worse, we were cheated. And we could not sell our wool. However, after liberation, the Central Committee always purchased the wool for a high price. All these helped us a lot.

Chairman: It is just the beginning. This will increase year by year. There are a lot of hidden natural resources in Tibet. From an economic point of view, it is not only that the Han help the Tibetans; it is mutual help. Just like the tea you drink, you do not get it free. You have paid for it in wool.

Panchen: Over the past several years, the whole country helped us a lot.

Chairman: We should help you. This kind of help is the same kind of help the USSR gives us. Our development will benefit them; your development will benefit our country. For example, there are rare metals in Xinjiang, and there are forests and iron mines in Mongolia. All these are good things for our country. Some of these mineral resources do not exist in the Han regions, but these things exist in the regions of minority nationalities. The Han cannot do without the minority nationalities. So you are not talking about the whole picture when you say only that the Han are helping minority nationalities.

Panchen: We have heard that there are iron ore and other kinds of ores in Tibet. However, in many places the land is not cultivated yet. At present, we have found coal mines near the Tangola Mountains. We will find more mines in the future.

Chairman: It is promising. You should be confident.

Panchen: We are confident of the development of Tibet. Today, we attended the meetings in the Central People's Government. Problems such as the establishment of the Preparatory Committee for the Tibet Autonomous Region, resolution of the unsolved problems inside Tibet, and assistance toward construction in Tibet have all been decided or answered. It is really good for the unity of Tibet and the development of Tibet in the future.

Chairman: These problems have been solved. These problems, plus what you said just now, give a summary of our work in Tibet after liberation. The peaceful agreement plays an important role in solving these problems. In the past, the Dalai was afraid of us. You too. Otherwise you did not have to flee to Xiangride [in 1950].

Panchen: In the past, we were tricked by the propaganda of the reactionaries. We worried because we did not know the truth.

Chairman: Yes, when I had a conversation with the Dalai yesterday, the Dalai said his elder brother is living abroad and won't come back, so what should he do? I said, "Do not be afraid of that. You have come back; you have done the right thing. He is afraid. It is okay for him not to come back. When he is not afraid, he can come back." Some people do not understand us. They want to watch us for eight or ten years to see how we are doing. Consequently, we must do good work for a long time. You will leave Beijing for Tibet on the 12th. It will take a long time to go back. I am wondering whether you will accept gifts or money from the masses during your trip?

Che Jigme: When we came, we got some gifts from the masses during the trip. We returned some of them. We gave others to the temples to let them do some good deeds.

Chairman: You can accept some gifts. Or you can take measures such as getting two yuan and giving back three yuan. Won't that be better? In the future, the country could compensate some of your expenses. If you do not collect money, the masses will appreciate it, because they could see the Buddha without spending money.

[Anonymous]: [in summary] Comrade Wang Feng reported to Chairman Mao that the Dalai and Panchen had written letters to Labrang Monastery (in Gansu) to stop them [the monastery and people] from giving gifts and from preparing to welcome the Dalai and Panchen with big expenses.

Chairman: This problem has been solved; this is very good. You solved the problem through good discussion with them. (to Panchen) You two and many members of the delegation came; you attended the meetings of the National People's Congress and the Political Consultative Congress; you have visited various places. In the future, maybe you will come every four years. Now the roads are open, so it takes only three months to make a round trip. You can attend the meetings without delaying your work. If it is like this time, when you have had to spend one year on your round trip, it is difficult to have these meetings.

Panchen: The Dalai and I had never come here to attend a conference. It is good for the unity and many other kinds of work in Tibet. In the future, we would like to come here often.

Chairman: When there is an airport in Xiangride, it will be really good.

Panchen: Yes.

Chairman: Your region was the place where apes changed to human beings. In order to survive, the apes gradually changed to human beings through physical work. You do not believe in this, do you?

Panchen: [answer redacted]

Chairman: So your yellow branch of the religion is different from other branches. Other religions do not believe in this. [Chairman continues]: Is this your second trip here?

Panchen: Yes. I came in 1951.

Chairman: How old were you in 1951?

Panchen: I was fourteen in 1951.

Chairman: You are eighteen this year. Where is your home town?

Panchen: Xunhua County.

Chairman: Is it in Labrang?

Panchen: No. But it is close to it.

Chairman: Are you going to Labrang? Are you going back to Xunhua this time?

Panchen: Yes.

Chairman: It is very good to go back to see your hometown. What is the language of the textbooks in elementary schools in Tibet?

Panchen: It is completely in Tibetan language. Chinese and English are electives.

Chairman: This is very good. (to Zhang Jingwu) In the past, I told you that after you got to Tibet you need to study Tibetan language, so how is it going?

Zhang Jingwu: We are studying right now, but we did not study hard. Only those people who attended training class learned well.

Chairman *(to Fan Ming):* Fan Ming, how is your study going? I will test you today. You should not only study the Tibetan written language but also learn to speak Tibetan.

Lhamön did not come this time, ask him to please come when he gets a chance. Please say hello to him for me when you get back.[26]

On another occasion when Mao was meeting with the Dalai Lama, he unexpectedly brought up an important political matter: the contentious issue of the Tibetan flag, which had been a source of major contention for the sitsab. Phünwang, who was translating that day, recalled his surprise,

> One day, Mao unexpectedly came to visit the Dalai at his residence at about 8 P.M. During their conversation, Mao suddenly said, "I heard that you have a national flag, do you? They do not want you to carry it, isn't that right?" After I translated Mao's words, the Dalai Lama asked me, "Who does he mean by 'they'?" Although I knew who he meant, I translated this back to Mao, who responded frankly that "they" meant Zhang Jingwu, Zhang Guohua, and Fan Ming.
>
> Since Mao asked this with no warning that the topic was to be discussed, the Dalai Lama just replied, "We have an army flag." I thought that was a shrewd answer because it didn't say whether or not Tibet had a national flag. Mao perceived the Dalai Lama was concerned by his question and immediately told him, "That is no problem. You may keep your national flag." Mao definitely said "national" flag (tib. gyedar). "In the future," he said, "we can also let Xinjiang have their own flag, and Inner Mongolia, too. Would it be okay to carry the national flag of the People's Republic of China in addition to that flag? Would that be all right?" The Dalai Lama nodded his head yes. This was the most important thing that Mao had told the Dalai Lama, and I was amazed to hear it.
>
> My mind was racing. I didn't know whether Mao had discussed this with other leaders in the Politburo or whether he mentioned it on his own. Since I had always paid great attention to the Soviet Union's nationality model, I was excited, because I took Mao's comment that Tibet could use its own flag to

26. Dui xizang gongzuo de zhongyao zhishi (wei chuban de shouji), n.d., transcript of meeting (emphasis added).

mean that China was contemplating adopting the Soviet Union's "republic" model, at least for these three large minority nationalities. That's why I thought it was something new and very important.

That night, I went to see Zhang Jingwu to tell him about this. Zhang Jingwu listened and then asked me, "When Chairman Mao said 'they,' who he was talking about?" I responded, "He explicitly said you, Zhang Guohua, and Fan Ming." Then he asked me whether he had said anything else in addition to mentioning their names. I said he hadn't. Just the names. It struck me as odd that Zhang paid more attention to the people mentioned by Mao than the issue.

Some time later I mentioned Mao's comment informally to Liu Geping. He understood the significance right away and responded the same way I did. He did not pay attention to who the "they" meant; instead he was interested in the issue. He said, "According to this, it is possible that in the future some nationalities like Tibet, Xinjiang, and Inner Mongol could get the same system as that of the Soviet Union, while the other smaller ones would get 'autonomy.'" He thought that would be wonderful. We both thought that the Central Government must have this idea if Mao said that. In subsequent years, however, I searched for written mention of this conversation about the flag in party documents, but I have never seen it mentioned.[27]

DEPARTURE FOR LHASA

In early March 1955, it was time for the Dalai Lama to return to Tibet. He had been receiving messages from Tibetans to return home; for example, in October 1954, he received the following appeal from Jenkhentsisum in the name of the Tibetan community in India:

> We beg Your Holiness to consider the concern felt over your long absence by Tibetans in Tibet and India and request Your Holiness to relieve people's anxiety by returning homeland quickly. We pray for your speedy and safe return, preferably via India so that sacred places in India may also be visited. Detailed petition following.
>
> Tibetan community in India
> Signed T. Shakappa [Shakabpa], Shakappa House
> Kalimpong

27. Goldstein, Sherap, and Siebenschuh 2004: 194–95. A Chinese transcript of Mao's 8 March 1955 meeting with the Dalai Lama (Dui xizang gongzuo de zhongyao zhisi [wei chuban de shouji], n.d.) indicates that the flag issue was raised by Mao, as Phünwang states, but apparently omits key parts of the exchange:

Chairman: . . . (to Zhang Jingwu and Wang Feng) Are they still using the flag of Tibet?

    Zhang: Yes. It is the flag of the army.

Chairman: Each nation has its own flag; is there a flag of Tibet?

    Dalai: Yes, it is used only on top of the barracks of the Tibetan army and when the Tibetan army marches outside. There are no other flags.

[imprint of three seals] [1 is unknown], Tibet Mahayana Monastery in Buddha Gaya [Bodhgaya], Tibetan Association[28]

Jenkhentsisum also sent Mao and Prime Minister Nehru (who was about to visit China) appeals on the same day. The one to Mao said,

Maotsetung, Chairman
people's republic of China
Peiping

Long absence of His Holiness from homeland is being highly felt by the people; therefore, we earnestly pray that facilities for His speedy return to homeland may kindly be provided. Both Dalai Lama and Panchen Lamas return journey may preferably be arranged via India to avoid tiresome overland journey. Petition following.
    Tibetan community in India
    Signed T. Shakappa [Shakabpa], Shakappa House
    Kalimpong
    [three seals] [1 is unknown], Tibet Mahayana Monastery in Buddha Gaya [Bodhgaya], Tibetan Association[29]

The Dalai Lama, as mentioned, had promised Tibetans before he left that he would not stay over a year, and the Chinese had agreed. So plans were made for him to leave in mid-March after a meeting of the State Council was held concerning Tibet.
    On 8 March, a few days before the Dalai Lama was to leave Beijing, he asked to visit Mao to say good-bye personally. When Mao heard this, he decided on the spur of the moment, to instead go to the Dalai Lama to say good-bye. The official Chinese account of this meeting again reveals Mao's sophistication and moderation and the Dalai Lama's enthusiasm with modernization and with being part of the Chinese nation.

Chairman Mao's Conversation with Dalai
8 March 1955 (Yu He Qiao Bridge)

Chairman: You are leaving, and I came to see you. Is everything settled about your trip back home? Is there anything that I can do to help?

Dalai: After we leave Beijing we plan to go back and visit places in the northwest. Now everything about the trip is settled, and there is nothing that we need to bother you with. If there is, I will ask for help.

Chairman: . . . We need to learn from the advanced nations and countries; we

28. Document provided from the library of Tsipön W. D. Shakabpa, dated 14 October 1954.
29. Ibid.

need to learn things useful for our nation. However, it does not mean that we should learn everything from other nations. We need to keep the characteristics of our own nation. . . . There are reasons why each nation in the world can develop itself over a long time. Each nation has its own strong points and characteristics. . . .

Our country is very backward; it is about one hundred years behind the advanced countries. Imperialists often bully us because we do not have large quantities of steel and machinery. We can only make a few cars, only one or two airplanes for teaching purposes. However, after three five-year plans, we will have laid the foundation of our industry.

I hear that after you have visited the northeast, you are very pleased with our industrial construction as assisted by the USSR?

Dalai: In the past, I heard only that the USSR gave our country a lot of selfless help, but I did not see what it was like and only tried to imagine it. This time, I have seen with my own eyes that the USSR is helping us selflessly. I want to go to their embassy to express my thanks to them.

Chairman: I heard this, and I feel you are very broad-minded. You do see things not only for Tibet but for the whole country. You are happy about good things in the whole country. This means that you are not thinking only about Tibet. You are very hopeful. You are younger than I am and want to take care of things all over the country. We need to do things well in China, and we have to be more broad-minded. We need to do things well in the world. This is a principle of Buddhism. The founder of Buddhism, Shakyamuni, spoke for the oppressed people in India. He believed in saving everyone from his or her own suffering, and in order to do it, he gave up being a prince and founded Buddhism. So you Buddhist followers and we communists work together to save the masses from their suffering. We have a common point here, [although] certainly we have different points. In inland China, there is a Guanyin Buddha. Her statue is made very beautiful, elegant, and kind. People believe in her, and think she is a goddess of enormous kindness. Is there a Guanyin in Tibet?

Dalai: There is the goddess Tara in Tibet. Her statue is also beautiful and kind, and she looks like a girl of fifteen or sixteen.

Chairman: The other day, you said that you would treat the Han cadres like your own cadres. That is right. Those Han cadres are in Tibet to help, not to replace Tibetans. The autonomous region rule should be real autonomous rule; it should mainly rely on Tibetan cadres. But in order to get the help of Han cadres, we will send a small number of Han cadres into the autonomous region. They will help you with all their hearts and souls. We have tried to tell those Han cadres who are sent to work in Tibet that they should help you with all their hearts and souls. In order to help, they may need to be prepared to sacrifice their lives, but they must do a good job, not a bad one. Some of them cannot understand this and do not like to work there. They want to come back every day. This means that they are still thinking about Han, not Tibetans. Another example is some of them try to give as few things as possible to Tibetans. All these are considerations for Hans only. Some of them have severe subjectivism and do things in a big hurry. They always think that other people are backward and do not like them. In fact, they forget that they themselves are backward too. At present, Han are a little advanced, but we developed from backwardness. In two thousand years, when people at that time look at us, they will feel we are very backward, just like we feel Confucius is backward. Confucius never saw cars, airplanes, and certainly he could not drive cars and planes; he could not hold meetings of people's representatives. In two thousand years, people at that time will feel we are backward. Society has to make progress.

You have solved a lot of specific problems this time, very good. How do you feel?

Dalai: Those of us here are very satisfied. The Kashag still has suspicions, because they are not clear about certain things.

Chairman: Very good. When you go back, explain things to them clearly. When the autonomous region is established, they will still have suspicions. They are mainly afraid that their interests will be hurt.

How are the two sitsab? Can we give them positions in the preparatory committee, or in the future, can we place them in the national Political Consultative Congress? When there are meetings, if they want to come, we welcome them; if they don't, it is fine. Anyway, we cannot forget them.

Since you are leaving, I came to see you. I have another thing to say. Any Han cadres who are sent to Tibet and cannot work with you or cannot unite with you, you tell me, and I will recall them.

Dalai: The chairman suddenly came here; I feel like in a dream. Through several talks with the chairman, I have experienced big changes in my thinking. When I go back, I will put these instructions into practice. If anything comes up, I will report directly to the chairman. In the meantime, please give me your instructions. Zhang Guohua and the other people are working in Tibet, and I will break with the [previous] situation of merely coping with them. Instead we will sincerely help each other and work hard together.

Chairman: We have big hopes for Tibetans. You can help us a lot in the future; you can be very helpful to the whole world. I have to make this point clear: the help between different nationalities is mutual help. Tibetans have given us big help politically. Things will get easy if different nationalities unite together. This time when you visited Beijing and other places, the Han people took you very seriously. Through our entertainment and welcome, we have shown that we

want to unite with you very well. Take national defense as an example; Tibet has given us big help. If you had chosen to cooperate
with the imperialists and made the Upper Yangtse (Jinsha) River
as the border with us and made us your enemies, things would have
been very difficult for us. Now that we are united together, things
are easier. This is why people of the whole China take you very seriously. People of the whole world also take you very seriously. Thus,
do not think that you have no capital. You do have capital, and you
have big capital. In the future, Tibet may be very helpful to us economically. Tibet used to be a vast sea; this was millions of years ago.
The crude oil we use now comes from the little creatures buried in
soil under the sea millions of years ago. So there may be a huge
amount of oil in Tibet; in addition, there are other mining resources
in Tibet. Once they are explored and dug out in the future, they
will be very useful to our country's construction.[30]

As Mao had done for him in their first meeting, the Dalai Lama reciprocated
and walked Mao out to his car.[31]

The Dalai Lama's recollection of this meeting with Mao is similar.

When I returned from China in 1955, I was in great spirits. . . . Mao Zedong
himself told me . . . , "Since you are poor at this moment, we are helping you,
but after twenty years you will improve and we will withdraw. At that time you
must help us." Mao Zedong himself told me this. He used to tell me such
things, strange things. He said, "In the old days Tibet was strong country, and
Tibetan soldiers came to China and kicked out the Chinese emperor, and the
emperor had to run away. Now these days you have declined, and so we are
helping you now."[32]

In a later interview, he added, "Chairman Mao praised Shakyamuni as well
as the goddess Tara. Shakyamuni he considered a great revolutionary."[33]

On the next day, 9 March, the Dalai and Panchen lamas attended a special meeting of the Seventh Plenary Session of the State Council to hear reports on Tibet and the resolutions on the issues settled in Beijing.[34] This
included the resolution on the PCTAR, together with resolutions on transportation and development.

The resolution on roads and transportation set up the Tibet Traffic Bu-

---

30. Zhonggong zhongyang wenxian yanjiu shi bian zhonggong xizang zizhiqu weiyuan hui
2005: 117–20.

31. Li 1996: 190–95. Two days later, on 10 March, Mao also visited the Panchen Lama to
wish him good-bye.

32. Dalai Lama, interview, 1994, Ann Arbor, MI.

33. Dalai Lama, interview, 2004.

34. All the reports and resolutions are presented in Xizang zizhiqu dangshi bangongshi
1998; and some in Union Research Institute 1968: 105–25.

reau to maintain and manage the Qinghai-Tibet and Kham-Tibet highways and authorized the purchase in 1955 and 1956 of 750 trucks and the creation of a truck-repair factory in Lhasa. It also stipulated that a spur of the Qinghai road be completed from Yangbajen (north of Lhasa) to Shigatse as well as a road from Shigatse to Gyantse.[35] The State Council also authorized forty-two million yuan for road construction in Tibet over the years 1955–57, in addition to that already stipulated for improvement and maintenance of the Qinghai-Tibet Road.[36]

The resolution on construction approved new funds and technical staff for a series of projects, such as a hydroelectric power plant in Lhasa and a technical team's investigation of the feasibility of building similar plants in Shigatse after the road there was completed. It also approved a small thermal electric plant to be built there. In addition, a leather factory was authorized to started in Lhasa, together with a small iron factory to produce things such as agricultural tools. Similarly, dams were authorized on the Lhasa and Nyanchu rivers to control floods and provide some irrigation for fields, and the "7-1" (1 July) State Farm in Lhasa was authorized to be improved through the provision of more equipment and technical staff. Funds were also allocated to the Cadre School in Lhasa to increase its size, as well as to the school in Shigatse, whose dormitory facilities were to be increased from two hundred to five hundred students. Finally, macadam roads were authorized for Shigatse and Lhasa; offices, for the Panchen Lama's Administrative Council in Shigatse; and a hostel for Lhasa, together with one million yuan, for the purchase of agricultural equipment in Tibet.[37]

In addition to these formal resolutions, Zhang Jingwu, Ngabö, and Che Jigme gave reports summing up the three years since 1951. Zhang Jingwu's report listed all the successes but clearly pointed out failures in the areas of Han chauvinism and disrespect for Tibetan religion and culture.

At the same time, the Central Committee issued instructions to the Tibet Work Committee in Lhasa (in March 1955) that emphasized, among other things, the continuing need for caution. Despite the completion of the two motor roads to Lhasa and the agreement to start the Preparatory Committee for the Tibet Autonomous Region, Mao told his officials in Lhasa to be cautious and go slowly, since conditions were still not appropriate to start to think of major reforms. And he told them to be careful not to encourage the Dalai Lama to do things that are too progressive, since there was a danger that he could become isolated from the people.

35. The road from Shigatse to Gyantse was opened for traffic on 20 October 1955 (Zhonggong xizang zizhiqu dangshi ziliao zhengji weiyuanhui 1990, entry for 20 October 1955).

36. Xizang zizhiqu dangshi bangongshi 1998: 42–43.

37. Xizang zizhiqu dangshi bangongshi 1998: 43–44.

Central Committee's Reply to Various Tibetan Questions

The Central Committee discussed Tibetan questions on 20 February 1955; the following are our replies:

(1) We basically agree to the direction of the work of the Tibet Work Committee for 1955 and have made some revisions and additions. We return the whole document to you and hope that you will study and carry it out according to the specific conditions in Tibet. You should also carry out our party's policies of making no haste in our work in minority regions and preventing arrogance.

(2) . . . When Dalai and Panchen visited Beijing this time, we reached initial agreements on the following: to establish the Preparatory Committee for Tibet Autonomous Region, to stop use of Tibetan currency, and to reorganize the Tibetan army. We have also settled a few historical problems. All these show that the Dalai and Panchen have made progress and have become closer to us. They have achieved results, and their doubts and suspicions have been reduced. All these are good. However, we must realize that this is only one step taken and not a big step. We are still faced with severe difficulties and obstacles and cannot become proud and become impatient in work and do risky things because of this progress. We cannot overestimate the current situation in Tibet. Our position in Tibet is still not very firm. In case something happens, we may be faced with big troubles. We cannot overestimate the faction of the left either. They are the left in their political attitude toward our motherland, but they are the right in the nature of their class. We cannot discuss questions of land reform and social reforms with them. Neither can we ask them to join the Communist Party. *Do not encourage them to be too progressive in their speech and action; they will isolate themselves from the masses that way and make us look very awkward.*

We should have sound understanding of the political role of Dalai and Panchen based on the supreme religious faith they both enjoy among Tibetans. Give them the right kind of care and encouragement. Do not encourage them to say or to do anything that hurts their religious customs. Even if they would like to say it or do it, try to persuade them not to in order to avoid any inconvenience or even danger to them.[38] Provide good security protection to them when they return to Tibet. Make sure that there is no slight carelessness and negligence in your work. The political task of the Tibet Work Committee is serious business. . . . [39]

As we shall see in the next chapter, the impact of this trip on the Dalai Lama

---

38. The Dalai Lama and many Tibetans in exile today contend that the Chinese did not let the Dalai Lama undertake reforms because they wanted to do it themselves. The evidence, as seen here and in other documents cited earlier, though, suggests that Mao and the Central Committee feared that the young and impressionistic Dalai Lama would try to impose change without first creating consensus and in the process alienate the elite and damage his stature. This, of course, could have negatively affected Mao's gradualist policy by diminishing the position of the Dalai Lama.

39. Dui xizang gongzuo de zhongyao zhishi (wei chuban de shouji), n.d. (emphasis added)

was enormous, but there was one discordant note. In one of their last meetings, Mao shocked the Dalai Lama when he said that religion was poison. The Dalai Lama explained,

> On the final day that I met Mao Zedong, he was so happy. He was sitting on a chair. He came close to me and asked me if there were any Tibetans who knew how to send telegrams. . . . He [Mao] talked about continual contact through telegrams, and he spoke very well about how to lead the people, how to have meetings, and how to gather the opinions. He gave me good advice, and I was happy. Right after that he said that religion is poison. [At] that I got a little scared. I thought, Oh, here is the real enemy of the religion. I used to keep notes, and that sent tingles through me. So I sort of kept my face turned away and wrote things down word for word.[40]

And in another interview about this, he said,

> In my last meeting, although the formal farewell meeting [was] already done . . . then he told me I think three things, three categories. One category [was that] after I return to Lhasa how to mobilize these kind of people and [that I should] listen to their views, but the decision should be in your own hand, and how to communicate with [the] public. Two, the best way to communicate directly with him [was] through telegraph, and then he said, "You should train some trusted Tibetans in these technological things." And then, three, he told me, "Your mind is scientific; that is very good; religion is poison." And [it was] quite dark when I was leaving and cold with Chairman Mao without his coat. He came up to my car, and he himself opened it. He himself was not very agile [laughs].[41]

But, notwithstanding the negative impact of this comment, the Dalai Lama's visit had surpassed even the Chinese side's wildest hopes. They had succeeded in what Fan Ming thought was an impossibility: they had succeeded in truly winning over the Dalai Lama. The Dalai Lama himself commented on this.

> When I returned from China I had some confidence that we could work with them. And with the help of the Chinese Communists, Tibet could be modernized. And I had more trust with those Communist Party members than the non–party members.
>
> Q: When you went back to Tibet you were feeling good, and everyone was feeling positive. What was the best you thought Tibet could get at that time?
> . . .
> Modernize Tibet and [have] sort of equal terms. To us, with Chinese help, to build Tibet, and to the Chinese we did not argue whether Tibet was an independent or separate nation or not. Phüntso Wangye [Phünwang] also had that feeling. He knows that Tibet is a separate nation, but we have to develop

40. Dalai Lama, interview, 1994, Ann Arbor.
41. Dalai Lama, interview, 2004.

our country, so for that the Chinese Communist were not like previous Chinese [i.e. they would help]. That is Phüntso Wangye's belief. He told me. The previous Chinese had very strong chauvinism, but the Communists were not like that, equal. And in fact worldwide revolution of the worker class, so national boundaries are not important. So with that belief there was no inconvenience, and we could work together to build a nation. So that was our aims and beliefs. So like that, Phüntso Wangye and some other party members became best friends of mine. Really.[42]

Mao had won a tremendous victory. The Dalai Lama was influenced greatly by what he had seen and learned in China and, for the first time since he had come to power in 1950, was beginning to develop a vision of a new Tibet and a commitment to exert influence on his government's policies. He was now eager to move forward in concert with the Chinese to create a modern Tibet that was part of and loyal to the People's Republic of China.

And so, after an amazing six months in Beijing and inland China, on 12 March 1955, the two lamas and their entourages set off for Qinghai Province to start their trip back to Tibet. It is the subject of the next chapter.

42. Dalai Lama, interview, 1995.

Chapter 21

The Return to Lhasa

The Dalai and Panchen lamas began their return trip to Tibet together, traveling to the Northwest, where they performed a religious teaching at Labrang, a famous yellow hat monastery in Gansu Province. It is reported that a crowd of over ten thousand Tibetans attended. One eyewitness recalled, with a touch of hyperbole, "It was so crowded my feet could not reach the ground."[1] Following this joint appearance, the two lamas, as they had done on the outbound trip to Beijing, returned by different routes. The Panchen Lama and his people went via the northwest (Qinghai-Tibet) road, and the Dalai Lama via the southwest (Sichuan-Tibet) road.

The Dalai Lama's trip took him first to the large city of Chongqing and then by train to Chengdu, where he arrived on 20 April. The plan was to spend a few days there and then go on to Tartsedo, the capital of Xikang Province and the beginning of ethnic Tibet. From Tartsedo he would travel through Chamdo to Lhasa. However, a large earthquake caused substantial damage to the road and forced the Dalai Lama to remain for several weeks in Chengdu, where his visit was marred by an unpleasant interaction with Li Jingquan, the first party secretary of Sichuan Province.

Whenever the Dalai Lama went to visit Chinese cities, the top officials, such as the governor and the first party secretary, always personally welcomed him if they were in town. On this occasion, however, the Dalai Lama noticed that the first party secretary of Sichuan was not present and asked about it. Phünwang recalled, "The Dalai Lama, as I said, was observant and noticed things, including the fact that Li Jingquan did not show up. He asked me and the Chinese officials who were responsible for the reception where Li

1. Phünwang, interview, 2000, Beijing.

was, but we passed it off by saying Li probably was out of town. The Dalai Lama, however, did not seem to believe what we told him."[2]

The Dalai Lama had observed correctly, and Phünwang and Xu Danlu (the government's liaison officer to the Dalai Lama for the trip) were lying to him.[3] They both considered Li's absence an insult that could endanger the overall success of the Dalai Lama's visit to inland China, and Xu, in fact, had been working behind the scenes to persuade Li to welcome him. He had failed, as the following account illustrates:

> When Xu Danlu arrived in Chengdu to prepare for the Dalai Lama's visit, he immediately reported to . . . the relevant departments about the Dalai Lama's schedule, arrangements, and issues that they should pay attention to.
>
> Xu Danlu noticed [in the course of this] that the name of the first secretary of the province was not on the list of leaders who would welcome the Dalai Lama, so he suggested that they should arrange for the first secretary to come also. [He then learned that] The relevant provincial department hadn't arranged this, because the first secretary was too busy. Xu Danlu was very worried about this. He . . . thought that they may not know the situation well and may not understand that this small thing [welcoming the Dalai Lama] was related to the big issue of united front work and nationality policy, and he was afraid that this trivial thing could harm the big issue of the unity of nationalities.
>
> While still in Beijing, Chairman Mao, Liu Shaoqi, and especially Premier Zhou had all gone to see the Dalai Lama themselves, so how could the first secretary of a province have any reason not to welcome the Dalai Lama? Also, Xu Danlu recalled that before he left to escort the Dalai Lama back to Tibet, Li Weihan had especially told him, "The Dalai Lama going back is different from when he came. Now he is a national-level leader [deputy director of the People's National Congress]. You have to arrange everything according to the relevant regulations of the Central Committee for welcoming ceremonies and parties in all locations [for a leader of his rank]."
>
> So Xu Danlu knew it would not be a trivial thing if the first secretary did not show up and decided to try his best to persuade him to welcome the Dalai Lama personally. Xu went directly to meet the first secretary and state all his concerns. The first secretary, however, did not listen and said, "The Dalai Lama is just a kid. Why am I required to go to welcome him?"
>
> Xu Danlu patiently explained, "Though the Dalai Lama is very young, he is the deputy director of the National People's Congress, so he is one of the leaders of the nation. Also, he is the religious head of the Tibetan area. If you can spare the time to meet him, it will benefit the [government's] work." The first secretary then made an excuse, saying, "I showed up to welcome him when he passed through our province going to Beijing. It is okay for me to meet him just once."
>
> Xu Danlu still patiently tried to persuade him, saying, "When he was in Bei-

2. Goldstein, Sherap, and Siebenschuh 2004: 200.
3. Xu was normally in charge of security for the Tibet Work Committee in Lhasa.

jing, Chairman Mao, Director Liu, and Premier Zhou all showed great respect to the Dalai Lama. They even went to see him personally." The hidden meaning of this was that since even Chairman Mao had gone to visit the Dalai Lama, how could you as a provincial secretary be so arrogant? However, the first secretary was even more unhappy when he heard this and said, "No matter what happens, I will not go. Just do whatever you like; and if you want to report this to the Central Committee, do so."

Xu Danlu then realized . . . it was useless to try any more persuasion. So he had to think of another way to strike a balance to avoid causing any trouble. He then said to the first secretary, "It's fine if you do not go. However, you should make an excuse by saying you are sick and during this period not meet anybody." The first secretary thought a little while and then agreed, "That is a good idea, so do it." Xu Danlu, however, reiterated, "You should not appear in public during this period. After a couple of days pass, then you may show up and say you are recovered. Don't cause the Dalai Lama to have any doubts."[4]

However, the second day after the Dalai Lama arrived, Li Jingquan made a prominent public appearance that was reported in the newspaper.

The Dalai Lama saw the picture in the newspaper so knew that the first secretary was not really sick. He was so angry at this that he threw the newspaper aside and went into his own room.[5]

Xu Danlu heard about this from the Dalai Lama's entourage and realized the first secretary had caused a big problem. He went immediately to the relevant department of the Government of Sichuan Province to discuss whether there was any other way to make up for this—to reduce the negative influence and eliminate the Dalai Lama's doubts. Xu Danlu was afraid that the Dalai Lama would think about this too much and perhaps think the warm welcomes he received from the Central Committee, Chairman Mao, and the other leaders were fake. If the Dalai Lama thought that way, all the work done with the Dalai Lama over the past half year would be totally wasted. This was, therefore, a very serious issue.

However, some comrades in the Government of Sichuan Province [still] did not take this very seriously and thought Xu Danlu was just making a big fuss, talking about this in a sensational way. "Is it really so serious that the first secretary did not go to welcome him personally? Who does he [Dalai Lama] think he is? If he were really a leader from the Central Committee, we promise we would have gone to welcome him."

Xu Danlu tried very hard [to convince them], but it was still no use. Xu was very worried and was wondering why some senior cadres within our party neg-

4. Li 1996: 280–83.
5. The Dalai Lama does not recall being angry at Li's snub or, in fact, the incident at all, but he does not deny it could have happened. Since both Phünwang and Li Weihai's book (which was based on documents and interviews) give almost identical accounts, there seems little doubt this occurred.

lected the united front and nationality work so much and did not realize its importance. . . .

[Xu Danlu now] called Beijing and reported what happened to Li Weihan. Li . . . immediately replied, "The first secretary is clearly wrong. The Dalai Lama now is the deputy director of the National People's Congress. Though he is not a member of the CCP and without any position in the party, he is one of the leaders of the nation. The first secretary is just someone in charge of the local organization of the party and is a local-level official, so when a leader of the nation comes, all the local leaders from the party and the political and military spheres should go to welcome him. The first secretary should choose another appropriate time to meet with the Dalai Lama and make up for all the bad influence."

Xu Danlu then worried a great deal about how to report these instructions to the first secretary. At that juncture, a call came from Beijing that changed things dramatically.[6]

Unlike Li Jingquan, the Central Committee took this so seriously that it had Premier Zhou Enlai make a detour to Chengdu on his return from the famous Bandong Conference in Indonesia. Xu Danlu was told to ask the Dalai Lama to stay for a few more days in Chengdu to meet the premier, and he agreed. The Sichuan Party Branch Office was also told to make preparations for his visit. As soon as they heard this, the Sichuan officials realized they had made a serious mistake and were in for criticism or worse, and went to Xu Danlu.

Now the relevant department of the province came to Xu Danlu asking, "How should we arrange the order of the leading comrades when welcoming Premier Zhou? Who will be the first, the first secretary or the Dalai Lama?"

Xu Danlu was very relaxed now and kicked the ball back, saying, "You had better get instructions from the first secretary." He deliberately said to them, "Do whatever you want. One is the deputy director and the other is the first secretary. It is okay whatever you want to do."

They [the working staff from the relevant departments] tried to ask for a compromise from Xu Danlu. They knew that the Dalai Lama was very upset that the first secretary had not welcomed him. When Premier Zhou came, the first secretary would definitely meet the Dalai Lama. If they did not arrange everything well, it would be a very embarrassing situation. They got very worried. One is a leader of the nation, and the other is the leader in charge of them directly. What should they do?

In the end, the first secretary made the decision. After consideration, he reluctantly said, "Okay, let the Dalai Lama be the first."

When Premier Zhou came to Chengdu, the Dalai Lama went to the airport with other leaders, including the first secretary, although they waited separately. The team to welcome Premier Zhou was headed by the Dalai Lama, and on

6. Li 1996: 283–84.

the left, a bit back, stood the first secretary. Then stood the governor of the province, . . . and so on. Premier Zhou appeared at the door of the airplane full of smiles and disembarked the airplane. . . .

When the first secretary saw Premier Zhou come down, he stepped out first and stretched his hand out to shake hands with Premier Zhou. However, Premier Zhou just gave him a glance and did not respond to him. Instead he reached out his hand to the Dalai Lama and shook the Dalai's hand very heartily and said very warmly, "Dalai Lama, I am so lucky to come back in time. Otherwise I would have had no chance to say good-bye to you! I came specially to say good-bye to you. How have you been recently? How is your health?" . . .

At that moment, the first secretary's face flushed. He did not know what he was supposed to do. Should he leave or stay? He knew that Premier Zhou had known about his attitude toward the Dalai Lama and had specially come to make up for his slight and prevent a negative impact falling on the party and government. The very warm and caring welcome by Premier Zhou toward the Dalai Lama was a silent criticism to him. Premier Zhou was giving face to the Dalai Lama to make up for his actions. . . .

The Dalai Lama said to Premier Zhou, "Premier, you have a rest today, and I will come to see you tomorrow." Premier Zhou shook his head and said, "How could that be? I will come to see you. It is a deal."

The next day, when Premier Zhou was going to see the Dalai Lama as promised, all the main leaders of the province heard about this, and all came. The first secretary was worried and said to Premier Zhou, "Premier, you decide if I should go." . . . The first secretary held his head down looking embarrassed. Then Premier Zhou said very seriously, "Why didn't you go to welcome him when the Dalai Lama came to Chengdu? What kind of a host are you! Now you want to see him, but it is too late!" Premier Zhou really got mad. He looked around at the other people and said, "You almost destroyed the work of unity and the close relationship with the Tibetan upper class, which was so hard for us to build up." The people all looked at Premier Zhou silently, and no one dared to say a word.

Premier Zhou tried to keep down his temper and then said to Li, "You need not go. Let me explain to the Dalai Lama."[7]

Phünwang recalled the Dalai Lama's meetings with Zhou.

[Zhou] stayed in Chengdu for three days. One day . . . Zhou made a special visit to the Dalai and talked with him for more than two hours. The Dalai Lama told Zhou that everything had gone very well on his trip to China and all officials, especially Mao, had treated him very well. In addition, he said, he was pleased with the discussions about establishing the Preparatory Committee for the Tibet Autonomous Region instead of the Military-Administrative Bureau. And he said that he was inspired by his visits to other cities and by seeing what was happening in China. Tibet, he said, was backward and its people poor. He

7. Li 1996: 283–84.

said he now understood clearly that there was a large gap between Tibet and China and that Tibet needed to gradually reform. Zhou replied, "Mao and I clearly know that all Tibetans believe in the Dalai Lama and respect him greatly. And your thinking is correct. However, when you go back to Tibet, it would be better not to do reforms immediately." I thought that Zhou felt that the Dalai Lama was young and impressionable, and so might act too precipitously and alienate the conservative religious and lay officials in Lhasa. . . .

At their second meeting, Zhou expanded on what he had said to the Dalai Lama. "Regarding implementing reforms in Tibet," he said, "you need to think very carefully. The Central Committee's policy is that stability is the priority. Now you have seen firsthand that China has undergone tremendous changes, and that by comparison, Tibet is backward. However, in Tibet the conditions for carrying out reforms are not yet sufficient. Therefore, things should be done carefully. If there is a big gap between the leaders' thought and the masses' thoughts, the reforms will not be successful. Only after the thoughts of the leaders and the masses are matched can reforms be carried out." Although Zhou said "masses' thoughts," I understood that he really meant the upper circles. The real masses would have been happy if the reforms ended the tax and corvée labor of the old society, but the aristocrats and monasteries would not be happy and might oppose reforms and create chaos in Tibet.[8]

The Dalai Lama then set off to Tartsedo, in Xikang Province. Xikang was part of what is called ethnographic Tibet, because it had not been part of political Tibet in recent times but was almost entirely composed of Khambas.[9] As the Dalai Lama passed through this Tibetan area, he gave many religious teachings and met many Tibetan leaders, conveying to them his thoughts on the future. He recalled,

From Tartsedo to Lhasa, at the larger towns I stayed for two or three days and gave teachings. There were gatherings of a several thousand [in the various places]. At that time what I was constantly saying was that the Chinese people have come to help us. I was very forceful in saying that with the help of the Chinese we must put our country in good shape. So for a month or two, at the important places, I said that. The Chinese were very friendly and very happy. When I used to meet a party member, I was quite glad. I used to ask around if the person was a party member or not. Then I used to feel quite relaxed and [found it] easy to speak with that person. Probably 1955 was the best year for that.[10]

The Dalai Lama's frame of mind at this time is also revealed in his recollection of meeting with Zhang Guohua in Kongpo, on his way back to Lhasa. "We met at Nyingtri, a sunny day I remember, in my tent. I told him, [on]

8. Quoted in Goldstein, Sherap, and Siebenschuh 2004: 201–2.
9. For a discussion of political and ethnographic Tibet, see Goldstein 1997.
10. Dalai Lama, interview, 2004, Dharamsala (English unedited).

the same route when I [was] coming from Tibet, from Lhasa, to Beijing [I was] full of suspicion, anxiety. Now I am coming back same route full of confidence and hope. I told him. So that is a fact at that time."[11]

Although some books have mentioned that on the return trip, Khambas appealed to the Dalai Lama for help against the Chinese, the Dalai Lama has denied this. He says the only person who said anything political was the famous Derge leader named Chagö Tomden. "I stayed there [with Chagö] in his room for two or three nights. [On] One occasion he came and he told me all Tibetans should be [in an] independent nation. . . . I never responded. Hesitant. I already know that that is [a] quite serious, dangerous topic."[12]

So except for this awkward moment, which the Dalai Lama passed off without comment, the final phase of the return trip also went well, and the Dalai Lama arrived in Lhasa on 23 June 1955, three weeks shy of a year since his departure.

For Mao, therefore, the trip was a resounding success. His gradualist strategy had set out to win over the Dalai Lama and then work down through him to transform Tibet and Tibetans. The visit to Beijing was Mao's chance to show the Dalai Lama that this was a new China and persuade him to become a genuine part of it. The Chinese were pleased to learn that the Dalai Lama was very intelligent, open to new ideas, and progressive in his outlook. Seeing a modern country made a deep impression on him and solidified his own prior feelings that Tibet had to modernize. Most important for Mao and the Central Committee was the Dalai Lama's acceptance of communism as an ideology and movement aimed at improving the life of common people. The idea that both Buddhism and communism sought to help the people to overcome their suffering was powerful and attractive and made it easier for him to see Tibet as part of an otherwise atheist state. The Dalai Lama also eagerly bought into the idea of nationality equality and the ideals of the Socialist International and felt comfortable interacting with Chinese Communist officials and leaders. On this trip, he came to consider himself for the first time as part of the Chinese nation—and, as we saw, actually asked to become a Communist Party member.

For the Dalai Lama, the trip was also a great success. At age nineteen, he had met the top leaders of China, including Mao, had been treated with great respect, and had seen and learned many new things. He now felt that Tibet could fit into the new China as an autonomous region run by Tibetans so consequently felt great optimism and hope for the future. The key question now was not so much should Tibet modernize and reform itself as part of

11. Dalai Lama, interview, 2004 (English unedited).
12. Dalai Lama, interview, 2004.

China? but How should he bring about greater consensus in Tibet among the elite to do this well?

BACK IN LHASA

After the Dalai Lama's return to Lhasa, an effort was made to communicate what had transpired in China to the Tibetan government officials who had stayed in Lhasa. Ngabö took the lead in this and gave a detailed report on the events and agreements. Shatra, a Tibetan lay official, recalled hearing this report.

> After they arrived, Ngabö gave a briefing for about a week [in the Tsidrung-lingka]. . . . He spoke about what happened from the time they first went down to China, including the discussions and the results, what was said, and so on. During the whole thing, Ngabö was the main person. Surkhang was there too, as was Ragasha, but Ngabö was the main speaker who related everything.[13] . . . He mentioned that they were able to get the Preparatory Committee for the Tibet Autonomous Region instead of the Military-Administrative Committee and that this was done by all three [Tibetan] units together, the Tibetan government, the Panchen Lama's entity, and the Chamdo Liberation Committee. So everyone was happy.
>
> Q: Did Ngabö say this was good achievement?
>
> Yes, Yes. It was presented as the accomplishment of His Holiness's visit. Since the Dalai Lama went and discussed these things, he said, we should work to do it. So he said that very strongly. He made everything very clear, saying that on such and such a month, on this date such and such happened, and so on. He was so precise that one wondered how could anyone remember so much.[14]

At about the same time, the Dalai Lama also made some political comments during a religious ritual, revealing some of his thinking about the future of Tibet. The Dalai Lama explained how this speech came about.

> But still, [I had] full confidence [when] I returned. . . . [I was invited] to do an Avaloketisvara initiation ritual (tib. cenrezi wangchen) at the Jenselingga Palace [in Norbulingka]. There, I mentioned some important policy matters. [I said] With full confidence, we are equal. [The] Chinese came to us as helpers, and we must utilize this opportunity [and] build our own country by ourselves. My statement of this, before I talked to the public, I discussed [it] with Fan Ming, and he also agreed. . . . [In the speech] I mentioned exactly Phüntso Wangye's point of view. Unity must be built on trust. Trust must come equally [with equality]. So I mentioned that with full confidence. So that was my peak.[15]

---

13. Surkhang actually explained the details of the agreement on the Tibetan army, which will be discussed below.

14. Shatra, interview, 1992, Lhasa.

15. Dalai Lama, interview, 2004.

In this speech, which was the first time the Dalai Lama publicly spoke about Tibet and the Chinese, he did not comment specifically on political issues such as the army or the currency, but the speech clearly projected a very positive image of the Chinese government and of the Chinese then living in Tibet. *This was a Dalai Lama very different from the one being represented to the U.S. and Indian governments.*

The speech made several points. Tibet was poor in its knowledge of secular affairs, so in order to develop and progress quickly it would be necessary to work closely with the Chinese. However, at the same time, the Dalai Lama emphasized that the Chinese were sent to Tibet to help Tibetans, and they were equal to the Chinese. The speech also explained that developing the secular sphere was important, because to be autonomous meant being able to do things themselves. And, he spoke positively about the Preparatory Committee for the Tibet Autonomous Region, in essence telling Tibetans not to worry about it. Everything, he said, would be done appropriately, according to the actual situation, step by step. Nothing would be implemented rashly, and they would learn more details later. The full translation of this part of his speech is presented here.

> Regarding [our] secular matters, they are not well managed, and the methods we use are weak. Therefore, you must improve these. The main thing is that we ourselves should strive vigorously and work hard. However, because of our lack of experience and work in secular matters, it is very difficult to be effective quickly, so it is important to rely on help from the Chinese [Han] nationality. In general, you should be friendly with [all] the nationalities, and in particular, you should be friendly with the Chinese nationality.
>
> Some people have the concept that the Chinese and the Tibetans are like lord and servant, but it is not like this. We have genuine nationality equality. For example, if a father had five children, even if there are differences in their knowledge and capability, they possess equal rights. So the Chinese nationality cadres living here came to help us because we couldn't manage secular matters well. They didn't come to be our lord. Also putting this help for us into practice should be done when the conditions are appropriate, according to the local situation and when all people want it. If the conditions are not appropriate, we have to be patient.
>
> The central government sent Chinese cadres here for the benefit of Tibet. They were not sent to cause trouble. So if some Chinese cadres have a kind heart but do something inappropriate for the local situation, it won't be beneficial. Therefore, you should not try to save face [for them] and should rather point out their error directly to advance the good and block the bad and reform them.
>
> As for the few Chinese cadres who have erred because of matters of principle, if there isn't any hope for them to become beneficial for Tibet, we can just send them back. As for Tibetan cadres, in the future we should be able to take our own responsibility; this is called autonomy. For example, in a monk's

household, if the people in the household could do all the work of the household [themselves], this is autonomy. If the people could not do their work and if it is done by hired people, this is not autonomy. Therefore, it is important to have Tibetan cadres, including monk and lay officials.

Among the current cadres, many think of religion and politics and the welfare of the people and work honestly. Last year, in order to manage the government's income well and address the welfare of the subjects, the government took back the management of the counties and their estates. I am very glad from the bottom my heart for the officials who made such a great accomplishment. If you serve religion and politics with sincere loyalty, even if you can't live in a hermitage and practice the dharma, it will be beneficial for both this life and the future life. In the future, all people should take responsibility and not think opposite of karmic law in this life and future lives.

Some people are concerned only with their private affairs. This is because they are too narrow-minded. You people all know that at one time, in order to achieve goals, some of the political people in charge [of Tibet] did everything [only] for money and gifts [bribes]. Therefore, government affairs were delayed and subjects were tortured and had to suffer, which caused more harm than benefit. So people should repent what they did and make a fresh start and improve themselves.

Some people are using the revolution [the coming of the Chinese] as a pretext to ignore native customs and habits, and they are acting in a disturbed manner and using crude conduct. This is wrong. That which is called revolution is not disorder (tib. gonju khunglung mepa). These actions [of leftists] should also be reformed.

If the monk and lay officials and [Communist] cadres have good internal unity, they can work effectively on government tasks. Among the cadres, you should point out the errors directly and promptly. It is important not to instigate and be deceitful. For example, if there is a big stone that one person cannot carry, four or five people can carry it. So if you can be friendly with your neighbors, you can help and save one another.

The monks in the monastic colleges (tib. tratsang) and [within these the] residential units (tib. khamtsen) and subresidential units (tib. mitsen) are also acting biased in favor of their own unit.

As for the new and old Buddhist sects, if they are not impure, all of the sects are the same, for they are seeking to achieve enlightenment. So there should not be any prejudice and unfriendliness among the sects. Similarly, regardless of the region, whether it is the center (Ü), the west (Tsang), the east (Kham), or the far west (Tö), all of us are Tibetans, so you should not be prejudiced, and you should have a strong unity.

I think there might be quite a few people who, because they don't know about the Preparatory Committee for the Tibet Autonomous Region, have doubts, but this Preparatory Committee for the Tibet Autonomous Region is going to be done only in accordance with the actual situation, through steady steps; it is not going to be done in a rash manner. You will gradually know about this in detail.

In short, the main characteristic of Tibet is that we have Buddhism, which is the life of all of us. So we should develop, restore, and spread it and try to preserve it for a long time. This is our principle. According to the combination of the two, the religious and the secular, all people should act in a way so as to be beneficial for this life and the future life.[16]

The Dalai Lama's "advice" was the first time he had actively tried to influence public opinion and public attitudes. Although the content was mild and rather general, it portrayed China and the Chinese cadres in Tibet as friends who had come to help Tibet progress. It also adhered to the advice that Mao and Zhou had given about not trying to impose change without first preparing the groundwork by bringing the elite along with him. Mao wanted the Dalai Lama to start to play a more active leadership role in developing a consensus in Tibet for change as well as for friendship with the Chinese, and this speech suggests that he was prepared to do that. The question was whether the Dalai Lama had the political skills and personality to be able to play such a role and become a key force in molding a new Tibetan outlook. Mao thought he could and had bet his money on him as China's best hope for winning over Tibetans, rejecting Fan Ming's alternative strategy. At this point his bet looked good.

Later, in December 1955, Mao and the Central Committee sent interesting instructions to the Tibet Work Committee in light of the new, more positive circumstances in Tibet. Having stabilized their position materially through the roads and solidified the left in Tibet, the Communist Party was now ready to start to try to win over the mass of the elite, which they considered the middle and the right.

Instructions on Certain Questions of Work in Tibet

3 December 1955

[To the] Tibet Work Committee:

We have done an overall study of the Tibet Work Committee's telegrams of 11 November, 13 November, and 17 November. The following are our instructions for the Tibet Work Committee:

Things in Tibet have changed a great deal in our favor since the Dalai and Panchen came to Beijing to attend the Conference of the National People's Congress last year and since the completion of the southern and northern roads. Under the new circumstances, we should work in a more active way, especially the united front work, so that we can maintain our progress, further get rid of the influence of imperialists and the Guomindang, isolate reactionaries, and lay a better foundation for our work among the masses for the establishment of the Tibetan Autonomous Region.

The chief task in our united front work is still to increase the forces of the

16. Cited in Tibetan in Alo Chöndze 1958: 18–21.

left [the progressives]. According to the changes during the past year, we can be sure that the Dalai has changed from the middle to the left. It proves that the policy of the Central Committee to win over the Dalai several years ago is correct. It also proves that our estimate that the Dalai would turn left was completely correct. This is a big victory for our party in our work in Tibet. To the Dalai, we should continue to give him our protection and help, and we should also help him to unify with the majority of the upper hierarchy. Do not encourage him to appear too left, too early, because we want him to avoid isolating himself from the masses. If we do these things, we will enable the Dalai to play a bigger role in Tibet.

Continue to carry out the same policy of protection of and assistance to Ngabö. Though he has certain weaknesses, he is still a strong force among the left, and we can rely on him. Try to educate him to develop a good relationship with those both above and below him, to negotiate more with different sides in his work, and to be cautious not to become isolated from the masses. It is the same policy in working with other members of the left. We must see that the forces of the left are increasing as a result of the changing situations. We need to discover and assist the growth of new forces on the left. In the meantime, we must also make good efforts to strengthen our work with the middle and the right, especially the work to win the middle, otherwise our forces on the left will always remain isolated. Change our past practice of dealing only with the progressive minority of upper hierarchy, and expand our united front work. Not only should we work to win the middle and the right, we should also assist the left to work in this area. Not only should we work very hard, we should also push them and teach them to work in this area.

Explain fully to the Dalai and Ngabö about the necessity and importance of working with the middle and the right. It is okay to let them know what we are prepared to tell the middle and the right. The goal of our united front work in Tibet is to strengthen the unity of the Tibetan nation, to oppose imperialists, to lay the foundation for the future social reforms, and to reform the feudal upper hierarchy. It is the same as our work inland. Not only do we need to carry out the socialist reforms of capitalist industry and commerce, we also need to reform the bourgeoisie gradually into members of the working class.

When we gradually carry out democratic reforms and socialist reforms in Tibet, we need to reform the upper hierarchy of priests and aristocrats gradually into citizens of a socialist society. This has mutual influence with and is an inseparable part of the discontinuation of the feudal system in Tibet through peaceful means. It is extremely tough and complex work to reform human beings, but it is our duty. According to our experience of working with the bourgeoisie and the upper hierarchy of minority groups, this reform of human beings is not only very important but also possible. In our united front work today, we should pay special attention to this question. For example, when we discuss the question of reforms with the feudal upper-hierarchy members, we should tell them the policy of the Central Committee is that reforms in Tibet should be carried out by the Tibetan people and those upper-hierarchy members who have contacts with the masses of Tibetan people. The Central Committee cannot make the determination for them about the reforms. The reforms will benefit people at different social levels. They will benefit the lives of the upper hierarchy and will not make them worse. We should spread those messages. . . .

Central Committee
3 December 1955[17]

But despite Mao's positive attitude toward the Dalai Lama and the obvious progress, not all Chinese cadres agreed that he was a progressive. We have already seen the attitude of Li Jingquan and his officials in Sichuan,[18] and in Tibet, Fan Ming continued to believe that relying on the Dalai Lama was futile. Fan, in fact, believed he was simply duping Beijing.

> In Beijing, the Dalai was elected the deputy chairman of the First National People's Congress, and the Panchen was elected the deputy chairman of the Chinese People's Political Consultative Conference. The problem of unification was solved. The Dalai was damned happy and tried to show how progressive he was—he loved the motherland, he was progressive, he even wanted to join the Communist Party! All these were false. You know all these. However, he fooled some people. They believed that the Dalai was a statesman, that he loved the motherland, et cetera. They believed that Dalai was truly a patriotic and progressive leader. . . .
> The Dalai deceived people by behaving in a leftist way. He [said he] believed in communism, he wanted to join the Communist Party, et cetera. He tricked the policy makers. The policy makers were tricked. There were rumors in Lhasa that we were holding the Dalai as a hostage. So we let the Dalai and Panchen return to Tibet soon. The Dalai was believed to be patriotic and progressive when he left for Tibet. So he had got himself a pretentious mask.[19]

Moreover, notwithstanding the Dalai Lama's support for the idea of secular change and for a Tibet autonomous region, many Tibetans remained vehemently anti-reform and anti-Chinese. They objected to accepting the Beijing changes, which they considered to have been forced on the Tibetan government. Like the sitsab earlier, they wanted Tibet to stay the way it was, without Chinese-socialist values and institutions replacing traditional ones. In fact, ideally, without Chinese at all. Mao's assessment that it would be difficult for even the Dalai Lama to reform Tibet without first increasing support for change among a larger portion of the elite and masses, therefore, was correct, and the Dalai Lama's enthusiasm for change was quickly balanced by a dose of conservative and nationalistic reality.

17. Dui xizang gongzuo de zhongyao zhishi (wei chuban de shouji), n.d.

18. Li, in fact, was about to hurriedly launch the full-scale democratic reforms in the Han and Tibetan areas of Sichuan that would precipitate the famous Khamba uprising at the start of 1956.

19. Fan Ming, interview, 1993, Xi'an.

One moderate official, Shatra, recalled his own negative reaction to the Beijing agreements.

> Now there were two matters that [Ngabö explained but] were not so satisfactory. I was not satisfied, and that I must tell you truthfully, right? One concerned the Tibetan paper currency that the central government was going to exchange [for Chinese currency] and then give a specified amount for the expenses of the local Tibetan government. The second concerned the amalgamation of the Tibetan army into the PLA and that . . . all the expenses for this would be borne by the central government.
>   . . . I was not satisfied. If this took place, then things would be pretty much gone. If one could not use one's own currency and if there were no Tibetan army, then there would be nothing Tibetan left. It immediately would become Chinese.[20]

Shatra's unhappiness with these two agreements was widespread. The army reform plan, in particular, immediately came under attack, because much of the officer corps and rank and file objected vigorously to the planned reductions. This is not surprising, since the head of the Trapchi Regiment was General Tashi Bera, a founding member of the anti-Chinese secret Namseling clique discussed earlier. Gyagpön Kedram, a noncommissioned officer in the Trapchi Regiment, recalled what happened when the Kashag tried to implement the plan agreed on in Beijing.

> After His Holiness returned [from China], there was a meeting for three or four days at the Tsidrunglingka [about the trip]. The Kashag minister Surkhang spoke about the Tibetan military. He said that because the Chinese central government is now going to guard the borders, there are too many Tibetan soldiers. So, he said, we agreed to retain only one thousand soldiers. Of this thousand, five hundred are for the Bodyguard Regiment, and the other five hundred are to be [Lhasa] police. There is no need to station troops in other regions.
>   In the old days, he said, there were three thousand Tibetan soldiers from the old regiments. The thousand soldiers to be retained will be chosen from this category. For the five hundred Bodyguard troops, members of the present Bodyguard Regiment will be selected. The remaining five hundred troops will come from the three thousand troops of the old regiments.
>   Regarding the other troops, [he said] I'm sure many soldiers will [want to] return home, so they should do so by all means. The officers and noncommissioned officers who don't want to leave [Lhasa] will be given nonmilitary work. For the regular soldiers, we will form a committee and give them some construction work or something. The thousand soldiers we keep will receive a salary that is more than what they are getting now. We [the Tibetan government] will give things such as grain, while the salary and uniforms will be given

20. Shatra, interview, 1992.

by the Central People's Government. Therefore, the talk is over, and gradually this must change.

At that time nobody said anything. But the four regiments in Lhasa, namely,
the Bodyguard Regiment, the Trapchi Regiment, the Ngadang Gyantse Regiment, and the Chadang Regiment, discussed this situation and agreed that for
His Holiness to be without proper bodyguards and soldiers to guard the land
at a time like this [would be terrible], and there was absolutely no need to make
such changes. At this moment the problem was that we had too few soldiers,
not too many. Therefore, we stood together in unity and would not leave His
Holiness. They decided they would absolutely not accept the changes. So we
then filed numerous petitions through the Tibetan government's military headquarters (tib. mag jigang). . . . But we did not get any answer from the Kashag.

So while we were waiting for an answer, we were wondering about the
changes and what was going to happen. Then His Holiness was invited by the
Karmapa Lama to visit his monastery at Tshurpu. At this time, three representatives from the Trapchi Regiment, the Gyantse Regiment, and the Chadang
Regiment were sent to Tshurpu Monastery to present our petition to the Dalai
Lama in person. In the petition, we stated the full content of the petition we
had sent to the Kashag and said that we had received no answer. We also said
that we were completely unified and stood shoulder to shoulder. And no matter what, during this difficult period, we could not leave [the army]. Moreover,
if the government was really having difficulty paying us our salary, we would
take no salary and would serve happily and respectfully, but we would not leave
and we would not change. This is what we petitioned.

At Tshurpu Monastery, Lord Chamberlain Phala treated the representatives
well, and while His Holiness was circumambulating, they were able to give him
the petition. Usually, when there is a face-to-face, out of channels (tib. dongshu) petition like this, there is some kind of punishment. [But this time] There
was no punishment, and within one to two months, the order came that there
were not too many Tibetan soldiers but too few, and there was no need to make
changes and things should be left as before. During this period the military
salary had not been paid to us by the Grain Office. However, after the decision, all [that was owed us] was given, and so everybody was satisfied and happy.
So that is the way we stayed on (as soldiers).[21]

What transpired behind the scenes during those two months is not known,
but the end result was that the Kashag and Dalai Lama backed down to the
Tibetan military on the main issue of reducing the army, although they did
make one change regarding uniforms. From the beginning, the Chinese had
been irritated by the British-style uniforms worn in Tibet; the Dalai Lama's
entire Bodyguard Regiment wore that style of uniform, and in other regiments the commanders wore that style, although the troops wore Tibetan
uniforms. This now ended with foreign uniforms being set aside. From then

21. Gyagpön Kedram, interview, 1992, Dharamsala.

on, the Bodyguard Regiment switched to wearing PLA garb, as did the commanders of the other regiments. Despite this, the troops in the other Tibetan units continued to wear Tibetan uniforms until 1959.[22]

Similarly, the plan to exchange Tibetan currency for Chinese currency was never implemented because of the same kind of resistance. In this case, the monasteries strongly opposed this change, and since they were the main bankers in Tibet, their strong opposition, in concert with the general views expressed above by Shatra, scuttled that reform. Tibet continued to print and use its own money until the uprising of 1959. On both of these issues the Tibetan government never openly said it would not enact them but simply stalled and did nothing. There was clearly still a very strong desire to hold on to these very visible symbols of Tibet's separateness from China.

The plan to start a preparatory committee for the Tibet Autonomous Region also generated anger and opposition and became one of main rallying cries for the reemergence of the anti-Chinese People's Association. We saw earlier that when the Dalai Lama was invited to Beijing, Alo Chöndze and others from "the people" asked that he not go to China and, when that failed, organized and sponsored a "long-life" ritual for him. Later in early 1955, when the Tibetan government was organizing its official welcoming-back delegations to go to Eastern Tibet to greet the Dalai Lama, Alo Chöndze, as he had done when the Dalai Lama returned from Yadong, asked permission to send a People's Association welcoming delegation and was permitted to do so. Then soon after returning to Lhasa, Alo, together with Bumdang Trunyi and Shigatse Lhabju, started to sign up members for a new people's association, which would again submit a petition to the Chinese. This will be discussed in the next volume, but it is useful here to cite a part of this petition, since it illustrates the strongly anti–Chinese nationalistic attitudes and views the Dalai Lama was facing with respect to reforming Tibet. This segment of society hated the Chinese and was implacably opposed to changing Tibetan traditional institutions.

> We Tibetan people make the following appeal because we oppose the Chinese Communists who are destroying all our customs and systems, and also because of their complete breach of the Seventeen-Point Sino-Tibetan Agreement signed by them. . . .
> But speaking about the present situation in Tibet we declare that our religion is facing a very grave crisis which has thrown us into the very deep valley of darkness and destruction. The Dalai Lama has been robbed of his political and religious powers. The Tibetan nation is facing as grave a danger as a candle light in a storm. The root cause of this crisis is the oppression of the Chi-

22. Shatra, interview, 1992.

nese Communists who have been forcing Communist ideas upon the Tibetan people, the most deplorable policy of violence practiced by the Chinese Communists, and the failure of the Chinese Communists to implement any of the promises made by them to the Tibetan people. In order to save our country from this dangerous future we have already, on a previous occasion, made a formal protest to the Chinese Government and the Dalai Lama.

Formerly, under the Dalai Lama, there were Regents, Kashag and the various other Government organizations which carried out the administration of the whole of Tibet. But since the occupation of Tibet by the Chinese Communists all the former organizations of the Government have ceased to function and the Chinese Communists have established a large number of illegal organizations in their place to carry out the administration. . . . Communists have not only increased administrative organizations but they have also established organizations such as the "Patriotic Youth League" and the "Chinese Schools", with the sole object of forcibly indoctrinating the youth of Tibet in Communism, and thus to destroy the culture and civilization of the nation. Moreover, in opposition to the will of the people, the Chinese Communists have destroyed the social system of Tibet in which political and religious life are joined together, and have also destroyed the religion of the Tibetan people. Therefore we, in the name of the people of Tibet, have come forward to appeal to the Dalai Lama.

We request that the Dalai Lama stop the organization of the "Patriotic Youth League", close the "Chinese Schools" and prevent the indoctrination of the Tibetan people in Communism by the Chinese Communists. We are now resolved not to accept the establishment of the proposed Regional Autonomous Government in Tibet as we already have the Government of the Dalai Lama. At the same time we also request the Chinese Communist Military Representative in Tibet to allow us to go to Peking to lodge this protest. If the Chinese Communists disregard the people's wishes, and by force, oppression and violence suppress the earnest appeal of the people, we, in the name of all the people of Tibet, are fully resolved to shed our blood and sacrifice our lives to oppose the Communists and we shall definitely not co-operate in any of the activities of the Chinese Communists in Tibet.[23]

And finally, as indicated earlier, Jenkhentsisum, the group of committed Tibetan nationalists in India, was not also beginning to expand its opposition activities in India but was moving to link up with anti-Chinese Tibetans in Tibet, especially the Namseling clique and Dalai Lama's own lord chamberlain, Phala. In the second half of the 1950s, this group would play an active role in opposing the Chinese presence in Tibet and thwarting the Dalai Lama's plan to work hand-in-hand with the Chinese to create a modern Tibet.

Consequently, if the changes agreed on in Beijing were the first test of the Dalai Lama's skill and resolve after his return from China, this was not

23. Cited without source in Patterson 1960: 112–14 (emphasis added).

a promising start. The advice and warnings that Mao and Zhou had given the Dalai Lama about the need for extreme care when initiating changes proved all too accurate, even for the things they in Beijing thought could be done. So while winning over the Dalai Lama was a tremendous victory for Mao, it obviously did not mean the end was in sight. The Dalai Lama would need to assert strong leadership to be able to win over the Tibetan elite and persuade them to accept the new Tibet he envisioned.

Chapter 22

Conclusions

The return of the Dalai Lama from his year-long trip to inland China marked the high-water mark in Sino-Tibetan relations in the 1950s. The Dalai Lama was deeply influenced by what he saw in China and by the attitudes of Mao and other Communist Party leaders, with whom he developed excellent rapport. Moreover, he became intellectually enamored with communism as an ideology and as a force for social and economic change and for improving the life of the poor Tibetan masses. He returned to Tibet filled with enthusiasm for developing and modernizing Tibet as a part of China. Mao had won over the Dalai Lama, and it seemed Tibet would now take its place as one of the most important national minority regions of the PRC, gradually being transformed into an autonomous region under the Dalai Lama's leadership.

China's success was the result of a carefully thought out and implemented strategy. From the beginning, it was obvious that incorporating Tibet would bring two diametrically opposite social and political systems face-to-face. The feudal, manorial estate–based socioeconomic system that was extant in Tibet was precisely the type of hereditarily oppressive elite system that the Chinese Communist Party was committed to overthrowing and had done so throughout the rest of China. In Tibet, however, Mao opted not to place "liberating the serfs" as an immediate priority. To the contrary, during the period of this history, traditional Tibetan society with its lords and manorial estates continued to function unchanged. Similarly, despite the presence of roughly twenty thousand PLA troops in Lhasa and Central Tibet, the Dalai Lama's government was permitted to maintain important symbols from its de facto independence period—its own army, its own flag, and its own currency—as well as to continue to collect its own taxes, arrest and punish its own criminals, try civil cases, unilaterally decide how to allocate its income, and promote and demote officials in its bureaucracy. Amazingly, even runaway serfs could still be caught and whipped with impunity. In the history of the PRC, the scale of this was, and still is, unique.

The architect and director of this moderate Chinese policy toward Tibet was Mao Zedong. His policy had minimal and optimal goals. The minimal goal was to liberate Tibet, whether or not Tibet's leaders agreed to become part of China. If need be, China would simply invade and take over Tibet militarily. Mao's optimal goal also took liberation as a given but laid out a much more ambitious, sophisticated, and nuanced strategic vision for Tibet, the prime focus of which was to incorporate it in a manner that created a stable, loyal Tibet that accepted its place as a part of China and willingly implemented socialist reforms. To achieve this transformation, Mao crafted a pragmatic "gradualist" policy and directly oversaw its implementation.

The first step in this strategy was to secure the "peaceful liberation" of Tibet, that is to say, to induce the Dalai Lama to sign an agreement that accepted Chinese sovereignty over Tibet and the arrival of thousands of Chinese troops and officials in Tibet. Mao deftly used a combination of carrot and stick tactics to achieve this, particularly making the carrot component extremely attractive to Tibet's leaders. The Dalai Lama and the Tibetan government would be allowed to remain in power and reforms would not be implemented without their agreement. However, since the Tibetan elite was clearly not interested in reforming Tibet, offering such terms meant that it could take years to transform Tibet. Mao accepted that reality, feeling that the long-term benefits of a peaceful transformation far outweighed the potential problems in quickly ending serfdom and the estate system.

China eventually was able to induce the Dalai Lama to send representatives to negotiate an agreement known as the Seventeen-Point Agreement. It also succeeded in persuading him to return to Lhasa to work under the agreement, despite the urging of many to flee into exile and denounce the agreement (e.g., the United States, his family, and many top officials, such as Namseling, Surkhang, and Shakabpa).

Peaceful liberation, however, was only the first step. The agreement established a legal framework for Tibet's status as part of the PRC and allowed Chinese troops and officials to enter Central Tibet peacefully, but it was not an end in itself. The second phase of Mao's gradualist policy focused on two related issues: (1) winning over the Dalai Lama and the Tibetan elite and, in concert with them, gradually implementing the Seventeen-Point Agreement so that ultimately socialist reforms and a new Tibet autonomous region would be created with their approval and (2) stabilizing the Chinese physical position in Tibet so that neither internal uprising nor external attack could dislodge them.

Mao's focus on the elite, especially the Dalai Lama, derived from his belief that the poor peasant masses in Tibet were not yet ready, nor would they be in the near future, to understand and accept class struggle. The powerful hold that religion and lamas had over them would be difficult to overcome, so China's best hope to incorporate Tibet in a positive manner was to work with and through the elite. Mao, in essence, was setting out to change nothing less than the elite's moral framework.

However, not everyone in the Chinese Communist Party agreed with Mao. Fan Ming considered an attempt to win over the Dalai Lama's feudal elite a hopeless task and advocated moving fast in tandem with the Panchen Lama to create demand for land reform among the serfs. His plan was to treat the Panchen Lama and his administration as separate and autonomous from the Tibetan government by giving them control over Back Tibet. Once the Panchen Lama controlled this area, the Panchen Lama would take the initiative and end the estate system and serfdom in his area. When the peasants under the Dalai Lama's government saw this going on beside them, they would demand the same for themselves, Fan was convinced, and this would compel the Dalai Lama to follow suit and disband the old system in his area.

Mao, however, rejected this strategy, believing that using the Panchen Lama in this manner would create such deep hatred of the central government on the Dalai Lama's side that Tibet could never be merged in the positive fashion he thought was important for China's long-term national interests. Tibet and China were at a unique juncture in their history, and it was critical to manage this transition carefully so that, in the end, Tibetans would become loyal citizens of socialist China. Gradualism and the Dalai Lama were the keys to accomplish this, so he insisted that cadres in Tibet, including Fan Ming, adhere to his gradualist program.

Setting out to transform the attitudes and perspectives of the Tibetan religious and feudal elite peacefully was a bold and ambitious undertaking, which Mao understood would require a combination of tact, flexibility, and time. Chinese officials in Tibet, therefore, were repeatedly instructed not to rush to change Tibet. The policy, in words and actions, was to move forward slowly and with great caution. The focus was to be first on the Dalai Lama and the more progressive and friendly segment of the elite and then on winning over more and more of the large undecided middle segment of the elite, while isolating and rendering insignificant the hard-line, anti-Chinese segment. The length of time this process would take depended on how successful Chinese tactics were in influencing the Tibetan elite, but Mao was willing to wait five or ten years or perhaps even longer to achieve this goal. His time commitment at this point was open-ended.

The Chinese officials in Lhasa, therefore, set out to develop cooperative and cordial relationships with the elite and to convince them that these officials had come to Tibet to help them modernize and develop Tibet, not to oppress and exploit them, as previous Chinese regimes had done. Projecting themselves as "new Chinese," the Tibet Work Committee made every effort to demonstrate respect for Tibetan religion, language, and culture in their speeches and behavior, including giving alms to all the monks in and around Lhasa.

However, while the Chinese were willing to proceed slowly in Tibet, they were not willing to do nothing. Their goal was clearly to transform Tibet in a way that would gradually replace the theocratic and feudal Tibetan autocracy with a Tibet autonomous regional government directly under the central government, although as mentioned above, they wanted to wait until the Dalai Lama and most of the Tibetan elite came to believe these changes were necessary. The Seventeen-Point Agreement, did not specify time frames, so when any of the seventeen points should be implemented was unspecified and depended on a subjective assessment of the conditions and attitudes in Tibet.

China's initial strategy in Tibet also had a practical dimension—stabilizing the PLA's physical position there as soon as possible. With no roads from inland China to Lhasa, the PLA initially had to depend entirely on Tibet for food. They were also vulnerable in the realm of military supplies, for should fighting break out, resupplying would require transportation by pack animals over long and difficult trails. Ending this dependency was a priority, and Mao authorized a crash program to build two roads to Lhasa, one from Sichuan Province and one from Qinghai Province. At the same time, he also ordered his troops in Tibet to make producing their own food a priority equal to that of road building. Beijing also shrewdly negotiated an arrangement with India whereby Chinese rice would be sent though Calcutta to Lhasa. But everything took time in Tibet, and it actually was not until December 1954 that these motor roads opened to traffic.

The Tibetan side, however, had no common voice and no clear strategy for dealing with their new status as part of the People's Republic of China. Within months of signing the Seventeen-Point Agreement, thousands of Chinese troops and officials entered Lhasa, and though virtually all of the elite saw the PLA as an army of occupation, not liberation, the Tibetan government had to decide how it would deal with the Chinese troops and cadres and with the Seventeen-Point Agreement, which had set out general guidelines for what Tibet could be as part of China. These guidelines, as mentioned, were vague and, in a few instances, somewhat contradictory, so there was considerable room for interpretation, maneuvering, and clarification. The future of the Dalai Lama, the Tibetan government, and Tibet's traditional institutions was likely to depend on how well the Tibetan government managed this.

In contrast to the Chinese, however, the Tibetan side developed no unified strategy. The two highest offices in the Tibetan government, the sitsab and Kashag, did not cooperate and utilized very different strategies and tactics. From the start, the two sitsab were hostile and confrontational toward the Chinese, trying not to cooperate on anything the Chinese proposed. They were angry at the Chinese occupation of Tibet and incensed by what, in their view, was the communists' hypocritical rhetoric about being "new" Chinese coming to help Tibet, when they had just launched a bloody invasion of Chamdo. And they were also angry at what they felt was Ngabö's negotiation of a badly flawed agreement. They considered Tibet independent and wanted, naively to be sure, at most an arrangement wherein the Chinese would withdraw virtually all their troops and officials and leave Tibet as it had been during the Qing dynasty era, that is, a loose protectorate of China.

The sitsab's attitudes reflected the majority attitude in Tibet, and they became Tibetan heroes for what was seen as standing up to the Chinese. However, their rhetoric and actions were driven by anger and emotion rather than a carefully calculated plan to negotiate with the Chinese to change the agreement or reinterpret responsibilities. Consequently, virtually every time the sitsab met with the Chinese leaders face-to-face, the meetings literally ended in yelling and screaming matches. Ignoring the reality that Tibet had lost the war and had signed an agreement accepting Chinese sovereignty, the sitsab seemed to think that telling the Chinese they were unwelcome in Tibet was a rational strategy for inducing them to change their policy.

The sitsab's understandable anger, but counterproductive behavior, encouraged opposition and led to the emergence, for the first time in Tibetan history, of a nonelite political organization that called itself the People's Association. And in turn, this led to increased unrest on the streets of Lhasa. As a result of this, the situation quickly deteriorated in Lhasa, and by March 1952, the city teetered on the edge of violence.

The Kashag, by contrast, had a different and pragmatic approach. They, too, were angry about what they saw as the Chinese occupation of their country, and they feared what the Communists might do to Tibet's religious and political institutions in the long run, but, having lost the war, they felt the best strategy was to take the Seventeen-Point Agreement at face value and, on the basis of its guidelines, strive to develop cooperative and cordial relations with the Chinese. Their strategy was to try to make the agreement work for Tibet's interests and welfare.

However, internally, the Kashag itself had different points of view. Ngabö, for example, thought that major reforms were inevitable, so it was best if Tibet took the initiative and implemented them itself. To paraphrase his metaphor, if one makes a hat for oneself it will fit just right, but if one does not and later has to wear a hat made for someone else, the fit will be poor. Several other ministers were also inclined toward moving ahead on reforms, but most opposed any unilateral radical changes. The Kashag, therefore, also did not develop a unified strategic position in regard to the Chinese and the agreement, preferring to deal with issues ad hoc as they arose. On the whole, the Kashag ministers realized reforms would have to be done but, despite

Ngabö's views, were hoping to be able to do them as slowly as possible. Nevertheless, they were clearly committed to working cordially with the Chinese and to living within the guidelines of the Seventeen-Point Agreement. Because of this, they felt the sitsab were pursuing a dangerous and unproductive course of action and tried to counterbalance the hostility and enmity projected by them. In turn, the sitsab did not trust the Kashag (especially Ngabö) and thus chose not to confide in or work together with them. At this time of extreme crisis, therefore, Tibet's two paramount offices, the Kashag and sitsab, were uncoordinated and pursued contrary trajectories.

A month or so after the first PLA troops arrived in Lhasa, the Chinese leadership exacerbated the situation by starting to pressure the Tibetan government to implement changes mentioned in the Seventeen-Point Agreement, for example, to open Lhasa's first primary school, to start the new Tibet Area Military Headquarters, to incorporate the Tibetan army under the PLA, and to create a new military-administrative committee. As was seen, these initiatives were poorly received by the Tibetan side, especially by the two sitsab, who were adamant about not changing the Tibetan army or starting a military-administrative committee. This also fueled the growth of the anti-Chinese People's Association. The Tibet Work Committee, therefore, had inadvertently done what Mao had admonished them to avoid at all costs, namely, moving too far too quickly without the cooperation of the elite. Mao responded in April 1952 by taking direct control over events in Tibet, ordering all decisions regarding Tibetans to be cleared first with Beijing. Mao and the Central Committee, from then on, directly managed affairs in Tibet.

The third key player at this time was the Dalai Lama. In theory he could have imposed a unified strategy on his officials and government, but in 1951 he was only sixteen years of age and was, by and large, disengaged from political affairs. Neither his own inclinations nor the advice of his entourage led him to take an active role in determining how Tibet should respond to the Chinese. As a result, he basically sat on the sidelines until events almost spun out of control in 1952, when the People's Association opposed the Chinese and the Chinese sand-bagged their positions and placed their troops on high alert in anticipation of an attack. Ultimately, as we saw, the Chinese and the Kashag appealed to the Dalai Lama to intervene, and, after considerable hesitation, he agreed to order the sitsab to step down and ban the People's Association. The Chinese, under instructions from Mao, now set aside all discussions about absorbing the Tibetan army and starting a military-administrative committee. They also compromised with the Kashag by allowing the sitsab, in essence, to retire with their full ceremonial status rather than be dismissed and also by not punishing any of the leaders of the People's Association. With the sitsab out of the picture, the Kashag now resumed its status as the highest office in the government, and the volatile situation quickly dissipated, ushering in a new period of cooperation with the Chinese.

In this new atmosphere, the Chinese organized popular youth and women's groups, new schools, a newspaper, and a series of tours to see inland China or study there or both. In the next two years more than a thousand Tibetans went to China on tours and to attend meetings, and roughly five hundred Tibetans went to the Nationalities Institute in Beijing to study. And within Tibet, over a thousand Tibetans were enrolled in new primary schools. On the Tibetan government's side, a reform organization headed by Ngabö was begun. He was not only the Kashag minister most trusted by the Chinese but also the one most trusted by the Dalai Lama, who frequently discussed political issues with him privately and who himself was in favor of reforms and modernization for Tibet. In 1953–54, therefore, the Tibetan government's Reform Assembly crafted new laws reforming interest rates, old loans, and the administration of counties. However, despite Ngabö's prominence after 1952, he did not have much skill as a political leader and was not able to change the attitudes of either the majority of less progressive officials or the people.

While this was occurring, on the Chinese side, Mao intervened to definitively end the machinations of Fan Ming, deciding in favor of the Southwest Bureau and the Dalai Lama. Fan Ming's defeat, although not known then by the Dalai Lama and the Tibetan government, meant Tibet potentially had time to work out changes and reforms its officials and people could live with.

In the midst of this new era of cordiality and cooperation, the Dalai Lama was invited to attend the first meeting of the National People's Congress in 1954. Many in Lhasa opposed his going, fearing that the Chinese would not allow him to return promptly, if at all, or would treat him with disrespect and disdain, or, even more ominous, would influence the attitudes and views of the young and impressionable Dalai Lama. However, he and the Kashag felt it was important to meet the leaders of China face-to-face. After much discussion and disagreement, the issue was deadlocked, and, as in the past, the fate of Sino-Tibetan relations came down to a divine lottery, which broke the deadlock and approved the trip.

The Dalai Lama was powerfully affected by what he saw in inland China and by the leaders he met. At one point he even asked to be allowed to join the Communist Party. Mao's improbable strategy of going slowly and winning over the Dalai Lama had turned out to be an amazing success. Tibet was now poised to enter the third phase of Mao's program by creating new administrative institutions in Tibet with the cooperation of the Dalai Lama—in this case moving to create a preparatory committee for the creation of a Tibet autonomous region. Everything seemed poised for Tibet to begin to move forward now socially, economically, and politically as an integral part of the People's Republic of China.

But notwithstanding the enthusiasm of the Dalai Lama and progressive officials such as Ngabö, implementing reforms in Tibet faced serious opposition. Many in Tibet, especially the monastic leaders and their monk official allies, opposed land reforms and the relinquishment of other symbols of Tibetan "independence" or distinctiveness, such as Tibet's use of its own currency. They read the Seventeen-Point Agreement to mean that unless they agreed to such changes, they did not have to go forward, so they felt justified in simply saying no.

Mao understood such attitudes still existed in Tibet and continued to support his gradualist strategy, even though the opening of motor roads in December 1954 secured the Chinese position in Tibet. As we saw, when the Dalai Lama left Beijing in March 1955, Mao and Zhou Enlai both counseled him not to let his enthusiasm lead him to move forward prematurely on changes his people were not ready to accept. They advised the Dalai Lama to work with patience and skill to coalesce public opinion for the reforms he would propose. Similarly, in December 1955, Mao reiterated the same message to the Tibet Work Committee in Lhasa.

But Tibet was a premodern state in 1951, with no institutions for propagandizing the people or influencing public opinion. The Tibetan government's perspective had been that politics was not the people's business, so the Dalai Lama had no ready indigenous Tibetan mechanisms to utilize to influence public opinion. Initially, as we saw, as soon as he returned to Lhasa in 1955, he expressed his "political" views during a religious teaching he gave, but if he was to change attitudes and mold a new consensus for his position, he would have to go beyond this and develop new methods of influencing public opinion, including perhaps replacing conservative officials with more progressive ones.

However, notwithstanding the optimism the Dalai Lama felt, the news that the Tibetan government in Beijing had agreed to end Tibetan currency, reduce the army, and establish a Tibet autonomous region generated instant anger and opposition in Lhasa similar to what had occurred in 1952. In Lhasa, the second anti-Chinese People's Association reappeared in 1954–55 under new leadership. It opposed the changes that had occurred since 1952 and especially objected to the forthcoming creation of the Preparatory Committee for the Tibet Autonomous Region. By the fall of 1955, it was challenging the Dalai Lama's view of a new Tibet and, by early 1956, was recreating the disturbances of the People's Association of 1952.

There were also complicating external forces the Dalai Lama would have to address. While the Dalai Lama was in China, a secret anti-Chinese resistance group emerged in India independent of the Tibetan government. Headed by his own older brother Gyalo Thondup and two other government officials, Shakabpa and Lobsang Gyentsen, Jenkhentsisum, as it was known, sought support from India and the United States and, in the second half of 1955, came to be linked with the anti-Chinese Namseling clique in Lhasa and the Dalai Lama's lord chamberlain Phala. It would become an important force opposed to the Chinese occupation of Tibet and to compromising solutions with China.

Similarly, far from Lhasa, in the heart of China, a major shift to the left was starting as Mao launched the Socialist Transformation Campaign in 1955. Mao, critical of the slowness of collectivization in China, now called for a rapid acceleration of the implementation of full communes. While this did not directly affect Tibet, since Mao continued to support his gradualist program there, it had major repercussions in Sichuan Province, where Li Jingquan implemented socialist reforms in the ethnic Tibetan (Khamba) areas precipitating a bloody uprising in 1956.

Finally, an important force in the 1950s was the U.S. government. It tried persistently in 1951–52 to induce the Dalai Lama to denounce the Seventeen-Point Agreement and flee into exile, in which case he would have been a valuable anti-communist voice in the Cold War in Asia. But as we have seen, the U.S. offer of support was too little to offset Mao's "carrot," even though Mao's offer required the acceptance of Chinese sovereignty. For most of the elite, particularly the more religious and conservative sectors, the idea of the Dalai Lama in exile was unacceptable. They believed that with the Dalai Lama in Tibet, Tibetan religion and culture could be preserved. By the end of 1952, therefore, it was clear that the Dalai Lama was not going to flee from Tibet, so an active U.S. interest in Tibet diminished. It remained quiescent until the end of 1955, when the United States again became interested in Tibet, this time with regard to unrest in Kham/Sichuan and the possibility of supporting a Khamba insurgency through the Dalai Lama's brother Gyalo Thondup.

Consequently, although the Dalai Lama returned in the summer of 1955 to a calm Tibet and was enthusiastic about modernizing Tibet and improving the lives of poor Tibetans, in the distance, dark storm clouds from several directions were already forming on the horizon. They would soon sweep into Tibet, challenging his hopes and views and calling into question his very understanding of the situation. How he, his leading officials, and the Chinese officials in Beijing and Lhasa would deal with this storm will be the focus of the next volume.

Lobsang Samden's 1952
Letter to Tsipön Shakabpa

[illegible]
[illegible]
[illegible]
[illegible]
[illegible]
[illegible]
[illegible]

Kashag's 1953 Edict
Reforming Debts in Tibet

This edict from the Kashag was issued in the Water-Snake year [1953] to the coun ties, the estates, the lenders, and the borrowers regarding analysis of the payments and the exemptions of grain loans taken from the government, the aristocrats, and the monastic estates.

THE ORDER

According to the plan submitted previously by the Reform Conference (tib. Legjö Jitso), loans were among the various kinds of reforms that should be put into practice. As a result of the obligation to send both taxes and soldiers [as a corvée tax] and, on top of that, failures in both their crops and animal husbandry, the poor serfs (tib. miser) had to take loans from the government, the aristocrats, and the monastic estates for their food and seed. They were [often] unable to repay the loans in autumn, which caused the interest to be added to interest for many years.

One debtor had to pay loans to many lenders, so the loans and the borrower became imbalanced, like the proverb "The sickle and mountain are imbalanced [a sickle is too small for cutting all the grass on a mountain]" (tib. risor gandzö). So even if they paid [the interest] from generation to generation, it was impossible for them to repay the loan [the principal], and, therefore, they became extinct [ceased to exist as a household]. So the poor taxpayer households (tib. tremi) had a very hard time physically and mentally during their entire lifetime.

Consequently, H.H. the Dalai Lama gave profound instructions that we should not let this continue and must implement a reform that gives relief to these poor people. So we don't have any choice but to adhere to these profound instructions and implement reforms as soon as possible.

We had sent an edict regarding the easy way for repaying money loans in the nomads' area in the far western (Tö) and northern areas, where there are no arable fields to be cultivated. For the remaining [areas] in Ü-Tsang, in the Water-Snake year we have also sent an edict (and printed copies of the edict) regarding making loans for sowing seeds, the rates of interest, and how to repay the loans taken before the Water-Dragon year [1952]. In this we said that we would clarify these in the future, and according to that [we are doing so below]:

[Loans of] government grain were meant for the happiness of the miser and charged only 10 percent interest (tib. gamgye jusur). Also, for these, adding the unpaid interest to the principal (tib. gyela gyegya) and imposing penalties for delaying the payment were not allowed. However, recently it seems that some (officials such as those in charge of the grain salary [tib. druphog] in Ü-Tsang, and the 10 percent lease fee of the grain of the Agriculture Department [tib. soley jubog], and barley for religious offerings [tib. chöndru], and the treasury offices in the Potala and Jokang [tib. tseshö chandzö], and the Shöl office) signed loan agreements with poor taxpayer miser that added interest on to the principal if the yearly interest due was not paid. Regarding this matter, all the loan agreements that have been made by all the successive officials must be analyzed, and all of the interest that was added on to the principal must be completely eliminated.

The principal and interest of the loans of the miser who are completely extinct [literally, have ceased to exist, but normally means have run away leaving their house and land] should not be imposed on either the new taxpayers who replaced them or their guarantors. All the principal and interest [on such loans] must be completely eliminated.

As for the taxpayer borrowers whose economic condition is good and who have the means to repay the loans but in the past have petitioned and received exemptions written on their petitions, they will not be exempt from repaying the loans now. And as for the rich households who willingly took the ownership of the fields that used to belong to the extinct subjects [subjects who ran away (or died out)] and guaranteed to pay the loans owed by the extinct subjects and to do the tax work, they will not have any exemptions. They must repay the principal and interest according to the agreements.

As to the loans that were taken newly from the Iron-Tiger year [1950] of the sixteenth sixty-year cycle to the Water-Dragon year [1952], if the borrowers and guarantors have become extinct, the payment and exemptions must be done as specified below. Otherwise, if the borrower and guarantor are still alive, he or she must pay all the principal and interest.

The borrowers from the middle class we have classified into three categories. With the exception of new loans taken after the Iron-Tiger year, all those old loans taken before the Earth-Ox year [1949] must be repaid and exempted as follows:

The best off of the middle-class (tib. dringrab) borrowers will be exempt by the amount of one-tenth of the principal [10 percent].

The medium middle class (tib. dringbar'bring bar) will be exempt by the amount of one-eighth [12.1 percent] of the principal.

The lowest of the middle class (tib. dringtha) will be exempt by the amount of one-fifth [20 percent] of the principal.

For all, the remaining principal must be paid at the rate of 10 percent interest.

If the borrowers still exist but are really poor, half of the principal will be eliminated, and the remaining principal must be paid according to the payment arrangement as follows:

> Those who owe from 10 to 100 khe of barley must pay one-tenth [10 percent] of the principal in interest each year.
>
> Those who owe from 100 to 200 khe of barley must pay one-twentieth [5 percent] of the principal in interest each year.
>
> Those who owe from 200 to 400 khe of barley must pay one-fortieth [2.5 percent] of the principal each year.
>
> Those who owe from 400 to 600 khe of barley must pay one-fiftieth [2 percent] of the principal each year.
>
> Those who owe from 600 to 800 khe of barley must pay one-eightieth [1.25 percent] of the principal each year.
>
> Those who owe from 800 to 1,000 khe of barley must pay one-hundredth [1 percent] of the principal each year.

For those who have more debt than that, the officials in charge of government grain must submit a plan for payment arrangements according to the law and the karmic law of cause and effect and according to the borrower's economic condition for repaying the loans.

In the future when you provide new loans, government grain is meant only for the miser under the government or aristocrats or monastic estates. Otherwise, it is strictly not allowed to lend government grain to government lay and monk officials and to the rich traders who want to take loans to make profit.

Furthermore, government grain must be lent to the taxpayer subjects evenly for both the food and seed they absolutely need, in accordance with their economic condition. When collecting the principal and the interest, they are absolutely not allowed to go against the original loan document and do the following things: When collecting a barley sample [of what is being paid], the people who measure the bags of grain (tib. bo), the house managers and the sweepers, may not measure it as rounded bo (tib. bokha tolen) [meaning the container must be filled just to the lip with grain, not heaped on top so that the payer is giving more that he owes]. And they cannot add a penalty for delaying the payment or add it to the principal, nor can they take food or money or eggs as gifts [bribes]. They are strictly not allowed to cause harm directly or indirectly by any means to the happiness of the subjects by using the above-mentioned pretexts. The subjects who want to take loans from the government's grain must also be grateful to the government and pay the yearly 10 percent interest on the principal.

In order to keep giving offerings and have the funds for rituals increase, not decline, the sponsors of the Three Great Monasteries (Drepung, Sera, and Ganden) and other monasteries have donated trust funds for offerings and for the expenses of the rituals performed in the monasteries. So we have informed the abbots and the representatives of the three great monastic seats that they must be well concerned about the well-being of their subjects without causing harm to the offerings and the rituals performed in the monastery.

We received a request from the monasteries saying that the private barley of the big labrang and the rich monk households should not be mixed in with the barley of the monastic common trust funds that are meant for the offerings and rituals. In the future, the Senior Monastic Council (tib. lachi) and the monastic officials must guarantee that such mixing [of private monk and monastery grain] will not happen again.

Concerning the funds given out by religious trust funds, the borrowers whose economic conditions are good and who have the means to repay the loans and who also have taken the loans through legal procedures, and the rich people who have taken the ownership of lands that used to belong to extinct households, will not have any exemptions. They must pay the principal and the interest according to the agreements.

As for the new loans [from religious trusts] taken since the Iron-Tiger year of the sixteenth sixty-year cycle [1950] and before the Water-Dragon year [1952], if a borrower has become extinct, his loan must be paid as listed below. For the remainder, the principal and the interest of the borrowers and guarantors who are alive must be repaid at the rate of 20 percent interest (tib. ngadru dro), because that barley goes for the offerings and for the performance of the rituals.

As for the middle of the middle class and the worst of the middle class, it [the interest] should be completely exempted, but we found that their yearly interest deficits [owed interest not paid] (tib. gyeche) were added on to the principal by changing the old agreement into a new one. Therefore, it is inconvenient for us to find out and separate the amounts of the deficit interest and the principal. And some people made a separate agreement for the interest deficit, so if we completely exempt the interest deficit, these people might suffer some loss.

Therefore, except for the loans taken since the Iron-Tiger year, the old loans taken before the Earth-Ox year have been classified into three different categories of economic conditions among the middle class as follows:

For example, if the principal was 100 khe and the interest deficit was 100 khe, when the deficit interest was added on to the principal, the total became 200 khe.

For the best middle-class borrowers whose interest deficit was not added on to the principal, they will be exempt for one-tenth (10 khe from 100 khe) of the principal and one-third (33 khe, 6 dre, and 4 phü from 100 khe) of the interest deficit. The total exemption will be 43 khe, 6 dre, and 4 phü. For the people whose deficit interest was already added on to the principal, they will be exempt for one-fourth of the total amount (50 khe from 200 khe).

For the medium middle-class borrowers whose interest deficit was not added on to the principal, they will be exempt for one-eighth of the principal (12 khe and 10 dre from 100 khe) and half (50 khe from 100 khe) of the deficit interest, and the total exemption will be 62 khe and 10 dre. For those whose interest deficit has already been added on to the principal, they will be exempt for one-third (66 khe, 13 dre, and 2 phü from 200 khe).

For the worst middle-class borrowers whose interest deficit was not added on to the principal, they will be exempt for one-fifth of the principal (20 khe from 100 khe) and two-thirds of the deficit interest (66 khe, 13 dre, and 2 phü from

100 khe). For those whose interest deficit is already added on to the principal, they will be exempt for half (100 khe from 200 khe).

If the borrower and the guarantor are both extinct, the loan will not be pursued, and both the principal and interest will be completely exempt from the taxable field.

If the borrower still exists, but if he is really poor and doesn't have the means to repay the loans, or if the borrower has died and only the guarantor exists and the interest deficit was not added on to the principal, the deficit interest will be completely exempted and half of the principal (50 khe from 100 khe) will be exempted.

For those interest deficits already added on to the principal, five-sixths (166 khe, 13 dre, and 2 phü) will be exempted. The remaining deficit will be paid according to the payment arrangement for a fixed number of years, starting from the Water-Snake year as follows:

The borrowers who owed from 10 khe to 100 khe must pay one-tenth per year.

Those who owed from 100 khe to 200 khe must pay one-twentieth per year.

Those who owed from 200 to 400 khe, must pay one-fortieth per year.

Those who owed from 400 to 600 khe must pay one-fiftieth per year.

Those who owed 600 to 800 khe must pay one-eightieth per year.

Those who owed 800 to 1,000 khe, must pay one-hundredth per year.

As for the borrowers who owed more than that, the lenders and the borrowers must make interest payment arrangements according to the law and the karmic law of cause and effect.

The payment arrangements made through the previous loan investigations and the payment arrangements made through the lawful agreement between the lenders and the borrowers will not be changed, and they can be paid and received as before.

For the taxpayer's fields that the lenders forcefully took away in lieu of the loan, regardless of there being a written agreement, exemptions must be made as much as possible from the principal according to his economic conditions. And the remainder must be paid through payment arrangements, and all of the taxpayer's lands must be returned to the owner from the harvest of the Water-Snake year [1953].

As for the fields that were handed over to lenders for a fixed number of years through mutual agreement as a replacement for a good amount of the payment arrangement, there is no need to make changed payment arrangements for the loan. For the number of years that are left, the lenders must reduce them as much as they can according to the economic condition of the borrowers. And the borrowers must make their own choice whether they want to take back the lands and make a yearly payment arrangement to the lenders.

In the future, if the borrowers agree to hand over fields to the lenders for a fixed number of years to repay their loans, they are allowed to do that. And it should be the replacement for a good amount of payment arrangement [i.e., must not undervalue the land]. Otherwise, the lenders are not allowed to take away the tax-payer's lands by force or take it away for good. So when the government, the aristocrats, and the monasteries make loans to all the subjects, they are not allowed to violate the Water-Snake year edict and the printed copies sent to the counties and the estates.

When the big and the small labrang, the monk's households in the monasteries, aristocrats, government officials, and other rich monks and laymen made loans, some of the borrowers who were the taxpayer subjects had quite a good living condition, and they took loans for doing business. For this type of loan and the new loans from the Iron-Tiger year [1950] to the Water-Snake year [1953], if the borrower and the guarantor are extinct, the payment and the exemptions must be done as listed below. Otherwise, the loans owed by the borrowers and guarantor who still exist must be paid according to 14 percent interest (tib. düngye dro).

As for the loans taken not for trading but for paying taxes, corvée soldiers, food, and seed, if the borrower's economic condition is good, the loans taken before the Earth-Ox year [1949] must be paid according to the mutually agreed payment arrangement.

For the old loans taken before the Earth-Ox year, the calculation is based on [several conditions], for example, if the principal was 100 khe and the interest owed was 100 khe and if the interest owed had been added on to the principal. We classified three different categories among the middle-class families.

For the best middle-class borrowers whose interest deficit was not added on to the principal, one-eighth (12 khe and 10 dre from 100 khe) will be exempted from the principal and half (50 khe from 100 khe) will be exempted from the interest deficit. If the interest deficit was already added on to the principal, one-third (66 khe, 13 dre, and 2 phü) will be exempted.

For the medium middle-income borrowers whose interest deficit was not added on to the principal, one-fifth (20 khe from 100 khe) will be exempted from the principal, and two-thirds (66 khe, 13 dre, and 2 phü) will be exempted from the interest deficit. The total exemption will be 86 khe, 13 dre, and 2 phü. For the interest deficit already added on to the principal, half (50 khe from 100 khe) will be exempted.

For the worst middle-class borrowers whose interest deficit was not added on to the principal, one-fourth (25 khe from 100 khe) of the principal will be exempted, and four-fifths (80 khe from 100 khe) from the interest deficit will be exempted. For the deficit already added on to the principal, two-thirds (133 khe, 6 dre, and 4 phü) will be exempted.

If the borrower and the guarantor are both extinct, the loan will not be pursued. For those who have the taxpayer's land, the principal and the interest will be completely exempted.

As for the borrowers who are really are poor and don't have the means to repay the loans, or if the borrower has died and only the guarantor is left, if the interest deficit was not added on to the principal, the deficit interest will be completely exempt, and four-fifths of the principal (80 khe from 100 khe) will be exempt.

If the interest deficit was added on to the principal, then they have to pay one-twentieth of the interest and principal together. The remainder is exempt (190 khe from 200 khe). Except for the above exemptions, the remaining interest deficit must be paid through yearly payment arrangement starting from the Water-Snake year as follows:

The borrowers who owed from 10 to 100 khe must pay one-tenth.

Those who owed from 100 khe to 200 khe must pay one-twentieth.

Those who owed from 200 khe to 400 khe must pay one-fortieth.

Those who owed from 400 to 600 khe must pay one-fiftieth.

Those who owed from 600 khe to 800 khe must pay one-eightieth.

Those who owed from 800 khe to 1,000 khe must pay one-hundredth.

As for the borrowers who owed more than that, the lenders and the loan takers must make interest payment arrangements according to the law and the karmic law of the cause and effect.

The payment arrangements made through previous loan investigations and the payment arrangements made through the lawful agreement between the lenders and the borrowers will not be reformed, and it [the loan] can be paid and received as before.

For the taxpayers whose lands were taken forcefully by lenders for loan payments, regardless of any written agreements to this, exemptions must be made as much as possible from the principal according to their living conditions. And the remaining loan must be paid through payment arrangement, and all of the taxpayers' lands must be returned to the owners from the harvest of the Water-Snake year [1953].

As for the land that was handed over to the lenders for a fixed number of years through mutual agreement as a replacement for a good amount of the payment owed, there is no need to make further payment arrangement for the loan. For the remaining years, the lenders must reduce the number of years as much as they can according to the economic condition of the borrowers. And the borrowers must make their own choice whether they want to take back the lands and make a yearly payment to the lenders.

In the future, if the borrowers agree to hand over the land to the lenders for a fixed number of years to repay their loans, they are allowed to do that, and it should be a replacement for a good amount of the payment owed. Otherwise, it is not allowed for the lenders to take away the taxpayer's land by force or take it away for good. So when the government, the aristocrats, and the monasteries make loans to all subjects, they are not allowed to violate the Water-Snake year edict and the printed copies sent to the counties and the estates.

The heads of the government, the aristocrats, and the monasteries must adhere to the above-mentioned points and make the exemptions on loans to one's own subjects. Furthermore, they must lend them new loans and voluntarily make more exemptions on paying the loans for many years, according to the economic conditions of the borrowers.

They must try their best to show concern and benefit for their livelihood, and are definitely not allowed to neglect the suffering of the poor and uneducated subjects who are unable to make accusations regarding their problems that would cause them to become extinct. The lenders of the government, the aristocrats, and the monasteries must make the right choice between taking and discarding.

If some lenders think about the happiness of the poor subjects and one's own present and future benefit and therefore make more exemptions than what we mentioned above, nothing is more beneficial for the happiness of the subjects than this kind of good deed. Therefore, the government will rejoice in it. All people must keep in mind the points of the edict, and this edict must be included in the catalog of the records in the county. On the date and month of the Water-Snake year [date and month not given].*

* From the original woodblock printed book, housed at the Library for Tibetan Works and Archives.

Agreement of the Secret Resistance Organization in India, 1954

Memorandum of agreement among the members of the secret meeting on the question of indeoendence [sic] of Tibet, dated the year, Wood Horse of the sixteenth Rabchung, month—date.*

We, the members of the secret meeting, undertake before our protecting deities, Lhamo, Norjin Daikpa Chansing, Dahla Woeden Karpo, Gyalchen Shugden, the following main points.

The country of Tibet is consisted of areas from Toe Shang Shung Bon area to the area of Gyamo Thakpa, and Toe Ngari Korsum, Bhar U-Tsang Rushi to Dokham Chushi Gangduk. The country was blessed by Lord Buddha and according to its prediction, it was known to be a place of Phakpa Chenre Zsi. The people of this country was peacefully regined [sic] from the time of Ngatri Tsepo to Tri Ralpa Chen and many rulers who initiated the religion, and set rules. From Domtom onwards many scholars worked and great progress was made on the teachings of Lord Buddha. Succession of Dalai Lama was unceased from Gedun Drupa. The fifth Dalai Lama was able to unite the land as one country, and till today the country under the duel government system had been achieved the freedom of religion and enjoying the fruit of the land. The government had been keeping good relations with all the neighboring government, but due to lack of political education in the land, no proper defense systems were established always setting examples of peaceful method all over the world. At such time, when in 1950, Tibetan year iron-tiger of Rabchung sixteenth,

---

* Mimeograph English translation of the Tibetan document. The Tibetan version was not available to this study. The English has not been corrected. The translation was obtained from the library of the late Tsipön Shakabpa.

the Chinese communists attacked Tibet without understanding the meaning of priest patron relation between the two governments. They claimed that Tibet was part of China and it must be liberated from the toke [*sic*, yoke] of imperialists. Special representatives were sent to New Delhi, India to meet the Chinese ambassador to explain that Tibet was an independent country and it wishes to remain as it was. While these negotiations were going on, a sudden attack by Chinese from different directions in mass scale and arrested the minister who was in-charge of political and defense along with his staff. Thereafter, the Government of Tibet appealed to the United Nations. His Holiness the Dalai Lama with a limited number of entourage left for Yatung. Still in consideration of our past relation of priest-patron, government sent representatives to China for talk. Chinese brought out a pre-prepared agreement of their own and coerced the Tibetans to sign it. The agreement mentioned that the position and power of the Dalai Lama would remain the same, there would be no change on the present system and China would not interfere, freedom of religion, culture, protection for the monasteries, all officials of the government would remain as before and all Tibetan territories from Dha Tsedo onwards would be given back to Tibet. For the time being, the Dalai Lama returned to Lhasa from Yatung.

In spite of the agreement, the Chinese began to bring in a large number of troops to Lhasa and other areas. They set up an autonomous state beyond Kongpo Gyamda, backed up the Telhun Labrang [Tashilhunpo] by permitting to set a private army, so many problems were created by not keeping up with the country's law, bought many houses and properties in the city of Lhasa under pressure. And used many vacant land without paying any tax. They also began establishing many new offices, indoctrinating all young people, in communist system, collecting grains by force from the Government, religious institutions and from the people, procuring so many animals from the nomads resulting gradually the number of animals, one hundred percent increase in food price because of influx of population, construction of motor roads from China, under the name of tour many Government officials, representatives of the monasteries, representatives of people were taken to China by force in spite of their unwillingness to go, and these were the reasons that the people began appealing to the Government and the Chinese. When the appeal was made in view of justice, the Chinese pressed for the resignation of the two Prime Ministers accusing they were the supporters of the Imperialist, and jailed five representatives of the people. Moreover, sudden invitation came to the Dalai Lama to visit China. The three monasteries and people of U and Tsang appealed that His Holiness is the heart and soul of the people and that he should not be taken to China. They ignored the appeal by the people and His Holiness was taken to China. People were put in a state of great grievance like fish taken out from the water on a land. People in their own country suffered so much that it was difficult to pass day and night under such frightening oppression. Still more, they announced that Political and Military office would be established and so many Chinese men and women were brought into Tibet. This was to accomplish their wish to genocide Tibetan people by bringing in Chinese because of Tibet's small population.

We have received so many letters from Tibet stating the Chinese atrocities in Tibet and pinning their hope on us, we are compelled to take up the matter in consideration of our religion, political affairs and our kinsfolk. We therefore, called out

meeting on 16th Rabchung, wood horse year, day 14th of fifth month, correspon-
ding to 14-7-1954 to discuss on regaining our independence. It was not a forced members to join the body but they were to voluntarily. In order to achieve our aim the
following signed people would agree to undertake the followings—

1. Till we accomplish our independence, we would sacrifice our lives and our
   wealth without ever retreating from difficulty and loss of moral. We would
   continue our effort year by year, even it takes a lifetime.

2. Effort should be made for the speedy return of His Holiness to the capital of Tibet.

3. At such important matter like this, all should unite to take up the question in hand whether it becomes successful or not. No one should blame
   each other, they should not depart from this due for self interest.

4. All discussions should be kept secret and they should not be permitted to
   reveal to outsiders. Shall undertake to bear all penalties should anyone be
   seen, heard and proofed.

5. Should any question arises as to a person's undesirable character, they
   should reveal it frankly without protecting a person for his embarrassment.
   All matters must be settled by self undertaking.

6. In case certain understanding arises among the members, members themselves should mediate between the parties and should never be publicized.
   Not only helping for one another, they should help others in order to win
   confidence in us.

7. When there are new entrees in this association, they should be examined
   thoroughly, even it takes a month or a year. When such candidate is approved by all members, he can enter this association with a guaranty by one
   the member.

8. Whatever the matter, great or small, each should express their opinion
   clearly. Then the matter will be discussed in meeting and decision taken.
   If votes arrive at equal numbers, whether it be on political or military, a
   Zendrill* would be made.

9. There may come on certain times that matters concerning the independence of Tibet cannot be discussed due to various reasons. They can be
   kept unrevealed for a time but eventually the cause and reasons must be
   explained at the meeting.

10. Our main political aim is that His Holiness would retain his leadership of
    the duel Government, all people in U, Tsang, Dokham, Amdo and Golok
    will have equal power in the administration of the country, which consists

* The following note appeared embedded in the agreement: Zsendril [sic] is made by rolling
two equal size of dough which contains the letter "Yes" or "No." The two round doughs are put
in a cup and rolled around before a deity (image or a thagka [sic] painting). The decision is
take on the one which cames out of the cup.

of education, health, improvement of people's living condition, freedom of speech, defense, freedom of various sects of religion. Whatever the best should be taken up. Such activities that hampers the progress should avoided so that the people may not be disappointed. We must ban all the activities of Communists and the atheists.

11. If there becomes necessary to add to the above points, we shall discuss on the matter.

In all time we are abide by the above memorandum and if anyone found to be dishonest it was needless to say that ills would fall upon you by the influence of the deities, not only during this lifetime but effects would befall upon you in your next life.

The following signators and their guarantors had undertaken that they would bear the responsibility if such incidents occur. . . .

List of Correct Tibetan Spellings

PHONETIC	ROMANIZATION
abra	a bra
adrung	a drung
alo	a lo
Alo Chöndze	a lo chos mdzad
Amdo	a mdo
Amdowa	a mdo ba
Andrug Gonpo	a 'brug mgon po
Andrutsang (Gompo Tashi)	a 'brug tshang (mgon po bkra shis)
Arotsang	a rog tshang
Ba	'ba'
babshib	'bab zhib
badzalaga	bar tsa lag ga
bag	sbag
bangla sersha shane	pang la gser sha bzhag nas
garsha gognyen mindu	dkar sha lkog mkhan mi 'dug
dale lama shane	ta la'i bla ma bzhag nas
jingdrü donglong mindu	bcings 'grol gtong long mi 'dug
Barkor	bar skor
barmi jey	bar mi byas
Batang	'ba' thang
Be Lhamo	dpal lha mo
bo	'bo
bokha tolen	'bo kha mtho len
bombola bombola sigi	dpon po lags dpon po lags zer gyi
bugdam	sbug dam

bugdam dzatsig	sbug tham rtsa tshig
bugdam dzadzig rimpoche	sbug dam rtsa tshig rin po che
Bumdang (Chömpe Thubden)	'bum thang (chos 'phel thub bstan)
Bumdan Trunyi	'bum thang drung yig
bünshib	bun zhib
Canglocen	lcang lo can
Canglocen (Yanchen)	kang lo can (dbyang chen)
chabsigang	chab srid khang
Chabtsom	chab tshom
Chadang	cha dang
Chagdrung (Lodrö Phüntso)	phyag drung (blo gros phun tshogs)
chambang	chab 'bangs
Chamdo	chab mdo
chandzö	phyag mdzod
cha ngamo	ja mngar mo
chantsö	phyag mdzod
Chayü	bya yul
Che	(1) the monastic college: byes; (2) che
Che Jigme	ce 'jigs med
Chenresig	spyan ras gzigs
Chenrezi	spyan ras gzigs
Chenrezi wangchen	spyan ras gzigs dbang chen
cheshung	byes gzhung
chibgyur chemmo	chibs sgyur chen mo
chödrö	chos 'khrol
Chogye Nyima	chos rgyal nyi ma
Chömpel Thubden	chos 'phel thub bstan
chöndru	chos 'bru
chöpön khempo	mchod dpon mkhan po
chöshi	chos gzhis
chöshu	chos zhugs
chösi nyiden	chos srid gnyis ldan
chötröl	chos 'khrol
chuba	phyu pa
Chunden Drokar	chos ldan sgrol dkar
chundru mimang thrötso	chu 'brug mi dmangs gros tshogs
Chushigandru	chu bzhi sgang drug
Chushul	chu shur
Ciso	spyi gso
Cöki Gyentsen	chos gyi rgyal mtshan
Coko Gyentsen	mtsho sgo rgyal mtshan
Dadang	da dang
Dadang	mda' thang
dagnyer	bdag gnyer
dagpo gyab	bdag po rgyag
Dakpo	dwags po

damaru	da ma ru
danag	zla nag
dangdzin	btang 'dzin
Dedön tshogpa	bde don tshogs pa
Dekyilingka	bde skyid gling pa
Denbul tshogpa	rten 'bul tshogs pa
Denlhün (Tsering Paljor)	ldan lhun (tshe ring dpal 'byor)
denshu	brtan bzhugs
denshu	gdan zhu
denshu shabten	rten bzhugs zhabs brtan
depön	mda' dpon
depön Tashi Bera	mda' dpon bkra' shis dpal rab
Derge sey	sde dge sras
Dewashung	sde pa gzhung
Diki Tsering	bde skyi tshe ring
dingja	lding bya
Dingqing	stong chen
Dingri	ding ri
Dingyön Surpa	lding yon zur pa
Ditru	sde phrug
dobdo	ldab ldob
doley labdra	ltogs sla'i slob gwra
domey jigyab	mdo smad spyi khyab
Dombor (Kyenrab Wangchuk)	gdong por (mkhyen rab dbang phyug)
dongshu	gdong zhu
dongtug tragbö drawo dül khagbe nosam thabgi dünpa drubar che	gdong gtugs drag pos dgra bo 'dul khag pas rno bsam thab kyis 'dun pas grub par byed
Dorgya linga	gtor rgyag gling kha
Dorjetra	rdo rje drag
Dorje Tseden	rdo rje tshe brtan
Dosenge	rdo'i seng ge
dotse	rdo tshad
Drakten	grags bstan
Drapchi	grwa bzhi
dre	bre
Drepung	'bras spungs
dringbar	'bring bar
dringrab	'bring rab
dringtha	'bring tha
droma dresi	gro ma 'bras sil
Drongtse	'brong rtse
drönyerchemmo	mgron gnyer chen mo
Drubthog Rimpoche	grub thob rin po che
Drubthola	grub thob lags
Drubtola	grub thob lags

drugö leygung	'bru bkod las khungs
drungtog	drung gtogs
druphog	'bru phogs
drurig dagnyer legung	'bru rigs bdag gnyer las khungs
dü	bdud
düjung	dud chung
dükhor wangchen	dus 'khor dbang chen
Dundrub Namgyal	don grub rnam rgyal
dung	dung
Dungchi Trokhang	drung spyi spro khang
Dunggar	dung dkar
düngye dro	bdun brgyad 'gro
Düsum Sanggye	dus gsum sang rgyas
dzadzi	rtsa tshig
dzadzig	rtsa tshig
dzasa	dza sag
Dzasag Gyaltakpa	dza sag rgyal stag pa
Dzasak Surkhang	dza sag sur khang
dzasa lama	dza sag bla ma
Dzayul	rdza yul
dzöbu	mdzod sbug
dzong	rdzong
Enda	brngan mda'
E Nyingkar	e nying mkhar
ga	ga
gadam dzadzi	bka' dam rtsa tshig
Gadang	ga dang
Gadang Shigatse Gyajong	ga dang gzhis rtse rgya sbyong
gadrang	dga' brang
gagö bu	bka' bkod pu'u
gamgye jusur	skam skyed bcu zur
gamja jusur	skam chag bcu zur
Gampala	gam pa la
Ganden	dga' ldan
Ganden Phodrang	dga' ldan pho brang
Ganden Tripa	dga' ldan khri pa
Ganden Tri Rimpoche	dga' ldan khri rin po che
gang	sgang
Gangtok	sgang thog
gangya	gan rgya
Ganzi	dkar mdzes
gashib	bka' zhib
Geda trulka	dge rtags sprul sku
Gelugpa	dge lugs pa
Gendün Chompel	dge 'dun chos 'phel
gendün mang	dge 'dun dmangs
gershi	sger gzhis

Giamda	rgya mda'
gomang	sgo mang
gombo	mgon po
gonju khunglung mepa	mgo mjug khungs lung med pa
gorchakpa	skor 'chag pa
Gowa Chöndze	go bo chos mdzas
gugpa utsu	lkugs pa u btsugs
Guja Kumbela	sku bcar kun 'phel lags
gülung	skul slong
günche	kun mched
gungö nyi tashidele	sku ngo gnyis bkris bde legs
gushab	sku zhabs
Gushri Tenzin Chögye	go shri bstan 'dzin chos rgyal
Gusung magar	sku srung dmag sgar
gutsab	sku tshab
Gyabing Chöndze	skyabs dbying chos mdzad
gyagpön	brgya dpon
Gyagpön Kedram	brgya dpon skal dgram
Gya kungdren drinjen phamare	rgya gung khren drin can pha ma red
ngü dayan sayu rdoyu re	dngul dayan sa g.yug rdo g.yug red
gyaling	rgya gling
Gyalo La	rgya lo lags
Gyalo Thondup	rgya lo don grub
Gyama ngüchu	rgya mo dngul chu
Gyambumgang	rgya 'bum sgang
gyami gyane yongdü	rgya mi rgya nas yong dus
kungdren kungdren sigi	gung khran gung khran zer gyi
gyami dayan dredü	rgya mi da yan sprad dus
bombola bombola sigi	dpon po lags dpon po lags zer gyi
gyami sarpa	rgya mi gsar pa
gyamju	skyabs 'jug
Gyantse	rgyal rtse
Gya pö	rgya bod
gyashi tonglang	brgya shi stong langs
gyatsa rangdag	skya rtsa rang bdag
gyatso	rgya mtsho
Gyawa Rimpoche	rgyal ba rin po che
Gyawa Rimpocheeeee!	rgyal ba rin po che
Lo chik le mashu ro nang!	lo gcig las ma bzhugs rogs gnang
Namgyang pheronang!	lam rkyang phebs rogs gnang
Gyaya Rimpoche	rgya ya rin po che
gye	dgyed
gyeba kembo	rgyas pa mkhan po
gyeche	skyed chad
gyedar	rgyal dar
gye gu dro	brgyad dgu 'gro
gyela gyegya	skyed la skyed rgyag

Gyentsen Phüntso	rgyal mtshan phun tshogs
Gyentsen Tempel	rgyal mtshan bstan 'phel
Gyetseluding	skyed tshal klu lding
gyoma	skyo ma
gyongdrag	gyong drags
Gyümed tratsang	rgyud smad grwa tshang
Horkhang	hor khang
Jagpori	lcag po ri
Jambey Trinley	'jam dpal 'phrin las
Janglocen	lcang lo can
jangshing	sbyang shing
Jaralingka	sbyar rag gling kha
Jarong jija (Tashi Dorje)	lcags rong spyi lcag (bkra shis rdo rje)
Jayan Dawa	'jam dbyang zla ba
jen	gcen
Jenkhentsisum	gcen mkhan rtsis gsum
Jenselingga	spyan gsal gling ga
Jetsun Dampa	rje btsun dam pa
jigyab khembo	spyi khyab mkhan po
Jija (Tashi Dorje)	spyi lcag (bkras shis rdo rje)
jimang	spyi dmangs
jimbang	spyi 'bangs
jiso	spyi so
jitso lapdra	spyi tshogs slob grwa
jögyur	bcos sgyur
Jokhang	jo khang
Jora	sbyor ra
jubo	bcu bogs
Jyekundo	skye rgu mdo
ka	ka
kadam	bka' dam
kadrung	bka' drung
ka ga	ka kha
kalön	bka' blon
Kamika Chöndze	dkar me khang chos mdzad
kandrön	bka' mgron
Kanting	mkhan po thing
Kapshöba	ka shod pa
Kargang (Phüntso Tashi)	bkar khang (phun tshogs bkra shis)
karma	skar ma
Karmapa	skar ma pa
Kashag	bka' shag
Kashag gi thawdro	bka' shag gi thugs spro
Kashag shöpa	bka' shag shod pa
Kashag Trungtsi Lhengye	bka' shag drung rtsis lhan rgyas
Katsab	bka' tshab
Kelsang Gyatso	skal bzang rgya mtsho

kha	kha
khadang	kha dang
Kham	khams
Khamba	khams pa
khamtsen	khang tshan
Khandrung Lhautara	mkhan drung lha 'u rta ra
Khargang Phüntso Tashi	bkar khang phun tshogs bkra shis
Kharna Depön	mkhar sna mda' dpon
khasey dingsey	kha gsal gting gsal
khata	kha btags
khe	khal
khembo	mkhan po
Kheme Dzasa (Sonam Wangdü)	khe smad dza sag (bsod nams dbang 'dus)
Khenche	mkhan che
Khenche Tempa Rapgye	mkhan che bstan pa rab rgyas
khenjung	mkhan chung
Khenjung Choepel	mkhan chung chos 'phel
Khenjung Chömpel	mkhan chung chos 'phel
Khenjung Lobsang Tsewang	mkhan chung blo bzang tshe dbang
Khenjung Thubden Lengmön	mkhan chung thub bstan legs smon
khensur	mkhan zur
Khentsab Lobsang Samden	mkhan tshab blo bzang bsam gtan
khijang kharis jiggyur	khyi spyang kha ris gcig gyur
khyebar mindu	khyad par mi 'dug
Kongpo	kong po
Kumbela	kun 'phel lags
Kumbum	sku 'bum
Kumbumthang	sku 'bum thang
Kunchok Pemo	dkon mchog dpal mo
Kundeling	kun bde gling
Kungo Tsipön	sku ngo rstis dpon
Kunkhyabling	kun khyab gling
Kusangla	kun bzang lags
Kyabying Sengchen Trulku	skyabs dbyings seng chen sprul sku
Kyenrab Wangchuk	mkhyen rab dbang phyug
Kyichu	skyid chu
Kyire	skyid ras
Kyitöpa	skyid stod pa
Labrang	bla brang
Labrang gyentsen thombo	bla brang rgyal mtshan mthon po
lachi	bla spyi
Lagong ngenda	la gong brngan mda'
Laja	bla phyag
Laja Losang Gyentsen	bla phyag blo bzang rgyal mtshan
Lajen gi drochen	bla phyan gi spro chen
lama-pombo	bla ma dpon po
lam rim	lam rim

lamyig	lam yig
Langdün	glang 'dun
Langdün (Pemala)	glang 'dun (pad ma lags)
leba drago	klad pa mkhregs po
legjö	legs bcos
Legjö Jitso	legs bcos spyi tshogs
Legjö Leygung	legs bcos las khungs
Legjö Tsondu	legs bcos tshogs 'du
leja	las bya
Leje labdra	las byed slob grwa
Lhadong shenka	lha gdong shan ka
Lhalu	lha klu
Lhalung Surje	lha lung zur spyi
Lhamo	lha mo
Lhamön (Yeshe Tsultrim)	lha smon (ye shes tshul khrims)
Lhamo Tsering	lho mo tshe ring
Lharigo	lha ri 'go
Lhatse	lha rtse
Lhatsun Labrang Chandzö	lha btsun bla brang phyag mdzod
Lhautara	lha'u rta ra
Lhautara Tsendrön (Tenzin Gyentsen)	lha'u rta ra rtse mgron (bstan 'dzin rgyal mtshan)
Lhawang Tobgye	lha dbang stobs rgyas
Lho Dzong	lho rdzong
Lhundrup	lhun grub
Lingor	gling skor
Ling Rimpoche	gling (rin po che)
Litang	li thang
Liu dzong	sne'u rdzong
Liushar	sne'u shar
Liushar (Thubden Tharpa)	sne'u shar (thub bstan thar pa)
Lobsang Dawa	blo bzang zla ba
Lobsang Samden	blo bzang bsam gtan
Lobsang Tashi	blo bzang bkra shis
Lobsang Trinley	blo bzang 'phrin las
Lodola	blo gros lags
Lodrö Chönzin	blo gros chos 'dzin
Lodrö Kesang	blo gros skal bzang
Losang Tashi	blo bzang bkra shis
Losang Yeshe	blo bzang ye shes
Loseling	blo gsal gling
Lukhangwa	klu khang ba
Ma Boje	ma po jie
Madrong	dmag drung
mag	dmag
Magar nyingpa	dmag sgar rnying pa
Magar sarpa	dmag sgar gsar pa

Mag jigang	dmag spyi khang
Magsi uyön lhengang	dmog srid u yon lhan khang
Magükhang	dmag khul khang
mang	dmangs
mang ja	mang ja
Maogi jingdrö dangne	Mao yis bcing bkrol btang nas
marla gyalor chasong	mar la brgya lor chags song
hamba tshando kabo	ham pa tsha mdogs kha po
ngörig gangga pharsong	dngos rigs sgang ga 'phar song
Maya (Tsewang Gyurme)	rma bya (tshe dbang 'gyur med)
Medrogonggar	mal gro gong dkar
Mei Dokham Chushigandru	smad mdo khams chu bzhi sgang drug
mendre	man dral
mendredensum	man dral rten gsum
meshing shagpa shane	me shing bzhag pa bzhag nas
kyigya bülong mindu	khyi skyag 'bud longs mi 'dug
dale lama shane	ta la'i bla ma bzhag nas
jingdrü donglong mindu	bcings 'grol gtong long mi 'dug
metok jangse	me tog lcang gseb
mibo	mi bogs
mije	mi brje
mimang	mi dmangs
mimang thrötso	mi dmangs gros tshogs
mimang throtsog	mi dmangs gros tshogs
mimang tshogpa	mi dmangs tshogs pa
mimang tsogpa	mi dmangs tshogs pa
mimang tsondu	mi dmangs tshogs 'du
Mindrubu (Thubden Gyebo)	smin drug sbug (thub bstan rgyal po)
Mingyula	mi 'gyur lags
miser	mi ser
miser gopa	mi ser 'go pa
mitsa yüügong	mi rtsa yul skong
mitsa yüügug	mi rtsa yul 'gug
mitsen	mi tshan
Mönlam	smon lam
Mönlam Chemmo	smon lam chen mo
Mönlom Chulenpa	smon lam chu len pa
Muru	rme ru
Nagatshang Lhamo Tsering	na ga tshang lha mo tshe ring
Nagchuka	nag chu kha
Namgye Tratsang	rnam rgyal grwa tshang
Namgye Wangdü	rnam rgyal dbang 'dud
Namru	gnam ru
Namseling (Penjor Jigme)	rnam sras gling (dpal 'byor 'jigs med)
Nanggang	nang gang
Nanggar (Ngawang Tsempel)	snang dkar (ngag dbang tshe 'phel)
Nanggarste	snang dkar rtse

Nangmagang	nang ma sgang
nangsen	nang gzan
nangsi	snang srid
Nangtsesha	nang rtse shag
Nangtsesha mipön	nang rtse shag mi dpon
Nathula	sna stod la
natsog thabgi dradülwar che	sna tshogs thabs kyis dgra brtul bar byed
nendrön	sne mgron
Ngabö	nga phod
Ngabö (Ngawang Jigme)	nga phod (ngag dbang 'jigs med)
Ngabö (Rinchen)	nga phod (rin chen)
Ngabö (Thudo)	nga phod (mthu stobs)
Ngadang magar	nga dang dmag sgar
ngadru dro	lnga drug 'gro
Ngagpa Khembo	ngags pa mkhan po
Ngamring	ngam ring
Ngari	mnga' ris
ngatsab	mnga' tshab
Ngawang Jigme	ngag dbang 'jigs med
Ngawang Jimpa	ngag dbang sbyin pa
Ngawang Rigdrol	ngag dbang rigs grol
Ngawang Tsemphel	ngag dbang tshe dpal
ngönshe	mngon shes
Ngopso Tashila	rngo bzo bkra' shis lags
ngüsang	dngul srang
Niu	sne'u
ngönjam jedzub	sngon 'jam rjes rtsub
Norbulingka	nor bu gling kha
Nortölinga	nor stod gling kha
Nyare gyejen	myang ral rgyal chen
nyeljang shogle	bsnyel byang shog lhe
nyengag	snyan ngag
nyerpa	gnyer pa
Nyertsang	gnyer tshang
Nyetang	mnyes thang
Nyetang lhachenpo	mnyes thang lha chen po
Nyima Gyalpo	nyi ma rgyal po
Nyima Trinley	nyi ma 'phrin las
nyingje	nying rje
nyingma	rnying ma
Nyingtri	nying khri
Nyiu	sne'u
pachog	pa lcog
Paldi	dpal di
Panchen Erdini	pan chen er ti ni
Panda Tobgye	spom mda' stobs rgyas
Pandatsang (Yambe)	spom mda' tshang (yur 'phel)

Panden	dpal ldan
pargang	par khang
pawo	dpa' bo
paysang	dpe bzang
pechawa	dpe cha ba
Pegaw Chöde	dpal 'khor chos sde
Pembar	dpal 'bar
Phala	pha lha
Phari	phag ri
phebsu	phebs bsu
phogang	phog khang
phogpön	phogs dpon
Pholhasey Gyurme Namgye	pho lha sras 'gyur med rnam rgyal
phü	phul
Phu Gyagpa	bu rgyag pa
Phündra	phun bkra
Phünkang Lhajam	phun khang lha lcam
Phünkang Sey	phun khang sras
Phüntsoling	phun tshogs gling
Phüntso Rabgye	phun tshogs rab rgyas
Phüntso Tashi	phun tshogs bkra shis
Phüntso Wangye	phun tshogs dbang rgyal
Phünwang	phun dbang
phusum pharma	bu gsum bar ba
po	spo
pö dedön tshogpa	bod bde don tshogs pa
pögi geyik jongdar dzindra	bod kyi skad yig sbyong brdar 'dzin grwa
pögyob tsogpa	bod skyob tshogs pa
pö leydön uyön lhengang	bod las don u yon lhan khang
Pomda Tobgye	spom mda' stobs rgyas
pöme tshogpa	bud med tshogs pa
Pö ranggyong jong	bod rang skyong ljongs
Potala	po ta la
Purang	spu hreng
Rabchung	rab chung
rabjung	rab chung
Radö Rimpoche	ra stod rin po che
Raga	rab dga'
Ragasha (Phüntso Rabgye)	rag kha shag (phun tshogs rab rgyas)
Ramagang	ra ma sgang
Ramba (Thubden Güngyen)	ram pa (thub bstan kun mkhyen)
rang gyong	rang skyong
ranggyong jong	rang skyong ljong
rangtsen tsangma	rang btsan gtsang ma
rapchung	rab byung
Reting (Labrang)	rwa sgreng (bla brang)
rimshi	rim bzhi

Rimshi Kharma	rim bzhi mkhar sna
Rinchen Drolma	rin chen sgrol ma
Rinzin	rig 'dzin
risor gandzö	ri zor ga 'dzol
Riwoche	ri bo che
Rong Phelung (Thubden Sampel)	rong dpal lhun (thub bstan bsam 'phel)
rupön	ru dpon
saden	sa rten
Sakya	sa skya
Sakya dakchen	sa skya bdag chen
Sakya daktri	sa skya bdag khri
Samada	sa ma mda'
Sambo (Tenzin Thundrup)	bsam pho (bstan 'dzin don grub)
Samjöla	bsam mchog lags
Samling	bsam gling
Samling (Söpal)	bsam gling (bsod dpal)
Samye Karme	bsam yas dkar me
Sandu (Rinchen)	sa 'dul (rin chen)
Sandutsang (Lo Gendün)	sa 'du tshang (blo dge 'dun)
Sandutsang (Rinchen)	sa 'du tshang (rin chen)
sane sishung	sa gnas srid gzhung
sangwe lungdrin	gsang ba'i rlung 'phrin
Sangye Yeshe	sangs rgyas ye shes
sarje	gsar rje
satsig	sa tshig
sawangchemmo	sa dbang chen mo
senampa	sras rnam pa
Senge Palden	seng ge dpal ldan
senril	zan ril
Sera	ser ra
Sera Che	ser ra byes
sermag	ser dmag
Seshin	zas zhim
Setrong Wangye	gser grong dbang rgyal
Shabden lhagang	zhabs brtan lha khang
Shakabpa	zhwa sgab pa
shagtsang	shag tshang
Shape Ngabö	zhabs pad nga phod
Shartsang Lama	shar tshang bla ma
Shasur	bshad zur
Shatra (Ganden Penjor)	bshad sgra (dga' ldan dpal 'byor)
Shatrom Para	sha khrom pa ra
Shatsela	shar rtse lags
Shelling (Tsewang Namgye)	shel gling (tshe dbang rnam rgyal)
Shenkawa	shan kha ba
Sherup Gyatso	shes rab rgya mtsho

sheyngo	zhal ngo
Shide	bzhi sde
shiga	gzhis kha
Shigatse	gzhis ka rtse
shimphar	zhib 'phar
Shina	bzhi sna
shi nga dro	bzhi lnga 'gro
Shingra shunggo	shing rwa gzhungs sgo
Shingsar (Lobsang Gelek)	zhing gsar (blo bzang dge legs)
shishung	gzhis gzhung
shoga	shog kha
shog ja	shog chag
Shöl	zhol
Shöl ga	zhol 'gag
Shölkang Jetrung (la)	zhol khang rje drung (lags)
Shölkang Sey (Sonam Dargye)	zhol khang sras (bsod names dar rgyas)
Shöl Pargang	zhol par khang
Shöl Parkhang	zhol par khang
shöpa	shod pa
Shopando	sho pa mdo
Shugola	shog bu la
shung choley namgye	gzhung phyogs las rnam rgyal
shungdru jidzökhang	gshung 'bru spyi mdzod khang
shungdzin	gzhung 'dzin
shungdzin phumpa silu	gzhung 'dzin bum pa sib blug
shung ganden podrang	gzhung dga' ldan pho brang
shungshi	gzhung gzhis
shungyupa	gzhung rgyug pa
shünu tshogpa	gzhon nu tshogs pa
si	srid
silön	srid blon
simjung gi thakor	gzim chung gi mtha' 'khor
simpön khembo	gzim dpon mkhan po
Simpön Khembo Rongtse Khembo	gzim dpon mkhan po rong rtse mkhan po
singga	gzim 'gag
sitsab	srid tshab
soley jubog	so las bcu bogs
Sonam Legung	bsod nams las khungs
Sonam Tobgye	bsod nams stob rgyas
Songtsen gambo	srong btsan sgam po
Sopal	bsod dpal
sopjö	bzo bcos
söpön khembo	gsol dpon mkhan po
sumtag	sum rtags
sung jör	gsung chos
Surjong Kashag	zur 'phyongs bka' shag

Surkhang (Wangchen Gelek)	zur khang (dbang chen dge legs)
Surkhang Depön (Lhawang Tobden)	zur khang sde dpon (lha dbang stobs ldan)
Surkhang Khenjung (Kherab Wangchuk)	zur khang mkhan chung (mkhyen rab dbang phyug)
Sursur Dzasa	zur zur rdza sag
Sursur Jigme	zur zur 'jigs med
tagor tshogpa	lta skor tshogs pa
Takla	Stag lha
Taktser Rimpoche	stag 'tsher rim po che
Taktra	stag brag
Taktse	stag 'tsher
Tak Tser	stag 'tsher
Ta Lama	ta bla ma
Talungdra	stag lung brag
Tangme (Kunchok Pemo)	thang smad (dkon mchog dpal mo)
Tangola	thang gu la
Tarchin	mthar phyin
Taring	'phreng ring
Taring (Rinchen Dolma)	'phreng ring (rinchen sgrol ma)
Taring Dzasa	'phreng ring dza sag
Tarkhang	tar khang
Tartsedo	dar rtse mdo
Tashi Bera	bkra' shis dpal rab
Tashilhunpo	bkra' shis lhun po
Tashilingpa	bkra' shis gling pa
tau khema	rta'u khal ma
tawu	rta'u
temo tö a	ltad mo ltos a
Tenzin Thundrup	bstan 'dzin don grub
Thamjö Sonam	dam chos bsod nams
Thando Rimpoche	dar mdo rin po che
Thangbe	thang spe
Tharchin	mthar phyin
Thondrup Namgyal	don grub rnam rgyal
Thönpa Khenjung	thon pa mkhan chung
Thubden Gyebo	thub bstan rgyal po
Thubden Lengmön	thub bstan legs smon
Thubden Ramyang	thub bstan rab dbyangs
Thubden Sangbo	thub bstan bzang po
Thubden Sangye	thub bstan sangs rgyas
Thubden Wangpo	thub bstan dbang po
thukdam	thugs dam
Tö	stod
Töba Khembo	stod pa mkham po
Tobgye Drüri	thob rgyal brul ri
Tö ngari	stod mnga' ris

Tö ngari kor sum	stod mnga' ris 'khor gsum
trag tra	mkhregs drags
Tranggo	'phrang sgo
Trapchi	grwa bzhi
tratsang	grwa tshang
tre	khral
treba	khral pa
tregang	khral rkang
trema	sran ma
trema gyangling	sran ma rgya gling
tremi	khral mi
Trendong (Che Jigme)	bkras mthong (ce 'jigs med)
Trendong (Jigme Drakpa)	bkras mthong ('jigs med grags pa)
Trendong Khenjung	bkras mthong mkhan chung
trenön	khral snon
trepa	khral pa
Tresur	bkras zur
Tride tsungtsen	khri sde srong btsan
Trijang Rimpoche	khri byang rin po che
trimdek	khrims 'degs
Trimön	khri smon
Trindor	'phrin rdor
Trinle	'phrin las
Trisam	khri zam
Tromo	gro mo
Trongdra	grong drag
trug dün dro	drug bdun 'gro
trunggo linga	drung 'khor gling kha
Trung ja	drung ja
Trung jilingka	drung spyi gling kha
trungtsi	drung rtsis
trungtsigye	drung rtsis brgyad
Trungtsinyi	drung rtsis gnyis
Trunyichemmo	drung gnyer chen mo
tsamba	rtsam pa
Tsang	gtsang
Tsangpo	gtsang po
tsang ranggyong jong	gtsang rang skyong ljong
Tsarong	tsha rong
Tseden Gongpo	tshe brtan mgon po
Tse ga	rtse 'gag
Tseja	rtse phyag
tseja gi druchen	rtse phyag gi spro chen
Tselabdra	rtse slob grwa
tsendrön	rtse mgron
Tsendrön Nanggar	rtse mgron snag dkar
tsenwang	btsan dbang

Tsenya truku	btshan nya sprul sku
Tsepön Shakabpa	rtsis dpon zhwa kha pa
Tsering Dolma	tshe ring sgrol ma
tseshö chandzö	rtse shod phyag mdzod
Tsesum Phunkhang	tshes gsum phun khang
tshab	tshab
Tshakur linga	tsha khur gling kha
Tsha Trunyi(la)	tsha drung yig (lags)
Tshatru Rimpoche	tsha sprul rin po che
Tshawa Khamtsen	tsha ba khang tshan
Tshecholing	tshe mchog gling
Tshomöling	tshe smon gling
Tshongpa gidu	tshong pa skyid sdug
tshopa	tsho pa
Tshurpu	mtshur phu
tsidrung gi yarkyi	rtse drung gi g.yar skyid
Tsidrunglingka	rtse drung gling pa
Tsigang	rtsis khang
Tsipön	rtsis dpon
Tsjchag Thubden Gyalpo	rtse phyag thub bstan rgyal po
Tsögo	mtsho sgo
Tsögo (Deyang)	mtsho sgo (bde dbyang)
Tsögo Sey	mtsho sgo sras
Tsondu	tshogs 'du
Tsondu Gyendzom	tshogs 'du rgyas 'dzoms
Tsondu Hragdu	tshogs 'du hrag bsdus
tsondzin	'tsho 'dzin
Tsongjö	tshogs mchod
Tsongjö sebang	tshogs mchod ser sbreng
Tsongkha	tsong kha
Tsuglagang	gtsug lag khang
Tülung	stod lung
Ü	dbus
udu	dbu gtugs
ula	'ul lag
üshung	dbus gzhung
Wangchen Gelek	dbang chen dge legs
Wangden Lhakpa	dbang ldan lhag pa
Wangye	dbang rgyal
Yabshi	yab gzhis
Yambe	yar 'phel
Yangbajen	yangs pa chen
Yangki	g.yang skyid
Yangpel Pandatsang	yar 'phel spom mda' tshang
Yeshe Gompo	ye shes mgon po
Yeshe Tsultrim	ye shes tshul khrims
Yeshe Yönden	ye shes yon tan

yiggyur	yig skyur
yig ja	yig cha
Yigtsang	yig tshang
Yiktsang	yig tshang
yogpo	g.yog po
yöle gyabla mi du	yol ba'i rgyab la mi 'dug
yügye	g.yul rgyal
Yuthok	g.yu thog
Yuthok (Dorje Yüdrön)	g.yu thog (rdo rje g.yu sgron)
Yuthok Dzasa	g.yu thog dza sag

REFERENCES

Ahmad, Zahiruddin. 1960. *China and Tibet, 1708–1959: A Resume of Facts.* Oxford: Oxford University Press.

———. 1970. *Sino-Tibetan Relations in the 17th Century.* Rome: Istituo Italiano per il Medico ed Estremeo Oriente.

———. 1975. "The Historical Status of China in Tibet." *Tibet Journal* 1, no. 1: 27.

Alo Chöndze, ed. 1958. *The Political Testament and Warning by H. H. the 13th Dalai Lama to His People in 1932 and an Advice by H. H. the 14th Dalai Lama to His People in 1955* [title is in English but text is in Tibetan]. Kalimpong: Tibet Mirror Press.

A lo chos mdzad (Alo Chöndze). 1983. *Bod kyi gnas lugs bden 'dzin sgo phye ba'i lde mig zhes bya ba* (The Key That Opens the Door of Truth to the Tibetan Situation: Materials on Modern Tibetan History). Australia: privately published.

Andrugtsang, Gompo Tashi. 1971. *Four Rivers, Six Ranges: A True Account of Khampa Resistance to Chinese in Tibet.* Dharamsala, India: Information and Publicity Office of His Holiness the Dalai Lama.

Anon. 1959. *Concerning the Question of Tibet.* Peking: Foreign Languages Press.

Aris, Michael, and Aung San Suu Kyi, eds. 1980. *Tibetan Studies in Honour of Hugh Richardson: Proceedings of the International Seminar on Tibetan Studies, Oxford, 1979.* Proceedings of Second Seminar of the International Association of Tibetan Studies. Warminister: Aris and Phillips.

Balestracci, Andrew. 1991. "Four Rivers, Six Ranges." *Himal* (March-April): 14–15.

Banerjee, Sudhansu Mohan. 1952. "A Forgotten Chapter on Indo-Tibetan Contact: A Further Review." *Calcutta Review* 23, no. 1: 32.

Barber, Noel. 1969. *From the Land of Lost Content: The Dalai Lama's Fight for Tibet.* London: Hodder and Stoughton.

Barnett, Robbie, and S. Akinar, eds. 1994. *Resistance and Reform in Tibet.* London: C. Hurst and Co.

Bawden, C. W. 1989. *The Modern History of Mongolia.* London: Keegan Paul International.

Beba, K. 1957. "Tibet Revisited." *China Reconstructs* 6: 9–12.

Beijing Review. 1992. "Tibet—Its Ownership and Human Rights Situation." *Beijing Review* 28 September—4 October, 9–42.

Bell, Charles. 1924a. "The Dalai Lama, Lhasa 1921." *Journal of the Royal Central Asian Society* 11, no. 1: 44–45.

———. 1924b. *Tibet, Past and Present.* Oxford: Clarendon Press.

———. 1928. *The People of Tibet.* Oxford: Oxford University Press.

———. 1931. *The Religion of Tibet.* Oxford: Clarendon Press.

———. 1946. *Portrait of a Dalai Lama.* London: Collins.

———. 1949. "China and Tibet." *Journal of the Royal Central Asian Society* 36, no. 1: 54.

Bka' shag. 1953. Rgyal khyab chab dbangs rnams la gzhung sger chos bcas nas 'bru bun gtong len sgrub chag dbye 'byed byed phyogs skor spyi khyab rdzong gzhis khag dang/ bun gtong byed po/ bun len mi ser bcas par rtsa 'dzin bka' tham bkod rgya. Manuscript, Library for Tibetan Works and Archives.

Bkras sgron, ed. 1992. *Bod kyi gsar brje'i lo rgyus* (The History of the Revolution in Tibet). Lhasa: Bod ljongs mi dmangs dpe skrun khang (Tibet People's Publishing House).

Blo gros chos 'dzin. 1986. "Rwa stag don rkyen skabs ngas bod dmag thengs gnyis pa dang mnyam du rwa sgreng don du bskyod skor" (Regarding How I Went Twice with the Tibetan Army at the Time of the Reting-Taktra Incident). In *Bod kyi rig gnas lo rgyus dpyad gzhi'i rgyu cha bsdams bsgrigs* (Selected Materials on the History and Culture of Tibet), vol. 8, ed. CMHC. Lhasa: Tibet Xinhua Publishing House.

Blo tshe (Lotse). 1965. "Li thang khul gyi lo rgyus" (A History of Litang). Handwritten manuscript.

———. 2001. *Bod chol kha gsum gyi ya gyal mdo khams sgang drug gi nang tshan li thang spo 'bor ra ba sgang du khe shing tsher lon jon ye bstan blo tshe nas so sos rgyal khab kyi don du shabs 'degs shus pa'i mi tshe'i lo rgyus tshangs pa'i thig shing bzhugs so* (The Life Story of How I Served the Nation, by Dukhe Shingtser Lönjön Yeten Lotse of Litang Pomporgang, Which is Part of the Six Ranges of Kham, Which Is One of the Three Provinces of Tibet). Darjeeling: Tibetan Refugee Self-Help Center.

Bod kyi rten 'bul tshogs pa. 1954. *Bod kyi rten 'bul tshogs pas rtogs zhib sbyangs brtson zhus pa'i spyi bsdoms snyan zhu* (Report of the Investigations of the Gift Presentation Delegation). Pamphlet. Beijing: Mi rigs dpe bkrun khang (Tibet Nationality Publishing House).

Bogoslovskij, V. 1978. "Tibet and the Cultural Revolution—a Russian View." *Tibetan Review* (August): 15–18.

Bradsher, Henry S. 1976. "Tibet Struggles to Survive." *Foreign Affairs* 47, no. 4: 750–62.

Brandt, C., B. Schwartz, and J. Fairbank. 1952. *A Documentary History of Chinese Communism.* Cambridge, MA: Harvard University Press.

Brauen, Martin, and Per Kvaerne, eds. 1978. *Tibetan Studies Presented at the Seminar of Young Tibetologists, Zurich, June 26–July 1, 1977,* ed. Martin Brauen and Per Kvaerne. Proceedings of First Seminar of the International Association of Tibetan Studies. Zurich: Völkerkundemuseum der Universität Zürich.

Brecher, Michael. *Nehru: A Political Biography* Oxford: Oxford University Press, 1969.

Bsam 'grub pho brang, Bstan 'dzin don grub. 1987. *Mi tshe'i rba rlabs 'khrugs po.* New Delhi: Sampho.

Bshad sgra (Shatra), Dga' ldan dpal 'byor. 1983. "Go min tang gi 'thus mi 'u krung shing taa la'i bcu bzhi pa'i khri 'don mdzad sgor yong ba'i skor gyi gnas tshul dum bu zhig" (Information about the Guomindang Representative Wu Zhongxin to the enthronement of the 14th Dalai Lama). In *Bod kyi rig gnas lo rgyus rgyu cha bdams bsgrigs* (Selected Materials on the History and Culture of Tibet), ed. CHMC, vol. 2, 82–92. Lhasa: Tibet People's Publishing House.

Bshad sgra (Shatra), Dga' ldan dpal 'byor, Chab tshom (Chabtsom) 'Chi med rgyal po, Sreg shing (Segshing) Blo bzang don grub. 1991. "De snga'i bod sa gnas srid gzhung gi srid 'dzin sgrigs gzhi" (The Administrative Structure of the Tibetan Local Government in the Past). In *Bod kyi lo rgyus rig gnas dpyad gzhi'i rgyu cha bsdams bsgrigs* (Selected Materials on the History and Culture of Tibet), ed. CHMC, vol. 13, 1–196. Lhasa: People's Publishing House.

Bull, Geoffrey. 1957. *When Iron Gates Yield.* London: Hodder and Stoughton.

———. 1967. *Forbidden Land: A Saga of Tibet.* Chicago: Moody Press.

Bullard, Monte R. 1985. *China's Political-Military Evolution.* Boulder, CO: Westview Press.

Bureau of His Holiness the Dalai Lama. N.d. *Tibet in the United Nation: 1950–1961.* New Delhi, n.p.

Burman, Bina Roy. 1976. "Thirteenth Dalai Lama's Plan for the Modernization of Tibet." *Tibetan Review* 11–12 (December): 12–14.

———. 1979. *Religion and Politics in Tibet.* New Delhi: Vikas.

Burridge, Kenelm. 1969. *New Heaven New Earth: A Study of Millenarian China's Tibet:* Oxford: Basil Blackwell.

Byams pa. 1985. "Zing slong jag pas shang dga' ldan chos 'khor nas mtshon cha 'don 'khyer byas skor" (Concerning the Bandit Rebels Taking Weapons from Ganden Chökhor Monastery in Shang). In *Bod kyi rig gnas lo rgyus dpyad gzhi'i rgyu cha bsdams bsgrigs* (Selected Materials on the History and Culture of Tibet), ed. CHMC, vol. 5, 222–28. Xining: Qinghai Xinhua Publishing Plant.

Bya ngos pa (Changöba), Rdo rje dngos grub. 1983. "Bod sa gnas srid gzhung gis 'thus mi tshogs pa btang nas mthun phyogs rgyal khab la g.yul rgyal bkra shis bde legs zhu ba dang 'go min rda hud' tshongs 'dur shugs pa'i don dngos" (Regarding the Tibetan Local Government Sending Delegates to Convey Congratulations for the Allied Victory in World War II and to Attend the Chinese National Constitutional Assembly). In *Bod kyi rig gnas lo rgyus dpyad gzhi'i rgyu cha cha bdams bsgrigs* (Selected Materials on the History and Culture of Tibet), ed. CHMC, vol. 2, 1–28. Lhasa: Tibet People's Publishing House.

Cammann, Schuyer. 1951. *Trade through the Himalayas: The Early British Attempt to Open Tibet.* Princeton, NJ: Princeton University Press.

Carlyle, Margaret, ed. 1953. *Documents on International Affairs, 1949–1950.* Oxford: Oxford University Press.

Caroe, Sir Olaf. 1960a. *Englishmen in Tibet: From Bogle to Gould.* London: Tibet Society publication.

———. 1960b. "Tibet: The End of an Era." *Royal Central Asian Journal* 47: 22–34.

Carrasco, Pedro. 1959. *Land and Polity in Tibet.* Seattle: University of Washington Press.

Cassinelli, C. W., and Robert B. Ekvall. 1969. *A Tibetan Principality: The Political System of Sa sKya.* Ithaca, NY: Cornell University Press.

Chab spel (Chape), Tshe brtan phun tshogs, and Nor brang o rgyan, eds. 1991. *Bod kyi lo rgyus rags rim g.yu yi phreng ba* (A Brief History of Tibet). Vol. 2. Lhasa: Tibet Xinhua Publishing House.

Chan, Victor. 1994. *Tibet Handbook: A Pilgrimage Guide.* Chico, CA: Moon Publications.

Chang, Jung, and Jon Halliday. 2005. *Mao: The Unknown Story.* London: Jonathan Cape.

Chang Kuo-hua. 1953. "A New Tibet Is Arising." *People's China* 10: 7–11.

Chapman, F. S. 1938. "Lhasa in 1937." *Geographic Journal* 91, no. 6: 304.

Chiang Kai-shek. 1959. "Message of President Chiang Kai-shek to Tibetans on March 26, 1959." *Free China and Asia* 6, no. 4: 3.

Chime Radha Rinpoche, Lama. 1981. "Tibet." In *Oracles and Divination,* ed. M. Loewe and C. Blacker. Boulder, CO: Shambhala Publications.

China, Information Office of the State Council of the People's Republic of. 1992. "Tibet—Its Ownership and Human Rights Situation." *Beijing Review* (September 28—October 4): 9–42.

CHMC (Culture and Historical Materials Committee of the Political Consultative Conference of the Tibet Autonomous Region), Bod ljongs chab gros rig gnas lo rgyus dpyad gzhi'i rgyu cha u yon lhan khang, ed. 1981. *Bod kyi rig gnas lo rgyus rgyu cha bdams bsgrigs* (Selected Materials on the History and Culture of Tibet). Vol. 1. Lhasa: Tibet People's Publishing House.

———, ed. 1983. *Bod kyi rig gnas lo rgyus rgyu cha bdams bsgrigs* (Selected Materials on the History and Culture of Tibet). Vol. 2. Lhasa: Tibet People's Publishing House.

———, ed. 1984a. *Bod kyi rig gnas lo rgyus rgyu cha bdams bsgrigs* (Selected Materials on the History and Culture of Tibet). Vol. 3. Lhasa: Tibet People's Publishing House.

———, ed. 1984b. *Bod kyi rig gnas lo rgyus dpyad gzhi'i rgyu cha bsdams bsgrigs* (Selected Materials on the History and Culture of Tibet). Vol. 4. Lhasa: Tibet People's Publishing House.

———, ed. 1985a. *Bod kyi rig gnas lo rgyus dpyad gzhi'i rgyu cha bsdams bsgrigs* (Selected Materials on the History and Culture of Tibet). Vol. 5. Xining: Qinghai Xinhua Publishing Plant.

———, ed. 1985b. *Bod kyi rig gnas lo rgyus dpyad gzhi'i rgyu cha bsdams bsgrigs* (Selected Materials on the History and Culture of Tibet). Vol. 6. Lhasa: Tibet Military Area Publishing House.

———, ed. 1985c. *Bod kyi rig gnas lo rgyus dpyad gzhi'i rgyu cha bsdams bsgrigs* (Selected Materials on the History and Culture of Tibet). Vol. 7. Lhasa: Tibet Military Area Publishing House.

———, ed. 1986a. *Bod kyi rig gnas lo rgyus dpyad gzhi'i rgyu cha bsdams bsgrigs* (Selected Materials on the History and Culture of Tibet). Vol. 8. Lhasa: Tibet Xinhua Publishing House.

———, ed. 1986b. *Bod kyi rig gnas lo rgyus dpyad gzhi'i rgyu cha bsdams bsgrigs* (Selected Materials on the History and Culture of Tibet). Vol. 9. Lhasa: Tibet Military Area Publishing House.

———, ed. 1990. *Bod kyi lo rgyus rig gnas dpyad gzhi'i rgyu cha bsdams bsgrigs* (Selected

Materials on the History and Culture of Tibet). Vol. 12. Lhasa: People's Publishing House.

————, ed. 1991. *Bod kyi lo rgyus rig gnas dpyad gzhi'i rgyu cha bsdams bsgrigs* (Selected Materials on the History and Culture of Tibet). Vol. 13. Lhasa: People's Publishing House.

————, ed. 1993. *Bod kyi lo rgyus rig gnas dpyad gzhi'i rgyu cha bsdams bsgrigs* (Selected Materials on the History and Culture of Tibet). Vol. 16. Lhasa: People's Publishing House.

Choudhury, Deba P. 1978. *The North-East Frontier of India, 1865–1914.* Calcutta: Asiatic Society.

Chowdhury, Jyotirindra Nath. 1967. "British Contributions to the Confusion of Tibet's Status." *Quest* 54: 35–36.

Christie, Clive. 1976. "Great Britain, China, and the Status of Tibet, 1914–21." *Modern Asian Studies* (October): 507–8.

Chu Wen-lin. 1969. "Peiping's Nationality Policy in the Cultural Revolution, Part I." *Issues and Studies* 5, no. 8: 12–23.

Chu sgang lo rgyus rtsom sgrig tshogs chung, eds. 2000. *Chu sgang lo rgyus* (The History of Chushigandru). Vol. 1. Delhi: Welfare Society of Central Dokham Chushi Gangdrug.

CIA, National Intelligence Survey. 1964. *Communist China,* section 23, *Weather and Climate,* part 5 — *Tibetan Highlands.* Carrollton, VA: Declassified Document Reference Service, Carrollton Press (September).

Clark, Leonard. 1954. *The Marching Wind.* New York: Funk and Wagnalls Company.

Clubb, O. E. 1964. *Twentieth Century China.* New York: Columbia University Press.

Cold War International History Project. 1995–96. *The Cold War in Asia.* Washington, DC: Woodrow Wilson International Center for Scholars.

Conboy, Kenneth, and James Morrison. 2002. *The CIA's Secret War in Tibet.* Lawrence: University Press of Kansas.

The Constitution of the People's Republic of China. 1983. *The Constitution of the People's Republic of China.* Beijing: Foreign Languages Press.

Corlin, Claes. 1978. "A Tibetan Enclave in Yunnan: Land, Kinship, and Inheritance in Gyethang." In *Tibetan Studies Presented at the Seminar of Young Tibetologists, Zurich, June 26–July 1, 1977,* ed. Martin Brauen and Per Kvaerne. Proceedings of First Seminar of the International Association of Tibetan Studies. Zurich: Völkerkundemuseum der Universität Zürich.

————. 1980. "The Symbolism of the House in rGyal-thang." In *Tibetan Studies in Honour of Hugh Richardson: Proceedings of the International Seminar on Tibetan Studies, Oxford 1979,* ed. Michael Aris and Aung San Suu Kyi. Proceedings of Second Seminar of the International Association of Tibetan Studies. Warminister: Aris and Phillips.

Craig, Mary. 1997. *Kundun: A Biography of the Family of the Dalai Lama.* Washington, DC: Counterpoint.

Dalai Lama. 1962. *My Land and My People: Memoirs of the Dalai Lama of Tibet.* New York: Potala Publications.

————. 1990. *Freedom in Exile: The Autobiography of the Dalai Lama.* New York: HarperCollins.

Dalvi, J. P. 1969. *Himalayan Blunder: The Curtain-Raiser to the Sino-Indian War of 1962.* Bombay: Thacker and Company.

Dangdai zhongguo congshu bianjibu (Modern China Editorial Department), ed. 1991. *Dangdai Zhongguo de Xizang* (Contemporary China's Tibet). Vol. 1. Beijing: Dangdai Zhongguo Chubanshe (Modern China Publishing House).

Das, Chandra Sarat. 1965. *Indian Pundits in the Land of Snow.* Calcutta: Firma K. L. Mukhopadhyay.

Das, Taraknath. 1929. *British Expansion in Tibet.* Calcutta: N. M. Raychowdhury and Co.

Dbus gtsang chos kha'i spyi khyab rgyun las khang (Standing Committee of the Ü-Tsang Association). 1988a. "Chu 'brug mi dmangs kyi sgrigs 'dzugs las 'gul la rjes dran lo rgyus snying don" (The Historical Essence Commemorating the People's Association of the Water-Dragon Year). *Dbus gtsang chos kha'i spyi khyab rgyun las khang (gi) dus deb* (Magazine of the Standing Committee of the Ü-Tsang Association) 1: 1–18.

———. 1988b. "Srid zur klu khang pa'i lo rgyus sa bon" (The History of the Ex-Sitsab Lukhangwa). *Dbus gtsang chos kha'i spyi khyab rgyun las khang (gi) dus deb* (Magazine of the Standing Committee of the Ü-Tsang Association) 1: 18–24.

Dbyin pha' thang. 1983. "Bod skyod thog ma'i dus kyi 'tsham 'dri'i byed sgo zhig dran gso byas pa" (Recollections of the Greetings When First Going to Tibet). In *Bod kyi rig gnas lo rgyus rgyu cha bdams bsgrigs* (Selected Materials on the History and Culture of Tibet), ed. CHMC, vol. 2, 224–50. Lhasa: Tibet People's Publishing House.

De Francis, John. 1951. "National and Minority Policies." *Annals of the American Academy of Political and Social Sciences: Report on China.* Philadelphia: American Academy of Political and Social Sciences.

De Gramont, Sanche. 1962. *The Secret War.* New York: G. P. Putnam's Sons.

Deng Xiaoping. 1957. *Report on the Rectification Campaign.* Beijing: Foreign Languages Press.

Department of State. 1949. *Policy Review Paper—Tibet.* Pamphlet. U.S. Department of State, Washington, DC.

———. 1956. "Unrest in Tibet." U.S. Department of State, Division of Research for the Far East, National Archives, Diplomatic Branch, Washington, DC.

Department of State, Office of Intelligence Research. 1948. "Tibet." Office of Intelligence Research Branch, National Archives, Diplomatic Branch, Washington, DC.

Dge rgyas pa, Bstan 'dzing rdo rje. 1990. "Kha bral ring lugs pas lha sar drag po'i ngo log zing 'khrug dngos su bslangs pa'i gnas tshul 'ga' zhig" (Some Information on Separatists Creating a Militant Uprising in Lhasa). In *Bod kyi lo rgyus rig gnas dpyad gzhi'i rgyu cha bsdams bsgrigs* (Selected Materials on the History and Culture of Tibet), ed. CHMC, vol. 12, 133–41. Lhasa: People's Publishing House.

Dhondup, K. 1984. *The Water-Horse and Other Years: A History of 17th and 18th Century Tibet.* Dharamsala, India: Library of Tibetan Works and Archives.

———. 1986. *The Water-Bird and Other Years: A History of the 13th Dalai Lama and After.* New Delhi: Rangwang Publishers.

Dolkar, Tseten. 1971. *Girl from Tibet.* Chicago: Loyola University Press.

Don grub rgya mtsho. 1989. "An Account of the History of Spo-smad Ka gnam Sde-pa." *Tibet Studies* (Lhasa) 1: 83–89.

Don khang, Skal bzang bde skyid. 1984. "Pan che sku phreng dgu pa mes rgyal nang khul du gsar phebs kyi snga rjes" (On the 9th Panchen Lama Coming to the Motherland). In *Bod kyi rig gnas lo rgyus dpyad gzhi'i rgyu cha bsdams bsgrigs* (Selected Materials on the History and Culture of Tibet), ed. CHMC, vol. 4, 1–32. Lhasa: Tibet People's Publishing House.

Dreyer, June Teufel. 1976. *China's Forty Millions*. Cambridge, MA: Harvard University Press.

Dui xizang gongzuo de zhongyao zhishi (wei chuban de shouji). N.d. (Important Instructions on Work in Tibet). Unpublished collection of documents.

Dung dkar (Dunggar), Blo bzang 'phrin las. 1981. *Bod kyi chos srid zung 'brel skor bshad pa* (On the Dual Secular and Religious Political System in Tibet). Beijing: Minority Publishing House.

————. 1991. *The Merging of Religious and Secular rule in Tibet*. Beijing: Foreign Languages Press.

Dunham, Mikel. 2004. *Buddha's Warriors: The Story of the CIA-Backed Tibetan Freedom Fighters, the Chinese Invasion, and the Ultimate Fall of Tibet*. New York: Jeremy P. Tarcher/Penguin.

Dutt, S. 1977. *With Nehru in the Foreign Office*. Calcutta: Minerva Associates.

Eekelin, W. F. van. 1964. *Indian Foreign Policy and the Border Dispute with China*. The Hague: Martinus Nijhoff.

Eftimiades, Nicholas. *Chinese Intelligence Operations*. Annapolis, MD: Naval Institute Press, 1994.

Epstein, Israel. 1977a. "Serfs and Slaves Rule Khaesum Manor." *Eastern Horizon* (Hong Kong) 16, no. 7: 21.

————. 1977b. "Visual Denunciation of Serf-Owner's Atrocities." *Peking Review* (Beijing) 29: 11.

————. 1983. *Tibet Transformed*. Beijing: New World Press.

Fairbank, John King. 1986. *The Great Chinese Revolution 1800–1985*. 1st ed. New York: Harper and Row Publishers.

Fan Ming. 1987. "Ba Wuxing Guoqi Gaogao di Chacai Ximalayashan Shang: Huiyi Zhonggong Xibei Xizang gongwei (Shiba Jun Duli Zhidui) Jing Jun Xizang" (Erecting the Five-Star National Flag on the Top of the Himalayan Mountains: A Memoir of the Entrance into Tibet by Tibetan Working Committee of the Northwest Bureau of CCP [the Independent Detachment of the Eighteenth Army]). Manuscript, 1–150. (A manuscript of an article published in shorter form in *Shijie wuji fengyunlu: Jinian heoping jietang Xizang sishi zhou nian* [Wind and Clouds on the Roof of the World: Commemorating the Fortieth Anniversary of the Peaceful Liberation of Tibet], ed. Wu Chen, vol. 1, 48–76 [Beijing: PLA Literature Publishing House, 1991]).

Fisher, Margaret, Leo E. Rose, and Robert A. Huttenback. 1963. *Himalayan Battleground*. New York: Praeger.

Ford, Corey. 1970. *Donovan of OSS*. Boston: Little, Brown.

Ford, Robert. 1950. "Tibet Radio Asks Aid against Reds." *New York Times*, 1 February.

————. 1957a. *Captured in Tibet*. London: Pan Books.

————. 1957b. *Wind between the Worlds*. New York: David McKay.

French, Patrick. 2003. *Tibet, Tibet: A Personal History of a Lost Land*. New York: Alfred P. Knopf.

Galbraith, John K. 1969. *Ambassador's Journal: A Personal Account of the Kennedy Years*. Boston: Houghton Mifflin.

Gao Ping. 2001. *Xiuzhu chuan zang gonglu qinliji* (Personal Experiences of the Sichuan-Tibet Road Construction). Beijing: China Tibetan Studies Publishing House.

Garver, John W. 2001. *Protracted Contest: Sino-Indian Rivalry in the Twentieth Century.* Seattle: University of Washington Press.

Gashi, Dorje Tsering. 1980. *New Tibet: Memoirs of a Graduate of the Peking Institute of National Minorities.* Dharamsala, India: Information and Publicity Office of His Holiness the Dalai Lama.

Gelder, Stuart, and Roma Gelder. 1964. *The Timely Rain.* London: Hutchinson.

Ginsburgs, George, and Michael Mathos. 1964. *Communist China and Tibet: The First Dozen Years.* The Hague: Martinus Nijhoff.

Goldstein, Melvyn. 1964. "Study of the *ldab ldob.*" *Central Asiatic Journal* 9: 123–41.

———. 1968. "An Anthropological Study of the Tibetan Political System." Ph.D. dissertation, University of Washington.

———. 1971a. "The Balance between Centralization and Decentralization in the Traditional Tibetan Political System: An Essay on the Nature of Tibetan Political Macrostructure." *Central Asiatic Journal* 15, no. 3: 170–82.

———. 1971b. "Serfdom and Mobility: An Examination of the Institution of 'Human Lease' in Traditional Tibetan Society." *Journal of Asian Studies* 30, no. 3: 521–34.

———. 1971c. "Stratification, Polyandry and Family Structure in Tibet." *Southwestern Journal of Anthropology* 27, no. 1: 64–74.

———. 1971d. "Taxation and the Structure of a Tibetan Village." *Central Asiatic Journal* 15, no. 1: 1–27.

———. 1973. "The Circulation of Estates in Tibet: Reincarnation, Land and Politics." *Journal of Asian Studies* 32, no. 3: 445–55.

———. 1978. "Adjudication and Partition in the Tibetan Stem Family " In *Chinese Family Law and Social Change,* ed. David Buxbaum. Seattle: University of Washington Press.

———. 1982. "Lhasa Street Songs: Political and Social Satire in Traditional Tibet." *Tibet Journal* 7, nos. 1–2: 56–57.

———. 1986. "Reexamining Choice, Dependency and Command in the Tibetan Social System: 'Tax Appendages' and Other Landless Serfs." *Tibet Journal* 11, no. 4: 79–112.

———. 1989. *A History of Modern Tibet, 1913–1951: The Demise of the Lamaist State.* Berkeley: University of California Press.

———. 1990a. "The Dragon and the Snow Lion: The Tibet Question in the Twentieth Century." In *China Briefing,* ed. A. J. Kane, 129–68. Boulder, CO: Westview Press.

———. 1990b. "Religious Conflict in the Traditional Tibetan State." In *Reflections on Tibetan Culture: Essays in Memory of T. V. Wylie,* ed. L. Epstein and R. Sherburne. Lewiston, NY: Edwin Mellen.

———. 1991. "Tibet: After the Fall of Chamdo." *Tibet Journal* 26, no. 1: 58–95.

———. 1997. *The Snow Lion and the Dragon: China, Tibet, and the Dalai Lama.* Berkeley: University of California Press.

———. 2003. "On Modern Tibetan History: Moving beyond Stereotypes " In *Tibet and Her Neighbours: A History,* ed. Alex McKay, 219–26. London: Edition Hansjoerg Mayer.

Goldstein, Melvyn, and Cynthia M. Beall. 1989. "The Impact of China's Reform Policy on the Nomads of Western Tibet." *Asian Survey* 28, no. 6: 619–41.

Goldstein, Melvyn, Dawai Sherap, and William R. Siebenschuh. 2004. *A Tibetan Revolutionary: The Political Life and Times of Bapa Phüntso Wangye.* Berkeley: University of California Press.

Goncharov, Sergei, John W. Lewis, and Litai Xue. 1993. *Uncertain Partners: Stalin, Mao and the Korean War.* Stanford: Stanford University Press.

Goodman, Michael H. 1987. *The Last Dalai Lama: A biography.* Boston: Shambhala Publications.

Gopal, Ram. 1964. *India-China-Tibet Triangle.* Lucknow: Pustak Kendra.

Gould, Basil J. 1941. *On the Discovery, Recognition and Installation of the Fourteenth Dalai Lama.* New Delhi: Government of India Press.

———. 1957. *The Jewel in the Lotus.* London: Chatto and Windus.

Goullart, Peter. 1957. *Forgotten Kingdom.* London: Readers Union.

Grasso, June, Jay Corrin, and Michael Kort. 1991. *Modernization and Revolution in China.* Armonk, NY: M. E. Sharpe.

Grunfeld, A. Tom. 1975. "Tibet: Myth and Realities." *New China* 1, no. 3: 17–20.

———. 1980. "Some Thoughts on the Current State of Sino-Tibetan Historiography." *China Quarterly* 83: 568–76.

———. 1985. "In Search of Equality: Relations between China's Ethnic Minorities and the Majority Han." *Bulletin of Concerned Asian Scholars* 17, no. 1: 54–67.

———. 1988. "Developments in Tibetan Studies in Tibet Today." *China Quarterly* 115: 462–66.

———. 1996. *The Making of Modern Tibet.* Armonk, NY: M. E. Sharpe.

Gup, Ted. 2001. *The Book of Honor.* New York: Anchor Books.

Gupta, Karunakar. 1971. "The McMahon Line 1911–1945—the British Legacy." *China Quarterly* 47: 524.

———. 1974. *The Hidden History of the Sino-Indian Frontier.* Calcutta: Minerva Associates.

Gyatso, Lobsang. 1998. *Memoirs of a Tibetan Lama.* Ithaca: Snow Lion Press.

Ha'o, Kong phu'u. 1986. "Sku tshab krang cin wu'u yi sku 'gram du las ka byed skabs" (Working at the Side of Representative Zhang Jingwu). In *Bod kyi rig gnas lo rgyus dpyad gzhi'i rgyu cha bsdams bsgrigs* (Selected Materials on the History and Culture of Tibet), ed. CHMC, vol. 9, 113–32. Lhasa: Tibet Military Area Publishing House.

Harrer, Heinrich. 1954. *Seven Years in Tibet.* New York: E. P. Dutton.

Harris, Claire, and Tsering Shakya. 2003. *See Lhasa: British Depictions of the Tibetan Capital 1936–1947.* Chicago: Serindia Publications.

Heberer, Thomas. 1989. *China and Its National Minorities: Autonomy or Assimilation.* Armonk, NY: M. E. Sharpe.

Hersberg, James G., ed. 1995. *The Cold War in Asia.* Vol. 6–7. Washington, DC: Woodrow Wilson International Center for Scholars.

Hilton, Isabel, ed. 1999. *The Search for the Panchen Lama.* New York: W. W. Norton.

Hoffmann, Helmut, ed. 1976. *Tibet: A Handbook.* Bloomington: Indiana University Press.

Information and Publicity Office of His Holiness the Dalai Lama. 1976. *Tibet under Chinese Communist Rule: A Compilation of Refugee Statements, 1958–1975.* Dharamsala, India: Information and Publicity Office of His Holiness the Dalai Lama.

International Commission of Jurists. 1959. *The Question of Tibet and the Rule of Law.* Geneva: International Commission of Jurists.

———. 1960. *Tibet and the Chinese People's Republic.* Geneva: International Commission of Jurists.

Jain, Girlal. 1960. *Panscheela and After: A Re-appraisal of Sino-Indian Relations in the Context of the Tibetan Insurrection.* New York: Asia Publishing House.

'Jam dpal gyal mtshan (Reting Dzasa), and Thub bstan snyan grags. 1986. "Rwa stag don rkyen nang gi bzhi sde smyung gnas bla ma" (On Shide's Nyungne Lama and the Reting-Taktra Incident). In *Bod kyi rig gnas lo rgyus dpyad gzhi'i rgyu cha bsdams bsgrigs* (Selected Materials on the History and Culture of Tibet), ed. CHMC, vol. 8, 83–95. Lhasa: Tibet Xinhua Publishing House.

Jamyang Norbu. 1994. "The Tibetan Resistance Movement." In *Resistance and Reform in Tibet*, ed. Robert Barnett and Shirin Akiner. London: Hurst and Company.

Jiangbian Jiacuo (Jambey Gyatso). 1989. *Banchan dashi* (Panchen, the Great Master). Beijing: Eastern Publishing House.

———. 2001. *Xüeshan mingjiang Tan Guansan* (The Famous General of the Snow Mountains: Tan Guansan). Beijing: China Tibetan Studies Publishing House.

Ji Youquan. 1993a. *Bai xue* (White Snow). Beijing: Material Resources Publishing House.

———. 1993b. *Xizang ping pan jishi—1959 panluan* (An Account of Putting Down the Rebellion in Tibet—the 1959 Rebellion). Lhasa: Tibet People's Publishing House.

Kapstein, Mathew. 1991. *The Long March: Chinese Settlers and Chinese Policies in Eastern Tibet.* Washington, DC: International Campaign for Tibet.

Karan, Pradyumna P. 1976. *The Changing Face of Tibet: The Impact of Communist Ideology on the Landscape.* Lexington: University of Kentucky Press.

Kar rgyal don grub. 1992. *Mdo khams cha phreng gi lo rgyus gser gyi snye ma* (The Golden Kernel of the History of Chadreng of Dokham). Dharamsala, India: Library of Tibetan Works and Archives.

Ka shod (Kapshöba), Chos rygal nyi ma. 1985. "Rgyal zur rwa sgreng dang stag brag dbar gyi don rkyen gang dran du bris pa" (All of My Recollections about the Conflict between the Ex-Regent Reting and Taktra). In *Bod kyi rig gnas lo rgyus dpyad gzhi'i rgyu cha bsdams bsgrigs* (Selected Materials on the History and Culture of Tibet), ed. CHMC, vol. 6, 1–113. Lhasa: Tibet Military Area Publishing House.

Ka shod (Kapshöba), Chos rygal nyi ma, and Lha klu (Lhalu), Tshe dbang rdo rje. 1983. "Lha sar bdyin ji'i slob grwa zhig btsugs pa dang thor ba'i bya rim" (The Sequence of Events regarding the Destruction of the English School That Was Started in Lhasa). In *Bod kyi rig gnas lo rgyus rgyu cha bdams bsgrigs* (Selected Materials on the History and Culture of Tibet), ed. CHMC, vol. 2, 55–72. Lhasa: Tibet People's Publishing House.

Khe smad (Kheme), Bsod nams dbang 'dus. 1965. "Don tshan bcu bdun bzhag skor gyi bka'slob dge'o" (Lecture on the Signing of the Seventeen-Point Agreement). Mimeographed copy of lecture given at the Tibetan Teacher's Training School, Dharamsala, India, 25 November 1965.

———. 1982. *Rgas po'i lo rgyus 'bel gtam* (Stories on the History of an Old Man). Dharamsala, India: Tibet Library.

Khren, bing. 1989. "Rgyal khab la rgyab gtod byas na pham nges yin" (One Will Definitely Lose If One Acts as a Traitor to the Nation). In *Gsar brje'i dran tho* (Revolutionary Memoirs), 72–98. Lhasa: Xinhua People's Publishing House.

Khreng (Cheng Bing), Tse-kri. 1981. "Chab mdo sa khul bcings 'grol gtong ba'i dmag thab" (The Battle to Liberate the Chamdo Region). In *Bod kyi rig gnas lo rgyus rgyu cha bdams bsgrigs* (Selected Materials on the History and Culture of Tibet), ed. CHMC, vol. 1, 208–50. Lhasa: Tibet People's Publishing House.

Khyung ram, Rig 'dzin rnam rgyal. 1986. "Nga'i pha khyung ram don grub rgyal por khrims chad phog pa'i lo rgyus" (The History of the Punishment of My Father, Khyungram Dondrup Gyebo). In *Bod kyi rig gnas lo rgyus dpyad gzhi'i rgyu cha bsdams bsgrigs* (Selected Materials on the History and Culture of Tibet), ed. CHMC, vol. 8, 132–39. Lhasa: Tibet Xinhua Publishing House.

Kirti sprul sku, ed. 1983. *Mdo smad pa dge 'dun chos 'phel gyi skor ngag rgyun lo rgyus phyogs bsdoms* (Oral History on Gendün Chompel). Dharamsala, India: Tibet Library.

Knaus, John Kenneth. 1999. *Orphans of the Cold War: America and the Tibetan Struggle for Survival.* New York: Public Affairs.

———. 2003. "Official Policies and Covert Programs: The U.S. State Department, the CIA, and the Tibetan Resistance." *Journal of Cold War Studies* 11, no. 3: 54–79.

Krang, Go hwa (Zhang Guohua). 1983. "Bcun bco brgyad pa bod skyod gnas tshul ngo ma bkod pa" (An Account of the Eighteenth Army Corps Going to Tibet). In *Bod kyi rig gnas lo rgyus rgyu cha bdams bsgrigs* (Selected Materials on the History and Culture of Tibet), ed. CHMC, vol. 2, 180–223. Lhasa: Tibet People's Publishing House.

Kra'o hreng dbying, ed. 1992. *Bod kyi gsar brje'i lo rgyus* (History of the Revolution in Tibet). Lhasa: Tibet Publishing House.

Kreng, ping (Cheng bing). 1981. "Bod dmag gi lo rgyus mdor bsdus" (Brief History of the Tibetan Army). In *Bod kyi rig gnas lo rgyus dpyad gzhi'i rgyu cha bsdams bsgrigs* (Selected Materials on the History and Culture of Tibet), ed. CHMC, vol. 4, 180–207. Lhasa: Tibet People's Publishing House.

Kru'u, zhi'u hran. 1989. "Lha sa'i dmag 'thab skor rjes dran byas pa." In *Gsar brje'i dran tho*, 60–71. Lhasa: Tibet People's Publishing House.

Kun bde gling (Kundeling), 'Od zer rgyal mtshan. 2000. *Mi tshe'i lo rgyus las 'phros pa'i gtam thabs byus snying stobs kyi 'bras bu* (The Results of the Spirit and Strategies in My Life History). 2 vols. Mysore, India: self-published.

Kun rtse (Kusantse), Bsod nams dbang 'dus. 1968. *Lhar bcas 'gro ba'i 'dren mchog gong sa skyabs mgon rgyal dbang sku phreng bcu bzhi pa bstan 'dzin rgya mtsho chen po mchog thog mar rtsad dpyod ngos 'dzin gdan zhu ji ltar zhus skor rang myong ma bcos lhug par bkod pa'i bden gtam rna ba'i dud.* Dharamsala, India: Tibetan government's Cultural Publishing House. (Alternative name for Khe smad.)

Laird, Thomas. 2002. *Into Tibet: The CIA's First Atomic Spy and His Secret Expedition to Lhasa.* New York: Grove Press.

Lamb, Alastair. 1960. *Britain and Chinese Central Asia.* London: Routledge and Kegan Paul.

———. 1964. *The China-India Border: The Origins of the Disputed Boundaries.* London: R.I.I.A.

———. 1966. *The McMahon Line, 1904–1914.* London: Routledge.

————. 1973. *The Sino-Indian Border in Ladakh.* Canberra: Roxford Books.

————. 1989. *Tibet, China and India, 1914–1950.* Hertingfordbury: Roxford Books.

Larsen, Knud, and Amund Sinding-Larsen. 2001. *The Lhasa Atlas: Traditional Tibetan Architecture and Townscape.* Boston: Shambhala Publications.

Levi, W. 1954. "Tibet under Chinese Communist Rule." *Far Eastern Survey* 23: 1–9.

Le Yuhong. 1982. "Bod zhi bas bcings 'grol skor gyi nyin tho gnad bshus" (Diary on the Peaceful Liberation of Tibet). In *Bod kyi rig gnas lo rgyus rgyu cha bdams bsgrigs* (Selected Materials on the History and Culture of Tibet), ed. CHMC, vol. 1, 117–69. Lhasa: Tibet People's Publishing House.

————. 1985. "Bod bskyod nyin tho gnad bshus" (Diary of Going to Tibet, part 1). In *Bod kyi rig gnas lo rgyus dpyad gzhi'i rgyu cha bsdams bsgrigs* (Selected Materials on the History and Culture of Tibet), ed. CHMC, vol. 6, 234–331. Lhasa: Tibet Military Area Publishing House.

————. 1986a. "Bod bskyod nyin tho gnad bshus (gnyis pa)" (Diary of Going to Tibet, part 2). In *Bod kyi rig gnas lo rgyus dpyad gzhi'i rgyu cha bsdams bsgrigs* (Selected Materials on the History and Culture of Tibet), ed. CHMC, vol. 8, 292–336. Lhasa: Tibet Xinhua Publishing House.

————. 1986b. "Bod bskyod nyin tho gnad bshus" (Diary of Going to Tibet, part 3). In *Bod kyi lo rgyus rig gnas dpyad gzhi'i rgyu cha bsdams bsgrigs* (Selected Materials on the History and Culture of Tibet), ed. CHMC, vol. 9, 165–235. Lhasa: Tibet Military Area Publishing House.

————. 1991. "Huiyi Tousheng heping Jiefang Xizang de licheng" (Recalling the Experiences of Participating in the Peaceful Liberation of Tibet). In *Xizang dang shi zi liao* (Resources for the History of the CCP) 2: 14–32.

Lha 'dzoms sgrol dkar. 1984. "Sku bcar thub bstan kun 'phel gyi skor" (On the Favorite, Thubden Kunpel). In *Bod kyi rig gnas lo rgyus dpyad gzhi'i rgyu cha bsdams bsgrigs* (Selected Materials on the History and Culture of Tibet), ed. CHMC, vol. 4, 135–64. Lhasa: Tibet People's Publishing House.

Lha klu (Lhalu), Tshe dbang rdo rje. 1981. "Mi dmangs bcings 'grol dmag lha sar bca' sdod byas rjes" (After the PLA Was Established in Lhasa). In *Bod kyi rig gnas lo rgyus rgyu cha bdams bsgrigs* (Selected Materials on the History and Culture of Tibet), ed. CHMC, vol. 1, 337–50. Lhasa: Tibet People's Publishing House.

————. 1983. "Nga'i pha lung shar rdo rje tshe rgyal dran gso byas pa" (Recollections of My Father, Lungshar Dorje Tsegyel). In *Bod kyi rig gnas lo rgyus rgyu cha bdams bsgrigs* (Selected Materials on the History and Culture of Tibet), ed. CHMC, vol. 2, 93–109. Lhasa: Tibet People's Publishing House.

————. 1984. "Rang nyid bskyod pa'i lam bur phyir mig rags tsam zhig bltas pa" (Looking Back a Little on the Path I Have Taken). In *Bod kyi rig gnas lo rgyus rgyu cha bdams bsgrigs* (Selected Materials on the History and Culture of Tibet), ed. CHMC, vol. 3, 26–49. Lhasa: Tibet People's Publishing House.

————. 1985. "Rwa stag gnyis kyi 'gal rkyen dang/rgyal zur rwa sgreng lha sar skong 'gug byed par bskyod pa'i brgyud rim" (The Dispute between Reting and Taktra and Bringing the Ex-Regent Back to Lhasa). In *Bod kyi rig gnas lo rgyus dpyad gzhi'i rgyu cha bsdams bsgrigs* (Selected Materials on the History and Culture of Tibet), ed. CHMC, vol. 5, 1–58. Xining: Qinghai Xinhua Publishing Plant.

————. 1993. "Yab gzhis lha klu'i khyim tshang gi lo rgyur skor" (On the History of the Yabshi Lhalu Family). In *Bod kyi lo rgyus rig gnas dpyad gzhi'i rgyu cha bsdams bsgrigs* (Selected Materials on the History and Culture of Tibet), ed. CHMC, vol. 16, 1–324. Lhasa: People's Publishing House.

Lha mo Tshe ring (Lhamo Tsering). 1992. *Btsan rgol rgyal skyob* (Opposing Suppression and Defending the Nation). Vol. 1. Dharamsala, India: Amnyemachen Cultural Research Center.

Lha'u rta ra (Lhautara), Thub bstan bstan dar. 1981. "Bod shi bas bcings 'grol 'byung thabs skor gyi gros mthun don tshan bcu bdun la ming rtags bkod pa'i sngon rjes su" (On the Events before and after the Signing of the Seventeen-Point Agreement for the Peaceful Liberation of Tibet). In *Bod kyi rig gnas lo rgyus rgyu cha bdams bsgrigs* (Selected Materials on the History and Culture of Tibet), ed. CHMC, vol. 1, 90–119. Lhasa: Tibet People's Publishing House.

———. 1984. "Ngas 'Lung shar don rkyen' nang zhugs pa'i gnas tshul" (An Account of My Involvement in the Lungshar Incident). In *Bod kyi rig gnas lo rgyus rgyu cha bdams bsgrigs* (Selected Materials on the History and Culture of Tibet), ed. CHMC, vol. 3, 60–70. Lhasa: Tibet People's Publishing House.

———. 1986a. "Tha'i ji khyung ram don grub rgyal po las zhabs gnas dbyung gis btson bcug rgyan 'bud btang skor" (Regarding the Demotion and Imprisonment of Khung Ram Dondrup Gyepo). In *Bod kyi rig gnas lo rgyus dpyad gzhi'i rgyu cha bsdams bsgrigs* (Selected Materials on the History and Culture of Tibet), ed. CHMC, vol. 8, 115–31. Lhasa: Tibet Xinhua Publishing House.

———. 1986b. "Gros mthun don tshan bcu bdun la ming rtags bkod pa dang lag len bstar rgyu'i skor gyi gnas tshul" (An Account of Signing and Putting into Practice the Seventeen-Point Agreement). In *Bod kyi rig gnas lo rgyus dpyad gzhi'i rgyu cha bsdams bsgrigs* (Selected Materials on the History and Culture of Tibet), ed. CHMC, vol. 9, 44–57. Lhasa: Tibet Military Area Publishing House.

Li Jue. 1991. "Huiyi heping jiefang xizang" (A Memoir of the Peaceful Liberation of Tibet). In *Shijie wuji fengyun lu* (Wind and Clouds on the Roof of the World), ed. Wu Chen, 16–47. Beijing: Jiefang junwenyi chubanshe.

Li Tieh-tseng. 1956. *The Historical Status of Tibet.* New York: Columbia University Press.

———. 1960. *Tibet Today and Yesterday.* New York: Bookman Associates.

Liu Xuecheng. 1994. *The Sino-Indian Border Dispute and Sino-Indian Relations.* Lanham, MD: University Press of America.

Liu Yuan, ed. 1983. *Xizang dashiji (1949–1981)* (Record of Major Events in Tibet [1949–1981]). Lhasa: Tibet People's Publishing House.

Li Weihai. 1996. *Lishi de yiye: Dalai Panchen Jinjing jishi* (A Page in the Book of History: The History of the Dalai Lama and Panchen Lama Going to Beijing). Beijing: Zhongguo shehui chubanshe.

Li Zhisui. 1994. *The Private Life of Chairman Mao.* New York: Random House.

Long, Jeff. 1981. "Going after Wangdu." *Rocky Mountain Magazine* (March-April): 36–42.

Lung shar (Lungshar), O rgyan rdo rje. 1984. "Rgyal zur rwa sgreng btson khang du bkrongs pa'i gnas tshul dngos" (A True Account of How the Ex-Regent Reting Was Killed in Prison). In *Bod kyi rig gnas lo rgyus rgyu cha bdams bsgrigs* (Selected Materials on the History and Culture of Tibet), ed. CHMC, vol. 3, 119–34. Lhasa: Tibet People's Publishing House.

MacFarquhar, Roderick. 1974. *The Origins of the Cultural Revolution: Vol. 1, Contradictions among the People, 1956–1957.* New York: Columbia University Press.

———, ed. 1993. *The Politics of China, 1949–1989*. Cambridge: Cambridge University Press.

MacInnis, Donald E. 1989. *Religion in China Today: Policy and Practice*. Maryknoll, NY: Orbis Books.

———, ed. 1972. *Religious Policy and Practice in Communist China*. New York: Macmillan.

Mackerras, Colin. 1994. *China's Minorities: Integration and Modernization in the Twentieth Century*. Oxford: Oxford University Press.

Mao Tse-tung. 1958. *On the Correct Handling of Contradictions among the People*. Beijing: Foreign Languages Press.

———. 1977a. "Criticize Great Hanism." In *Selected Works of Mao Tse-tung*, 87–88. Peking: Foreign Language Press.

———. 1977b. "On the Policies of Our Work in Tibet—Directive of the Central Committee of the Communist Party of China." In *Selected Works of Mao Tse-tung*, 74–75. Peking: Foreign Languages Press.

Marchetti, Victor, and John D. Marks. 1975. *The CIA and the Cult of Intelligence*. New York: Dell.

Maxwell, Neville. 1970. *India's China War*. London: Jonathan Cape.

McCorquodale, Robert, and Nicholas Orosz, eds. 1994. *Tibet: The Position in International Law*. London: Serindia.

McGranahan, Carole. 2001. "Arrested Histories: Between Empire and Exile in 20th Century Tibet." Ph.D. dissertation, University of Michigan, Ann Arbor.

McKay, Alex. 2001. "'Kicking the Buddha's Head': India, Tibet and Footballing Colonialism." *International Journal of the History of Sport* 2, no. 2: 89–104.

———, ed. 2003. *The History of Tibet: The Modern Period: 1895–1959, the Encounter with Modernity*. Vol. 3. London: RoutledgeCurzon.

Mdo mkhar, Phun tshogs rab rgyas, et. al. 1954. "1953 lo'i rgyal khab dbu brnyes rten 'brel mdzad gzigs tshogs pa'i tshogs gtso nas rgyang sgrags rlung 'phrin thog gungs pa'i legs sbyar" (Broadcast speech by the 1953 delegation attending the National Day holiday celebration). Beijing: Nationalities Publishing House.

Mehra, Parshotam. 1956. "India, China and Tibet, 1950–54." *India Quarterly* 12: 3–22.

———. 1958. "Tibet and Russian Intrigue." *Royal Central Asian Journal* 45, no. 1: 32.

———. 1967. "Beginnings of the Lhasa Expedition: Younghusband's Own Words." *Bulletin of Tibetology* 4, no. 3: 9–18.

———. 1969. "Tibet and Outer Mongolia vis-à-vis China, 1911–1936." In *Studies in Asian History: Proceedings of the Asian History Congress, 1961*, ed. K. S. Lal, 240. New York: Asia Publishing House.

———. 1976. *Tibetan Polity 1904–1937: The Conflict between the 13th Dalai Lama and the 9th Panchen Lama*. Wiesbaden: Otto Harrassowitz.

Meng, C. Y. W. 1930. "Miss Liu's Mission to Tibet." *China Weekly Review* 6 (September): 22–24.

Michael, Franz. 1982. *Rule by Incarnation: Tibetan Buddhism and Its Role in Society and State*. Boulder, CO: Westview.

Mirsky, Johnathon. 1990. "The Secret Massacre." *Observer*, 12 August, 17.

Mitter, Jyoti P. 1964. *Betrayal of Tibet*. Bombay: Allied Publishers.

Moraes, Frank. 1960. *The Revolt in Tibet*. New York: Sterling Publishers.

Morrow, Michael. 1970. "Super Secret Missions: CIA Spy Teams inside Red China." *San Francisco Chronicle*, 4 September, 24.

Moseley, George. 1966. *The Party and the National Question in China.* Cambridge, MA: MIT Press.

Mullik, B. N. 1971. *My Years with Nehru: The Chinese Betrayal.* Bombay: Allied Publishers.

Mullin, Chris. 1975. "The CIA: Tibetan Conspiracy." *Far Eastern Economic Review* (5 September).

———. 1976. "How the CIA Went to War in Tibet." *Guardian,* 19 January.

Nakane, Chie. 1984. *Map of Lhasa.* Tokyo: Institute of Oriental Culture, University of Tokyo.

Neame, Maj. Gen. P. 1939. "Tibet and the 1936 Lhasa Mission." *Journal of the Royal Central Asian Society* 26, no. 2: 245.

Ngabö, Ngawang Jigme. 1989. Tape recording of a speech before the Tibet People's Congress. 30 August, Lhasa. Private distribution.

Ngagpo, Jigme. 1988. "Behind the Unrest in Tibet." *China Spring Digest* (January/February): 22–32.

Nga phod, Ngag dbang 'jigs med (Ngabö, Ngawang Jigme). 1989. "Rang skyong ljongs kyi skabs lnga pa'i mi dmags 'thus tshogs kyi tshogs 'du thengs gnyis pa'i thog gnang ba'i gal che'i gsung bshad" (Important Speech at Second Session of the 5th People's Congress of the Autonomous Region). *Bod ljongs nyin re'i tshags par,* 31 August, 1–6

Niemi, M. L. 1958. "Recent Trends in Chinese Communist Control of Tibet." *Far Eastern Survey* 27: 104–7.

Norbu, Dawa. 1974. "Who Aided Khambas and Why." *Tibetan Review* 6/7 (July/August): 19–23.

———. 1979. "The 1959 Rebellion: An interpretation." *China Quarterly* 77.

———. 1985. "An Analysis of Sino-Tibetan Relationships, 1245–1911: Imperial Power, Non-coersive Regime and Military Dependency." In *Soundings in Tibetan Civilization,* ed. Barbara Nimri Aziz and Matthew Kapstein. New Delhi: Manohar.

———. 1987. *Red Star over Tibet.* New Delhi: Sterling Publishers.

———. 1991. "China's Dialogue with the Dalai Lama 1987–90: Prenegotiation State or Dead End?" *Pacific Affairs* 64, no. 3: 351–72.

Norbu, Jamyang. 1986. *Warrior of Tibet: The Story of Aten and the Khambas' Fight for the Freedom of Their Country.* London: Wisdom Press.

Norbu, Thubten Jigme, and Heinrich Harrer. 1960. *Tibet Is My Country.* London: Hart Davis.

Norbu, Thubten Jigme, and Colin M Turnbull. 1968. *Tibet.* New York: Simon and Schuster.

Office of Tibet. 1994. *Tibet Briefing.* Pamphlet. New York: Office of Tibet.

Paljor, Kunsang. 1977. *Tibet: The Undying Flame.* Dharamsala, India: Information and Publicity Office of His Holiness the Dalai Lama.

Panchen Lama. 1988. "On Tibetan Independence." *China Reconstructs* (January) : 8–15.

Panikkar, K. M. 1955. *In Two Chinas: Memoirs of a Diplomat.* London: George Allen and Unwin.

Patterson, George. 1958. "Kalimpong: The Nest of Spies." *Twentieth Century* 163: 527.

———. 1959. *Tragic Destiny.* London: Faber and Faber.

———. 1960. *Tibet in Revolt.* London: Faber and Faber.

———. 1963. *Peking versus Delhi.* London: Faber and Faber.

———. 1990. *Requiem for Tibet.* London: Aurum Press.

Peissel, Michel. 1972. *The Secret War in Tibet*. First American Edition. Boston: Little, Brown.

Pemba, Tsewang Y. 1957. *Young Days in Tibet*. London: Jonathan Cape.

People's Association. 1952. Petition manuscript. Ü-Tsang Association, Dharamsala, India.

Phun rab, Rin chen rnam rgyal. 1984. "Gzhung bla'i dbar thog ma'i 'gal ba yong rkyen" (How the Dispute between the Tibetan Government and the Panchen Lama First Started). In *Bod kyi rig gnas lo rgyus dpyad gzhi'i rgyu cha bsdams bsgrigs* (Selected Materials on the History and Culture of Tibet), ed. CHMC, vol. 4, 123–32. Lhasa: Tibet People's Publishing House.

Phun tshogs tshe ring. 1992. *Rwa stag gi don rkyen dang de'i ngo bo'i skor gleng ba* (About the Reting-Taktra Dispute). Lhasa: Tibet People's Publishing House.

Phu pa, Tshe ring stobs rgyas. 2000. *Mdo stod chu bzhi sgang drug bod kyi bstan srung dang blangs dmag gi lo rgyus* (The History of the Chushigandru Volunteer Defenders of the Faith). New Delhi, India: Central Committee of Dhoto Chushi Gandrug.

Phur (bu) lcog (Phurbucho). 1935. *Lhar bcas srid zhi'i gtsug rgyan gong sa rgyal ba bka' drin mtshungs med sku phreng ba . . . gsum pa chen po'i rnam thar rgya mtsho lta bu las mdo can brjod pa ngo mtshar rin chen phreng ba zhes bya ba'i gleg bam stod cha cha sa*. Vols. 1 and 2. Lhasa: hand printed by woodblock.

Prouty, Fletcher L. 1972. "Colorado to Koko Nor: The Amazing True Story of the CIA's Secret War against Red China." *Denver Post*, 6. February 6, 11–17.

———. 1973. *The Secret Team: The CIA and Its Allies in Control of the United States and the World*. Englewood Cliffs, NJ: Prentice-Hall.

Puncog Zhaxi. 2001. "My Experiences during the Peaceful Liberation of Tibet." *China's Tibet* 12, no. 3: 14–15.

Rahul, Ram. 1962. "The Structure of the Government of Tibet, 1644–1911." *International Studies 3*, no. 3.

Rgyal mtshan phun tshogs. 1986. "Nga mdo spyi'i las byar skyod skabs kyi gnas tshul 'ga' zhig" (Some Information on When I Went as Part of the Staff of the Government of Eastern Tibet). In *Bod kyi rig gnas lo rgyus dpyad gzhi'i rgyu cha bsdams bsgrigs* (Selected Materials on the History and Culture of Tibet), ed. CHMC, vol. 9, 13–29. Lhasa: Tibet Military Area Publishing House.

Richardson, Hugh E. 1945. *Tibetan Précis*. Calcutta: Government of India Press.

———. 1980. "The Rva-sgreng Conspiracy of 1947." In *Tibetan Studies in Honour of Hugh Richardson: Proceedings of the International Seminar on Tibetan Studies, Oxford, 1979*, ed. Michael Aris and Aung San Sui Kyi. Warminster: Aris and Phillips.

———. 1984. *Tibet and Its History*. Boulder, CO: Shambhala Publications.

———. 1986. *Adventures of a Fighting Monk*. Bangkok: Tamarind Press.

———. 1993. *Ceremonies of the Lhasa Year*. Edited by Michael Aris. London: Serendia Publications.

Rlas, Ying he'e yi. 1989. "Bod du zing 'khrug zhod 'jags gtong bar bskyod pa'i gnas zin" (On How the Revolt in Tibet Was Quelled). In *Gsar brje'e dran tho* (Revolutionary Memoirs), 147–60. Lhasa: Bod ljongs mi dmangs dpe skrun khang (Tibet People's Publishing House).

Rnam gling (Namseling), Dpal 'byor 'jigs med. 1988. *Mi tshe'i lo rgyus dang 'brel yod sna tshogs* ([My] Life History and Other Related Things). Dharamsala, India: Library of Tibetan Works and Archives.

Rnam rgyal dbang 'dus. 1976. *Bod ljongs rgyal khab chen po'i srid lugs dang 'brel ba'i drag po'i dmag gi lo rgyus rags bsdus* (A Brief History of the Tibetan Nation's Political and Military System). Dharamsala, n.p.

Rositzke, Harry. 1977. *The CIA's Secret Operations: Espionage, Counterespionage, and Covert Action.* New York: Reader's Digest Press.

Rubin, Alfred P. 1967. "Review of *The McMahon Line.*" *American Journal of International Law* 61: 827.

———. 1968. "The Position of Tibet in International Law." *China Quarterly* 35: 130.

Rwa sgreng mkhan po, 'Jam dpal rgya mtsho. 1985. "Bod dmag gis rwa sgreng du spel ba'i spyod ngan" (The Bad Actions of the Tibetan Army in Reting). In *Bod kyi rig gnas lo rgyus dpyad gzhi'i rgyu cha bsdams bsgrigs* (Selected Materials on the History and Culture of Tibet), ed. CHMC, vol. 5, 78–91. Xining: Qinghai Xinhua Publishing Plant.

Schram, Stuart R. 1965. *The Political Thought of Mao Tse-tung.* New York: Praeger.

Schurman, Franz. 1968. *Ideology and Organization in Communist China.* Berkeley: University of California Press.

SCMP. 1960–77. *Survey of China Mainland Press.* Hong Kong: American Consulate General.

Selden, Mark, and Victor Lippit, eds. 1982. *The Transition to Socialism in China.* Armonk, NY: M. E. Sharpe.

Sen, Chanakya. 1960. *Tibet Disappears.* London: Asia Publishing House.

Sga gra'u dpon, Rin chen tshe ring, Chab mdo drug yig, and Blo bzang dbang 'dud, eds. 2000. *Chu sgang lo rgyus* (The History of Chushigandru). Vol. 1. Delhi, India: Welfare Society of Central Dokham Chushi Gangdrug.

Shah, A. B. 1966. *India's Defense and Foreign Policies.* Bombay: Manaktala.

Shakabpa, Tsepon W. D. 1967. *Tibet: A Political History.* New Haven, CT: Yale University Press.

Shakya, Tsering. 1999. *The Dragon in the Land of Snows.* New York: Columbia University Press.

———. 2003. "The Genesis of the Sino-Tibetan Agreement of 1951." In *The History of Modern Tibet*, vol. 3: *The Modern Period: 1895–1959, the Encounter with Modernity,* ed. Alex McKay, 589–606. London: RoutledgeCurzon.

Shan kha ba (Shenkawa; Shasur), 'Gyur med bsod nams stobs rgyal. 1990. *Rang gi lo rgyus lhad med rang byung zangs* (My True History). Dharamsala, India: Library of Tibetan Works and Archives.

Sharlho, Tseten Wangchuk. 1992. "China's Reforms in Tibet: Issues and Dilemmas." *Journal of Contemporary China* 1, no. 1: 34–60.

Shar rtse (Pebola), Ye shes thub bstan. 1983. "Rgyal zur rwa agreng do dam srung bya byed ring gi gnas tshul srong por bkod pa" (An Account of the Detention of Ex-Regent Reting). In *Bod kyi rig gnas lo rgyus rgyu cha bdams bsgrigs* (Selected Materials on the History and Culture of Tibet), ed. CHMC, vol. 2, 110–25. Lhasa: Tibet People's Publishing House.

Sheehan, Neil. 1967. "Aid by CIA Put in the Millions: Group Total Up." *New York Times,* 19 February, 27.

Shelvankar, K. S. 1962. "China's Himalayan Frontiers, India's Attitude." *International Affairs* (London) (October).

Shên Tsung-lien and Liu Shen-chi. 1973. *Tibet and the Tibetans.* New York: Octagon Books.

Sheridan, J. E. 1966. *Chinese Warlord: The Career of Feng Yü-hsiang.* Stanford: Stanford University Press.

Sinclair, William Boyd. 1965. *Jump to the Land of God. The Adventures of a United States Air Force Crew in Tibet.* Caldwell, OH: Caxton Printers.

Singh, Amar Kaur Jasbir. 1988. *Himalayan Triangle.* London: British Library.

Sinha, Nirmal Chandra. 1967. *Tibet: Considerations on Inner Asian History.* Calcutta: Firma K. L. Mukhapadhyay.

Skal ldan. 1985. "Tsha rong zla bzang dgra 'dul gyi skor" (Concerning Tsarong Dasang Dramdü). In *Bod kyi rig gnas lo rgyus dpyad gzhi'i rgyu cha bsdams bsgrigs* (Selected Materials on the History and Culture of Tibet), ed. CHMC, vol. 5, 249–93. Xining: Qinghai Xinhua Publishing Plant.

Sle zur, 'Jigs med bdang phyug. 1984. "Taa bla bcu gsum pa gshegs rjes bod kyi chab srid dus babs" (Political Times after the Death of the 13th Dalai Lama). In *Bod kyi rig gnas lo rgyus rgyu cha bdams bsgrigs* (Selected Materials on the History and Culture of Tibet), ed. CHMC, vol. 3, 1–26. Lhasa: Tibet People's Publishing House.

Smith, R. Harris, OSS. 1972. *OSS: The Secret History of America's First Central Intelligence Agency.* Berkeley: University of California Press.

Smith, Warren. 1989. *China's Tibet: Chinese Press Articles and Policy Statements on Tibet, 1950–1989.* Cambridge: Cultural Survival.

———. 1996. *Tibetan Nation: A History of Tibetan Nationalism and Sino-Tibetan Relations.* Boulder, CO: Westview Press.

Snellgrove, David, and Hugh E. Richardson. 1968. *A Cultural History of Tibet.* London: George Weidenfeld and Nicolson.

Snow, Edgar. 1968. *Red Star over China.* New York: Grove Press.

Sreg shing, Blo bzang don grub. 1983. "Go min tang gi 'thus mi hong mu'o sung taa la'i bcu gsum pa'i dgongs rdzogs mchod sprin spro 'bul du yong ba'i gnas tshul thor bu" (An Account of the Coming of the Guomindang Representative Huang Musung to Give Condolences on the Death of the 13th Dalai Lama). In *Bod kyi rig gnas lo rgyus rgyu cha bdams bsgrigs* (Selected Materials on the History and Culture of Tibet), ed. CHMC, vol. 2, 73–81. Lhasa: Tibet People's Publishing House.

Stag lha (Takla), Phun tshogs bkris (Phüntso Tashi). 1995. *Mi tshe'i byung ba brjod pa* (On My Life Experiences). 3 vols. Dharamsala, India: Library of Tibetan Works and Archives.

Stoddard, Heather. 1985. *Le mendiant de l'Amdo.* Paris: Société d'ethnographie.

Strong, Anna L. 1960. *When Serfs Stood Up.* Peking: New World Press.

Sun Tzu. 1991. *The Art of War.* Trans. Thomas Cleary. Boston: Shambhala Publications.

Takla, T. N. 1969. "The Revolution Betrayed: Notes on Some Early Tibetan Communists." *Tibetan Review* (June-July).

Ta la'i bla ma (Dalai Lama). 1963. *Ngos kyi yul dang mi mang* (My Land and My People). Darjeeling: Freedom Press.

Tambiah, Stanley. 1976. *World Conqueror and World Renouncer: A Study of Religion and Polity in Thailand against a Historical Background.* West Nyack: Cambridge University Press.

Taring, Rinchen Dolma. 1986. *Daughter of Tibet*. London: Wisdom Publications. Originally published 1970.

Teichman, Eric. 1922. *Travels of a Consular Officer in Eastern Tibet—together with a History of the Relations between China, Tibet and India*. Cambridge: Cambridge University Press.

———. 1939. *Affairs of China: A Survey of the Recent History and Present Circumstances of the Republic of China*. London: Methuen Publishers.

Teiwes, Frederick C. 1993a. "The Establishment and Consolidation of the New Regime, 1949–1957." In *The Politics of China, 1949–1989*, ed. Roderick MacFarquhar, 5–86. Cambridge: Cambridge University Press.

———. 1993b. *Politics and Purges in China*. 2nd ed. Armonk, NY: M. E. Sharpe.

———. 1999. *China's Road to Disaster: Mao, Central Politicians, and Provincial Leaders in the Unfolding of the Great Leap Forward, 1955–1959*. With Warren Sun. Armonk, NY: M. E. Sharpe.

Terrill, Ross. 1993. *Mao: A Biography*. First Touchstone Edition. New York: Simon and Schuster.

Thomas, Lowell, Jr. 1950. *Out of This World: Across the Himalayas to Tibet*. New York: Greystone Press.

———. 1959. *The Silent War in Tibet*. New York: Doubleday.

Thub bstan sangs rgyas (Thubten Sanggye). 1982. *Rgya nag tu bod kyi sku tshab don gcod skabs dang gnyis tshugs stangs skor gyi lo rgyus thabs bral zur lam zhes bya ba dge'o* (Concerning the History of the Establishment of the First and Second Tibetan Bureau Office in China). Dharamsala, India: Tibetan Library.

Tokan, Tada. 1965. *The Thirteenth Dalai Lama*. Tokyo: Center for East Asian Cultural Studies.

Tsering, Diki. 2000. *Dalai Lama, My Son: A Mother's Story*. New Delhi: Penguin Books India.

Tsering Wangyal. 1994. "Sino-Tibetan Negotiations since 1959." In *Resistance and Reform in Tibet*, ed. Robert Barnett and Shirin Akiner. London: Hurst and Company.

Tshe ring don grub, ed. 1989. *Gsar brje'i dran tho* (Revolutionary Memoirs). Lhasa: Xinhua Press.

Tshe ring don grub, and O rgyan chos 'phel, eds. 1991. *Bod ljongs spyi bshad* (On Tibet). Vol. 3. Lhasa: Tibet People's Publishing House.

Tung, Rosemary. 1980. *A Portrait of Lost Tibet*. New York: Holt, Rinehart and Winston.

Union Research Institute. 1968. *Tibet: 1950–1967*. Kowloon, Hong Kong: Union Research Institute.

United Nations. 1959. "Official Records." Paper presented at the Fourteenth Session, Plenary Meetings, United Nations, General Assembly.

U.S. Department of State. 1949. "Policy Review Paper—Tibet." Washington, DC.

———. 1974. *Foreign Relations of the United States, 1949, the Far East: China*. Vol. 9. Washington, DC: Government Printing Office.

———. 1983. *Foreign Relations of the United States, 1951, Korea and China*, part 2. Vol. 7. Washington, DC: Government Printing Office.

———. 1985. *Foreign Relations of the United States, 1952–1954, China and Japan*, part 1. Vol. 14. Washington, DC: Government Printing Office.

———. 1996. *Foreign Relations of the United States, 1958–1960, China*. Vol. 19. Washington, DC: Government Printing Office.

U.S. Information Agency. 1955. "Documents on Contemporary China, 1949–1975." National Archives, Diplomatic Branch, Washington, DC.

U.S. Office of Strategic Services (OSS), Research and Analysis Bureau. 1943. "Survey of Tibet." National Archives, Diplomatic Branch, Washington, DC.

Wang, Furen, and Suo Wenqing. 1984. *Highlights of Tibetan History.* Beijing: New World Press.

Wang Jiawei and Nyima Gyaincain. *The Historical Status of China's Tibet.* Beijing: China Intercontinental Press.

Wang Xiaoqiang. 1994. "The Dispute between the Tibetans and the Han: When Will It Be Solved?" In *Resistance and Reform in Tibet,* ed. Robert Barnett and Shiren Akiner. London: Hurst and Company.

Wang Xiaoqiang and Bai Nanfeng. 1991. *The Poverty of Plenty.* London: Macmillan.

Wangyal, Phuntsog. 1974. "The Revolt of 1959." *Tibetan Review* (July-August).

———. 1975. "The Influence of Religion on Tibet's Politics." *Tibet Journal* 1, no. 7: 84.

Wei Jing. 1989. *100 Questions about Tibet.* Beijing: Beijing Review Press.

Weissman, Steve. 1973. "Last Tangle in Tibet." *Pacific Research and World Empire Telegram* 4, no. 5: 1–18.

Weissman, Steve, and John Shock. 1972. "CIAsia Foundation." *Pacific Research and World Empire Telegram* 3, no. 6: 3–4.

Welch, Holmes. 1972. *Buddhism under Mao.* Cambridge, MA: Harvard University Press.

Wignall, Sydney. 1957. *Prisoner in Red Tibet.* London: Hutchinson.

Wis, kha'. 1984. "Cun bco brgyad pas bod skyod kyi las 'gan dang du blangs pa'i skor bkod pa" (Concerning the Eighteenth Army Corps Getting the Responsibility to March into Tibet). In *Bod kyi rig gnas lo rgyus rgyu cha bdams bsgrigs* (Selected Materials on the History and Culture of Tibet), ed. CHMC, vol. 3, 326–88. Lhasa: Tibet People's Publishing House.

Wise, David. 1973. *The Politics of Lying: Government Deception, Secrecy and Power.* New York: Vintage Books.

Wise, David, and Thomas B. Ross. 1964. *The Invisible Government.* New York: Random House.

Woodcock, George. 1971. *Into Tibet: The Early British Explorers.* London: Faber and Faber.

Woodman, Dorothy. 1969. *Himalayan Frontiers. A Political Review of British, Chinese, Indian and Russian Rivalries.* New York: Praeger.

Wu Chen, ed. 1991. *Shijie wuji fengyun lu: Jinian heping jietang Xizang sishi zhou nian* (The Wind and Clouds on the Roof of the World: Commemorating the Fortieth Anniversary of the Peaceful Liberation of Tibet). 3 vols. Beijing: PLA Literature Publishing House.

Wylie, Turrell V. 1959. "A Standard System of Tibetan Transcription." *Journal of Asiatic Studies* 22: 261–67.

Xizang zizhiqu dangshi bangongshi (Party History Office of the Tibet Autonomous Region), ed. 1998. *Zhou Enlai xu xizang* (Zhou Enlai and Tibet). Beijing: Zhongguo zangxue chubanshi (China Tibetology Publishing House).

Ya Hanzhang. 1986. *Taa la'i bla ma'i rnam thar* (Biography of the Dalai Lamas). Xining: Mtsho sngon Publishing House.

———. 1991. *The Biographies of the Dalai Lamas.* Beijing: Foreign Languages Press.

———. 1994. *Biographies of the Tibetan Spiritual Leaders, Panchen Erdenis.* Beijing: Foreign Languages Press.

Yang, dbyi kran (ch. Yang Yizheng). 1986. "Bod dmag khul khang thog mar 'dzugs skabs dang 'mi dmangs tshogs 'du' zer ba rdzus mar 'thab rtsod byas pa'i gnas tshul" (Information on the False People's Association and the Establishment of the Tibet Military Area Headquarters). In *Bod kyi lo rgyus rig gnas dpyad gzhi'i rgyu cha bsdams bsgrigs* (Selected Materials on the History and Culture of Tibet), ed. CHMC, vol. 9, 58–85. Lhasa: Tibet Military Area Publishing House.

Ye shes tshul khrims. 1986. "Rwa sgreng don rkyen nang ngas sgrubs pa'i bya ba 'ga' zhig" (Some of My Actions in the Reting Incident). In *Bod kyi rig gnas lo rgyus dpyad gzhi'i rgyu cha bsdams bsgrigs* (Selected Materials on the History and Culture of Tibet), ed. CHMC, vol. 8, 60–83. Lhasa: Tibet Xinhua Publishing House.

Yin Fatang. 1992. "Deng xiaoping yu xizang heping jiefang" (Deng Ziaoping and the Peaceful Liberation of Tibet). *Xizang dangshi ziliao* (Selected Materials on the History and Culture of Tibet) 1: 1–10.

Yuan Sha and Aiming Zhou. 2001. "The 17-Article Agreement and things related to it." *China's Tibet* 12, no. 3: 6–11.

Zhang Guohua. 1983. "Jun bco brgyad pa bod skyod kyi gnas tshul ngo ma bkod pa" (A Firsthand Account of the Advance into Tibet of the Eighteenth Army). In *Bod kyi rig gnas lo rgyus rgyu cha bdams bsgrigs* (Selected Materials on the History and Culture of Tibet), ed. CHMC, vol. 2, 180–223. Lhasa: Tibet People's Publishing House.

Zhao Shenying. 1995. *Zhongyang zhuzang daibiao—Zhang Jingwu* (Zhang Jingwu—the Central Committee's Representative in Tibet). Lhasa: Xizang renmin chubanshe (Tibet People's Publishing House).

———. 1998. *Zhang Guohua jiangjun zai Xizang* (Commander Zhang Guohua in Tibet). Beijing: Zhongquo zangxue chubanshe.

Zhaxi Puncog. 2001. "My Experiences during the Peaceful Liberation of Tibet." *China's Tibet* 12, no. 3: 12–15.

Zhonggong xizang zizhiqu dangshi ziliao zhengji weiyuanhui (Committee for Collecting Materials on the Party History of the Chinese Communist Party of the Tibet Autonomous Region), ed. 1990. *Zhonggong xizang dangshi dashiji (1949–1966)* (Chronology of Major Events of the Chinese Communist Party in Tibet, 1949–66). Lhasa: Xizang renmin chubanshe (Tibet People's Publishing House).

———, ed. 1995. *Zhonggong xizang dangshi dashiji (1949–1994)* (Chronology of Major Events of the Chinese Communist Party in Tibet [1949–1994]). Rev. ed. Lhasa: Xizang renmin chubanshe (Tibet People's Publishing House).

Zhonggong zhongyang wenxian yanjiu shi bian zhonggong xizang zizhiqu weiyuan hui (Central Committee of CCP's Anchwal Research Office and the Party Committee of the Tibet Autonomous Region), ed. 2005. *Xizang gongzuo wenxian xuanbian (1949–2005)* (Selected Documents on Work in Tibet [1949–2005]). Beijing: Zhongyang wenxian chubanshe.

Zhonggong zhongyang wenxian yanjiu shi; zhonggong xizang zizhiqu weiyuanhui; zhongquo zangxue yanjiu zhongxin (Literature Research Office of the Central Committee, the Party Committee of the TAR, and the China Tibet Studies Center), ed. 2001. *Mao Zedong Xizang gongzuo wenxuan* (Selected Literature of Mao Zedong on Tibet). Beijing: Zhongyang wenxian chubanshe and zhongguo zangxue chubanshe (Central Literature Press and China Tibet Studies Publishing House).

Zhongguo zangxue yanjiu zhongxin keyan chu zhuban (China Tibetology Research

Center, Science Research Department). 1993. *Mao zedong zang minzu wengao* (Documents by Mao on the Tibetan Nationality). Manuscript. Beijing.

Zhou Jin, ed. 1981. *Tibet: No Longer Medieval.* Peking: Foreign Languages Press.

Zhwa sgab pa (Shakabpa), Dbang phyug bde ldan. 1976. *Bod kyi srid don rgyal rabs* (Political History of Tibet). Vol. 2. Kalimpong: Shakabpa House.

INDEX

Thondup's views on, 374; and initial
Chinese strategy for Tibet, 179, 182–
83, 206; and initial Tibetan strategy for
Chinese occupation, 190n46, 200; and
Military-Administrative Committee, 308;
and Military Area Headquarters, 303;
and Panchen Lama's return to Tibet,
387–89, 422; and People's Association,
330–31, 333–43, 345, 359; and road
construction, 414; and Seventeen-Point
Agreement, 109–11, 110nn55,57, 217–
18, 223–24, 223n41, 224n45; and sitsab,
171–77, 341–42, 350–51, 353–55, 357–
58, 360–65, 361nn33,34; and Tibet
Work Committee, 294–95, 297–300,
303, 344, 396; and Trimön house
(Lhasa), 172, 244–45; welcome reception for, 171–72, 171nn8,9, 177, 187
Zhang Jinsun, *496*
Zhang Jun, 284
Zhang Lan, *496*

Zhang Yintang, 187, 266–67, 266n4
Zhang Zongxun, 281
Zhao Fan, 436n18, 490
Zhou Enlai, xxx; and Dalai Lama's Beijing
visit, 490–91, 505, *506*, 524–28, 533,
540, 548; and Fan Ming–Southwest
Bureau conflict, 428; and Gao Gang,
436; and Ngabö's negotiations with
Beijing, 151; and Panchen Lama, 286;
and Shakabpa mission, 43
Zhou Renshan, 273
Zhu Dan (Gyalo Thondrup's wife), 236, 238,
240, 377, 464
Zhu De, xxx; after arrival of PLA Advance
Force, 206; and Chinese National Day
celebration, 217; and Dalai Lama's
Beijing visit, 490–92, 505; and Ngabö's
negotiations with Beijing, 151; and
Panchen Lama, 274–76; and public
schools, 400; and Shakabpa mission,
42n5

Text:	10/12 Baskerville
Display:	Baskerville
Compositor:	Integrated Composition Systems
Indexer:	Sharon Sweeney
Cartographer/Illustrator/:	Bill Nelson